Strategy: Analysis and Practice

John McGee
Howard Thomas
David Wilson
Warwick Business School
University of Warwick, UK

The McGraw·Hill Companies

London   Boston   Burr Ridge, IL   Dubuque, IA   Madison, WI   New York   San Francisco   St. Louis   Bangkok   Bogotá   Caracas   Kuala Lumpur   Lisbon   Madrid   Mexico City   Milan   Montreal   New Delhi   Santiago   Seoul   Singapore   Sydney   Taipei   Toronto

Strategy: Analysis and Practice
ISBN 0-07-7107055
ISBN 13 9780077107055

Published by McGraw-Hill Education
Shoppenhangers Road
Maidenhead
Berkshire
SL6 2QL
Telephone: 44 (0) 1628 502 500
Fax: 44 (0) 1628 770 224
Website: www.mcgraw-hill.co.uk

British Library Cataloguing in Publication Data
A catalogue record for this book is available from the British Library

Library of Congress Cataloging in Publication Data
The Library of Congress data for this book has been applied for from the Library of Congress

Publishing Director: Catriona King
Acquisitions Editor: Kate Mason
Senior Development Editor: Caroline Howell
Sales and Marketing Director: John Donovan
Marketing Manager: Marca Wosoba

Text Design by Fakenham Photosetting Limited, Fakenham, Norfolk
Cover design by Fielding Design
Printed and bound in Spain by Mateu Cromo

ISBN (This edition) 0-07-7107055
ISBN 13 (This edition) 9780077107055
ISBN (Text and Cases edition) 0-07-71070 63
ISBN 13 (Text and Cases edition) 9780077100 62

Dedication

To our colleagues, past and present, who have shaped our thinking;
To our students past and present who have contributed more than they know;
And to Jenny, Jo and Lynne who have always inspired us.

Brief Table of Contents

Detailed Table of Contents

Preface

The origins of this book grew out of the teaching and the research of the authors recognising that the field of strategy was one of the most central, yet most contested areas of management knowledge. Rather than contribute to the seemingly endless debate about what strategy is (and is not) we chose to write about it in what we hope is a refreshing, analytical, inclusive and accessible way. It is refreshing and analytical, because we are ourselves animated by the topics it embraces and we hope this enthusiasm shows in the text and in our analysis of strategy. It is inclusive and accessible because we have tried to develop a systemic view of strategy which gives breadth and depth to an overall understanding of strategy and its processes.

We hope readers will notice that this text includes some very different approaches to strategy, from viewing strategy as economic analysis to it being embedded in social and broadly contextual processes. Yet we try to blend these approaches in one systemic framework which we present in Chapter 1. As we wrote the various sections of the book we recognized that, far from being incommensurable, different approaches to strategy resonated with each other more than we had realized. It was not so much that paradigms were incommensurable, but rather that approaches could be viewed as being complementary if one highlighted the linkages between them.

We have also tried to be eclectic in the range of topics we have included under the term 'strategy'. Readers may be surprised to find chapters on governance, learning or process improvements in a book about strategy, but we realized as we constructed our framework that we could not talk about strategy in any way holistically without reference to these topics. So, we have tried to seek fit and 'complementarities' (to use the jargon of strategy) between paradigms and approaches and we have tried to be as inclusive as possible in the range of topics we feel contribute toward a more holistic view of strategy. We hope this will enthuse readers more than it may confuse.

It was quite a process and a journey for ourselves in getting to the product you are about to read. The three authors had taught strategy and had researched and written about it in quite different ways. When we came to write together, we discovered commonalities that we had not seen before and which were able to inform the construction of our systemic framework.

Many contemporary authors in strategy have developed a rather dismissive approach to the work that has preceded their own perspectives. Indeed, the field of strategy has been strongly characterised by the almost total substitution of one frame of reference for another as time has progressed. For example, models of rational planning have, over a few decades, been dismissed and ignored by later writers who emphasized a more emergent or politically shaped view of strategy. Whilst we certainly do not want to slow the intellectual progression of this exciting field by ignoring these paradigmatic shifts, we feel that such shift are, in practice, difficult to spot, characterised as much by latest fad and fashion as they are by the substitution of one theoretical lens for another. So marked are these fashions and fads that many authors have published books simply listing the various perspectives that can be taken toward strategy. Rather grandiosely, these have sometimes been called 'schools of thought', but they do not bear scrutiny as such. They are simply ways of looking at strategy, some of which have become fashionable and some of which have not. In this book, therefore, we set out to see if we could weave together in a coherent way what had previously been cited as incommensurable theoretical approaches to the field and we have deliberately avoided the schools of thought approach. Some may feel this is an overly conservative or, even, wrong-headed approach, but our own experience would tell us otherwise. Our students, too, appreciate the linkages and cross-references we make to different epistemologies, as they try and make sense of strategy and develop the field alongside us. What has emerged is a text which we feel has the following defining characteristics:

♦ **Strong emphasis on strategy in practice:** An innovative approach which is informed by academic research but remains highly practical and 'hands on'. Dedicated chapters on Risk Management, Managing Strategic Change, Strategy and the Learning Organization and Corporate Governance.

♦ **An analytical approach to strategy:** A thorough study of competitive advantage provides students with the level of analysis fundamental to understanding business and corporate level strategy.

♦ **An understanding of the link between strategy, knowledge and technological change, and value and performance**. Value and value-based management is shown as central to strategic management. Three themes are treated explicitly because they are particularly close to the core of strategic management thinking. These are (i) performance assessment; (ii) organizational knowledge, learning and value innovation; and (iii) total quality management and customer value.

♦ **A range of contemporary and relevant cases throughout:** Illustrative case examples and end of chapter cases offer insights into a variety of globally recognized companies such as easyJet, Benetton, Deutsche Post, Airbus, Samsung, Disney, Dell and more.

◆ **A section of longer cases in the Text and Cases Edition** places strategy into a variety of contemporary international contexts and offer students the opportunity to analyse strategic decisions across an array of international businesses including BSkyB, Ikea, Honda, Shell, Nike, and Nokia.

◆ **Clear and well-developed pedagogy:** An introduction to each part orients the student to the landscape of the chapters that follow. To aid learning, each chapter introduces its themes and concepts, and leads the student through the topic with key terms highlighted in bold for easy reference. Case Examples contained within the chapters provide illustrations of strategy in practice within real organizations, and at the end of each chapter, a summary and assignments draw together the overarching themes and test understanding. A concluding Chapter-end Case Study encourages the student to analyze how some of the concepts raised in the chapter can be applied within an organization. See the Guided Tour for more information.

◆ **An unparalleled range of supporting resources**- the book is accompanied by an Online Learning Centre website, www.mcgraw-hill.co.uk/textbooks/mcgee, which provides a range of resources for lecturers and students. Lecturers will find PowerPoint presentations, lecture guides, and case study notes to assist them in teaching with the textbook. The student area contains a wealth of extra resources including test questions; help with studying cases, guide answers to the end of chapter assignments questions and more. For more information see our guide to *Technology to enhance teaching and learning* on the following pages.

Like all books, in the writing, it has had its glory moments and its days of drudgery. But we are pleased that the idea with which we began – to try and examine a holistic approach to strategy – was not dismissed as we progressed with the writing. Indeed the reverse was true. We became more committed to the approach as we wrote. And it proved useful, both to ourselves and to our students at all levels from undergraduate to post-experience. As authors, we could be argued to represent something of an eclectic approach. We have tried to synthesize the perspectives and epistemologies of three very different scholars, one who began in mathematics and statistics, a second in economics and a third in organization theory. At least at this level of analysis, we are an example of the inclusive approach to strategy that we present in this book. The final judgement will, of course, be with you, the reader. We hope you enjoy your journey through its pages and, in the process, become as enthusiastic about this area of study as we remain. Happy reading.

John McGee
Howard Thomas
David Wilson   **January 2005**

List of cases

At the end of each chapter from Chapter 3 onwards, you will find a case study that explores the themes and concepts covered on the preceding pages, with study questions. The following cases are featured:

1. The Harder Hard Sell (Ch 3)

There are significant new challenges facing the advertising industry: traditional methods of advertising seem no longer to work – does this mean that the potential to differentiate consumer products and services is diminishing?

2. Made in Japan (Ch 4)

Japan is threatened by competition from low-cost Chinese competitors. What implications does this have for Japanese firms and their competitive advantages? Is it possible for firms to locate in several different countries so as to gain from local comparative advantage without suffering from the disadvantages? In other words can they have their cake and eat it? What can national governments do about this?

3. The Novotel Value Chain (Ch 5)

The strategy of a hotel chain is displayed in its value chain. This shows how the configuration of the value chain relates to competitive advantage and illustrates the importance of the coordination and integration of the different elements in the value chain.

4. Mobile Telephone and the move from 2G to 3G (Ch 6)

The advent of a new technology requires a new business model. This describes how a business model is derived from strategy and the way new technology changes the business model. The example illustrates how the business model is directly derived from the underlying competitive strategy. It also demonstrates how successive technology platforms do require different business models

5. How Dell Keeps from Stumbling (Ch 7)

How supply chain management can be the key to strategy and to sustained competitive advantage. Dell's strategy is well known for its management of suppliers but what is less well known is the direct impact this has on its value proposition to customers.

6. Brand extension with Jacuzzi – Armani (Ch 7)

Should luxury-goods firms go into the hotel business? This case discusses how brands can form the basis for a diversification strategy. It also looks at Armani's businesses in terms of the core competences that underpin a luxury brand. The case allows discussion of the limits to brand strength and also the extent to which luxury brands depend on their founders, such as Giorgio Armani.

7. Stelios Haji-Ioannou (Ch 8)

How important is the entrepreneur? An interview with Stelios shows how his personality and drive is reflected in easyJet's business strategy and operational processes. But is leadership the same as strategy? And how does Stelios compare with other entrepreneurs e.g. Anita Roddick in chapter 21 and Giorgio Armani in chapter 6?

8. Old Dogs, New tricks (Ch 9)

Conventional thinking now holds that conglomerates are undesirable and that industrial restructuring should lead to more highly focused business portfolios. This is examined in the context of major German manufacturing companies. How much notice are industrial giants such as Siemens and Hoechst taking of the antipathy of international investors for industrial diversification?

9. The Battle for the Magic Kingdom: Comcast's bid to acquire Disney (Ch 10)

Comcast, America's biggest cable company, has launched an audacious hostile bid for Disney. The timing is shrewd, for Michael Eisner, Disney's boss, is under attack for poor governance and disappointing results. This illustrates the difficulties faced by hostile bids but also the way in which their targets need to organize their defences.

10. International law firms: getting the right global balance (Ch 11)

London firms want to be more global; New York firms want to be more profitable. Ultimately, more big global law firms will probably emerge to provide services for the international marketplace. But the legal profession does not look as if it will go the way of accounting, with just a few firms dominating the market everywhere.

11. How good is Google: the challenges faced by the search engine (Ch 12)

Will Google become one of the few valuable Internet survivors, joining Amazon and above all eBay? Google the new-age advertising agency makes money, but it is Google the search engine that builds the consumer brand that makes the ad agency powerful. Google's board has decided to bring Google to the stock market next spring in an effort to translate the search engine power into money. But, does Google really have a viable strategy?

12. Browser Wars: Netscape's new Gecko browser challenges Microsoft (Ch 12)

Remember the browser wars, when Netscape and Microsoft fought for dominance of the web? In the end, Microsoft prevailed by bundling its browser with its Windows operating system. Now a new browser war is under way, as software firms compete to provide the browsers for 'information appliances' such as set-top boxes, handheld computers and smart phones. Such devices are still in their infancy, but they are widely expected eventually to outnumber PCs. So the stakes in this new browser war are high. And this time round, the battlefield looks very different.

At the end of the Text and Cases edition of this book, you will find a selection of longer cases to explore.

Guided Tour

Part openers

At the beginning of each part, the authors introduce the topics and themes covered throughout the five Parts of the text.

Chapter introduction

Each introduction section indicates the key ideas that will be discussed within each chapter, linking the chapter to those surrounding it and explaining how the ideas fit together.

Key terms

These are highlighted throughout each chapter and a list of terms at the end of each chapter provides key points for ease of reference.

Case boxes

Each chapter contains a number of brief examples in Case Boxes that serve as illustrations of strategy in action. The examples provide useful insights that highlight the strategy decisions under discussion in the chapter.

Figures and tables

Each chapter provides a number of figures and tables to help you to visualize the various economic models, and to illustrate and summarize important concepts.

End of chapter summary

This briefly reviews and reinforces the main topics you will have covered in each chapter to ensure you have acquired a solid understanding of the key topics.

Assignments and questions

These questions encourage you to review and apply the knowledge you have acquired from each chapter and can be undertaken to test your understanding.

End of chapter cases

Longer case examples at the end of each chapter provide students with more in-depth discussions of organizations through which to explore the ideas from the chapter and apply their strategic decision making skills.

Case section

The case section at the back of the text and cases book provides a range of case studies from a variety of industries and organizations, offering students real business situations around which to explore, analyse and critique strategy in action.

Technology to enhance learning and teaching

Visit www.mcgraw-hill.co.uk/textbooks/mcgee today

Online Learning Centre (OLC)

After completing each chapter, log on to the supporting Online Learning Centre website. Take advantage of the study tools offered to reinforce the material you have read in the text, and to develop your knowledge of marketing in a fun and effective way.

Resources for students include:

- Student test questions testing your grasp of the concepts in the book
- A guide to how to interpret case studies
- Glossary of key terms from the textbook
- Further reading suggestions for research and assignments
- Chapter by Chapter Learning objectives
- Suggested answers to the end of chapter assignments
- Web links and more

Also available for lecturers:

- Case study teaching notes to support the cases in the textbook
- Lecture outlines to assist lecturers in teaching with the new book
- PowerPoint slides for presentation
- PowerPoint slides for print
- Figures and tables from the textbook
- A Guide to how to teach using case studies
- Tutorial exercises, essay questions and guide answers
- Further mini case study updates, exercises and solutions

For lecturers: Primis Content Centre

If you need to supplement your course with additional cases or content, create a personalized e-Book for your students. Visit www.primiscontentcenter.com or e-mail primis_euro@mcgraw-hill.com for more information.

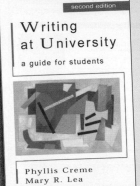

Study Skills

Open University Press publishes guides to study, research and exam skills, to help undergraduate and postgraduate students through their university studies.

Visit www.openup.co.uk/ss/ to see the full selection.

Computing Skills

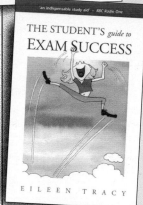

If you'd like to brush up on your Computing skills, we have a range of titles covering MS Office applications such as Word, Excel, PowerPoint, Access and more.

Get a £2 discount off these titles by entering the promotional code **app** when ordering online at www.mcgraw-hill.co.uk/app.

Acknowledgements

Our thanks go to the following people who have helped us during the writing of this textbook:

Duncan Angwin, Sue Bridgewater, Derek Condon, Ben Knight, Tanya Sammut-Bonnici and Chris Smith for their invaluable assistance in preparing the text, and to Duncan Angwin, Stephen Hodge, Ian Maude, Robert Salter, Tanya Sammut-Bonnici and Bridgette Sullivan-Taylor for creating new case material.

We also thank the McGraw-Hill team who have encouraged and motivated us, channeled our enthusiasms and focused our efforts – Max Elvey, Caroline Howell, Catriona King, Kate Mason and Melissa Rosati.

Our thanks go to the following reviewers for their comments at various stages in the text's development:

Andy Adcroft, University of Surrey
Veronique Ambrosini, University of Cranfield
Lisa Barton, University of Cardiff
Bruce Cronin, University of Greenwich
James Cunningham, NUI Galway, Republic of Ireland
Leanne Cutcher, University of Sydney, Australia
David Jennings Nottingham Trent
Judith Jordan, University of the West of England
David Lal, Robert Gordon University
Lester Lloyd Reason, Anglia Polytechnic University
Nick Potter, University of Birmingham
John Rudd, Aston University
Shafeek Sha, Rhodes University, South Africa
Gordon Smith, University of Plymouth
Iraj Tavakoli, University of Brighton

We would also like to thank Judith Jordan, of the University of the West of England, for her work in developing the support materials that accompany this textbook, and for her helpful advice as the book developed.

Finally, we thank the following individuals and organizations that granted permission for material to be reproduced within the textbook:

The Economist Newspaper Limited
INSEAD
John Wiley and Sons, Inc.
Palgrave Macmillan
IMD
The Telegraph Group Limited
Ivey Publishing
Institute of Directors
Professor Bernard Taylor, Henley Management College
Elsevier
Kogan Page Publishers
Blackwell Publishing
Westburn Publishers
Simon and Schuster Publishers
Rosalind Beere, Trinity College Dublin
Peter McNamara, University College Dublin
Centre for Asian Business Cases
Harvard Business School Publishing
Professor Ashok Som, ESSEC Business School, Paris

Every effort has been made to obtain permission from copyright holders to reproduce material within this textbook and to acknowledge these sources correctly. We would be pleased to hear from copyright holders whom it has not been possible for us to contact.

Part 1

An introduction to strategy

Part contents

In this part you will find the following chapters:

Introduction

This section forms the key introductory theme music both to the concepts of strategy and to the orientation of this book. In the opening two chapters we try to cover both the basics of strategy – what it is and how we might conceive of it analytically – and how strategy and organization can interact, mutually influencing what happens in practice. This section also presents our own theoretical model (depicted in Figure 1.6) which attempts to show how quite often disparate perspectives on strategy (for example planning, performance, execution and feedback) can be seen as a coherent system. In this respect, these opening chapters form the essential foundation of the book and help inform all the sections and chapters that follow. Each section is a breakdown of the overall framework (Figure 1.6). You will see that at the beginning of each section of the book we have depicted which parts of the systemic framework are being emphasized and addressed. The final chapter of the book then attempts to reassemble these component parts into our overall view of strategy and the strategy process.

Chapter 1 points out the contested terrain of strategy, in particular its various definitions and descriptions. Showing how different perspectives on strategy developed, the chapter then provides examples and techniques for assessing strategy. Beginning with planning, the chapter outlines the basics of the planning process and shows the basic analytical tools which can help underpin future plans and trajectories. Taking the perspective that a large proportion of strategy researchers have viewed it largely as a question of alignment (or fit) of the organization with its environment, the chapter covers the various positioning tools and perspectives that can help determine future actions (strategies). Knowing where the organization is positioned in relation to its operating environment allows strategists to plan either for achieving a better (more competitive) position or to try to make it more difficult for others to enter the market and compete. The chapter concludes its analysis of planning by looking at the public face of strategic planning for many organizations. This public face is captured in the notions of goals and mission. A few examples of mission statements shows how such goal-oriented statements can be the overall guide of strategic decisions taken in the organization. Such guiding can take the form of a statement about future economic positioning (we want to be number one in the industry) or can take the form of expressed values (we want to be seen as environmentally friendly and socially responsible).

Nevertheless, we know some curious things can happen when planned strategies are implemented. As the popular expression has it, there can be many a slip between cup and lip. The rest of Chapter 1 and all of Chapter 2 then deal with these questions of what happens when we view strategy as embedded in a particular organizational context. For example, viewing an organization as a constellation of resources (people, knowledge, financial and so on) reveals that some organizations are better endowed with such resources than others. They have more people with more skills and knowledge and are able to resource strategic decisions to a greater extent than other organizations. Taking this perspective leads us to the resource-based view of the organization and we discuss this in some detail.

Similarly, we know that strategy is not always a linear process. By this we mean that strategy is not necessarily a long period of thinking (planning) followed by a long period of acting (implementation). In many cases, strategists implement decisions without much (or, sometimes, any) planning. Decisions emerge from an organization, driven by a wide range of influences such as history (what strategists have done in the past), organizational values (the way we do things around here) and knee-jerk reactions to external threats. Planning, if it exists at all, is then retro-fitted to the process. This debate over whether strategic decisions are planned or emerge is covered in detail in Part 1.

Chapter 2 hinges around what many researchers have termed the more 'process' views of strategy. Taking the view that planning a trajectory is necessary but not sufficient to ensure strategic decisions follow automatically, the chapter shows how animation is as important as orientation for strategists. Animation examines the interplay between strategic intention and how managers interpret the environment, providing a context in which organizational members can become enthused and committed to a particular set of tasks.

The chapter also examines in detail debates over the appropriate levels of analysis we might adopt to understand strategy. In particular, recent work has stressed the importance of relatively micro approaches (what managers think, do and say) over the more macro approaches (level of competition, industry characteristics). Taking the individual as pivotal, the chapter shows how we can conceive of strategy as being essentially a process of individual *interpretation* of events and actions. This view has gathered momentum over recent years and it draws on classic work in the 1950s and 60s about behavioural theories of the firm as well as classic work on strategic decision making in the 1970s and 80s. The point of such debates is that, ultimately, strategists have to make a choice between the extremes of voluntarism and determinism. Determinism implies that all managerial action is shaped and, in the extreme, pre-determined by the context in which they operate. Voluntarism is the opposite view, arguing that strategists can act freely and without environmental constraints. Depending on which perspective you take (or what mixture of each), your view of how strategy processes actually work will be completely different.

Finally, Chapter 2 emphasizes the important role of history. Where an organization and its members have been in the past will have an influence upon its present activities. The longer an organization has been in operation, the longer will be its history of strategic decisions and it is likely to have built up a substantial repertoire of standard responses and actions to particular situations. Organizations can easily become programmed to the degree that they are more accurately described as a collection of ready-made solutions looking for new problems, rather than there being any proactive approach towards taking strategic decisions. Having read both chapters, you should then re-visit Figure 1.6. Here you will recognize both the detail and the bigger pictures of strategy. We have tried to show these as a dynamic and self-reinforcing model that also acts as a frame and as a lens to the rest of the book.

Chapter 1

The concept of strategy

Introduction

Why another book on strategy? Given the huge number of books on the subject, an initial conclusion might be that all that needs to be communicated has already been written. There is some truth in this statement if one assumes that the nature and definitions of strategy are pretty well aligned no matter which authors are consulted, or if one assumes that the theoretical and practical aspects of understanding strategy are uncontested. However, congruence in any of these areas is very difficult to find. Strategy remains one of the most contested and ill-defined concepts in management theory. As Magretta (2003) states:

> . . . of all the concepts in management, strategy is the one that attracts the most attention and generates the most controversy. Almost everyone agrees that it is important. Almost no-one agrees on what it is.

This book will acknowledge some of the key debates concerning how scholars and practitioners have viewed and practised strategy, but it will not dwell in great detail on either the historical development of the field or on the intense debates which have emerged from five or so decades of theoretical and empirical work. This has indeed been achieved in many textbooks on strategy already (see, for example, Hussey 1998 for a conventional history of strategy, and Cummings and Wilson 2003 for a relatively less conventional mapping of the field). Our intention here is to review briefly some of the key shapers and characteristics of the field and then to see to what extent it is possible both to acknowledge and to combine competing perspectives to create a more holistic approach to understanding strategy. This book analyses the meaning of strategy by breaking it down into its component parts, namely: its *external logic* – how the organization positions itself relative to its external context; its *internal logic* – the levels of the organization at which strategy has different meanings and what distinctive resources and competences it must acquire; its *performance over time* – distinguishing between achievement of long-term objectives, meeting milestones along the way, and preserving short-term stability; and, finally, its *managerial requirements* – the role of general managers and how strategy is planned, managed, monitored and maintained. The next section tries to clarify what we mean by strategy in this book by building upon and trying to synthesize the approaches of key works in the field.

1.1 Key definitions of strategy

In a conference at Harvard Business School in 1963, Cook (reported in Bower 1982) argued that 'the charter of business policy is to focus on the life and death issues of central interest to top management . . . to help top management to deal with these issues effectively, profitably and morally'. Legge (2003), in her chapter on strategy as organizing, points out when discussing Henry Mintzberg's (1994) work that, in general, 'if you ask someone to define strategy, you will likely be told that strategy is a plan or something equivalent – a direction, a guide, a course of action into the future, a path to get from here to there'. Of course, Mintzberg *et al.* (1998) argue that this definition of **intended strategy** fails to recognize strategy as an emergent process, which is best seen as a pattern in a stream of decisions. Strategy, for Mintzberg, is what emerges from actions rather than something planned in advance or in anticipation of future contexts. We explore this planned versus emergent aspect of strategy in later sections of this chapter.

Prahalad and Hamel (1990), have also been very instrumental in influencing how we view strategy. They conceptualized strategy in terms of **strategic intent**, which they define as providing an overarching strategic direction. Strategic intent is, in essence, about winning in a competitive game. This leads to a focus on strategy as a process for reinforcing intent by developing the core competences of a corporation, and leading and managing change.

They also propose the viewpoint of 'strategy as stretch and leverage', in which the strategist sees the advantage of breaking the strategic frame and leveraging the critical core competences in an innovative and distinctive manner. Indeed, the concept of strategy as innovation is dominant in their current thinking and they stress the need for strategists to embrace radical innovation and innovate to stay in front of the competitive game. Their thinking in this respect mirrors that of Christensen (1997) who has discussed the role of the disruptive innovation and the new economy in shaping strategy in the evolving competitive landscape.

Perhaps the definition of strategy that is most common in the field is that attributed to the renowned Harvard business historian Alfred D. Chandler in his landmark book *Strategy and Structure*. The Chandler (1963) definition characterizes strategy as:

> *the determination of the basic long-term goals and objective of an enterprise and the adoption of courses of action and the allocation of resources necessary for carrying out these goals.*

This is the classical view of strategy, very much rational in analysis and following militaristic traditions, including those specified in the Japanese strategy book authored by Sun Tzu entitled *The Art of War* (1990). Quinn (1980), in an equally famous book entitled *Strategies for Change: Logical Incrementalism*, follows Chandler's case study tradition and talks about strategy in a more process-oriented way. Quinn's definition is:

> *the pattern or plan that integrates an organization's major goals, policies and action sequences into a cohesive whole. A well-formulated strategy helps to marshal and allocate an organization's resources into a unique and viable posture based on its relative internal competences and shortcomings, anticipated changes in the environment and contingent moves by intelligent opponents.*

Porter (1987), the Harvard Business School strategy professor, who has also had a tremendous influence on the field of strategic management and competitive strategy, picks up the themes of being different and achieving strategic coherence in organizational strategy. He argues, therefore, that competitive strategy is about being different (i.e. effective strategic positioning). It means deliberately choosing a different set of activities to deliver a unique mix of value. However, a strategic position is not sustainable unless there are trade-offs with other positions. Trade-offs create the need for choice (making strategic decisions) and protect against repositioners and straddlers. Strategy is about combining activities that are complementary and reinforcing. This strategic 'coherence' among many activities is fundamental not only to achieving competitive advantage, but also to the sustainability of that advantage. It is harder for a rival to match an array of interlocked activities than it is merely to match a particular sales force approach, match a process technology or replicate a set of product features. Positions built on a series of coherent activities are far more sustainable than those built on individual activities.

Although the previous definitions might seem at odds with one another (even mutually exclusive in some cases, for example between planned and emergent strategies) there are some common elements which we can identify to help us clarify the analysis a little. Common elements in these viewpoints include the following:

- Strategy as a means of establishing organizational purpose.
- Strategy as a definition of the competitive domains of the firm and the organizational context.
- Strategy as a response to the complexity of external opportunities and threats and internal strengths and weaknesses in order to achieve sustainable competitive advantage.
- Strategy as a way to define managerial tasks and processes with corporate, business and functional perspectives.
- Strategy as a system involving a coherent, unifying and integrative systematic pattern of decisions.
- Strategy as a definition of the economic and non-economic contributions which the firm intends to make to its stakeholders.
- Strategy as an architecture to develop the distinctive competences of an organization.
- Strategy as a vehicle for determining investments in tangible and intangible resources to develop the core capabilities which lead to sustainable advantages.
- Strategy as an expression of strategic intent; stretching the organization to innovate, leverage resources and develop new skills.

These common elements form the backbone of this book. They include the economic analysis of strategy to help plan and inform strategic decisions (Part 2); the analysis of strategy as both a feature of organizational positioning and capabilities, especially in a changing context of globalization and the new economy (Part 3); the analysis of strategy as a series of processes in which decisions have to be implemented and put into practice and which require an understanding of how organizations and individuals change and develop (Part 4); and a view of strategy as monitoring, improving and developing, helping data feedback into the next wave of strategy formulation (Part 5). Complex though all these factors are, the basics of strategy are relatively easily summarized and described. We examine these in the next section.

1.2 The basics of strategy

Figure 1.1 depicts the main basic dynamics and key factors to be taken into consideration when we begin to examine what we mean by strategy. At the most basic level, we mean that actions and decisions need to be analysed and taken in order for the organization to survive and thrive as conditions develop and change around it. These conditions (the external environment in Figure 1.1) comprise a wide range of factors. They include characteristics of the industry (for example the typewriter industry is today completely different from when electronic typewriters were state of the art); characteristics of the market (this may change from being benign to highly competitive and back again); sustainable development is now something all strategists have to consider and political conditions may change the context of business and government markedly (the impact of global terrorism, for example). We take each of the key factors and examine them in more detail in the following sections.

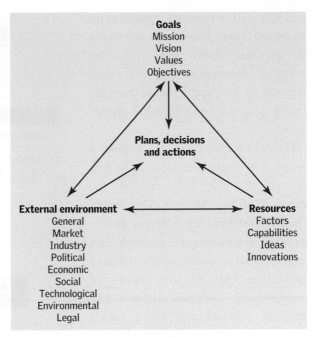

Figure 1.1 The basic dynamics of strategy

1.2.1 Plans, decisions and actions

The notion of planning heralds the beginnings of strategy. Many authors, such as Quinn (1980) and Cummings and Wilson (2003), have traced the military genesis of the term strategy from the Greeks and the Macedonians. The word 'strategos' began as a term describing a commanding role in the army (a general, for example) and by the time of Alexander the Great (330 BC) had become the word which described the successful deployment of troops to overcome the enemy and to the system of governance which facilitated this planning. It is this combined notion of planned deployment and governance which pervades the planning schools of strategy. Authors such as Ansoff (1965; 1972), building on the earlier work of the Stanford Research Institute, epitomize the translation of this planning orientation to the strategic conduct of business and the view of the general manager as a 'strategist' (coining the phrase 'strategic management' in 1972).

Most of today's organizations have some form of corporate plan or strategic plan and some form of planning process. In terms of Figure 1.1, strategic planning is the process by which the firm organizes its resources and actions in relation to an **external environment** in order to achieve its **goals** or **objectives**. This is usually a formal rather than an informal process, the key elements of which are outlined in Figure 1.2.

Planning is conducted in a very hierarchical and formal manner. It is typically top down with the direction and energy being supplied by top management. The process is iterative and the cycle is repeated (typically) on an annual basis. Planning horizons are in practice about three years in Western companies but this does depend on the length of product life cycles and the life of capital equipment.

Formal analysis would go through a number of stages in sequence. The first is typically the statement of the **mission** of the business. This would then be followed by a review of the external environment in which, for example, the economics of the industry would be assessed, the nature of markets and customers analysed, and broader political and social trends identified. In parallel there would be a review of the **internal environment** of the organization. This covers basic strengths and weaknesses, core competences and capability assessments. Based on these, views of the strengths and weaknesses and opportunities and threats (the well-known SWOT analysis which covers the reviews of the internal and external environments) are used as a starting point for formulating the

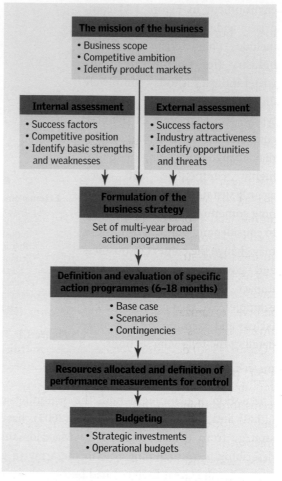

Figure 1.2 A typical planned, formal process of strategy formulation

strategy. From the basic business strategy will come a definition of the specific action programmes required to put the strategy into practice. This is what is usually called the business plan although the way in which this term is used varies widely between firms. This business plan is then submitted to an investment committee (this also goes under a variety of names) for resource allocation along with definition of performance milestones. After the investment expenditures are agreed, budgets are specified and agreed throughout the organization.

However, any person who has had experience of the above process in action in any organization may well have a wry smile on their face as they read the above seemingly rational and militaristic procedure. Great in theory, but never happens in practice might summarize their feelings. According to Mintzberg and Waters (1985) some strategies may be planned, at least in their first stages, but many more just simply *emerge* in an organization without being consciously intended or being deliberate acts. We might make sense of the *pattern* of these actions later and call them a strategy, but we do so with the luxury of hindsight. We construct a logic which was never intended in the first place. **Emergent strategies** can be seen as responses to unexpected opportunities and problems and are usually developed from the locations at which

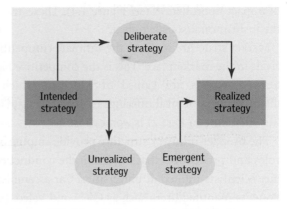

Figure 1.3 Intended and emergent strategies

business-level strategies are usually implemented, i.e. within business units and not at corporate headquarters. The pure definition of emergence requires the absence of any intentions. This is too strong for most occasions but, as Mintzberg and Waters (1985) observe, organizations come close to pure emergent strategies when an environment directly imposes a pattern of actions on them.

Quinn (1980) developed logical incrementalism as a way of explaining the combination of longer-term plans and targets with evolutionary, learning-based patterns of movement on the way (patterns of decisions which emerge). This is an attractive explanation because it seems to combine rational resource allocation thinking with practical learning by doing. Quinn argues that 'properly managed, it is a conscious, purposeful, pro-active, executive practice'.

The twin lenses of intentions and emergence are useful tools with which to analyse strategy since neither as a pure form is likely to be observable. Instead there is a continuum on which different blends can be seen. Figure 1.3 illustrates intentions being formulated as deliberate strategies, some of which come to fruition. But we also see a simultaneous pressure from circumstances producing a stream of emergent (but purposeful) thinking. **Realized strategy** is a blend of intentions and emergence which can be interpreted by reference to the strength of pressure from the external environment – a kind of environmental determinism.

1.2.2 The external environment

The external context of strategic decisions is very broad ranging. In principle, it can include anything and everything that might have an effect on decisions. We could include governments, international trade organizations, buyer and supplier markets, competitors, trade associations, civil servants, and the impersonal progression of science and technology. In order to provide some structure to this variety of influences, we can think of three regions of impact upon firm A (*see* Figure 1.4). These are market structure, industry structure, and the institutional/social context.

Market structure includes the intimate competition for the customers' attention between rivals in the marketplace. This is the competitive battleground within which the firm's long-term objectives are gained or lost and which provides the basis for assessing the distinctiveness of rival offerings to customers. It is here that competitive advantage (which we will define in Part 2) is won or lost.

The broader industry structure provides inputs of traded goods, knowledge and technical rules and procedures that condition the conduct of firms. Thus, pharmaceutical firms will hire scientists trained at universities. Car assemblers such as Ford and GM buy from components manufacturers such as GKN and Valeo. Industry trade associations stipulate rules of conduct and may conduct joint research. Distribution channels act across the board as intermediate customers and sometimes as powerful buyers in their own right. This industry structure has a deep impact on the underlying economic possibilities open to the participants in the market structure.

The broader institutional and social structure sets out the rules of the game in terms of what is morally, legally and ethically possible as well as setting the political terms of reference within which firms are obliged to operate.

These regions represent zones of influence for firms. Most influence is exercised within the market structure and least within the broad institutional context – at least as a general rule. However, firms see it as at least possible that they might shape the rules of the game by seeking to promote changes at various levels. But firms might also see their sphere of

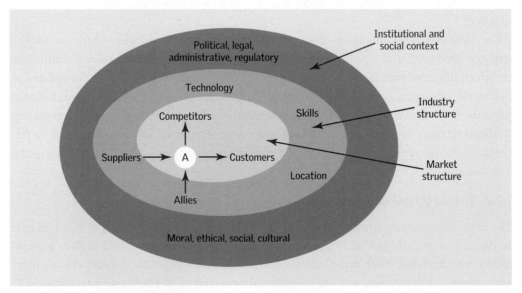

Figure 1.4 The external environment

influence as tightly focused within their market environment and subject, without any recourse, to powerful forces from elsewhere. One way for firms to assess exposure to forces within this broad context is through a PEST analysis. This is an analysis of political, economic, social and technological forces. Occasionally, specific aspects of dealing in particular national legal systems (for example) can be added to this analysis, but for simplicity they are excluded in the following description. Figure 1.5 provides an illustration of the variety of forces that can be identified via a PEST analysis.

In order to make sense of this 'shopping list' some analysis is needed to identify the really significant influences. This involves assigning probabilities and possible outcomes to each event and calculating an 'expected value' (technically the probability multiplied by the outcome). In practice this requires considerable judgement because many of the events can only be described in qualitative terms and because managers may have little, or very partial, information on each factor. We need also to identify ways in which the probabilities of the events and the outcomes of the events might be moderated by management action.

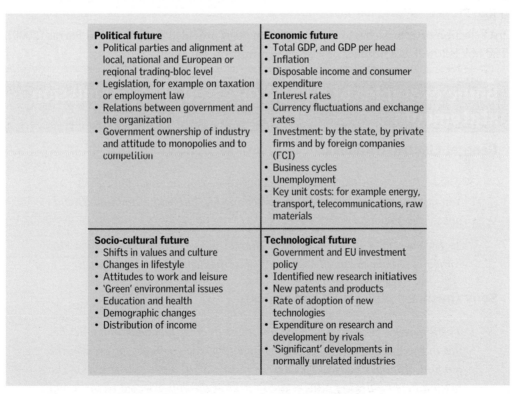

Political future
- Political parties and alignment at local, national and European or regional trading-bloc level
- Legislation, for example on taxation or employment law
- Relations between government and the organization
- Government ownership of industry and attitude to monopolies and to competition

Economic future
- Total GDP, and GDP per head
- Inflation
- Disposable income and consumer expenditure
- Interest rates
- Currency fluctuations and exchange rates
- Investment: by the state, by private firms and by foreign companies (FCI)
- Business cycles
- Unemployment
- Key unit costs: for example energy, transport, telecommunications, raw materials

Socio-cultural future
- Shifts in values and culture
- Changes in lifestyle
- Attitudes to work and leisure
- 'Green' environmental issues
- Education and health
- Demographic changes
- Distribution of income

Technological future
- Government and EU investment policy
- Identified new research initiatives
- New patents and products
- Rate of adoption of new technologies
- Expenditure on research and development by rivals
- 'Significant' developments in normally unrelated industries

Figure 1.5 An example of a PEST Analysis

1.2.3 Goals

As Quinn (1980) observes, goals (or objectives) are statements about 'what is to be achieved and when results are to be accomplished'. Goals do not address the question of *how* these objectives are to be achieved. They are basic statements of desired future objectives.

To communicate goals, organizations typically provide detailed statements of their strategic intent and their major goals in the form of **mission statements**. These are often criticized for their vacuity – indeed, one test of a good mission statement is said to be if employees can recite it without ironic laughter breaking out. It is possible to characterize two approaches to mission statements. One expresses mission in terms of *philosophy* and *ethics*, thereby widening the band of actors that are relevant to the long-term future of the company and capturing the notion of stakeholders. It also captures those forms of corporate behaviour that have implications for the social good and which are not reflected in the pricing mechanisms in marketplaces. The second approach expresses mission as *strategy*, an intellectual discourse that defines the firm's commercial *rationale* and *target markets*. Overall, mission is supposed to answer the question, What is our business and what should it be?

A selection of approaches to mission statements is provided by Collins and Porras (2000). The box below lists a number of well-known mission statements.

Some examples of goals expressed through mission statements

General Electric (rationale)

The first step is for the company to define its destiny in broad but clear terms. You need an overarching message, something big, but simple and understandable. (Jack Welch)

To become No. 1 or No. 2 in every market we serve and revolutionize this company to have the speed and agility of a small enterprise. (Jack Welch)

Sony (business philosophy and ethics)

*The difference between our efforts and those of other Japanese companies lies not in the level of technology, or the quality of the engineers, or even in the amount of money budgeted for development (about 5 per cent of sales). The main difference lies in ... the establishment of mission-oriented research and proper **targets**. Many other companies give their researchers full freedom. We don't; we find an aim, a very real and clear **target** and then establish the* *necessary task forces to get the job done ... once the commitment to go ahead is made, **never** give up. This pervades all the research and development work at Sony.*

Mission as business objectives

To build a car for the great multitude ... (Ford, Henry Ford 1907)

To change the image around the world of Japanese products as poor in quality. (Sony, Akio Morita 1950)

To make my little Newport store the best, most profitable variety store in Arkansas within five years. (Walmart, Sam Walton 1945)

To become a $1 billion company in four years. (Walmart, Sam Walton 1977)

To double the number of stores and increase the dollar volume per square foot by 60 per cent by year 2000. (Walmart, Sam Walton 1990)

To build the airplane (the 747) even if it takes the entire resources of the company. (Boeing 1969)

Less well-known mission statements also reflect and try to tap into the values of potential customers. Consider the mission statement from Don Hewitson.

Don Hewitson's wine bar: The Cork & Bottle

A MISSION STATEMENT
'LIFE'S TOO SHORT TO DRINK BORING WINE'

Nowadays most wine can be relied upon to be an agreeable tipple. None of the gut-searing acidic whites or over-ripe, jammy oxidised reds which were all I could afford when I arrived in Blighty in 1972. Elton John was on Top Of The Pops with 'Rocket Man' that very day ... and the charts have gone down the tubes ever since!

BUT ... and it is a 'big' BUT. In the desire for squeaky clean wines at as cheap as possible prices, have we thrown the baby out with the bathwater? I didn't develop a passion for wine in order to drink virtually the same taste sensation every time ... I love the bewildering variety of styles and flavours.

STUART WALTON, in his excellent book 'YOU HEARD IT THROUGH THE GRAPEVINE' (Aurum Press £9.99) sums up the desire for conformity brilliantly by blaming the High Street.

'What has happened in the last few years . . . is the wholesale mediocratisation of wine in the UK . . . As monotony begins to set in, there is the Safebury' wine-buyer at the door, cheque-book in hand and ready to spread this monotony all over the UK high street.'

These wines can be avoided, especially when you are a small operator in a business striving for globalisation. There are thousands of wine producers out there, in all countries, with no interest in producing bland, boring wines. Even if they make wines in sufficient quantities to satisfy the High Street chains, they are not prepared to shave their costs to fit supermarket price points. These days supermarkets invariably require a major financial contribution (a fee to be on their shelves, although they do put it a little less like the Kray twins, it's basically the same approach to business).

My suppliers wouldn't recognise a 'marketing budget' if they fell over one! They are my mates. I trust them implicitly. They are a disparate bunch of individuals dedicated to producing the best wines possible . . . I'll drink to that!

Salut Don

This is a 'Mission Statement' written on the inside page of an eight-page pamphlet entitled *Wines To Go* – an order form for customers. The Cork & Bottle is a very well-known wine bar in Leicester Square, London, founded by an Australian whose original mission was to bring Australian and New Zealand wines to the British drinking public. It represents an approach to mission statements which is very different from those illustrated earlier. For one thing it is included in a selling/marketing document which is to be read by potential customers. But the main difference lies in the style and content of the narrative. It sets out clear values which are intended to engage with potential customers who share the same values (the charts have gone down the tubes since Elton John's 'Rocket Man') and the statement also acts as both an assessment of the competition (supermarket wines) and as an ethical comment upon them ('like the Kray twins'). Finally, the statement tells the consumer something about the way in which the supply chain is managed (trust – 'they are my mates'). It is also considerably longer than most mission statements, making it suitable for inclusion in a leaflet, but not as useful as a single-sentence strap line to describe the whole organization.

1.2.4 Resources

During the 1980s, the view that organizational resources were important became known as the **resource-based view** (RBV). Its arguments are deceptively simple. An organization has, develops or acquires a range of competences which can then be mobilized by strategists to gain an advantage on the competition. The origins of this way of thinking about strategy can be traced back to Penrose (1959). She adopted what was then something of a unique stance against the conception of the firm by her fellow economists, who had concentrated on conditions external to the firm (such as demand) as drivers of strategy and growth. Penrose took the opposite view, arguing that an organization can be viewed as a collection of resources (in her case she focused particularly on the entrepreneurial resource) which are the drivers of strategy and growth rather than external factors.

In the late 1950s, this was a radical view, but by the time Andrews (1980) had talked about identifying corporate competence and Prahalad and Hamel (1990) had published their article on the core competence of the organization, the RBV had become established. The argument is that strategists can build and mobilize resources which, if unique enough, can bring huge rewards to the organization. One of the most famous examples of this is the 3M Corporation. This organization valued the capacity of its staff to innovate, allowing them up to 25 per cent of company time in which to experiment, regardless of whether the outcome was successful or not. The result of one of these experiments was the Post-It note. Born from an adhesive which did not stick very well (in an organization dedicated to finding better and stronger adhesives) the idea looked initially doomed. But a use for this low-grade adhesive was found by attaching it to small pieces of paper. It could be stuck to paper and other delicate products as a marker, or with a note scribbled on it, and could be removed years later without damaging the paper.

Curiously, no customers were begging 3M or any other organization to produce such sticky notes. In terms of pure economics, there was no *demand* to drive creation of the product. Rather, 3M had produced something that customers did not even know they needed (yet). Here is a core competence according to Prahalad and Hamel (1990). It is the ability to produce something customers need but have never imagined. Conceiving of the firm as a collection of competences allows strategies to be planned 'inside–out'. That is, from the inside of the organization, out to its external environment (markets and industries). In turn, feedback from customers and demand could identify additional competences which might be needed (and may indicate which current core competences might be redundant).

Prahalad and Hamel (1990) define core competences as:

> the collective learning in the organization, especially how to co-ordinate diverse production skills and integrate multiple streams of technologies . . .

For example, Honda's core competence in engine and power trains gives it a clear advantage in car, motorcycle, lawnmower and generator businesses. There are three characteristics of a core competence. Competences should:

- provide potential access to a wide variety of markets;
- make a significant contribution to the perceived customer benefits of the end product;
- be difficult for competitors to imitate.

Prahalad and Hamel (1990) argue that very few organizations are likely to build world leadership in more than five or six competences. Firms may have many capabilities (more than 20 or 30) but they have not aggregated these into the key four or five competences needed for success and growth. Not knowing what are an organization's core competences can create difficulties for strategists. For example, they may outsource a function or operation not realizing that they have saved some costs at the expense of losing a core competence. Prahalad and Hamel (1990) cite the example of Honda, which would never outsource its manufacturing or design to an outside company, versus Chrysler, which has done so. Honda has preserved its core competence in engine and power trains while Chrysler has not. Of course, it is difficult to devise an effective outsourcing strategy if the core competences of the organization have not previously been identified. The crown jewels of the company could easily be outsourced this way in what might seem like a simple (and rational) cost-saving exercise.

So Figure 1.1 provides the basic factors in understanding strategy. Core competences (resources) allow strategists to have strategic intent (goals). These are orientated toward the external environment (market or socio-economic conditions) and these become organizational goals which are often communicated to stakeholders by means of mission statements. However, conceptualizing strategy is a little more complicated than these three factors (important thought they are). The next sections show how we can build upon Figure 1.1 to understand strategy a little more fully.

1.3 Towards a systemic concept of strategy

In this section, we will develop a concept of strategy that builds on Figure 1.1 and which guides the rest of this book. Strategy, as a topic of study, concentrates very much on the situational problems of the general manager (or top management team or CEO). Strategy is different, then, from a more general theory of organizations. It is more specific and more focused than general organizational theories. The general manager's job is to diagnose what is critical in complex business situations and to find realistic solutions to strategic and organizational problems. To solve problems, the general manager must be capable of understanding and using the knowledge from each of the organization's functional areas to provide a holistic 'total business' (systems) perspective on issues pertaining to strategic management. In addition, the general manager must be able to analyse competitive situations within industries in order to understand the sources of the firm's competitive advantage. We see strategy as determined and constrained by the underlying economic and political conditions which prevail in an industry or country, as well as by the resources available to management.

In consequence, we believe that a strategist (or the strategic team) must focus on understanding the specific *context* of the strategic problem. He or she must have an intuitive feel for defining the boundaries of the problem and the issues to include in any analysis. A strategist must also recognize the interrelationships between all the organizational functions, activities and processes, and be able to frame the problem by recognizing the influence not only of history but also of the future on the problem context. The strategist must be willing to act, must have a bias for action and be equally willing to accept the consequences – be they success or failure of the strategies he or she chooses. Therefore, unashamedly, we present in this book a conception of strategy which focuses on the role and the perspective of the general manager.

That said, it is important to develop a discussion about strategy around an appreciation of some of the theories which contribute to current strategic thinking and which help to outline managers' cognitive frames and interpretations of strategy. It is important to understand how these theories develop, how they have evolved and what problems they either seek to solve or begin to explain. What follows, therefore, is a very brief review of the main theories in the strategy field as a basis for showing how they are reflected in the development of the strategic framework and strategic systems model which are the basis for this book.

As noted earlier, the Chandler definition of strategy is the guiding principle underlying the so-called classical or rational view of strategy. A range of other eminent academics, including March and Simon (1958), Cyert and March (1963), Mintzberg (1994), Alchian (1950), Henderson (1973), Williamson (1975), Pascale (1984) and others, personify the main viewpoints in the field of strategy. The so-called **evolutionary view** emphasizes competitive processes of natural selection and environmental determination; survival is everything and nature is the optimiser. In this world, strategy can be a delusion and 'economy is the best strategy'. On the other hand, the so-called **strategy processual** or **organizational process** view of strategy expresses a more agnostic view about a market's ability to produce satisfactory outcomes, which we explain more fully in Chapter 2. In this view, both organizations and markets are sticky and messy, and strategies emerge slowly with much confusion and in small steps. Strategic behaviour is embedded and entrenched in cultures, routines and standard operating procedures. In this view, strategy is programmed by the DNA of organizations. An alternative and more recent viewpoint, focusing on the **strategy-as-systems perspective**, has room for managers and organizations to look forward and make effective plans, in contrast with the agnostic and even nihilistic stance of the evolutionary and strategy process perspectives. The systemic view is drawn principally from the work of organizational sociologists such as Granovetter (1985) and rests on notions of social embeddedness. Embeddedness maintains that people's economic behaviour is embedded in a network of social relations that may involve their families, the state, their professional and educational backgrounds, even their religion and ethnicity. Such influences are absent from the restricted environment of the classical and processual approaches but may find some expression in the evolutionary view.

These viewpoints are largely mutually exclusive but practising strategists in organizations would recognize their presence in strategy as practised. However, there is a new approach which has gained recent significant support. This is the resource-based view attributed to economist Edith Penrose. In this view, the emphasis is on those resources and competences that are distinctive to the organization and are the fundamental underpinning of their marketplace positioning. In this world, competition is a contest for the acquisition of skills and competences and other intangible assets. This represents a theory of core competences (to use the words popularized by gurus Gary Hamel and C.K. Prahalad) that provides linkages between the classical, processual and systemic views. By virtue of its focus on tacit and intangible resources, it links directly with new theories of knowledge management and is the basis for a new knowledge-based view of strategy advanced by Nelson and Winter (1982) and others, in which superior knowledge is likely to be the most valuable resource of all.

Our observation of many of these writers is that they err on the side of conventional rationality, the classical model, and provide the reader with little guidance about how to interpret the changing world of technology and globalization in which we live and the way in which organizations form strategic positions in this world. We observe also that strategizing in the real world is something of a caricature in conventional writing with little attention paid to providing realistic appreciations of the forces at work. It is obvious that the drivers of change have been new structures of scientific knowledge, the internationalization of experience in a time of rapid media access to diverse cultures and the acceleration of technological change in post-industrial society. Thus, we see strategy as marked increasingly by an eclecticism and multicultural nature and a post-industrial, high-tech, internationalistic context. For example, the US and the UK are essentially post-industrial service economies; Asia is entering the industrial stage with specialized industries but markets that are almost entirely international. Structural change is endemic in the world economy and even the largest corporations are caught up in the ebb and flow of outsourcing, refocusing new technologies and intangible, human capital. This is in sharp contrast to the world of the rationalist, where strategy is the preserve of top management and the approach is strategy-as-planning, where organizations are efficient, rational resource-allocation mechanisms designed to achieve competitive advantage and economic rents.

What we propose in our conceptual strategic model is a much more blended, balanced and systemic view of the world. It is a treatment of strategy that builds on the roots provided by the classical model (after all, there is still virtue in rationality) that reflects the modern resource-based and knowledge-based view but uses all the available lenses and viewpoints of strategy and strategic thinking to interpret, make sense and provide a basis for strategic decisions.

As a motivating example to illustrate of the use of multiple viewpoints in framing strategy, we attempt to make sense of Honda's strategic behaviour in the celebrated case of its entry into the US motorcycle marketplace. This has been extensively discussed in the strategy literature but its very familiarity enables us to make the point convincingly. The classical view held that Honda's successful entry was a masterpiece of rational economic calculation, so much so that Boston Consulting Group, in a celebrated report, laid out their view about the importance of market share objectives and economies of scale and experience in the motorcycle industry. They used this argument as a benchmark in providing advice to the British government in its own attempts to revitalize the failing British motorcycle industry in the mid 1970s. The opposing explanation of Honda's success was the processual view advanced powerfully by Richard Pascale. He maintained that Honda's successful entry was, indeed, a masterpiece of strategic thinking but rather of flexible, quick incremental adjustment to the marketplace realities and emergent thinking in framing their ongoing strategy. Honda management did not know what they were taking on but learned very quickly. The broader, all-encompassing systemic view holds that it is not the Japanese management of Honda that determines the strategy, nor is it simply a version of 'muddling through', but it is the local US management of Honda that works out how the game has to be played. Indeed, Honda USA becomes embedded in the network of American social and business relationships, albeit with a very distinctive Japanese flavour. In particular, Honda, like all auto/motorcycle companies, worked out that they face the same industry conditions of scale economies, access, capacity, persistent entry by newly industrializing countries and trends towards commoditization. Although, while Honda may have found short-term distinctiveness in the US market, in the end it will find that this will erode and the only strategy available to it over the long term will be to 'economize', i.e. keep its costs low and its options open.

This commentary on Honda exemplifies the need for contemporary strategic thinking to move away from the purely rational or planned view towards a more eclectic view that embraces the emergent, incremental or processual approaches with a stronger respect for the power or markets and institutions – primarily governments – to shape the behaviour of corporations. Corporate behaviour is neither simply rational nor simply determined by its various environments. Any strategic model has to capture the increasing complexity of modern corporate life by, first, providing alternative lenses (perspectives, theories and rules of thumb) through which to see the world and, second, by articulating a way of telling the strategy story so that the reader can see how organizations frame their strategic positioning in their drive for long-term strategic successes. Thus, the centrepiece – our strategy story – is the juxtaposition of intangible resources at the firm level with imperfectly competitive markets in the context of ever more dynamic and intrusive environments involving globalization and rapid, disruptive technological change. We now move on to a discussion of the strategy systems framework which defines the structure and context of this book.

1.3.1 The strategy systems framework

Figure 1.6 shows the conceptual framework and the logic underlying the approach taken to understanding strategy in this book. It argues that the various models, definitions of strategy and frameworks provided in the book are vehicles for thinking about strategy and policy and carrying out a dialogue about strategic options. In essence, our strategy story is conceptualized in terms of a strategy map, which motivates the strategy team and leads to a discussion of strategy options in a broad, systemic fashion. We believe, following Cummings and Wilson (2003), that:

> strategy frameworks, images or maps help people to do their own mapping, thereby kick-starting an oscillating thinking/acting or strategising process, which instils a momentum that brings other choices and possibilities to the fore. It may not get people 'down the mountain' in a straight line but it gets things moving and, when things move, other things come into view.

In short, the interaction between the general map and the mapping of a particular course of action orientates and animates, and no course is likely to be taken effectively without a measure of each of these things. Cumming and Wilson (2003) go on to propose that strategy is an art in the following terms:

> It is argued that the art of strategy lies both in the combination of frameworks, images or maps and the choice of their focus (e.g. big picture versus certain detail) toward mapping an organization's particular course.

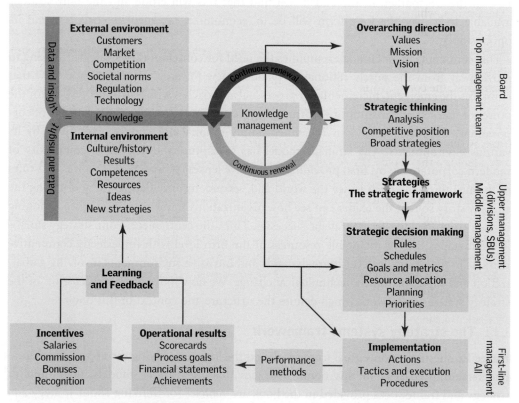

Figure 1.6 A systemic model of strategy

As we shall see, our framework in Figure 1.6 interacts as an organizing framework with strategic processes of animation and orientation (see our introduction in Chapter 2) to produce a preferred strategy for an organization.

What follows now, therefore, is an articulation of the elements of Figure 1.6, recognizing that it is a map and a system model. It 'animates and orientates' the problem of strategy and invites debate and dialogue among those strategists taking part in the strategy process. Note that each of the elements in the diagram (e.g. overarching direction or strategic thinking) encompasses a set of issues and generally poses a specific question. For example, the notion of the overarching direction of an organization begs the question, What do we want to be?

Let us follow through with each of these elements and describe what is going on in each of the boxes.

Overarching direction

Understanding the firm's overarching direction is critical. The general question being asked here is What does the organization want to be? The organization must develop a long-term vision of what it wants to be and take into account the company's culture, reputation, competences and resources in addressing that question. The vision is the core ideology of the organization, which provides the glue that binds the organization together. It encompasses a set of core values that address questions such as why the company exists and what it believes in. The core values may include such things as honesty and integrity, hard work and continuous self-improvement, strong customer service, creativity and imagination. On the other hand, the core purpose is to do with the company's reason for being – in Walt Disney's case, it is simply stated as being to make people happy or, in Hewlett Packard's case, to make a technological contribution to the advancement and welfare of humanity. Purpose, in this sense, is very close to the mission of the organization and, as stated earlier, the vision is the core ideology that binds the organization together. Collins and Porras (2000) argue that what they describe as 'big, hairy, audacious goals' improve long-term vision – for example, Stanford University's statement in the 1940s that they wanted to become 'the Harvard of the West' or Boeing's vision in the 1950s of becoming the 'dominant player in aviation and bringing the world into the jet age'. Thus, a vision breaks down into a more flexible set of aspirations, perhaps sub-goals, which are defined in both qualitative and quantitative terms (e.g. long-term growth or profit), and these aspirations tend to be refreshed more frequently than the overall vision.

Strategic thinking

This element of the strategic concept advances a holistic and integrated view of the business. It asks the question of how, through analysis and strategic positioning, the firm will answer the question, Together, how will we do that?

What we seek to understand here is the relationship between the firm's positioning, resources and capabilities, and organization. We seek to ensure here that the firm's strategy is such that the elements complement and reinforce each other, i.e. the strategies are cohesive. In other words, a co-ordinated framework of high-level enterprise strategies is developed to achieve the vision. This brings together the best strategic thinking and analysis and widely communicates one strategic viewpoint to get everyone pulling in the same direction and to discourage unproductive behaviour.

The agreed enterprise strategy is then broken down into a range of strategies that position the organization in its markets and in its various functional activities (e.g. product strategies, distribution strategies, etc.). They emphasize strategic options and positions, and highlight them in a framework such that they work together. Obviously, strategic thinking requires a whole range of techniques and tools. These include a determination of the broad goals of the organization, thus answering the question, What is most important? Analysts and strategists also have to understand the sources of value creation through revenue drivers, cost drivers and risk drivers.

In other words, strategic thinking begins with a good business model that analyses the economic relationships central to achieving the organization's purpose. These include value creation and analysing industry dynamics – perhaps using the 'five forces' framework developed by Porter (1980). The firm must also recognize the distinctiveness of its own resources and capabilities, because these core capabilities are often long-lasting and provide the linkage with a firm sustaining superior performance over the long run. Porter's (1980) framework is shown in Figure 1.7.

In terms of new entrants, there can be threats from, for example, low barriers to entry, where it is fairly easy for an organization to start trading and enter the market. Equally, if brand identity is weak (say in a commodity product) then the threat of new entrants is likely to be high. Barriers against these threats can be high capital cost of entry (for example, it is very costly to set up a new pharmaceutical manufacturing and R&D organization from scratch) or the development of economies of scale (where bigger and older companies will always benefit from economies of scale and new entrants will not). Substitutes can present a threat if, for example, the cost of a customer switching from one product to that of the substitute is low. Not surprisingly, these are known as switching costs. The lower the switching costs, the greater are the threats from substitution. Substitution can also occur via price. A substitute product at a much lower price (and a

Figure 1.7 Porter's five forces: the elements of industry structure

product which customers will value just as much) will pose a large threat to the company charging higher prices for similar products. Commodity products, such as washing powders, and white consumer goods are examples where customers will switch relatively easily to a lower price product.

Buyers can exert power. If a small number of suppliers serve a large number of firms, then the concentration of supplier power is relatively high. If the reverse situation holds, and there are many suppliers for a few firms, then supplier power is low. In the former case, buyer power is low; in the latter, buyer power is high. An example of the latter case can be found among the large supermarkets worldwide, which exert so much power over their suppliers that they can sometimes charge a premium for stocking and displaying items on their shelves (wine is an example).

Supplier power is really the opposite of buyer power. Where the switching costs of firms in the industry are high, they will not decide lightly to change suppliers. In this case, suppliers have relatively high levels of power over those organizations. However, new suppliers entering the market will have a potential substitution effect and reduce existing levels of supplier power. The relative threat of forward and backward integration will also affect supplier (and buyer) power. For example, if a firm decides it can manufacture its own raw materials (rather than buy from a supplier) then the balance of power between supplier and firm will be changed radically in favour of the firm and to the disadvantage of the supplier.

This kind of framework is useful for picturing the dynamics of an industry but such frameworks do not tell the whole story. They are relatively static frameworks which make a number of assumptions, not least that all players will have perfect knowledge (everyone is aware of the extent of their power or the threat they pose) and will always exercise the power they have. To inject a more dynamic perspective, these frameworks should be seen as one part of a greater process. The strategist has to recognize the source of the power balances or imbalances, but having done that he or she needs to drill deeper into the analysis to analyse not only the sources of such threats and power but also the impact of each on the strategy process. This explains why the five forces model, central to many scholars' strategy frameworks, is only a part of the systemic model presented here. We will be referring to Porter's model again in Chapter 5, where we will use it to explore competitive advantage in more detail.

Strategies: the strategic framework and product goals

In its simplest terms, a strategy consists of a set of goals and a set of policies or actions to achieve those goals. Goals answer the question of what is most important for the organization. The strategy and process also encompass the strategic planning process, which varies from organization to organization in levels of familiarity. However, the most important element in strategic planning is to link the strategic framework and broad goals as guides and allow each of the divisions or sub-units of the organization to develop their own strategies in a co-ordinated fashion. That is, responsibility for strategy formulation should be devolved to the sub-units or entities within the business which have responsibility for products and services. The individual managers running those units are the ones who know the products and services, the product markets and the presence of other competitors in the marketplace. They can then develop a statement of what strategic positioning the organization should reasonably adopt at that level. The role of top management is to co-ordinate those strategies in an enterprise sense, so that it fits the overall strategic framework defined by the vision and the overarching direction of the organization.

Strategic programming

This focuses on the answers to questions such as Who, when and how much? In other words, assuming broad strategies are agreed, an operating plan must be developed to attack such issues as day-to-day priorities, organizational roles and responsibilities, and resource allocation with regard to budgets and systems development. Obviously, this leads to the development of a clearer, tactical plan.

Tactics and execution

This phase of the strategy process answers the tasks of 'Let's get organized and let's do it, and do it right!' In other words, the tactical part of the operating plan fills in the gaps about division plans, unit plans and individual goals, and develops performance metrics at each level, so that monitoring of those plans can be undertaken. The executive focuses not only on the monitoring of performance and targets but the ability to adjust plans quickly and rapidly as new ideas and challenges are developed within the organization.

Performance measurement and purpose

In any organization, there must be a linkage to performance. The feedback that is necessary for any organization in re-framing its strategy in a sensible way is the answer to the question, How do we do a check of performance against targets and cost? Performance metrics are extremely important – they highlight issues such as progress towards goals and, more importantly, how certain tasks and certain strategies can be adjusted better and faster and how change can be incorporated most effectively within the context of the organization.

Information and analysis: the internal and external environment

Obviously, changing the organization through performance monitoring and strategy adjustment is but one process in a series of feedbacks and feedback loops which are absolutely necessary in analysing information about both internal and external environments. In the external environment, we have to question what is happening around us; there must be a process of data gathering and development of insight and knowledge about such issues as new technology and its impact on the business, and the potential impact of regulation and legislation on the activities of the company. The underlying national economic and macroeconomic conditions are also important in setting the global economic context for the organization and, at a more micro level, framing intelligence and analysis about competition, the nature and changing shape of markets and customer needs and opinions. Obviously, key success factors in this external environment enable the firm to focus on appropriate product renewal and generate knowledge and insight about new products and ideas. In the context of the internal environment, the firm needs to analyse and identify its key resources and capabilities and evaluate their impact on competitive advantage. For example, a company's culture and the history of its development can provide a source of competitive strength as in the case of Johnson & Johnson (J&J), which is regarded by many as an extremely ethical and well-run pharmaceutical company. That perception is a result of J&J's strong culture, its history and the strength of its financial resources over a long period of time. Internal analysis also requires a process of continual investigation, discovery and criticism, leading to new ideas, new product concepts, updated financial results and updated metrics. Information about organizational strengths and weaknesses can, in turn, lead to the continual renewal of the strategy process.

Feedback of results and incentives

Kaplan and Norton (1992) have developed processes known as a balanced scorecard for monitoring operational financial results within the organization. Figure 1.8 depicts this scorecard in its simplest form (it is used elsewhere in this book in greater detail; *see*, for example, Chapter 14).

The balanced scorecard attempts to answer questions about progress towards goals and identifies any operational results which can be fed back to continually improve organizational processes. The balanced scorecard also contains an incentive structure which answers the question, What's in it for me? Clearly, if incentives such as salaries, commission and bonuses can be co-aligned with strategic objectives, the employee recognition will lead

Figure 1.8 The balanced scorecard
Source: adapted from Kaplan and Norton (1992).

to employee loyalty and a strong alignment between individual objectives, organizational objectives and organizational strategy.

In summary, the strategy concept presented here in Figure 1.6 is a map, a framework and a virtuous circle, at the core of which is a process of knowledge management which trades upon analysis of the external and internal environment, analysis of performance, analysis of strategies and competitive updating of values and mission in order to achieve a process whereby the organization is engaged in a continual debate about how it can improve and how it can frame its strategy so that the organization itself fits in a dynamic sense with its current and future strategic position.

1.4 Summary

This chapter has outlined the contested terrain of strategy. The field is full of competing definitions. In order to move beyond a battle of definitions, we have attempted to build a framework which helps show how strategy 'works' rather than debating exactly what it 'is'. Complex though this model might appear at first sight, it provides a framework which the following chapters of this book outline in greater detail.

For example, a solely economics-based perspective would examine the dynamics of *matching the internal environment* of the firm *with its external environment*. As Figure 1.6 makes clear, this is only part of the process – but is an important part. Strategists who do not consider the implications of internal and external do so at their peril. Thus, Part 2 of this book describes in detail the essential elements of this process. In order for strategists to make decisions, they need a detailed appreciation of both the micro- and the macro-economic characteristics of the firm and its environment. But such analysis cannot stand alone. We have already seen in this chapter how values, mission and vision communicate an organization's strategic stance to its wider audience, most importantly its customers. Getting this wrong (as when Gerald Ratner famously called his company's jewellery products 'crap') can seal the demise of the firm no matter how sophisticated the economic analysis has been. In one sentence, Ratner's was doomed.

This chapter has also highlighted the importance of analysis. Strategists are faced with a range of options and rarely are faced with simple go or no-go decisions. Therefore, the skill of *thinking strategically* cannot be overemphasized. Strategists need to be aware not only of the options they face, but also the trade-offs they make, for example, by choosing one course of action over another. This can be a problem for many organizations. Consider Volkswagen's decision to position the Skoda (which it acquired) as a quality mid-range car available in medium to high performance ranges as well as diesel, petrol and dual fuel. What seemed initially like a good decision – to beef up the brand and reputational image of Skoda (Skoda jokes were legendary: what do you call an open-top Skoda? Answer – a skip!) – backfired on Volkswagen since the trade-off this decision produced was to reduce demand for the equivalent Volkswagen products (the Golf and Passat). Skodas were selling at the expense of the firm's existing products. Part 3 of this book examines these sorts of analysis and thinking problems both from the domestic viewpoint (what is our strategic position?) and in the global context (how do we take strategic decisions in an international environment?).

Strategies do not exist independently of organizations, however. The notion of a small number of policy makers sitting in a darkened room formulating key decisions which they then unleash on an unsuspecting organization is a fond and inaccurate characterization. First of all, making strategic decisions involves a wide range of stakeholders and interests which are both internal and external to the organization. Their influences shape and often control what happens. Second, strategies have to be put into practice. They have to be implemented. Moreover, they have to be implemented in often large and complex social environments, which have the convenient label 'organizations' or 'firms' but which contain very high levels of social, individual, elite and irrational behaviours. Organizations are social environments and not solely economic machines. What managers do and how people behave matters. Hence, Part 4 of this book examines in detail the question of strategic acting. It looks at how strategic decisions can be formulated relatively easily but can run into difficulties once managers start to try to implement strategic decisions. The ways in which they organize, oversee and govern decisions matter. Putting decisions into practice means organizations and people are faced with often significant levels of change and new learning. Managers neglect these aspects of strategy (which have often been dismissed as the softer, intangible aspects of strategy) at their peril. Resistance to change and an inability to learn will ensure the death of an organization independently of whether or not it is in a fierce or benign environment. Internal barriers to strategy are just as important as external competitive threats, for example.

Finally, strategies (and organizations) need continuous renewal. Putting decisions into practice is one thing. Knowing and measuring how they have performed and knowing why are completely different skills and processes. Part 5 of this book examines the important questions of performance. How do decision makers know they made the right, or the wrong, decision? This part discusses such topics as performance, quality and process improvements as well as operational results such as financial statements, achievement of stated objectives and process goals. In turn, we view these performance metrics as helping the feedback process into the next set of strategic decisions which managers will take in the future. In this sense, performance metrics also help the learning process and the development of new capabilities as well as the abandonment of old capabilities which might no longer be useful for future strategies.

Before looking at the next parts of the book, it is important to place some of the above arguments in their organizational contexts. The following chapter raises some questions about what happens when 'strategies meet organizations' and provides more detail about the contextual aspects of organization. We would view Chapter 2 as essential pre-reading to Part 4 of this book.

Key terms

Emergent strategy *11*

Evolutionary view *19*

External environment *9*

Goals *9*

Intended strategy *6*

Internal environment *10, 14*

Mission/mission statement *10*

Objectives *see* Goals

Organizational process view *19*

Realized strategy *11*

Resource-based view *16*

Strategic intent *see* Intended strategy

Strategy-as-systems perspective *19*

Strategy processual view *19*

Organizational process view *19*

When you have read this chapter, log on to the Online Learning Centre website at www.mcgraw-hill.co.uk/textbooks/mcgee to explore chapter-by-chapter test questions, further reading and more online study tools for strategy.

Further reading and references

Alchian, AA (1950) 'Uncertainty, evolution and economic theory', *Journal of Political Economy*, **58**, pp. 211–21.

Andrews, KR (1980) *The Concept of Corporate Strategy*, Irwin, Homewood, Il.

Ansoff, HI (1965) *Corporate Strategy*, Penguin, Harmondsworth.

Ansoff, HI (1972) 'The concept of strategic management', *Journal of Business Policy*, **2**, **4**, Summer.

Bower, JL (1982) 'Business policy in the 1980s', *Academy of Management Review*, vol. 7, no. 4, 630–8.

Bower, JL (1986) *Managing the Resource Allocation Process*, Harvard Business School Press, Boston, MA.

Chandler, AD (1963) *Strategy and Structure: Chapters in the History of the Industrial Enterprise*, MIT Press, Cambridge, MA.

Christensen, C (1997) *The Innovator's Dilemma: When New Technologies Cause Great Firms to Fail*, Harvard Business School Press, Cambridge, MA.

Collins, JC and Porras, JI (2000) *Built to Last: Sucessful Habits of Visionary Companies*, Random House, New York.

Cummings S, and Wilson, DC (eds) (2003) *Images of Strategy*, Blackwell, Oxford.

Cyert, RM and March, JG (1963) *A Behavioral Theory of the Firm*, Blackwell, Oxford.

Granovetter, M (1985) 'Economic action and social culture: the problem of embeddedness', *American Journal of Sociology*, **91**, **3**, pp. 481–510.

Henderson, BD (1973) *The Experience Curve Reviewed*, Boston Consulting Group, Boston, MA.

Hussey, D (1998) *Strategic Management: From Theory to Implementation*, 4th edition, Butterworth-Heinemann, Oxford.

Kaplan, RS and Norton, DP (1992) 'The Balanced Scorecard: Measures that Drive Performance', *Harvard Business Review*, Jan–Feb.

Legge, K (2003) 'Strategy as organising', in S Cummings and DC Wilson (eds) *Images of Strategy*, Blackwell, Oxford.

Magretta, J (2003) *What Management is*, Profile Books, London.

March, JG and Simon, HA (1958) *Organizations*, Blackwell, Cambridge, MA.

Mintzberg, H (1994) *The Rise and Fall of Strategic Planning*, Prentice-Hall, Englewood Cliffs, NJ.

Mintzberg, H and Waters, J (1985) 'Of strategies, deliberate and emergent', *Strategic Management Journal*, **6**, pp. 257–72.

Mintzberg, H, Lampel, J and Ahlstrand, P (1998) *The Strategy Safari: A Guided Tour Through the Jungle of Strategic Management*, Prentice-Hall, Englewood Cliffs, NJ.

Nelson, RR and Winter, SG (1982) *An Evolutionary Theory of Economic Change*, Harvard University Press, Cambridge, MA.

Pascale, R (1984) 'Perspectives on strategy: the real story behind Honda's success', *California Management Review*, **14**, **3**, pp. 47–72.

Penrose, E (1959) *The Theory of the Growth of the Firm*, Blackwell, Oxford.

Porter, M (1980) *Competitive Strategy*, Free Press, New York.

Porter, ME (1985) *Competitive Advantage*, Free Press, New York.

Porter, ME (1987) 'From competitive advantage to corporate strategy', *Harvard Business Review*, May–June, pp. 2–21.

Prahalad, CK and Hamel, G (1990) 'The core competence of the organization', *Harvard Business Review*, May–June.

Quinn, JB (1980) *Strategies for Change: Logical Incrementalism*, Irwin, Homewood, Il.

Sun Tzu (1990) *The Art of War*, Sterling Publishing, New York.

Williamson, OE (1975) *Markets and Hierarchies: Analysis and Antitrust Implications*, Free Press, New York.

Chapter 2

Strategy and organization

Introduction

The traditional concepts of strategy outlined in Chapter 1 largely emphasize the dominance of models that highlight the positioning of organizations in relation to their competitive and operating environments. This is certainly an important part of understanding strategic management, but it only tells part of the story. Our eclectic model (see Figure 1.6) emphasizes other key aspects of strategy, locating processes in a wider context, both organizational and societal. This chapter is concerned with the interfaces between strategy and organization. It looks at issues of the *strategy process* – how managers enact and interpret the world around them – and the **organizational** *context* in which such processes take place. Practice focuses on where and how strategic intent has to be formulated, implemented and processed through an organization. Strategy, as a refined and often rarified concept, has to be translated by managers before it can be put into practice. This chapter deals with the key aspects of this translation process and outlines ways of **interpreting strategy** from this perspective.

Translation covers a wide area of topics as well as a wide variety of levels of analysis, ranging, for example, from looking at what managers do when they make strategic decisions to the wider context of organization, such as structure, culture, organizational politics and inter-organizational relations. We shall briefly introduce these concepts in this chapter and expand on each in later chapters (see Part 4).

De Wit and Meyer (1999) provide some useful guidelines for differentiating between strategy content, process and context. They generally define each as:

- *Strategy content:* basically the 'what' of strategy. This means defining what strategic decisions are about (for example, a new product or service) and what their intention is (for example, cost reduction or profit maximization). The content perspective also addresses such questions as where are we going (what are the long term goals?) and what is the scope of the business (what are we going to do?).

- *Strategy context:* the 'where' of strategy. This is the set of factors that comprise the setting for a strategy. This includes the internal context of the organization as well as the characteristics of the external context in the operating environment (such as the nature of inter-organizational relations or the influence of government agencies).

- *Strategy process:* the 'how' of strategy. This details who is involved in the process and when activities take place. It is the story, the drama and the list of players in the strategy as well as the characteristics of the process itself (for example, continuous or discontinuous, short or drawn out over time).

2.1 Linking organization and strategy

The positioning models of strategy introduced in Chapter 1 are deceptively simple. In turn, they can be made sense of by managers in an equally simple way, ignoring the nuances which may lie in the way of thinking and **acting strategically**. As Michaud and Thoenig (2003) point out, a good strategy model is one which is easily readable, can be understood quickly by managers, is transparent to organizational members and outsiders. The philosophy here is that simple is best. The best performances come from adopting and implementing simple models that can be easily understood throughout the organization. Thus, multiple views on strategy and nuances of interpretation are to be avoided as far as possible.

Yet with this view comes a paradox. If all organizations have access to the same models of strategy and to the same external consultants that prescribe best practices, which they distribute in the manner of a cure-all, then what is to differentiate them? Where is the source of competitive advantage, since most organizations will follow similar routes based upon models of best practice and effective strategic positioning?

The answer seems to lie in how managers both interpret such models and how they put strategies into practice in organizations. In short, when strategy meets organization, the actions and processes that ensue have a large impact on the extent to which strategy is effective, competitive and ultimately successful. How managers think and act matters as much as the models that may have informed strategy in the first place.

2.1.1 Thinking and acting strategically

Strategic management, like many other management sub-disciplines, favours dualisms to make conceptual distinctions in the models it uses. These can take many forms, such as competition versus co-operation, or strategy versus structure. While they are useful thinking devices, such dualisms tend to mask the extent to which they are really not polar extremes at all, but are inextricably interrelated. Structure is as much a part of process as process is a part of structure. And certainly, competition and co-operation both inform one another and are part of one another, rather than existing as separate entities. In the same way, the terms thinking and acting strategically are also interrelated and blend together in the strategy process.

The primary reason for focusing on **strategic thinking** and acting is that simply focusing on strategy content (strategic positioning) is insufficient to guarantee desired outcomes (for example, securing a competitive advantage). Consider Porter's five forces model, for example (Porter 1980). This is one of the most well-used and well-described tools for assessing a firm's competitive position. Informed largely by economic models of the firm, the five forces model assesses a firm's position in regard to such factors as the power of suppliers and customers, the ease with which substitution can take place and the barriers to entry for new competitors. The compelling argument from this analysis is that strategic content should be guided by the nature of the interrelationships among the forces and the firm (allowing, for example, a choice of generic versus specialist strategies or quality and customer service strategies). As in many economic models, however, the assumptions that have to be made in order for the analysis to work are fairly heroic and increasingly questionable. For example, the five forces model assumes:

◆ Independence among all the factors.

◆ Organizations can formulate strategies 'at arm's length' in relation to rivals, customers and suppliers.

◆ Structural advantage is the sole key to competitive success (the more a firm has relative power over customers, suppliers etc., the greater is its competitive advantage).

◆ Even where such structural advantages occur, firms can always act to exercise such power without any constraints.

◆ The individual organization is the key unit of analysis.

Even at a common-sense level of analysis, not all of the above assumptions can hold true. Even within the same organization, Chief Executives report severe difficulties in gathering enough information to assess and to mobilize their own operating companies. Looking outside their own organizations to try to implement a forces model is even harder and less realistic.

So what really goes on when managers run with the strategic baton? This chapter begins to unpack this question – the practice of strategy in organizations.

2.1.2 **Animation and orientation**

At the most basic level, the practice of strategy in organizations is chiefly about defining strategic aims – formulating ambitions and visions (**orientation**). It is also about encouraging and ensuring the various parts of the social system, which is the organization, are mobilised, act in concert with strategic ambitions and contribute to implementation (**animation**). Figure 2.1 illustrates this concept.

Of course, no one believes strategy is as simple as that, but the basic principles of animation and orientation are powerful ideas to begin with (Cummings and Wilson 2003). Everyone knows the story of the group who were lost in the Alps seemingly without a map when one member of the group found a tattered map in a little-used pocket. This find increased morale and animated the group to walk until they were able to orientate themselves by finding familiar bearings. So far so good – but the map was one of the Pyrenees. The value of the map was akin to a strategic framework such as those discussed in Chapter 1. However, what mattered most was this individual's ability to achieve focus and direction, even with the wrong map. The symbolic nature of the framework appears as important as its accuracy in this respect (*see* Weick 1987).

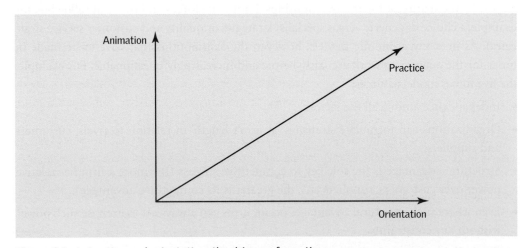

Figure 2.1 Animation and orientation: the drivers of practice

In terms of the strategy model that guides this book (*see* Figure 1.6), animation coincides with the concept of continuous renewal. The interplay between strategic intention and how managers interpret the environment provides a context in which organizational members can become enthused and motivated around a particular set of tasks. Orientation coincides with concepts such as strategic thinking, looking at the broad range of strategies available to decision makers and the processes of analysis undertaken to decide on strategic direction. Orientation embraces values, mission and vision. Orientation is thus inextricably linked with future direction, and all the uncertainty this involves. It is through such statements of future intent (such as we want to achieve 35 per cent market share in two years) that individuals in the organization are motivated to try to achieve. They become animated and oriented towards a particular future or future desirable states of affairs. This is a simple statement to make but a remarkably difficult process to achieve in practice and later sections of this book will explore these social processes of animation and orientation in greater depth (*see* Part 4).

As we argued in Chapter 1, the model of strategy we embrace is eclectic, systematic, attempting to place a resource-based view of the organization in a wider context of cultural, technological and structural changes. How managers interpret and decode the context they inhabit influences the strategies they might choose and colours the desired future states they may articulate. Orientation is thus a combination of interpretation and planning. Equally, the resources at a manager's disposal (either within or outside the organization) will influence the extent to which the manager can successfully animate people and arrange resources around them to achieve desired future states. We examine some of the key interrelationships between context, organization and interpretation in the following sections.

2.2 Context, organization and managerial interpretation

Many authors have called for a view of strategic management that is highly micro, focused on an activity-based view of what managers do (*see*, for example, Johnson *et al.* 2003). The intention is to try to relate what happens in the day-to-day activities of individuals in organizations to strategy processes and outcomes. Some authors go further and argue that the analysis of talk and conversations of all individuals in organizations (not just managers) is relevant for the study of how strategies are formulated, supported and implemented (*see*, for example, Samra-Fredericks, 2003). While we agree that some micro-activities in organizations may reveal a level of analysis previously overlooked by 'traditional' strategic management, such a perspective is nevertheless highly reductionist. As Balogun *et al.* (2003) argue, while micro-perspectives may reveal more about the deeply rooted nature of individual activity (and routines) in organizations, there is a simultaneous need to understand breadth and macro levels of analysis. They argue that if we are to understand any possible relationships between changing forms (structures) of organizations and the characteristics of strategy, we must adopt a broad and more systems-based view of the interactions between context, organization and individual action.

Such a systems perspective is a guiding principle of this chapter. Reductionism allows us to see the detail. It allows us to observe, follow and dissect the activities of individuals as they go about their day-to-day activities and we can learn a great deal about human behaviour in organizations this way, but this prevents us seeing the overall picture. Reductionism, however, can never provide a complete explanation of the strategy process. A more systemic view allows us to move across levels of analysis and across the patterns of organization which any organism adopts in relation to its wider environment (Capra, 1982). In this way we can emphasize the relational aspects of management practice and organizational context.

All organizations are essentially complex systems which interact with their environments. In the case of living systems (such as a species of animal) the relationships between the system and its environment can be characterized by the term structural coupling. That is, a series of interactions between the living system and its environment trigger a set of responses in the living system, resulting in structural and processual changes. These changes can be viewed as the way in which the organism learns, develops and adapts. The same process holds true for complex social organizations. Figure 2.2 shows the main systemic adaptation and strategy processes that help keep the organization aligned with its environment. Managers in organizations *interpret* the environment. They then have to communicate this interpretation among others in the organization. They may have to build a strategic vision (an ideal goal to aim for) and they may also have to create a new language that can be shared by all organizational members in order to close any gaps between ambition and action. Interpretation and communication allow *strategic options* to be outlined. These are the key choices among a number of possible courses of action which managers might take. Having decided on a course of action, a number of decisions have to be taken in order to *implement* the chosen strategy. In turn, the actions taken by an organization may have an impact on the environment and perhaps modify it slightly. The process then recycles.

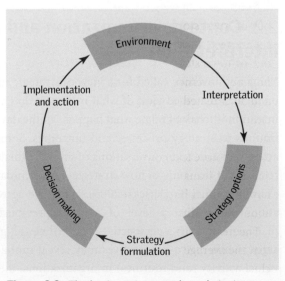

Figure 2.2 The basic systems cycle and strategy

The ways in which managers interpret the environment and instigate changes in their organizations is a fundamental part of the strategy process. Getting this interpretation wrong will increase the risk of demise for the organization and getting it right will increase the chances of growth and success. The following example of Tesco illustrates this point and also shows how the strategic actions of an organization can, in turn, influence and change the operating environment.

Tesco's retail strategies

Tesco (along with other big supermarket chains) has changed the way we shop and the ways we think about shopping. Sensing that 80 per cent of the population have most of the things we want, shopping no longer is a necessity where trolleys are filled to sustain a family for a week, but is a process which happens every two or three days. Many shoppers no longer write lists for the weekly shop, but rely on impulse purchases instead. Recognizing this change in the environment, Tesco moved towards creating the 'shoppable shop' and moved away from competing on volume (stack 'em high) or on price (Sainsbury's is currently the only supermarket competing on low price, perhaps an indication of its poor market position). Tesco now emphasize the shopping experience. Getting the store laid out so customers can get in, shop and get out in the shortest time possible has become a priority. In addition, customers want a one-stop shop. Tesco responds. Almost 50 per cent of the average Tesco store is given over to non-food items such as clothes, homeware and CDs so that the customer does not have to go elsewhere to buy them.

Another change in the 'environment' has been customers' reluctance to drive to large out-of-town stores. Consequently, Tesco are moving back into smaller (less than 2000 square feet) local stores, effectively operating as a corner shop (the average size of an out-of-town store is 50 000 square feet). In another interpretive move, Tesco sensed the organic movement very early – almost before consumers knew what the word meant – and formulated a strategy of providing an uncontaminated, ethically and physically clean food chain. Organic produce now permeates almost all Tesco foodstuffs. In turn, the effects on the consumer (the customer environment) have been marked. Consumers demand more local shops: Tesco sells more DVDs than HMV, more shampoo than Boots and its £4 jeans outsell Levi's, Gap and Wrangler put together. Tesco's strategic actions have modified both the shopping experience of consumers and also their expectations about the quality and type of goods on offer in their stores.

The next environmental challenge for Tesco (and other supermarkets) is the estimate that the average Sunday lunch travels 26 234 miles to the table (e.g. beans from Zambia, chicken from Thailand and carrots from Spain). Cheapest source production is coming under pressure from an increasing number of lobbying groups, including customers, so, according to the simple systems model, Tesco managers will have to interpret these signals correctly and adjust their retail strategies accordingly, perhaps towards a more 'locally produced' initiative.

Source: original data, and the *Observer*, 18 January 2004.

Beer (1981), in his cybernetic view of the firm, crystallizes the systems perspective into five different levels of analysis, showing in each case how the physical analogies of a living organism can be equated with organizational processes. Table 2.1 summarizes this view.

It can be seen from Table 2.1 that 'strategy' can be found in virtually all of Beer's (1981) levels of analysis. The common conception of strategy as being akin to the 'brain' of an organism, telling the rest of the body what to do, is located at levels four and five. Yet, as we have seen from Chapter 1, 'strategy' also comprises controls, monitoring, measurement and procedures and these span levels one to three in Beer's hierarchy. The argument proposed by Beer is that for an organization to be viable (co-exist with and adapt to its environment) all five levels should be present and active. We argue here that the understanding of strategy needs to go beyond a simple understanding of senior management control and direction setting and embrace a broader organizational perspective of tactics, control and execution. The systemic perspective facilitates such a broad perspective.

Nevertheless, the systems view also cannot tell the whole story. While it can show how each level of analysis is important within its own right and that, combined, the levels provide an understanding of complex systems, it makes some rather heroic assumptions about the role of managers, the availability of information and managers' abilities to interpret correctly and communicate effectively under suboptimal conditions of certainty. We explore these issues in the next section.

Table 2.1 The five levels of analysis of the systems view

Level of system	Physical analogy	Function	Organizational analogy
Level one	Muscles, organs	Action and movement	Operational processes
Level two	Spinal cord	Processing and transmission of signals	Information systems and technologies
Level three	Pons/medulla	Autonomic control	Controls embedded in operational processes
Level four	Ganglia, diencephalon (brain connections)	Sensing, arousing and monitoring	Assessing risk and opportunity
Level five	Cortex	Cerebral control and protection	Strategic management processes

Source: adapted from Bell *et al.* (1997).

2.3 **Managerial agency and practice**

The previous parts of this chapter run the risk of making managers seem all-important and pivotal agents of practice and change. In other words, the assumption is that strategy all comes down to managers correctly interpreting an environment 'out there' and taking actions to align their organizations in an optimal interrelationship with that environment. Such a view is equally true of micro-perspectives on the strategy process, since they also give almost absolute primacy to **managerial agency**. The assumption is that understanding micro-practices will reveal more pieces in the strategy jigsaw is equally flawed in this respect.

Many authors, especially in recent years, have suggested that the operating environment of organizations has become increasingly deterministic. However skilfully managers interpret their environments, ultimately strategy is determined by conditions and events external to the organization and outside the direct control of managers or their organizations. Taking this perspective, we could include authors such as Bettis and Hill (1995); Hamel and Prahalad (1996); Hill *et al.* (1998). They argue that the simple feedback loops in systems theory, or the assumptions of perfect knowledge on the part of managers, have been surpassed by changes in what they term the 'competitive landscape' facing organizations. There are two principal drivers of this new landscape – information technology and globalization. Key features are:

◆ hypercompetition;

◆ blurring of traditional industry boundaries;

◆ greater knowledge intensity;

◆ greater reliance on knowledge as a strategic asset; and

◆ discontinuous change.

Table 2.2 The new competitive landscape and shifts in strategic emphasis

From	To
General, formal strategies ⟶	Local, customized solutions
Strategy content ⟶	Strategy process and context
Identifying tangible routines ⟶	Managing intangible assets
Certainty seeking ⟶	Understanding the dynamics of uncertainties
Competition ⟶	Collaboration
Vertical structures ⟶	Network and clusters
Learned organizations *(distinctive competence)* ⟶	Learning organizations *(open to change and the developments of new competences)*

Source: adapted from Cummings and Wilson (2003).

The result is to make traditional models of competitive advantage questionable (such as Porter's five forces) and to render anachronistic traditional efficiency-oriented vertical organizational structures. It also brings into question to what extent managers can act as 'perfect' interpreters of environmental signals and as 'perfect' communicators of strategy within their organizations. Cummings and Wilson (2003) argue that there has been a shift of emphasis from one on strategy content to a focus on contexts and processes. Table 2.2 summarizes some of these changes of emphasis.

From this competitive landscape perspective, strategy is firmly rooted in processes where flexibility, knowledge creation and retention and collaboration within and between organizations are of primary importance (Cummings and Wilson 2003). Performance benefits are likely to be the result of effective combinations of strategy content, process and context and from interlinked systems and practices. Performance benefits are less likely from an organization becoming 'distinctively competent' – in other words, excellent at what it currently does (*see* Table 2.2) since such distinctiveness will soon be eroded in the new competitive landscape.

The majority of the abundant literature on strategy and strategic management tends to emphasize the positioning of organizations in relation to their competitive and

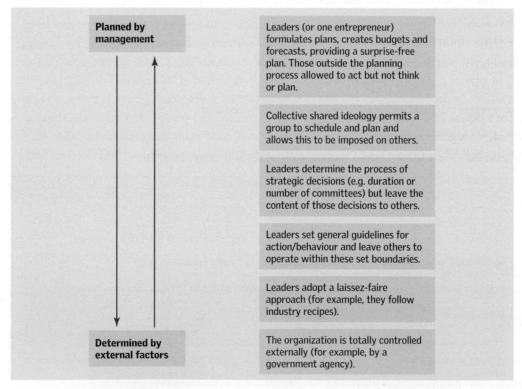

Figure 2.3 Planned versus externally determined strategies: some example characteristics

operating environment. This is certainly an important part of understanding strategic management, but it only tells part of the story. The other parts of the story concern the *strategy process* and the *context* in which such processes take place.

Managerial agency as the sole influence on strategy is certainly questionable in a number of other respects. So far, we have seen that we can make cases for environmental determinism and for managerial choice within a systemic framework. As we saw in Chapter 1, much of the work by Henry Mintzberg and his colleagues sheds light on the middle ground between determinism and choice. As Mintzberg and Waters (1985) argue, strategies do not always come about as a direct result of managerial action. Nor do they come about as a direct result of environmental determinism. Instead, they emerge as a pattern one can detect in a number of strategic decisions made over time in any organization. This emergent pattern in a stream of decisions – taken under conditions of uncertainty – is what we call strategy. It is the interplay between environmental determinism and managerial agency. Mintzberg and Waters (1985) distinguish between planned and emergent strategies:

> **Planned strategies** *are deliberate and are planned as intended in advance.*

> **Emergent strategies** *are patterns which are realized in a stream of decisions, often in the absence of (or in spite of) managerial intentions.*

Obviously, many strategies fall in between these polar extremes of planned versus emergent. Andrews (1987) suggests that, in practice, the only fully planned strategies that can be observed in organizations amount to little more than financial planning statements. Figure 2.3 illustrates a range of planned versus externally determined strategies.

One of the key features of the above debates about managerial agency is that managers have a degree of choice in the strategies they formulate and pursue. As Child (1972) recognized, managers are rarely so constrained by external conditions that they have no discretion to act at all. They simply have varying limits to the autonomy of their actions. Michaud and

	Short term	Long term
External pressure perceived as strong	Mercenary organization	Organic organization
External pressure perceived as weak	Fragmented organization	Self-sufficient organization

Figure 2.4 Strategic orientation
Source: adapted from Michaud and Thoenig (2003).

Thoenig (2003) have characterized how organizational types might emerge over time depending on what degrees of autonomy managers have and to what extent they try to formulate strategies for long-term effectiveness or for short-term gain. Their theoretical arguments owe much to Vincent's (1996) book *La Chair et le Diable* (*Flesh and the Devil*), which has not been translated from the original French. The basic argument is that organizational typologies emerge over time depending on how managers think and act strategically. These typologies can be represented for illustrative purposes in a simple matrix, as in Figure 2.4.

2.3.1 The fragmented organization

Here, managers have been typically exposed to quite benign and calm external contexts. Over time, their strategic thinking and acting has led to the embedding of relatively bureaucratic organizational features. Specialized sub-units have built up, each with its own short-term perspective and each pitched against the other sub-units for resources and senior management attention. Such an organization is fragmented in the sense that there is little incentive to think longer term or to engage in innovation or renewal. In many ways the organization distances itself from the immediacy of the competitive marketplace. Internal co-operation among sub-units is very restricted and formalized and standardized procedures take the place of individual or co-operative initiatives. Referring to Table 2.2, such an organization has become *learned* (very good at what it presently does) but is one which has difficulties in *learning* (changing and developing what the organization does and how it does it). Individuals in the organization have no incentive to change. Examples of such organizations would include many public sector organizations (prior to privatization) and financial services organizations, especially banks, which had a long history of such strategic thinking.

2.3.2 The self-sufficient organization

Here, we have an organization typified by perhaps years of managers facing a benign environment, but is also characterized by managers who think strategically in a particular way – they assume they can find the resources needed for innovation and renewal within their organizational boundaries and can change incrementally towards more longer-term goals. Such an organization may be equally bureaucratic as the fragmented stereotype. However, the key difference is that managers get around specialization and fragmentation by ad hoc and informal processes. Improvisation and informal processes drive strategic thinking. There is strong emotional attachment by individuals to the organization, although strategy may still be imposed from the top rather than be fostered at other levels in the hierarchy. This is an organization characterized by 'in' groups and 'out' groups. Those who are members of the 'in' groups (often informal groups) are those who can influence strategy longer term and can bestow upon themselves privileges which are invisible to the 'out' groups. Examples would include many professional organizations, including universities and further education establishments in the UK.

2.3.3 The mercenary organization

Typified by a threatening and turbulent external context, managers in these organizations permanently seek short-term changes by exploiting the current situation. There are no assumptions that the required skills and knowledge reside within the organization's boundaries, with a readiness to recruit and employ individuals who can bring such needed skills within the organization. In this way, the structure of this organization permanently changes as sections are closed and abandoned in favour of new ones which suit the market more closely. Strategic thinking in these kinds of organization is very much like that of the mercenary soldier. Temporary clusterings of skilled individuals make policy 'on the hoof' as market conditions demand and individual managers (mercenaries) can join or leave the organization at any time. The key to innovation and change is to be found in the engagement of these professionals and the skills they bring with them from outside the organization. Such an organization attracts weak loyalty and, therefore, strategy is inevitably short term in its focus. Nevertheless, such an organization demands strong bonds of co-operation to get the job done. It is also likely to operate in a context where there may be common standards or benchmarks for performance. Examples of such organizations would include many management or professional consulting firms as well as many project-based organizations.

2.3.4 The organic organization

The environment is unstable and perhaps threatening. Competition, regulation and technological changes are all around. Yet, this organization is populated by managers who think and act strategically in very different ways from the mercenaries described above. In this organization socialization and loyalty to the organization are extremely high. Co-operation between people is high and is perhaps seen as something of a normative process (e.g. a moral duty). While there may be differentiated sub-units in the organization, there is mutual loyalty between them. There is also a prevailing assumption that the required skills and knowledge reside inside the organizational boundaries rather than outside them (as in the mercenary organization). As Michaud and Thoenig (2003: 32) note, there is a sense of a shared adventure in such organizations, where cognitive channels spread rapidly across the sub-units to provide a strong and relatively unified organizational culture. Such features allow senior managers to capture ideas and embryonic suggestions made at lower levels in the organization. Internal networks and communities are strongly in evidence and provide a sound platform for longer-term thinking. In more extreme cases, managers may have developed, over time, a community of language and expression unique to the organization in which to express and to short-cut complex ideas and suggestions. In the terminology of organizational cultures, these organizations exhibit strong, cohesive cultures that allow longer-term strategic thinking even in the face of highly turbulent environments

2.4 Summary

In this chapter, we have mapped out the complex terrain where strategies meet organizations. The ways in which managers interpret their environment shapes and influences the ways in which they think and act strategically. They will orientate themselves towards problems and opportunities in different ways, depending on their perspectives and will attempt to animate enthusiasm, support and resources accordingly. Over time, such patterns of strategic thinking and acting become embedded in the infrastructure of the organization and this can lead to the emergence of quite distinct organizational stereotypes.

There are large questions over what are the appropriate levels of analysis to interrogate managerial practice. In this chapter, we have described some of the key levels and the debates each has engendered. These range from a highly focused perspective on the micro-practice of strategy – observing and recording what individual managers do in the strategy process – to a much more macro-level of analysis – showing how the wider context, the organization and managerial interpretation co-exist in a systems model. From this perspective the micro cannot be understood separately from the macro and vice versa.

Finally, the perhaps over-rational and deterministic perspectives of the systems view can be counterbalanced by the consideration of planned versus emergent perspectives. That the majority of strategies seem to err towards emergent processes may come as no surprise to those who participate in strategic decision making. However, even emergent strategies appear to have characteristics which typify them and which, once appreciated, can be of immense help to scholars and practitioners alike.

The sub-themes raised in this chapter (for example, decision making, **strategy and practice**, organizational design and embedded routines) are discussed in greater detail in Part 4 of this book.

Key terms

Online **LearningCentre**

When you have read this chapter, log on to the Online Learning Centre website at www.mcgraw-hill.co.uk/textbooks/mcgee to explore chapter-by-chapter test questions, further reading and more online study tools for strategy.

Further reading and references

Andrews, KR (1987) *The Concept of Corporate Strategy*, 3rd edition, Irwin, Homewood, Illinois.

Balogun, J, Huff, AS and Johnson, P (2003) 'Three responses to the methodological challenges of studying strategizing', *Journal of Management Studies*, **40**, 1, pp. 197–224.

Bell, TB, Marrs, FO, Solomon, I and Thomas, H (1997) *Auditing Organizations Through a Strategic-Systems Lens*, KPMG Peat Marwick LLP, London.

Beer, S (1981) *Brain of the Firm: The Managerial Cybernetics of Organization*, Wiley, Chichester.

Bettis, R and Hill, M (1995) 'The new competitive landscape', *Strategic Management Journal*, **16**, pp. 7–19.

Capra, F (1982) *The Turning Point: Science, Society and the Rising Culture*, Bantam Books, New York.

Child, J (1972) 'Organizational structure, environment and performance: the role of strategic choice' , *Sociology*, **6**, pp. 1–22.

Cummings, S and Wilson, DC (eds) (2003) *Images of Strategy*, Blackwell, Oxford.

De Wit, B and Meyer, R (1999) *Strategy Synthesis: Resolving Strategy Paradoxes to Create Competitive Advantage*, International Thomson Press, London.

Hamel, G and Prahalad, H (1996) 'Competing in the new economy', *Strategic Management Journal*, **17**, pp. 237–42.

Hitt, M, Keats, B and de Marie, S (1998) 'Navigating in the new competitive landscape: building strategic flexibility and competitive advantage in the 21st century', *Academy of Management Executive*, **12**, 4, pp. 22–42.

Johnson, G, Melin, L and Whittington, R (2003) 'Micro strategy and strategizing: towards an activity-based view', *Journal of Management Studies*, **40**, 1, pp. 2–22.

Michaud, C and Thoenig, J-C (2003) *Making Strategy and Organization Compatible*, Palgrave Macmillan, Basingstoke.

Mintzberg, H and Waters, JA (1985) 'Of strategies deliberate and emergent', *Strategic Management Journal*, July/Sept, pp. 257–72.

Porter, M (1980) *Competitive Strategy: Techniques for Analysing Industries and Competitors*, Free Press, New York.

Samra-Fredericks, D (2003) 'Strategizing as lived experience and strategists' everyday efforts to shape strategic direction', *Journal of Management Studies*, **40**, 1, pp. 141–74.

Vincent, JD (1996) *La chair et le Diable*, Odile Jacob, Paris.

Weick, K (1987) 'Substitutes for strategy', in J Teece (ed.) *The Competitive Challenge*, Ballinger, Cambridge, MA.

Part 2

Economic analysis for strategic decisions

Part contents

In this part you will find the following chapters:

Introduction

The logic of Part 2 parallels the logic employed by the strategy analyst. The operation of markets and the nature of supply and demand conditions provides an economics calculus and a toolkit (Chapter 3). There is a context broader and more extensive than markets that we conventionally call the macroeconomy. This (in Chapter 4) shapes and conditions the behaviour of organizations and organizations spend much time and effort in understanding how to cope with or even defy these powerful economic forces. This macroeconomic perspective allied with the microeconomic toolkit gives us the basis for the concept of competitive advantage (Chapter 5). Competitive advantage is the cornerstone of strategy analysis specifically and for strategic thinking generally. It conveys the notion of competitive success in the sense of providing superior (relative to competitors) benefits to customers while earning above average profits (again relative to competitors). Strategy is the pursuit of success and the economic logic expressed in this section gives us an economic language for defining the nature of success. Therefore, this Part should be read as a whole, understanding that competitive advantage is the analytical key to strategy.

Chapters 3 and 4, taken together, present an outline of the basic economic principles that are required in order to understand the detail of strategic management. Economics is a very broad subject, ranging from microeconomics (the organization of markets and the behaviour of firms and individuals), through macroeconomics (the study of whole economies and the determinants of national income, growth etc.), to international trade (the exchange of goods and services by people in different economies). The basic economics in these chapters represent a bare minimum of economics sufficient to gain an understanding of strategic management. For readers who really want to read further in economics we recommend reading McAleese (2004).

Chapter 3 covers the basic economic concepts that are used in strategic management. These include:

- Cost analysis, opportunity cost and economies of scale and scope.

- Market and firm demand and price and income elasticities.

- Competition and rivalry including monopoly, imperfect competition and generic strategies open to firms.

These concepts are fundamental to the way in which economists describe the operations of markets and the operation of the competitive market process. These concepts apply equally to the understanding of the way in which costs arise in the firm and the way in which firms interpret the markets around them. Thus, this chapter presents cost analysis, demand analysis (the analysis of the demand conditions that face individual firms), and analysis of markets and the way in which they operate and the discretion that firms have in their participation in markets. Cost and demand analyses lay the basis for understanding from where cash flows of firms come. Markets are the basis for understanding competition.

The markets perspective in Chapter 3 indicates how strategists need to have an eye to the fit of their organization with its immediate operating environment. Competitors, substitutes and markets can be capricious and their impact immediate. Therefore, a main theme for the strategist is the exploration of the impact of the external economic 'context' on company performance. The strategist is looking to differentiate between those economic forces that are so powerful as to be irresistible and those market conditions that can be conditioned by the choice of appropriate strategy. It is common to observe that economists emphasize the power of markets over organizations whereas organizations adopt strategies for the very purpose of defying environmental pressures and imposing themselves on markets.

The immediate operating environment usually refers to markets for goods and services and to industries – those elements in the supply chain that combine to deliver products and services into final markets. Often overlooked, however, are the apparently more distant influences of an organization's context (such as the impact of government policies or the actions of a regulator). These are present in the deeper context that comprises the infrastructure of government, civil administration, the law, and social custom and practice that shapes the behaviour of businesses and consumers. This deeper context is covered in Chapter 4. The fit of an organization with its environment goes beyond its understanding of the market context of business. All firms and organizations in general are sensitive to events in the wider economy. Even with no change in the strategy of the firm, major changes in its performance and prospects will occur for macroeconomic reasons beyond its control. Whereas the firm might reasonably hope to condition and control its markets, the macroeconomy is typically beyond control but has to be factored into the firm's plans and expectations for the future.

Chapter 4 covers the fundamentals of aggregate demand and supply and the implications for GDP, inflation and unemployment. It also examines the causes and effects of business cycles and what in a global economy causes booms and slumps to come to an end. It goes on to consider issues concerning the sustainability of strong economic growth, especially in emerging markets. The chapter concludes by considering national competitive advantage and the link with company competitive advantage. It also explores issues of uncertainty and risk, and some of the forward-looking strategies business might adopt to limit the effects of exposure to risk. How might uncertain and volatile economic factors (for example, exchange or interest rates) be incorporated into strategic thinking?

Equipped with a microeconomic toolkit and a sense of how to analyse the economic environment, Chapter 5 introduces the key notion of competitive advantage. This is the foundation stone for any strategy analysis. It is a powerful intellectual construct that is used universally. The idea of competitive advantage is gained through the denial of perfect competition, the economist's competitive ideal explained in Chapter 3. Whereas perfect competition leaves no room for individual firms and their strategies, the whole idea of strategy is built on the presence of imperfections in markets. This starting point for strategy is explained in Chapter 5 and further explored in other basic concepts: industry analysis (often referred to as the Porter five forces analysis), the generic competitive strategies and the value chain. Moving from these foundations for strategy analysis, the rest of the chapter introduces a more practical flavour. If we understand the idea of competitive advantage as a key attribute that is specific to the firm, then we have the beginnings of a description of strategy. We describe a template for describing and identifying a strategy – how would you recognize a strategy if you saw one? Whereas competitive advantage is an external positioning concept, strategy also needs to say something about the internal disposition of resources and assets as well. The internal logic of strategy is shown in the strategy cycle and cost analysis is reflected in the value chain. The latter is extremely well known, being another product of Porter's analysis (1985). The strategy cycle illustrates the significance of the balance between internal resources, external market positioning and financial performance. The value chain builds directly on the cost analysis of Chapter 3 and enables us to identify a picture of the internal asset structure and activity structure of the firm. The chapter concludes with a template for a practical overview of strategy – a self-testing of your firm's strategy IQ. This can be turned into a simple questionnaire for assessing the strategy of your own firm or of any firms of which you have some knowledge. By the end of this chapter we will see the significance of competitive advantage for the study of strategy and for strategy making in firms.

Part 2 provides the economic rationale for strategy, a toolkit for analysing strategy, a language for conducting the strategy discourse, and a set of strategy tools. Part 3 goes on to describe how the idea of competitive advantage is translated into practice in a variety of different situations.

Chapter 3

The microeconomics of strategy[1]

Introduction

One of the key questions raised in Chapters 1 and 2 is that of the 'fit' of the organization with its environment. For many years, the question of to what extent does an organization need to 'match' the demands of its environment has been debated. Strategists have long argued that there are significant performance pay-offs from an organization which is in tune with its operating environment. For example, the five forces model (see Chapter 1 and later in Chapter 5) identifies key factors in the operating environment of an organization. There may be high levels of competition or the threat of competition may be relatively benign. On the other hand, the threat of substitution may be high and the switching costs of

---

[1] This chapter is written jointly with K.G (Ben) Knight.

consumers may be relatively low. This means that, in a competitive industry, strategists will have to ensure that the structures and processes of their organizations are flexible enough to undertake rapid changes should the environment become difficult (new organizations enter easily with substitute products, for example).

This seemingly obvious truism – that structures and processes should be increasingly flexible and open to change as environmental conditions become more turbulent – is actually more difficult to analyse and enact in practice. There have been two broad approaches to addressing this key question of organizational fit; one from organization theory and the other from economics. The debate in organizational theory is summarized below and Chapter 3 and the rest of Section 2 then go on to show how a microeconomic analysis can help develop and deepen this organization–environment question.

Organization–environment fit

The key question addressed by organization theorists was: How do organizations adapt successfully to different levels of environment uncertainty? For example, a beer or lager distribution organization operates in a relatively certain environment. Fluctuations in demand for beer are incremental and take place over a long period of time. Beer is also a difficult product to substitute. On the other hand, oil companies and airlines face highly uncertain environments as operating conditions can change rapidly (e.g. terrorist activities, shifting demand patterns) and substitution can be quick and easy (e.g. low-cost airlines).

Building on the work of Burns and Stalker (1961) conducted in England and Scotland, Lawrence and Lorsch's (1967) study of a sample of American organizations facing different levels of uncertainty revealed that two factors were key to sustained performance – differentiation and integration. **Differentiation** refers to the breadth and diversity of individuals' perspectives in departments (broad or narrow; focusing on functional aspects only, for example, versus seeing a broader picture beyond the function). It also refers to the degree of formal structure in a function or department. **Integration** refers to the extent to which functions or departments collaborate. It is also an index of the quality of that collaboration. Lawrence and Lorsch (1967) found that different departments in organizations faced different levels of uncertainty. For example, they found that research and development (R&D) departments faced uncertainties over long time horizons and R&D strategies had to be extremely goal-directed. Sales departments faced uncertainties over short time periods (weeks, not months). In successful firms, R&D departments were structured informally and the sales departments were formally structured but were very socially orientated. The Lawrence and Lorsch study concluded that organizations perform better when the levels of differentiation and integration match the levels of uncertainty in the environment.

Burns and Stalker (1961) had shown earlier that another response to environmental uncertainty lay in the way an organization was structured overall. They depicted two extreme types of structure, **mechanistic** (centralized, formal, with strategic decisions made only by a small number of top managers) and **organic** (decentralized, informal, with strategic decisions made where the relevant expertise lay in the organization). They concluded that organizations which adopt organic structures performed better (were able to innovate, change and thrive) when the environment was highly uncertain. They also found the reverse was true. Mechanistic organizations perform well in very stable and predictable environments.

Both studies provided a firm foundation for a contingency view of strategy and organization which persists today. However, as Rosenfeld and Wilson (1999: 358) point out:

> there has been a growing body of disquiet over the simplicity of this contingent 'fit' between structure and environment ... environmental characteristics do not wholly fashion organization structures ... managers have choices within certain limits to carve out their own organizational designs and processes ...

This debate about to what extent managers have autonomy over the strategic decisions they take can be read in detail in Child (1972; 1997), where he introduces the concept of 'strategic choice'. Managers are not wholly constrained by their environments according to Child. But the premise is clear, whether one takes a wholly or a partially contingent view:

> Environments and organizations are closely interlinked and the nature of those linkages seems to affect organizational performance.

The perspective of the strategist

For the strategist, therefore, it is essential to analyse such organization–environment relations. They both affect where strategic decisions are taken in the organization (centrally or not) and influence the likely success of their outcomes. Despite this apparent 'Eureka' moment in organization theory, there has been no significant precision and identification of what exactly those environmental variables might be. Which organizational factors are the basis of highly uncertain environments and vice versa? The answers from organization theory remain too broad for the strategist. There is an urgent need for further detail and the identification of key variables. It is here where microeconomics comes to the rescue. It drills deeper than organization theorists attempted to do.

Chapters 3 and 4 present an outline of the basic economic principles that are required in order to understand the subject of strategic management. Economics is a very broad subject, ranging from microeconomics (the organization of markets and the behaviour of firms and individuals), through macroeconomics (the study of whole economies and the determinants of national income, growth etc.), to international trade (the exchange of goods and services by people in different economies). The basic economics in these chapters represent a bare minimum of economics sufficient to gain an understanding of strategic management.

A main theme in both chapters is the exploration of the impact of the external economic 'context' on company performance and the aspects of the business environment over which strategic 'actions' have limited control. Context usually refers to markets for goods and services and to industries – those elements in the supply chain that combine to deliver products and services into final markets. Behind this there is a deeper context that comprises the infrastructure of government, civil administration, the law, and social custom and practice that shapes the behaviour of businesses and consumers. As the book progresses you will see that the theme of strategic management is how the firm can position itself against these economic forces in order to survive and prosper.

This chapter covers the basic economic concepts that are used in strategic management. These include:

◆ Cost analysis, opportunity cost and economies of scale and scope.

◆ Market and firm demand and price and income elasticities.

◆ Competition and rivalry including monopoly, imperfect competition and generic strategies open to firms.

These concepts are fundamental to the way in which economists describe the operations of markets and the operation of the competitive market process. These concepts apply equally to the understanding of the way in which costs arise in the firm and the way in which firms interpret the markets around them. Thus, this chapter presents cost analysis, demand analysis (the analysis of the demand conditions that face individual firms), and analysis of markets and the way in which they operate and the discretion that firms have in their participation in markets. Cost and demand analyses lay the basis for understanding from where cash flows of firms come. Markets are the basis for understanding competition.

3.1 Strategy, markets and macroeconomy

Although there are rival and contrasting views of strategy (set out in Chapter 5), understanding the past and present performance of a company is a key input to strategy making. Skilful analysis of a company and its business environment enables the *separate* effects of factors external and internal to the firm to be carefully identified. Accurate diagnosis of the state of a company is essential for effective competitive strategy, because strategic action is inevitably constrained by a whole host of external events over which managers have no control. For example, the economic crisis that occurred in Asia in 1997/8 derailed the strategies of many companies, not just in the Asian region. The globalization strategy of major Korean companies such as Samsung was thwarted both by the scale of the domestic recession in Korea and the uncontrollable movement of the Korean exchange rate. The impact of these external shocks on the financial position of Samsung and many other companies in the Asian region made it impossible for them to carry out their overseas investment strategy. In late 1997, Samsung were forced to close a new excavator factory and to shelve expansion plans for their electronics factory in the UK.

The effect of this crisis was not confined to Asia. Many non-Asian firms lost large export orders. The Prudential saw its single premium sales drop from £49 million to £9 million in 1997/98. Many EU-based companies with large Asian projects were hit. For example, in the UK the Midlands-based CAD had been commissioned by an Indonesian conglomerate to design and develop a sophisticated multi-purpose vehicle for the Asian market. The crisis in Asia, and in Indonesia in particular, meant that the project could not be completed, with catastrophic consequences for CAD.

Similarly, the 'technology crash' heralded by the collapse in the prices of technology stocks on the NASDAQ in May 2000 signalled the end of the technology boom of the 1990s and led to a significant slowdown of the world economy. In particular, telecommunications companies found themselves to have substantially overinvested in licences for new technology communications, resulting in excessive debt burdens on balance sheets without compensating increases in consumer demand. Most of these companies had still not recovered by late 2003.

The identification of these 'contextual' constraints and an awareness of the severity of their impact on the firm are clearly important. Managers take 'actions' to influence the 'context' in which a firm works, but to do this effectively managers have not only to know what *should* be done, but also to be sensitive to what *can* be done. Recognizing the limitations of strategic 'actions' is fundamental to success. Economic analysis helps us in achieving this understanding of the business environment, so this chapter introduces some key concepts that are used in this stage of the strategy process.

This chapter explores these issues using the example of two real-life manufacturing companies which, for the sake of anonymity, we will call PaperCo (Company A) and MetalCo (Company B). PaperCo and MetalCo operate in different market sectors and

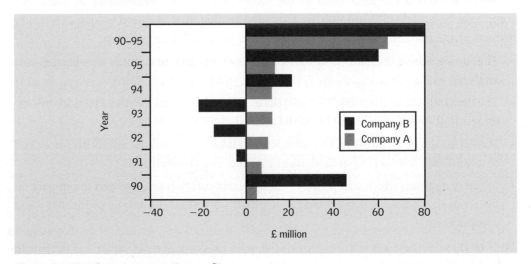

Figure 3.1 Total pre-tax operating profit

produce different goods. MetalCo is a metals manufacturer selling its product to the engineering and vehicle sectors, while PaperCo is a papermaker supplying packaging products to the food industry. The financial performance of these companies over a five-year period in the 1990s is shown in Figure 3.1.

Note that over the five-year period as a whole, the profit performance of MetalCo is significantly better than PaperCo. Both companies are of similar size in terms of capital employed and sales, so that this superior performance is mirrored in the rates of return on both capital and sales. However, it is also clear from Figure 3.1 that there are substantial differences in the pattern of profits over time. PaperCo shows a steady increase in its profits while MetalCo experiences a much more variable performance. Indeed, in three of the five years, MetalCo made a loss, and our view of the comparative performance of these companies in these three years would be completely different from the analysis of the whole five-year period. (The reason the data ends in 1995 is that MetalCo was taken over by a larger company and there is no separate financial data for the years since 1995.)

One explanation for these differences is variation in managerial competence and in particular in strategic capability. Anticipating the discussion in Chapter 5 we set out here the definition of competitive advantage:

> *Delivering superior value to customers and in doing so earning an above average return for the company and its stakeholders.*

One measure of its existence is the ability of a company to outperform its sector rivals. Both PaperCo and MetalCo enjoy substantial competitive advantage in their respective market sectors and this is reflected in their financial performance. Both are in the top 25 per cent of companies operating in their separate market sectors.

How, then, could the differences in the long-run financial performance of these two companies be explained? Economic analysis suggests that, first, we need to look at four key features of the market 'context' in which these two firms sell their products:

- The supply side of the market, which tells us how costs arise and which we will label **cost analysis**.

- The demand side of the market, which tells us how value is perceived and paid for by customers and which we will label **demand analysis**.

- Market rivalry, which tells us how competition takes place and the effects on prices and costs and which we will label **analysis of markets and competition**.

- Industry analysis, which tells us the economic configuration of firms and the impact on the strategic choices that they make and which we will label **analysis of industry and competition**.

The first three of these key features provide the main headings of this chapter and the fourth is discussed in Chapter 5.

Now consider the following simple profits equation:

Profits = total revenue − total costs

The supply side mostly focuses on the cost element of the profits equation, while the demand side and market rivalry mainly deal with revenue issues such as price, sales volume and market share. However, as we shall see, costs are also influenced by sales volume and hence demand and rivalry issues. Analysis of industry and competition assesses the combination of forces that leads to greater or lesser profitability. Note how in our approach to understanding the economic concepts we indicate how the nature of markets affect the way competition works through the interaction of buyers/consumers in the marketplace. But we also show that the economic configuration of the firms in the industry also affects competition by virtue of the cost structures and the nature of their resources and capabilities that condition the competitive offerings that they wish to make.

3.2 Cost analysis

The firm needs to examine the implications of its decisions for the costs of the business – the links between decision making and costs is central to an understanding of long-run cost position and competitiveness. The guiding principle is the idea of **opportunity cost.** This is defined as:

> *The sacrifice of alternatives foregone in producing goods or services.* (Seldon and Pennance 1965, p. 253)

For example, the cost of capital for project A is the return foregone by taking project X rather than project Y. It is not simply the cash cost of the funds required for project X. For an individual, the opportunity cost of a new car might be the benefits forgone by not extending the house. For a company, the opportunity cost of expansion into North America might be the return foregone by not investing in China. The notion of opportunity cost rests on the fact of scarcity, that resources are limited in relation to the possibilities that exist. Without scarcity there would be no concept of cost and indeed economics and economic thinking would be irrelevant.

The strength and pervasiveness of the concept of opportunity cost leads us into an understanding of **relevant costs**: the costs associated with a decision are those costs that are directly affected by and are changed by a decision. The significance of this is that costs are decision-specific and therefore are unlikely to be routinely available from those costs reported in the annual accounts for the purposes of reporting to shareholders. Accounting costs are typically backward looking and relate to the firm as a whole whereas relevant costs are decision-specific and relate to future costs. Management accounting strives to bridge this gap by taking a future perspective, although, by its nature, it cannot, in setting budgets, anticipate the characteristics of decisions that are relevant for future costs.

Many costs arise directly from the scale (volume) of operation of a business. The term **cost structure** refers to the technical conditions of production in the markets in which PaperCo and MetalCo operate. The critical issue is the balance of costs between **fixed costs**, which do not vary with output (for example, the cost of machines or buildings or R&D spending), and **variable costs**, which do (for example, labour costs or raw material costs). Table 3.1 sets out the definitions of these different cost concepts together with an example of the impact of different levels of output

Figure 3.2 depicts a cost function that shows the relationship between average total cost and output. It shows how average costs vary with output. Note the shape of the average cost relationship. Average total costs fall and are at the minimum value when output is Q1. The fall in average total costs occurs (arithmetically) because of the fall in average fixed costs (*see* Table 3.1 above).

The shape of cost curves depends critically on the specification of the relevant time period. Economists make a simple but very powerful distinction between the **short run** and the **long run**. The short run is the (short) time within which the fixed factors of production cannot be changed. For example, the nature of a factory and the characteristics of its production lines cannot normally be changed within a period of weeks or even months. However, over a longer period, say five years, the factory can be remodelled and the production lines rebuilt to take advantage of new technology and new working processes.

Short-run cost behaviour has two important characteristics. These are captured in the **law of diminishing returns**. This says that as additional amounts of variable factors of production are added to fixed factors (e.g. factory, production lines), unit costs of output will first decrease up to a point, but will then increase (*see* Table 3.1 above). The first part of this arises

Table 3.1 Cost definitions and cost mechanics

Fixed cost:	Costs which do not vary with output
Variable cost:	Costs which vary with output
Total cost:	Fixed cost + Variable cost
Average total cost:	Total cost ÷ Output
Average fixed cost:	Fixed cost ÷ Output

1 Output	2 Total fixed cost	3 Total variable cost	4 Total cost	5 Average total cost (4 ÷ 1)	6 Average variable cost (3 ÷ 1)	7 Average fixed cost (2 ÷ 1)
100	300	100	400	4.00	1.00	3.00
250	300	200	500	2.00	0.80	1.17
400	300	300	600	1.50	0.75	0.75
500	300	400	700	1.40	0.80	0.60
560	300	500	800	1.43	0.89	0.53

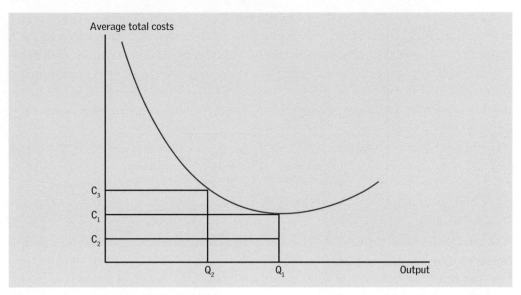

Figure 3.2 Short-run average total costs

because the fixed costs (associated with the fixed factors of production) remain constant as output increases. Therefore unit costs will fall (see Table 3.1 above) and we see the importance of attaining the 'right' volumes of output where average costs are minimized. The second part arises because the fixed factors imply capacity constraints on output that might in part be offset by applying more variable factors but at lower efficiencies (such as overtime rates and higher machinery maintenance costs). Thus, output can only be expanded at higher **marginal costs** (marginal cost is the cost of producing one extra unit of output).

In the long run, all factors of production are variable. For the firm this implies investment decisions that pose the question of how much should we invest (in fixed factors such as production lines) so as to minimize the cost of production in the long term. Figure 3.3 depicts a long-run cost curve that exhibits a range in which increasing returns to scale takes place (to Q_1), a range of constant returns (Q_1 to Q_2), and a range of decreasing returns to scale (beyond Q_2). In this figure the point Q_1 is called the **minimum efficient scale of output (MES)**.

Note that the horizontal axis is the designed scale of the plant whereas in the short-run curve (Figure 3.2) it is the actual volume of output. Figure 3.4 places the short- and long-run curves together. The short-run curve shows the costs that arise given the capital that is actually invested at that scale of plant design. Actual costs will reflect the intensity of use of that invested plant as well as the benefits of having a plant designed for that level of operation. You can, of course, imagine a situation in which the plant has been designed and built to too great a scale (e.g. because of errors in forecasting demand) and the actual short-run cost curve results in very high unit costs because the fixed costs are far too high. In Figure

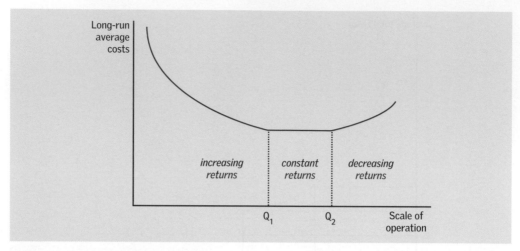

Figure 3.3 Long-run average costs

3.4 you can see that a demand forecast Q_f would require Plant B to be constructed and if the forecast was correct then Q_f would be produced at the minimum point of the short-run cost curve. If, however, demand actually turns out to be Q_a then this has to be produced from Plant B (although Plant A would have been preferable). You can see from inspection that the cost of producing at this level from Plant B is higher than from Plant A. Economies of scale derive specifically from an optimal combination of factors of production and they can be quantified from conventional capital budgeting (net present value) calculations. It is important to recognize that the short-run cost curves (Figure 3.2) represent actual costs identifiable as cash outflows. By contrast the long-run costs should be seen as *planning costs*.

Companies that have cost functions with substantial returns to scale have a strong incentive to sell and produce the large-scale output at Q_1 in Figure 3.3. If they fail to produce Q_1, average total costs will rise and this will damage their financial performance. A common source of scale economies is the opportunity to spread the fixed costs of capital, such as physical equipment, e.g. plant and buildings, or R&D spending. Scale economies usually arise from the efficient use of these fixed *firm-level resources*. There are other sources of *plant* scale economies arising that also have an impact on average variable costs. Large-scale production enables specialization of labour (see the section below on sources of economies of scale) to take place, increasing the productivity of the labour force and reducing average labour costs. It also enables the producer to place large orders with suppliers and negotiate quantity discounts that lower average material and component costs.

PaperCo and MetalCo are both in this category. Their technology is heavily capital-intensive and, as a result, they both benefit from large-scale economies, so Q_1 is their large optimal level of output. In the long term, they are both successful in reaching this optimal scale, so they both appear in the top 25 per cent of their sector's performance, so they enjoy

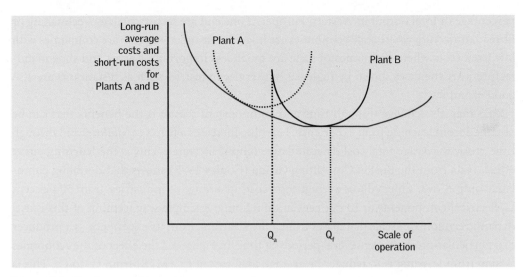

Figure 3.4 Short-run and long-run average costs

a competitive advantage over their competitors as a result of their effective use of *resources*. Although this may be a critical issue in explaining the financial performance of many companies, especially in slow-growing sectors of any economy, it is not crucial to the explanation of the differences between our selected companies PaperCo and MetalCo. This is therefore not the reason for the superior long-run performance of MetalCo. On the other hand, note that in the short-run PaperCo is clearly better able to achieve the optimal scale more consistently. We explore the reasons for this later in this chapter.

Note that economies of scale are much more important in heavy manufacturing industries in which there are substantial capital requirements. Table 3.2 shows the MES (the minimum efficient scale of output – *see* Q_1 on Figure 3.3) for various industries expressed as a

Table 3.2 MES as percentage of EU production

Cellulose fibres	16.00
Aerospace	12.20
Refrigerators	11.00
Steelmaking	10.00
Agricultural machinery	6.60
Cigarettes	6.00
Shoes	0.08
Carpets	0.03

Source: Pratten (1988): Emerson (1988); EU Commission (1997).

percentage of total output in Western Europe. At one end are sectors such as steelmaking or fibre manufacture where scale economies are huge. At the other extreme are companies with low fixed costs where economies of scale are much less important. Carpet and shoe manufacturers are the cases shown in Table 3.2 but service industries such as restaurants are also good examples.

MES may also change through time and an important reason is the benefits that can be obtained from learning from experience. Learning increases a firm's *capabilities* and through time reduces average total cost as cumulative output increases. This is the **learning curve effect**. Data from the Boston Consulting Group (Conley 1975) shows that doubling cumulative output over time reduces average total costs in a range of industries, from 30 per cent in electrical components to 10 per cent in oil refining. A simple way to think of this is as a dynamic economy of scale that arises from a firm learning from its experience as a producer of a particular product over several periods of time. In Figure 3.2 the effect of the economies arising from learning is to reduce the average total cost at Q_1 (MES) from C_1 to C_2. This is another potent cause of differences in cost and profitability, but again is not important to the differences observed in PaperCo and MetalCo.

Another source of superior financial performance is the ability of a firm to exploit **economies of scope**. Economies of scope exist when the cost of joint production of two outputs is less than the cost of producing each output separately (Panzer and Willig 1981). In terms of Figure 3.2 economies of scope arise when the average cost of a single product is lowered by its joint production with other products in a multiproduct firm. When output for each product is at Q_1 (so scale economies for each product are fully exploited), it is possible for average costs at C_2 to be even lower than C_1, if the economies of scope are also fully exploited. In practice, these scope economies can be important. A study (Pratten 1988) of the cost effects of halving the number of products made by each producer in a selection of EU industries shows impacts that range from +3 per cent in carpet manufacture to +8 per cent in motor vehicles. These scope economies may arise from the opportunity to leverage a *core capability* arising from knowledge and learning, organization or management skill, so as to reduce the average total cost of all products produced in a multiproduct firm. A good example is the expertise that arises from technical and scientific knowledge within the firm. Exploiting this distinctive expertise by innovation and product diversification lowers the average total cost of all products. Pharmaceutical manufacture and steel production are both sectors where this kind of cost economy is important. Scope economies can also arise from efficient use of *resources*, for example, where a number of related goods are produced using a common process. Car manufacture of a range of models is an example and part of the reason for the significant scope economies found in Pratten's study. Another source of scope economies arises from spreading the fixed cost of a network over a wider range of products. Commercial banks, for example, incur a large fixed cost from their branch networks. If they spread this cost over a large range of related corporate and retail financial products, the average total cost of each product is reduced. In the area of microelectronics it is possible to realize economies of scope between software and hardware products. Open systems require knowledge of how hardware and software products can be integrated across different vendors' systems. Specifically, software knowledge is essential to design hardware and vice versa (Langowitz 1987). However, there are limits to the economies that scope can offer. Eventually, as the demands for sharing know-how increase, bottlenecks in the form of overextended scientists, engineers and other technical personnel occur.

PaperCo and MetalCo are both able to exploit economies of scope – and do so. Hence, they build competitive advantage and appear in the top 25 per cent of profits performance in their separate industries. However, for reasons outside their strategic control, scope economy opportunities are much larger in Company B, MetalCo. Its core technical competence has more uses and markets, so its product range is much larger than A's, whose core capability is in a tightly demarcated niche. This is the source of the difference in their long-run performance.

A final issue of importance on the supply side in explaining differences in financial performance between industries and firms is supplier power (see the later discussion in this chapter, section 3.4). Powerful suppliers drive up costs and this has an impact on profits. PaperCo and MetalCo are in industries in which suppliers are generally weak, with one major exception: all companies in both industries are heavy users of energy, the suppliers of which have considerable market power.

3.2.1 Sources of economies of scale

The division of labour

Economies of scale figure prominently in modern discussion of the appropriate size of industrial plants. The phenomenon itself has long been recognized and Adam Smith provided the first classic description after witnessing pinmaking processes in the eighteenth century:

> ... one man draws out the wire, another straightens it, a third cuts it,
> a fourth points it, a fifth grinds it at the top for receiving the head;
> to make the head requires two or three different operations:
> to put it on is a peculiar business, to whiten the pins is another;
> it is even a trade by itself to put them into the paper; and the important
> business of making a pin is, in this manner, divided into about
> eighteen distinct operations, which, in some manufactories, are
> all performed by distinct hands ... I have seen a manufactory of this kind
> where ten men ... could, when they exerted themselves, make among them ...
> upwards of forty-eight thousand pins in a day ... But if they had all wrought
> separately and independently, and without any of them having been educated

to this peculiar business, they certainly could not each of them have made
twenty, perhaps not one pin in a day . . . (Adam Smith, *An Inquiry into the Nature*
and Causes of the Wealth of Nations, 1776)

In this famous passage Adam Smith describes an improvement in labour productivity in excess of 15 000 per cent. He is describing the **division of labour** (also called **specialization**) which came to Britain with the Industrial Revolution of the eighteenth and nineteenth centuries, bringing with it the development and organization of specialized factory trades and an increase in the use of machinery. In Smith's view, these great increases in the productivity of labour were due directly to three consequences of the division of labour: an increase in the dexterity and skill of individual workers due to specialization in one trade; the saving of time lost in moving labour from one type of work to another; and (in his words) '*the invention of a great number of machines which facilitate and abridge labour, and enable one man to do the work of many*.'

The passing of two centuries has not diminished the force of Adam Smith's observations. The assembly line of an automatic plant provides a classic illustration of the impact of labour specialization. The extent of specialization depends technically on the scale of automation and the amount of capital invested in machinery. The greater the automation, the more can a worker specialize in one operation, e.g. 'a left wheel nut tightener' (*see* Scherer 1970). At a rate of output of 500 cars per day, the left wheel nut tightener can be fully employed. But in a smaller plant where output is only 250 cars per day he will be idle for half the time and may be assigned other jobs. However, this inspires losses in his efficiency as he moves to another work location (or as the work flow is re-routed to come to his position) or as he changes his mental gear and finds the correct tool and adopts a different work technique. In general, larger firms can enjoy more specialization than smaller ones but in any event the extent of the division of labour is restricted by the size of the market.

Identical principles apply in the use of specialized machinery. Machines can be designed to perform a range of specific tasks at high speed with great reliability, and considerable savings in time and labour. Such machinery is of little value to the small-scale producer because they cannot be scaled down to his output levels and would be idle for much of the time. Likewise, their preparation for a production run requires much set up time and costs which are only recouped over long production runs. In general, smaller firms must use slower, more labour-intensive machine tools. Nowhere is this more sharply illustrated than in the comparison between the labour productivity of Japanese motorcycle factories (about 200 bikes per man year) and the factories of North America and Western Europe (about 20 bikes per man year) (Boston Consulting Group 1975). Due in part to their privileged access to the large and growing Japanese and Asian markets in the 1950s and 60s, the Japanese industry developed a scale of automation unknown in other countries where the market was more specialized and limited in size.

The benefits of division of labour are fairly obvious and can be summarized thus:

◆ increase in output at lower unit costs;

◆ increased use of machinery;

◆ increased possibility of improvement and quality control;

◆ the saving of time and tools through the avoidance of moving labour from place to place or the need to own general purpose equipment.

For the individual worker there are also several advantages, for instance hours of work may be shortened and work may be lightened (although productivity gains may have to be shared among the entire workforce). Against this there are problems arising from the loss of traditional skills and pride in workmanship and monotony and strain imposed by the speed of the production line. For the firm there are clear difficulties that arise from the complexity of administration of such large units of production and the risk of failure of production from whatever cause when production is concentrated in one plant.

However, there are consequences to the large-scale adoption of this doctrine of specialization. These are reviewed in Chapter 19. The adoption of the doctrine of specialization and economies of scale has important consequences for the firm in that they develop hierarchical management structures appropriate for the management of specialized tasks but much less so in terms of flexibility and in terms of the costs of adversarial labour relations resulting from specialization.

The cube law

Along with specialization of labour and of capital equipment goes the capital cost savings on large items of machinery due to the operation of the so-called **cube law**. The volume of a vessel (which for process plant determines the volume of output) is roughly proportional to the cube of its radius while its surface area (where the cost is to be found) is proportional to the square. Thus, as the volume capacity of a plant increases, the material requirements and hence its capital cost tend to rise as the two-thirds power of the output capacity. There is considerable empirical support for the existence of this 'two-thirds rule', which is used by engineers in estimating the cost of new process equipment (Moore 1959; Haldi and Whitcomb 1967).

Economies of massed reserves

Another benefit of size comes from the **economy of massed reserves** (*see* Robinson 1958). This rests on the law of large numbers on which the entire insurance industry is based. To preserve continuity of production, the firm must insure itself against the consequences of machine breakdown by maintaining a reserve of excess capacity. The larger the firm and the more identical (or similar) machines it uses, the smaller the proportion required of spare capacity. Such economies exist for stockholding, financial assets, labour, and service department staffing.

Firm-level economies of scale

We should also distinguish between scale economies achievable at the plant level and those achievable at the level of the firm itself. Division of labour and the operation of the cube law each apply at the level of the plant. The economy of massed reserves can apply at both levels. Generally, it is relatively easy to specify and estimate the scale economies at plant level because they rest on technical, engineering considerations. Firm-level economies are more difficult to identify with such clarity and are, surprisingly, more difficult to achieve. But, as we shall see in later chapters, they are, in theory at least, the basis for much merger activity.

The costs incurred by the firm as distinct from the plant can be grouped broadly as: managerial and administrative; research and development; transportation and distribution; and marketing. Where the firm operates many plants, and particularly when there is some degree of horizontal and/or vertical integration, then the firm-level economies can be of great potential significance. Administrative economies can arise through the traditional division of labour and substitution of labour by capital-intensive equipment; for example, word processing equipment replacing typists, automatic document coding and transferral replacing clerks. Financial economies are available by reducing the level of stocks and work in progress relative to the rate of production. Marketing economies are available in advertising to mass markets and using a common sales force to purvey a product line. Risks can be spread in R&D by managing a portfolio of projects rather than a single or few projects. The pooling of risks arises through pooling financial resources across markets with different cyclical characteristics.

Barry Supple (1977) has placed economies of scale in the context of business history and development of large-scale enterprise:

> the specific factors responsible for this trend to large-scale enterprise have varied markedly. The economies of scale in their conventional sense – the unit cost reduction derived from large accumulations of capital equipment, advanced and expensive technology, specialization of functions, bulk purchasing and distribution – played an obvious part ... At the same time, however, the emergence of the giant firm was also a function of financial considerations (stock market buoyancies in particular increased the probability, and profitability, of mergers and flotation) and of market vicissitudes and ambitions. The desire to protect investments and market shares, the ambition to secure market control and stability of sales, the pressure to mitigate competition and to expand sales and profit margins – all illustrate the range, from defensive to offensive, of policies involved, as well as the overall importance of market strategies in the history of large-scale enterprise. And, in the event, many of the most spectacular instances of big business (with Courtaulds, Lever Brothers, Austin Morris) rested as much on product differentiation as on 'pure' cost advantages.

Supple's comments reinforce the earlier statement that the size and the nature of the market place some limits of the extent to which unit costs can continue to fall. Apart from market size, there are other limitations to the extent of economies of scale.

The first relates to the way in which specialized but indivisible units of equipment dovetail in the production process. At some point a stage is reached at which further cost reductions are not possible because all units of equipment are being used at their optimum rates. Any expansion of output in units less than that required for replication of existing equipment will cause unit costs to rise.

A second set of assertions about the management process is probably more significant in bringing potential technical economies to an end. The general hypothesis is that the management of sufficiently large units entails rising unit costs. One variant of this ascribes the problem to the relatively fixed input of senior management time as the scale of operation grows. The cost of communication rises very rapidly, usually evidenced by large numbers of middle managers, staff and so on. The consequence of these managerial and co-ordination problems is upward pressure on costs until diseconomies of large-scale management eventually overpower the technical economies of scale. A concrete analogy is the rise in transport and distribution costs as production is increasingly centralized to obtain production economies. To service a network of distribution points from one central production point entails higher distribution costs than the servicing of smaller numbers of distribution points from a number of decentralized production facilities.

The organization of large-scale management has become highly specialized. Specialized staff functions that supply information for decision making to line executives have been used quite effectively. Communication spurred on by rapid technological developments has been simplified and cheapened beyond our recent expectations. Control techniques based on management accounting, budgetary control and cash flow analysis have been brought to a high state of perfection. Information technology and systems permit the storage, retrieval and analysis of vast amounts of information. These changes in the technology of management, together with more sophisticated views of organizational structure, allow the management of large-scale enterprise to become more and more effective.

Notwithstanding the state of the managerial art, the potential for achieving cost savings through larger plant and from size has often been frustrated by circumstances (for some early examples, *see* HMSO 1978). Examples include the difficulty of phasing out obsolete plant in the steel industry in the face of slow-growing demand and political difficulties. The motor industry in Europe also has a large number of plants in relation to the numbers of cars produced. Similarly the merging of the manufacturing facilities of the aircraft industry and the development of a coherent commercial strategy has taken undue time. However, scale economies are not always frustrated by practical difficulties. More encouraging results have been seen in electricity generation, the restructuring of the bearings industry, and the change of scale in the brewing industry. The limits to the realization of technical economies might be summarized as follows:

- diseconomies of scale in distribution;
- the complexity of large-scale management which requires high investment cost and accumulated experience to reduce it;
- the need to maintain product differentiation and flexibility in the face of changes in tastes;
- the industrial relations problems in managing large plants.

3.3 Demand analysis

The demand side of the market is also relevant to an understanding of the 'deep structure of markets', which is so critical to company performance. The first issue is the degree to which market-level product demand is responsive to changes in price.

Figure 3.5 shows a downward sloping relationship of demand with product price. This market 'demand curve' shows that price increases reduce the volume of demand and vice versa. We could measure the degree of responsiveness of demand to a change in price as the:

$$\frac{\text{Change in quantity demanded}}{\text{Change in price}}$$

which is the slope of the demand curve, or by:

$$\frac{\% \text{ change in quantity demanded}}{\% \text{ change in price}}$$

The latter is the measure preferred by economists who call it the **own price elasticity of demand**. Since demand falls when price is raised and vice versa, real life estimates of the price elasticity are generally negative. Some examples are shown in Figure 3.6.

What factors influence the elasticity? Clearly, as is evident from Figure 3.6, necessities such as basic foodstuffs and fuel are likely to have a low elasticity and demand is therefore relatively insensitive to changes in price. One further important matter is the availability of substitutes for the product. If substitutes are readily available, an increase in price

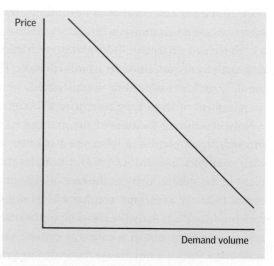

Figure 3.5 Market demand curve

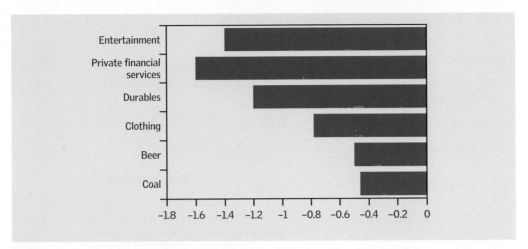

Figure 3.6 Luxuries, necessities and substitutes: market price elasticities of demand (% change in sales ÷ % change in price)
Source: Deaton (1975).
Copyright 1975, with permission from Elsevier.

will have a much larger impact on demand. Petrol, for example, has no close substitutes. If you own a petrol-driven car you have no alternative to petrol and, hence, the elasticity of demand for petrol will be low. This market-level demand relationship gives rise to an aspect of the market environment over which companies have no direct control. It has to be managed. A particular problem arises with products with a very low elasticity. Petrol is one and beer, where firms are concerned, is another. Products like this are an attractive source of revenue for a government. An increase in the rate of tax raises prices, but has little effect on the volume of sales. Because of this, raising the rate of tax has a strong positive effect on tax revenue. The result, from the firm's point of view, is that political forces over which they have no control significantly alter market prices and severely constrain its pricing strategy.

What about the firm-level relationship of price and demand? A crucial issue here is the homogeneity of the product and the ability of the individual firm to differentiate its output from others through branding, thereby reducing the threat of substitute products. If the product is difficult to differentiate, the firm will face a highly elastic **demand curve**, whatever the industry-level relationship looks like.

In the extreme case in which the product is completely homogeneous, the firm will face a horizontal demand curve, as shown in Figure 3.7, so that if an individual firm raises its price above P_1, it will attract no customers. If it lowers its price, it is overwhelmed by demand. The firm in this case is a passive actor with absolutely no power over the market for its products. This is a key feature of perfect competition, in which the individual firm is a price taker with absolutely no impact on prices. In the more normal case, where some differentiation is possible, perhaps by product branding or through service excellence, the firm is able to exercise

Figure 3.7 Firm and market demand curves

some market power and secure a degree of control, though this will be conditional on the market dominance of its customers. This market power extends not only to price (raising it), but also to the price elasticity, as Figure 3.5 shows. Branding secures the attachment of the buyer to the individual product, so that an increase in its price will have a less adverse effect on demand, because there is less substitution into alternative products available from other firms in the same market.

A good illustration of these concepts is a branded food manufacturer, such as Heinz or Nestlé, operating in the EU or the US. It is possible for these manufacturers to brand the product and hence secure a price premium and improve profitability, and this is what they have done. Since branding also has the helpful effect of reducing the price elasticity, the extra profit margin they get is sustainable over time. However, these benefits are increasingly problematic for the branded food manufacturers, because of the growth in supermarket retailing and hence the growth in the buying power of their customers. Large retailers promote their own brands, weakening the manufacturer's brand and, as a result, demand large quantity discounts from branded food manufacturers which need the supermarket outlet for their products. Clearly, the changing balance of power on the demand side of the market challenges the sustainability of an individual business's competitive advantage, even when they successfully brand their products.

In the case of companies PaperCo and MetalCo, both sell a difficult-to-differentiate product to powerful industrial users. As a result, it is difficult for either to secure premium prices and the profits that go along with them. This is characteristic of all firms in their markets so, in the sector ranking of profitability, both appear in low profitability sectors (PaperCo in paper packaging for the food industry and MetalCo in metal manufacture). Some global data for this is shown in Figure 3.8.

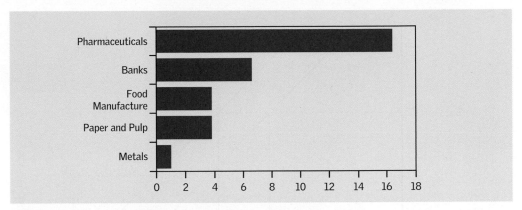

Figure 3.8 Return on revenues (%) in the Fortune Global 500, 2001
Source: Fortune (www.fortune.com).

A further reason for the relatively poor sectoral profits performance of PaperCo and MetalCo is the result of the weak effect of long-run increases in national income on the demand for these products. Both PaperCo and MetalCo have their customer base in the rich industrial economies of North America and the EU. In these markets, the share (or intensity, as it is sometimes called) of the products produced by companies A and B in the total national sales of all products is falling. They produce manufactured products and this sector's share of total sales is declining, while the service sector is expanding. Many manufacturing markets suffer as a consequence of mature and saturated markets. We can measure the response of market-level sales to changes in the long-run income of a country by calculating the long-run income elasticity of demand. This is an analogous concept to 'price elasticity. The long-run income elasticity of demand is:

$$\frac{\% \text{ change in long-run quantity demanded}}{\% \text{ change in long-run national income}}$$

Generally, this is a positive number, so increases in national income shift the market demand curve upwards, as shown in Figure 3.9, where the initial curve D_1 is shifted to a new curve D_2 as a result of an increase in income. Since the curve has shifted up, more will be demanded at each price. At a price of P_1, for example, the quantity demanded will increase from Q_1 to Q_2. If national income falls, the opposite happens and the quantity demanded falls.

Where the income elasticity is high, firms will experience large increases in market demand when long-run income increases, and vice versa when it is low. In the mature economies of the EU and the US, the long-run income elasticity of demand is higher in service markets such as tourism or media providers, but low in engineering and food, which are the end users of the output of PaperCo and MetalCo. The result is a progressive decline in the share of GDP produced in the manufacturing sector and a rise in the service

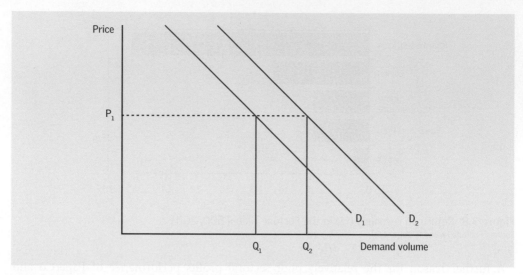

Figure 3.9 Market demand curve and changes in national income

sector's share. Note also the link between the long-run income elasticity and financial performance. Figure 3.8 shows that most of the high-performing sectors are service providers or manufacturers of high-tech products such as pharmaceuticals, while the traditional manufacturing sectors do relatively badly. What makes it worse for the manufacturers A and B is that in an earlier stage of economic development, the long-run elasticity was a good deal higher. In this period, substantial capacity was installed to meet the large long-run growth in demand. Reduction of this capacity in a stagnant manufacturing market is a slow business and this often leaves substantial surplus capacity (refer back to the earlier discussion in this chapter of long-run and short-run costs). This can greatly increase the intensity of market rivalry, driving down prices and contributing to the weak financial performance we see in Figure 3.8.

The long-run income elasticity of market demand is clearly an important feature of markets and a key influence on financial performance. It is also largely out of the strategic control of individual firms.

3.3.1 Demand analysis in practice

Demand analysis is important in two ways: (i) it provides a framework for analysing price and other influences on the sales of the firm's products, and (ii) it provides a baseline for pricing products, and marketing generally, and for forecasting and manipulating demand.

Demand analysis is built around the price–quantity relationship and the many ways in which this relationship is manifested. It is easy to see how important price and volume are to the firm. Price and quantity together determine sales revenue. Sales volume dictates production volume and the scale of production operations together with the capital required

Figure 3.10 Price-volume and return on capital

for production and for working capital. Thus, volume and price fundamentally drive cash flow, profits and return on capital (*see* Figure 3.10). Consequently, the extent to which price can influence volume is of great importance to the firm.

In understanding how return on capital is driven it is helpful to consider those characteristics that shape demand (market characteristics in Figure 3.10) and how the firm's decisions can affect the outcome. We will see below and in later chapters that one of the enduring problems for a firm is how to avoid its activities being totally dictated by market conditions and for its own decisions to provide it with some distinctiveness in markets and therefore some ability to earn profits beyond the minimum rate of return required merely to stay in business. In this section we consider the following:

- elasticities and the implications for revenues;
- individual versus market demand;
- final demand versus derived demand;
- producer versus consumer goods;
- durable versus perishable (non-durable) goods.

Price elasticity and revenues

Consider a product whose initial price is P_1 and whose initial sales volume is Q_1. If price is reduced to P_2 and volume increases to Q_2 (following the downward sloping demand curve of Figure 3.5) we can see that on the original volume Q_1 a lower price is being earned and there will be a loss in revenue equal to $(P_1-P_2)Q_1$. But this is to some extent offset by the extra revenue $P_2(Q_2-Q_1)$. The larger the extra volume from the price cut, the more likely it is that revenue will be greater. Thus, the higher the price elasticity, the larger will be the new revenue. At the other end of the scale, if the elasticity is zero then no extra volume is created, and revenue will fall. When the price elasticity is one, the price effect on the original volume $((P_1-P_2)Q_1)$ – i.e. a fall in revenue – is exactly offset by the extra sales revenue arising from the volume increase $P_2(Q_2-Q_1)$. Table 3.3 shows the general relationship between revenues and price elasticity.

Individual demand versus market demand

The demand curve for a market or any group of consumers is obtained by summing the demand curves of all the individuals concerned. This is done by summing all the quantities demanded at each price level. This submerging of individual differences may matter little if we are concerned solely with predicting total market demand at given price levels. The more stable the individual demand curves are, the easier is the task of forecasting. But, from the point of view of the pricing policy of the firm, matters are not so simple. Price is just one, albeit an important one, of the many instruments with which the product is marketed. Others include distribution channels, advertising and promotion, and support from one's own sales force and also from retailer sales activity. To direct this marketing effort effectively it is helpful to be able to define a target market on which the marketing effort can be focused. So the concept of market segmentation is likely to be useful, i.e. the concept of individual and group differences within the overall market demand curve. A firm may choose to treat its market in a uniform manner, spreading its marketing efforts far and wide in order to bring as much of the market within its orbit as possible. This would normally require uniform pricing and mass advertising campaigns. Alternatively the firm might choose to adopt different price policies for different groups or segments in the market. A high price policy might be indicated for one segment and a low price for another. The success of this approach depends on the two segments being unable to communicate and/or trade with each other and being able to set up a black or grey market (such as happens with UK-sourced cars and European-sourced cars).

Table 3.3 Elasticity and revenue

Elasticity	Effect of price fall	Effect of price rise
Infinite (perfectly elastic)	Sell as much as can be produced	Sell nothing
Greater than 1 (elastic)	Larger sales revenue	Smaller sales revenue
1	Constant sales revenue	Constant sales revenue
Less than 1 (inelastic)	Smaller sales revenue	Larger sales revenue
Zero (perfectly inelastic)	Fall in revenue proportional to fall in price	Increase in revenue proportional to increase in price

In economic terms a market is a group of buyers and sellers who are in sufficiently close contact for the transactions between any pair of them to affect the terms on which the others buy and sell. The existence of individual or group differences cannot be exploited if there is close contact between buyers. Firms can choose to exploit the differences in individual demand curves by pursuing product policies that enable the firm to apply a different 'offer' to different segments. Thus the offer of a standard car to the mass market would result in a price level that would enable those with low price sensitivity (low price elasticity) to buy at prices lower than their reservation price (the highest price that would keep them in the market). To avoid this loss of revenue firms devise product range policies that enable different product characteristics to be directed towards different segments. Thus, higher-income purchasers can be directed towards more expensive cars with more accessories and a higher quality build. Lower-income purchasers would correspondingly be directed to less well equipped and built cars. The bigger the product range, the more the firm can cover the breadth of the market and keep potential customers within its range of offerings. But there is an extra cost of marketing and a potential loss of economies of scale in production as variety of models is increased.

Final demand versus derived demand

When demand for a product is tied to the purchase of another product then this demand is said to be *derived*. The demand for steel is in part derived from the demand for cars and the demand for bricks is derived from the demand for houses. These are instances where the product whose demand is derived is a component part of the final product. Sometimes complementary consumption patterns cause dependence in demand. Thus the demand for film is complementary to the demand for cameras. However, the distinction between final and derived demand should not be pressed too far because in some sense all demand is derived. The demand for golf clubs is derived from a demand for leisure; the demand for washing machines is derived from demand for laundry services. Certainly demand for all producer goods (as distinct from consumer goods) is derived, and so is the demand for labour.

Derived demand is generally supposed to have less price elasticity than final demand. This is attributable to dilution of the cost of the component by other component products whose prices are sticky. It used to be reckoned that a 10 per cent rise in the price of steel would cause only a 1 per cent increase in the cost of a car if all other costs remained unchanged. However, this would be a characteristic primarily of the elasticity in the short run. In the longer term there is the possibility of substitution of one raw material or component part by another. As the possibilities of substitution increase then the price elasticity increases. Thus, glass fibre may rival steel in some applications in ship and boat building: aluminium can displace copper; and synthetic rubber can replace natural rubber.

Some products are so closely tied to the parent products that they have no distinctive demand determinants of their own – television aerials, for example. Here the elasticity will be very low indeed in the short run but such cases of fixed proportions between the parent and component products are rare. More commonly there is considerable leeway for substitution at the margin as well as more than one parent use for the product. In very many instances there is a multitude of parent uses for a product and it becomes impossible to characterize demand in terms of particular final demands. Small electric motors have no final demand of their own but to analyse their demand in terms of their thousands of parent uses would be impossibly tedious. Sulphuric acid and many other chemicals are further examples and integrated circuits provide a contemporary example.

The distinction between derived and final demand is important in understanding the determinants of demand for individual products, and where there is a stable proportional relation between the component and its parent then forecasting of demand can be done by reference to the parent.

Producer goods versus consumer goods

This distinction in some ways is parallel to that between final and derived demand. However, this distinction concentrates attention on who makes the purchase decision rather than the relationship, whether technological or economic, between the component and its parent product. There are two reasons usually cited for expecting purchase decisions made for producer goods to be qualitatively different from those for consumer goods. Buyers are expected to be professional and, hence, more expert. Their motives for buying are expected to be purely economic and not influenced by non-monetary considerations.

It is doubtful whether the distinction between producer and consumer goods can always be maintained. How does one distinguish between cars sold to companies and those sold to private individuals? In addition it is not at all clear that producer goods are evaluated in a cold-eyed professional way. There must be thousands of purchases by any one firm that are incidental in their impact on costs and are purchased with speed and convenience without expensive evaluation. This of course leaves the door open for the human element in purchasing which is supposed to be so characteristic of final consumers.

Durable goods versus perishable (non-durable) goods

By definition durable goods are not completely consumed at the time of their purchase; they yield a stream of services over time (typically measured in years rather than months). They include both consumer and producer durables. The sale of durables can be seen as replacing that part of the existing stock of durables that has worn out (i.e. replacement demand), and as that which is really new (i.e. an expansion of demand). Thus, if the existing stock of cars is 100 of which 10 wear out each year, and the normal growth in demand is 5 each year, then car production (and sales) would be 15, two-thirds of which is to meet replacement demand. If there is now an increase in demand for car stock of 3 units (less than a 3 per cent increase) then production must rise to 18 (a 20 per cent increase) in order to meet this increase. Relatively modest increases in demand for a stock of durables can thus result in large fluctuations in production.

In general, the demand for durable goods fluctuates differently and more violently than the demand for perishable products. The further down the chain of production, the more violent is the cutback in production when final demand falls. If economic activity were to contract by 1 per cent it would not be surprising to see contractions of 10 per cent or even 20 per cent in the output of the steel and metals industries. The volatility of demand for durables is not the only salient feature. Both replacement and expansion have quite distinct sets of demand determinants. When the demand for transportation as a whole goes up, then production tends to take some time to respond and used car values go up relative to scrap values. Then the scrapping rate falls and thus replacement demand also falls. So an increase in demand may initially extend the life of the existing stock and reduce replacement demand. Conversely, if the public desire fewer cars then the scrapping rate accelerates as used car prices fall relative to scrap prices. The most important factor determining replacement demand is the rate of obsolescence that determines prices in second-hand car markets. There are two elements in obsolescence. One is purely financial and requires a comparison of capital costs and running costs of a new car with the scrap value and running costs of the old car. In general, running costs rise with age to a point where the difference in running costs between new and old becomes larger than the required capital outlay. Physical deterioration lies behind these calculations and is an obvious component of obsolescence. However, it is rarely the only factor in replacement decisions. When replacement takes place before the financial criterion is satisfied then in some other way the services of the new car are more highly valued than the services of the (apparently cheaper) old car. For consumer durables, and perhaps also for producer durables as well, style, convenience and youth play an important role in demand.

The determinants of expansion demand for durables are not, in principle, very different from those for perishables but in practice are much more complicated. The key to durables lies in their length of life and the purchase decision is marked by the buyer's difficulty in assessing the future. The buyer has to assess whether they can afford to operate it, whether its services will command a suitable price in the future, whether its price will rise or fall if they postpone their purchase and so on. For durable goods, not only present prices and incomes but also their trends and the buyer's optimism are proper variables to consider. Expectations about technological change are also critical. Should one wait for prices to fall as technology improves (e.g. computers and video games) or might important savings be lost through delay?

Case box: No End of Luxury

THE terrorist attacks on September 11th 2001 reverberated even in the world of fashion. Department stores closed their spring-collection orders, the spring 2002 New York Fashion Week was cancelled for the first time ever, and LVMH's net income for the 2001 financial year plummeted from €722m in 2000 to just €10m. After a recovery in late 2002, misfortune struck again in 2003: war in Iraq, the SARS epidemic in Asia and a persistently sluggish economy in Japan. Tourists around the world are responsible for around a quarter of the world's luxury purchases, so anything that lessens international travel hurts the industry.

Yet this apparent vulnerability to world events is actually a sign of strength. The world of luxury is truly global, with all the commercial opportunities that implies: as people get richer, they spend proportionately less on necessities and more on luxuries. This has long been true in Japan, whose fashion-conscious people account for a quarter of the world's luxury-goods sales. That is why corporate analysts anxiously examine the state of the Japanese economy: any change will have an effect on the share prices and sales of luxury-goods houses. And because most Japanese prefer to buy their luxury goods abroad (where prices are up to 40% lower than at home), any change in the value of the yen against the dollar and euro matters too.

But looking a little farther ahead, it is clear that other Asian countries, and particularly China and India, will follow where Japan has led. Between them, those two countries make up more than a third of the world's population, and already the luxury labels of Europe and America are rushing to set up flagship stores in Beijing and Shanghai (though not yet in India). According to the Boston Consulting Group, China already accounts for 5% of the world luxury market – the same share, it is worth remembering, as post-communist Russia.

This suggests that the luxury labels need not fear a shrinking market. They may, however, need to fear a changing market. In the days of Christian Dior, who in 1947 launched his elegant 'New Look' of small waists and full skirts, a fashionable woman would never dream of mixing that look with something designed for the masses. Nor would fans of Coco Chanel, even though in the 1920s, when materials were in short supply, Miss Chanel had more or less invented 'poor chic' by using jersey knit, a fabric previously used for men's underwear.

Yet today it is perfectly acceptable for a smart woman (or man, for that matter, though women outnumber men by four-to-one in their shopping forays) to mix a Chanel or Prada jacket with a pair of blue jeans. The female fashion fad of the moment is the Ugg shoe, an ugly but supremely comfortable sheepskin boot originally made for Australia's surfers, male and female, when they get out of the water. It is perfectly acceptable to wear Uggs with just about everything. Fashion has become democratised, and a market that once belonged entirely to high-fashion brands is being invaded by low-price competitors, from the Gap to Hennes & Mauritz, a Swedish ready-to-wear chain which over the past 57 years has exported its H&M logo to 17 other countries.

The most impressive competitor, however, is Zara, a Spanish company operating in 46 countries, which has shortened the fashion cycle to the point where it no longer exists. By having 200 in-house designers and by controlling the whole process from textile mill to retail shop, Zara can put new items in its 626 stores twice a week. Moreover, it ruthlessly removes its lines – even

Developing nicely
Contribution of China, Russia and India to total sales of luxury-goods companies, %

Source: Merrill Lynch
(Reprinted courtesy of *The Economist*)

the best-selling ones – every three weeks or so. The result is that Zara always has fresh styles, and its customers never feel out of fashion. Perhaps companies such as LVMH, Gucci, Prada and Armani should start to worry.

Yet a Zara sweater or skirt will never be the equal of one by Missoni or Dolce & Gabbana. As long as customers want quality, the high-fashion brands will be safe. Calamities notwithstanding, there still seem to be plenty of people who can afford prices that give the high-fashion brands gross margins of 50–60% on clothes and 80% on leather goods.

Could the internet threaten the luxury brands? There are sites such as bluefly.com that discount their wares heavily, but undiscounted sales by the brands' own sites have been somewhat disappointing. Salvatore Ferragamo used to offer its clothes and accessories on LVMH's eluxury.com site (where Dior's 'latest blonde shoulder bag' sells for a mere $1,280), but the company pulled out. 'Our consumers didn't want internet buying,' says the company's boss, Ferruccio Ferragamo.

What may make a difference is a better way to get clothes to fit. Suran Goonatilake, 'entrepreneur-in-residence' at the London College of Fashion, is the founder of Bodymetrics, a company that uses three-dimensional scanning to get an exact measure of a person's body. At the moment the system is being tested at Selfridges, a store in London's Oxford Street, where customers are being advised which clothes to try according to the print-out. Clothing sizes vary not just from country to country but from manufacturer to manufacturer, so Bodymetrics could be a boon both for the buyer and the manufacturer alike – even for the creative people, who tend to design for clothes horses rather than for normal human beings.

Art, no craft

Yet fashion cannot be reduced to a set of measurements. Some designers insist that fashion is not art. Instead, it is 'design' because, like architecture, it has a function. By contrast, this survey would argue that the best designers, from Balenciaga to Alexander McQueen, are as creative as any painter or sculptor, and even when they borrow from the past they add something new. Indeed, because the designer's medium is the human body, fashion is surely interactive art at its best.

But it is not yet art for the masses, whatever the efforts of Zara and of the talented Isaac Mizrahi, who now works for America's downmarket Target chain. That is not to demean those efforts. After all, when the materials are cheap, it becomes technically more difficult to design good-looking clothes. Nor is it to demean the masses, whose fashion choices are generally limited by price. Instead, this survey would simply praise the self-selected elite who choose to spend their time and money on the kind of clothes and accessories that are plainly luxury rather than necessities. If, for the narrow-minded, that qualifies them as irresponsible wastrels, so what? In an often ugly world, they provide some welcome style.

So forget the threat to luxury brands from the 'democratisation' of fashion and the pressures of mass-market competition. The chances are that as long as human beings apreciate art, and as long as there are enough rich people to pay for it, the world of luxury and high fashion will prosper. Let the designers indulge their fantasies. Today's fantasy becomes tomorrow's fashion, and the-day-after-tomorrow's discard. Hence the paradox that keeps us fascinated: fashion, by definition, is temporary – but it is always with us.

Source: 'No End of Luxury', *The Economist*, 6 March 2004.
© The Economist Newspaper Limited, London (6 March 2004).

Questions for discussion

1 Explain how markets for high fashion products work. In particular, who are the principal customers and what are the driving forces behind their purchases.

2 How are fashion markets affected by external events such as (i) terrorist attacks and (ii) changes in supply markets such as cost inflation?

3 What are the business risks of being in these markets?

3.4 Analysis of markets and competition

This section assesses how competition takes place and, in particular, how this is reflected in the different types of competition already mentioned in the previous section. This section looks explicitly at the way in which markets affect the nature of competition and firms' strategic choices. Contrast this with the discussion in Chapter 5 which deals with supply side characteristics usually referred to as industry structure. Market structure (the analysis of markets and competition) and industry structure (the analysis of the economic configuration of firms and their chains of supply) should be seen together as drivers of strategic choice.

The critical market-level influence on firm performance is the form and intensity of rivalry between the existing firms in a market. The economist's approach to market structure and the form and extent of rivalry is to use a taxonomy based on the number of firms in each industry. Figure 3.11 illustrates the economist's approach to market structure.

At one extreme, we have perfect competition, in which products are not differentiable, rivalry is intense and no firm has the power to alter market prices. In such a market the price is determined at the market level by the forces of supply and demand so from the firm's point of view the price of its product is given. The forces of competition limit strategic discretion and drive profits down to the 'normal' level, i.e. a level insufficient to attract new entrants to the market. Markets for agricultural products such as wheat or barley are often viewed as perfectly competitive, because no single producer can alter the market price. Perfect markets are not common. Firms have a huge incentive to adopt strategies which avoid the 'strategic hell' of perfect competition. The exploitation of scale economies is one route through which market power might be obtained and a measure of strategic discretion secured.

Another route by which the 'strategic hell' of perfect competition can be avoided is by product differentiation. Economists often exemplify this by using the example

Market structure	Number of firms	Degree of differentiation	Comments
Perfect competition	many	zero	Fragmented, commodity-like
Monopolistic or imperfect competition	many	some	Multiple niches, localized competition
Oligopoly – undifferentiated	Some to very few	low	Commodity-like with scale economies, e.g. steel
Oligopoly – differentiated	Some to very few	high	Strategic imterdependence, large segments
Dominant firm	One to very few	high	Price leadership, high entry barriers, competitive fringe
Monopoly	single	Not applicable	Natural monopoly due to very high scale economies

Figure 3.11 Market structure: the broad spectrum for competition

of advertising. Advertising is a feature of product differentiation and is characteristic of oligopolistic markets. The producer faces a downward sloping demand curve. The effect of advertising is that it shifts the demand curve out and it probably, and more importantly, steepens the slope of the curve (this means it reduces the price elasticity). This is intuitively sensible; if a product is desired because of its inherent features or quality, price will be less important – you remember the quality long after you have forgotten the price. Consequently the business is taken further away from the perfect competition 'nightmare' of a horizontal demand curve and price taking.

At the other extreme, we have a **monopoly** in which one firm supplies the whole market. Technically a monopoly exists when there is a single seller of a product. As a consequence the monopolist's demand curve is the market demand curve and is thus downward sloping. The monopolist therefore has pricing power, knowing that price reductions expand the market and vice versa. Typically, such markets exhibit low price elasticity and it is therefore in the interest of the monopoly to restrict output, gain higher prices and thereby increase revenues (a straightforward application of Table 3.3). Monopolies (as opposed to dominant firms – see below) exist because of very large economies of scale such that the MES (minimum efficient scale of output/plant size) is greater than the market size. Therefore, there is room for only one efficient firm – as in electricity generation and in water supply. These so called **natural monopolies** are controlled by governments to avoid them exploiting their customers – control is either in the form of public ownership or through regulation (e.g. competition regulators such as Ofcom or Ofwat in the UK – these are offices that regulate the behaviour of the telecommunications and water industries respectively).

Dominant firms may also have de facto monopoly positions. Usually they have risen to dominance over their competitors through superior product differentiation which serves as a highly effect deterrent to entry by new competitors and imitation by existing competitors. The dominant firm enjoys significant market power, is able to fix prices and hence enjoys a high degree of control over its market environment. Patents such as that secured by the UK pharmaceutical company Glaxo in the market for ulcer drugs confer this kind of market power. A high level of market power enables the monopolistic firm to earn higher profits than the competitive firm, as Glaxo did with Zantac in the 1980s and until 1997. There may be a few dominant firms (e.g. three or four), in which case one usually observes very large segments each of which being dominated by a particular player (as in pharmaceuticals where each therapeutic class is dominated by one player).

At a lower level of concentration of competition we have oligopolistic markets, in which a few firms compete against each other, and **monopolistic competition**. Most economists would regard these intermediate cases as the norm. In the monopolistic competition case, there are many firms each with small market shares, but each is able to differentiate its product to some degree and to obtain modest control over its prices and other aspects of its strategy, to build competitive advantage over other players. The restaurant business in a big city such as London or Singapore is a good example of monopolistic competition.

In oligopolistic markets, there are fewer players – perhaps as many as ten, each able to gain competitive advantage by exploiting scale economies, by product differentiation and so on. There are numerous examples of this kind of market including, for example, the global car market and the EU steel market. In both of these cases, a handful of firms compete against each other. This competition could be muted because of collusion between firms aimed at reducing rivalry. Although this collusion is possible and gives market control to all colluding producers, improving both the financial performance of both individual firms and the sector as a whole, it is sometimes difficult to create and to sustain, and is usually illegal.

Some oligopolies are essentially undifferentiated and intense price competition can occur. The large size of the players is determined by large scale economies as in steel or in automobiles and this is the kind of market that confronts both companies PaperCo and MetalCo. Each firm knows that in this case, effective strategic management may create competitive advantage, but also each needs to be aware that its rivals may copy any strategic move. Other oligopolies are much more differentiated, such as the toiletries markets where the degree of product innovation and differentiation is very high and creates sustainable differences between competitors. In both cases the degree of strategic independence is very high, i.e. the strategic moves of one competitor can have an immediate discernible effect on its rivals. This leads to 'gaming' behaviour and a very careful calculation of the risks of precipitating too much competition.

As well as the rivalry from existing players, it is important to take account of the threat of new entrants. This is technically known as '**contestable markets**'. In the case of PaperCo and MetalCo, the threat of new entrants is very low because of the huge entry costs. These arise from the large fixed costs of installing plant, as well as the costs of acquiring the key competencies of these businesses. The existence of static and dynamic scale economies arising from learning curve effects also create market barriers for incumbent firms. In other sectors, this may not be the case.

Case box: **The slumping price of salmon**

'Economics is giving salmon farming more trouble than science is.' This is a common refrain in business. Scientific and engineering problems can usually be solved but business and economic problems are endemic and rarely go away. In this instance the concern is with the salmon farming industry in the Scottish Highlands which has grown and now employs 1500 people but its future looks precarious.

Periodic health scares have claimed the headlines but many believe that the technology is there to reduce health risks to low levels. But the main problem is that supply has been growing faster than demand. Scottish farmed salmon production has grown swiftly from 32 000 tonnes a year in 1990 to 145 000 tonnes in 2002 and output from Norwegian and Chilean fish farms has grown similarly. Wholesale prices have fallen from around £2.70 per kilo in 2000 ($9 a lb) to less than £2.20 a kilo now. Smaller fish farms have been going bust for even large firms have been finding conditions difficult. Graeme Dear, managing director of Dutch-owned Marine Harvest (Scotland) Ltd which produces about 30 per cent of Scottish farmed salmon says, 'Probably no one is making an acceptable return.'

Mr Deare needs price to recover enough to justify the cost of a new ship equipped with seawater tanks whose purpose is to transport live fish to processing factories nearer the markets. This could add 24–48 hours to the salmon's shelf life and this would give Marine Harvest a competitive advantage. But it will cost £1 million a year. Smaller fish farmers cannot afford this so the industry looks likely to consolidate as well as shrink. The industry has a record of mechanization and computerization of feeding but, as cost pressures are prolonged, the larger operators will be looking to gain more efficiencies by grouping their cages together into bigger units.

In addition the industry is under fire from rod fishermen and from conservationists. Rod fishermen blame the falling numbers of wild salmon in Scottish rivers on the parasites that accompany fish farms. Conservationists complain that fish farms kill off sea-bed life beneath them. They both argue that the industry needs more regulation, which would put up costs and reduce profits even more.

Source: adapted from 'Salmon a-slumping', *The Economist*, 17 January 2004, p. 25.

Questions for discussion

1 Explain the mechanisms of supply and demand that are causing these problems for fish farmers.

2 What remedies do farmers have available to them?

3 How would you expect an industry like this to develop over time?

So far in this chapter we have:

◆ Provided a checklist of the key elements of the 'deep structure' of a firm's product market, which we need to consider when explaining differences in the financial performance of firms both within and between markets.

◆ Explored the extent to which these features are outside the strategic control of the firm and, hence, the extent to which effective strategic action is constrained by the business environment.

◆ Illustrated these ideas with respect to two companies. Although there are significant differences in their long-run financial performance, it is clear that they have a very similar 'deep structure'. However, there are differences, of which the most important is the greater opportunity for MetalCo to exploit economies of scope. These arise for reasons largely outside the control of the two businesses and are not the result of effective strategic 'actions'.

As well as the differences in the long run, Figure 3.1 also shows very significant short-run differences between PaperCo and MetalCo. In PaperCo, profits increase steadily and continually, whereas in MetalCo there are large fluctuations with losses made in the middle years. If an appraisal of MetalCo's performance were done in the single year 1993, it would show a very adverse relative position, although it has the superior financial performance in the long run. Why?

The answer is not to be found in the 'deep structure' of the market environment of the two companies but in the wider macroeconomic environment and in its particular impact on each of them. The macroeconomic environment refers to economic forces operating at both the national and the global level, to which all markets are sensitive. Of particular importance is the annual rate of growth of Gross Domestic Product (GDP). GDP is the total amount of all goods and services produced within a national economy or within the global economy (world GDP). It can be measured at the current prices of goods and services to obtain *nominal* GDP or at a single and constant set of prices to obtain a measure of *real* GDP. When GDP increases or decreases, this affects the market demand curve. If GDP growth increases, this shifts the demand curve upwards, increasing the demand at the price P_1 in exactly the same way as shown in Figure 3.9. Similarly, a slowdown in GDP growth shifts it downwards. Why? The answer is that if GDP growth increases (or decreases), there will be an equivalent increase (or decrease) in national income, and this affects the market demand for all products. The impact on market demand is measured by the *short-run (annual)* **income elasticity of demand**, which is defined as:

% change in short-run quantity demanded

% change in short-run national income

Some estimates for the rich industrial economies of the Organization for Economic Co-operation and Development (OECD), which includes both the EU and North America, are shown in Figure 3.12.

Not surprisingly, given the reasoning above, the short-run income elasticity of demand is always a positive number. Note, however, the differences between market sectors. The food sector to which PaperCo in Figure 3.1 supplies its product has a very low short-run income elasticity, while MetalCo in Figure 3.1 is a metals company that supplies 70 per cent of its product to the highly income elastic vehicles sector. The simplest explanation for this difference in volatility is that final consumers are able to postpone their purchases of new vehicles in the short run. They do not and cannot postpone their purchases of food. Food is non-durable and cars are a durable good (recall the earlier discussion of durable and non-durable goods in this chapter). In a nutshell, booms and slumps in GDP have a much greater effect on the quantity demanded in MetalCo's markets.

Why does the greater sensitivity of sales in MetalCo's markets affect its financial performance? Recall from the analysis of Figure 3.2 that if scale economies are important to both of these companies and if they fail to maintain their production at the minimum cost level (Q_1 in Figure 3.2), the average cost of production will rise above C_1 (to, say, C_3 if sales fall to Q_3). This will drive down profits. In years where GDP growth is low or even negative (as in 1993), costs will rise in MetalCo. It is also the case that in recession years (in which GDP growth is negative), prices are driven down in MetalCo's markets so, not surprisingly, its profitability suffers for reasons totally outside its control. What happens in the macroeconomy severely constrains MetalCo's scope for strategic action. In PaperCo's case, its products are used in the low short-run income elasticity food sector, so there are only very small fluctuations

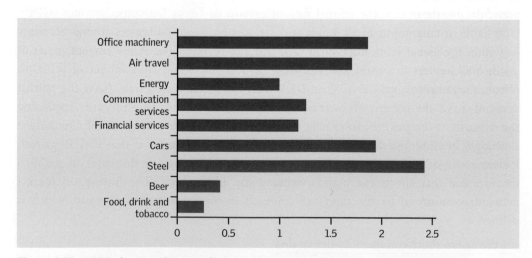

Figure 3.12 OECD short-run income elasticity (% change in 'real' sales/% change in GDP)
Source: KG (Ben) Knight (1999).

in output volumes, costs and also prices. Short-run movements in GDP growth have little effect on its financial performance.

Given the obvious importance of these uncontrollable shocks in the macroeconomic environment to the performance and strategy of individual companies, it is important to understand the workings of the macroeconomy and, in particular, the factors which cause GDP growth to rise and fall. It is also important to scan information sources, to select signals that help to build scenarios of the future. Scenario approaches are discussed in Chapter 14.

3.5 Summary

This chapter has introduced the basic microeconomic concepts that we use in strategic management, namely the basic principles of cost and demand analysis and an understanding of the nature of competition. The discussion in the chapter has given a managerial interpretation of these ideas. By contrast, in a conventional economics textbook you will find the discussion framed in terms of the nature of competitive markets and the government policy implications for fostering efficiency in markets. The concepts in this chapter are used both by economists and by managers. Economists use them to provide a basis for understanding the efficiency of competitive markets whereas managers are more interested in the implications for decision making. This theme is continued in the next chapter where we look at the macroeconomic concepts that condition strategic decisions.

We continue to build on these economic concepts in the chapters that follow. Chapter 4 focuses on the macroeconomy and the way in which this sets out the broad economic backdrop to the operations of firms. Chapter 5 takes the idea of imperfections in markets and the striving for entrepreneurial profits to develop an economic perspective of strategy that sees competitive strategy as a set of firm-specific imperfections around which a long-term business can be developed and defended. Chapter 6 follows directly from the industry analysis and generic strategies of Chapter 5 to create a deeper understanding of the meaning of competitive advantage and the market positioning competitive strategies. Chapter 7 extends this theme into an assessment of the characteristics of resources and capabilities that underpin competitive position in markets. Chapter 8 explicitly introduces time into the analysis and asks how industries change over time, what the implications for strategy are and what kinds of practical problem and opportunity are presented.

Key terms

Analysis of industry and competition *60*
Analysis of markets and competition *60*
Contestable markets *87*
Cost analysis *60*
Cost structure *62*
Cube law *69*
Demand analysis *60*
Demand curve *73*
Differentiation *56*
Division of labour *68*
Durable goods versus perishable goods *80*
Economies of scope *66*
Economy of massed reserves *69*
Final demand versus derived demand *79*
Fixed costs *62*
Income elasticity of demand *89*
Individual demand versus market demand *78*
Integration *56*

Law of diminishing returns *62*
Learning curve effect *66*
Long run *62*
Marginal cost *63*
Mechanistic *56*
Minimum efficient scale (MES) *63*
Monopolistic competition *86*
Monopoly *86*
Natural monopoly *86*
Opportunity cost *61*
Organic *57*
Own price elasticity of demand *72*
Producer goods versus consumer goods *80*
Relevant costs *61*
Short run *62*
Specialization *68*
Variable costs *62*

Recap questions and assignments

To build your strategic awareness, use the framework of this chapter to analyse the financial performance of an organization that you are familiar with. It may be an organization in which you have worked, or a well-known company that you can research online. Alternatively, you might choose an organization featured in one of the case studies in the book.

1 Are economies of scale or scope important?

2 Does your strategic 'action' take full advantage of economies of scale and scope?

3 What is the 'deep structure' of the demand side of the organization's markets and what form of market rivalry does the company have?

4 How exposed is the company to local and global macroeconomic shocks, especially to fluctuations in GDP?

5 Is its financial performance the same if you compared your chosen company to another operating in the same markets?

6 If not, why not?

In particular, try to isolate those factors outside management control which affect the financial performance of your chosen company and which constrain the scope for strategic action to build competitive advantage.

Guide answers to these questions are given on the Online Learning Centre.

Online
*Learning*Centre

When you have read this chapter, log on to the Online Learning Centre website at www.mcgraw-hill.co.uk/textbooks/mcgee to explore chapter-by-chapter test questions, further reading and more online study tools for strategy.

Case 1 **The harder hard sell**

More people are rejecting traditional sales messages, presenting the ad industry with big challenges

It may have been Lord Leverhulme, the British soap pioneer, Frank Woolworth, America's first discount-retailer, or John Wanamaker, the father of the department store; all are said to have complained that they knew half of their advertising budget was wasted, but didn't know which half. As advertising starts to climb out of its recent slump, the answer to their problem is easier to find as the real effects of advertising become more measurable. But that is exposing another, potentially more horrible truth, for the $1 trillion advertising and marketing industry: in some cases, it can be a lot more than half of the client's budget that is going down the drain.

The advertising industry is passing through one of the most disorienting periods in its history. This is due to a combination of long-term changes, such as the growing diversity of media, and the arrival of new technologies, notably the internet. Consumers have become better informed than ever before, with the result that some of the traditional methods of advertising and marketing simply no longer work.

Ad spending grew rapidly in the late 1990s, but in 2000 – just as the technology bubble was about to burst – it soared by more than 8% in America, which represents about half the world market. The following year it plunged by 8%. Spending is up again, according to ZenithOptimedia, which has long tracked the industry. It forecasts that worldwide expenditure in 2004 on major media (newspapers, magazines, television, radio, cinema, outdoor and the internet) will grow by 4.7% to $343 billion. It will be helped by a collection of big events, including the European football championship, the Olympic Games and an election in America. Historically, when there is an upturn in advertising expenditure, it tends to rise faster than the wider economy. So, provided economic growth can be sustained, ad spending may continue to pick up.

How will the money be spent? There are plenty of alternatives to straightforward advertising, including a myriad of marketing and communications services, some of which are called 'below-the-line' advertising. They range from public relations to direct mail, consumer promotions (such as coupons), in-store displays, business-to-business promotions (like paying a retailer for shelf-space), telemarketing, exhibitions, sponsoring events, product placements and more.

These have become such an inseparable part of the industry that big agencies now provide most of them. Although some are less than glamorous, marketing services have grown more quickly than advertising. Add in the cost of market research, and this part of the industry was worth some $750 billion worldwide last year, estimates WPP, one of the world's biggest advertising and marketing groups.

As ever, the debate in the industry centres on the best way to achieve results. Is it more cost-effective, for instance, to employ a PR agency to invite a journalist out to lunch and persuade him to write about a product than to pay for a display ad in that journalist's newspaper? Should you launch a new car with glossy magazine ads, or – as some carmakers now do – simply park demonstration models in shopping malls and motorway service stations? And is it better to buy a series of ads on a specialist cable-TV channel or splurge $2.2m on a single 30-second commercial during this year's Super Bowl?

Such decisions are ever harder to make. Although a Super Bowl ad is still cheaper than in 2000, in

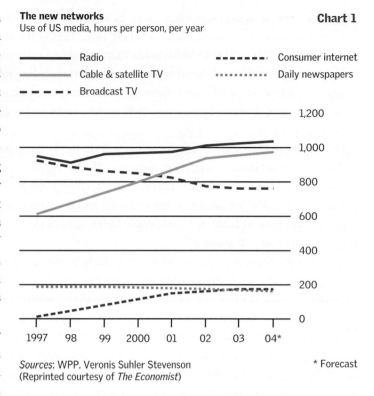

The new networks
Use of US media, hours per person, per year

Chart 1

Sources: WPP, Veronis Suhler Stevenson
(Reprinted courtesy of *The Economist*)

* Forecast

general network-TV pricing has risen faster than inflation – even though fewer people tune in. Changes in TV-viewing habits, however, are only part of a much wider shift in the way media is consumed, not least because it has become more fragmented and diverse.

For a start, people are spending less time reading newspapers and magazines, but are going to the cinema more, listening to more radio and turning in ever-increasing numbers to a new medium, the internet (see chart 1).

After the technology bust it was easy to dismiss the internet. But the phenomenal success of many e-commerce firms, such as Amazon and eBay, shows that millions of people are becoming comfortable buying goods and services online. Many more are using the internet to research products, services and prices for purchases made offline. Some 70% of new-car buyers in America, for instance, use websites to determine which vehicle to buy – and often to obtain competing quotes from dealers.

Google that

Such consumers can be targeted by internet advertisers and, in some cases, their responses accurately measured. A surge in online advertising is being led by paid-for text-links dished up by search engines such as Google and Yahoo! The response rate from people clicking on paid links can be as low as 1% – about the same as direct mail, which remains one of the biggest forms of advertising. But there is an important difference: internet advertisers usually pay only if someone clicks on their link. This is the equivalent of paying for the delivery of junk mail only to households that read it.

How are companies and the advertising industry responding to these trends in media consumption? Some people do not believe they amount to a sea-change, while others are simply hoping it will not come to pass on their watch, reckons Sir Martin Sorrell, WPP's chief executive.

Nor is it the only significant force he sees at work. New markets, such as China, are becoming increasingly important for advertisers, especially multinationals. But these markets can have very different characteristics. Clients are also more concerned than ever about getting value for money. What will increasingly matter, says Sir Martin, is not what it costs to put an ad in front of 1,000 people (a traditional industry measure), but 'how effective is that cost-per-thousand?'

At the same time, negotiating advertising deals is becoming tougher because of consolidation, both among clients and among media owners. This could favour the big, integrated agencies. In May, WPP won a contract to handle all the advertising and marketing for HSBC, after the international banking group decided that parent companies and not their individual agencies should bid for the $600m it spends on such services every year. Samsung, a big South Korean electronics firm, is also expected to appoint a single group.

Nevertheless, the smaller agencies believe they can still compete by being more nimble. 'There is definitely a change in the landscape,' says Jane Asscher, chairman of 23red, a London-based agency that describes itself as 'media-neutral' in its choice of outlets for campaigns. Ms Asscher believes that consumers are becoming far more sophisticated in their reaction to all forms of advertising and marketing, so smarter ways have to be used to reach them.

During the slump, some companies tried different forms of advertising and liked the response they got. 'There's lots of ways to skin a cat today,' says Scott Goodson, founder of StrawberryFrog, an agency based in Amsterdam that specialises in international campaigns. While his firm still uses traditional media, such as TV and print, it is often in conjunction with other techniques, such as 'viral'

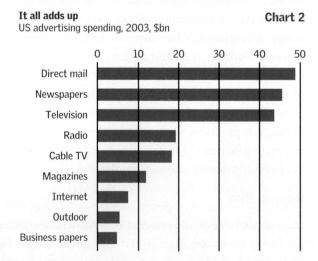

It all adds up
US advertising spending, 2003, $bn

Chart 2

Sources: PwC/IAB Internet Ad Revenue Report; McCann Erickson
(Reprinted courtesy of *The Economist*)

marketing. This means trying to spread the message by word of mouth – still considered the most powerful form of advertising. Sometimes that involves using the internet for e-mail messages containing jokes, film clips and games, which recipients are encouraged to pass along to friends.

No one knows just how important the internet will eventually be as an advertising medium. Some advertisers think it will be a highly cost-effective way of reaching certain groups of consumers – especially for small companies operating in niche businesses. But not everyone uses the internet, and nor is it seen as particularly good at brand building. Barry Diller, the head of InterActiveCorp, believes network TV is a great place to promote his company's websites, such as Expedia, his online travel agency, and LendingTree, a consumer lender. Unlike bricks-and-mortar businesses, web-based firms do not worry if their ad is being seen by lots of people in towns where they have no shops. They just want people to remember their website address – or at least enough of their name to be Googled.

So far, the internet accounts for only a tiny slice of the overall advertising pie (see chart 2), although it has been growing rapidly. A joint study by the Interactive Advertising Bureau and PricewaterhouseCoopers found that internet advertising revenue in America grew by 39% to $2.3 billion in the first quarter of 2004, compared with the same period a year earlier. Internet ad revenues are now back above what they were at the height of the tech boom.

And Google and Yahoo! have yet to unleash the full potential of their technology. Google, which already places text ads on other people's websites and splits the revenue with them, recently began testing a system to distribute display ads as well, in effect increasing its role as a sort of online ad agency.

Others are honing new techniques. As part of a recent campaign for American Airlines, the online edition of the *Wall Street Journal* used 'behavioural targeting' to estimate how likely readers were to be frequent-flyers based on how much interest they paid to travel-related stories and columns. The targeted readers were presented with American Airline ads, and not just when they were reading travel stories. According to Revenue Science, a New York company that developed the targeting system, the results were dramatic: the number of business travellers who saw the ads more than doubled.

The potential for advertising on the internet is tempting more firms to join the fray. For instance, Microsoft is working on a search system with the intention of leapfrogging Google. Microsoft and others see that as more types of media, including music and films, start to be distributed over the internet, there will be more opportunities for online operators to put advertising messages in front of consumers.

Indeed, the makers of personal video recorders (PVRs) recently announced that their new machines will be capable of downloading music and films from the internet, as well as from TV. Many advertisers dread PVRs because they can be used to 'time shift' viewing, allowing viewers to record their own schedules with greater ease than existing video recorders. Several studies have shown that users think one of the machine's most-appealing features is the ability to skip past ads. The providers of internet-based content might be able to slip in those ads in other ways than traditional 30-second commercials, perhaps through sponsorship deals or as display ads on the websites which PVR owners will use to select their programming.

Bombarded

People are tiring of ads in all their forms. A recent study by Yankelovich Partners, an American marketing-services consultancy, says that consumer resistance to the growing intrusiveness of marketing and advertising has been pushed to an all-time high. Its study found 65% of people now feel 'constantly bombarded' by ad messages and that 59% feel that ads have very little relevance to them. Almost 70% said they would be interested in products or services that would help them avoid marketing pitches.

It has been calculated that the average American is subjected to some 3,000 advertising messages every day. If you add in everything from the badges on cars to slogans on sweat-shirts, the ads in newspapers, on taxis, in subways and even playing on TVs in lifts, then some people could be exposed to more than that number just getting to the office. No wonder many consumers seem to be developing the knack of tuning-out adverts.

'Consumers are getting harder to influence as commercial clutter invades their lives,' says a recent report by Deutsche Bank. It examined the effectiveness of TV advertising on 23 new and mature brands of packaged goods and concluded that in some cases it was a waste of time. Although in the short-term TV advertising would lead to an incremental increase in volume sales in almost every case, there was only a positive cash return on that investment in 18% of cases. Over a longer term the picture improved, with 45% of cases showing a return on investment. Not surprisingly, new products did better than older ones. The study concluded that 'increased levels of marketing spending were less important than having new items on the shelf and increasing distribution'.

The effectiveness of advertising is a hugely controversial area. Conventional wisdom in the industry is that sales may well increase for a certain period even after the advertising of a product ends. But there comes a point when sales start to decline and it then becomes extremely expensive to rebuild the brand.

This supports the idea of continuous advertising. But some people in the industry believe the conventional wisdom is no longer true. When America's big TV networks reached prime-time audiences of 90% of households, they were a powerful way to build a brand. Now that those audiences might be as low as one-third of households, other ways of promoting a brand have become more competitive. Moreover, many clients never really embraced continuous advertising: when times get tough, just as they did after 2000, one of the first things many companies cut is their ad budget.

Robert Shaw, a visiting professor at the Cranfield School of Management in Britain, runs a forum in which a number of big companies try to monitor the 'marketing payback' from advertising. The return from traditional media was, he says, 'never terribly good'. Generally under half of ads provide a return on their investment. And there can be various reasons why ads influence sales, other than their direct effect on consumers. For instance, if a producer announces a multi-million dollar ad-campaign, then retailers are often persuaded to increase deliveries. This can result in a 'distribution effect' that leads to additional sales.

Some companies have profited from re-allocating their spending across different media, adds Mr Shaw. But it is a tricky business to determine what works best. For many companies, and especially the media-buyers who purchase space and slots for ads, greater media diversity and the arrival of the internet has made a difficult job much tougher.

Soap stars

Some big spenders have already made clear choices. With an annual budget of more than $4 billion, America's Procter & Gamble (P&G) is the biggest advertiser in the world. Ten years ago about 90% of its global ad spend was on TV. Now the figure is much smaller. Last year the company launched a non-prescription version of Prilosec, an anti-heartburn medicine. It was one of the most successful brand launches in the company's history, according to Jim Stengel, P&G's global marketing officer. But only about one-quarter of the marketing spend on Prilosec went to TV. The rest was spent on other forms of marketing, such as in-store promotions.

P&G, which helped to launch TV soap operas as a new way to market goods, is now looking once again for novel ways to reach consumers. Three years ago it set up an operation called Tremor to recruit an army of several hundred thousand American teenagers. It uses them to discuss ideas about new products and to help spread marketing messages. In return, the teenagers get to hear about and use new things before many of their peers.

Getting trendsetters to buy (or be given) new products in order to influence a broader market is hardly a new idea. So-called 'early adopters' are a similar group, much sought-after by consumer-electronics companies in order to give their new products a good start. But there is a wider group which marketers sometimes call 'prosumers'; short for proactive consumers. Some people in the industry believe this group is the most powerful of all.

Euro RSCG, a big international agency, is completing a nine-country study of prosumers, which it says can represent 20% or so of any particular group. They can be found everywhere, are at the vanguard of consumerism, and what they say to their friends and colleagues about brands and products tends to become mainstream six to 18 months later. They also vary by category, says Marc Lepere, Euro RSCG's chief marketing officer: a wine prosumer, for instance, will not necessarily be a prosumer of cars.

Such people often reject traditional ads and invariably use the internet to research what they are going to buy and how much they are going to pay for it. Half of prosumers distrust companies and products they cannot find on the internet. If they want to influence prosumers, says Mr Lepere, companies have to be extremely open about providing information.

Despite all of these complications, many in the advertising business remain sanguine. For Rupert Howell, chairman of the London arm of McCann Erickson, which is part of the giant Interpublic group, the industry's latest downturn was the third he has experienced. As it did from the others, he says, the industry is emerging a little wiser. But, he insists, 'the underlying principles haven't changed'. Even the arrival of new media, like the internet, does not spell the demise of the old. Indeed, as he points out, TV never killed radio, which in turn never killed newspapers. They did pose huge creative challenges, but that's OK, he maintains: 'The advertising industry is relentlessly inventive; that's what we do.'

Source: 'The harder hard sell', *The Economist*. 26 June 2004, pp. 83–5.
© The Economist Newspaper Limited, London (26 June 2004).

Case Questions

1 Why is it that traditional methods of advertising 'simply no longer work'? What is it about changes in consumer demand that contribute to this phenomenon?

2 Assess the potential of internet players such as Google and Yahoo! to influence and change the way in which the advertising industry operates.

3 What response do you think advertisers should make to the claim that 'consumer resistance to the growing intrusiveness of marketing and advertising has been pushed to an all-time high'? Does this mean that the potential to differentiate consumer products and services is diminishing?

4 What advice would you offer to an advertising agency such as McCann Erickson and to a major advertiser such as P&G?

Further reading and references

Besanko, D, Dranove, D and Shanley, M (2000) *Economics of Strategy*, 2nd edition, John Wiley & Sons, New York.

Boston Consulting Group (1975) *Strategy alternatives for the British motorcycle industry*, HMSO, London.

Burns, T and Stalker, GM (1961) *The Management of Innovation*, Tavistock, London.

Chandler, AD (1990) 'The Enduring Logic of Industrial Success', *Harvard Business Review*, March/April, pp. 130–40.

Child, J (1972) 'Organizational structures, environments and performance: the role of strategic choice', *Sociology*, **6**, pp. 1–22.

Child, J (1997) 'Strategic choice in the analysis of action, structure, organization and environment: retrospect and prospect', *Organization Studies*, **18**, **1**, pp. 43–76.

Conley, P (1975) *Experience Curves as a Planning Tool*, Boston Consulting Group (pamphlet).

Deaton, A (1975) 'The Measurement of Income and Price Elasticities', *European Economic Review*, Vol. 7, pp. 261–74.

Duncan, R (1972) 'Characteristics of Organisational Environments and Perceived Environmental Uncertainty', *Administrative Science Quarterly*, **17**, **3**.

Economist, The (1999), November, pp. 27–35 and p. 122.

Emerson, M (1988) *The Economics of 1992*, Oxford University Press.

European Commission (1997) 'Economies of Scale', *Single Market Review*, Subseries V, Volume 4, Office for Official Publications of the European Communities, Luxembourg.

Fahey, L and Narayanan, VK (1986) *Macroenvironmental Analyses for Strategic Management*, West, New York.

Haldi, J and Whitcomb, D (1967) 'Economies of Scale in Industrial Plants', *Journal of Political Economy*, **75**, **4**, August, pp. 373–85.

Her Majesty's Stationery Office (1978) *A Review of Monopolies and Mergers Policy*, cmnd 7198, London.

Langowitz, N (1987) 'Sun Microsystems Inc. (A)', Harvard Business School Case 9–686–133, June, revised.

Lawrence, PR and Lorsch, JW (1967) *Organization and Environment: Managing Differentiation and Integration*, Irwin, Homewood, Illinois.

McAleese, D (2004) *Economics for Business*, 3rd edition, Prentice Hall, London.

Moore, FT (1959) 'Economies of Scale: Some Statistical Evidence', *Quarterly Journal of Economics*, May, pp. 232–45.

Panzer, JC and Willig, ND (1981) 'Economies of Scope', *American Economic Review*, **71**, pp. 268–77.

Porter, M (1980) *Competitive Strategy*, Free Press, New York.

Porter, ME (1985) *Competitive Advantage*, Free Press, New York.

Porter, ME (1986) 'What is strategy?' *Harvard Business Review*, Nov/Dec, pp. 61–78.

Pratten, C (1988) 'A Survey of the Economies of Scale', in *Research on the Costs of Europe*, Vol. 2, Office for Official Publications of the European Communities, Luxembourg.

Robinson, EAG (1958) *The Structure of Competitive Industry*, University of Chicago Press.

Rosenfeld, R and Wilson, DC (1999) *Managing Organizations: Text, Readings and Cases*, McGraw-Hill, Maidenhead.

Seldon, A and Pennance, FG (eds) (1965) *Everyman's Dictionary of Economics*, JM Dent & Sons, London.

Scherer, FM (1970) *Industrial Market Structure and Economic Performance*, Rand McNally.

Supple, B (1977) *Essays in British Business History*, OUP.

Teece, DJ (1980) 'Economies of scope and the scope of the enterprise', *Journal of Economic Behaviour and Organisation*, **1**, pp. 223–47.

Chapter 4

The macroeconomics of strategy[1]

Introduction

This chapter focuses on the influence on businesses of changes taking place in the external context of both the market and the macroeconomy. This involves not just the systemic impact of external forces but also, and in particular, the way these forces are augmented and mediated by public policy. The chapter covers the fundamentals of aggregate demand and supply and the implications for GDP, inflation and unemployment. It also examines the causes and effects of business cycles and what in a global economy causes booms and slumps to come to an end. It goes on to consider issues concerning the sustainability of strong economic growth, especially in emerging markets. The chapter concludes

Chapter contents

---

[1] This chapter was written jointly with K.G (Ben) Knight.

brewing in the UK and in the EU as a whole and the adoption of an exit strategy by some UK brewers.

As part of its strategy Interbrew acquired the brewing activities of Whitbread in May 2000. Like many UK brewers, Whitbread were anxious to divest themselves of their brewing interests and focus on their more profitable leisure business for the reasons set out above. It was an attractive acquisition for Interbrew not least because Whitbread held the UK franchise for the Stella brand, which is owned by Interbrew.

Similar motivations lay behind the acquisition in August 2000 of Bass, a much larger player in the UK market. The sale of Bass to Interbrew was referred to the UK Competition Commission (www.mmc.gov.uk) by the European Commission. In January 2001 the Competition Commission ruled against the acquisition of Bass on the grounds that it would leave the two top players in the sector (Interbrew and Scottish and Newcastle) with 59 per cent of the UK market which the Commission deemed too large a market share since both would have 'a common interest in raising operating margins' and driving up prices paid by consumers. This decision was a serious blow to Interbrew's strategic ambitions.

As well as national competition regulators, the European Union has its own increasingly active transnational competition regulator. The regulator is a key feature of the EU's programme of economic integration.. The process of EU integration has been driven by a desire to create a larger (US-size) home market for EU business. The first stage was to remove all tariff barriers between member countries in order to encourage the growth of trade within the EU, and this is exactly what has happened, with intra-EU trade as a percentage of total EU trade growing by 20 percentage points between 1974 and 2001. In addition there has been a huge growth in cross-border mergers and acquisitions especially in the run-up to the introduction of the euro in 1999 and also in 2000. Although this process has slowed down since 2000, the European Commission is still keen to ensure that this process of pan-European consolidation does not lead to unwanted accumulation of market power and that the EU maintains a high degree of domestic market rivalry. One area in which the EU competition regulator is actively exerting its influence to limit the market power of producers is in the EU car market, and this has serious implications for the strategy of the EU car-makers.

4.2 The basics of macroeconomics

It is not just a matter of understanding the market context of business. As we saw in Chapter 3, all firms and industries are also sensitive to events in the wider economy. This is true in any economy irrespective of its geographical location or stage of development. The extent of exposure for each industry differs little across countries. As we also saw in Chapter 3, booms and slumps in GDP lead to major changes in the rate of growth of sales and output at both the market sector and firm levels. These feed through to financial performance and, although they have to be managed, are totally outside the control of the individual firm or its managers.

Hence, even with no change in the strategy of the individual firm, major changes in its performance and prospects will occur for reasons outside its direct control. If the threat of adverse developments is to be minimized and the benefit of the opportunity afforded by favourable conditions is to be maximized, these macroeconomic factors need to be taken into account by managers. Chapter 3 suggests that the first critical question to be considered is: what causes the short-run fluctuations in GDP growth which have such a significant impact on firm-level performance?

4.2.1 Short-run fluctuations in GDP

Initially we will focus on national economies. Goods and services in any national macro-economy as a whole are produced to meet demand, not necessarily immediately, but eventually. Hence, the normal cause of booms and slumps in GDP is fluctuations in the volume of demand for goods and services in the economy as a whole (**aggregate demand**). If aggregate demand goes up, so does GDP, and if it goes down, GDP again follows suit.

This can be seen from Figure 4.2, which shows the close relationship of changes in aggregate demand and output (GDP) for the rich OECD (Organisation for Economic

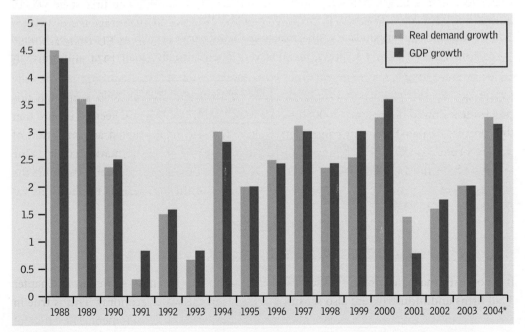

Figure 4.2 Boom and slump in practice: demand and output in industrial economies (annual % growth)
Note: * = estimated.
Source: OECD.

Co-operation and Development) economies of the EU, North America and the Pacific Rim as a whole. This accounts for nearly two-thirds of world GDP. The match between demand growth and GDP growth is not perfect and, where it is not, there will be changes in the stocks of finished goods. If GDP growth exceeds demand growth, for example, stocks rise. When demand growth exceeds GDP growth, stocks fall, as they did in 1994. However, there is clearly a close correspondence between changes in GDP and in aggregate demand and it is this correspondence which we explore next.

What is 'aggregate demand'? It is the total demand for goods and services from all sources in the national economy. Where does the demand originate? Economists identify the following sources of aggregate demand:

1 The demand for consumer goods, both durable (such as cars) and non-durable (such as food), and services by all households resident in the national economy. In most economies this constitutes the biggest source of demand. In the UK, for example, just over 50 per cent of aggregate demand originates from this source and this is very typical of the OECD economies.

2 Demand for investment goods (buildings, plant and machinery) and services by private companies. This varies in importance across economies but is rarely less than 10 per cent of the total aggregate demand for goods and services and in some countries (e.g. the economies of East Asia) can be as high as 25 per cent.

3 Demand for export goods, e.g. pharmaceuticals and services such as tourism, by foreign customers. As Figure 4.3 shows, in some very open (usually small) economies heavily

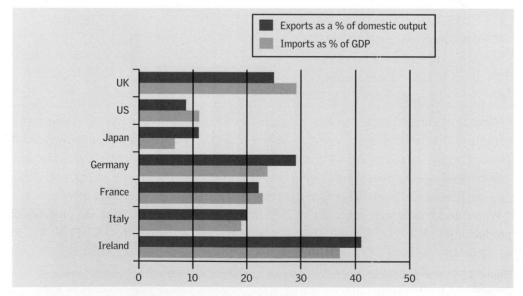

Figure 4.3 Indicators of macroeconomic openness 2003
Source: OECD.

engaged in trade (e.g. Ireland) this can be very high but in the average OECD economy around 25 per cent of the demand for goods in industrial economies comes from this source. In the very large and more self-sufficient economies such as Japan and the US (which together account for over a third of world GDP), the proportion is much lower.

4   Demand for goods and services by the government. This arises from public spending on defence, education, health and so on. It does not include 'transfer payments' (such as state pensions), i.e. payments made to individuals by the government using funds raised from other citizens, because these funds are used by households and hence are included in consumer demand. The share of the government in aggregate demand for goods and services also varies a lot but the 15 per cent level found in the UK is very typical of the industrial economies as a whole.

5   In calculating the aggregate demand for a country's output, account must also be taken of the extent to which demand is met by overseas production, i.e. imports. Increases in imports reduce the level of aggregate demand for home produced goods and vice versa if imports fall. Figure 4.3 also gives an indication of the share of imports in various countries. The most obvious feature here is that the share of imports as a percentage of demand is lowest in the larger more self-sufficient countries such as Japan and the US and highest in a small economy such as Ireland.

Aggregate demand for goods and services in any economy is therefore the sum of each of these sources of demand:

$C + I + G + X - F$ where

> C = *consumer demand by households*
> I = *investment demand by firms*
> G = *public sector demand*
> X = *exports to other economies*
> F = *imports from other economies*

What determines the level of aggregate demand for goods and services in any national economy? The first and most important answer is the level of aggregate income (wages and salaries *plus* profits) received by all firms and all households in the economy. The government's income is derived from the same source via taxation. In the case of exports, what counts is the income of firms and households in the overseas economies where exports are sold.

Where does this income come from? The most important source is from the proceeds of producing goods and services in the national economy as a whole, i.e. from GDP! We started by wanting to explain GDP and the explanation ends up with GDP!! Not surprisingly, economists refer to this as the **circular flow of income** and this is shown in Figure 4.4.

Figure 4.4 shows the interaction between the three fundamental macroeconomic processes described above, namely:

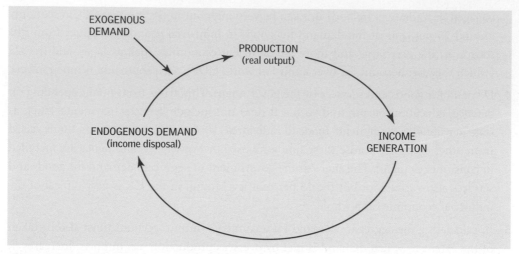

Figure 4.4 The circular flow of income

1 the national production of goods and services;

2 the income generated by this production of goods and services; and

3 the disposal of income to create the aggregate demand for goods and services which completes the circle.

Each of these processes feeds back on the others. Production in an open economy (i.e. one which engages in international trade) would not occur without demand, which in its turn would not happen without income, which depends itself on the production of goods and services. The demand that arises from the circular flow of income is called **endogenous** by economists. It refers to the demand (spending) that arises in the home economy from income earned from the home production of goods and services. Note that some of this income is lost to the home economy because it is spent on imports produced in other economies. Economists call this loss of income a **leakage** from the circular flow of income of any national economy.

Demand, however, can also arise from other sources and this offsets the leakage which arises from imports. This type of demand is called **exogenous** because it does not arise from *within* the circular flow of income but rather from *outside*. It can come from outside the home economy, i.e. from exports of goods and services to the outside world, or from within the domestic economy as a result of spending changes driven by forces other than changes in current income, especially the important spending changes which result from changes in wealth and/or in the level of borrowing.

Changes in any component of aggregate demand can cause fluctuations in GDP. History has taught us that the key drivers of the circular flow of income and the changes observed in GDP are shocks to aggregate exogenous demand. There are many exogenous shocks to aggregate demand which can lead to changes in GDP. In all cases, demand originating in the private sector (consumer demand and investment) and in exports plays a crucial role, not least because in most economies this is at least 80 per cent of the total demand for goods and services. However, there is also a role for government in stimulating exogenous demand. Note this in the examples set out below.

Among the many examples of potent causes of change in the volume of exogenous demand are changes in the following.

The cost and availability of credit

Easy, cheap credit increases consumer spending at any income level. This causes an increase in exogenous demand. The result of this is an increase in output. If, on the other hand, credit becomes more expensive, aggregate demand falls (or increases by less) and this will cause output to fall (or increase by less). In 1999 US interest rates rose to slow down the US economy. The problem is that in 2000 this slowdown happened rather more quickly and dramatically than the monetary authorities thought, so a correction was required. In 2001 onwards US interest rates fell several times to stop the slowdown turning into a severe slump.

Rises in interest rates are sometimes also used to reduce capital outflows and stabilize exchange rates which are under pressure. This is the recent experience of many Asian and Latin American economies and severe recession is the result as demand falls. In November 1998 interest rates in Rio were 49 per cent as the Brazilian government attempted to maintain the real/$ parity! Unsuccessfully as it turned out, so rates fell in 1999 but remain high in 2004. Changes in the interest rate also change the cost of finance as well as the opportunities for gain from financial investment. This has an important effect on both real fixed investment and stockbuilding. When the interest rate rises, firms cut back their fixed investment because borrowing is dearer and financial investment is a more attractive alternative. This response is not, however, immediate. Stockbuilding, in contrast, responds more quickly. Increases in the cost of finance encourage de-stocking, especially of finished goods. When this happens output falls directly.

Changes in wealth

Changes in wealth affect the take-up of credit opportunities by consumers. Increases in wealth encourage consumers to borrow, especially when interest rates are falling. The most important source of wealth for many consumers is equity in houses. When house prices rise, as they did in the UK in the mid 1980s and again in 1999–2004, households experience an increase in wealth, enabling them to increase debt without increasing their debt/wealth ratio. Since additional wealth also encourages greater consumer confidence, increased consumer demand results and output rises. The whole chain of events is reversed when house prices stabilize and then fall as they did in the period 1989–95. This both causes and lengthens a recession because it makes consumers reluctant to increase their spending even when interest rates fall. This was a persistent feature of the UK until 1996/97 when house prices, and hence household wealth, started to rise. Similar effects can occur through changes in the value of non-housing wealth. Rising share prices were profoundly important in explaining the strong growth of private sector demand and GDP in the US from 1992 to 2000. In the opposite direction, falls in the value of shares in Japan, for example, contributed to the slump in consumer demand in 1993 and the subsequent poor and volatile performance of the Nikkei share price index has held back consumer demand and contributed to the difficulty Japan has experienced in getting a strong recovery underway even when base interest rates fall to 0.5 per cent. Falls in world stock markets in 2001 and 2002 also triggered these kinds of 'wealth effects' and contributed to reduced confidence, lower demand and global slowdown despite lower interest rates.

Changes in government spending

Increases in government spending (current or capital) increase aggregate demand, and output increases. This is an important means through which the government can influence the economy. The Japanese government adopted this approach to ending recessions in 1993/4 and 1996 and also in 2000/2001. It is an important reason for the relatively (compared to other G7 economies) strong performance of the UK in the years 2000–2004.

Changes in tax rates

Cuts in income taxes increase consumer spending because they increase net household income and, if government spending is not cut, aggregate demand rises as well. Cuts in the US tax rates in 2001 were intended to boost consumer spending to stop a prolonged recession. Further cuts in both personal and corporate tax rates will have the same effect. In contrast, increases in personal or corporate tax rates have the opposite effect, reducing consumer and investment demand.

Changes in the exchange rate

One critical driver of exogenous aggregate demand is the exchange rate, which sets the price of one currency in terms of another: e.g. if the £/$ rate is 1.50 it tells us the number of US dollars needed to buy £1 – i.e. $1.50. The exchange rates are fixed daily across the world. Changes in the exchange rate have a big effect on cross-border spending, i.e. on exports.

Table 4.1 Exchange rate arithmetic

	$P^x_£$	$P^x_$$	$P^f_$$	$P^f_£$	
£1 = $2	100	200	300	150	strong £
£1 = $1	100	100	300	300	weak £

Exchange rates also impact on imports, i.e. on leakages from the circular flow of income, so they also impact on the endogenous demand arising from the circular flow of income. The effect is shown in Table 4.1. $P^x_{\pounds}$ is the price of exports in the home currency (£ in this example) and $P^x_{\$}$ is the price in export markets. What is the effect of a change in the exchange rate when the home price remains the same (£100 in Table 4.1)? When the exchange rate is £1 = \$2, the price in the export market is \$200, but when the exchange rate depreciates to £1 = \$1, the price in the export market falls to \$100. This fall in price increases export sales and leads to faster export volume growth. $P^f_{\$}$ is the price of imports in the overseas currency and $P^f_{\pounds}$ the price charged in the home market. When the exchange rate falls, the price paid in the home market goes up, benefiting the domestic producer who sells more at the expense of the now dearer imported product, so leakages from the circular flow of income fall. As a result, GDP also goes up.

If the exchange rate goes up (appreciates), exactly the opposite happens. Table 4.1 shows that prices in export markets rise when the pound is stronger. This rise will reduce export volume and hence exogenous demand. Note also the fall in import prices, which increases both import volume and the level of leakages from the circular flow of income.

There are many examples of the effect of exchange rates on exogenous demand and GDP. An increase in the exchange rate, such as that which occurred in the UK between 1996 and 2000, reduces trade competitiveness and exports. It also increases import leakages from the circular flow of income. This reduces the demand for domestically produced goods and output growth falls as a result.

If the exchange rate falls, the opposite happens. The strong growth of the euro-area economies in 2000 was a direct result of the fall in the euro after its introduction in 1999. The depreciation of the Korean won and other Asian currencies in 1997/98 had the same effect on those economies in 1999/2000.

Why does the exchange rate change? The exchange rate is determined in the foreign exchange market and reflects the forces of both supply and demand in that market. The drivers of supply and demand in the foreign exchange (FOREX) market are set out in Table 4.2.

If the demand for home currency rises, the exchange rate also rises (appreciates). What causes this to happen? An increase in the demand for home assets is a common driver.

Table 4.2 Drivers of supply and demand in the FOREX market

Demand for home currency rises (falls) if:
- Exports rise (fall)
- Demand for home assets from overseas investors rises (falls)

Supply of home currency rises (falls) if:
- Imports rise (fall)
- Demand for overseas assets from home investors rises (falls)

This will happen if home interest rates rise, increasing the desire for overseas investors or home-based investors to deposit their money in the home economy. Similarly, if foreign interest rates fall, the impact on investor behaviour will lead to a rise in the exchange rate of the home economy. An increase in exports from the home economy will lead to increased demand for the home currency by foreign buyers, which appreciates the exchange rate. A decrease in imports has the same effect because home residents who want less foreign currency to pay for the imports decrease the supply of home currency in the FOREX market. Test your understanding of these ideas by filling in the blank boxes in Table 4.3. Use arrows to indicate the direction of change.

Knowledge of these relationships helps a business to anticipate government policy, especially with respect to interest rates. Rises in interest rates will take place if a government wants to stabilize exchange rates that are under downward pressure. The idea is to increase the demand from international investors for home assets by increasing the interest rate on them. As noted above, this is the experience of many Asian and Latin American economies.

In summary, booms can only occur if there is an increase in the aggregate demand for goods and services. Similarly, slumps would not happen if the aggregate demand for products did not fall. From a business strategy point of view it is important to keep track of movements both in aggregate demand and in the key determinants of these movements, and to relate this to knowledge of the macroeconomic exposure of the business and its markets.

4.3 Aggregate supply and the end of booms

It is evident from Figure 4.2 that booms end. At the beginning of the 1990s the boom in the OECD economies ended with a bump. Why? The answer to this question is usually found on the supply side of the macroeconomy. At the peak of a boom, shortages of machine capacity begin to appear. Supplies of key skilled labour diminish. As a result, output growth slows down because firms cannot keep up with the growth in demand.

Table 4.3 Exchange rates in the FOREX market

	Demand for £ by overseas residents	Supply of £ by UK residents	£/euro (price of pounds/euros)
Home interest rate down			
Foreign interest rate down			
Current balance of payments worsens			
Home inflation rate up			

In addition to these purely physical constraints there are other effects which bring booms to an end. Emerging supply shortages drive up input (labour and raw materials) prices and this raises costs and hence inflation, i.e. the rate of increase of prices goes up.

This is the idea that underlies the so-called *Phillips curve* which is depicted in Figure 4.5. A boom causes a fall in unemployment from U_1 to U_2. Employers experiencing recruitment difficulties, especially of skilled workers, will bid up their wage offers. To prevent a loss of workers, others will follow suit. Workers will be in a stronger bargaining position to drive up wages. In short, an acceleration of the rate of wage inflation from W_1 to W_2 will occur. Since labour costs are a very significant part of the average costs of production incurred by firms, any increase in the rate of wage inflation will have a positive effect on the rate of price inflation. There may also be other more direct routes that lead to higher prices. For example, through, the increase in profit margins that occurs in booms in GDP growth. The evidence from upturns in Europe and North America is that even in historically inflation-prone economies such as the UK, France and Italy, the growth in inflation is much more muted in the 1990s, so there is now much less inflation at all stages of the business cycle.

The result is that inflation no longer takes off as it did in the 1970s and, more spectacularly, in the hyperinflations afflicting parts of Eastern and Central Europe in the early 1990s. One reason for this slowdown in inflation is the much lower rate at which imported raw material and energy prices are rising. Other factors may also impinge on the relationship depicted in Figure 4.5, such as prices and incomes policy of the kind still very much in use in Ireland, the strength of trade unions, the rate of growth of labour productivity, and so on. You should try to think through the effects of changes in these factors. The impact of higher inflation on a boom is reinforced by the response of governments and central banks.

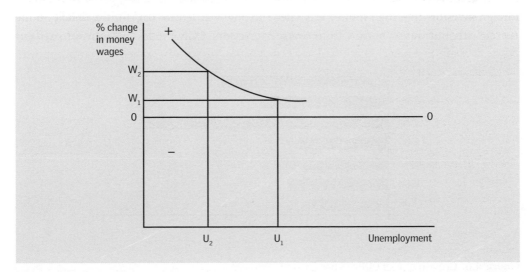

Figure 4.5 The Phillips curve

Banks that target the rate of inflation will tend to drive up interest rates to contain an expected rise in inflation. A rise in the rate increases the costs of borrowing, hence reducing private sector and overall aggregate demand. This slows down GDP growth and brings the boom to an end and brings inflation down to hit the target rate.

A further factor that sometimes brings a boom to an end arises from the effect of a boom on the overseas balance of payments. Rapid growth in output increases income through the circular flow mechanism and this causes an increase in a country's imports to take place. At the same time, the strong pressure of demand can lead to a reduction in exports as home producers seek to meet burgeoning home demand. Hence the balance of trade (exports − imports) worsens.

In fact, this is key to understanding the crisis in the East Asian economies in 1997. This region of the world, almost without exception, grew exceptionally fast throughout the 1990s. So successful were these economies that the World Bank promoted the idea of an 'East Asian Miracle' and urged other emerging economies to look to East Asia to find the ingredients for successful long-run performance.

Figure 4.6 shows GDP growth across the world and it indicates just how successful East Asia was in the period up until 1997 (note that the only OECD country which compares with East Asia is Ireland). However, this rapid growth in GDP led to strong growth in imports and a slowdown in exports, especially in Thailand. The effect on the current account (i.e. where trade flows are recorded) of the balance of payments was substantial deficits. Normally, as you can see from the analysis of exchange rate movements above, this deficit should lead to a fall in the demand for Asian currencies and an increase in their supply in FOREX markets. As a result the exchange rate should have fallen but most of the region's economies had fixed their exchange rates against the US dollar, partly to persuade foreign investors that their money was safe. The only way left to 'pay' for the deficit on the current account was to borrow from overseas investors. Only modest incentives to achieve

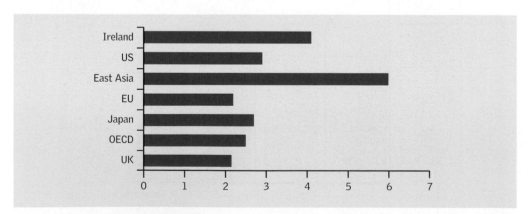

Figure 4.6 Growth of real GDP (% per annum) 1980–97
Source: World Bank.

this were necessary since the international financial community also believed a 'miracle' was happening and lending to East Asian economies was a 'good bet'.

You can see in Figure 4.7 (which also shows the position of Mexico in 1994 when similar events occurred as a result of the same rapid GDP growth) the impact on the overseas debt position of various Asian economies. Much of the debt was short-term lending by East Asian banks from OECD financial institutions which lent it on to local companies to fuel the boom (*see* Figure 4.8).

Problems started (in Thailand) in 1997 when a GDP-boom-driven 'bubble' in the property market burst. Property developers had borrowed heavily and overinvested in projects on which they could not secure a short-run return. Several went out of business with an adverse effect on the poorly regulated banking sector. The ensuing loss of confidence led to a flight of foreign investors and irresistible downward pressure on the exchange rate. This contagion spread to other Asian economies, causing a stock market crash throughout the region. The flight of foreign investors caused exchange rates to fall, as suggested by your answers in Table 3. As a result the US dollar value of East Asian debt soared which, combined with the stock market crash, led to dramatic falls in GDP growth in 1998 (*see* Figure 4.9) as reductions in wealth and increasing debt hit exogenous aggregate demand growth. One exception to these events was Hong Kong, where the monetary authorities were able to resist the downward pressure on the HK dollar by using some of Hong Kong's huge reserves of foreign currencies, including US dollars.

However, the fall in the exchange rate also brought relief to most of the East Asian economies so that by mid 1999 the boost to international competitiveness led to significant increases in GDP being reported in several economies in the region. This emphasizes the important role often played by the exchange rate as a 'shock absorber'.

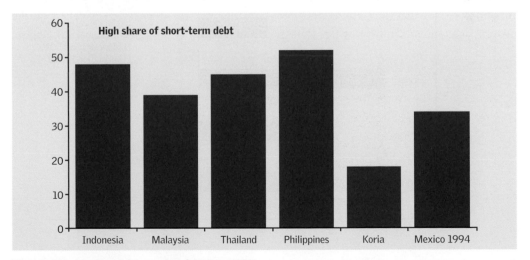

Figure 4.7 Foreign debt as a % of GDP in 1997
Source: World Bank.

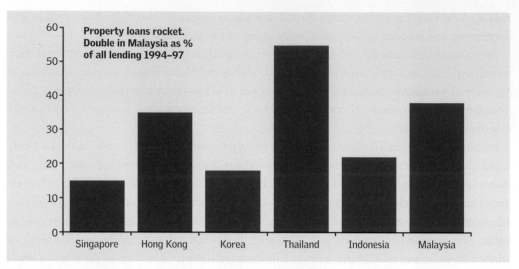

Figure 4.8 Growth in bank lending (% points of GDP) 1991–97
Source: World Bank.

The Asian experience illustrates the importance of **balanced growth** in the emerging economies. Balanced growth implies a growth in the aggregate demand for goods and services that is in line with the growth in aggregate supply, not only of physical assets such as machines and labour (i.e. 'resources'), but also in capabilities such as skill and knowledge, some of which arise from the large learning curve effects evident in emerging economies. More rapid growth in demand is a characteristic of emerging economies where there are few slow-growing mature markets, but if this proceeds at a pace which is faster than aggregate

Figure 4.9 GDP growth in Asia 1997/8 (%)
Source: World Bank.

supply, the impact on imports, especially of the capital goods necessary for sustained development, creates financial pressures that are difficult to manage.

The Asian crisis also reflects the development and interdependence of the global economy. Rapid growth in the region would not have been possible without the huge inflows of both long-term (i.e. investment in fixed assets) and short-term (i.e. investment in financial assets) capital from the OECD economies. The growth in global financial markets and the global strategies of large transnational and largely OECD-based businesses are crucial here. Also important is the issue of interdependence. Crisis in Asia carried an important threat for the OECD economies. It had obvious effects on global financial stability but also impacted on global trade and hence global GDP growth. It required the governments of the OECD economies to take an increasingly global view and to take on board the global implications of their domestic policies. This is exactly what happened in 1998 when OECD interest rates were cut at a time when most commentators expected them to rise. The effect was to create OECD markets for goods and services produced not only in the OECD but also in the non-OECD world.

4.4 **National competitive advantage and long-run macroeconomic performance**

One central feature of the fast-growing economies in Asia is a high degree of **national competitive advantage**, especially in international trade. They have, as a result, achieved strong trade performance and this is reflected in the big increase in their share of world trade, notably in manufacturing goods, which represent 60 per cent of world exports and which is the fastest growing global product market.

Of course, no nation actually engages in international trade itself. This is done by the individual businesses operating in a nation state and competing in the global markets for their products. A competitive economy is, hence, one in which the average business located in the economy enjoys global competitive advantage. Note the emphasis on *average*. Even in the most uncompetitive economies there are still firms with **competitive advantage**. There just are not many of them. Similarly, there are laggards in the most competitive nation states, but not many. What follows from this link is that competitive advantage is not simply to do with a 'natural' endowment of resources, but can be created by policy at *both* company and national level. Company-level global competitive advantage can be facilitated by a favourable political–economic context, but there is still a role for company-level strategic 'actions' in building both *company and national* competitive advantage.

What determines **national competitiveness**? The lessons of the extensive research (including Porter) into this topic emphasize four crucial interdependent factors:

- High levels of investment in 'factors of production' and innovation.

- Effective production and effective business.

- A supportive home market.
- Maintaining domestic competition and maximizing 'external' economies.

Case box: **The Big Mac index**

The world economy looks very different once countries' output is adjusted for differences in prices

HOW fast is the world economy growing? How important is China as an engine of growth? How much richer is the average person in America than in China? The answers to these huge questions depend crucially on how you convert the value of output in different countries into a common currency. Converting national GDPs into dollars at market exchange rates is misleading. Prices tend to be lower in poor economies, so a dollar of spending in China, say, is worth a lot more than a dollar in America. A better method is to use purchasing-power parities (PPP), which take account of price differences.

The theory of purchasing-power parity says that in the long run exchange rates should move towards rates that would equalise the prices of an identical basket of goods and services in any two countries. This is the thinking behind *The Economist's* Big Mac index. Invented in 1986 as a light-hearted guide to whether currencies are at their 'correct' level, our 'basket' is a McDonald's Big Mac, which is produced locally in almost 120 countries.

The Big Mac PPP is the exchange rate that would leave a burger in any country costing the same as in America. The first column of our table converts the local price of a Big Mac into dollars at current exchange rates. The average price of a Big Mac in four American cities is $2.90 (including tax). The cheapest shown in the table is in the Philippines ($1.23), the most expensive in Switzerland ($4.90). In other words, the Philippine peso is the world's most undervalued currency, the Swiss franc its most overvalued.

The second column calculates Big Mac PPPs by dividing the local currency price by the American price. For instance, in Japan a Big Mac costs ¥262. Dividing this by the American price of $2.90 produces a dollar PPP against the yen of ¥90, compared with its current rate of ¥113, suggesting that the yen is 20% undervalued. In contrast, the euro (based on a weighted average of Big Mac prices in the euro area) is 13% overvalued. But perhaps the most interesting finding is that all emerging-market currencies are undervalued against the dollar. The Chinese yuan, on which much ink has been spilled in recent months, looks 57% too cheap.

The Big Mac index was never intended as a precise forecasting tool. Burgers are not traded across borders as the PPP theory demands; prices are distorted by differences in the cost of non-tradable goods and services, such as rents.

Yet these very failings make the Big Mac index useful, since looked at another way it can help to measure countries' differing costs of living. That a Big Mac is cheap in China does not

The hamburger standard

	Big Mac price in dollars*	Implied PPP[†] of the dollar	Under (−)/ over (+) valuation against the dollar, %		Big Mac price in dollars*	Implied PPP[†] of the dollar	Under (−)/ over (+) valuation against the dollar, %
United States	2.90	–	–	Aruba	2.29	1.41	−21
Argentina	1.48	1.50	−49	Belarus	1.37	1021	−53
Australia	2.27	1.12	−22	Bulgaria	1.85	1.03	−36
Brazil	1.70	1.86	−41	Colombia	2.35	2241	−19
Britain	3.37	1.54[§]	+16	Costa Rica	2.61	390	−10
Canada	2.33	1.10	−20	Croatia	2.42	5.14	−17
Chile	2.18	4.83	−25	Dom. Rep.	1.32	20.7	−54
China	1.26	3.59	−57	Estonia	2.27	10.2	−22
Czech Rep.	2.13	19.5	−27	Fiji	2.35	1.47	−19
Denmark	4.46	9.57	+54	Georgia	1.90	1.26	−34
Egypt	1.62	3.45	−44	Guatemala	2.01	5.52	−31
Euro area	3.28**	1.06[††]	+13	Honduras	1.98	12.4	−32
Hong Kong	1.54	4.14	−47	Iceland	6.01	151	107
Hungary	2.52	1.83	−13	Jamaica	1.88	39.0	−35
Indonesia	1.77	5,552	−39	Jordan	3.65	0.89	26
Japan	2.33	90.3	−20	Kuwait	7.33	0.74	153
Malaysia	1.33	1.74	−54	Latvia	2.00	0.38	−31
Mexico	2.08	8.28	−28	Lebanon	2.84	1483	−2
New Zealand	2.65	1.50	−8	Lithuania	2.26	2.24	−22
Peru	2.57	3.10	−11	Macau	1.40	3.86	−52
Philippines	1.23	23.8	−57	Macedonia	1.84	32.8	−36
Poland	1.63	2.17	−44	Moldova	1.93	7.93	−33
Russia	1.45	14.5	−50	Morocco	0.26	0.82	−91
Singapore	1.92	1.14	−34	Nicaragua	2.19	11.9	−25
South Africa	1.86	4.28	−36	Norway	5.18	12.2	79
South Korea	2.72	1,103	−6	Pakistan	1.90	37.9	−34
Sweden	3.94	10.3	+36	Qatar	0.68	0.85	−77
Switzerland	4.90	2.17	+69	Saudi Arabia	0.64	0.83	−78
Taiwan	2.24	25.9	−23	Slovakia	1.98	22.8	−32
Thailand	1.45	20.3	−50	Slovenia	2.42	166	−17
Turkey	2.58	1,362,069	−11	Sri Lanka	1.41	48.3	−51
Venezuela	1.48	1,517	−49	Ukraine	1.36	2.50	−53
				UAE	0.67	0.84	−77
				Uruguay	1.00	10.3	−65

*At current exchange rates
[†]Purchasing-power parity
Average of New York, Chicago, San Francisco and Atlanta
[§]Dollars per pound
**Weighted average of member countries
[††]Dollars per euro

Sources: McDonald's; The Economist.

in fact prove that the yuan is being held massively below its fair value, as many American politicians claim. It is quite natural for average prices to be lower in poorer countries and therefore for their currencies to appear cheap.

The prices of traded goods will tend to be similar to those in developed economies. But the prices of non-tradable products, such as housing and labour-intensive services, are generally much lower. A haircut is, for instance, much cheaper in Beijing than in New York.

One big implication of lower prices is that converting a poor country's GDP into dollars at market exchange rates will significantly understate the true size of its economy and its living standards. If China's GDP is converted into dollars using the Big Mac PPP, it is almost two-and-a-half-times bigger than if converted at the market exchange rate. Meatier and more sophisticated estimates of PPP, such as those used by the IMF, suggest that the required adjustment is even bigger.

Weight watchers

The global economic picture thus looks hugely different when examined through a PPP lens. Take the pace of global growth. Anyone wanting to calculate this needs to bundle together countries' growth rates, with each one weighted according to its share of world GDP. Using weights based on market exchange rates, the world has grown by an annual average of only 1.9% over the past three years. Using PPP, as the IMF does, global growth jumps to a far more robust 3.1% a year.

The main reason for this difference is that using PPP conversion factors almost doubles the weight of the emerging economies, which have been growing much faster. Measured at market exchange rates, emerging economies account for less than a quarter of global output. But measured using PPP they account for almost half.

Small wonder, then, that global economic rankings are dramatically transformed when they are done on a PPP basis rather than market exchange rates. America remains number one, but China leaps from seventh place to second, accounting for 13% of world output. India jumps into fourth place ahead of Germany, and both Brazil and Russia are bigger than Canada. Similarly, market exchange rates also exaggerate inequality. Using market rates, the average American is 33 times richer than the average Chinese; on a PPP basis, he is 'only' seven times richer.

The way in which economies are measured also has a huge impact on which country has contributed most to global growth in recent years. Using GDP converted at market rates China has accounted for only 7% of the total increase in the dollar value of global GDP over the past three years, compared with America's 25%. But on PPP figures, China has accounted for almost one-third of global real GDP growth and America only 13%.

This helps to explain why commodity prices in general and oil prices in particular have been surging, even though growth has been relatively subdued in the rich world since 2000. Emerging economies are not only growing much faster than rich economies and are more intensive in their use of raw materials and energy, but they also account for a bigger chunk of global output if measured correctly. As Charles Dumas, an economist at Lombard Street Research, neatly puts it, even if a Chinese loaf is a quarter of the cost of a loaf in America, it uses the same amount of flour.

All measures of PPP are admittedly imperfect. But most economists agree that they give a more accurate measure of the relative size of economies than market exchange rates – and a better understanding of some of the dramatic movements in world markets. The humble burger should be part of every economist's diet

Source: 'Food for thought', *The Economist,* 29 May 2004, pp. 75–6.
© The Economist Newspaper Limited, London (29 May 2004).

Questions for discussion

1 Draw up a list of strengths and weaknesses of market exchange rates versus purchasing-power parity for assessing the relative size of different national economies.

2 In assessing a foreign country as a place in which to make investments in plant and machinery, what specific advantages would you get from the use of a PPP approach?

3 The PPP approach suggests that one country (such as Britain) has its currency overvalued against the dollar whereas another country (such as Brazil) has its currency quite heavily undervalued. What does this imply about the relative strength of these two economies and their competitiveness in world markets?

4.4.1 High levels of investment in 'factors of production' and innovation

In competitive economies, the typical firm invests heavily in new products and processes. This enables the firm to produce better and cheaper products and to do so in effective ways. Product innovation is part and parcel of building new markets and the creation of competitive advantage in them. Process innovation is necessary to produce high-quality products in a cost-effective way.

One necessary condition for innovation to take place is a high level of investment in new plant infrastructure and in human capital. Porter calls this the '**factor conditions**' necessary for building national competitive advantage. 'Factors' are factors of production and refer to the resources of capital and labour. Excellence in 'factor creation' is a feature of the fast-growing Asian economies. Consider the facts shown in Figure 4.10. The high level of investment (approximately twice the level of the average OECD economy) in new plant and infrastructure facilitates the rapid diffusion of new up-to-date technologies and speeds up the introduction of new 'state of the art' products. Note that this high level of investment is helped by substantial flows of inward investment from the rich OECD countries and by the very high levels of savings in the region (meaning proportionately less consumption expenditure), which have also grown to a point at which savings as a share of GDP are over twice the level of the OECD countries as a whole.

A high level of investment in fixed capital is necessary for a globally competitive business and for a fast-growing economy, but it is not sufficient. It is also necessary to invest in human capital. A further feature of the East Asia region, emphasized in the research conducted by the World Bank, is a high level of investment in human capital – that is, in the education and training of the workforce. If effective use is to be made of high levels of investment in physical capital, it is important to have a well-educated and trained labour force. This is especially important to securing the innovation benefits of fixed investment. Modern products and processes, even of basic goods such as textiles, require a skilled, flexible and trained labour force.

The World Bank calculates that between 26 and 56 per cent of the growth of GDP experienced in the region (the 56 per cent figure refers to Hong Kong) is the product of high levels of human capital investment. In contrast, the comparative position of the UK within Western Europe, notably in the provision of vocational education, is very weak. Part of this investment, especially on the vocational side, is carried out by business but, clearly, a nation's government has a critical role to play in building both company and national *capabilities*. Ensuring that a nation's workforce is both highly numerate and literate is a basic and essential requirement of any publicly provided or privately sponsored education system.

The reason government's role is so important is because of the presence of the significant market failures in the provision of education. To understand the concept of market failure, refer back to Chapter 3 where the market demand and supply curves are explained. It is shown again in this chapter, in Figure 4.11. The simple idea underpinning the market demand curve is that an increase (or decrease) in price will decrease (or increase) the quantity demanded in the market. In Figure 4.11 recall the market supply curve which implies that an increase in the price of products increases the willingness of producers to increase their supply.

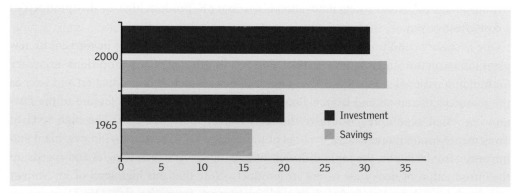

Figure 4.10 Savings and investment in East Asia as % of GDP
Source: World Bank.

In the market the interaction of demand and supply decisions will lead to a price of P_1, with Q_1 being sold and produced. If price were above P_1 at, say, P_2, more would be supplied (Q_3) than could be sold (Q_2), so price would fall to P_1. The opposite would happen if price were below P_1. Competitive market forces rule. If firms succeed in building market power (for example, a monopoly created by merger and/or acquisition), the price can be driven above the market level of P_1, as we saw in Chapter 3.

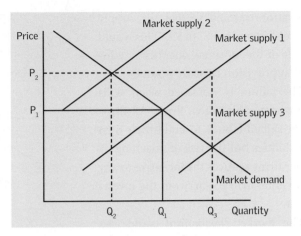

Figure 4.11 Markets and market failure

The market supply curve assumes an underlying relation between costs borne by the firm and the willingness to supply goods. However, the only costs the firm takes into account are the *private* costs of capital, labour, materials, etc. which it bears itself.

However, from society's point of view, there may be important social costs or benefits which the firm does not take into account in its decision making. For example, a firm may pollute a river through its production. In this case, the Market supply curve 1 in Figure 4.11 does not reflect these extra social costs arising from producing the firm's product. On the other hand, Market supply curve 2 does include these pollution costs and it suggests that the price of the polluting product should be P_2, with an amount sold of Q_2. Clearly, the market solution at P_1 and Q_1 leads to significant overproduction. In other words, the market *fails*, because the price charged and the quantity sold in the free market do not reflect all the costs and benefits of production.

Market failure also occurs when there are important social benefits that the private provider does not take into account. A good example is the provision of education and training. Business needs a highly trained and educated labour force and this is also key to long-run macroeconomic success. However, if the provision of education and training is left to the market, there will be substantial underprovision. This is shown in Figure 4.12. DD_1 represents the demand curve associated with the private benefits received from education /training. But there are social benefits that accrue additionally and the real demand curve should be DD_2. Thus, the market fails because it provides less education than it should, viz. $Q_2 - Q_1$. Note that the price effect, $P_2 - P_1$, depends on the slope of the supply curve. If there are economies of scale in education/training, the supply curve could be flat and the price effect could be zero or very small, but the quantity effect (underprovision of education) would be correspondingly larger. One way of dealing with this is for government to provide subsidies for education/training so that the supply curve shifts from SS_1 to SS_2. This would result in the 'optimal' quantity of education provision closer to point Q_2.

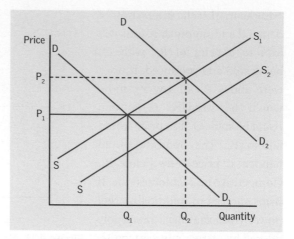

The failure is worsened when skills are transferable across firms. All firms want skilled labour to build their own capabilities but the risk of poaching by other firms reduces the incentive to any individual firm to carry out the investment.

The market mechanism could also fail in the provision of education and training because there is a missing

Figure 4.12 Market failure in education and training

market. The missing market is a capital market to finance investment by individuals in their own education and training. As a result of this failure, there is a lower level of investment in human capital than is socially and economically desirable and lower than is needed to build company and national competitive advantage. This problem arises because the providers of capital (for example, banks) have no reliable information to enable them to distinguish individuals who are good risks from those who are bad risks. This phenomenon is called **adverse selection**.

The solution to these market failures is some form of government intervention to correct the market failure. Taxes, for example, are often used to correct for the failure to take into account the social costs in private production. Taxes on tobacco are a good example. Smoking damages health and, as a result, causes social costs to be incurred. In the case of social benefits generated by education and training, direct provision by the state, or subsidies to private providers, reflect the social benefit to the economy. To overcome the missing capital market, grants or cheap loans could be given to individuals and businesses to enable them to invest in education and training. However, whatever is done, the key requirement is that the government recognizes its critical role in the provision of human capital and that business understands the motivation for this outside intervention in the operation of the market.

> *Building a highly skilled and well-educated labour force is essential to competitiveness at both the business and national levels, but it is not enough.*

Factor creation in the form of skilled labour facilitates innovation and upgrading, which is fundamental to the creation of company and national competitive advantage. A further necessary condition for rapid innovation to take place is a high level of expenditure on research and development. Examine Figure 4.13, which shows spending on R&D as a percentage of GDP in a number of large OECD economies. In Japan, R&D spending is almost at US levels and has increased between 1981 and 2000 at an impressive rate. Look at the UK for a contrast. The differences in performance shown in Figure 4.13 reflect the different rates of innovation by the business sector, especially in manufacturing firms. This performance contributed to the competitive advantage of the Japanese nation relative to European nations, and

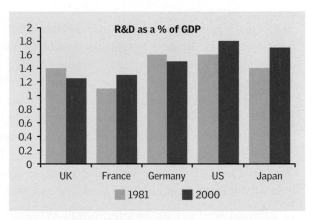

Figure 4.13 R&D as % of GDP
Source: OECD (www.oecd.org).

the strong growth in GDP it achieved in the 1960–90 period. It enabled Japanese industry to increase its share of non-American patents taken out in the US from 1.9 per cent in 1958 to 41.3 per cent in 1988. Over the same period, the UK share fell from 23.4 per cent to 10.8 per cent. It is also important that there is a match between education, training and R&D. Porter (1990) writes, 'To support competitive advantage, a factor (like skilled labour) must be highly specialized to an industry's particular needs'.

> *A high rate of innovation is a key element in business policy and a central ingredient of competitiveness, both in the firm and in an economy.*

Case box: Is outsourcing/offshoring bad for the economy and bad for jobs?

Contrary to what John Kerry and George Bush seem to think, outsourcing actually sustains American jobs

In February 2004 the president's chief economic adviser, Gregory Mankiw, once Harvard's youngest tenured professor, attracted a storm of abuse. He told Congress that if a thing or a service could be produced more cheaply abroad, then Americans were better off importing it than producing it at home. As an example, Mr Mankiw uses the case of radiologists in India analysing the X-rays, sent via the internet, of American patients.

Republicans and Democrats both rebuked Mr Mankiw for approving of jobs going overseas. The White House gave Mr Mankiw only lukewarm support – unsurprisingly, since George Bush recently signed a bill forbidding the outsourcing of federal contracts overseas. And the Democratic presidential contenders? The Wisconsin primary early in 2004 was dominated by the subject of jobs, and the failure of the Bush administration to do enough to protect them from going off to India. Democrat presidential hopefuls such as John Edwards and John Kerry have also seemed very protectionist, using language that criticizes American bosses of betraying American workers by moving jobs overseas, presumably to boost returns for fat-cat investors.

The business lobby seems to be in disarray. 'Tech jobs are fleeing to India faster than ever,' moans the cover of *Wired*. Watch *Lou Dobbs Tonight*, America's main business show, and every factory-closing is hailed as proof of America's relentless 'hollowing-out' at the hands of dark forces in China, India and indeed the White House. Strangely, no mention is made of the fact that a pretty tiny proportion of all jobs lost actually go overseas.

So what is really happening? *The Economist* suggests three themes.

- Although America's economy has, overall, lost jobs since the start of the decade, the vast majority of these job losses are cyclical in nature, not structural. Now that the economy is recovering after the recession of 2001, so will the job picture, perhaps dramatically, over the next year.
- Outsourcing (or 'offshoring') has been going on for centuries, but still accounts for a tiny proportion of the jobs constantly being created and destroyed within America's economy. Even at the best of times, the American economy has a tremendous rate of 'churn' – over 2 million jobs a month. In all, the process creates many more jobs than it destroys: 24 million more during the 1990s. The process allocates resources – money and people – to where they can be most productive, helped by competition, including from outsourcing, that lowers prices. In the long run, higher productivity is the only way to create higher standards of living across an economy.
- Even though service-sector outsourcing is still modest, the growing globalization of information-technology (IT) services should indeed have a big effect on service-sector productivity. During the 1990s, American factories became much more efficient by using IT; now shops, banks, hospitals and so on may learn the same lesson. This will have a beneficial effect that stretches beyond the IT firms. Even though some IT tasks will be done abroad, many more jobs will be created in America, and higher-paying ones to boot.

In the absence of an obvious jobs recovery since the downturn in 2001, it is perhaps not surprising that the myth arose that the American economy was being buffeted by structural, not cyclical, forces. Yet it nevertheless is a myth – as three notable economists, William Baumol, Alan Blinder and Edward Wolff, point out in a recent book (*Downsizing in America: Reality, Causes and Consequences*, Russell Sage Foundation).

Churning, they point out, has being going on in the American jobs market for years, and 'the creation of new jobs always overwhelms the destruction of old jobs by a huge margin.' Between 1980 and 2002, America's population grew by 23.9 per cent. The number of employed Americans, on the other hand, grew by 37.4 per cent. Today, 138.6 million Americans are in work, a near-record, both in absolute terms and as a proportion of the population.

Of course some firms wither – Reynolds Tobacco's workforce shrank by nine-tenths between 1980 and 2002 – but others grow: Wal-Mart's by 4,700 per cent. During the 1990s, about a quarter of all American businesses shed jobs in a typical three-month period, equivalent to 8 million jobs. Yet jobs created greatly outnumbered these, to the tune of 24 million over the decade.

The process leads to incremental shifts that can have profound cumulative consequences for some sectors of the economy. In 1960 only 1 in 25 workers was employed in the business-services and healthcare industries. Today, 1 in 6 is. In terms of output, manufacturing has risen, but, thanks to that productivity spurt, these goods are produced by fewer people – 12 per cent of the workforce, less than half the proportion of three decades ago.

Instead of focusing on jobs lost to the globalization of information technology, Catherine Mann of the Institute for International Economics in Washington looks at globalization's power to reduce prices and so help spread new technology, new practices and job-creating investment through the economy. She uses the example of cheaper IT hardware, one of the main aspects of globalization in the 1990s. Most of the drop in prices for PCs, mainframes and so on was caused by the relentless advance of technology; but she still thinks that trade and globalized production – all those Dell Computer factories in China, for instance – was respon-sible for 10–30 per cent of the fall in hardware prices. These lower prices led to higher American productivity growth and added $230 billion of extra GDP between 1995 and 2002, equivalent to an extra 0.3 percentage points of growth a year.

Will the trend lead to jobs going overseas? You bet, but that is not a disaster. For a start, America runs a large and growing surplus in services with the rest of the world. The jobs lost will be low-paying ones, such as bank tellers and switchboard operators. Trade protection will not save such jobs: if they do not go overseas, they are still at risk from automation.

By contrast, jobs will be created that demand skills to handle the deeper incorporation of information technology, and the pay for these jobs will be high. The demand for computer-support specialists and software engineers, to take two examples, is expected by the Bureau of Labour Statistics (BLS) to double between 2000 and 2010. Demand for database admin-istrators is expected to rise by three-fifths. Among the top score of occupations that the BLS reckons will see the highest growth, half will need IT skills. As it is, between 1999 and 2003 (that is, including during the recession) jobs were created, not lost, in a whole host of white-collar occupations said to be particularly susceptible to outsourcing.

Yes, individuals will be hurt in the process, and the focus of public policy should be directed towards providing a safety net for them, as well as ensuring that Americans have education to match the new jobs being created. By contrast, regarding globalization as the enemy, as many politicians do, is a much greater threat to America's economic health than any Indian software programmer.

Source: summarized and adapted from 'The great hollowing-out myth', *The Economist*, 19 February 2004.

Questions for discussion

1 Outline the case in favour of outsourcing.
2 Under what conditions would the above reasons not hold good?

4.4.2 **Effective production and effective business**

A second requirement for achieving global competitiveness is achieving effective production. Partly this is about achieving low-cost production through the exploitation of scale and scope economies. That requires the speedy adoption of both production technologies (investment) and production management techniques, which result in high levels and strong growth in input productivity. The World Bank Report on East Asia attributes a third (on average) of the high GDP growth in the region to the effects of rapid improvement in the productivity of all the inputs used in production.

Effective production is not just about low costs. It is also about putting in place the conditions that create competitive advantage at the business level. Porter's 'diamond' analysis identifies the importance to national competitive advantage of firm strategy and structure, and in particular the organizational frameworks which facilitate the development of firm-level competitive advantage. He also emphasizes that no single managerial system is universally appropriate, so that '*competitiveness in a particular industry results from the convergence of the management practices and organisational modes favoured in the country*'. A key issue here is the way management practices encourage commitment and effort from the entire labour force.

National competitiveness requires business to be effective in its use of inputs and to be focused on the development of its own competitive advantage.

4.4.3 **A supportive home market**

This third ingredient is given especial importance in Porter's 'diamond':

> *Nations gain competitive advantage in industries where the home market gives their companies a clearer or earlier picture of emerging buyer needs, and where demanding buyers pressure companies to innovate faster and achieve more sophisticated competitive advantages than their foreign rivals.* (Porter, 1990)

A good example is Denmark's global expertise in windmills for electricity generation. In part, this reflects the 'green' preferences of Danish consumers, but it also reflects local rural community preference for small-scale, local electricity generation. Another example is the competitive advantage of Italian textile and footwear manufacturers. The home market preference for well-designed, innovative and well-crafted clothes and shoes has put pressure on Italian manufacturers to meet the demanding home consumer and this has contributed to their global competitive advantage. Other examples can be found in Porter (1990).

4.4.4 **Maintaining domestic competition and maximizing 'external' economies**

The fourth key ingredient in building a competitive economy noted by Michael Porter (1990) is the responsibility of government for maintaining high levels of domestic competition and, hence, low levels of **horizontal integration**. Horizontal integration is the process of merger in which firms producing the same products come together, thus reducing the degree of competition in the market. As we saw in Chapter 3 market concentration of this kind leads to another form of market failure arising from the growth of market power, which enables firms to charge higher prices than would prevail under competitive conditions. Porter draws attention to the large number of rivals producing the same product in Japan (*see* Figure 4.14) in the period of greatest economic success. Similarly, McAleese (2004) shows that the dominance of large firms in the UK is over three times the rate found in Japan. In Sweden it is nearly seven times the Japanese rate. Domestic rivalry also pressurizes companies to innovate and improve, and hones the skills necessary for successful international competition and this helps explain, in part, the international competitive success of Japanese business.

In apparent contradiction, Porter also emphasizes the need to maximize those business synergies which require a high degree of inter-firm co-operation. These synergies, or **'agglomeration economies'** as economists call them, arise from the location of firms in 'clusters'. These clusters create benefits for all the firms in the cluster which lower their costs and increase their competitive advantage. Porter uses the success of the Italian footwear industry as an example to support his argument. Italian designers and manufacturers of shoes, of leather and leather-working machinery have formed 'clustering' relationships which involve a high degree of co-operative interaction along vertical supply chains. Porter remarks that '*Close and ongoing interchange with suppliers and buyers is integral to the process of creating and sustaining competitive advantage in international competition.*'

A high degree of horizontal competition and of vertical co-operation leads to global competitiveness.

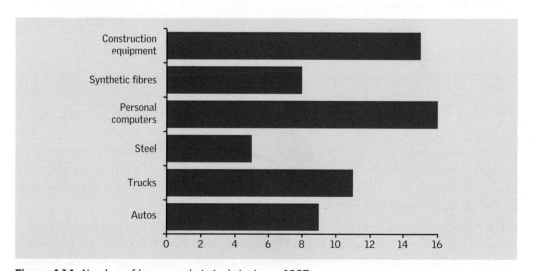

Figure 4.14 Number of home market rivals in Japan 1987
Source: Porter (1990) p. 82. Reprinted with permission of The Free Press, a division of Simon and Schuster Adult Publishing Group. Copyright © 1990 by Michael E. Porter. All rights reserved.

Knowledge of these four requirements for the creation of national competitive advantage is helpful to globalizing businesses, which need to take a long view of the markets in which they plan to locate. When the markets of interest are in the emerging economies, statistical forecasting of the future development of the macroeconomy is difficult, if not impossible. Therefore, in order to make useful judgements about long-run prospects, it makes sense to identify the key determinants of long-run economic success and to benchmark the markets of interest, in terms of their local performance, against these determinants.

Next we explore in more detail the way in which business can use other economic information as part of a strategy to build competitive advantage over its rivals.

4.5 Macroeconometric forecasting and business

Here we examine further the link between business and macroeconomic performance and explore further the implications for business strategy. As we have seen, effective strategy requires an insightful understanding of the macroeconomic environment. In part, this is needed to evaluate and explain past and current performance and this is what we have emphasized so far. However, strategy is about future actions, so a forward-looking view of the macroeconomic environment is also needed. One simple way to do this is to access one of the many published macroeconomic forecasts and to use that. A number of websites are available which contain the kind of forecasts that businesses need. Some of these websites are listed below:

- http://www.imf.org
- http://www.worldbank.org
- http://www.oecd.org
- http://www.niesr.ac.uk

How are these forecasts prepared? A starting point for most forecasters is to look at past experience and use this as a guide to the future. One simple approach would be to collect past information on a particular economic variable (for example, exchange rates), explore its statistical properties and forecast the future time path from this information. The problem with this approach is that it fails to use all the available information, since no attempt is made to link the behaviour of one economic variable with other variables. For example, we know from earlier in this chapter that the link between a nation's interest rates and its exchange rate is critical.

The solution adopted by most forecasters, including the forecasts that can be found in the websites listed above, is to build a macroeconometric model capable of use for forecasting purposes. A macroeconometric model consists of a set of equations that identify the links between macroeconomic variables. It will use all the macroeconomic links discussed before in this chapter and many others as well. One of the basic relationships in a macroeconometric model is that between aggregate demand and GDP. It assumes GDP growth is driven by growth in aggregate demand. It will be accompanied by a set of relationships that set down the variables that cause aggregate demand to change. The interest rate, for example, will feature as a determinant of both consumer demand and investment demand. Share prices and wealth will figure as drivers of consumer demand. Past experience is used to measure the impact of variables on each other. The objective of the model builder is to construct a set of relationships capable of explaining past history.

How do forecasts derived from macroeconometric models of this type perform? The answer is 'not very well'. In an article in the *Financial Times* in 1995, Professor John Kay reviewed the performance of 34 UK forecasts of GDP growth in the years after 1987. He found that the forecasts tended to cluster around an average value, but the average seldom forecasted accurately. He found all the forecasts in 1993 and 1994 were significantly below the actual growth rate, while the opposite was true in 1991 and 1992. A more recent OECD study of forecasts of both GDP growth and inflation for seven countries after 1974 found the same. Detailed results of this exercise can be found in McAleese (2004, Chapter 16).

Why are the published forecasts so notoriously inaccurate? The most important reason is that the models are constructed using past experience. They have to make a number of strong assumptions:

◆ *Links observed in the past continue in the future.* For example, assuming that interest rates will continue to influence investment, as they have done in the past, may not be correct. Cuts in interest rates may not stimulate investment if there is a crisis of business confidence.

◆ *The strength of the relationships embodied in the links in the model stays the same.* This may not be true. Increases in wages tend to follow increases in prices, but the size of the effect is a lot less now than in the 1970s and 1980s, so twenty-first-century inflation of prices will tend to be overestimated in a macroeconometric model which uses 1970s and 1980s data for its estimate of the strength of the link.

◆ *There are no events for which there is no historical experience.* This is clearly not true. When the price of oil quadrupled in the 1990s, forecasts of both inflation and GDP growth across the world were in error, because none incorporated a historical experience of a change of this magnitude.

◆ *Historical data exists and is a good representation of what has happened in the past.* This is especially problematic in emerging markets, where historical data is scarce and where the collection of statistics is at a rudimentary stage. Macroeconometric forecasts are unlikely to be accurate.

What can be done when uncertainty about the macroeconomic future cannot be eliminated by the use of a forecasting model? One solution is simply to accept that the risk is endemic and has to be managed as far as possible by shifting the risk to another party (at a price).

This is what is done when businesses are exposed to exchange rate risk. This may happen because they have a contract to buy a product (for example, raw materials) from an overseas supplier that wants to be paid at some time in the future in an overseas currency. Given the volatility of exchange rates and the notorious difficulty of forecasting movements in the rate, the business cannot predict what the cost of the purchase in the home currency will be at the date of payment. The simplest solution is to 'buy forward' – to enter into a contract with a bank to supply overseas currency at an agreed rate on the date of the payment to the overseas supplier. There will be a cost associated with this forward contract, but it eliminates risk and obviates the need to forecast the exchange rate between the home and the overseas currency. The problem is that forward markets of the kind we see for exchange rate dealings do not exist in many other areas where macroeconomic risk is critical to strategy.

Another solution is to adopt a signalling approach, that is, to use signals that past experience has said are good predictors of the future. This is a good solution to the problem for OECD-based businesses (for example, retailers such as Wal-Mart and Carrefour) seeking to pursue a global strategy. How do they select suitable emerging markets in which to build a presence? There are no reliable long-run forecasts of future macroeconomic performance to guide their decision. What could they do? One solution is to search in the national economies they wish to target for some of the favourable signals set out earlier in this chapter.

The failure of macroeconometric forecasting models to provide a *single* accurate view of the future does not mean these models have no role in strategy. Planning models using this deterministic approach to the future are not the only option for strategic 'actions' that need to be informed by some kind of forward-looking assessment. Another solution is to assess the historical impact of exogenous macroeconomic changes on the individual firm *and* its market(s). This assessment needs to be built upon the same econometric foundations, using the same statistical methodology, as embodied in the macro model.

This extended macroeconometric model enables the creation of a variety of 'what if' scenarios of market prices, volumes and so on. These scenarios set out the impact of a wide variety of uncontrollable shocks from the macroeconomic environment on the business. These shocks need to be managed so this methodology helps to establish some of the limits of strategic action. These scenarios could explore, for example, the impact of different home exchange rates or different rates of growth of world trade over a five-year period. This is no longer difficult. Ten years ago, economists needed up to six weeks to run a full five-year scenario on a mainframe computer. Now relatively inexperienced users can do this in seconds on a PC. It is a simple matter, once the model is built, to use it to think. (This is what you are asked to do in the tasks that accompany this chapter.)

4.6 Summary

A useful proposition with which to end this chapter is:

> *Businesses that do not understand their economic environment make strategic errors, sometimes catastrophic ones, especially if they do not know that booms and slumps are bound to end!*

This chapter is not intended to turn you into an economist. On the other hand, it is critical for managers to be sensible, practical economists because macroeconomics plays such a significant role and has such a direct impact on firms. The argument in Chapters 3 and 4 directs attention to the uncontrollable nature of economic forces and the contextual constraints that it imposes on managerial discretion. This chapter has detailed some of the major forces in the macroeconomy so that managers can, through analysis, understanding and preparation, be able at least to anticipate the pressures on the firm. There are two main themes here. The first considers the nature of the business cycle and the demand and supply characteristics of boom and bust. A well-informed and prepared firm might be able to take strategic decisions contra-cyclically so as to avoid herd behaviour in merely following the economy. The second theme is the nature of national competitiveness and the relation of firms to this. Much of the infrastructure of the economy falls within the range of government spending. Thus, the fortunes of firms in any economy are going to be dependent in part on the ability of governments to foster national competitiveness. But firms also need to respond to these pressures themselves in forming their own strategies so as to mitigate the undesirable effects of economic misfortunes.

All businesses are sensitive to macroeconomic shocks outside their control and have to find ways in which to manage them. Strategic 'actions' need an understanding of the contextual links between an individual company, its markets and GDP growth in both the home and export markets. Exchange rates play a particularly important role for the company that trades outside its own home market but also for those who face competition from imports and whose business is sensitive to GDP fluctuations in its own home economy. It also requires an understanding of how economies in general work and also of the particular economies in which the business's markets are located.

At this point you should read the case box below. This summarizes the dramatic changes that are taking place in Deutsche Post (the German Post Office). This reflects the huge amount of privatization and deregulation that has been taking place across Europe over the last 20 years or so. Privatization has often been associated with diversification (please consult Chapter 9 on corporate strategy for this), with acquisitions (*see* Chapter 10) and with internationalization (*see* Chapter 11). Insights into Deutsche Post can be gained from each of these perspectives but in the context of this chapter the issue of 'fair' competition is raised. Is the growth of Deutsche Post subsidized by a protected home market? From this case, identify the concerns that the EU might have and that its main competitors might have. What would be persuasive grounds on which Deutsche Post might defend itself, or on which its competitors might have a good case? Try also to identify the economic logic on which such a broad expansion of services might be sustained.

Case box: Logistical challenge

Not long ago, Deutsche Post was merely Germany's national post office. Now it wants to be the world's top logistics company

Twice bitten, thrice shy? Not, seemingly, Germany's growing army of shareholders. In the past few weeks, Germans have been inundated with advertisements for 'yellow shares' in the national post office, Deutsche Post. Those who still have shares from offerings by Deutsche Telekom and its internet subsidiary, T-Online, sold amid much hype in the spring, are nursing losses. Yet Germans (as well as a fair number of foreigners) are eager for more. They have been rushing to subscribe to the 25–29 per cent of Deutsche Post that is due to be floated on 20 November 2000, raising somewhere between €5.8 billion ($5 billion) and €7.4 billion.

Whether Deutsche Post will prove a good investment will depend largely on the success of a transformation brought about by its chairman Klaus Zumwinkel. Mr Zumwinkel, who likes to spend his spare time climbing mountains, spent 16 years at McKinsey, a consultancy, before taking over the post office in 1990. He has not only turned a sleepy, loss-making utility into a proper business; he has also tried to turn Deutsche Post from a national post office into an international logistics giant, delivering not just letters, but anything from anywhere to anywhere else, at any time.

Over the past two years, the growth of Deutsche Post and the expansion of its activities have been remarkable. In 1998, mail accounted for almost three-quarters of its turnover, with express parcels making up the rest. In the first half of this year, mail, though still the biggest of the company's four divisions, accounted for only 35 per cent of sales. Parcels' share was about one-sixth. The rest (i.e. almost half) was split evenly between new divisions for logistics and financial services. Equally striking, the share of sales coming from foreign operations leapt from a mere 2 per cent in 1998 to 28 per cent in the first half of this year. By next year, says Mr Zumwinkel, it will be 40 per cent, thanks to the acquisition earlier this year of a majority stake in DHL, a courier.

To bring about this transformation, Mr Zumwinkel has been buying companies left, right and centre. Since the start of 1999 Deutsche Post has bought, besides DHL, a clutch of other logistics firms: Danzas, a Swiss company; the European operations of Nedlloyd, a Dutch firm; America's Air Express International; and Sweden's ASG. The growth of the financial-services operation began when Deutsche Post took Germany's state-owned Postbank (which already operated in post offices) under its wing. To this deposit-taker has now been added a lender, with the acquisition of DSL, another state-owned bank, which mainly provides finance for new buildings.

There remain three main obstacles for Deutsche Post to overcome if it is to succeed. The first is the long-delayed opening of Europe's national postal monopolies to competition. From 2003 the European Union plans to limit national post offices' monopoly to items weighing less than 50 grams, and to open direct mail and outbound international mail up to full competition.

Some incumbent post offices, especially those in Britain and France, are resisting fiercely. But the Germans are more enthusiastic: in two years' time the monopoly in Germany, already down to 200 grams, is due to drop to 100, well below the limit in other European countries. Analysts reckon that, after TNT Post Groep, a privatized Dutch firm, Deutsche Post is Europe's second-most efficient post office. So it should have less to fear than most from competition. Indeed, it should be well-placed to pinch business from other mail and logistics firms if it gets the chance. And in any case, Mr Zumwinkel points out, a cut in the monopoly from 200 to 100 grams will expose only around 7 per cent of mail sales to competition. 'Maybe we'll lose 1–2 per cent of profits,' he says. 'But on the other hand, we can win market share in other countries.'

The second big challenge is tougher: integrating its huge clutch of recently acquired businesses. Until this is done, the reorientation of Deutsche Post will be incomplete. Although the mail business accounts for only around a third of sales, it still brings in more than 75 per cent of profits. The company's aim is to cut this to 50 per cent by 2004. If this goal is to be met, new acquisitions will have to be woven quickly and successfully into its existing structure.

The third challenge, wrapped as it is in a thick legal mist, is harder to judge, but potentially the most hazardous. Critics of Deutsche Post say that it has, in effect, received illegal state aid in the form of high, government-controlled charges for its domestic mail monopoly, and that it has used these monopoly profits to subsidize its expansion into other markets. The company also stands accused of predatory pricing in its parcels business, which began to turn a profit only last year, after more than a decade of subsidized losses. The European Commission is investigating these and other allegations. The German government and Deutsche Post strenuously deny them.

Should Deutsche Post be required to 'repay' state aid, Mr Zumwinkel insists, the effect on its profits would still be slight. Maybe so. The biggest repayment of state aid ever demanded was €227 million, from Air France in 1995, and in that case the subsidy was explicit. Even something on that scale would scarcely dent Deutsche Post. Nonetheless, an adverse EU ruling would be damaging beyond its one-off blow to the bottom line, because it would show Mr Zumwinkel to be less sure-footed than he has looked so far. With no doubt second and third tranches of yellow shares still to be sold, it could even make investors less eager next time around. For now, though, they seem happy to trudge behind Deutsche Post's determined boss.

Source: 'Logistical Challenge', *The Economist*, 18 November 2000, p. 78.
© The Economist Newspaper Limited, London (18 November 2000).

Key terms

Adverse selection *126*

Agglomeration economies *131*

Aggregate demand *107*

Balanced growth *118*

Circular flow of income *109*

Competitive advantage *119*

Endogenous *110*

Exogenous *110*

Factor conditions *123*

Horizontal integration *130*

Leakage *110*

National competitive advantage *119*

National competitiveness *119*

Recap questions and assignments

1 Within an economy, what are the main effects of the following on its GDP growth, the rate of price inflation and unemployment?

  (a) A fall in the home rate of interest.

  (b) A decrease in the rate of income tax or social security contribution rates.

  (c) An increase in the rate of indirect tax (e.g. VAT).

  (d) A rise in government spending on (i) health and (ii) defence.

2 Access the Virtual Economy Model software available on the website www.bized.ac.uk. Click on 'Virtual Worlds' and then on 'Virtual Economy'. Go to the 4th floor and click on the selected variable model variant. Change the rate of VAT to 20% and record the effects you observe. Reset the model and then explore the effects of a 10% increase in health expenditure and defence spending. Are there any differences and, if so, why ? Finally, explore the impact of a fall of 1% in the home interest rates using the model in its full variant.

3 What are the impacts on the exchange rate of the various changes you have made in the Virtual Economy model? Explain the results you obtain.

Online LearningCentre

When you have read this chapter, log on to the Online Learning Centre website at www.mcgraw-hill.co.uk/textbooks/mcgee to explore chapter-by-chapter test questions, further reading and more online study tools for strategy.

Case 1 **Made in Japan?**

How are Japan's manufacturers faring against low-cost competition from China?

Japan's manufacturing has been steadily moving overseas, most obviously to China. Among the reasons: wages in Japan are much higher, by a factor of between 20 and 30 times. Look more closely, however, and China is far from being the only threat facing Japan's manufacturers. Individual Japanese companies talk as much about competitors in America and Europe as they do about China. Some are most concerned about the technological prowess of South Korean firms such as Samsung and Hyundai.

Many Japanese companies are raising their game, using a range of strategies to fend off low-cost competition from overseas. Some of them are fortunate because they start from positions of relative strength. Leading firms such as Toyota and Canon have developed integrated manufacturing systems that are far more sophisticated and complex than rivals can manage. In other sectors, companies have learned how best to protect trade secrets that have long made them competitive, often bringing back home activities that might otherwise risk exposure to rivals. And most big firms believe that they can keep an edge in future by continuing to invest in new generations of products.

Japan's weak spot is in low-cost, mass production, which has been steadily leaving for lower-wage countries (just as it has also been seeping out of Western Europe and America). There are only rare examples of Japanese companies trying to compete from a domestic base in the low-cost arena. One is Suzuki Motor. Its latest hit is a stripped-down budget scooter that costs one-third as much as regular scooters. Designed for urban short-distance drivers, it has eliminated some parts, such as rear suspension, once thought essential. Clever though this is, low-cost manufacturing in Japan is likely to be limited to niche products; Suzuki admits its efforts could be 'a useless struggle' against an inevitable tide.

Although they interfere less than they once did, Japan's bureaucrats are concerned by the prospect of manufacturing, especially high-tech manufacturing, going abroad. Surely, the thinking goes, if one Japanese company builds a plant in China, and the technology is copied, then all of the firm's Japanese rivals will face cheap competition? Hidetaka Fukuda, who oversees information technology for the Ministry of Economy, Trade and Industry, says that METI stepped in earlier this year to persuade NEC, an electronics giant, to sell its plasma-display business to local rival Pioneer, rather than a foreign investor, as a way to keep its technology in Japan. Mr Fukuda says that he is currently in similar negotiations with roughly ten other companies that might otherwise transfer technology abroad.

Sometimes cheap labour is not the prime motive for moving abroad. For instance, carmakers and construction-machinery makers say they have set up overseas simply in order to follow customer demand. Honda, Japan's second-largest carmaker after Toyota, says that, by building plants close to its markets, it can reduce production times, distribution costs and currency losses. Research facilities are set up overseas in order to tailor cars to meet regional needs, such as sports-utility vehicles in America with extra towing capacity, rarely required in Japan. Manufacturing techniques, such as welding methods, continue to be refined at home.

Indeed, many manufacturers are responding to competition by keeping core technologies secret and at home, while moving low-value-added production and assembly operations abroad. For instance, Toshiba, Japan's biggest chipmaker, is racing to develop high-end chips, and says it is determined not to repeat past mistakes. Initially it co-operated with South Korean chipmakers in basic DRAM memory chips, which have since become commodities, only to find its rivals overtaking it far more swiftly than it had expected.

Others have discovered additional virtues in making things at home. Two years ago Kenwood's new boss, Haruo Kawahara, shifted production of mini-disc players from Malaysia back to Yamagata, Japan. This 'in-sourcing' has raised profits in several ways, which highlight three long-standing advantages of the Japanese approach to manufacturing: specially trained workers, low defect rates and 'lean' processes that hold down inventory costs and boost production flexibility.

Unlike Kenwood's Malaysian workers, who come and go frequently, workers in its Yamagata factory stick around long enough to master several different tasks. A typical Yamagata worker can quickly do four or five steps in the assembly process before handing over to another worker, whereas employees in the Malaysian plant did one step each. These days it takes four employees to put together a mini-disc player in Yamagata, compared with 22 Malaysian workers before the move. The Japanese plant takes up 70 per cent less space, while the defect rate has fallen by 80 per cent.

Mouldy business

An under-appreciated, but critical, sector of Japanese manufacturing is the country's mould-makers. Tiny, secretive firms generally consisting of less than a handful of workers, these craftsmen usually work in what look like dim, grimy, oversize garages, filled with worn machines and piles of scrap metal. Industrial moulds are used to create the shape and form of almost anything that can be picked up, from ballpoint pens and toys to mobile-phone and satellite parts. The work is highly specialized. Many mould-makers, now in their 50s and 60s, started learning their trade when they were children.

The best firms, clustered around Ota, Shinagawa and Sumida wards in south and east Tokyo, make moulds, often prototypes, for the top international names in cars and consumer-electronics – and even for NASA, America's space agency. 'Mould-making technology lies at the base of all manufacturing. If this were to start disappearing, it would be a danger sign for Japanese manufacturing,' warns Mr Kinoshita.

Opinion is split as to whether warning lights are now flashing. Since 1990, almost 40 per cent of mould-makers in Sumida have gone out of business (and only one new one was set up), while more than a third of the remainder had no work at the start of the year, says Yukio Ouchi, an economic commentator who has studied more than 4,000 mould-makers. This reflects a broader trend. One street in Ota, once filled with top-notch mould-makers and other small manufacturers, initially dubbed 'bankruptcy street' was subsequently renamed 'suicide street', reflecting growing pressure from loan sharks.

Kazuo Hori, president of Koyo Seiko, a mould-maker mainly for ballpoint pens, says he has lost almost half his business, mostly to China, over the past year or so. Though some big manufacturers are coming back because quality is higher at home, many mould-makers have gone bust during their absence. More disturbing is a recent trend in which unscrupulous Japanese manufacturers steal mould designs to send to cheaper Chinese makers.

Still, there are bright spots. Business is booming for mould-makers that specialize in car parts and mobile phones. Despite the overall decline, many of the best firms have managed to hang on, says Mr Ouchi. Diversification helps. Tohru Izumi, boss of Izumi Kanagata, counts every Japanese carmaker and, since the late 1990s, an increasing number of foreign carmakers, such as BMW and Jaguar, as recipients of car-audio panels made from his moulds.

Which bits of Japanese manufacturing will survive and flourish will depend on managers' ability to identify, hold on to, and improve, Japan's inherent strengths. In an influential recent article, 'A Twenty-first-century strategy for Japanese manufacturing' (published in Japanese in *Bungei Shunju* in November 2003, translated in *Japan Echo* in February 2004). Takahiro Fujimoto, a professor at Tokyo University, said it is too simple to suggest that Japan should focus on high-value-added production. What Japanese manufacturers really excel at, he argued, are 'products whose functions require many components to be designed in careful detail and mutually adjusted for optimal performance'. This requires close teamwork within a company, as well as co-operation with suppliers.

The Japanese way

This ability to meld different skills and technologies is a common feature among top Japanese manufacturers in several sectors. For instance, successful photocopier companies, such as Canon and Ricoh, combine precision mechanics, advanced chemical processes for toner inks, and servicing skills. Cars, too, are all about mixing different technologies. 'There is no "core" technology in cars,' says Mitsuo Kinoshita, chief production control and logistics officer at Toyota, Japan's top carmaker, which last year overtook America's Ford to become the second-largest seller of cars. For example, he explains, it is not enough to perfect a hybrid system (which combines an engine that runs on petrol with an electric motor) in the laboratory: an equal amount of expertise is needed to make sure it works when actually placed in a car.

It is hard, says Masahiro Sakane, president of Komatsu, Japan's biggest construction-machinery maker, to come up with fresh business models that exploit mixed technologies.

Yet doing this well produces rewards. Komatsu added information technology, such as global-positioning systems (GPS), to hydraulic excavators three years ago to combat theft, and help machinery-rental firms track how much fuel individual excavators had left in their tanks. Yet this has also unexpectedly helped raise sales of Komatsu's excavators in China, where the beginnings of a credit crunch are emerging – banks consider excavators with GPS easier to seize as collateral against soured loans.

One company in an excellent position to see how Japanese manufacturers are faring is Omron, which makes a range of sophisticated sensors and scanning devices that get used on other manufacturers' assembly lines. Omron sells these devices not only to Japan's domestic manufacturers, but also to firms building overseas plants in China (among other countries). Factories in China are upgrading their methods, and are buying more Omron devices to help. Factories in Japan, however, are hardly standing still.

One Omron product that is popular in both China and Japan is a scanner that inspects the substrate of printed-circuit boards for minute imperfections. In China, placing one of these scanners at the end of the line is good enough: defective products can be discarded before the rest are shipped to customers. In super-efficient Japan, however, detecting flawed products so late is seen as shamefully wasteful. So Omron has made a new system for Japanese clients that networks several substrate scanners together. Complex software gives a warning when aberrations start to appear – and then immediately pinpoints which machine needs tweaking.

Canon firing

Canon, which has a high-tech product line ranging from precision photocopiers, to optical components for digital cameras, to expensive equipment for making semiconductors and flat-panel television screens, is a good example of how Japanese firms are regrouping in the face of competition from abroad. Fujio Mitarai, its boss, said earlier this year that over the next three years, 80 per cent of Canon's global capital spending will be in Japan. Among other investments, it is building a high-end digital camera factory in Oita prefecture and a new research centre near Tokyo.

Canon is hardly naive about the benefits of outsourcing: 42 per cent of its worldwide production is overseas. To maintain its technological edge and high profit margins, however, it must balance low-cost manufacturing abroad with the high-tech precision it achieves in Japan. Mr Mitarai told *The Economist* recently that he has a rough cut-off rule for allocating investment: anything for which labour comprises more than 5 per cent of production costs can be done in China or some other low-wage country. Because Canon continues to invest in R&D, Mr Mitarai reckons there should be plenty left to do profitably in Japan. For instance, labour accounts for only 2 per cent of the cost of its lithographic steppers, which are used in making semiconductors and fetch around $22 million each.

Few of Japan's manufacturing bosses, however, are as relaxed as Mr Mitarai is about China. In Japan's vast electronics sector, for example, digitization has forced business leaders to think long and hard about China's changing role. The rapid spread of new digital devices – such as DVD players, mobile phones and digital cameras – has allowed China to do something much simpler than moving from easy technologies to harder ones. Instead, it has actually leap-frogged the harder stuff (i.e. analogue devices) to get to newer and easier digital products.

Manufacturers in China would have a dreadful time producing good conventional film cameras, for example, because of the complex optical, chemical and mechanical processes that must be mastered. But Chinese factories have little trouble assembling digital cameras: all they need to do is to obtain advanced components from Japan that are pre-designed to work in harmony when snapped together.

This combination of digital diffusion and Chinese expansion is driving two profound changes among Japan's electronics firms. First, it has widened an important split between makers of many final consumer products (such as Sony, Sharp and Matsushita's Panasonic brand) and the scores of focused Japanese firms that feed materials, components and equipment into the process. The second, related, change is a rapid erosion of the barriers that have long allowed Japanese manufacturers to protect their trade secrets.

Because China and other low-wage countries need their inputs to make digital products, Japan's focused suppliers and equipment-makers have been doing especially well. They boast large global market shares in specialized niches: ceramics and other fine materials for semiconductors, tiny motors for hard drives and other digital equipment, a range of sophisticated machines for making liquid-crystal display panels, and so forth.

The big consumer electronics companies, by contrast, make a wide range of both components and final products. China's growing production base and the spread of digital products thus presents the big firms with a confusing mix of threats and opportunities. They have lately been enjoying brisk global demand for mobile phones, digital cameras and DVD recorders, along with a rising appetite for flat-panel TVs and other higher-end home electronics. Yet they face tough competition and must rely on cost cutting and a steady stream of new models to maintain profit margins that are already low. They must keep shifting production to China, therefore, to keep up with one another.

Looking Sharp

The rapid movement of manufacturing to South Korea, Taiwan and China is, in turn, forcing Japanese firms to think much harder about which technologies to protect and which activities to leave in Japan. Since much of their edge depends on closely held trade secrets, this is becoming ever more difficult.

Earlier this year, Sharp opened a new 'sixth-generation' plant to make flat panels for televisions in Kameyama, Mie prefecture, which cranks out panels much bigger than those made in fifth-generation plants. Sharp (and rival Samsung) is pushing the frontiers of this technology. Designing a new plant requires the sorting out of dozens of complex steps, each with its own specialized equipment, all of which must work seamlessly to churn out delicate panels with almost no defects. Sharp's reward is good profits at the relatively uncontested high end when it introduces bigger flat-panel TVs from newer and more efficient plants.

Nearly all of the important suppliers to Sharp are Japanese. That has been great news for Mie prefecture, which has been reinvigorated by a cluster of over 50 firms that have built facilities there to be closer to Sharp's Kameyama plant. Unfortunately for Sharp, however, its suppliers also work closely with its rivals, many of them Taiwanese. By the time the paint had dried in Kameyama, imitators in Taiwan were already cobbling together their own sixth-generation plants.

Sharp goes to great lengths to slow its rivals down. When a machine breaks down, engineers now try to fix it in-house rather than telling the supplier – just to keep equipment-makers in the dark about any problems that might occur on the machines they have sold to Sharp's competitors. For the same reason, the company quietly rewrites the software on some equipment once it is installed.

The cumulative effect of many such small steps is to defend Sharp's global market position from erosion, at least for now. Other Japanese manufacturers have absorbed this and other lessons. Having invented lean manufacturing, they are not about to let low-cost rivals have it all their own way.

Source: 'Manufacturing in Japan', *The Economist*, 10 April 2004, pp. 65–7.
© The Economist Newspaper Limited, London (10 April 2004).

Case Questions

1   What actions could and should the Japanese government take to cope with the threat of low-cost competition?

2   Based on this case study, what do you think is Japan's comparative advantage? What implications does this have for Japanese firms and their competitive advantages?

3   Is it possible for firms to locate in several different countries so as to gain from local comparative advantage without suffering from the disadvantages? In other words, can they have their cake and eat it? What can national governments do about this?

Further reading and references

McAleese, D (2004) *Economics for Business*, 3rd edition, Prentice Hall. Once again we recommend this excellent introductory text on economics, Parts 2 and 3 of which provide a much more complete analysis of the macroeconomic environment than could be provided in this chapter.

Porter, ME (1990) *Competitive Advantage of Nations*, Macmillan, London.

World Bank (1993) *East Asian Miracle*, Oxford University Press, New York.

Useful websites

www.bized.ac.uk

Provides excellent supporting material including a glossary of economic terms and the 'Virtual Economy', which is a computer-based model of a real-life macroeconomy. You can carry out a variety of experiments to build your understanding of the concepts developed in this chapter.

The macroeconomic environment changes rapidly so it is important to keep up to date with events. There are many websites which provide up to date information on the macroeconomic context of strategy and which employ many of the concepts developed in this lesson. Examples of the best are:

www.imf.org
www.oecd.org
www.worldbank.org
www.niesr.ac.uk

Chapter 5

Industry analysis and competitive strategy

Introduction

In this chapter we introduce the basic ideas of competitive strategy and indicate some of the issues involved in turning them into practicable propositions. The basic concepts are industry analysis (often referred to as the Porter five forces analysis), the generic competitive strategies, the value chain, and the main sources of competitive advantage. The foundations for these ideas were explained in Chapter 3. Moving from these foundations for strategy analysis the rest of the chapter introduces a more practical flavour. If we understand the idea of competitive advantage as a key attribute that is specific to the firm then we have the beginnings of a description of strategy. We describe a template for describing and identifying a strategy – how would you recognize a strategy if you saw one?

Whereas competitive advantage is an external positioning concept, strategy also needs to say something about the internal disposition of resources and assets as well. The internal logic of strategy is shown in the strategy cycle and cost analysis is reflected in the value chain. The latter is extremely well known being another product of Porter analysis (1985). The strategy cycle illustrates the significance of the balance between internal resources, external market positioning and financial performance. The value chain builds directly on the cost analysis of Chapter 3 and enables us to identify a picture of the internal asset structure and activity structure of the firm. The chapter concludes with a template for a practical overview of strategy – a self-testing of your firm's strategy IQ. This can be turned into a simple question-naire for assessing the strategy of your own firm or of any firms of which you have some knowledge. By the end of this chapter we will see the significance of **competitive advantage** for the study of strategy and for strategy making in firms.

5.1 Analysis of industries and competition

In Chapter 3 perfect competition is presented as the benchmark by which economists and others such as government departments and regulators judge the efficiency of markets. In general, markets are seen as efficient if they are perfect in their principal characteristics, demonstrating price competition, ease of entry and exit, and wide distribution of relevant knowledge. Conversely, individual firms see it as in their own interest to have specific knowl-edge that enables them to build unique assets and offer distinctive products for which they can charge a price premium. In other words, firms have an interest in constructing imper-fections that favour them in the marketplace. Firms may also have a joint interest in colluding together to create collective imperfections by which they can artificially limit com-petition and charge higher prices than otherwise. This is not the subject of this book but there is a very considerable literature on these monopolistic practices and the ways in which governments pursue pro-competitive policies in order to make industries more efficient and markets more competitive. Firms actually compete on two levels. One level is in the market-place where customers compare rival offerings and make choices and, in doing so, prices emerge from these market processes. Firms also compete through their plans and invest-ments for the future and, in doing so, they construct assets that they hope will be sufficiently distinctive for them to offer distinctive products. Thus, the R&D activities of pharmaceutical firms is intended to create new and unique products that can be protected by patents and which can then be sold as unique high-priced products in the market. Industry analysis is the analysis of assets, resources and capabilities that set out the basic economic conditions under which firms collectively operate (the 'industry context') and which condition their individual abilities to create distinctive individual positions in their industries.

For example, Ford and Toyota operate in the automobile industry. They share some common operating characteristics such as significant economies of scale in assembly operations, a largely common knowledge basis and technology characteristics, and a set of competing products that compete more on price than on product differences. To some extent they share common economic characteristics. However, they each conduct R&D and other development activities in order to gain points of difference versus each other. Toyota might claim a distinctive way of organizing its manufacturing activities with beneficial effects on quality and reliability. Ford might claim a better organization of distribution and servicing activities with beneficial consequences for the way in which consumers experience the service process. This mixture of common economic characteristics coupled with attempts at individual differentiation comprises the content of industry analysis. As we have seen in the section on cost analysis (Chapter 3), the nature of economies of scale in an industry (such as automobile assembly) affects the number of potential competitors in an industry (the greater the minimum efficient scale, the fewer competitors that can survive). Thus, the economic characteristics of the industry shape the nature of competition in the market by affecting the number of players (in this example). More generally, the economic characteristics of an industry are shaped by the investment and planning decisions of firms, and the extent to which firms can sustain uniqueness affects the way in which competition then plays out in the marketplace.

5.1.1 Porter's five forces

Industry analysis is best known as Porter's **five forces** (introduced initially in Chapter 1). This was first popularized by Michael Porter in his path-breaking *Competitive Strategy*, first published in 1980. Figure 5.1 shows the celebrated diagram of the five forces of competition, namely: rivalry, threat of entry, supplier power, buyer power and threat of substitutes. These are the five fundamental forces that determine the 'attractiveness' of the industry, a term which is a surrogate for industry profitability. Thus the weaker/stronger are these forces then the more/less attractive will be the industry taken as a whole and the larger/smaller will be its overall profitability. On the whole, the more attractive the industry, the more likely it is that participants will enjoy 'good' profits.

The supply chain

The heart of the five forces diagram is the horizontal line. Porter draws this as a force diagram with all the arrows pointing towards the central box, which represents the industry in question measured in terms of the competitors present. Alternatively this can be shown as a **supply chain** representing the build-up and flow of goods to the final customer. Thus, for the food industry, goods flow from the farm, to food ingredients companies (such as flour milling), to food manufacturers (such as cake and bread manufacturers), to wholesalers, to supermarkets, and then to final consumers. At each stage of the supply chain there is an industry that invests in assets, that accumulates **fixed** and variable **costs** and then prices its goods to the next stage of the chain. The difference between its revenues and its material

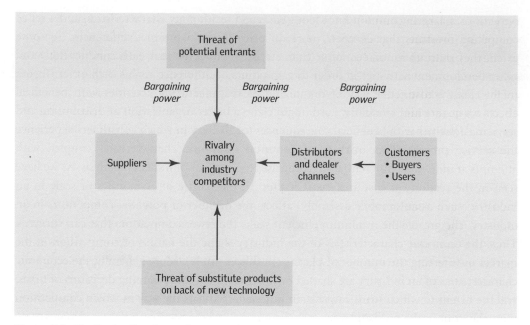

Figure 5.1 The Porter five forces framework
Source: Porter (1980), *Competitive Strategy*. Reprinted with permission of The Free Press, a division of Simon and Schuster Adult Publishing Group, from *Competitive Strategy* by Michael E. Porter. Copyright © 1980, 1998 by The Free Press. All rights reserved.

costs is its added value, i.e. the value it adds to its material input costs.[1] This added value can be partitioned into three parts: labour costs, capital costs and profits. The more attractive the industry, the greater is likely to be the value added, including also the profits, and vice versa. Where perfect competition is the norm, prices will tend to converge downwards and profits will fall to a level that is the minimum rate of return on capital that will enable the capital to be retained in the industry. If profits fall below this there will be pressure to withdraw capital and place it in more profitable employment. If profits are higher then there will be an incentive for more capital to enter the industry. This is the basic mechanism behind the **threat of entry** in Figure 5.1.

The threat of entry

At each stage of the supply chain there is an industry that can be analysed in terms of the five forces. Firms considering investment in an attractive industry will make an entry calculation. This takes the form of a conventional capital investment decision with three components. The revenue stream depends on prices that can be charged (taking account of the price elasticity of demand) and the volumes attainable. The costs depend on the unit costs of production and access to available economies of scale, scope and learning, and on

[1]   Economists use the difference between revenue and materials costs as the definition of value added (being the value added to materials by the actions of the firm). However, many business analysts use 'value added' in a much more intuitive sense to mean profitability.

the level of marketing and other costs of getting the product to markets. Finally, the capital cost of the investment needs to be reckoned. If any of the cost elements (expressed in cost per unit of output) are higher than those of the incumbents and if the prices relative to incumbents are lower, then the potential entrant faces 'entry barriers', i.e. its profit margins are lower than those of the incumbents and it faces a cost disadvantage or barrier. If the cost disadvantages are high in relation to the profit margins then they serve as an effective barrier to entry. If for other reasons, such as access to technology or to distribution systems, the entrant is effectively barred from entry then we say that entry is *blockaded*.

The power of suppliers and buyers

Suppliers have a natural interest in raising their prices at your expense. To the extent that they succeed, they enhance their margins at your expense. Under what conditions might this happen? Where there are relatively few suppliers you may not have many alternatives to an aggressive supplier. Where the supplier is providing a product that is very important to the eventual performance of your own product, they might be able to charge a 'premium' price. Where you are accustomed to using a particular product there may be costs of *switching* from this product to an alternative. This provides a price umbrella for the supplier in his negotiations with you. If there are no substitution possibilities then price can go up. For example, if as an electricity generator your power stations are configured around coal supplies and conversion to other supplies such as gas or oil are only longer-term possibilities, then coal suppliers have bargaining power. OPEC, in pricing oil, has to be aware that an overaggressive pricing policy provides incentives for its customers to convert to other fuels and/or to invest in energy saving.

The analysis of buyer power is identical. The greater the relative concentration of buyers, the less important is your product to the buyer; the more your product can be substituted by others, the less is your bargaining power and the greater is their bargaining power. In the UK the celebrated example of this is the power of supermarket chains over food manufacturers. The larger and more powerful the chain, the more it can force down its input prices. However, the principal defence of the manufacturer vis-à-vis the supermarket is its ability to differentiate its products. Thus, the more distinctive is Nestlé's Nescafé brand, the less will Tesco be able to force its price down. Nestlé's calculation could be that customers will come into the store having already decided to buy the Nescafé brand regardless of any price differentials between Nescafé and other brands including the supermarket's own brand. However, if Tesco could legitimately conclude that customers respond principally to Tesco's own branding and will therefore buy whatever Tesco put on the shelves (especially its own brand) then Tesco's buying power is strong and it will be more able to treat Nestlé and its other suppliers as providers of commodity products. The threat of vertical integration can be very effective in disciplining suppliers. Some retailers, such as Marks & Spencer, have an own-brand policy that is a form of quasi-vertical integration that leaves strategic power effectively with the retailer. Conversely, the distinctiveness of luxury-brand purveyors such as Louis Vuitton and Gucci has enabled many of these players to invest in their own captive distribution and retailing systems so that they can extract every drop of the product differentiation premium for themselves (see the Louis Vuitton case study).

The balance between supplier power and buyer power is a key issue in business. Very often the biggest threat to your margins comes not simply from your competitors but from the adjacent (and sometimes even the more remote) parts of the supply chain. The biggest threat to food manufacturers probably comes from retailers. In the personal computer business the power in the supply chain lies upstream with the suppliers of components, that is, with Microsoft's operating systems and other software, and with Intel and its microprocessors. Estimates in Harvard Business School's case studies on Apple in the 1980s suggested that more than half of all the profits made in the personal computer industry supply chain were earned by Microsoft and Intel (Yoffie 1992). Thus, the location of power along the supply chain is a key issue in understanding how profits can be earned. The case box on Dell in Chapter 7 shows how a strategic innovation downstream, close to the customer, has been able to create a defensible and profitable position in spite of the power of Microsoft and Intel.

The threat of substitutes

The pressure from substitutes tends to be longer-term pressure. If you conceive of the product from your industry as having a certain benefit–cost ratio to the immediate customer then pressure from substitutes can be calibrated in terms of alternative benefit–cost ratios. A simple but powerful example concerns the substitution of fibre optic cable for coaxial cable in telecommunications in the 1980s. Fibre optic cable offered so many more benefits at relatively low marginal cost that the costs of investing in entirely new cabling systems could very quickly be earned back. Most technological changes can be assessed in the same way, trading off the added benefits, the added costs and the required investments. Complications arise when the products involved are components within larger systems. The increased use of modularity of electronic components and the standardization of electronic interfaces has increased the incentives for substitution. Another problem arises when the scale and scope of substitution is so large as to effectively disrupt the existing supply chains. The advent of photocopying, the laser printer, and the personal computer demonstrate that there can be system-level substitutions that cause industries and supply chains to transform.

Note the similarity and the difference between threat of entry and **threat of substitutes**. Both are about the entry of new capacity into the industry and into the set of competitors. However, entry is essentially about imitation and the entry of new competitors to take advantage of the existing attractiveness of the industry. Substitution, however, is about new dimensions of competition and the ability of new ways of competing to displace existing ways. New entrants reckon to be able to exploit the existing value proposition to customers, whereas substitute products expect to be able to change the value proposition.

Competitive rivalry

The intensity of competition is the fifth force in our list. This is regarded by economists as the first force in that it is the prototype of competitive force present in all economic text-books (this was summarized in the Chapter 3). The propositions follow from our earlier discussion of perfect competition. Thus, competition will be the stronger (and profits the lower) the more competitors there are and the more commodity-like are the products. In addition, the supply–demand balance directly affects the market price. In declining markets prices fall as excess supply chases deficient demand. The more the cost structure is fixed rather than variable, and marginal costs are therefore low, the more room there is to cut prices before contribution margins become negative. This explains why capital intensive industries with low marginal costs suffer so much in recession. Prices can keep falling as long as cash flows remain positive – remembering that the capital costs are sunk (for example, Eurotunnel) and fixed costs are programmed over a time period – so the only discretionary policy is to place price somewhere above marginal cost. In extreme cases cash flows might remain positive (and sufficient to pay cash costs including interest payments on capital) while accounting losses could be very high.

5.1.2 **Strategy as imperfections**

Many writers have emphasized that strategy is, in the end, a practical matter, as is manage-ment studies in general. However, the long-run nature of strategic decisions and their inherent complexity, coupled with the uncertainty attached to futurity, means that there can be a substantial pay-off to strategic thinking. Strategic thinking places a premium on good understanding and use of concepts. Strategy was always recognized to centre on resource allocation decisions that determine the long-term capability of organizations in relation to choices about how and where the organization intends to compete. The foundation for stra-tegic thinking requires an understanding of the nature of markets (see Chapter 3 for a detailed explanation). Perfectly competitive markets are characterized by free entry, perfect information and identical commodity-like products. The consequence of such 'perfect' competition is that price is the only competitive variable, that firms are essentially identical and, therefore, that there are no supernormal profits to be had. Profit is sufficient to provide a normal return on capital and any profits above this will be transitory, either through random shocks or because competition erodes the profit benefits of new initiatives. Thus, the perfectly competitive world is not conducive to super profits ('rents') and does not provide much incentive to entrepreneurial behaviour.

However, imperfections in markets do provide the possibility for **rents** and rent-seeking activities. Imperfections could be differences in information about production possibilities, or consumer ignorance about product benefits. Some imperfections are market-wide, in that monopoly might prevail, perhaps because of government edict, or because of natural economies of scale, or perhaps through cartels. These imperfections are associated with rents, because prices can be held artificially high without (much) fear of competition. The worldwide wave of privatization and deregulation is usually marked by lower prices and greater competition. Figure 5.2 portrays the differences between the conditions under which perfect competition obtains and competitive advantage exists.

Imperfections can be firm-specific. Thus, a pharmaceutical company may, through its R&D activity, develop specific, proprietary knowledge that results in new products that cannot be imitated without a significant time lag. An office equipment company might establish a worldwide service system that allows it to give 24-hour service response to clients. Competitors can only imitate after substantial delay. **Firm-specific imperfections** enable firms to be different from their competitors and to expect this difference to be sustainable over a non-trivial time span. If firms can be different, and if customers value such differences, then these firms can earn supernormal profits, at least for a time. In economic terms, this is the essence of strategy. Firms create advantage by creating assets and positions that are distinctively different from those of their competitors. The essence of these firm-specific imperfections lies, first, in the creation of different assets (either tangible or intangible) and, second, in the creation of distinctive, defensible positions in their chosen product markets. The '**positioning**' school (which could be known as the **market-based view**) focuses primarily on the latter, with analysis of the nature and dynamics of competitive advantage. The **resource-based view** is concerned with the former.

Figure 5.2 Perfect competition versus competitive advantage

What industry analysis does is to create a framework within which all the possible ways in which imperfections arise can be identified, assessed and analysed. The next section looks at how these firm-specific imperfections can be described as generic types of strategy.

Case box: **Profitability of UK retailers**

It is a commonplace to observe that British supermarket groups are much more profitable than their counterparts elsewhere in Europe or North America – isn't it? The companies themselves do not agree, and claims and counter-claims fly around like confetti ... Several factors make comparisons inherently difficult. One factor is that the UK groups are all publicly owned, while many of the continental firms are still private. Definitions of profit, and the motivation to declare a higher or lower figure are different. If you want to please the stock exchange, you tend to declare high profits; if you and your family will be paying income tax on the sum, you may want to minimize it.

Another factor is that accounting conventions vary, in particular in relation to the treatment of goodwill, and amortization of property costs. Sums arising from the purchase of goodwill are amortized against the profit and loss account over 20 years in France; in the UK they will usually be written off immediately to reserves. In France, store assets (land and buildings) are depreciated over a 20-year period, while in the UK this has not until recently been true. The argument in Britain was that because of the high quality of the buildings, they would not decline very quickly in value over time, and the residual asset would have a high resale value. This was clearly not true after the collapse of the property market in the early 1990s, and increasing criticism from analysts eventually led some retailers to acknowledge the validity of the argument. First, Morrison and Asda, then later all the others, agreed from the mid-1990s to depreciate their freehold and long-lease buildings. This reduced profits in the first few years ...

With these preliminaries, we can look at some actual figures. There are (at least) two ways of analyzing profitability: margin on sales, and return on capital employed (ROCE). It turns out that they produce different patterns. With return on sales, which critics most often quote, it is clear that UK supermarkets appear to have an advantage. The profit margins on sales in Britain rose steadily over the decades until the early 1990s, and have consistently been above those for Continental and US operators. Over the period 1988–93, the average operating margin for six French supermarket groups was 2 per cent. For six British groups, the average was over 6 per cent (Burt and Sparks, 1997). Adjustment of the British figures to take account of the differences in accounting treatment mentioned above (and certain other factors), will bring the UK figures down to around 4 to 5 per cent, but the French figures will still be significantly lower at 1–2 per cent. Almost all the US supermarket chains have been nearer the French than the British levels (though in general, US and Continental margins have been rising through the 1990s, while UK rates have been falling).

These comparisons have aroused most attacks from critics. They claim that the UK margins are the result of massive buying power exerted by the supermarkets groups. And the use of oligopoly power to impose on consumers a higher-than-normal price level. It is virtually impossible to compare price levels across countries, and it is also the case that there are large and powerful buying groups in many other countries. The British firms tend to be more centralized than some Continental competitors, and to use a single fascia; this should help in reducing costs. It may also be that British firms are more experienced and more skilful in using their buying power to extract better terms from suppliers.

Other possible explanations for higher British margins flow from lower costs:

◆ British companies have a lead in applying IT to logistics. Their distribution systems are centralized, with deliveries to a small number of company warehouses. Such efficiencies are reflected, for example, in fewer days' stockholding: an average of 20 days in the period 1988–93 for British firms, compared with 35 for French (Burt and Sparks, 1997).

◆ Labour costs are lower in the UK, both because of lower social costs borne by employers, and because in Britain the proportion of part-time labour in supermarkets is higher than elsewhere.

◆ The significantly higher level of own-label penetration in British supermarkets means that the average cost of goods sold is lower than in the rest of Europe, and the gross margin higher.

On the other hand, the costs of buying sites and of building superstores are considerably higher than in other countries; not all cost comparisons favour the British. Another element in the difference between British margins and those of Continental and US operators is the nature of competition in the different markets. Price plays a much more important role in both the USA and in Continental Europe than in Britain, for whatever reason.

When we turn to ROCE, we see a different picture. A study of the years 1988–93 showed an average ROCE for six French companies of 19 per cent, and for six British companies of 21 per cent. A later analysis (Deutsche Morgan Grenfell, 1998) compared store groups in Britain, France, Belgium, and the United States. The results from 1991–7 were consistent, and 1997 showed:

ROCE per cent
Six British companies   16
Nine US companies   21
Eight French companies   20
Three Belgian companies   24

Any comparison of ROCE across countries shows that even the best British supermarket groups are at best similar to their rivals, but certainly not more profitable. The higher capital investment needs servicing by higher margins.

Source: Seth, A and Randall, G (1999), pp. 215–16.
Reproduced with permission of Kogan Page Ltd.

> **Questions for discussion**
>
> 1 Are the British supermarkets more profitable than their European and US counterparts?
>
> 2 Using the industry analysis framework, why might you expect the profitability of retailers to be different on average in different countries?
>
> When you have read Chapter 6 and the section on the Business Model, you can answer the following questions.
>
> 3 Do British supermarkets operate on a different business model than their rivals?
>
> 4 On what basis would you judge whether a different business model was sustainable or not?

5.2 **Generic strategies**

Porter's five forces and the various sources of imperfections are summarized in Figure 5.3. These powerful economic forces on industries, supply chains and markets suggest that firms can have substantial problems in identifying and responding to the competitive pressures that surround them. However, we have seen some examples where firms very deliberately set out to countervail these forces and create space within which they can earn profits at a higher rate than their industry confrères. This is the essence of strategy, the creation of space within which discrete and distinctive actions can secure improved positioning within markets and greater performance. Using the basic economic models popularized by Porter, we can see that competitive position can be improved in two basic ways. A firm might enjoy cost advantages that its rivals will find difficult to imitate. Or a firm might create a differentiated product that its rivals might find difficult to imitate. The essence of perfect competition is that imitation will be easy, not too costly, and speedy. Any differences that emerge will be competed away very quickly. The introduction of an extra feature on a car (such as a rear parking sensor) is generally easy to copy. However, to offer hybrid motors (electric plus gasoline such as in the Toyota Prius) is much more difficult to copy in terms of quality, cost and speed of imitation. Firms with distinctive cost advantages will typically have built up economies of scale and scope over a long period of time and rivals may find it difficult to attain the same low costs. The very well known report on the British motorcycle industry (BCG 1975) identified huge scale economies in Japanese motorcycle factories leading, for example, to labour productivity figures of around 500 bikes per man year compared to the traditional craft-based production processes of European and US producers whose labour productivity was around 18 bikes per man year. This kind of cost advantage is inherently difficult to replicate and would take a very long time even if it were judged sensible to try to emulate.

The other main dimension of strategic choice revolves around the notion of **scope**. We have described **economies of scope** as arising when the average cost of a single product is lowered by its joint production with other products in a multi-product firm. This is based on the indivisibility of certain resources. For example, knowledge is indivisible in the sense that it cannot be divided into pieces, some of which you choose to use or have and some of which you choose not to use or have. Knowing about aluminium means that you will have knowledge relevant to airframe manufacture and to pots and pans. Economies of scope arise when your knowledge or other indivisible resource can be applied in multiple directions without using up that resource. Thus scope becomes interesting strategically. A firm may choose to operate with broad scope (such as Ford in the automobile assembly industry covering a very wide product range and covering also the whole globe). Conversely, a firm may choose to operate

Figure 5.3 Behind the competitive forces

on a very narrow scope (such as Morgan Cars which covers only a particular part of the sports car market). The choice of broad scope suggests a calculation about available economies of scope in such a fashion that once chosen it is a commitment that cannot readily be reversed. The choice of narrow scope suggests an alternative calculation, that the benefits of assets and other resources and capabilities focused and dedicated to specific ways creates differentiation and/or cost advantages of a different sort. Figure 5.4 illustrates these generic strategies.

Generic strategies represent typologies that illustrate the type and range of strategic options that are available in principle. Thus, within the brewing industry, over time it is possible to see some brewing companies as low-cost players relying on size of brewing plants to reduce costs to the lowest possible levels. Other brewers would see themselves as offering a wide range of differentiated products (e.g. cask-conditioned beer). Many well-known breweries are comparatively quite small and offer only a small range of 'real ale' products. Historically, most brewers were small local operations producing cheap and cheerful low-cost products. These typologies are useful in understanding the nature of the strategic options that face firms but they do not in themselves provide prescriptions for strategic choice. Choice depends on the ways in which an individual firm can deploy advantages from cost, differentiation and scope – the key dimensions of the generic strategies box.

Figure 5.4 Porter's generic strategies
Source: Porter (1980) Chapter 2. Reprinted with permission of The Free Press, a division of Simon and Schuster Adult Publishing Group, from *Competitive Strategy* by Michael Porter. Copyright © 1980, 1998 by The Free Press. All rights reserved.

5.3 **Sources of competitive advantage**

The idea of a generic strategy is a powerful foundation for understanding how competitive strategies are in practice articulated and implemented. A generic strategy is a simple typology that captures the essential economic forces at work in a market (the demand side) and in an industry (the supply side). Porter suggested that there are three generic strategies to choose from, and each business unit can have its own strategy. According to Porter, a business can strive to supply a product or service more cost-effectively than its competitors (cost leadership), it can strive to add value to the product or service through differentiation and command higher prices (differentiation), or it can narrow its focus to a special product market segment which it can monopolize (focus). Not following any of these strategies characterizes a firm as being 'stuck in the middle'. The choice of generic strategy should be based on the firm's business unit's strengths and weaknesses, and a comparison of those with the strengths and weaknesses of competitors.

If a firm can become the lowest-cost producer in the industry then **cost leadership** may be the most appropriate strategy to pursue. Cost reduction should be continuous, so that the cost differential with competitors is maintained, and should involve all stages of the value chain. It can be achieved by methods such as proprietary access to cheaper inputs or technologies, or by positioning to exploit any experience effects. Typically, these come with market share, so the control of a large share of the market is likely to be necessary. Where there are limited opportunities to build efficient plant, the second, third or other low-cost producers may also be able to achieve above average performance. Moreover, because of the reliance on economies of scale and the like, cost leadership is likely to be more sustainable in the long run if relatively stable, no-frills products of reasonable quality are involved. For the same reason, cost leadership strategies are more appropriate in relatively stable environments. The typical staffing and administrative requirements of a cost leader are also distinct. Unskilled personnel can undertake much of the workload, and technocrats such as scientists and engineers are not required on any large scale, particularly where commodity products are involved. Similarly, cost control is of the utmost importance, and very developed formal systems are often encountered.

If cost leadership is not a feasible option, but the firm is able to differentiate its products along some attributes which customers value, and the cost of doing so is lower than the extra revenue envisaged, then **differentiation** may be the appropriate strategy to pursue. Porter defines differentiation in terms of the ability to charge higher prices, and not on the basis of the product's attributes *per se*. It can be based, therefore, on either product innovation or marketing. In order to pursue a differentiation (value added) strategy, an accurate picture of the target market will have to be obtained to ensure that there are sufficient ways in which to differentiate the product, and that the marketplace can be subdivided – and is willing to pay for the differentiation. An effort will then have to be made to avoid imitation, and this typically involves a regular redefinition of the basis of differentiation. For the same reason, it would be desirable for the differentiation to be based on a mix of features and activities rather than a simple product feature or service, and for it to involve many parts of the value chain. Added protection from imitation may also be possible by linking into the value chains of suppliers and buyers. Differentiation, whether innovation or marketing based, is more appropriate in dynamic industry environments, in which it can help to avoid, at least in the short run, potentially more costly forms of competition such as price cuts. However, as it often involves new technologies and unforeseen customer and competitor reactions, it also contributes, in turn, to environmental unpredictability. As far as staffing and administrative requirements are concerned, differentiation typically requires the employment of experts, and the establishment of mechanisms to facilitate the co-ordination of these experts, who may work in different functional departments.

If it is not possible to access the entire market on the basis of either low cost or differentiation, a defensible niche may still be available to provide above average performance. Marketing to such a niche would again involve a choice between low cost or differentiation but, this time, if the niche is well chosen, the scope of the market would enable the firm to advance on more limited cost and differentiation capabilities. In principle, a *focus* strategy exploits the differences in cost behaviour in some segments, or the special needs of the buyers in those segments, so it is only available where such segments are poorly served by the broadly targeted competitors and, of course, only sustainable for as long as the niche can be defended. The difficult point for the focuser is reached when the niche has been exhausted, at which time they may be tempted, out of a false sense of security derived from their success within the narrow scope of the niche, to target the broader market. This can have catastrophic consequences.

From the above discussion it should be evident that each generic strategy makes its own demands on the organization in terms of skills and administrative structure, and is more appropriate in different sets of circumstances. Nevertheless, a firm pursuing one strategy would act foolishly if it did not act to gain from elements of the other strategies too, as long as this did not detract it from its chosen strategy. A differentiator, for example, should pursue all cost reduction which does not sacrifice differentiation, and a cost leader could differentiate until this started to cost too much. However, when a firm confuses its primary goal and source of competitive advantage, and pursues both cost reduction and differentiation indiscriminately (or not at all), then it is said by Porter to be 'stuck in the middle'. This, he said, is an unenviable strategy because, in general, cost leadership and differentiation are inconsistent in principle, and there will typically be a cost leader, differentiator, or focuser that will be able to compete better than the firm stuck in the middle in any one segment of the market. Firms with such a (lack of) strategy, Porter said, typically end up stuck in the middle because they find it difficult to make the necessary choices.

There are a few cases, however, in which cost leadership and differentiation are not mutually inconsistent, at least in the short run. This may occur, for example, when the firm pioneers a proprietary innovation (whether a product, service or process) that enables it to reduce cost and at the same time differentiate successfully. With the appropriate barriers erected, it may be possible to exploit such an innovation for a considerable period of time. Similarly, cost leadership and differentiation may also be pursued together when costs are largely determined by market share, and control of a considerable share enables the firm to use the extra margin to differentiate and still remain the cost leader. The same may be possible if there are interrelationships between industries that a competitor may be able to exploit while others are not. In any case, the profitability of a 'stuck in the middle' company may remain adequate in the medium term in a high-growth environment (as this sustains inefficiencies), in a particularly attractive industry, or if the firm faces similarly stuck in the middle competitors.

Porter's claim that *no* firm should be stuck in the middle has, however, received critical attention and a lot of effort has gone into interpreting and questioning this advice. J.S. Sainsbury, the retailer ('Good food costs less at Sainsbury's'), is often cited as proof that a stuck in the middle strategy can be viable and successful (Cronshaw *et al.* 1990) because Sainsbury exhibits both low cost and differentiation. Gilbert and Strebel (1991) distinguished between one-dimensional and outpacing strategies, and suggested that the latter are designed for being stuck in the middle. The crux of this debate is that there exists no reason to imply that a low-cost base should necessarily be coupled with lower prices, or that a differentiated product should be coupled with premium prices. The low-cost base could simply be used to earn higher margins or, indeed, a differentiated product could be priced low enough to achieve a higher volume of sales (pricing differentiated products low enough to gain entry into a new market is only a temporary strategy which can lead to no competitive advantage, so it is of no relevance here). The underlying cause that leads to the overlap has been identified by Mathur (1988), who observed that whereas differentiation is an output concept, cost leadership is relevant to both inputs and outputs. Finally, some of the most common dangers to sustainability that are inherent in each of the strategies are shown in the tables in Chapter 6.

It is common to hear protests that generic strategies are too simple. But this is to miss the point. Generic strategies are intended to capture and portray the essential underlying economic forces. What firms do is to interpret these in the context of their own circumstances and formulate more or less complex strategies accordingly. Criticism has also focused on the lack of market orientation in the generic strategies matrix (Figure 5.4). Also missing is government and its frequently very significant role in the operation of markets. However, typologies and generics are not intended to be an accurate portrayal of the world – that is the role of the strategist in practice. Thus, the Ansoff diversification matrix is another generic strategies matrix. This sets out to define appropriate types of strategy for the marketing of new or existing products to new or existing markets. This attracted much attention because it drew the distinction between horizontal and vertical integration and conglomerate styles. These are pure types of strategy (like cost, differentiation and focus) that are applied in specific ways according to circumstances. Porter's generic strategy approach enables us to focus on the essence of strategy, which is to seek out and defend competitive advantage, a unique strategic position. This chapter and the one that follows goes behind the three generic strategies to examine the nature of strategic positioning so as to capture a sustainable competitive advantage.

5.4 Describing strategy

We are now in a position to set out the key headings under which we can describe an organization's strategy. The basic paradigm is set out in the strategic concepts framework introduced in Chapter 1 and is further developed in Figure 5.5.

Step 1 requires a description of the underlying mission of the organization and the objectives (including financial performance) that it wants to achieve over a defined time horizon. This includes coverage of mission and vision statements, the notion of strategic intent, and an assessment of stakeholders and shareholders (as discussed in Chapter 1).

Step 2 describes the scope of the organization – in which product markets does it choose to compete? Firms obviously cannot compete in any and every market. They must make some choices. However, the logic for making choices is not obvious in itself. Firms might choose to compete in closely related markets where, for example, the technologies and production methods are similar, where distribution channels are common, or where there are common customers for a range of products. But such 'relatedness' or 'synergy' can be difficult to define or achieve and some firms have preferred to adopt more conglomerate-style approaches where the chosen businesses are apparently very diverse (*see*, for example, Hanson plc and Tomkins in the UK). Another facet of scope is geographic markets.

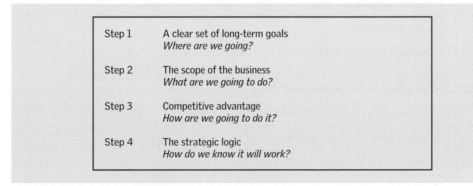

Figure 5.5 Describing strategy

Should one restrict the focus to the home market? Or are there arguments for adopting a more multinational posture? Ansoff's (1965) famous diversification matrix shows the different types of diversification. The grounds for making diversification (that is, scope) decisions are treated more formally in Chapter 9 on corporate strategy, in which business portfolio choices are analysed.

Step 3 articulates the benefits that the firm can bring to its customers and to itself by its positioning within its chosen product markets. Why should the customer buy this product? Why should he or she buy from us? What value can we gain from making this proposition to the customer? These are all ways of describing the nature of the competitive advantage that the firm can achieve.

Our definition of competitive advantage is:

> *Delivering superior value to customers and in doing so earning an above average return for the company and its stakeholders.*

This has implications for positioning choices in product markets. This takes us into Step 4, the strategic logic behind competitive advantage. This has two parts. The first is the positioning logic – the market-based logic which underpins our competitive advantage ambitions (*see* Figure 5.6). The second part is the resource-based logic that states why we think our intentions and actions about resources and capabilities will lead to the products and services that can be positioned in markets in the desired way (*see* Figure 5.7).

Listing the sources of advantage in this way gives us one way of focusing on the resources and capabilities that are needed. In this language we use resources to refer to tangible assets,

- Statement of competitive intent.

- The outward evidence of competitive advantage.

- Combination of:

  - superior delivered cost position

  - differentiation advantage

  - protected niches.

- Differences in positional advantage cannot be exploited profitably unless they can be seen to provide *direct benefits* which:

  - are perceived by a sizeable customer group

  - their customers value and are willing to pay for

  - cannot be readily obtained elsewhere both now and in the foreseeable future.

Figure 5.6 Positional advantage

Resources:

• Distribution coverage

• Financial capacity

• Shared expertise with related businesses

• Low-cost manufacturing and distribution systems

• Production capacity

• Ownership of raw material sources

• Long-term supply contracts

Capabilities:

• Specialized knowledge

• Customer service orientation

• Design expertise

• Application experience

• Trade relationships

• Ability to utilize relevant technologies

• Systems design capability

• Fast, flexible response capability

Figure 5.7 Resources and capabilities as sources of advantage

'Our strategy is to dominate the UK market for inexpensive widgets by being the low-priced manufacturer selling through mass market channels. Our low price in these channels will generate high volume and because there are economies of scale in the production of widgets, will make us the low-cost producer enabling us to achieve favourable margins even with a low price.'

Low price → High volume and market dominance → Lower costs than competitors → Low price

Figure 5.8 A simple strategic logic

Case box: **Tesco**

A decade ago Tesco was the modern equivalent of a music hall joke. But now it is a Tesco which is laughing – all the way to the bank … at the end of the seventies Tesco began discarding the 'pile it high sell it cheap' philosophy on which the chain had been built … then it discovered what much of British industry has been learning; that people are often prepared to pay for better quality, are often more concerned with service than with price and there's often more profit in worrying about the feel of quality and service than in bribing the customers with low prices. The transformation of Tesco is a remarkable success story.

Source: D. Powell (1991) *Counter Revolution: The Tesco Story*, Grafton Books, London.

Questions for discussion

1   Use the frameworks in Figure 5.5, 5.6 and 5.7 to compare the 'old' Tesco strategy with its new strategy.

2   What do you think is the impact on the cash flows?

3   What would a balanced scorecard show?

This example is not intended to provide you with enough detail to answer the questions in depth. Instead we are looking for your ability to capture the essence of retailing (you can use any company example at all) in the language of the strategy frameworks.

and capabilities to refer to intangibles such as knowledge, organization and management skills. More recently there has been much attention paid to the notion of '**core competence**' – an amalgam of the languages of resources and capabilities. We define core competence as the underlying capability that is the distinguishing characteristic of the organization. We explore these ideas further in Chapter 7. Putting together the market-based logic of positioning and the resource-based logic we should be able to make a simple statement of the underlying strategic logic. Figure 5.8 provides an example.

5.5 The internal logic of competitive strategy

Industry analysis and the generic strategies approach gives us useful frameworks for thinking about the external logic of strategic decisions (see also Chapter 1). This enables us to complete the first stage of an assessment of **strategic position**, the impact of strategy on the external environment. We proceed in this section to examine the role of internal resources and capabilities with regard to strategy, and in particular the way in which they are captured within the value chain, i.e. that part of the supply chain that is owned and controlled by the firm.

First we look at a map of the interaction between the external world and the internal world of the firm. This is explicit about the nature of strategy over time and asks about the inherent stability or instability of strategy – the strategy cycle.

5.5.1 **The strategy cycle**

Strategy is concerned with fashioning success in the long term, hence there is a performance dimension to the market-based view and the resource-based view. This is demonstrated in Figure 5.9 which shows how the real economy[2] of the firm (the creation of resources and capabilities and the positioning within product markets) interacts with the financial economy of the firm. The top line shows schematically the transformation of 'raw' assets (people, knowledge, and money) into resources and capabilities customized to create goods and services for the chosen product markets. The 'output' of the real economy is cash flow conditioned by the scale of the competitive advantage achieved.

Competitive advantage has two dimensions: the extra value over competitors that customers receive, and the extra value in terms of real profits that are taken back into the firm. These profits, contained within the cash flow, are partitioned between those that are returned to shareholders and debt holders, and those that are retained internally. The returns to shareholders and bondholders as dividends and interest payments serve to maintain the value of the firm in financial markets through two mechanisms. The first is the market value as represented by the share price, which itself is determined through the price/earnings ratio by dividends and by shareholder expectations about future profitability. The second is the credit rating (for example, an AAA rating by Standard & Poors on the New York Stock Exchange) which influences the interest rates a company will have to pay for any new debt issues. Through these mechanisms the value of the firm and its financial capacity are established. Coupled with internal liquidity, this represents the ability of the firm to reinvest in resources and capabilities.

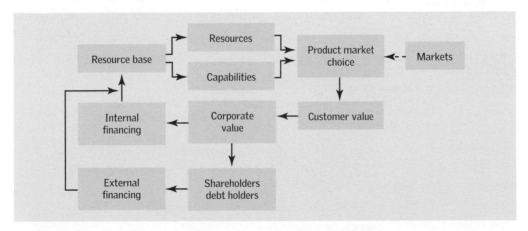

Figure 5.9 The strategy cycle

---

[2] The 'real' economy is the trade in goods and services as opposed to the 'financial' economy.

We can see the possibility of a virtuous circle whereby the firm enjoys competitive advantage and superior profitability, has the financial capacity to reinvest in its assets, capabilities and competences, from which it can further enhance its competitive advantage and its profitability, and so on. We can see also the possibility of a vicious spiral in which competitive disadvantage and poor profitability could be matched with limited financial capacity and consequent inability to reinvest to restore competitive advantage and so on.

A key role for top management is to manage this balance between the firm's real and financial economy. The dynamics of markets and companies is such that there is rarely a balance; rather, there is continuous adjustment of the key decision variables so as to maintain competitiveness in markets, maintain cash flows, and maintain financial capacity. In this sense we see the firm as taking 'actions' to influence the 'context' in which it works in order to achieve superior 'performance' (*see* Figure 5.10). Context in this language has external dimensions, such as markets and industry membership, and internal dimensions, such as its assets and its organization structure and processes. Strategy, thus, has a focus on actions to affect performance directly and indirectly through context.

The strategy cycle demonstrates (in the top line of Figure 5.9) the conversion of basic *resources* into customized assets which we will call **capabilities**. The ability of a firm to create customer value and corporate value (line 2 of Figure 5.9) depends on the match that can be made between internal resources and capabilities and the opportunities and risks endemic in the external environment. There is an important distinction to be made between resources and capabilities. Resources are typically inputs into the real economy of the firm. They include finance, skills of individual employees, purchased components and items of capital equipment, and anything else purchased on open markets. Resources on their own do not provide a distinctive characteristic to the firm. To obtain a distinctive strategic position the firm also requires specific capabilities that enable the combination,

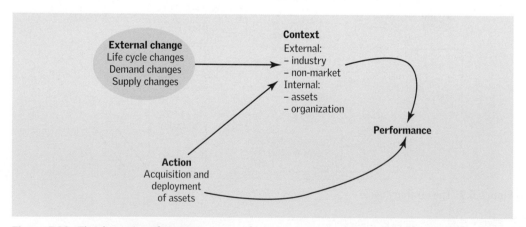

Figure 5.10 The dynamics of strategy

development and co-ordination of basic resources. Capability (often called competence) is the capacity to perform tasks or activities and distinctive capabilities (or core competences) are the capacities to perform these tasks in a sufficiently distinctive way so as to create unique strategic positions (see Figure 5.7), as explored further in Chapter 7.

5.5.2 The value chain

We have seen that the supply chain forms the basic spine of the five forces analysis. It contains all the activities required to bring the final product or service to the customer. Along the way many different firms or businesses have their own activities along the supply chain. Each firm has its own **value chain**, a subset of the supply chain. Figure 5.11 is Porter's classic picture of the value chain. It has two parts. The lower part contains those activities (labelled primary activities) that are organized in sequence, just like a production line. Thus, inbound logistics is the first step, leading to manufacturing operations, then outbound logistics, marketing and sales, and eventually service. This is a caricature and each firm's value chain will contain different headings according to the nature of the operations. These categories can be described as follows:

- *Inbound logistics.* Activities associated with receiving, storing, and disseminating rights to the product, such as material handling, warehousing, stock management and the like.

- *Operations.* All of the activities required to transform inputs into outputs and the critical functions which add value, such as machining, packaging, assembly, service, testing and so on.

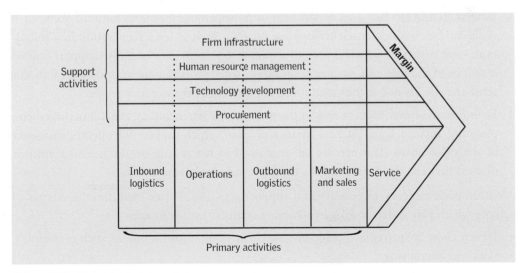

Figure 5.11 The generic value chain
Source: adapted from Porter (1985).

◆ *Outbound logistics.* All of the activities required to collect, store and physically distribute the output. This activity can prove to be extremely important both in generating value and in improving differentiation, as in many industries control over distribution strategies is proving to be a major source of competitive advantage – especially as it is realized that up to 50 per cent of the value created in many industry chains occurs close to the ultimate buyer.

◆ *Marketing and sales.* Activities associated with informing potential buyers about the firm's products and services, and inducing them to purchase by personal selling, advertising and promotion, and so on.

◆ *Service.* The means of enhancing the physical product features through after-sales service, installation, repair and so on.

The second part of the value chain is the upper section which contains all the overhead service elements (labelled support activities) required by the firm. In Porter's picture he named four elements: firm infrastructure, human resource management, technology development and procurement.

1 *Procurement.* This concerns the acquisition of inputs or resources. Although technically the responsibility of the purchasing department, almost everyone in the firm is responsible for purchasing something. While the cost of procurement itself is relatively low, the impact can be very high.

2 *Human resource management.* This consists of all activities involved in recruiting, hiring, training, developing, rewarding and sanctioning the people in the organization.

3 *Technology development.* This is concerned with the equipment, hardware, software, technical skills and the like used by the firm in transforming inputs to outputs. Some such skills can be classified as scientific, while others – such as food preparation in a restaurant – are 'artistic'. Such skills are not always recognized. They may also support limited activities of the business, such as accounting, order procurement and so on, and in this sense may be likened to the value added component of the experience effect.

4 *Firm infrastructure.* This consists of the many activities, including general management, planning, finance, legal, external affairs and so on, which support the operational aspect of the value chain. This may be self-contained in the case of an undiversified firm or divided between the parent and the firm's constituent business units.

Within each category of primary and support activities, Porter identifies three types of activity which play different roles in achieving competitive advantage:

◆ *Direct.* These are activities directly involved in creating value for buyers, such as assembly, sales and advertising.

◆ *Indirect.* These are activities that facilitate the performance of the direct activities on a continuing basis, such as maintenance, scheduling and administration.

- *Quality assurance.* These are activities that insure the quality of other activities, such as monitoring, inspecting, testing and checking.

The value chain is another generic framework that permits a range of applications and analyses. It permits the analyst to decompose the firm's activities into broad categories (as above) and increasingly into finer categories. Thus, operations might be refined into sub-components and assembly; marketing and sales into market research, product development, sales force and so on. The usefulness of this is to be able to identify those activities that are the source of the competitive advantage and to be able to locate them within the value chain. For example, if Intel's competitive advantage is product performance and this is derived (at least in large part) from R&D activities, then this can be isolated within the value chain and measured, compared to competitors, and provided with support.

Competitive advantage is often quite subtle in its manifestation and in its sources. Cost advantage might arise from the way in which every single activity in the value chain is linked to the others and managed for efficiency. The story of the low-cost airlines such as easyJet, RyanAir and SouthWest Airlines is about system management of the costs as well as focus on driving down each cost component. Differentiation may be delivered as a service quality perception driven by the way in which each element of service delivery is managed systematically, along with all other elements, in order to differentiate the product. The case exercise at the end of the chapter illustrates this for the hotel chain Novotel.

The Novotel example shows how the value chain can be a powerful tool in diagnosing and explaining how the management of competitive advantage takes place within the firm. The interrelationships between the elements of the value chain provide an important explanation of the nature of competitive advantage in large, complex organizations. Such organizations typically are rich in tacit knowledge. This is the kind of knowledge that you call upon to ride a bicycle. We all know how to do this – but it is impossible to explain it. Similarly, large corporations are used to making links between complex and far-flung activities, and between related and unrelated technologies. This is a glue that binds these companies together and makes it impossible for others to imitate quickly. The 'hidden' part of the value chain is these linkages that contain the tacit knowledge. In the Novotel example we can see how the authors use Novotel's own management processes to describe how the elements of the chain are linked together. The way this glue works determines the level of vertical integration, i.e. those elements of the supply chain that can be brought within the value chain and within the firm, and those that should remain outside the firm. The guiding principle is that when the costs of internal transactions (making the glue work properly) exceed the costs of buying outside, then the firm should source outside its boundaries. This glue is part of the core competence that we will be discussing in Chapter 7. We turn now to the issues of cost analysis and outsourcing.

The value chain and cost analysis

The value chain provides a good basis on which to conduct a cost analysis. Its principal advantage is that the elements of the value chain are already organized around those issues that are important in driving competitive advantage and profitability. Porter was therefore able in his 1985 book to make very strong links with the array of literature and practice on cost cutting that was already available. A criticism of the cost analysis literature was the difficulty of defining the correct units of analysis, an issue which the value chain solved brilliantly at a stroke!

Therefore a normal cost analysis procedure can take place with the following stages:[3]

1 Define the value chain in terms of those elements that relate to the sources of competitive advantage. Key considerations are:
   - The separateness and independence of one activity from another.
   - The importance of an activity in relation to competitive advantage and to the margin.
   - The dissimilarity of activities in terms of requiring different cost drivers.
   - The extent to which there are differences in the way competitors perform activities (i.e. where there are differences there are potential advantages to be gained).

2 Establish the relative importance of different activities in the total cost of the product. This means assigning costs to each activity based on management accounts or other customized analysis procedures. The distinctions made in Chapter 3 about fixed and variable costs sunk costs, and cost allocations are really significant issues at this stage. Errors in cost analysis can lead to significant misunderstanding of the what contributes to profits and how valuable a competitive advantage is.

3 Compare costs by activity and benchmark against competitors. The comparison is not in terms of how big are the costs but how different are they from efficiency benchmarks and from competitor standards.

4 Identify cost drivers. These are the forces that move costs up or down. Planned scale of activities is a driver of overall plant cost and so also is degree of capacity utilization. A driver of sales force costs might be product range – if the range is too small, costs will be high. Another driver will be geographical concentration of customers and another might be sales communication methods (face to face or remote teleconferencing). For labour intensive activities critical drivers might be wage rates, speed of production line and defect rates. It is the understanding of cost drivers that signifies how well you understand the nature of your business. One needs to look behind the obvious in order to identify the fundamentals.

5 Identify linkages between activities. As we see from the Novotel example, interrelationships may be very many in number – the critical cost drivers may seemingly relate to

---

[3] This section draws on Grant (2002), Ch. 7.

another activity entirely. We will see in later chapters a comparison between Xerox and Canon in the photocopying industry. Xerox found that its service costs were driven by design complexity and manufacturing inefficiencies. Grants observes that:

> *the optimisation of activities through the value chain has become a major source of cost reduction, and speed enhancement has become a key challenge for computer integrated manufacturing.* Grant (2002, p. 271)

6 Identify opportunities for reducing costs. By identifying areas of obvious inefficiency (i.e. deviations from designed machine performance standards) and of deficiencies against competitive benchmarks, opportunities for cost reduction become evident. Very often the option is posed of contracting outside the firm for components or services. Some firms have subcontracted entire IT departments. Currently European firms are outsourcing their call centres to India. The automobile companies are going through an extensive process of outsourcing. The Ford Fiesta plants in Cologne outsource fully made-up doors (as a subsystem) to plants adjacent to the Ford plant.

Value chain in summary[4]

The value chain concept thus helps to identify cost behaviour in detail. From this analysis, different strategic courses of action should be identifiable in order to develop differentiation and less price sensitive strategies. Competitive advantage is then achieved by performing strategic activities better or cheaper than competitors.

To diagnose competitive advantage, it is necessary to define the firm's value chain for operating in a particular industry and compare this with those of key competitors. A comparison of the value chains of different competitors often identifies ways of achieving strategic advantage by reconfiguring the value chain of the individual firm. In assigning costs and assets it is important that the analysis be done strategically rather than seeking accounting precision. This should be accomplished using the following principles:

- operating costs should be assigned to activities where incurred;
- assets should be assigned to activities where employed, controlled, or influencing usage;
- accounting systems should be adjusted to fit value analysis;
- asset valuation may be difficult, but should recognize industry norms – particular care should be taken in evaluating property assets.

The reconfiguration of the value chain has often been used by successful competitors in achieving competitive advantage. When seeking to reconfigure the value chain in an industry, the following questions need to be asked:

- How can an activity be done differently or even eliminated?

---

[4] See Channon (2005).

◆ How can linked value activities be reordered or regrouped?

◆ How could coalitions with other firms reduce or eliminate costs?

5.6 Strategy making in practice

5.6.1 Intended versus emergent strategies

As we saw in Chapter 1, strategic management deals essentially with four questions:

1 How do we develop and formulate strategy?

2 How do we make choices between strategic options?

3 How do we put the strategy into operation and sustain it over time?

4 How do we manage the processes of strategic change and strategy renewal?

The first question raises issues of intended and planned strategies (typically top-down) versus emergent strategies, which arise from experience and learning and where the emphasis is on knowledge that is distributed throughout the organization, versus accidents, serendipity and 'muddling through', within which strategy is very much the junior partner to flexibility, operations expertise, tactical acumen and speed of response.

The second question focuses on the nature of data and information required, the analytical processes used and how trade-offs are made. It confronts the logic approach of economic and quantitative models with the uncertainty and risk endemic in long-term decisions and raises questions about criteria for decision making and the nature and role of organizational influences.

The third question is widely regarded as the key to superior performance. This view is based on the nostrum that ideas are cheap but action is difficult. However, we argue throughout this book that these questions are linked and, for example, difficulties in implementation are partly (if not largely) to do with over-ambition and error in the first two parts. Nevertheless, implementation is distinctively difficult. It is complex in the range and the depth of detail making operational planning and control highly complex. It often requires the adoption of path-breaking new knowledge beyond the known best practice. Thus it is clear that matters may not proceed as expected and contingencies have to be anticipated. If operational matters were clear-cut and lacked complexity then it would almost always follow that the strategy would lack distinctiveness and competitive advantage would not be attained. The points at which competitive advantage are delivered are generally through specific operations and activities. Where these are unique, or at least new to the firm, successful implementation is clearly not assured. The issue of sustainability is to be seen in similar fashion. Keeping ahead of competitors involves continuous reinvestment and reappraisal of key operations. Thus, the firm is continually having to prospect into new territory in order to keep ahead, with all the risks and uncertainties that this implies. These issues are all taken up in detail in Part 4 of this book.

The fourth question has provided significant employment and fee income for consultants. Referring back to the strategy cycle diagram (Figure 5.9), we observed that strategies get out of date and performance suffers when markets change faster than organizations can respond. This gives rise to the need for strategic change and renewal. The management of strategic change has been one of the central practical and theoretical issues of the last 25 years. The era since 1979 has been one of radical external change resulting in radical changes to the business portfolios and activities of firms and to their traditional ways of doing business. The most common management responses have been to divest businesses and product lines in order to refocus on sustainable core businesses in which competitive advantage can be pursued. The pressures for internationalization have been very strong and companies have used acquisitions, alliances and organic growth in order to enter new markets. This combination of retrenchment plus expansion has obliged firms to undertake major programmes of change in which these changes in strategy have had to be matched by internal changes in organization structure and habitual ways of doing business (culture), and management processes have also had to be adapted and re-engineered.

5.6.2 Assessing progress

Bearing in mind the complexities arising from the proposition that at least part of your strategy may in practice be emergent or accidental (see Chapter 1), there is nevertheless a need to assess progress against your intentions. This section suggests a number of questions that you can use to judge the underlying logic of a strategy and the validity of the fundamental planning process.

Judging a competitive strategy

1 What does the customer really want and is willing to pay for?

2 What is the economic logic of the industry and how is it changing?

3 What are the key forces for change and how are we planning to take advantage of them?

4 What is the company's competitive advantage (business idea) that makes it unique?

5 How can it gain this competitive advantage?

6 How are the competitors likely to react?

You can see that these questions are closely related to our description of strategy in the strategy cycle.

How good is the strategic thinking?

 1 Is strategy clearly articulated:

- in product-market terms?
- with measurable objectives?
- with clear milestones?
- specific on source of competitive advantage?

2 Is it evident that strategy has been created with reference to the external environment?

3 Does strategy provide a clear guide to resource allocation?

4 Are business unit strategies clearly stated and linked to corporate strategy?

5 Is strategic planning linked to operational decision making?

6 Is the budgeting process subservient to the strategic planning process?

Points 1 to 6 relate directly to the content of the strategy and the way it is linked up and down the organization to its main systems and processes.

7 Is strategy consciously set by senior management?

8 Is the company's culture and value system conducive to strategic thinking?

9 Is strategy widely understood by division and middle level managers?

10 Is the concept of strategy understood by those providing 'strategy inputs'?

Points 7 to 10 bring in managers and management and provide a basis for asking how strategy processes and the values in the company actually support the production of 'good' strategy content.

Ten questions for judging a strategic plan

1 Will a high-quality business position result?
- At the end of the planning period we should feel good about the character and quality of our achievement, that is, a strong foundation and competitive position, and attractive financial results.

2 Is it clear what we want to have in our value chain?
- What will we invest in and what will we discard? Resource priorities should be focused in order to develop a healthy portfolio and a value chain of activities that can be managed with economies of scale and scope.

3 How are we anticipating and managing change to our advantage?
- The environment is changing rapidly: how will competitors respond and what are we planning to do?

4 Are the assumptions sound?
- Major changes in volume, share or margins should be firmly based on plans that support such changes, taking into account market realities and competitor reactions.

5 Are there specific concrete ideas driving the plan?
- Avoid 'hollow' plans that are superficially attractive but lack a solid idea capable of good execution.

6 Is there a sustainable competitive advantage?
- What is it that is going to result in superior performance over time and will warrant investment?

7 Is the implementation clear and specific?
- The organization must be able to understand, accept and carry out the key actions involved.

8 Are the financial results achievable?
- Is cash generation evident within an appropriate time frame with clear milestones identified?

9 Are the necessary resources identified?
- The plan must be within the existing capabilities of the company or have identified how these will be obtained.

10 Will the organization be able to adapt to the plan and its implementation?
- How much change in current operations and motivation of key managers will be required for successful achievement?

5.6.3 Assessing progress: the balanced scorecard

A critical element in successful strategy implementation is an appropriate performance measurement system (we develop this theme at greater length in Chapter 18). Conventional accounting systems often do not provide the critical information required by management to assess the company's progress to achieving its strategic vision and objectives because of their focus on reporting the past rather than assessing the future consequences of decisions made now. The **balanced scorecard** is a performance measurement system developed by Kaplan and Norton (1992) which, although including financial measures of performance, also contains operational measures of customer satisfaction, internal processes, and the company's innovation and improvement activities. These are seen collectively as the key drivers of future financial performance and individually as key success factors.

The balanced scorecard examines a business from the four important perspectives of:

- How do customers see the firm?
  (*customer perspective*)

- What does the firm excel at?
  (*internal perspective*)

- Can the firm continue to improve and create value?
  (*innovation and learning perspective*)

♦ How does the firm look to shareholders?
(*financial perspective*)

This approach avoids information overload by restricting the number of measures used so as to focus only on those seen to be essential – the key success factors.[5] The balanced scorecard presents this information in a single management report and therefore brings together often disparately reported elements of the firm's strategic position such as short-term customer response times, product quality, teamwork capability, new product launch times and the like. As a result, the approach guards against suboptimization by forcing management to examine individual operational measures systematically and comprehensively.

A typical scoreboard is illustrated in Figure 5.12. From this you can see how management can translate its general mission statements into the four perspectives, each of which contains a series of specific measures. The precise scorecard design should reflect the vision and strategic objectives of the individual company. The key point is that the scorecard approach

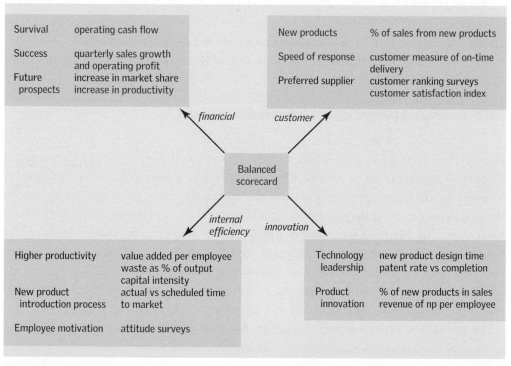

Figure 5.12 Balanced scorecard example

---

[5]   The term '**key success factors**' is widely used but rarely defined. In the next two chapters we will provide a useable definition, but for this chapter just think of it as referring to the range of competitive advantages evident in an industry from which firms make profits.

puts strategy and corporate vision, rather than financial reporting, as the key driver of performance management design (see Chapter 1). This is consistent with the development of corporate transformation techniques, cross-functional organizations, customer–supplier interrelationships and other major corporate programmes that are designed to have major effects on business performance.

> *Question: Using Figure 5.12 and the previous case box examples on Tesco and the profitability of UK retailers, try to create a balanced scorecard for Tesco (or any other major retailer).*

The case box below is included here for you to look at a specific characteristic of retailing, namely capital intensity, and ask, how does this affect the way we look at a business and how, therefore, does it affect the way in which we judge progress over time?

Case box: Capital intensity in retailing

A distinctive feature of the UK supermarket industry has been that it is far more capital intensive than in other countries. This stems, first, from certain aspects of the property market in the UK. Britain is a small country, and land for development is scarce and therefore expensive. During a long period of rising prosperity and therefore of increased demand it has become more scarce (as Mark Twain noted, 'They've stopped making it'). In these circumstances leases always contain regular, upward-only rent reviews. Ownership of commercial sites is concentrated among institutional investors, who are interested only in their capital gains and revenue streams. British leasehold law allows the lessor to recover all rent due from the head lessee, even though the lease may have been assigned, often many times. The original lessee may thus find that – when the latest tenant has defaulted, and even if the premises are shuttered – the owner will pursue him for all rent owing. British supermarket companies have therefore concentrated almost entirely on freehold properties.

Further, the planning authorities have insisted on high building standards, so the cheap, large sheds of Continental or US hypermarkets are not an option for UK grocers. One estimate suggests that a US supermarket can be built for half the cost of its UK equivalent.

High investment is also needed for the IT systems on which a modern retail chain depends. It would be impossible to run a group of several hundred stores, each with 20 000 or more SKUs (stocking units) without a formidably effective IT system. All the UK chains have invested hundreds of millions of pounds over the years on IT.

Finally, compared with France at least, UK retailers have to fund more of their own working capital. In France, the large food retailers take at least 90 days credit from their suppliers; in Britain, the figure is nearer 30 days. UK food manufacturers may feel that they are supplying their retail customers with much of their working capital along with their products, but the situation is much worse in Continental Europe.

High capital investment has been forced on the UK chains, and has dictated much of their strategy; they *have* to achieve higher margins. Their drive for efficiency has led them inexorably to the superstore format (seemingly unique to Britain, because of the market size and population density), and to take over much of the distribution chain themselves. Return on capital, the ultimate measure of profitability, shows that they achieve results similar to their rivals elsewhere but the route is different – higher margins and higher capital intensity.

Source: adapted from Seth and Randall (1999), pp. 226–7.
Reproduced with permission of Kogan Page Ltd.

Questions for discussion

1   How does capital intensity affect the way in which profits are earned?
2   What does this imply for strategic decisions such as store expansion and pricing?

5.7 Summary

This chapter, along with Chapters 3 and 4, provides a foundation for the strategy analysis that comes in Part 3. In this chapter we have introduced the idea of competitive advantage as a firm-specific imperfection that is the foundation and cornerstone of all strategy analysis. Strategy cannot be understood without this concept and it cannot exist without it existing in practice. Without competitive advantage we are consigned to the 'strategic hell' of perfect competition in which profits are elusive, products are commodities and firms are creatures of their environments. With competitive advantage, firms can be different, managers and managements can exercise choice and discretion, and entrepreneurial profits are possible. With competitive advantage we can have strategic choice. We can observe industries in which the participants can pursue similar or different strategies. Above all, with diverse and changing consumers firms can be entrepreneurial in constructing new value propositions. The ways in which competitive advantage can be deployed in different strategic clothes is the subject of the next section of seven chapters. The way the practice of strategy is carried on in the pursuit of competitive advantage is the subject of the six chapters of Part 4.

Alongside the idea of competitive advantage we have introduced some other well-known ideas. Generic strategies provide a typology of strategies based on competitive advantage. The value chain gives us a framework for identifying and analysing the internal disposition of assets, resources and activities. The balanced scorecard enables us to relate performance outcomes to these strategy ideas. We have also looked at some practical ways of categorizing strategy and assessing a firm's progress in setting out its own strategic thinking.

Key terms

Balanced scorecard *177*

Capabilities *168*

Competitive advantage *148*

Competitive rivalry *153*

Core competence *166*

Cost leadership *160*

Differentiation *160*

Economies of scope *157*

Firm-specific imperfections *154*

Five forces *149*

Fixed costs *149*

Generic strategies *159*

Key success factors *178*

Market-based view (MBV) *154*

Positioning *154*

Power of suppliers and buyers *151*

Rents *153*

Resource-based view (RBV) *154*

Scope *157*

Strategic position *166*

Supply chain *149*

Threat of entry *150*

Threat of substitutes *152*

Value chain *169*

Recap questions and assignments

1 Undertake a strategy audit of a business with which you are familiar. How attractive is the industry in which it competes? What strategies seem to be available in this industry? How would you describe the strategy of your selected business (Cheat: use Figure 5.5)?

2 Choose two companies in the same industry – preferably direct competitors – and compare the configuration of their value chains. Expain how these relate to their competitive positioning.

3 Do a SWOT analysis for your chosen business. Explain why you have chosen each of the key items.

Online
LearningCentre

When you have read this chapter, log on to the Online Learning Centre website at www.mcgraw-hill.co.uk/textbooks/mcgee to explore chapter-by-chapter test questions, further reading and more online study tools for strategy.

Case 1 **The Novotel value chain**

Figure 5.13 captures some of the key elements in the Novotel value chain. Each of the elements of the chain is important in itself for service delivery. But also most of them interact with other elements.

To expand further on the *hospitality concept*, one would need to describe intangibles such as 'greeting', 'welcome for the traveller' and personal warmth. It lends a relevant insight into the nature of the management task in services to reflect on the robustness of internal systems and processes to deliver these service elements to the customer on a routine basis. Indeed, Novotel use the layout of their hotel (part of *Service Design*, the first lower half (primary) activity in column 1) to lead the customer immediately to the 'hospitable' public spaces of bar and restaurant, which are always on the entry floor adjacent to reception.

Marketing (lower half, column 2) is extensive, sophisticated and linked closely to *distribution systems*. Novotel operates within both the individual and corporate business and leisure markets. Its special promotions and advertising themes (column 2, lower half) address these different segments. For example, Dolphi, a baby dolphin, is the marketing and promotional symbol for children's events worldwide. However, although all *locations* worldwide (column 1, lower half) will use the co-ordinated symbol and marketing materials for this (or any other) segment, general managers at different locations and in different countries will tailor promotions to local holidays and lifestyles.

Partnership programmes (column 2, lower half) are common nowadays. Novotel links them with deepening *relationship marketing* (column 2, top half). Particularly noteworthy are the supplier partnership programmes, linked with purchasing and learning efficiencies (see *firm infrastructure* and *procurement* in top half of value chain), delivering both scale and scope economies. An example of this would be an agreement to purchase televisions from a sole *preferred supplier worldwide* (column 1, top half) – a recent innovation at Novotel where local purchasing had been common. The television (or any other) supplier would be expected to develop a reciprocal relationship through utilizing their customer's hotels for corporate travel purposes (column 3). *Purchasing efficiencies* are thus linked to *internal and external relationship marketing* (see linkages between columns 1, 2 and 3 in top half).

The *hospitality concept* is further implemented by other key elements in *Service Delivery* (column 4). *Staff exchanges* (column 4, lower half) (between countries, locations and type of customer mix) contributing to *multi-culture* (column 1, top half) are essential to the philosophy of 'welcome'. They provide a means of motivating staff in an industry where labour turnover is typically high (column 4, top half – *staff retention*) and service delivery is dependent on the quality of the service encounter, to which staff motivation is crucial (column 4, lower half – *responsiveness* etc.). It also ensures an international mix of hotel staff to interact sympathetically with an international client mix.

_Spanning labels (top): HIGH EXPERIENCE EFFECTS (eg. site selection, hotel construction) · EFFECTIVE MANAGEMENT OF LINKAGES · PURCHASING SCALE EFFICIENCIES_

	SERVICE DESIGN	MARKETING	DISTRIBUTION	SERVICE DELIVERY	SERVICE MONITORING & ENHANCEMENT
FIRM INFRA-STRUCTURE	– Central design unit – NPD	– Global branding & positioning – Image management	– Central systems – Accor HQ	– Academie Accor – G M autonomy	– Flat reporting structure – WAR ROOM – Transfer of best practice
HRM	– HOSPITALITY CONCEPT – Core values – Multi-culture	– Relationship marketing (internal & external) – Incentive programmes	– Relationship-building	– Superior recruitment & selection – TRAINING – Superior staff retention	– Extensive training – Skills grading
TECHNOL DEVELPT	– Customer interface – Service needs – Rapid roll-out of new specifications	– Software & systems development	– Global reservation systems – Network linkages – Dedicated suppliers (global)	– Unique service features	– Process development
PROCUREMENT	– Standardization – Worldwide global best suppliers – High quality components & features	– Media selection placement & negotiation – Market research	– Dedicated software/systems	– Best available inputs – EOS	– Continuous enhancement & upgrading

	– Tight design specifications
	– Global coverage
	– 3-star
	– Features:
	  – hotels
	  – rooms
	  – restaurants
	– Layout
	– Locations
	– Image
		– Corporate travel management
		– Partnership programmes
		– Special promotions
		  – segmentation
		– Advertising themes
		  – for segments
		– Materials
		  – brochures
		  – give-aways
		– Campaign mgt.
		– Pricing
		– Supplier partnerships
		– Personal relationships with suppliers
			– Geographic network
			– Best locations
			– Centralized systems
			– Corporate agency network
			– Travel agency network
			– Availability
			– Rapid response/ timelines
			– Capacity utilization
			– Vertical & horizontal integration
				– Staff multi-skilling
				– Staff exchanges
				– Transferability of staff & skills
				– Languages
				– Responsiveness to customer requirements
				– Interface mgt.
				– High service recovery
				– Attractive styles/ appearance (people & hotels)
					– High quality controls
					– High conformance
					– Standard setting/quality measures
					– Skills – testing & banding/ grading
					– Extensive supplier training
					– Directors Clubs
					– Progress Groups (all staff levels)
					– 'Progress Novotel'
					– Customer surveys/feedback
					– Staff surveys/feedback
					– Staff empowerment
					– 'Pilot Case'
					– 'Quick' meetings
					– Refurbishment

Figure 5.13 Value chain for Novotel
Source: McGee and Segal-Horn (1997).

However, the more interesting elements of the Novotel offering for the purposes of this discussion are the management processes which enable the standardized service levels to be delivered at all locations worldwide.

Since hotel design and guest bedrooms are standardized, basic housekeeping and maintenance functions can in turn be standardized (see all *Service Design* and *Firm Infrastructure* elements in Figure 5.13). That means that training of staff in all basic functions may be simplified and the procedures for training can be themselves standardized (see all *HRM* and *Service Delivery* elements). Indeed, one of the features of the Accor Group (Novotel's parent) is the 'Academie Accor' set up in 1985, as the centre for all staff training within the Group. It's 'campus' is located on the site of Group corporate headquarters just outside Paris. From there, all training is designed and delivered. This standardized approach to the core service concept places special requirements on the staff as the key medium for delivery of consistent service standards wherever the customer is staying. Standardized procedures and centrally designed training programmes are one of the core mechanisms for securing such consistency (columns 4 and 5).

Taking the notion of consistency one stage further, the Novotel senior management developed a new approach to staffing in the hotel sector which is described as 'multi-skilling'. The idea behind multi-skilling is to develop staff as a team able to perform tasks and work as needed in a flexible manner. Obviously, this would have many advantages for hotel management, not least in smoothing the need for certain types of staff at peak bottleneck periods of the day or evening. Pressures on checking-in or checking-out at reception and getting rooms cleaned while guests are at breakfast are common bottlenecks dramatically affecting patterns of staffing. With the Novotel approach to flexible skilling and team working, a new pattern is emerging. Flexible working patterns have broken down some of the staff demarcation normal within the hotel industry. Reception and front-of-house activities (e.g. showing guests to rooms) may be carried out by the same staff as serve in the restaurant at peak mealtimes or perform housekeeping or room-cleaning tasks at other times of the day. The benefits of this to the firm have been enormous in a reduction of core staff levels and a more resourceful workforce. However, maintaining universal quality standards as the chain grew rapidly over a 25-year period became more and more problematic, especially when many new staff were recruited from other hotel groups with different working practices.

A system to monitor standard procedures was introduced in 1987 which became known as the '95 Bolts'. This system was intended to be, and duly became, a template for learning. It was a hierarchical system, centrally-designed and centrally-driven. It emphasized structural elements of service and was authoritarian in both concept and style. It was about managerial direction and control. The 'Bolts' were 95 points or regulated systems applied to the 13 main points of staff/customer interaction. These key service encounters or 'moments of truth' included: reservation, arrival/access, parking, check-in, hall, bedroom, bathroom/WC, evening meal, breakfast, shops, bar, outdoor games/swimming-pool and check-out. Each of these key interaction points were divided into a series of compulsory directives for staff, e.g. how to set out a bedroom, lay a place setting in the restaurant or welcome a guest. A booklet containing the 95 Bolts was issued to all staff and was a mainstay in induction for new staff. Monitoring of standards was carried out by an internal team of inspectors who visited each hotel approximately twice each year. They functioned in the same way as 'mystery shoppers' in that they made reservations, arrived, stayed and departed incognito. On completion of their stay they would make themselves known to the General Manager (GM) for review and discussion. Percentage grades were awarded and recommendations made. The 95 Bolts, while helpful to control and consolidate after a period of rapid growth, gradually became over-rigid and procedural in orientation and was replaced by a more adaptive system in 1992.

Source: McGee and Segal-Horn (1997).

Case Questions

1 Describe Novotel's strategy using the 'Describing strategy' framework (above).

2 What are its competitive advantages?

3 How does the value chain configuration help us to understand how the competitive advantages are managed and delivered?

Further reading and references

Andrews, KR (1980) *The Concept of Corporate Strategy*, Irwin.

Ansoff, H (1965) *Corporate Strategy*, Penguin.

Boston Consulting Group (1975) *Strategy alternatives for the British motorcycle industry*, HMSO, London.

Buchelle, RB (1962) 'How to Evaluate a Firm', *California Management Review*, Fall.

Chandler, AD (1962) *Strategy and Structure: Chapters in the History of the Industrial Enterprise*, Cambridge, MA, MIT Press.

Chandler, AD (1977) *The Visible Hand: The Managerial Revolution in American Bussiness*, Harvard University Press, Cambridge.

Channon, DF (2005) 'Value chain analysis', in J McGee and DF Channon (eds) *Encyclopedic Dictionary of Management*, 2nd edition, Blackwell Business, Oxford.

Cronstraw, MJ, Davis, E and Kay, J (1990) 'On being stuck in the middle – good food costs less at Sainsbury's', *Proceedings of the British Academy of Management Annual Conference*, Glasgow.

De Geuss, A (1988) 'Planning as Learning', *Harvard Business Review*, **66**, **2**, pp. 70–4.

Eccles, RG and Nohria, N (1992) 'Strategy as a language game', from *Beyond the Hype: Rediscovering the essence of management*, Harvard Business School Press.

Gilbert, X and Strebel, P (1991) 'Developing competitive advantage', in H Mintzberg and JB (1991) *The strategy process: Concepts, contexts, cases*, Prentice-Hall, Englewood Cliffs, NJ, pp. 82–93.

Grant, RM (2002) *Contemporary Strategic Analysis: Concepts, Techniques and Applications*, 4th edition, Blackwell Business, Oxford.

Hamel, G and Prahalad, CK (1993) 'Strategy as stretch and leverage', *Harvard Business Review*, March/April.

Hamel, G and Prahalad, CK (1994) 'Competing for the Future', *Harvard Business Review*, July/Aug, pp. 122–8.

Kaplan, RS and Norton, DP (1992) 'The balanced scorecard: measures that drive performance', *Harvard Business Review*, **1**, Jan/Feb.

Mathur, S (1988) 'How Firms Compete: A New Classification of Generic Strategies', *Journal of General Management*, **14**, **1**, pp. 30–57.

McGee, J and Segal-Horn, S (1997) 'Global competences in service multinationals', in H Thomas, D O'Neal and R Alvarado (eds) *Strategic Discovery: Competing in New Arenas*, J Wiley & Sons, pp. 49–77.

Mintzberg, H (1987) 'Crafting Strategy', *Harvard Business Review*, **65**, **4**, pp. 66–75.

Mintzberg, H (1994) *The Rise and Fall of Strategic Planning*, Prentice Hall.

Mintzberg, H (1993) 'The Fall and Rise of Strategic Planning', *Harvard Business Review*, Jan/Feb, pp. 107–14.

Mintzberg, H and Waters, J (1985) 'Of strategies, deliberate and emergent', *Strategic Managment Journal*, **6**, pp. 257–72.

Porter, M (1980) *Competitive Strategy*, New York, Free Press.

Porter, ME (1985) *Competitive Advantage*, New York, Free Press.

Porter, ME (1986) 'What is strategy?' *Harvard Business Review*, Nov/Dec, pp. 61–78.

Porras, JI and Collins, JC (1996) *Built to Last*, Century Books, New York.

Quinn, JB (1980) *Strategies for Change: Logical Incrementalism*, Irwin.

Rumelt, R, Schendel, D and Teece, D (eds) (1994) *Fundamental Issues in Strategy*, Boston, MA, Harvard Business School Press.

Seth, A and Randall, G (1999) *The Grocers: the rise and fall of the supermarket chains*, Kogan Page.

Sloan, AP (1983) *My Years at General Motors*, Doubleday.

Whittington, R (1993) *What is strategy and does it matter?* Routledge.

Yoffie, DB (1992) 'Apple Computer 1992', Harvard Business School Case Study, revised August 1994, 9–792–081.

Part 3

Strategy analysis

Part contents

Introduction

Part 2 set up the economic logic that gives us the tools for analysing and formulating strategy. The key concept introduced here is essentially the logic of competitive advantage supported by specific frameworks such as industry analysis, generic strategies and the value chain. The strength of these concepts lies in the way of thinking about strategy. These are intellectual constructs — they are not cookbooks into which one uncritically feeds data. They apply in different ways to different contexts. By themselves they have limited interest. Their value lies in the way in which they can be applied in different circumstances. Part 3 contains a variety of different contexts for which specific strategies have to be formulated.

Chapter 6 articulates the nature of strategic positioning. We call this the market-based view and others have called it the activity-based view. What strategic positioning is about is what activities have to be pursued in chosen markets so as to gain competitive advantage. Positioning is about the deployment of cost and differentiation-based advantages. It is about the identification of distinctive cost strategies and distinctive differentiation strategies. In practice we see the need for detailed analysis of markets and industries, first, to see what the 'rules' are and how to play them but, second (hopefully) to see how we might innovate with our strategies so as to break the rules and get ahead. In industry terms this means understanding how we can be better than our competitors. In market terms it means understanding what the customer wants. Strategy is about value creation and value analysis is an important element of this chapter.

Chapter 7 steps back into the firm and asks what capabilities are needed for the desired positioning to be achieved. This has become known as the resource-based view often captured in the term 'core competence'. This approach to strategy has become very widespread but suffers from a high degree of subjectivity and lack of agreement about terminology and definitions. This chapter sets out to review some of the main contributions and to indicate a basic language to which we might all subscribe. Core competence, like competitive advantage, is an intellectual construct that is useful because it can be deployed in a wide range of situations. The chapter goes on to examine how competence-based competition can be conducted in practice and suggests some practical ways of relating these ideas to value creation.

Following Chapters 6 and 7 we should now have the ability to develop our own strategic theory of the firm comprising both a view of competitive advantage and core competence *and* the way in which they support and complement each other.

Chapter 8 adds a number of important practical dimensions to the strategic theory that has come from Chapters 6 and 7. Basically it introduces the timeline in the form of life cycle analysis – a notable deficiency of Porter-style work is its static character with only a nodding acknowledgement of the importance of dynamics. In exploring different parts of the time line, going from embryonic stages to decline, the chapter picks out some salient issues. First, we discuss entrepreneurs and start-ups – individualism and idiosyncrasy of both people and events but subject to some overarching strategy context. Second, we examine entry strategies, where we look at the extraordinary difficulty of gaining a foothold in attractive industries in the teeth of organized opposition. Third, we look at turnarounds. These come about typically (but not exclusively) when differentiation advantages have been competed away, the strategy is worn out, and performance is not acceptable. This chapter sets out to put strategic thinking into practical contexts, suggesting as we go along how elements such as personal leadership may be crucial.

Chapter 9 shifts the focus from the single business to the multibusiness portfolio. This is the arena of corporate strategy where the task of the corporate centre is to choose what portfolio it wants and to design and manage the organization structure and its management processes. There are other key tasks: the mission statement and the choice of strategic objectives are discussed in Chapter 1. Managing performance is mentioned in many places but Chapter 18 is devoted to the analysis and measurement of performance. In Chapter 9 the key issue is the way in which the portfolio creates value. This revolves around the economies of scope that we introduced and discussed in Part 2, often called synergy by practitioners and relatedness by analysts and academics. Depending on how synergies arise, there are implications for the fit of strategy and structure and for the styles by which the organization is managed. These are discussed in Chapter 9 and also recur throughout Part 4.

Chapter 10 continues the corporate-level theme with mergers and acquisitions (M&A). These are the biggest and riskiest decisions that most companies make. Mistakes can destroy a company but companies can also grow and prosper very quickly. This chapter lays out the context for M&A decisions and explores in some detail the planning of an acquisition and then its implementation. M&A is a highly controversial area: the risks are very high, the rewards are enticing, but the track record of companies is very varied with perhaps more glaring failures than conspicuous successes. But remember that we said strategy is about risk – a theme we return to in Chapter 14.

Chapter 11 introduces the international domain. This again is controversial and risky (you should be getting used to the idea that these are defining characteristics of strategy) because of the difficulties inherent in moving out of one's home base to international markets and to international suppliers. Globalization is presented in its specialized meaning as global standardization (e.g. the 'world car'). This forms the basis for discussion of the two con-trasting strategies of global standardization versus local differentiation. These are a replay of our old friends cost and efficiency on one hand, and differentiation on the other. Not sur-prisingly, therefore, there is the possibility of combining globalization and localization into a joint approach characterized as 'transnational'. Some think this is just a theoretical possi-bility but it has led to widespread discussion about the nature of the multinational firm. The chapter concludes with a profile of the 'flagship firm', a concept originated by Alan Rugman in which he portrays how some international firms can sit at the nexus of opposing forces – international versus local forces, global customers versus global suppliers, and different host governments. Overall the theme for the international company is how to blend and balance host-country-specific advantages (CSAs) with firm-specific advantages (FSAs).

Chapter 12 uses the 'new economy' as a rallying cry. This rests on the observation that information technology and knowledge intensity, driven by highly successful R&D pro-grammes over the last forty years, have transformed the cost conditions and demand conditions to which we became accustomed on the old manufacturing-based economy. Cost structures have become predominantly fixed cost in nature with vanishingly small variable costs. Markets have been transformed by the flood of new products that have redefined the elements of consumer leisure time and the patterns of consumer expenditure. Also signifi-cant (but quite how much is not yet known) is the emergence of a consumer phenomenon based on standardization and complementarity.[1] Customers increasingly and consciously buy products that conform to known standards and that technically complement their existing products and the products that other people have (one buys a new 'Wintel' computer because your Windows-based software and that of your friends will run on it). This means that we are increasingly buying products because other people have them.[2] It also results in very large, quasi-monopolistic market positions for some companies (e.g. Microsoft), dependency positions for others so that, for example, one is obliged to buy Microsoft's operating systems, and expensive market failures for others (On-Digital versus BSkyB). Business risk has risen markedly in these conditions. Strategies have to be adapted to these specific conditions. Maybe, also, these industries are becoming a bigger proportion of the whole economy. Chapter 12 and some of the case studies at the end of the book discuss the reasons why these new economy characteristics have taken hold and indicates how new economy strategies represent significant adaptations to the strategies common in the traditional manufacturing economy.

The chapters cover the areas depicted below in the strategy resources concepts map and the strategy process concepts map (introduced in Chapters 1 and 2 of this book). The shaded boxes represent the primary focuses of this part of the book. The non-shaded boxes are covered in other parts of this book. The degree of shading in the boxes reflects the degree to which these topics are covered here and also indicates the interconnections explored in each chapter.

The maps show that this section concentrates heavily on resource concepts but only lightly on process concepts. Notably this section says little about 'direction', taking it largely for granted and leaving it mainly to the introduction in Part 1 and to the discussions in Part 5. Throughout this part there are references and allusions to process issues. Sometimes the organization structure issues are covered in some depth. Overall, however, process issues are covered in detail in Part 4 but the allusions herein are important in setting the stage.

---

[1] Strictly speaking it is a re-emergence: it was well known back in the nineteenth century as a characteristic of utilities (e.g. railways and the telegraph) but in a sense was forgotten as manufacturing-style cost conditions became pervasive in the twentieth century.

[2] This is characteristic of fashion products as well, where the benefit is psychological rather than practical.

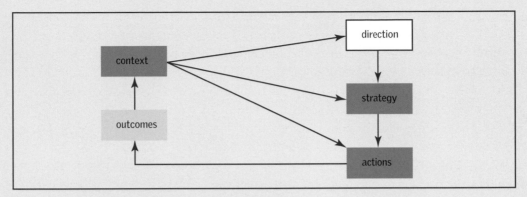

Figure 6.00a Strategy resources concepts map
Based on Figure 1.6.

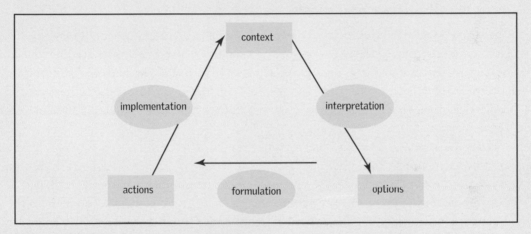

Figure 6.00b Strategy process concepts map
Based on Figure 2.2.

Chapter 6

Competitive strategy: the analysis of strategic position

Introduction

This chapter sets out the essence of strategy as the denial of perfect competition and the search for firm-specific advantages that we call competitive advantage. Chapter 3 developed the economic concepts that underpin the operation of markets. These concepts give us the frameworks and the language for analysing markets and costs. Chapter 4 set out the large-scale macro forces that can shape the fortunes of firms. In Chapter 5 we saw the fundamental importance of the idea of competitive advantage. In this chapter we set out the basic framework of competitive strategy and how it enables us to analyse the **market-based view** that is, as its name suggests, the **positioning** of the firm in its markets versus competitors. The central pillar of this is *competitive advantage*. Chapter 8 presents the *resource-based view*.

Chapter contents

This focuses on the distinctive nature of the resources and capabilities that are required to produce competitive advantage. The central pillar of this is *core competence*. Chapter 8 concludes by relating the ideas of competitive advantage and core competence to managerial tools such as SWOT analysis, PEST analysis, and critical success factor analysis.

Much of this chapter is built upon Porter's original description (1980) of generic competitive strategies, where strategies are characterized as being cost or differentiation based on the one hand or narrow versus broad focus on the other hand (see Figure 6.1). This derives directly from the economist's view of strategy as explained in Chapter 5, where competition can be seen as cost based at one extreme and pure differentiation based at the other extreme. It also includes fundamental ideas of **economies of scope** (from Chapter 3) that are reflected in the vertical axis of Figure 6.1. This idea of a generic strategy is a powerful foundation for understanding the nature and variety of competitive strategies. A generic strategy is a simple typology that captures the essential economic forces at work in a market (the demand side) and in an industry (the supply side). Porter suggested that there are three generic strategies to choose from, and each business unit can have its own strategy. According to Porter, a business can strive to supply a product or service more cost-effectively than its competitors (cost leadership), it can strive to add value to the product or service through differentiation and command higher prices (differentiation), or it can narrow its focus to a special product-market segment which it can monopolize (focus). Not following any of these strategies characterizes a firm as being 'stuck in the middle'. The choice of generic strategy should be based on the firm's business unit's strengths and weaknesses, and a comparison of those with the strengths and weaknesses of competitors.

Generic strategy ideas are pervasive in strategy analysis but not for their operational value. They provide a sound conceptual framework from which more operational ideas can be developed. This chapter develops the ideas of cost advantage and differentiation advantage beyond the introduction given in the previous chapter. It then goes on to look at two powerful grouping concepts – markets segments and strategic groups. The former is well developed in marketing and is explored here for its basis for differentiation strategies and for pricing and value capture. Strategic groups is the idea of industries within industries. It is useful in trying to understand complex industry structures. But it is also valuable in looking ahead to ways in which industries might evolve.

Figure 6.1 Porter's generic strategies
Source: Porter, 1980 Chapter 2. Reprinted with the permission of The Free Press, a Division of Simon and Schuster Adult Publishing Group, from *Competitive Strategy* by Micheal E Porter. Copyright © 1980, 1998 by the Free Press. All rights reserved.

Industry transformation looks at bigger, more revolutionary changes in structure. Finally, we look at business models. This phrase has become current in the new world of e-business, being used to show how the internet creates new rules and new ways of making profits – hence the ideas of new business models.

All of the ideas in this chapter contribute to the way in which the firm positions itself in markets to gain competitive advantage. The concepts and frameworks can be deceptively simple, even generic. But the applications require care with data and with interpretation. Above all, application requires a strong grasp of what the competitive strategy concepts are and how to think through their implications. This chapter should be powerful in helping you turn concepts and frameworks into tools for strategic thinking.

6.1 Industry analysis and competitive strategy: the market-based view

In this section we develop the market-based view in some more detail. Building on Chapter 4, we look at cost analysis, especially at the nature of economies of scale and learning effects, as the basis for cost leadership strategies. We consider further the nature of advantage and the different forms in which it can be seen. Finally, we look at some practical advice when formulating competitive strategy.

6.1.1 Cost advantage

The microeconomics of strategy is built initially on an understanding of the nature of costs. Cost for economists is essentially opportunity cost, the sacrifice of the alternatives forgone in producing a product or service. Thus, the cost of a factory building is the set of houses or shops that might have been built instead. The cost of capital is the interest that could have been earned on the capital invested, had it been invested elsewhere. In practice, money prices may not reflect opportunity costs because of uncertainty, imperfect knowledge, natural and contrived barriers to movements of resources, taxes and subsidies, and the existence of externalities (spillover effects of private activities on to other parties; for example, pollution imposes costs on more than just the producer of pollution). Opportunity cost provides the basis for assessing costs of managerial actions, such as in 'make or buy' decisions, and in all those situations where alternative courses of action are being considered.

Costs are also collected and reported routinely both for purposes of stewardship and for control. The behaviour of these costs in relation to the scale of output is of much importance. We see, for example, that break-even analysis is based on the extent to which costs vary in relation to output (in the short term) or are fixed in relation to output. The distinction between fixed and variable costs has implications for the flexibility a firm has in pricing to meet competitive conditions. Thus, one would always wish to price above variable cost per unit in order to maintain positive cash flow. Fixed costs in this example are **sunk costs**;

they are paid and inescapable, and the only relevant costs are those that are affected by the decision under consideration. It is the behaviour of costs in the long term that has strategic implications for firms and for the structure of industries. The long term is the time horizon under consideration and affects what is considered to be 'fixed'. In the very long term, all economic factors are variable, whereas in the very short term, nearly all economic conditions are fixed and immutable. An economy of scale refers to the extent to which unit costs (costs per unit of output) fall as the scale of the operation (for example, a factory) increases (in other words, as more capital-intensive methods of operation can be employed).

In Figure 6.2 we can see that Plant 1 exhibits increasing returns to scale or, simply, economies of scale. By contrast, Plant 2 shows decreasing returns to scale, diseconomies of scale. The strategic significance of economies of scale depends on the minimum efficient plant size (MES). This is important in relation to market size. The higher the ratio of MES to market size, the larger the share of the market taken by one plant, and the more market power that can be exercised by the firm owning the plant.

Table 6.1 contains estimates of the ratio of MES to market size for various industries in the US and the UK. It is evident, for example, that the refrigerator industry will be much more *concentrated* than the shoe industry (it will have many fewer players) because economies of scale are so much bigger in relation to the market size.

The major sources of economies of scale are usually described as:

♦ Indivisibilities and the spreading of fixed costs.

♦ The engineering characteristics of production.

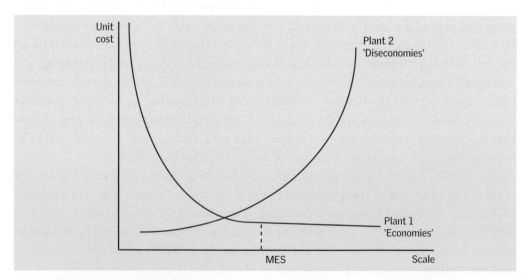

Figure 6.2 Minimum efficient plant size

Indivisibility means that an input cannot be scaled down from a certain minimum size and can only be scaled up in further minimum size units. Thus, costs per unit diminish after the initial investment until a further new block of investment is required. The original examples of 'specialization' (the term coined by Adam Smith) were often engineering in nature. As volumes go up, it is usually cheaper to make work tasks more specialized – as exemplified dramatically in Henry Ford's mass production assembly line operations in the first decade of the last century. Economies of scale also arise because of the physical properties of processing units. This is exemplified by the well-known cube-square rule. Production capacity is usually determined by the volume of the processing unit (the cube of its linear dimensions), whereas cost more often arises from the surface area (the cost of the materials involved). As capacity increases, the average cost decreases, because the ratio of surface area to cube diminishes. (For a full discussion of economies of scale, *see* Besanko, Dranove and Shanley (2000) Chapter 5.)

These general principles apply to functional areas other than production. In marketing, there are important **indivisibilities** that arise out of branding and the creation of reputation effects. There are important scale effects in advertising, as the costs of campaign preparation can be spread over larger (for example, global) markets. Research and development requires substantial minimum investments – another indivisibility – in advance of production, and the costs of R&D therefore fall as sales volumes increase. Purchasing in bulk exhibits economies of scale, in that the price per unit falls as the number of purchased items goes up. Sometimes this is because of monopolistic buying power (for example, supermarkets in

Table 6.1 Minimum efficient scale for selected industries in the UK and the USA

Industry	% Increase in average costs at ½ MES[1]	MES as % of market	
		UK	USA
Cement	26.0	6.1	1.7
Steel	11.0	15.4	2.6
Glass bottles	11.0	9.0	1.5
Bearings	8.0	4.4	1.4
Fabrics	7.6	1.8	0.2
Refrigerators	6.5	83.3	14.1
Petroleum refining	4.8	11.6	1.9
Paints	4.4	10.2	1.4
Cigarettes	2.2	30.3	6.5
Shoes	1.5	0.6	0.2

[1] This gives a measure of the sensitivity of costs across the range of plant sizes.

Source: Scherer and Ross (1990) *The Economics of Mutiplant Operations*, Tables 3.11 and 3.15.

the UK). But each purchase does have a certain element of fixed costs attached to it (writing contracts, negotiation time, setting up production runs) and these may be significant.

The **experience curve**, sometimes called the **learning curve**, has similar strategic implications. The experience curve is an empirical estimate of the proportion by which unit costs fall as experience of production increases. An 80 per cent experience curve arises when costs fall to 80 per cent of their previous level after production has doubled (see Figure 6.3). Strategically, this means that a firm which establishes itself first in the market and manages to build a cost advantage by being twice the size of its nearest competitor would have a 20 per cent production cost advantage over this competitor if an 80 per cent experience curve existed. Experience and learning effects arise where there are complex, labour-intensive tasks. The firm can facilitate learning through management and supervisory activities and coaching. It can also use incentives to reward learning.

In general, economies of scale and experience effects provide the basis in terms of cost advantage for those strategies that depend on cost leadership. The objective of cost leadership strategies is to realize a price discount to the customer and/or a margin premium that reflects the size of the cost advantage. Cost advantages are also available through vertical integration and the exercise of buying power.

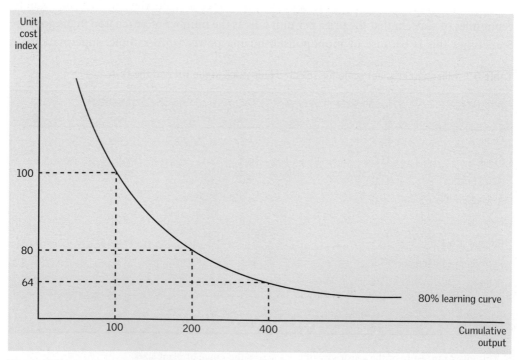

Figure 6.3 The learning curve
Source: Besanko *et al.*, 2000, p. 197. Reprinted with permission of John Wiley and Sons Ltd.

The example in Figure 6.4 is taken from a case study on Du Pont's attempt in the 1970s to dominate the market for titanium dioxide in the USA by virtue of its superior cost position. The cost advantage is based on economies of scale, on experience effects, on vertical integration, and on lower raw material prices. In total, the cost advantage over typical competitors is around 40 per cent. As a result, the competitors were unable to stop Du Pont building scale-efficient new plant to take advantage of market growth – a classic example of a pre-emptive strategy. Similar arguments lay behind the analysis of the rapid growth of Japanese companies in the 1970s. Significant economies of scale gave the opportunity for lower prices, the building of market share, even lower costs, and the gradual dominance of markets. In general, the analysis of **first mover advantage** relies on the existence of significant scale and experience effects, a price-sensitive market, and the willingness to commit capital ahead of competition.

6.1.2 **Differentiation advantage**

We first encountered product differentiation in Chapter 3, where we saw that it was a characteristic of imperfect markets where 'non-price' strategies are important. Product differentiation is the act of making products different from one another. This might involve tangible differences such as quality, reliability, performance or design. Alternatively (or in addition) it might be based on intangible elements such as reputation and branding.

	Ilmenite Chloride	Rutile Chloride *1972 cents/lb*	Difference
From exhibit 3	18.80	21.50	2.70
Less depreciation	−3.00	−2.50	−0.50
Capital charge	6.80	5.60	1.20
	22.60	24.60	−2.00
Learning effect	−4.75	0.00	−4.75
Scale effect	−3.75	0.00	−3.75
Integration effect	−1.30	0.00	−1.30
Capacity effect	1.30	1.00	0.30
Cost per lb	14.10	25.60	−11.50

capital charge   =   investment requirements per lb multiplied by hurdle rate (say 15%)
learning effect   =   79% learning curve and double the experience
scale effect   =   85% doubling effect and twice the scale
capacity effect   =   differences in capacity utilisation

Figure 6.4 Du Pont's calculation of its cost advantage
Source: Du Pont in Titanium Dioxide (A), Harvard Business School case 9-385-40 (1984) exhibits 2 and 3.

Thus, Subaru's cars might be differentiated on the basis of their performance characteristics as attested by their success in motor sport. But Mercedes would rely heavily on accumulated reputation in addition to other tangible differentiators such as build quality.

Differentiation[1] requires the investment of resources – typically time, capital cost and higher variable costs – in a risky bet that the customer will respond to the differentiated product by buying it at a premium price and/or more frequently. The bet is risky because the attempt to differentiate might fail:

1 product quality might fail to improve as a result of the product development activity;

2 a competitor does it better (for example Jaguar is involved in an attempt to catch up with the differentiation power of the German brands BMW and Mercedes);

3 customers fail to respond to the new proposition (see, for example, the failure of laser disks in the consumer electronics market);

4 the costs of differentiation might be in excess of the gains from differentiation – the capital costs and any higher variable costs might not be offset by the new price–volume combination. The classic case of this is IBM's attempts to differentiate its personal computers from the stream of IBM-compatible new entrants in the 1980s. IBM offered a new operating system, OS2, but the benefits of this were not apparent to customers who preferred to stay with the Microsoft DOS system that had become the industry standard.

Successful differentiation makes the market less perfect (see the discussion in Chapter 3) because the firm that has created the differentiation has in fact created a firm-specific imperfection. Product differentiation is therefore the process of creating a competitive advantage by making the product (or service) different from those of rivals to the extent that superior performance results.

In Table 6.2 we can see that there are different bases for cost advantage and differentiation advantage. Cost leadership typically requires large (mass) markets in which minimum efficient plant sizes can be reached. Differentiation, by contrast, prospers in market segments in which different customer needs can be identified and products designed for those needs. The approaches to the market are distinctive. Cost leadership is accompanied by price (low price) strategies, whereas differentiation is based in non-price strategies. Different competences are also indicated. Cost leadership is usually manufacturing and procurement based, whereas differentiation activity is marketing based and R&D intensive. Michael Porter argued, controversially, that firms could not do both and if they tried they would get '**stuck in**

---

[1] It is important to distinguish product differentiation from differentiation as applied to organization structure. The building blocks of organization structure are differentiation and integration. In this context differentiation is the way in which a company allocates people and resources to different organization tasks – the greater the number of functions and activities, the higher is the level of differentiation (*see* p. 56).

	Cost leadership	Differentiation
Cost advantage	Scale and scope	None required
Differentiation advantage	Low (price strategies)	High (non-price strategies)
Market segmentation	Low (mass market)	High (many markets)
Distinctive competences	Manufacturing and buying	Marketing, R&D

Table 6.2 Comparison of cost and differentiation strategies

the middle'. However, his position clearly depends on a particular view of the competences that support cost and differentiation positions. The case box (below) describes the emergence of the scale economy brander in the food processing industry.

Case box: **The scale economy brander**

The consumer packaged goods industries (including the food processing industry) enjoyed halcyon days in the 1960s when manufacturers were dominant. This was a period when mass markets in processed foods were growing quickly, retail distribution was highly fragmented, economies of scale were available, and processing technologies were proprietary. These substantial economic advantages were buttressed by the creation of mass marketing systems comprising national media advertising, national sales forces and increasingly sophisticated marketing support services. The visible output of this business system was the brand, the repository of guarantees to the customer of product qualities arising from proprietary technology. The creation of the brand was subject to many economies of marketing scale, and fostered scale economies available elsewhere in the system. The brand was the visible symbol of the manufacturer's strength, and was the visible barrier to entry behind which grew a series of oligopolies earning monopoly rents. There were seven entry barriers around these brand positions:

1 National sales force and distribution: 'filling up the backroom and stealing shelf space'.
2 Listing muscle: fragmented retailers felt they had to stock the leading brands on manufacturers' terms.
3 Intensive media advertising bought at preferential rates and defrayed across large volumes.
4 Superior product quality arising from proprietary processing technology and/or from consumer perceptions.
5 Low-cost processing either from superior technology or from scale economies.
6 Sophisticated support services, e.g. market research, product management support structure, advertising skills.
7 Discounts on raw material purchases based on volume.

Branding economics was all about premium prices, consumer pull and economies of scale. The association of market share and profitability was well attested in this regime of the scale economy brander. Behind the brand lay a technology edge and a new management structure and style – the style of the marketing company.

These marketing companies came in two forms. The first was the multinational major branders (e.g. Unilever, BSN, Heinz). These were multinational companies operating multiple, related consumer goods businesses across the world, with strong perceived product differentiation accompanied by strong branding. These companies have been traditionally multi-domestic in character as opposed to global (Porter 1986) or transnational (Bartlett and Ghoshal 1989) (see the discussion in Chapter 11 on the nature of international advantage).

The second was the national major branders (e.g. St Ivel). These were nationally based and focused companies with very high levels of marketing support for a product range which, by the standards of the multinationals, were more limited.

Source: McGee and Segal-Horn, 1992.

Questions for discussion

1 Why was it possible for scale and differentiation effects to be simultaneously present?

2 What effect do you think this could have on the pattern of competition?

Sources of differentiation advantage

Product differentiation opportunities arise from the physical characteristics of the product, from the technological foundations of the product, and from the nature of customers and markets. As a shorthand we can observe that 'quality' reflects the physical characteristics of the product; 'innovation' captures the technological dimension; and 'customer responsiveness' reflects market and customer factors. If we correlate these with the tangibility/intangibility dimension we can see Table 6.3 describing the arena in which product differentiation works.

Table 6.3 is a simple representation of the complexity of differentiation. However, you can see the elements that can make up differentiation. Performance and reliability of products (such as durable goods, computers, cars, washing machines) are obvious characteristics but

Dimensions of differentiation	Tangible	Intangible
Quality	Performance and Reliability	Reputation
Innovation	New functional attributes New usage patterns	Modernity
Customer responsiveness	New distribution system	Brand Relationship management

Table 6.3 Dimensions of differentiation

ones which can be imitated. However, reputation is less easily gained and less easily lost. So a Rolls-Royce reputation for automobile quality may linger for a long time even if the objective data on tangible characteristics might suggest that others have long since caught up.[2] Innovation allows for a reshaping of the way in which the product works and the way in which customers use the product. Thus laptop computers are an innovation sitting alongside the desktop alternatives but operating in different ways and places and requiring different technical solutions. Sometimes innovation captures a style (which we have called modernity) that reflects lifestyle choices. Thus, architectural innovation may have tangible effects on the nature of buildings but much of the benefit may be felt in the feel, style and texture of the space. The (high) fashion industry is one where intangibles are predominant and functionality unimportant. Customer responsiveness captures the extent to which products have value because of the degree and style of interaction between buyer and seller. Dell Computers offer the lesson that product features are not all-important. Michael Dell's innovation was to identify that customers valued close interaction between buyer and seller through the distribution system. Dell's competitive advantage rests on the closeness of links to the customer and the entire business is about creating the logistics that give the customer maximum choice and timeliness of choice.

Dell Computers is a good example of how differentiation advantages can be built in self-reinforcing pyramids. Dell innovated, created a new tangible marketing and distribution process, and has also created an enviable reputation and brand name. The more diverse the bases and dimensions of differentiation, the more powerful will be the differentiation effect. As a result companies that are successful at this (see the scale economy branders above) become infused with the differentiation culture. Witness, or example, how the scale economy branders such as Procter & Gamble, General Foods, Unilever and others are known as marketing companies despite their very considerable talents in manufacturing and other non-marketing functions. The prime source of advantage is differentiation secured through core competences (see Chapter 7) in marketing.

Differentiation covers many approaches to the customer. It might rest on a broad market appeal or it might rely on narrow market niches in which it offers highly specific solutions for customers. Figure 6.5 suggests a methodology by which you can begin an assessment of the market and the potential for differentiation. In looking at the product and customer dimensions in this figure you are trying to work out whether this is a market in which common needs prevail or where there is a diversity of needs. Where you might identify commonality and make your differentiation investments accordingly, you are open to the niche player who might target a niche in your market to which a more specific and valuable customer proposition can be made. In mature markets this process of continuous segmentation

---

[2] This is *not* true of the Rolls-Royce reputation for aero engines which continues to be high on both tangible and intangible dimensions.

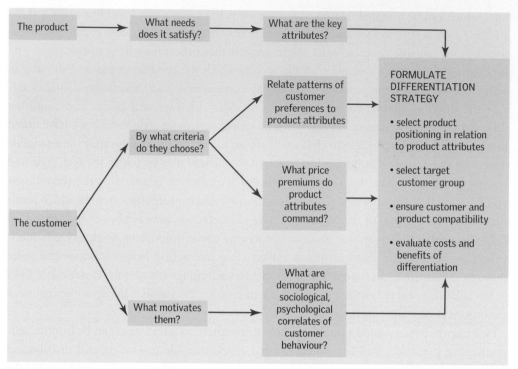

Figure 6.5 Identifying differentiation potential
Source: Adapted from Grant, 2002, p. 287.

allows smaller firms to chip away at the bigger but broader positions of the market leaders. Conversely a niche play is susceptible to innovation by large players such that the niche offer is swept up in a bigger and better offer that covers many segments. The decline of small and medium-size retailers is testament to the ability of large retailers to provide an unmatchable price proposition together with different differentiation propositions.

6.1.3 Competitive advantage

In the case examples on retailing in Chapter 5 we drew the connection between strategy choices and profitability. We argued that strategy choices are resource allocation decisions that enable the firm to create distinctive assets and capabilities (this is the language of core competences, as we shall see below). These enable the firm to create imperfections in markets that are specific to itself and therefore the firm can capture the benefits of this positioning in terms of higher prices or lower costs or both. Figure 6.6 illustrates the point. A successful strategy can earn superior financial returns because it has an **unfair advantage**, that is, it creates, exploits and defends firm-specific imperfections in the market vis-à-vis competitors. We deliberately use the term unfair advantage as a colloquial simile for competitive advantage in order to underline that such advantages are achieved in the face of organized opposition, both from competitors that wish to emulate your success and from customers that will exercise bargaining power to achieve lower prices.

Figure 6.6 Firm-specific imperfections as the source of profits

In theory, competitive advantage is the *delivering of superior value to customers and, in doing so, earning an above average return for the company and its stakeholders.* These twin criteria impose a difficult hurdle for companies because competitive advantage cannot be bought by simply cutting prices or by simply adding quality without reflecting the cost premium in higher price. Competitive advantage requires the firm to be sustainably different from its competitors in such a way that customers are prepared to purchase at a suitably high price. Classic perfect competition works on the basis that all products are so alike as to be commodities and that competition takes place solely on the basis of price. The search for competitive advantage is the search for differences from competitors, and for purchase on the basis of value (that is, the offer of an attractive performance-to-price ratio). Competitive advantage is a statement of positioning in the market and consists of the following elements:

- A statement of competitive *intent*
- Outward evidence of *advantage* to the customer
- Some combination of:
  - superior delivered cost position
  - a differentiated product
  - protected niches
- Evidence of *direct benefits,* which:
  - are perceived by a sizeable customer group
  - these customers value and are willing to pay for
  - cannot be readily obtained elsewhere, both now and in the foreseeable relevant future

The sustainability of competitive advantage depends on the following:

- *Power* – maintaining the levels of commitments in resource terms relative to competitors
- *Catching-up* – ease of copying and nullifying the advantages
- *Keeping ahead* – productivity of one's own continuous search for enhanced or new advantages
- *The changing game* – rate of change of customer requirements
- *The virtuous circle* – the self-sustainability and mutual reinforcing of existing advantages

Economists argue that competitive advantages are by their nature temporary in character and therefore decay quickly. This is to argue that product markets and the market for underlying resources is reasonably competitive. Indeed, much of the analysis of competitive advantage is concerned with assessing just how defensible, durable and large the advantages can be. The Porter five forces framework (Porter 1980) (*see* Figure 5.1) provides a useful basis for categorizing and understanding the industry economics that lie behind competitive advantage and Figure 5.3 summarizes the competitive forces. Notice that the barriers to entry shown in Figure 5.3 are, in essence, the competitive advantages that are available in the industry. They represent the cost premiums that entrants would have to pay in order to enter the industry and compete on equal terms. In other words, these are the imperfections that the incumbents have created (or are the beneficiaries of). It is important to note that the barriers to entry may be generic, meaning that the incumbents do not have advantages over each other, but have a shared advantage with a shared rent. Or the barriers may be firm-specific, implying that different

Supplier/buyer power	**Barriers to entry**
• Relative concentration	• Scale economies and experience
• Relative importance of product to the provider and the user	• Product differentiation
• Credible threat of vertical integration	• Capital requirements
• Substitution possibilities	• Switching requirements
• Control of information	• Access to distribution
• Switching costs	• Scale-independant cost advantages
	• Level of expected retaliation
Intensity of rivalry *High if . . .*	**Pressure from substitutes**
• Several equally strong players	• Benefits not product features
• Low/no growth in market	• Sideways competition
• High fixed costs and cyclical demand	• Comparative price/performance
• Few chances for differentiation	• Comparative technology life cycle
• Large-scale capacity increments	• What business are you in?
• Different 'culture' or players	• Backing by rich competitor
• High strategic stakes	
• Major exit barriers	

Figure 6.7 Behind the competitive forces

incumbents are protected by different advantages and are themselves different from one another. Barriers are also entrant-specific in that different potential entrants have different assets and therefore different ways in which they might compete.

Figures 6.8 and 6.9 show a reworking of Porter's generic strategy table (Figure 6.1) to emphasize that the three routes to advantage are potentially reinforcing. Figure 6.9 outlines

Figure 6.8 Three major routes to competitive advantage

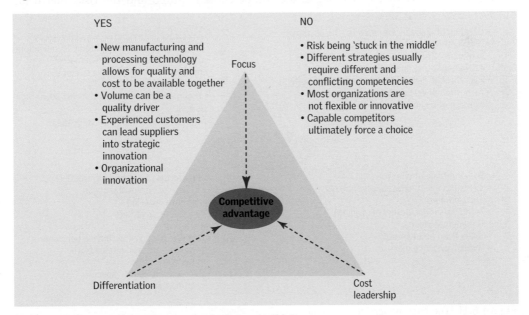

Figure 6.9 Is more than one generic strategy possible?

Figure 6.10 The differentiation strategy

the arguments for and against more than one generic strategy. The argument rests on the point that the different strategies require different resources and capabilities and, therefore, different organizational forms and cultures. The alternative argument suggests that new technologies are leading to more similarities in the strategies.

Figures 6.10, 6.11 and 6.12 summarize the generic strategies in terms of the essence of the strategy, the nature of its advantages, the competences required and the risks that it has

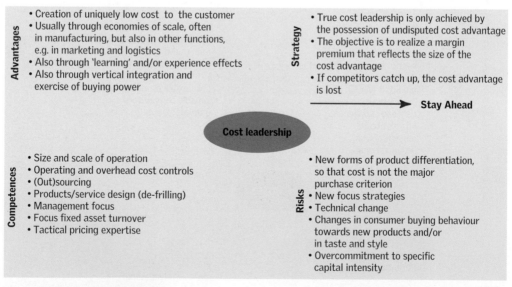

Figure 6.11 The cost leadership strategy

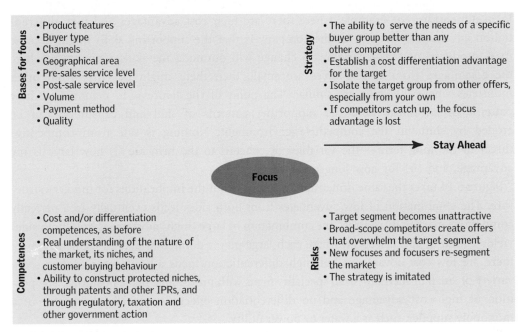

Figure 6.12 The focus strategy

to face. This should reinforce the idea that strategy is about making a commitment and about the deliberate calculation and taking of risk.

Figure 6.13 shows the implications of composite differentiation and cost strategies. The figure arrays cost advantage against a composite differentiation and

Figure 6.13 How industry dynamics shape competitive threats

focus dimension. For example, where there are high cost advantages and high differentiation advantages, the risk for the company is that the supporting skills might become mass produced or that technological change will outmode the skills. Conversely, where the advantages from both sources are small, then there might be entry from other industries where the skills are similar. The point of the figure is to demonstrate how patterns of advantage (and the supporting patterns of skill and capability) can be eroded by shifts in the competitive environment. Nothing is safe from competitive threat in the long term – the variables of concern to the firm are (i) how large is my advantage, and (ii) for how long can I retain it?

Figure 6.14 takes the same dimensions and draws out the implications for industry structure. The combination of low advantages from both sides leads eventually to a perfectly competitive market. By contrast, the combination of large (high) advantages from both sides yields a kind of specialization, where each large player dominates a large segment. Where there are low-cost advantages but high differentiation/focus advantages, we often see a variety of small or medium-sized speciality firms with protectable niche positions. The position of high-cost advantage and no differentiation effects is typically the profile of a monopoly supplier, such as a water or power utility.

Industries and firms differ markedly in the size and shape of the advantages that are available. In Figure 6.15 we array the number of advantages against the size of the advantages. The point of origin is the perfectly competitive solution, where there are very few

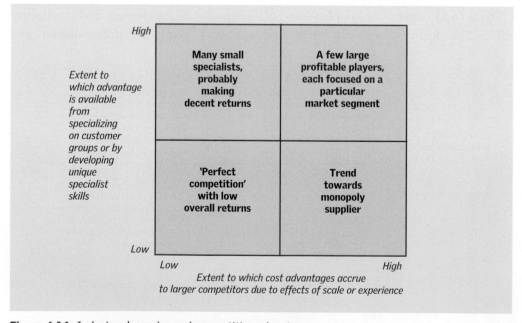

Figure 6.14 Industry dynamics and competitive advantage

advantages and/or the advantages are extremely small. The typical comparison is between the 'blockbusters' and the 'inch by inch' polar alternatives. The blockbuster situation arises where there are very few, usually one or two, sources of advantage, but these are very large in size. The prescription pharmaceuticals industry is like this. Its sources of advantage are research and development (including product registration) and sales force. But products are protected by patent and are typically price insensitive in the markets, so the advantages are huge. Perhaps more typical in most situations is the pattern of multiple sources, but each being of small consequence – the inch by inch situation. This would be typical of much of retailing, where there are a great many ways to compete through choice of product ranges, locations, sourcing policy, staff training and skills, and so on. A more dramatic example is Formula One racing, where the racing teams are very close to each other in terms of performance, but performance does depend on myriad different dimensions. What Formula One does demonstrate is that it is possible for the compounding of many different sources of small advantage to result in predictable and sustainable differences between teams. The source of performance differences here lies in the way in which the resources and capabilities are systematically managed – another resource-based argument.

Read the case box on the video gaming industry and interpret the rules of the game in terms of Porter's five forces analysis. Do this for the original rules of the game and for the new rules that Sony is trying to establish. What benefits is Sony expecting to gain? How would you expect its competitors to react?

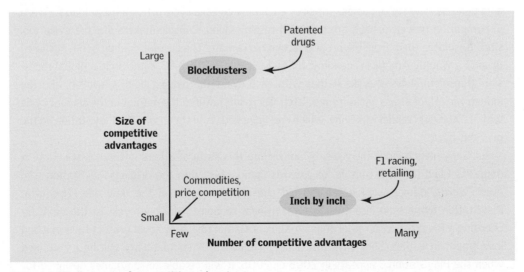

Figure 6.15 Degrees of competitive advantage

Case box: Changing the game in video gaming industry

Something funny is going on in the video gaming business. Sony, the market leader, is changing the technological and business rules that have defined this cut-throat industry for two decades. By doing so, it hopes both to improve its fortunes – earlier this year the company admitted that its revenues and profits had unexpectedly plunged – and to fend off a challenge from Microsoft, which launched its first games console, the Xbox, in 2001. Though motivated by Sony's self-interest, these new rules are also good news for consumers, whether they are seasoned gamers or occasional players, since they impose some stability on a volatile and cyclical industry.

The existing rules are simple: every five years or so, console-makers release new consoles that are far more powerful than the previous generation. The current crop consists of Sony's PlayStation 2, Microsoft's Xbox and Nintendo's GameCube. The PlayStation 2, launched in March 2000, is the most successful by far, with over 60 million units sold, compared with around 15 million units each for the Xbox and GameCube. Just as shaving companies make money on blades rather than razors, the industry works by selling consoles at knock-down prices and making a profit on the games. A game typically costs $50, around $10 of which is passed from publisher to console-maker as a licence fee.

The result is a regular 'console cycle', as one generation succeeds the next. At the end of each cycle, gamers abandon their old consoles and buy new ones, and the whole process starts again. Games written for one console do not work on another, so they also have to buy a completely new set of games. But since each new console cycle offers a great leap forward in computing power, gamers are prepared to play along. Console-makers like the cycle too, since it isolates them from the broader economic climate. The current gaming boom occurred despite a wobbly American economy; the last but one, in 1991–93, came amid a global recession. Console-makers also like it that with each cycle, the playing field is levelled, and the industry in effect starts again from scratch. Microsoft entered the market in the current cycle with its Xbox; its model was Sony, which had launched its first console, the PlayStation, in the previous cycle.

But Sony has changed the rules, by subverting this state of affairs in three ways. First, it made its PlayStation 2 console 'backwards compatible' with the original PlayStation – in other words, games written for the old console also work on the new one. This gave PlayStation owners an incentive to remain loyal to Sony from one cycle to the next. By choosing a PlayStation 2, rather than an Xbox or GameCube, they could protect their existing investment in games. Sony says this policy of backwards compatibility will be maintained when the PlayStation 3 appears in 2005 or 2006: it will be able to run games designed for previous consoles. Since each generation is so much more powerful than the last, this trick is relatively easy to pull off by getting a console to impersonate, or emulate, its less powerful predecessors.

Next, Sony did not kill off the PlayStation when it launched the PlayStation 2, but instead cut its price and aimed it at new, more price-sensitive markets. In 2002, Sony sold 20 million PlayStation 2s and 4 million PlayStations – compared with sales of about 6 million each for the Xbox and GameCube. In other words, successive console cycles are starting to overlap.

Sony's third move is intended to extend this trend still further. It has just launched the PSX, a home-entertainment device that combines a PlayStation 2 with a DVD recorder, a hard-disk based video recorder, satellite and analogue TV tuners, and photo-album and music playback features. As well as cutting down on spaghetti-like wiring behind the TV, this jack-of-all-trades is the first example of Sony's new strategy to combine its games consoles with other consumer-electronics devices. By throwing in PlayStation 2 functionality with other devices at a small premium – made easier by Sony's recent cramming of a PlayStation 2 on to a single chip – it hopes to broaden the market and appeal to people who would not normally dream of buying a stand-alone games console. 'Once they get it down to a single chip, then economies of scale come in, and the potential for integrated devices becomes very real,' says Nick Gibson of Games Investor Consulting.

Playing to win

Together, these three moves have the effect of damping the industry's cyclicality, maintaining loyalty and widening ownership. They also make life more difficult for Microsoft, which is expected to be Sony's chief rival in the next cycle. The Xbox, which was launched more than a year after the PlayStation 2, could never have caught it up in sales. Instead, it was widely seen as Microsoft's trial run for the next round, in which the Xbox 2 will battle the PlayStation 3 on more equal terms. Sony's strategy changes that calculation. As the winner of the previous cycle, it has the most to gain by trying to reduce the industry's cyclicality, in order to maintain its dominance. By overlapping console cycles and spreading the PlayStation 2 into a range of other devices, it hopes to make the coming fight between the Xbox 2 and the PlayStation 3 just one front in a larger battle on a wider landscape. Indeed, says Toby Scott of *Games Analyst*, an industry publication, it now makes sense to consider the PlayStation's collective market share across multiple console cycles. Since Microsoft is now under pressure to make the Xbox 2 backwards compatible too, the next cycle will arguably not start from scratch after all.

That does not mean the console cycle is dead. But it will matter less, which is good news for consumers. In the old days when consoles were killed off and there was no backwards compatibility, says Mr Scott, 'gamers were the playthings of manufacturers'. The changing dynamics of the industry now mean that buying a console, particularly late in the cycle, is much less dangerous than it used to be. If you buy a console this Christmas, in short, you are much less likely to end up getting stuck with a turkey.

Source: 'Changing the Game', *The Economist*, 4 December 2003.
© The Economist Newspaper Limited, London (4 December 2003).

6.2 **Strategic market segments**

In Chapter 3 we saw that the basis for market segmentation lies in the existence of different responses to price (and other marketing variables) by individuals or groups of individuals. Earlier in this chapter we saw how differentiation activities are intimately related to the existence of market segments. One of the most creative endeavours in strategy making has been the seeking out of new markets or market niches to which customized products can be directed. In general we can see that a market can be divided into **strategic segments** based on product range and on associated price differentials. Figure 6.16 illustrates the general case.

Customers are faced by an **offer curve** that summarizes the range of options open to them. This shows what groups of customers exist for each combination of product performance and price. Thus, group A is content with a low product specification and a correspondingly low price. Group B is the larger segment, where both the product specification and price are higher. Group C is higher still on both counts, the premium market. Given this offer curve, firms would be unwilling, in general, to offer a product at point X for two reasons. First, it does not fall into any of the established segments A, B or C. Second it falls above the offer curve, meaning that it is overpriced for that level of product performance. Another way of putting it is to say that at that price the product is under-specified. The shape of the offer curve depends on customer price sensitivities – how much are they prepared to pay for extra product performance? It also depends on the cost characteristics of the product. Thus, the premium product may require different product development routines, and specialized attention in production and marketing. The existence of only a small market for the premium product is likely, due to the high costs

Figure 6.16 The offer curve

involved and the level of the minimum price that has to be charged in order to make a profit. Innovation in the market can transform the offer curve, as shown in Figure 6.16. The innovation, for example, could be due to cost reductions in product development and manufacturing so that lower prices can be charged. A good example is the way the Lexus intruded on the premium car market in Europe and the USA by creating its own version of a premium offer at lower prices than Mercedes. The unfair advantage was the application of the Toyota production system to the Lexus (which is Toyota's premium brand), giving Toyota considerable cost advantage over Mercedes.

Another way of looking at strategic segmentation is to compare price and differentiation patterns across a market. Figure 6.17 suggests a pattern of locations along which the price differentiation trade-off takes place. Starting from point A you can charge relatively higher prices for modest increases in differentiation. This, however, flattens out so that a plateau is achieved around point B, where the price is relatively stable whatever the level of differentiation. This implies a stable price point at which product changes make little difference. Eventually the plateau is broken because differentiation differences are so large as to be able to command higher prices. In this example point C represents a journey through progressively steep trade-offs where customers are prepared to pay disproportionately high prices for modest changes in differentiation. This locus of trade-offs enables us to locate different market positioning strategies. Around point A but below the curve we could see low-cost strategies being deployed. Around point C but above the curve we could see premium-quality strategies. Below the curve and to the right of the mass market located at B we could see a combination of low-cost and high-quality strategies in region D. Although strategies

Figure 6.17 Strategic segmentation

around A, B and C are stable and consistent in relation to each other, the offerings in D have the potential to destabilize the market.

6.2.1 **Identifying segmentation variables**

The bases for segmentation have always been major issue for companies. The conventional approach is to look at the characteristics of buyers and the characteristics of products, as in Figure 6.18. This is a very well known approach and is probably more useful for identifying existing patterns of segmentation than for discovering new and untested segments. Figure 6.18 should remind you of the earlier section on differentiation because the drivers are very much the same in each case. This is to be expected, but what is difficult to do is to develop new bases for segmentation and differentiation. However, the more that all competitors follow the same logic, the more likely they are to end up with the same kinds of strategies. By definition these will cancel out and competitive advantage will be elusive.

The end-of-chapter case study describes the move from 2G standards in mobile telephony to 3G standards. This describes the value proposition of the 3G service, the differentiation required and the segmentation on which it is based. 3G allows for internet connection to mobile telephones, whereas the 2G standard has become almost a commodity-style offer.

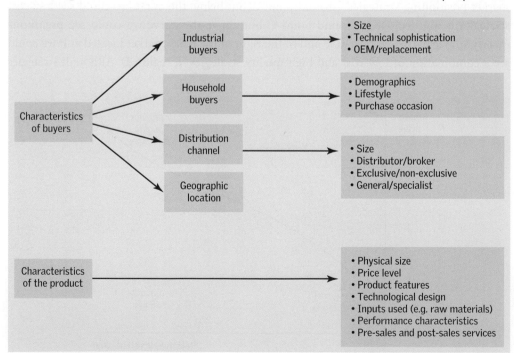

Figure 6.18 Bases for segmentation
Source: Grant, 2002, p. 121.

You should use this example to think about how new technology and development of standards require effective segmentation and differentiation for success.

The analysis of strategic segments leads towards the firm's choice of pricing strategy. In assessing pricing options the firm is essentially concentrating on issues of *value*; that is. how to price in order to gain value to the firm while still delivering value to the customer. The next section addresses this.

6.2.2 **Value creation and value analysis**

The concept of value is central to economics and to the understanding of competitive advantage. The **theory of value** in economics deals with the determination of final market prices (as opposed to factor prices, which are determined by the theory of distribution).

Perceived benefit and consumer surplus

If you buy a car for $15 000 but it is worth $20 000 to you in terms of the services it renders, then you are better off by $5000. This is known as the **consumer surplus**. Given a choice of cars with identical service values, you would (rationally) buy the cheaper car – this would save you money and increase your consumer surplus. The idea of consumer surplus is a profit idea – it is the 'profit' that the consumer makes from a purchase. If the 'consumer' was a firm buying a machine for $15 000 but as a result lowering its costs by $20 000, the value created by the purchase (i.e. the profit) is $5000.

In tabular form:

> *Perceived gross benefit*
> > *less   user costs*
> > *less   transactions costs*
> = *Perceived net benefit*
> > *less   price paid*
> = *Consumer surplus*

Value maps

A firm must deliver consumer surplus to compete successfully. **Value maps** illustrate the competitive implications of consumer surplus analysis. The vertical axis shows the price of the product and the horizontal axis shows quality or performance characteristics of the product. Each point corresponds to a particular price–quality combination. At any time, the series of price–quality combinations available to consumers is shown by an upward-sloping schedule, an indifference curve. The slope shows the trade-off between price and quality; the steeper the slope, the higher the extra price to be paid for increased quality. This is an 'indifference' curve because at each point on the curve the consumer surplus is the same. Above the curve is lower consumer surplus, because prices are higher. Below the curve is higher consumer surplus because prices are lower. Without any innovations in product or process, any firm wishing to price below the indifference curve to gain volume will do so at the expense of profit. Genuine innovation might enable a competitor to make a different 'offer' in the form of a new indifference curve below the original one. This will offer higher consumer surplus, will divert volume towards the new competitor and take volume and profit away from the non-innovating competitor.

   This is illustrated in Figure 6.19 by the luxury car market in the USA (the example is taken from Besanko *et al.* 2000). When the Japanese luxury automobiles Lexus, Infiniti and Acura were introduced in the late 1980s they offered comparable quality to Mercedes but at lower prices. Not surprisingly they gained market share. Eventually the Japanese firms increased prices and Mercedes lowered price, converging on a new and lower indifference curve. Overall the consumer gained – consumer surplus increased. The suppliers would have benefited if their costs had fallen by at least an equivalent amount.

Value creation and pricing

As goods move along the supply chain and into and along the firm's value chain, economic value is created. Firm A in Figure 6.20 illustrates the different value creation packages:

◆ Consumer surplus is benefit less price paid: B – P

◆ Firm profit (or producer surplus) is price paid by the consumer less costs: P – C

◆ Total value created is consumer surplus and firm profit: B – C

◆ Value added (as measured in the national accounts and used as a measure of output of the economy) is technically firm profit less costs of raw materials: P – RM

The firm's pricing decision can be seen as critical in partitioning total value between consumers and firms. A high price claims more for the firm, giving less to the consumer and running the risk that Firm B, for example, might opt for lower prices and attract volume

Figure 6.19 Value maps

Figure 6.20 Pricing, consumer surplus and profit

away from Firm A. With similar costs competitive forces will move the market towards a common price level P. However, if Firm B is innovative and reduces costs to C_1, then it has the option of various prices below P, such as P_1 or P_2. The choice of price depends on the price elasticity of demand.

Pricing, price elasticity, costs and profits

Table 6.4 illustrates the interactions between **price elasticity** for the firm (not the market) and type of advantage – differentiation (benefit) or cost. The four boxes tell different stories:

- With a cost advantage and high price elasticity, it pays to underprice competitors to gain share.
- With a differentiation (benefit) advantage and high price elasticity, it pays to maintain price parity and let the differentiation advantage increase volume and thereby pull profits through.
- With cost advantage and low price elasticity the best option is a margin strategy whereby prices are maintained and profits are increased through the margin benefit.
- With a differentiation (benefit) advantage and low price elasticity, a margin strategy is again indicated where prices can be substantially raised because of the low elasticity and high benefits – profits accrue through increased margins with only small volume offsets.

In setting prices the task is to create a competitive advantage by (i) creating unique value to consumers (best possible consumer surplus) and (ii) creating above average profits for the firm. If every firm were like Firm A in Figure 6.20, there would be no competitive advantage. If one firm can innovate and create lower costs (like Firm B) or higher benefits, then a competitive advantage is possible for a range of possible prices depending on the price elasticities

Table 6.4 Pricing, advantage and profits

	Cost advantage	Differentiation (benefit) advantage
High price elasticity	SHARE STRATEGY Underprice competitors to gain share	SHARE STRATEGY Maintain price parity and let differentiation gain share
Low price elasticity	MARGIN STRATEGY Maintain price parity and gain profits through high margins	MARGIN STRATEGY Charge price premium relative to competitors

of demand and the type and scale of advantage available to the innovating firm. In this situation Firm B would wish to identify the '**break-even price elasticity**', that is the elasticity that would enable it to identify the borderline between a share strategy and a margin strategy.

6.3 Strategic groups

In the same way that there are segments on the demand side, there are groups on the supply side. We call these **strategic groups**. From Figure 6.14 you can see that we have arrayed differentiation characteristics against cost characteristics to obtain a map of different locations for firms within an industry. In this case we looked in terms of the consequences for profits for firms in different locations. The dimensions of this matrix are strategic choices and thus difficult to change and difficult to imitate. Strategic groups are configurations of this kind. They represent substructures within an industry that enable us to identify groups of firms with similar strategies.

A strategic group is formed when:

> *A firm within a group makes strategic decisions that cannot readily be imitated by firms outside the group without substantial costs, significant elapsed time, or uncertainty about the outcome of those decisions.* (McGee and Thomas, 1986, p. 150)

Strategic groups are based on the notion of **mobility barriers**, the sources of which are illustrated in Table 6.5:

> *Mobility barriers are a corollary to the existence of strategic groups. They are factors which deter or inhibit the movement of a firm from one strategic position to another and, more generally, the expansion of firms in one group to a position held by another group. Therefore a mobility barrier is essentially a limitation on replicability or imitation. It acts like an entry barrier, but it acts for the group within the industry rather than for the industry as a whole.*
>
> *A group structuring carries no meaning without costs attached to the imitation of strategy by other firms. Mobility barriers thus reflect the decisions of firms and*

Table 6.5 Sources of mobility barriers

Market-related strategies	Supply and cost characteristics	Characteristics of firms

Product line
User technologies
Market segmentation
Distribution channels
Brand names
Geographic coverage
Selling systems
	Economies of scale:
	  production
	  marketing
	  administration
	Manufacturing processes
	R&D capability
	Marketing and distribution systems
		Ownership
		Organisation structure
		Control systems
		Management skills
		Boundaries of firms:
		  diversification
		  vertical integration
		Firm size
		Relationships with influence groups

Source: McGee and Thomas (1986) *Strategic Management Journal*, p. 151.

are a way of defining the set of key strategies available to a firm. The essential characteristic is relative cost advantage over all other competitors. The remedy for cost disadvantage of this kind probably involves investment expenditure on tangible or intangible assets with significant elapsed time before the investment comes to fruition. Moreover, the investment expenditures are irreversible ... and there will typically be considerable uncertainty attached to the outcome of the investment expenditures. (McGee and Thomas, 1986, p. 153)

6.3.1 The implications of strategic groups

Groups may exist for many different reasons. Investments in distinctive assets and therefore in competitive advantage are risky investments and firms may have quite different risk aversion postures. Thus, strategic positions, which are the outcome of patterns of decisions over time, can be seen in terms of return–risk trade-offs calculated ex ante. Corporate structure may also affect the nature of strategic groupings. Business units can vary considerably in their relationship with their corporate parents and may pursue different goal structures in ways that lead to strategy differences (see Sjostrom 1995). More generally, the historical development of an industry bestows differential advantages on firms depending on their timing of entry (first mover advantages versus follower advantages), geographical location (country-specific advantages), and sheer luck. Whatever the historical genesis of strategic groups, the essential characteristic is similarity along key strategic dimensions. The patterns of similarity and the extent of variety in an industry will have consequences along three dimensions:

1 the structure of the industry and its evolution over time;

2 the nature of competition; and

3 implications for relative performance of firms.

Industry structure analysis is intended to identify the nature and range of profit-earning possibilities for the participants. There are benchmark but simple models of perfect competition and monopoly (see Chapter 3), but the real interest lies in oligopolistic market structures within which different groups of firms may behave in systematically different ways protected (at least for a time) by their mobility barriers. Figure 6.14 illustrates the variety of structural types. Where there are significant opportunities available for both cost and differentiation there will be firms or groups of firms with different strategies and differing expansion paths. This becomes more important as the concept of industry becomes more fluid as entry conditions change, as boundaries become flexible and as 'new' industry groupings are formed (e.g. new media industries, new electronic commerce industries). Industry definition is in itself a form of classification process. Strategic group analysis provides a more fundamental basis for assessing future strategic possibilities and the emergence of new industry boundaries.

Strategic groups affect the nature of competition. Because of their structural similarities, firms in the same group are likely to respond in the same way to disturbances from outside the group and to competitive activities within the group. Here we can see oligopolistic interdependence at work on the basis of ability to imitate the moves of rivals. The interdependence here does not arise from targeting the same customers (although this may be a consequence of similar strategies) but stems solely from the possession of structural similarities.

The ability to explain the relative performance of firms is a central theme in strategic management research. Wide variation in profitability is characteristic of many industries and means that industry structural characteristics are not likely to be a good or stable predictor of profitability. However, mobility barriers (i.e. strategy differences) can explain persistent differences in profit rates between groups in an industry. Porter (1979) argued that the pattern and intensity of inter-group competition and the consequences for profitability in the industry depends on three factors:

1 *The number and size distribution of groups.* Other things held constant, the more numerous and more equal in size are the strategic groups, the higher is the rivalry. On the other hand, if one strategic group constitutes a small portion of an industry while another is a very large portion, then strategic asymmetry is likely to have little impact on rivalry since the power of the small group to influence the large group is probably low.

2 *The strategic distance between groups.* This is the degree to which strategies in different groups differ in terms of the key strategic decision variables. The greater this distance, the more difficult tacit co-ordination becomes and the more vigorous rivalry will be in the industry.

3 *The market interdependence between groups.* Diversity of strategies increases rivalry between groups the most, where market interdependence is high. However, those

strategic groups that possess high mobility barriers are relatively more insulated from rivalry. On the other hand, when strategic groups are targeting very different segments, their effect on each other is much less severe.

Profits may be differentially affected across strategic groups for other reasons:

- There may be differences in **bargaining power** that some strategic groups may have towards customers and/or suppliers. These differences may be due to differences in scale, threat of vertical integration or product differentiation following from differing strategies.

- There may be differences in the degree of exposure of strategic groups to *substitute products* produced by other industries.

- There may be great differences in the degree to which firms *within* the group compete with each other. While mutual dependence should be fully recognized within groups that contain few firms, it may be difficult to sustain if there are numerous firms in the strategic group or if the risk profiles of the firms differ.

There are also firm-specific factors that influence profitability within a group:

- *Differences in firms' scale within the strategic group.* Although firms within the same strategic groups are likely to be similar in the scales of their operations, differences in scale *may* exist and may work to the disadvantage of smaller firms in the group where there are aspects of the strategy subject to economies of scale.

- *Differences in the cost of mobility into a strategic group.* If there are absolute cost advantages of being early in establishing brand names, locating raw materials, etc., a later entrant in a specific strategic group may face some disadvantages with respect to established firms. Timing is in this case a factor that may impact profit differences. This may also be the case if an established firm also possesses assets from its operations in other industries that could be jointly utilized.

- *Ability of the firm to execute or implement its strategy* in an operational sense. Some firms may be superior in their ability to organize and manage operations, develop creative advertising themes, make technological breakthroughs with given inputs of resources and the like. While these are not structural advantages of the sort created by mobility barriers, they may be relatively stable advantages if the market for managers, scientists and creative personnel is imperfect. Those firms in a group with superior abilities to execute strategies will be more profitable than others firms in the same group.

6.3.2 Strategic mapping

It is convenient and conventional to turn the multidimensional concept of strategic groups into a practical tool by drawing **strategic maps**. These are two-dimensional replications of the larger group structure within which the important strategic dimensions can be seen and through which key opportunities and threats can be depicted. The key steps in this process are (following Fiegenbaum *et al.*, 1990, and Fiegenbaum and Thomas, 1990):

1 choice of the strategy space (industry);

2 choice of organizational levels to be incorporated (corporate, business or functional);

3 identification of the variables which best capture firms' strategies;

4 identification of stable time periods;

5 clustering of firms into strategic groups.

The main issue concerning choice of strategic space relates to the identification of the boundaries of the 'industry'. The concept of industry is fuzzy but in practice we often over-rely on Standard Industrial Classification (SIC) codes. However, these mirror product variation and are typically bounded by nationality. The term strategic space is used as an alternative to industry to indicate that the relevant criterion for choice is competitive interaction.

When choosing the organizational level at which to analyse firms' strategies one must not simply focus on business level characteristics such as product and geographical scope, and relative emphasis on cost versus differentiation. Corporate parenting can provide a significant element of the eventual competitive advantage and it would be an oversimplification to exclude corporate effects. Similarly, functional strategies such as advertising intensity and sales force characteristics can be critical investments in support of the business strategy.

On the identification of the variables representing firms' strategies it is common to argue that there are a small number of dimensions that capture the essence of strategy differences between firms and between groups. This suggests that it is entirely possible to adopt a pragmatic approach. Typically an in-depth case study can reflect the views of industry participants, can give peer group judgements on competitors' strategies, and can also give the analyst a database for independent judgement. The alternative is to use clustering and other statistical techniques to determine, de facto, what groups exist and then to interpret the groupings using independent data on strategy dimensions. This is typically the route taken by academic researchers.[3]

---

[3] A number of different methods exist for clustering firms into groups. Analysis of empirical research indicates that most researchers use cluster analysis. Once strategic variables have been identified, researchers generally use clustering techniques to form groups so that homogeneity is at its maximum internally and at its minimum externally. There is considerable debate about the nature of cluster analysis; see Ketchen and Shook (1996) for a review of the way it has been used in strategy research. The advantage of cluster analysis is that it indicates the distance that exists between strategic groups and between companies within the same strategic group. The distance between groups can be considered as approximating the height of mobility barriers while the distance between firms can be used as a basis to analyse the differences between them. The main difficulty with cluster analysis is that it identifies clusters regardless of the presence or absence of any underlying structure (Ketchen and Shook, 1996). Then there remains the question of how to describe and empirically validate the dimensions that the analysis reveals.

Much research in strategic management has studied industry change over long periods of time. This contrasts with research in economics where the emphasis has been much more on cross-section, relatively short-period studies. When studying strategic groups longitudinally there is a problem about identifying the nature of change and the way it affects the groupings. The typical approach is to think in terms of '**punctuated equilibria**'. Periods of stability are punctuated by periods of change within which strategies are changed, new positions taken up, and rivalry adjusts in response. Firms' strategies and industry structure are seen in equilibrium during each strategic time period. When the equilibrium ends (maybe because of exogenous shocks in the environment or alternatively triggered by autonomous firm actions), some firms change their strategies, new strategic groups are formed and others disappear. Statistical techniques can be used to identify the relatively stable sub-periods within which strategic groups are identifiable (see Bogner, Thomas and McGee 1996) and the transition points or periods from one equilibrium to the next.

6.3.3 **Strategic groups in practice**

We illustrate these points by looking at a study of the food processing industry in Europe at the time of the enactment of the European Single Market Act 1987–1992 (McGee and Segal-Horn 1990 and 1992). This looked across conventional market (national) boundaries and asked how the industry might evolve given the exogenous legislation shocks to the industry.

The practical question concerned the possible emergence of a pan-European food industry from the existing mosaic of separate nationally focused industries, i.e. transnational companies emerging from multidomestic structures. This possibility was mooted in the context of the Single European Act, conceived in 1987 for implementation by 1992. This was expected to reduce the costs of access to separate European markets and, along with expectations about increasing homogeneity of consumers across Europe, constituted external triggers for structural change.

The approach to this was to develop a model of '**strategic space**' on to which the prospective movements of firms could be mapped. A historical overview enabled the identification of periods of stability and the conditions causing breaks between periods. On the basis of this history, key variables were identified as the basis for strategic group identification. These were market scope (territories covered), marketing intensity and brand strength, manufacturing focus, and R&D intensity (the latter two were not statistically validated). These were used to identify the strategic group configuration in 1990, enabling the identification of at least four distinct groupings. However, the real interpretive power of the configuration lay in the specification of the mobility barriers between the groups. The strategic space idea is the converse of the strategic group, i.e. why is there no group present in a particular location on an n-dimensional map. The first possible answer is that some spaces are currently infeasible and the asset structures implied by that space are competitively dominated by other asset structures. The second possible answer is that some spaces have never been entered because the construction of the implied assets was not thought to be competitively viable. This second insight allowed the analysis of certain empty spaces to suggest that certain assets could technically be constructed (e.g. European marketing systems and brands) and that changing market conditions might yield a pay-off for those new asset structures.

Thus the strategic group/space analysis allowed the juxtaposition of a changing market situation in Europe with a lowering of mobility barriers between existing groups and the empty spaces. The conclusion drawn is that certain kinds of new asset structures of firms are very likely to be constructed and that these will fall into two or three key new groups. The processes by which this might happen can be identified, including a wave of mergers and acquisitions. The consequences for competition both in the transition period and for a period of subsequent stability can be analysed, although the time period over which the transition will take place could not be identified. The analysis is distinctive in that it is almost entirely prospective in character, laying out a framework for analysing future change in the industry.

Figures 6.21, 6.22, 6.23 and 6.24 summarize the analysis. Figure 6.21 shows the existing strategic group structure in the late 1980s. Figure 6.22 summarizes the mobility barriers that protect each group. Figure 6.23 contains the strategic space analysis and Figure 6.24 shows the authors' conjectures about the group configuration in 2000. The dimensions of the matrix are key strategic decisions faced by firms in this industry, namely geographical coverage of the EC (representing internationalization strategy) and marketing intensity (representing brand focus). The map distinguishes different kinds of brand players, national versus European in scope, and cost-based own-label suppliers.

The authors conclude:

First, two major new strategies are likely to emerge, the pan-European own label supplier and the pan-European brander. Second, the strategic space analysis tells us something about the pathways to achieving these positions. Third, it also tells us something about the nature of competition both en route and in the new structure. This approach does not tell us how long the process of change will take, nor does it say

Figure 6.21 European food processing industry strategic groups, late 1980s
Source: McGee and Segal-Horn (1990) *Journal of Marketing Management*. Reproduced with permission of Westburn Publishers Ltd.

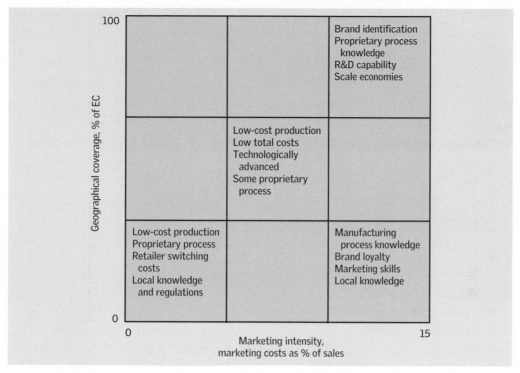

Figure 6.22 European food processing industry mobility barriers, late 1980s
Source: McGee and Segal-Horn (1990) *Journal of Marketing Management.* Reproduced with permission of Westburn Publishers Ltd.

who will be the winners and losers. It does, however, say a great deal about the characteristics of the winners and losers. (McGee and Segal-Horn, 1990, p. 190)

After the passage of time since this paper was written, it is interesting to reflect on the extent to which the pan-European brander space has been occupied. At that time it seemed like an attractive space since it offered economies of scale across a European market that was showing signs of converging consumer tastes, developing its logistics networks and creating fewer larger factories. In the 1990s it becomes clear that Unilever, Nestlé and Mars were beginning to focus on just such a strategy (Johnson and Scholes 1999, p. 129).[4]

Strategic group maps do not have to be historical and therefore 'backward-looking'. History is important in developing an understanding of the nature of mobility barriers and the time and cost involved in investing to overcome them. However, one can assess the present and make forward-looking conjectures. For example, Figure 6.25 is a speculative map constructed in 1996 of retail banking in 2000 in order to assess the implications of new

[4] Note that the Pan-European group emerges with lower marketing/sales ratios because transnationals (and trans-regionals) save costs by eliminating duplication of marketing costs across country markets.

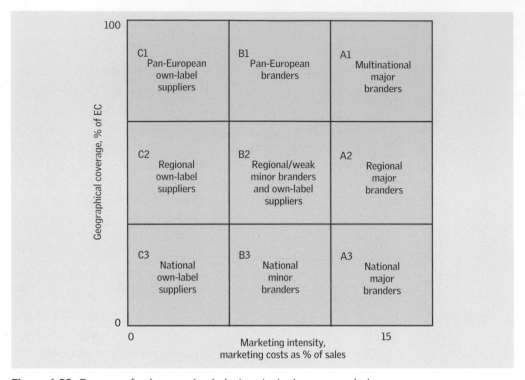

Figure 6.23 European food processing industry strategic space analysis
Source: McGee and Segal-Horn (1990) *Journal of Marketing Management*. Reproduced with permission of Westburn Publishers Ltd.

possibilities such as banking through the internet. The two strategy dimensions are degree of vertical integration and brand novelty. Traditional banks have a 'complete' value chain and do everything in-house whereas the new e-banks focus for the most part on electronic distribution and sub-contract everything else such as cheque processing. The new e-banks have enormous brand novelty indicated by the plethora of 'cute' names such as Egg, Goldfish and Smile. Thus, we have two utterly distinct groups. The first question to ask is, are these groups highly rivalrous, or is the emergence of the new group merely indicative of a new market segment? This poses a degree of threat to traditional banks which need to ask whether they can remain where they are with some strategic adaptation such as opening of new electronic channels of distribution in parallel to their existing channels (viz. the High Street). Or should they seek to develop some brand novelty? Or perhaps deconstruct their integrated value chains into separate upstream and downstream businesses? Or is there a different dimension on which they can play, for instance TV banking? For the new e-banks the question is, to what extent is this strategic group defensible? Should a highly deconstructed value chain be supported by a series of alliances to secure access to best-in-class highly complementary activities?

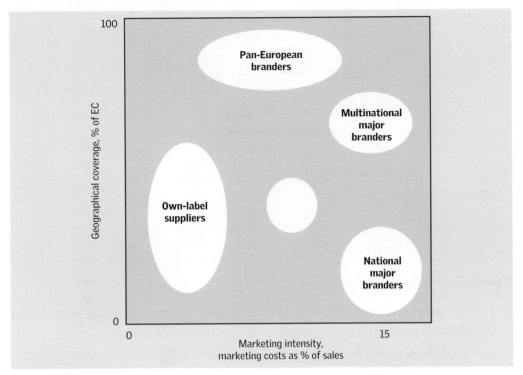

Figure 6.24 European food processing industry strategic groups, 2000
Source: McGee and Segal-Horn (1990) *Journal of Marketing Management*. Reproduced with permission of Westburn Publishers Ltd.

These two examples demonstrate some key themes:

1 Strategic group analysis enriches our discussion of the nature of strategic choice.

2 The formation of groups reflects strategy innovations and risky decisions.

3 The stability of group structures over time tells us, through mobility barriers, about sustainability.

4 The nature of mobility barriers forces us to think about the investments that underpin market position and competitive advantage. It points us towards the nature of resources and the idea of core competences.

Any analysis of group structures leads very quickly from history to predictive ability. The essence of strategic decision is investment in distinctive assets against an uncertain future and therefore strategy innovations and industry evolution are closely linked. Innovation disturbs the industry equilibrium and foreshadows the emergence of new ways of competing and new group structures. Ex ante analysis of possible strategy innovations gives an indication of new strategy dimensions and therefore the nature, pattern and intensity of future rivalry. The pay-offs from this approach can be summarized in terms of interpretation, framework and language, viz.:

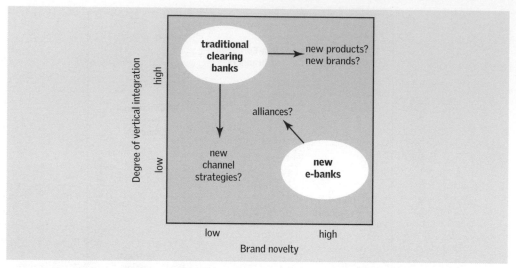

Figure 6.25 UK retail banking, 2000

1 a richer *interpretation* of current industry structures and the interaction of firm asset (tangible and intangible) structures with intra-industry competition;

2 a conceptual *framework* for analysing change over time and across industries;

3 a *language* for interpreting change in terms of asset structures of firms and the ensuing effects on competition in the long run.

6.4 **Industry transformation**

It is common to observe that change is endemic and many consulting firms have been very successful in promoting programmes of strategic change. However, many also note that strategies by their nature are not things that one changes readily or frequently. Strategies involve investment in lumpy and sticky assets without the comfort of knowing that mistakes can be easily undone. Nevertheless, markets and industries do evolve and grow. Growth very often is continuous and cumulative, especially when research and development follows cumulative trajectories. The experience of the last quarter of a century shows that new knowledge has very often moved sideways into adjacent industries and done an excellent job of unsettling long-held beliefs and strategies. Thus, new materials such as plastics have undermined the steel industry and the coming of the internet has caused major changes in distribution industries. So are there any patterns in the way in which industries are transformed? In what ways does Porter's famous picture of the five forces change systematically? Figure 6.26 suggests the major possibilities.

The principal **industry transformation** routes, as a result of which the five forces are reconfigured, are:

1 redefining the market

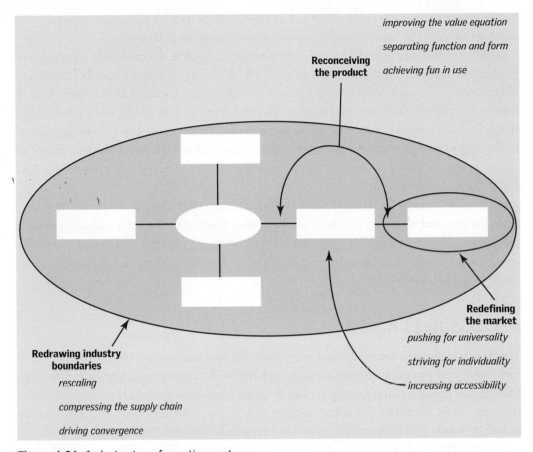

Figure 6.26 Industry transformation routes

2   reconceiving the product

3   redrawing the industry boundaries

Market redefinitions involve changing the relationship with the customer. At one level firms may seek universality, that is, striving to get a wider take-up of their products across hitherto distinct market segments. This is the approach typically taken in internationalization and we could say that Coca-Cola has succeeded in achieving a universal market. The opposite approach is individualization with segments of one person – an approach typical in modern electronic and internet-based industries. Most redefinition strategies have some element of higher accessibility involving major changes in logistics and distribution.

Rethinking the role of the product is also an attempt to capture changes that are taking place in the psychology of consumers. There have been fundamental and controversial changes in the nature of drinks on offer to young people (alco-pops, for example), where the producers have been trying to tap into the rapid changes that are taking place.

Similarly, sports cars are being redefined as toys for the retired. Product changes typically involve changing the value equation (benefit–cost ratio to the customer).

Redrawing industry boundaries stems from major changes in the underling economics of production and of the supply chain in general. The drivers of change are usually rescaling to obtain economies, and driving convergence and eliminating variety to the same end. A simple way of reducing costs has been to outsource more and more but this in itself is not strategic – it is more a rebalancing of the location of costs along the chain. More significant is the compressing of the supply chain, where new technology raises the possibility of changing the nature of the operations in the chain with the effect of changing the product and its cost characteristics.

In Chapter 5 and in this chapter we have often referred to the 'economic model' that captures the essential economic characteristics and cash flows of the firm. In assessing strategic position we wish to be able to relate the intended strategic position and the nature of the competitive advantage to the performance of the firm. In the next section we introduce the idea of the **business model**.

6.5 **Business model**

This is a widely used term intended to provide the link between an intended strategy, its functional and operational requirements, and the performance (typically cash flows and profits) that is expected. It usually applies to single businesses where a specific competitive strategy can be identified but it can also apply to those multi-business portfolios that are linked by strong synergies and therefore have common or similar strategies.

Chesbrough and Rosenbloom (2002) cite their experience in turning up 107,000 references to 'business model' on the World Wide Web while only finding three citations in the academic literature. In the usual practitioner sense, a business model is the method of doing business by which a company can sustain itself – that is, generate revenue. The business model spells out how a company makes money by specifying where it is positioned in the value chain. A more precise definition has been offered by the consultants KM Lab (2000): 'business model is a description of how your company intends to create value in the marketplace. It includes that unique combination of products, services, image and distribution that your company carries forward. It also includes the underlying organization of people and operational infrastructure that they use to accomplish their work.'

Chesbrough and Rosenbloom (2002) describe the functions of a business model as:

◆ to articulate the value proposition

◆ to identify a market segment

◆ to define the structure of the value chain

◆ to estimate the cost structure and profit potential

- to describe the position of the firm within the supply chain
- to formulate the strategic logic by which the firm will gain and hold advantage

The simple Du Pont accounting identities are a good starting point for identifying a business model. Thus:

$$\pi = (p - c)Q - F$$

and

$$NA = WC + FA$$

where

π is profits
p is price
c is variable costs
Q is quantity sold
F is fixed costs
NA is net assets
WC is working capital
FA is fixed assets

An intended strategy should have specific effects on the variables in these equations. For example, a cost leadership strategy would be expected to reduce variable costs, to increase fixed costs, and to increase fixed assets – according to the economies of scale available. Accordingly, profits and return on investment (π/NA) will be expected to increase because the rise in fixed costs and fixed assets due to the investment will be more than offset by the increase in contribution margin $(p - c)$. A more ambitious business model might also specify a price reduction that will result in a volume increase through the medium of a high price elasticity and no imitation by competitors. The validity of such an assumption about lack of competitor response depends on judgements about competitor cost levels and their willingness to sacrifice margin for volume.

Similarly, a differentiation strategy would be expected to raise both costs and prices. Costs would go up because of the variable costs (such as quality and service levels) and fixed costs (such as advertising and R&D) of differentiation. Prices would be expected to increase disproportionately if the value to customers was sufficiently high to make the product price inelastic. This business model then calls for a higher margin game, offset to some degree by higher fixed costs. A more ambitious model might also aim for a volume increase on the basis of higher product 'value' stimulating demand (a rising demand curve rather than a negatively sloped one).

What the business model does is to articulate the logic of the intended strategy in terms of the specific operations that have to take place. With this detailed plan the consequences for cash flows can be determined and the link between (intended) strategy and (expected) performance can be established. Beyond the obvious benefit of quantifying the strategic logic of the firm, the business model also enables sensitivity testing and risk analysis. In the case of the cost leadership example the intention might be to reduce variable costs by a target percentage. The implications of a shortfall in cost reduction can easily be calculated and expressed in terms of the percentage change in profits in relation to a given percentage shortfall from the target cost reduction. Where the business model calls for price changes, the implications of competitor imitation or non-imitation can also be calculated.

In practice a business model can be articulated in terms of detailed plans and budgets that provide guidance to managers relating to their operational responsibilities. The logic that drives plans and budgets lies within the business model. The business model itself is the mechanism through which a business intends to generate revenue and profits. Figure 6.27 shows a schematic (Yip, 2004) that describes the process from inputs to customers – in many ways this is simply a restyled value chain. This should not be surprising – the value chain is an activity map on to which can be placed assets and costs. Figure 6.28 shows an application to the existing mobile telephony business (*see* end of chapter case study). The merit of this is the explicit nature of the choices made and from this the implications for cash flows will follow. A different example is shown in Figure 6.29. This describes the leasing operations of a London bank. This shows clearly the performance dimensions at the top of the figure. Shareholder value is decomposed into components such as market share, price and costs. The bottom of the figure shows the drivers of the cash flows, starting with characteristics such as flexibility and moving upwards to a higher level of aggregation to customer satisfaction and brand strength from which the cash flows stem directly. This is an unusual picture of a business

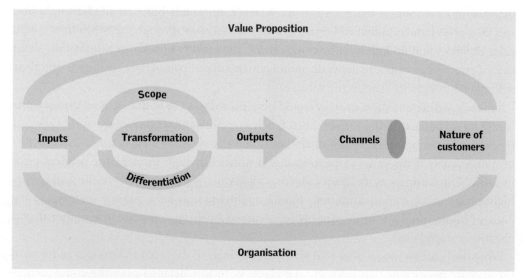

Figure 6.27 Elements of a business model
Source: Yip, 2004.

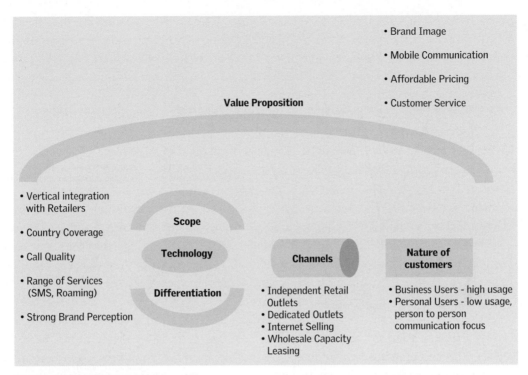

Figure 6.28 The 2G business model
Source: Puri, 2004.

model because it is not faithful to the value chain idea – only selected activities are shown. You should look at this and ask yourself (i) is this likely to be an accurate model if some variables are excluded? (ii) not all the variables are observable and quantifiable – does this matter? and (iii) what extra information would you require (hint: consider sensitivity analysis)?

6.5.1 **Commitment and sustainability**

The business model has become a standard part of the business lexicon to indicate the way cash flows are underpinned by a strategic logic. For the business model to be genuinely useful it needs to reflect the sustainability and defensibility of its strategic position and the nature of the commitment that is required in the strategic assets of the firm. Recall the strategy cycle (Figure 5.9) and note that the top line requires a balancing of resources and assets with the market position. The resource and asset component of this is discussed in the next chapter. Sustainability of the strategic position is to do with the imitability (or otherwise) of the competitive advantage. The five forces model gives an indication of the overall attractiveness of the industry – attractiveness means the degree to which the profits of the industry players are protected from erosion by the five competitive forces. More specifically, sustainability is to do with the insulation of the net cash flows (and the net present value of

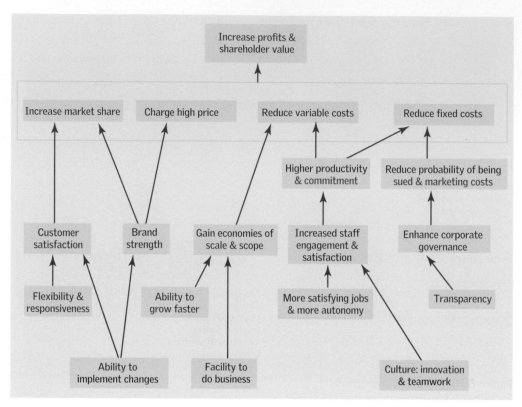

Figure 6.29 London bank: leasing business model
Source: Tello, 2004.

the firm) from attack by any individual competitor. A failing of the generic five forces model is its inability to move beyond the industry on average or in general. Sustainability analysis involves analysing potential responses by competitors and potential entrants and the impact of those actions on the degree of competition and on the cash flows that are generated by the competitive advantage of the incumbent firm. Richard Rumelt invented the term **isolating mechanisms** to refer to the economic forces that limit the extent to which a competitive advantage can be neutralized or duplicated. Isolating mechanisms are to the firm what entry barriers are to an industry – they are the forces that inhibit other firms from competing away profits from incumbent firms. There are different approaches to identifying and classifying isolating mechanisms (*see* Rumelt 1984; Ghemawat 1991, 1994a, 1994b; Yao 1988). Besanko *et al.* (2000) put them in two distinct groups.

Impediments to imitation

These isolating mechanisms prevent firms from imitating and/or surpassing the resources, competences and strategic assets that underpin the incumbent's advantage. Thus, many firms compete in the executive car markets but few, if any, can match the approach of BMW and Mercedes. Note, however, the concerted efforts of Audi, Jaguar and Lexus to do so. In the soft drinks industry Coca-Cola has been unrivalled in fostering its brand name as a symbol of uniqueness. These impediments include legal restrictions, superior access to inputs or to customers, and intangible barriers (resource-based) to imitating the incumbent's core competences.

Early mover advantages

Once a firm establishes a competitive advantage then certain economic forces can protect its position. We saw earlier in this chapter the example of Du Pont in titanium dioxide. Its first move pre-empted the market by establishing a requirement for sufficiently large size to attain competitive costs that there was insufficient room in the market for followers. Similarly, Microsoft's position as the effective standard in the personal computer industry (see Chapter 13 for an analysis of network effects) has meant that no follower has been able to create a value proposition for consumers such that they would be willing to incur the costs of switching to a new (and presumably much improved) standard. These impediments are all related to market size and scale economies, and also to technological change and the creation of legally recognized or de facto standards.

Firms usually analyse isolating mechanisms through a process of competitor analysis (*see* Channon, 1988). This can take a variety of forms but usually contains a number of common headings:

- Identifying which competitors to track
  - existing direct competitors
  - new and potential entrants
- Establishing a competitor database
  - surveying sources of competitor intelligence
  - collecting data regularly and systematically
  - building and using the database
- Analysing competitor strategies
  - functional strategies
    - marketing
    - production/operations
    - R&D
    - financing strategy
  - business unit strategies
  - corporate/group objectives
  - long-term financial capability

Competitor analysis is capable of giving insight into ways in which the incumbent's core competences might be imitated or outflanked. Sometimes this can be done by direct observation of the activities of competitors and making appropriate inferences. A longer-range warning might come from studying the stated and sometimes covert intentions of significant competitors. Thus, Citibank and Chase Manhattan might have credited the possible appearance of HSBC[5] as a global competitor as it began its move out of its Hong Kong base in the early 1980s. It is now bigger than Chase.

These ideas are captured in the case box below, which discusses changes in the business model for large pharmaceutical companies.

Case box: Big trouble for Big Pharma

Why Big Pharma urgently needs a new business model

When GlaxoWellcome and SmithKlineBeecham announced their merger in 2000 to form GlaxoSmithKline (GSK), the world's second-largest drug firm, its new boss, Jean-Pierre Garnier, said that the merged firms would be 'the kings of science.' This week GSK unveiled its crown jewels: a full pipeline of compounds in research and development, the result of a £2.6 billion ($4.5 billion), 16,000-researcher-strong effort. 82 new drugs and 20 vaccines are in development, 44 of them moving into later-stage trials. Yet if Mr Garnier hoped that these numbers would impress his shareholders, he had to think again: GSK's share price actually fell on the news. Like investors in many other big drug firms, GSK's shareholders have little confidence that many of its new compounds will earn them a cent anytime soon. Of the 20 drugs that GSK plans to put into final-phase human testing in the next three years, the chances are, on current industry averages, that less than half of them will make it to market.

Next, consider Merck. On November 20th, news that the firm was stopping development of a diabetes drug after finding tumours in lab mice was met with dismay – and a wave of selling that knocked 11% off the firm's already-battered share price. With another vaunted project – an experimental anti-depressant – also failing last month, Merck's near-term pipeline now looks horribly empty. Even an upbeat profit forecast for next year, on December 3rd, did not cheer investors much.

Merck and GSK are not alone. In 1998–2002, according to Lehman Brothers, Big Pharma firms launched on average 59 drugs per year. In 2002–06, reckons Lehman, they will launch just 50 per year. Moreover, as many patents for the industry's existing products expire in the next five years, competition from generic-drug makers will threaten $30 billion (one-fifth) of annual sales in America alone, says AT Kearney, a consultancy.

When the drugs don't work

Big Pharma now faces two big challenges. First, control costs better. Stuart Walker, head of the Centre for Medicines Research International, reckons that total industry spending on R&D

---

[5] Formerly the Hong Kong and Shanghai Banking Corporation.

will reach $50 billion this year, over 25% up on 1998. Sales and marketing overheads have soared, too. In the past four years, says Dean Hart, head of North American sales at Takeda, a Japanese drug firm, the number of sales representatives employed by drug firms in America has risen by 54%, to 90,000. Each rep costs on average $200,000 a year. Sales, general and administrative expenses account for 17% of a typical big American firm's revenues, says Christopher White of AT Kearney. In the drug industry, such overheads (even excluding the big American sales forces) account for 33% of revenues. Standard management practices such as consolidating procurement, outsourcing personnel and finance functions and automating transaction processing all compare poorly with other industries, says Mr White. Many firms still make pills in-house, a job perhaps better done by a contract manufacturer.

But the tougher challenge is to improve the productivity of R&D. As Mr Walker points out, it is not just the number of new products that has fallen in recent years, but also their originality. Less than 30% of drugs launched last year were first or second in their class. The proportion was far higher in the late 1990s. Roughly 40% of R&D spending by Big Pharma is now on 'line extensions' – improving existing drugs, not creating entirely new ones.

Many big drug firms have begun to license more of their technology and products from outside companies, especially biotechnology start-ups: having slumped in recent years, the value of biotech firms is now rising again. Novartis has set up a big R&D centre in Cambridge, Massachusetts, in part to better position itself to collaborate with outside academics. Eli Lilly's InnoCentive subsidiary runs a website where problems confronting drugmakers, such as how to generate a particular compound in chemical synthesis, are posted to be tackled by more than 25,000 registered problem-solvers as far afield as Russia and China. For a reward of $10,000–100,000, the firm gets a solution that would have cost more time and money to solve itself.

Others hope to improve the way they manage in-house R&D. Wyeth is encouraging its researchers to perform their tasks better by changing how it pays them. Unusually for the industry, its scientists get to share a bonus pool which depends, in part, on how many new drugs they launch each year. There used to be a temptation for Wyeth's early-stage researchers to throw their work 'over the wall' before it was ready to the scientists who run clinical trials, says Robert Ruffolo, the firm's head of research. Because early-stage researchers now share incentives with later-stage scientists, the later-stage researchers have begun to 'pull' the development of the most promising compounds forward. A corresponding 'push' from early-stage workers hastens the process. GSK fundamentally reorganised its R&D in 2001, splitting its more creative arm into smaller 'centres of excellence', and enlarging the arm that enjoys economies of scale. Mr Garnier claims that his 'best of both worlds' strategy is now paying off.

The industry's bloated overheads appear to be driving its decisions on the sort of drugs it seeks to develop. Like a supermodel who will not get out of bed for less than $10,000 a day, Big Pharma has decided that it is simply not worth investing in anything but a blockbuster.

This means that lesser, albeit interesting, compounds fall by the wayside. An oft-quoted figure from the Tufts Centre for the Study of Drug Development puts the average cost of bringing a new drug to market at $897m. But as F.M. Scherer, an economist, points out, this is an average cost for big firms producing drugs for chronic diseases. Other firms can bring drugs for other complaints – infectious diseases or rare conditions, say – to the market for around $100m–200m.

Big Pharma also needs to do something about its poorly trained, generalised sales force, which is simply not equipped to chase smaller, more specialised markets. Most sales calls end, at best, with just a few seconds of a doctor's time, laments Mr Hart of Takeda. Some reps do not even make it past the reception desk before dropping off their free samples. Drug firms lag behind other industries in the way they use information technology to discriminate between profitable and unprofitable customers. Only one in five drug companies invests in any sales force training beyond initial courses offered to recruits. Who, after all, needed to bother with trifles such as training and IT when, without much effort, a drug such as Lipitor, Pfizer's cholesterol-lowering medicine, was making sales of $8.6 billion last year alone?

Can Big Pharma achieve transformation without changes at the top? The bosses of big drugs firms have been horribly slow to grasp the enormity of their problems. Until recently, Merck's boss, Raymond Gilmartin, has been reluctant to license much technology from outside, instead putting his faith in the firm's own scientists. With Merck's in-house R&D now struggling, it will be no surprise if Mr Gilmartin's head is the first to roll.

Source: 'Big Trouble for Big Pharma', *The Economist*, 4 December 2003.
© The Economist Newspaper Limited, London (4 December 2003).

6.6 Summary

This chapter has examined the notion of competitive advantage from the viewpoint of establishing and defending strategic position in the marketplace. This requires a deep understanding of the economic drivers of the firm, its essential cost position, its approach to differentiating itself in the market from its competitors, and its chosen position in the market in terms of ability to exploit natural economies of scale and scope. We have also looked at what competitive advantage means to customers and to firms and the ways firms have of understanding their positions in terms of strategic market segments (on the demand side) and of strategic groups (on the supply side). This leads to an understanding pricing and value and the sustainability of value over time. Any competitive strategy has to be turned into action – the notion of the business model is the way in which the firm's individual theory of its business (its competitive strategy) is turned into cash flows. A proper understanding of the business model leads to an appreciation of how the strategy might be sustained into the future (sustainability).

In the next chapter we turn our attention to the assessment of strategic capability, those core competences that underpin competitive advantage and are the target of the firm's strategic investment programmes.

Key terms

Bargaining power *225*

Break-even price elasticity *222*

Business model *234*

Consumer surplus *219*

Early mover advantages *239*

Economies of scope *196*

Experience curve *200*

First mover advantage *201*

Indivisibilities *199*

Industry transformation *232*

Isolating mechanisms *238*

Learning curve *200*

Market-based view *195*

Mobility barriers *222*

Offer curve *216*

Positioning *195*

Price elasticity *221*

Punctuated equilibria *227*

Strategic groups *222*

Strategic maps *225*

Strategic market segments *216*

Strategic space *227*

Stuck in the middle *202*

Sunk costs *197*

Theory of value *219*

Unfair advantage *206*

Value maps *219*

Recap questions and assignments

1 Read the case box on the video gaming industry and interpret the rules of the game in terms of Porter's five forces analysis. Do this for the original rules of the game and for the new rules that Sony is trying to establish. What benefits does Sony expect to gain? How would you expect its competitors to react?

2 Read the case box that discusses changes in the business model for large pharmaceutical companies. Identify the original business model by which these companies have traditionally earned high profits. Why has this model become unsustainable? Is this because industry forces have gradually eroded the traditional imperfections upon which firms could build their profits? Or, alternatively, have there been significant shifts in the business environment that have outdated their strategies. Define the new business model. What are its risks?

Online
Learning Centre

When you have read this chapter, log on to the Online Learning Centre website at www.mcgraw-hill.co.uk/textbooks/mcgee to explore chapter-by-chapter test questions, further reading and more online study tools for strategy.

Case 1 **Mobile telephony and the move from 2G to 3G standards**

The 3G business model

The transition from 2G to 3G business model is not a radical step change. With the introduction of WAP and GPRS services, the 2G business model is continually evolving. The proposed 3G business model is the culmination of this evolution. Of course business models are dynamic, like strategy, and will continually alter with rapid technology introduction (Yip 2004).

The 3G business model is muddied by the number of services that an operator can offer. The 3G platform allows enhanced data services and therefore the complexity of the service offering is increased. Obviously, since 3G is essentially offering 2G services, part of the business model stays the same; however, many new business models need to be amalgamated with this existing voice telephony model.

The 3G business model identifies two distinct uses a mobile operator may offer its customer base: a provider of communication and a mobile exchange. The network operator must try to provide the characteristics that will make each of these offerings successful in the marketplace and build a business model that will be sustainable.

3G as communication provider

The role of the communications provider is to allow customers to send and receive communications over the mobile network to which they are connected.

- **The value proposition** – in this case, is similar to that in the 2G case. Mobility and convenience of communication is clearly an advantage to the customer. The value proposition is enhanced by a strong brand image that confers the psychological risk reduction of branding on the customer. The newest entrant to the market, 3 UK, may suffer from this as they have no particular brand image at present. Negative publicity over network problems will further disadvantage the company, which has obviously spent millions in trying to build a brand. Although Vodafone and Orange may hold premium place in the branding stakes, it is important to realize that a branding strategy needs to be aligned with the customers you intend to target. Vodafone's premium position may be a disadvantage if pressure on call charges increases. Customers are looking to pay the least they can for what is now viewed as a commodity market and Vodafone's perceived higher prices may put customers off.

- **Differentiation** – is the step that operators must take if indeed they are to price calls higher than competitors. In the 2G world, Vodafone (and to a certain extent O_2) was able to create the impression that its network was of higher quality and dropped less calls than T-Mobile and Orange. These factors lead business customers and other high-value users to subscribe to the Vodafone connection as being the premium network. In the world of 3G, voice will be the main driver and to protect revenues operators must establish a differentiation between themselves and competitors. Handset range is a potential differentiator. 3 UK has suffered badly from being unable to provide customers with a handset range that meets the standards of the newest 2G phones. 3G phones need significant improvement in aesthetics and battery power if they are to be considered a viable alternative to the current crop of 2G phones. The average customer is looking for a phone that can be considered a fashion accessory and it could take some time before 3G phones reach this stage (Morrison 2003). Another strong avenue of differentiation must be customer service. T-Mobile ploughed millions of pounds into the renovation of the customer service department before and after rebranding from One2One. One2One was always associated with poor levels of customer service and high levels of churn. Rebranding meant that T-Mobile was focusing on new market segments and customer services had to be of industry standard before marketing to these customers could occur.

◆ **The channels of distribution** – are also not greatly changed for this particular 3G offering. Independent retailers offer an excellent way of getting phones to market and do not require the expense of building expensive prime-located stores. Carphone Warehouse dominate this market and more than 27 per cent of customers say that it would be the first place they would go if they wanted to find out more about their phone (ICM Research 2003). Interestingly, dedicated retailers Orange and Vodafone, which have invested large sums in building up the branding of their stores, come second and third in the poll. O_2 and T-Mobile stores lag further behind after a string of independents such as The Link and Phones 4 U. The findings show that the companies that lead the branding stakes are also foremost in the minds of customers when they are thinking about their phones. Vodafone and Orange consistently score higher on brand awareness surveys than other networks and customers automatically think of these brands when they want to make changes to the way they use their phones (Wolff Olins 2004).

Preferred mobile phone retailers

Retailer	Percentage of customers
Carphone Warehouse	27%
Orange shops	18%
Vodafone shops	16%
The Link	16%
Phones 4 U	9%
O_2 shops	5%
T-Mobile shops	5%

Source: ICM Research, 2003.

◆ **Segmentation of customers** – is an extremely important stage that requires operators to begin thinking in different ways. Operators must think of the consumer base as different sub-groups, which can be characterized by different needs, some of which will overlap. Remembering that voice is very much the main driver, tariff plans must be altered to accommodate the needs of a majority of these groups. In August 2003, 51 per cent of customers on 3 UK admitted to voice and SMS being the primary reason they purchased a new phone and connection (Deutsche Bank 2003). An analysis of the market shows that there are many types of users, each with different usage patterns of voice and SMS products. By mapping these on to axes we can see which particular services operators will have to target when putting together tariffs to appeal to these different segments. The business community can be seen as a large range of users that primarily use voice services but may be high users of text messages as well. Users in an older demographic can be considered low users of either service, with mobility and convenience being their main concern. The main group of users relates to customers in a middle-age demographic, but even this must be segmented. Traditional users continue to use their handset as a voice-calling instrument and do not use other services heavily. Prepay customers look to receive more calls and send more SMS messages, while the upwardly mobile users are high-worth customers that use their phone for all occasions. Between these groups are students, who look to minimize payments by sending SMS messages, and children under 15, who may have parental limits on the amount they spend. It must be remembered that there are many other variables to be considered when deciding tariff and this analysis is simply a guide.

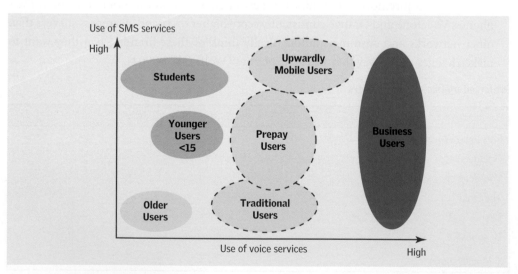

3G voice and SMS services segmentation

Other segmentation factors

Factor	High-end user	Low-end user
Handset style	Upwardly mobile user	Older user
Price sensitivity	Prepay user	Business user
Interconnect allowances	Upwardly mobile user	Older user
International options	Upwardly mobile user; students	Younger users

Source: Puri, 2004.

Case Questions

1 Describe the strategy being followed to move to the 3G standard.

2 What are the bases for differentiation and segmentation? Try to describe these in terms of Tables 6.3 and 6.5 and Figure 6.18.

3 Is there anything novel about the approach described here?

4 Can you suggest alternative, new ways for differentiating innovative products?

Further reading and references

Bartlett, C and Ghoshal, S (1989) *Managing Across Borders*, Hutchinson, London.

Besanko, D, Dranove, D and Shanley, M (2000) *The Economics of Strategy*, (2nd edition), John Wiley & Sons, New York.

Bogner, WC, Thomas, H and McGee, J (1996) 'A Longitudinal Study of the Competitive Positions and Entry Paths of European Firms in the US Pharmaceutical Market', *Strategic Managment Journal*, **17**, **2**, pp. 85–107.

Chesbrough, H and Rosenbloom, RS (2002) 'The role of the business model in capturing value from innovation: evidence from Xerox Corporation's technology spin-off companies', *Industrial and Corporate Change*, **11**, **3**, pp. 529–55.

Deutsche Bank (2003) 'European Wireless Review', May, Deutsche Bank Equity Research, London.

Economist, The, 'Big Trouble for Big Pharma', 4 December 2003.

Fiegenbaum, A and Thomas, H (1990) 'Strategic Groups and Performance: The US Insurance Industry 1980–84', *Strategic Management Journal*, **11**, pp. 197–215.

Fiegenbaum, A, Tang, MJ and Thomas, H (1990) 'Strategic Time Periods and Strategic Group Research: Concepts and an Empirical Example', *Journal of Management Studies*, **27**, pp. 133–48.

Ghemawhat, P (1989) 'Du Pont's Titanium Business (A)', Harvard Business School Case Study 9–390–112.

Ghemawat, P (1991) 'Commitment: the Dynamic of Strategy', Free Press, New York.

Ghemawat, P (1994a) 'Du Pont in Titanium Dioxide (A)', Harvard Business School Case Study 9–385–140.

Ghemawat, P (1994b) 'Capacity Expansion in the Titanium Dixoide Industry', *Journal of Industrial Economics*, XXXIII, December, pp. 145–63.

Grant, RM (2002) *Contemporary Strategy Analysis*, 4th edition, Basil Blackwell, Oxford.

HMSO (1978) *A Review of Monopolies and Mergers Policy*, cmnd 7198, London.

ICM Research (2003) 'Do People Want More from their Mobiles?', ICM Research Review, July, pp. 3–4, ICM Research, London.

Johnson, G and Scholes, K (1999) *Exploring Corporate Strategy*, Prentice Hall, Hemel Hempstead.

Ketchen, DJ and Shook, CL (1996) 'The Application of Cluster Analysis in Strategic Management Research: An Analysis and Critique', *Strategic Management Journal* **17**, pp. 441–58.

Kitchen, S (2000) 'Connections in the Wireless World', Warwick Business School, September.

KM Lab (2000) www.Kmlab.com/4Gwarfare.html, 20 June.

MacMillan, I and McGrath, RG (1997) 'Discovering New Points of Differentiation', *Harvard Business Review*, July/August, pp. 3–11.

McGee, J and Thomas, H (1986) 'Strategic Groups: Theory, Research and Taxonomy', *Strategic Management Journal*, **7**, **2**, pp. 141–60.

McGee, J and Segal-Horn, S (1990) 'Strategic Space and Industry Dynamics', *Journal of Marketing Management*, **6**, **3**, pp. 175–93.

McGee, J and Segal-Horn, S (1992) 'Will There Be a European Food Processing Industry?' in S Young and J Hamill (eds) *Europe and the Multinationals: Issues and Responses for the 1990s*, Edward Elgar.

McGee, J and Channon, DF (eds) (2005) *The Encyclopaedic Dictionary of Strategic Management*, 2nd edition, Blackwell Publishing, Oxford.

Miller, D (1992) 'The Generic Strategy Trap', *Journal of Business Strategy*, **13**, **1**, pp. 37–42.

Morrison, D (2003) 'Calling up a New Strategy', *New Media Age*, October, pp. 24–7.

Porter, ME (1979) 'The Structure within Industries and Company Performance', *Review of Economics and Statistics*, **61**, May, pp. 214–27.

Porter, ME (1980) *Competitive Strategy: Techniques for Analysing Industries and Competitors*, Free Press, New York.

Porter, ME (1985) *Competitive Advantage*, Free Press, New York.

Porter, ME (1986) *Competition in Global Industries*, Harvard Business School Press, Boston.

Puri, R (2004) 'Mobile Telephony: The Move from 2G to 3G Standards', Warwick Business School, September.

Rumelt, RP (1984) 'Towards a Strategic Theory of the Firm', in RB Lamb (ed.) *Competitive Strategic Management*, Prentice-Hall, pp. 566–70.

Rumelt, RP (1991) 'How much does industry matter?' *Strategic Management Journal*, **12**, pp. 167–85.

Scherer, FM and Ross, D (1990) *The Economics of Multiplant Operations*, Harvard University Press, Boston.

Sjostrom, C (1995) 'Corporate Effects on Industry Competition: a Strategic Groups Analysis', unpublished doctoral dissertation, University of Oxford.

Tello, M (2004) 'Opportunities in the Leasing Market for London-based Banks', Warwick Business School, September.

Wolff Olins (2004) 'Significance of Mobile Branding', Wolff Olins Orange Case Study, April, Wolff Olins Brand Consultancy, London.

Yao, D (1988) 'Beyond the reach of the invisible hand: impediments to economic activity, market failures, and profitability', *Strategic Management Journal*, Special Issue, **9**, pp. 59–70.

Yip, G. (2004) 'Using Strategy to Change your Business Model', *Business Strategy Review*, **15**, **2** (Summer), pp. 17–24.

Chapter 7

Competitive strategy: the analysis of strategic capability

Introduction

In setting out to understand strategic management we are in effect building our own strategic theory of the firm. The usual starting point of this endeavour is provided in Chapters 5 and 6, which describe the behaviour of firms in markets, the nature of competition, and the search for unique and sustainable market positions. To attain competitive advantage is to open the door to higher profits, other things being equal. This chapter sets out the internal agenda for the firm seeking to create competitive advantage. What resources and capabilities should the firm create and protect that will be the critical underpinning of its desired competitive advantage? In common parlance this is the concern with 'core competences'. In the academic discourse this is the **resource-based view** (RBV) of the firm in which it is recognized that firms are internally heterogeneous and in effect possess unique clusters of resources. Thus firms in the same industries and markets will very likely have different strategies and different performance levels. Critics of the **market-based view** (MBV) have argued that it is nonsensical to place the MBV at the centre of strategy making, leaving the inside of the firm to operate as a black box. Some, therefore, use the RBV to place the firm, rather than the industry or the market, at the centre of strategy making. However, the emphasis of this chapter is that the RBV and the MBV provide complementary perspectives on how to compete and jointly provide the basis for a strategic theory of the firm.[1]

7.1 **The resource-based view in theory**

Economists see the firm as a bundle of productive resources, where resources are defined as inputs into the firm's operations so as to produce goods and services. In this view resources are generic and specific categories are not suggested, but typical examples include patents, capital equipment, and skilled and unskilled human resources. Strategists go further and distinguish **capabilities** from **resources**. A capability is the ability to perform a task or activity that involves complex patterns of co-ordination and co-operation between people and other resources. Capabilities would include research and development expertise, customer service and high-quality manufacturing. Skills, by contrast, are more specific, relating to narrowly defined activities such as typing, machine maintenance and book-keeping.

Strategists are interested in those resources and capabilities that can earn **rents** (a surplus of revenue over cost). These collectively are known as **strategic assets** or **core competences**[2] and are a subset of but distinct from those other resources and capabilities that do not distinctively support the competitive advantage. The strategic task for the firm is to sustain these rent streams over time by creating and protecting the competitive advantage and the strategic assets that together underpin them. The inherent value of the strategic assets for the firm depends on the ways in which the firm combines, co-ordinates and deploys these assets in concert with the other firm-specific and more generic resources and capabilities.

The internal economy of the firm can be seen as sets of discrete activities (e.g. a product line), each of which leads to market positions and each of which is supported by assets of resources and capabilities. *Similar* activities (for example the Ford Mondeo and Ford Focus product lines) share some common strategic assets and some common generic assets. This sharing can lead to economies of scale (if different components share the same production line), to economies of scope (where products might go through common distribution

---

[1] However, this is to ignore important contributions such as the theory of the growth of the firm by Edith Penrose (1954) and the evolutionary theory of Nelson and Winter (1982).

[2] But note that there are many other labels, such as distinctive capabilities from Selznick (1957), that are and have been current.

channels), and experience effects. *Complementary* activities require dissimilar sets of strategic assets which would then require degrees of co-ordination (for example marketing activities and production activities). The skills of co-ordination and internal co-operation are in fact high-level capabilities with considerable strategic significance.

In the real world of uncertainty and imperfect information the firm may have (and usually does have) considerable problems in knowing which particular configurations of its strategic assets will maximize profits. Managers do not have perfect knowledge of future states of the world, of alternative actions that could be taken, or of the pay-offs from adopting various alternatives. Moreover, the way a manager chooses to allocate resources will be a function of past personal experience, the firm's experience, values, biases and personality. Accordingly, even if two managers were given identical bundles of resources they would use them in different ways. The result is that a firm's set of resources and capabilities will diverge from those of its competitors over time. Managers in competing firms in the same markets do not face the same sets of choices – rather, they have different menus with different choices. The future, as firms sees it, is to a greater or lesser degree uncertain and unknowable and their capacities for addressing the unknowable are diverse. Further, no amount of information gathering can resolve this fundamental uncertainty of what the future will hold.

Case box: **The game of chess**

If the theory of chess were really fully known there would be nothing left to play. The theory would show which of the three possibilities (white wins, tie or black wins) actually holds and, accordingly, the play would be decided before it starts … human difficulty necessitates the use of incomplete, heuristic methods of playing, which constitute 'good' chess; and without it there would be no element of 'struggle' and 'surprise' in the game.

Rationality and full information would give us the ability to solve well-specified problems like chess. The initial resources (i.e. whether you start with white or black) would fully determine the outcome. Furthermore, no one would read or write books on how to play chess well, because all the optimal moves would already be known. In practice, people differ widely in their ability to play chess and many find that studying books on chess ('rules' for winning) improves their play. People rely on heuristics, on search, on experience and on training to aid their decisions. Such individuals can learn better heuristics and search patterns from books and can improve their performance.

If we assume in both chess and in strategy that no one knows all the 'rules' then there can exist rules for riches that can benefit many participants. Indeed, half the firms in any industry could improve their status by becoming average. Neither in chess nor in strategy is there a fully fledged theory with optimization procedures in place. Participants have therefore to make progress by adopting heuristics (or intellectual constructs) that help them make sense of the possible varieties of moves and counter-moves. There cannot exist simple nostrums or simple rules for riches that apply universally.

Thus, strategy making is a long way from the simplistic assumptions of the economic model. Strategies tend to be unique and idiosyncratic and simplistic theories for success are usually 'magic theories', i.e. theories which explain everything but predict nothing.[3] Nor are there simple rules for riches, i.e. there are no automatic rules that provide benefits in the long run. The case box above uses the game of chess as an analogy.

This means that strategic management is not captured in the form of a strategic theory of the firm in a way that enables equations to be identified, data collected and analysed and simple rules be inferred. Strategic management is much more eclectic and diverse. Contexts external to the firm and internal to the firm are highly idiosyncratic. This places a premium on the ability to diagnose situations and formulate options. The specific routes to high performance are many and varied and not readily susceptible to simple generalizations. This goes some way to explaining why the RBV is widely seen as lacking specificity and definable concepts, and having no traceable connection to real performance improvements.

7.2 The language of the resource-based view: what is core competence?

In Chapter 5, we introduced the resource-based view with a figure similar to Figure 7.1. The top line of this diagram shows how the firm's investment programmes are directed towards the creation and development of resources and capabilities, and that these underpin the positional advantage from which superior value can be delivered to customers. The bottom line shows the value and financial consequences, in terms of the capacity of the firm to finance its investment programmes. The resource-based view focuses on the resources and capabilities of the firm, asserting that it is the distinctiveness of these that enables **sustainable positional**

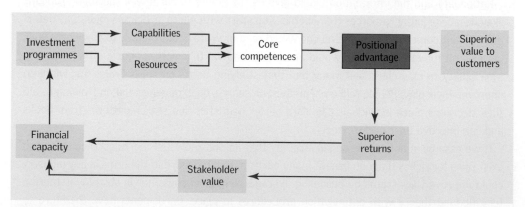

Figure 7.1 Competitive advantage and core competence

[3] Lave C and J March (1993) *An Introduction to Models in the Social Sciences*, University Press of America, NY.

advantages to be constructed. The added element in this diagram is the presence of core competences as representing those resources and capabilities that are distinctive to the firm. As a result, competitive advantage is seen as the joint product of core competences and positional advantage. What many writers observe is that imperfections in the resource and capability markets are more in number and larger in size than those in product markets. This places the burden on firms to pay attention to the underpinnings of competitive advantage in resource and capability terms. What many writers have also observed is that markets are changeable and even volatile, but it is quite difficult to get firms to change their internal cultures and processes quickly enough to keep pace with market changes.

Here we follow Grant's (1991 and 1998) lead in using 'resources' to describe inputs that can in general be purchased on open markets and customized for use by the purchasers. Thus, production capacity might be generally available, but will be configured for specific use by each purchaser. The activities of individual purchasers may lead to imperfections in supply markets. For example, a company may seek to monopolize certain raw materials through acquisition, or maybe through offering long-term supply contracts. But, on their own, few resources are immediately productive. By contrast, the 'capabilities' described here are firm-specific. They are developed internally against the specific needs and ambitions of each company. They often depend on tacit knowledge, are path-dependent in that they emerge and develop over time, and are not in the form of assets that can be traded. These resources and capabilities have individual characteristics, but a large part of their value-in-use to a firm is related to their configuration and their co-ordination. Figure 7.2 compares typical resources and typical capabilities (we introduced their distribution in Figure 5.7 on p. 165). The distinctiveness of the firm's specific set of resources and capabilities is a function of which resources to acquire and what capabilities to develop (the *configuration* issue), the way in which each of these is developed (the *firm-specificity* issue), and the way in which they are internally managed to create positional advantage (the *co-ordination* issue).

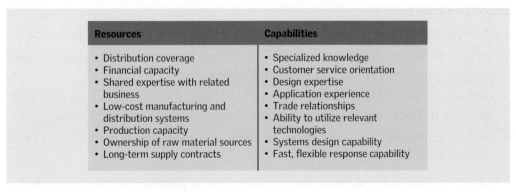

Resources	Capabilities
• Distribution coverage • Financial capacity • Shared expertise with related business • Low-cost manufacturing and distribution systems • Production capacity • Ownership of raw material sources • Long-term supply contracts	• Specialized knowledge • Customer service orientation • Design expertise • Application experience • Trade relationships • Ability to utilize relevant technologies • Systems design capability • Fast, flexible response capability

Figure 7.2 Resources and capabilities

7.2.1 Prahalad and Hamel on core competence

The language of assets, resources and capabilities can be confusing. The Grant (1998) distinction between resources and capabilities is as easy a distinction as any to maintain. However, it is laborious to keep referring to strategic resources and capabilities as those that systematically and uniquely underpin the competitive advantage relative to those other resources and capabilities that do not. Thus it is attractive to refer to these as core competences, the language popularized by Prahalad and Hamel in the *Harvard Business Review* (1990). They provided an unusual metaphor:

> *The diversified corporation is a large tree. The trunk and the major limbs are core products, the smaller branches are business units; the leaves, flowers, and fruit are end products. The root system that provides nourishment, sustenance, and stability is the core competence. You can miss the strength of competitors by looking only at their end products, in the same way you miss the strength of a tree if you look only at its leaves ...*
>
> *Core competences are the collective learning in the organization, especially how to coordinate diverse production skills and integrate multiple streams of technologies.*

7.2.2 BCG and capabilities-based competition

Prahalad and Hamel's approach is to define core competence as the combination of individual technologies and production skills that underlie a company's product lines. Sony's core competence in miniaturization allows it to make everything from the Sony Walkman to video cameras and digital cameras. Honda's core competence in engines and powertrains allows it compete from lawnmowers to racing cars. But this latter example shows a difficulty in their approach in that Honda's dealer network would be invisible – because of the focus on competences that lead directly to products. A development of their idea is contained in a Boston Consulting Group paper in 1992[4] on 'capabilities-based' competition. This contained four basic principles:

1 the building blocks of strategy are not products and markets but business processes;

2 competitive success depends on transforming these key processes into strategic capabilities that consistently provide superior value to the customer;

3 companies create these capabilities by making strategic investments in a support infrastructure that links together and transcends traditional strategic business units;

4 because capabilities necessarily cross functions, the champion of a capabilities-based strategy is the chief executive officer.

[4] Stalk, G, P Evans and L Shulman (1992) 'Competing on Capabilities', *Harvard Business Review*, March/April.

This approach has the real merit of focusing on business processes as the integrative glue that binds together the various lower-level ingredients and on the investments that are required to make this effective. Unfortunately, the continued use of capabilities makes for some confusion. The essence of the idea here is that these business processes should connect to real customer needs. Things are only strategic when they begin and end with the customer because that is where value is sensed and created. The box below is an extract from the same paper and summarizes the five dimensions on which a company's strategic resources and capabilities should aim to outperform the competition.

- ◆ **Speed:** the ability to respond quickly to customer or market demands and to incorporate new ideas and technologies quickly into products
- ◆ **Consistency:** the ability to produce a product that unfailingly satisfies customers' expectations
- ◆ **Acuity:** the ability to see the competitive environment clearly and thus to anticipate and respond to customers' evolving needs and wants
- ◆ **Agility:** the ability to adapt simultaneously to many different business environments
- ◆ **Innovativeness:** the ability to generate new ideas and to combine existing elements to create new sources of value

Source: Stalk, Evans and Shulman, 1992.

Boston Consulting Group present this discussion in the language of strategic capabilities in an attempt to avoid an overuse of competences, which is a feature of the Prahalad and Hamel approach.

7.2.3 Amit and Schoemaker on strategic assets

A similar approach can be seen in another classic paper from the same era. Amit and Schoemaker (1993) build on the resource and capability language to create 'strategic assets'. By resources they mean stocks of available factors of production that are owned and controlled by the firm. Capabilites refer to the firm's capacity to deploy resources, usually in combination, using organizational processes to effect a desired end. They are information-based, tangible and intangible processes that are firm-specific and are developed over time through complex interactions with each other and with the firm's resources. Unlike resources, capabilities are based on developing, sharing and exchanging information through the firm's human capital – as information-based assets they are often called 'invisible assets'. The authors describe 'strategic assets' as:

> the set of difficult to trade and imitate, scarce, appropriable and specialised resources and capabilities that (underpin) the firm's competitive advantage.

In practice it is difficult to draw clear distinctions between the core competences of Prahalad and Hamel, the capabilities-based competition of Boston Consulting Group, and the strategic assets of Amit and Schoemaker. They all convey the sense of firm-specific assets that are typically process and information based and intangible in character.

There are other assets and activities in the value chain, notable complementary assets that, when linked to strategic assets (core competences), are necessary for the existence of the competitive advantage.

Figure 7.3 The asset triangle

Thus, a research-based pharmaceuticals company such as Merck or SmithKlineGlaxo would identify research expertise as a core competence but would regard management of government regulations as a complementary asset, essential but not unique. Many other assets and activities in the firm can be classified as 'make-or-buy', that is, the firm makes a financial calculation as to make or buy. Figure 7.3 distinguishes 'strategic assets' from 'complementary' assets and 'make-or-buy' assets. Strategic assets are those that are truly distinctive and unique to the firm and provide the underpinning of positional advantage in product markets. Complementary assets are those assets that are jointly required with the strategic assets in order to produce and deliver the product or service. Thus, product development might be a strategic asset, but production capacity is required for product trials and for product adaptations, even though that capacity is not unique to the firm. These assets are sometimes called **co-specialized assets**, in that they are complementary to the specialized assets and (lightly) customized to interface with them. Make-or-buy assets are those that you choose to include in the assets portfolio solely on the basis of financial calculations. For example, the decision to own or lease company cars might be made solely on financial criteria, because there are no strategic implications. In principle, if there are no strategic implications (which means that there is no need to customize the assets for specific purposes), then there will, in general, be a free outside market. This in turn generally means that the market is able to supply cheaper than is possible internally. You can see from this that the pressure to outsource can be very high and depends critically on the characteristics of supply markets.

7.2.4 **Core competence = distinctive capability = strategic asset**

In this chapter we propose to follow the terminology shown in Figure 7.1. This means that we follow the definition of resources and capabilities as discussed by Grant (1998) and that we use the term 'core competences' to cover the capabilities language of Boston Consulting

Group and the strategic assets approach of Amit and Schoemaker. This language of core competences is nevertheless abstract and hard to put into practice. This reflects the idiosyncratic and unique nature of the strategic problems faced by individual firms. But it also reflects the need to have a clear concept upon which to base strategic thinking. The two building blocks of strategy (identified so far in this book) are competitive advantage and core competence. They are both intellectual constructs. Each relies on situational characteristics for their application in practice. Each provides a way of thinking so that strategists can develop a 'theory in use' that applies to their own situation. Gary Hamel (1994) has attempted to codify the idea of core competence further. He offers the following essential characteristics of a core competence:

1   A competence is a bundle of constituent skills and technologies rather than a discrete skill or technology and a core competence is the integration of a variety of individual skills.

2   A core competence is not an asset in the accounting sense of the word. A factory, a distribution channel or brand cannot be a core competence but an aptitude to manage that factory, that channel or that brand may constitute a core competence.

3   A core competence must make a disproportionate contribution to customer-perceived value. The distinction between core and non-core competence thus rests on a distinction between the relative impacts on customer value.

4   A core competence must also be competitively unique. This means either that (i) a competence is held uniquely by one firm in the competitive set or that (ii) a competence that is ubiquitous across an industry must be held at a superior level in the firm (for example, powertrains are ubiquitous in the automobile industry but one could argue that Honda has unique strength in this area and thus it is a core competence for Honda).

5   From the corporate (multi-business) perspective[5] a core competence should provide an entrée into new markets. A particular competence may be core from the perspective of an individual business, but from a corporate perspective it will not be core if there is no way of imagining an array of new product-markets issuing from it.[6]

The language of core competence has become widespread. Core competence and competitive advantage together have become the central conceptual terms in the analysis of competitive strategy. We define core competence quite simply as:

> *the underlying capability that is the distinguishing characteristic of the organization.*

♦   It is the way we do things.

♦   It is how we organize the way we do things.

---

[5]   See Chapter 9 for an explanation of the way in which competitive advantage should be deployed across multiple businesses within one company.

[6]   For an excellent example, see the case study Canon: Competing on Capabilities, HBS in the text and cases version of this book.

◆ It is how we *communicate* systematically this knowledge and build upon it.

◆ It is understanding the difference, and building bridges, between tangible and intangible assets, tacit and explicit knowledge, and individual and team knowledge and skill.

More formally, we define core competences as:

> *the set of firm-specific skills and cognitive processes directed towards the attainment of competitive advantage.* (McGee and Segal-Horn, 1997)

Core competence is a fundamental concept in our understanding of what strategy making is. It is *only* through core competence that the firm attains competitive advantage and is therefore the mainspring of sustainable distinctiveness. But it is also the lens through which the world is seen and interpreted. Different firms (and people) see different things in their environments and this is a function of their inheritance and their experience. In the same way, firms (and people) differ in the way in which they see themselves and therefore in their understanding of what they might achieve. In this way we can see core competences as the link between managerial cognition and the economics of the firm (*see* Figure 7.4). The key tasks of a strategy analyst are interpreting the external environment, understanding the dynamics of markets and of competition, and understanding the internal dynamics of one's own organization. Core competences provide the links to these economic assessments through a clarity of perception about the shared values and beliefs in the firm (often explicit in the mission statement), through tacit knowledge and understandings (that are possibly unique to the firm), and through flexible routines and recipes that enable non-standard challenges to be comprehended.

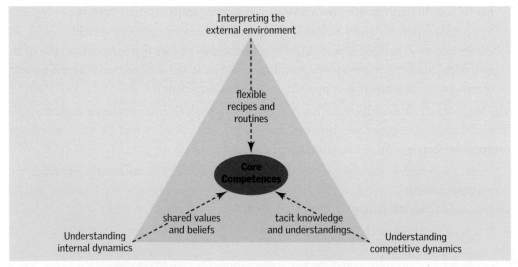

Figure 7.4 Core competences as the link between managerial cognition and the economics of the firm
Source: McGee and Segal-Horn, 1997.

7.3 **Related issues and the management of core competences**

There are some mistakes that managers make very frequently. The first is to assume that acquiring and leveraging generic resources will be a major source of advantage in a new market. Advantage requires some degree of difference between firms and this requires the construction of assets that are unique to the firm. Another common mistake is to overestimate the transferability of specific assets and capabilities to a new product market. Assets are unique to the firm in relation to the use for which they have been designed. New uses require some degree of further customization or re-adaptation. Even where the firm has constructed unique assets, it is easy to overestimate their capability to compete in highly profitable markets. This is merely to say that strategic choices are highly risky. Even if one can create a distinctive asset base it does not necessarily follow that customers will like the product offering that follows. Through this observation, you can see that competitive advantage is a composite of a resource-based view and a market-based view. Both are necessary: neither is necessary and sufficient on its own.

7.3.1 **Resource leverage**

Managers often neglect ways of creating advantage from a resource-based perspective. It is common to see firms paying much attention to the detail of product positioning in attempts to create those pieces of unique advantage that can make a difference. However, attention to the resource side can have significant pay-offs. For example, the approach of the Japanese automobile assemblers, especially Toyota,[7] show the benefits from rearranging the supply chain in such a way that essential customer values such as reliability can be fundamentally changed. There are five ways in which management can **leverage** its resources so as to create the conditions under which a core competence can emerge.[8] The idea of leverage (a much-used word of strategists) is to focus attention and effort an a specific object to the exclusion of rival objects so as to create a desired outcome. The exercise of leverage requires clear strategic intent and the possession of the relevant assets and competences.

Concentrating resources: convergence and focus

Convergence is the idea of focusing resources on few rather than many objectives and focus itself prevents the dilution of resources being applied to a specific target. The basic principle is the concentration of resources and the avoidance of dissipation of effort.

---

[7] See 'Competitive Advantage the Toyota Way' by Gary Fane, Reza Vagheti, Cheryl Van Deusen and Louis Woods, *Business Strategy Review*, 14, 4, 51–60, Winter 2003.

[8] This is taken from Gary Hamel and CK Prahalad (1993) 'Strategy as Stretch and Leverage', *Harvard Business Review*, March/April.

Accumulating resources: extracting and borrowing

Extraction is the ability to surface resources and capabilities that exist within the firm but might be lying concealed or dormant. The capacity to draw from the stockpile of resources is a facet of the ability to learn. Borrowing resources is the ability to tap into the resources of other companies. A simple example is the use of one company's basic research as an input to another company's commercialization. Thus Sony commercialized the transistor that was pioneered by Bell Laboratories. As Hamel and Prahalad (1993) point out:

> *Increasingly, technology is stateless. It crosses borders in the form of scientific papers, foreign sponsorship of university research, international licensing, cross border equity stakes in high-tech start-ups and international academic conferences. Tapping into the market for technology is a potentially important source of resource leverage.*

Complementing resources: blending and balancing

Blending resources is similar to what we called co-specialization (above). How resources fit together in planned and unplanned ways gives the possibility to transform the value of resources while using them. Blending requires integrative skills such as technological integration, functional integration and new product development. The blending of functional skills is a new way of restating the nature of general management. This traditionally has involved the integration of functions such as production, marketing and R&D. Balancing requires the firm's resources and capabilities to be able to support a business model. Unbalanced firms would have gaps such that resources and capabilities would be required from others for a sustainable revenue stream to be achieved. A balanced firm may benefit from tapping into the resources of others but has a defensible position on its own.

Conserving resources: co-opting and shielding

Conserving resources simply means retaining resources so that they are reusable – the basis for economies of scope. The issue is how to retain knowledge in the memory banks so that it is addressable and recyclable to other activities. Co-option has the same theme as recycling but involves collaborative efforts to work collectively towards new standards or new products. Shielding resources is about not wasting non-renewable resources (such as cash) on difficult targets. Attacking competitors directly in their home markets is an example of a difficult target where the probabilities are more of failure than of success. The example of Canon taking on Xerox in plain paper copying is a classic example. Xerox's R&D budgets were very much higher than those of Canon, but Canon chose to compete in areas where the Xerox business model was weak, e.g. small machines, third-party distribution systems and machine reliability.[9]

---

[9] See the case study Canon: Competing on Capabilities, HBS in the text and cases version of this book.

Recovering resources: expediting success

Pace is a significant dimension of performance. The faster the cycle time from investment through to sales, the quicker that resources can be renewed and redeveloped (see Figure 7.1, where the strategy cycle indicates the process). The speed at which Japanese automakers and motorcycle manufacturers operated gave these companies higher cash flows than their Western counterparts but also more up-to-date products and a greater ability to respond to changing markets.

7.3.2 Identifying intangibles

The expression 'intangible' is being applied more and more frequently to resources and to capabilities. For our purposes it refers to the following:

- Intellectual property rights of patents, trademarks, copyright and registered designs
- Trade secrets
- Contracts and licences
- Databases
- Information in the public domain
- Personal and organizational networks
- The know-how of employees, advisers, suppliers and distributors
- The reputation of products and of the company
- The culture of the organization

Richard Hall conducted a study of the relative contribution of intangible resources and capabilities to business success.[10] Some of the results are summarized in Tables 7.1, 7.2 and 7.3. Table 7.1 summarizes the average weightings for each intangible drawn from the above list. Hall found that the results were common and systematic across a wide sample of companies. Four factors stood out as most important namely, company reputation, product reputation, employee know-how and organization culture. By contrast, intellectual property rights and trade secrets were by far the least significant. Table 7.2 unpacks the employee know-how factor seen in Table 7.1. Here CEOs were asked which business function was the most important contributor to employee know-how. Operations scores highly because of the high tacit content of know-how (learning by experience). In contrast, in finance, know-how has a large external knowledge content, which means that skills can be formalized and transferred. The importance attached to sales and marketing by both manufacturers and retailers is to be expected, whereas the contribution of technology is quite modest.

---

[10] Richard Hall (1992) 'The Strategic Analysis of Intangible Resources', *Strategic Management Journal*, 13, 135–44.

Table 7.1 Relative importance of intangible resources in overall business success

Ranking (1 = highest, 2 = lowest)	Average weight (crucial = 10, insignificant = 1)
1 Company reputation	8.6
2 Product reputation	8.4
3 Employee know-how	8.1
4 Organization culture	7.9
5 Networks	7.1
6 Specialist physical resources	6.1
7 Databases	6.0
8 Supplier know-how	5.8
9 Distributor know-how	5.3
10 Public knowledge	5.2
11 Contracts	4.7
12 Intellectual property rights	3.2
13 Trade secrets	2.9

Sample size = 95
Source: Hall, 1992. © Copyright 1992, John Wiley and Sons Ltd. Reproduced with permission.

Table 7.2 Percentage of CEOs quoting the function as the most important area of employee know-how

	Total sample	Manufacturing	Retailing
Operations	43	27	8
Sales and marketing	29	46	46
Technology	17	18	31
Finance	6	0	15
Other	5	9	0
Total	100	100	100

Source: Hall, 1992. © Copyright 1992, John Wiley and Sons Ltd. Reproduced with permission.

Table 7.3 Replacement periods

	Average replacement period (years)
Company reputation	10.8
Product reputation	6.0
Employee know-how	4.6
Networks	3.4
Supplier know-how	3.1
Databases	2.1
Distributor know-how	1.6

Source: Hall, 1992. © Copyright 1992, John Wiley and Sons Ltd. Reproduced with permission.

Table 7.3 looks at the time it takes to replace an intangible asset. The question posed was, How many years would it take to replace the *particular resource* if you had to start from scratch? This gives an indication of protection from new entrants depending on the transferability of existing reputation. Reputational resources dominate this list. Company reputation, in particular, gives strong incumbents a significant advantage. By contrast, much know-how can be replaced or rebuilt over quite a short period (around three years), suggesting that speedy imitation is quite probable in most situations.

The importance of reputation suggests that it should receive constant management attention. The distinction between company and product is interesting, implying, first, that attention to both is probably necessary and, second, that in multi-business companies the corporate name could have a significant halo effect across businesses and product lines. The experience of companies such as Sony, Hewlett-Packard and IBM provide good examples of this. The high scores for employee know-how support the idea of invisible assets that are information and experience rich. This is clearly fertile ground for the development of core competences. In Table 7.1 the term culture has a specific meaning: it refers to ability to manage change, ability to innovate, teamworking ability, participative management style, perception of high quality standards, and perception of high standards of customer service. These are also ingredients that are information and experience rich.

7.3.3 What determines the value of a core competence?

Figure 7.5 summarizes the conditions that determine the value of a core competence (strategic asset). The basic foundations of value are *imitability*, *durability*, *substitutability*

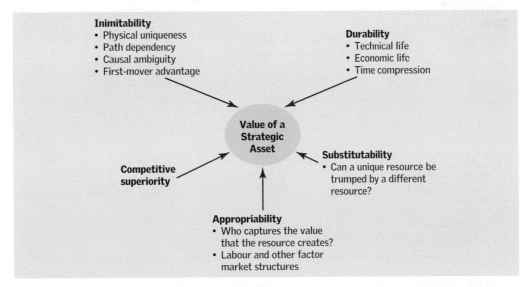

Figure 7.5 Value of a core competence
Source: Peteraf, 1993.

and *appropriability*. The ability of competitors to imitate your assets is in part to do with *physical uniqueness*. More subtle issues around inimitability are:

♦ **Path dependency** – cumulative learning and experience over time, which is difficult to replicate over short periods.

♦ **Causal ambiguity** – not really knowing what it is that is the important element in a complex asset.

♦ **First-mover advantage** – the pre-emption of a market by being the first to create scale efficient assets.

Substitutability is often an unknown, in that new technologies can emerge which very quickly outdate older solutions. For example, the battle between satellite and cable television systems is still raging – substitutability is high, but it is not clear which standard will prevail. Appropriability is an important but subtle issue. A central question about a strategic asset is: Who can capture the value that is created? Is it the firm? Could it be the skilled technicians? Might it be patent owners? Perhaps there are long-term supply contracts?

7.4 Linking core competence to competitive advantage

The resource-based view (RBV) is not a theory in its own right. But coupled with the market-based view (MBV) it enables the strategist to link the firm's internal behavioural

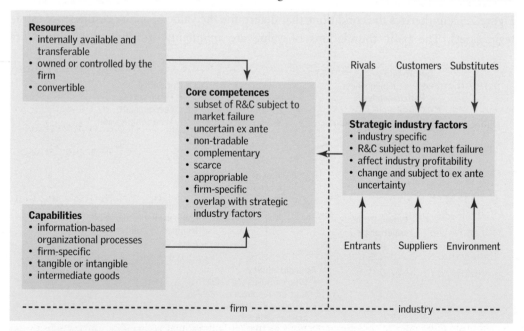

Figure 7.6 Strategic industry factors and core competences
Source: Amit and Schoemaker, 1993.

decisions and organizational choices with the need to secure a defensible positional advantage in the market. RBV and MBV together provide a theory-in-use for the strategist. Figure 7.1 shows the link between RBV and MBV as a juxtaposition of core competence and competitive advantage. Amit and Schoemaker (1993) went a stage further. Their full model is shown in Figure 7.6, adapted only to use the phrase core competence for strategic asset. The extra dimension (compared to Figure 7.1) provided here is contained in the phrase 'strategic industry factors'. These are the sources of market imperfections that firms can capture as elements in their competitive advantage.[11]

From our earlier discussion of industry analysis and Porter's five forces we obtained a general description of the characteristics of an industry. Porter's model provides five generic characteristics and others have suggested more, such as government and deeper environmental variables. Other ad hoc analyses have developed over the years, particularly the idea of key success factors (KSFs). Later in this chapter we suggest a way of using KSFs in practice, but in general KSFs can be seen as those elements in the industry that are deemed as *important* for customers. Strategic industry factors are a way of articulating KSFs as those elements in the industry and in the market that are subject to market failure and therefore where firms can provide them they will have an advantage. Using our language of advantage, these factors are those firm-specific imperfections that represent competitive advantage. Amit and Schoemaker synthesize contributions from many writers in producing this list of characteristics that apply to strategic industry factors.

1   They are determined through a complex interaction among industry rivals, new entrants, customers, regulators, innovators, suppliers and other stakeholders.

2   They are strategic in that they are subject to market failures and may be the basis for competition among rivals.

3   They are known ex post but not ex ante; in particular, not all aspects of their development and interactions with other factors in the market will be known or controllable.

4   Their development takes time, skill and capital: they may be specialized to particular uses.

5   Investments in them are largely irreversible (i.e. sunk costs).

6   Their pace of accumulation is affected by own prior knowledge and experience and that of rivals (i.e. path dependent) and cannot be readily increased (doubling the investment will not usually halve the time).

7   Their value to any particular firm will depend on its control of other factors – the complementarity property.

---

[11] Economists often refer to these imperfections as market failures, that is, inabilities to trade in these factors in perfect markets. Our view of competitive advantage as firm-specific imperfections in the market rests on this notion of market failure.

You will observe that this list is similar to, and is a development of, the discussion in section 5.1, where we discussed the essential ingredients of strategy. In examining Figure 7.6 you will see that the list of core competences has similarities to the list of strategic industry factors. This is not an accident, nor is it an error. The difference is that firms seek to design their core competences in anticipation of their usefulness in creating and sustaining an intended competitive advantage. The strategic industry factors are those imperfections in the market that have succeeded. The core competences are ex ante in nature; they are intentions. The strategic industry factors are ex post, those characteristics that have actually worked in the market to produce competitive advantage.

7.4.1 Competence-based competition in practice

In 1977 Dan Bricklin, an MBA student at the Harvard Business School, developed on his Apple computer a type of 'electronic blackboard' that allowed him to display a grid of numbers linked together by formulae. His professor told him (allegedly) that it had no future as a product. Why? Because software was (and is) easily imitated. There was virtually no entry barrier. There were established firms selling mainframe languages to do pro-forma calculations. Moreover, the Apple was a mere toy! What was wrong with the professor's reasoning?

In 1973 one of the authors wrote a case on the Japanese motorcycle industry. The final discussion question asked, Should Honda enter the emerging global automobile business? It was a 'giveaway' question – anyone who said 'yes' flunked, because markets were saturated, efficient competitors existed in Japan, the USA and in Europe. Honda had little or no experience in automobiles and it had no automobile distribution system or access to one. In 1985 his wife drove a Honda! What was wrong with this answer?

This was a common fault in the strategy analyses of that period. Why was it that Canon could beat Xerox? How did Komatsu manage to beat Caterpillar? The fault lay in the lack of a proper resource-based perspective. There are three parts in an answer to this question: strategic intent, strategic innovation and core competences.

Strategic intent

Strategic intent has a particular meaning in encouraging people to go beyond 'business as usual'. It appeals to the resource language that we reported above, particularly the sense of concentration, convergence and focus, and to the idea of resource leverage.

It has been argued that US firms seeking strategic fit have often found themselves overtaken by firms, especially the Asian conglomerates, driven by long-term visions of the future, which are then relentlessly and ruthlessly pursued with *strategic intent*. Companies such as CNN, Honda, NEC and Sony have succeeded (according to this argument) because of their sustained obsession with achieving global dominance in their industries. This obsession has been labelled strategic intent (Hamel and Prahalad 1989). The significance of this is that the intent of these companies was out of proportion to their existing resources and capabilities.

Table 7.4 The Xerox position in 1980

	Xerox
Technology	Leading edge product technology: 7000 patents
Distribution	Worldwide direct sales: 7000 in USA, 5000 in Europe, 3000 in Japan
Financing	Leasing
R&D investment	$600 million p.a.
Manufacturing	Worldwide network of plants
Scale	Market share = 90%
Image	Photocopy = Xerox

Source: Ackenhusen (1992) 'Canon: Competing on Capabilities', case study.

This gap between ambition and resources is known as **strategic stretch**. These companies had to expand and adapt their current stock of resources and create new ones. They were more concerned with 'leveraging' resources than with achieving **strategic fit** between their current resources and their industry environments.

Strategic intent can thus be used as a psychological target which provides a focus that all members of the organization seek to adopt. Becoming the industry leader or dominating a specific segment are frequent missionary goals. The fundamental focus of the firm's strategy commits well beyond its current resource profile. The prophecies can therefore become self-fulfilling provided that employees have faith in their leadership and that, in many cases, the existing industry leaders fail to recognize that the challenge is on. The logic of expansion coupled with economies of scope provides an economic basis for justifying strategic intent. However, there are limits to economies of scope which arise when industries and markets require more variety than the fixed factors that sustain scope effects can support.

Strategic intent implies a stretch beyond current resources, capabilities and means. But for those companies that have adopted this style it became a necessity and was not a luxury.

Table 7.5 How Canon rewrote the rules of the game

	Xerox existing business	**Canon's new rules**
Customer definition	Medium/large companies	Small companies/individuals
Use pattern	Centralised copying	Decentralised
Product	High copy volume features	Utility, value for money
Distribution	Own sales force	Office products dealers
Service	Own network	By dealers
Financing	Lease	Sale
Technology	Leading edge dry toner	Low cost liquid toner

Source: Ackenhusen (1992) 'Canon: Competing on Capabilities', case study.

Strategic innovation

Strategic investments are bets against an unknowable future. These bets often require technical progress and substantial investment in R&D and in new products. In 1980 Xerox had a stranglehold on the copier industry. IBM were poised to enter, attracted by Xerox's huge profits. Canon also had an interest in fine optics and precision mechanics on the basis of their existing camera business. On whom would you have bet? Table 7.4 shows the Xerox hand.

The barriers to entry were formidable. In IBM's favour was their own large scale that meant it could probably afford to spend as much money as Xerox (but note that Kodak had had the same thoughts earlier without too much success). Canon had no obvious points of superiority given the nature of the market and the strategic industry factors that were present at that time. The idea of strategic innovation is to rewrite the rules of the game. Table 7.5 catches the essence of what Canon did to outflank Xerox and one can do similar analyses to show how Komatsu outflanked Caterpillar by changing the point of competition from quality to cost and reliability, and how Honda managed to enter the global automobile industry by emphasizing quality.

Strategic innovation leads to a new form of competitive advantage, a different conception of the required core competences and a different business model through which the cash could be seen to flow. In the case of the Apple computer and Dan Bricklin's spreadsheet invention, the spreadsheet became the killer application that placed the new Apple personal computer on millions of desks by appealing to a similar sense that Canon identified – the customers' wish to have desktop capability.

Figure 7.7 Matching resources and markets: linking the inside and the outside

Core competence

The core competences in each of these examples were created by investments in the operational and organizational infrastructure of the strategic innovators. The new capabilities spawned through these investments were linked across business units and the learning and experience of diverse business units was captured and leveraged across the company. Canon's distinctive management processes (compared to Xerox) were high levels of decentralization, strong internal co-ordination processes and external co-operation. Canon exemplified the value of external co-operation through importing knowledge from strategic alliance partners and joint ventures The complex core competences that arose could be described as (i) a high pace of learning and innovation, (ii) a long-term approach to developing capabilities, and (iii) the systematic transfer of competences across businesses and into new businesses.

The risks associated with the Japanese approach – most of the examples have been Japanese companies – is that an overdependence on a resource-based perspective can lock you into your own view of the world, away from changing markets and customer preferences. In an earlier discussion of the strategy cycle in Chapter 5 we commented on how Marks & Spencer became trapped in their own conception of the world just as the textile market became more fashion conscious, new entrants were appearing and product offers were changing rapidly (the strategic industry factors were obviously in a process of change).

How do we balance the inside view with the outside view? Figure 7.7 summarizes inside and outside perspectives and the links between them. The firm is driven by the link of resources and capabilities through strategic intent to core competences. This is the crux of the firm's intended strategy culminating in the match between core competences and competitive advantage. A failed strategy would have empty boxes in the middle of the diagram. The core competences are captured in products which have to match customer functionality. The dynamics of the process are shown by strategic innovation which through 'newgame' strategies match with and/or drive industry development.

The demand side, the outside, is captured by the link between industry structure through strategic industry factors to competitive advantage. Industry structure has multiple industry factors and competitive advantages associated with it. The firm's task is to identify one of the set and match with it – this implies a set of customer functionalities to be satisfied. The dynamics are captured through industry development and other exogenous factors.

The design of the firm's theory-in-use is shown by the strategic fit between core competences and competitive advantage. The practical present-day fit is shown by the fit between product range and customer functionality. The dynamic fit is between strategic innovation and industry development. Lack of fit in the short term can be a result of (i) the requirements of the outside moving too quickly for the inside to keep pace, or (ii) by the strategic drive from the inside missing its targets. There may be a short-term fit that erodes because the dynamic linkages through innovation and industry development do not work properly.

7.4.2 **The role of learning**

When we compare product markets and resource markets, we can see that fundamentally competition is a contest for the acquisition of skills. Moreover, competition in product markets is a superficial expression of the more fundamental competition over competences. Looked at in this way, the dynamics of markets, of industries and of firms is about 'learning' rather than technical theories of product market evolution; hence, all the current concern with the 'learning organization' and with 'knowledge management'. Core competences arise through the collective learning of the firm, through accumulated experience with the coordination of diverse production skills and the integration of multiple streams of technology. Prahalad and Hamel (1990) take the proposition further. They argue that core competences span across businesses and products within a corporation – they can support several products or businesses. Thus, they argue that the narrow focus of strategic business units is dysfunctional. It is also clear that core competences have temporal dominance over products. They evolve slower than the products that they make possible, or core competences support several generations of essentially the same product classes. Figure 7.8 suggests a framework within which all these strands can be seen. The focus of the diagram is on the way in which the resource-based view is becoming accepted as the genesis of advantage in the firm, but also reflects the modern debate about the contribution of learning and knowledge to our understanding of how firms compete. Chapters 16 and 19 take this discussion further.

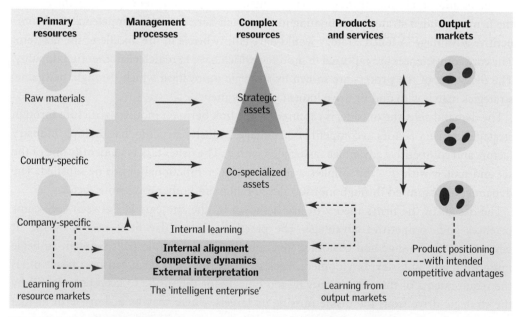

Figure 7.8 A synthesis of positioning, the resource-based view and learning
Source: McGee and Segal-Horn, 1997.

7.5 **Competitive strategy in practice**

We start from the premise that there can be great differences between the abilities of firms to succeed – there are fundamental inequalities between most competitors. This contrasts with the conventional economics textbook view of perfect competition that holds that firms are essentially similar, if not the same, and that over time their performances will converge on a minimum rate of return on capital. Less efficient firms will be obliged to exit and the more efficient firms will be subject to imitation. But the competitive strategy view of the firm is that understanding and manipulating the factors that cause these inequalities, so as to give the firm a sustainable competitive advantage, largely govern long-term business success. These factors vary widely; so different businesses, even within the same industry, often need to be doing different things. Thus, there are many strategies open to firms. The usual starting point is to recognize that strategy is the outcome of the resolution of several different, conflicting forces. These are summarized in Figure 7.9. Society has expectations of its business organizations. Owners, managers and other implementers of strategy have their own personal values and ambitions. The company has strengths and weaknesses, and the industry context offers opportunities and threats. The traditional top-down view of strategy is encapsulated in the *strategic planning view*. This involves deciding on long-term objectives and strategic direction, eliminating or minimizing weaknesses, avoiding threats, building on and defending strengths, and taking advantage

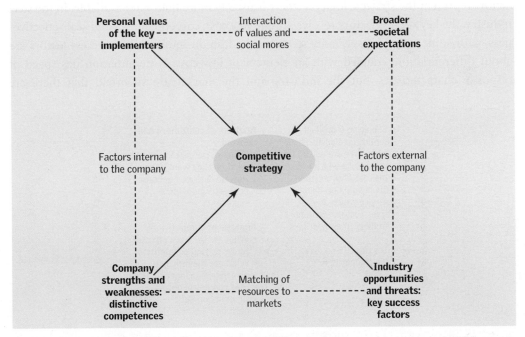

Figure 7.9 An overview of the influences on competitive strategy

of opportunities. But, from reading this chapter, it should be clear that given the strategic direction, the key strategic decision is product market selection. This should be based on the existence of long-term viable business opportunities (not merely the existence of growing markets), together with the prospect of creating the relevant core competences. Viable business opportunities depend on:

◆ The existence of valuable market segments.

◆ The existence of a sustainable positional advantage.

◆ The creation of the appropriate strategic assets.

In conducting the assessment of viable business opportunity, the term *key success factors* is often used. Intuitively, this means 'What do we have to do to succeed?' We can put some analytical flesh on these bones. Figures 7.10 and 7.11 illustrate the process (see Grant 1991). There is a set of key questions to ask:

◆ Is there a market?

◆ Do we have some advantage?

◆ Can we survive the competition?

These lead us into two pieces of analysis: the analysis of customers and demand, and the analysis of competition (summarized in Figure 7.10). Figure 7.11 shows how these can be put together to identify key success factors in three different industries. The key success factors represent the strategic logic(s) (there is usually more than one) available. In the steel industry, the key success factors revolve around low cost, cost efficiencies and scale effectiveness, with some scope for speciality steels. In the fashion industry, key success factors are about differentiation, coupled with an element of low cost. Differentiation has speed of response characteristics, but the industry and the market are so broad that there are

Figure 7.10 Identifying key success factors

Industry	What do customers want? (analysis of demand)	How do firms survive competition? (analysis of competition)	Key success factors
Steel	Customers include automobiles, engineering, and container industries. Customers acutely price sensitive. Also require product consistency and reliability of supply. Specific technical specifications required for special steels.	Competition primarily on price. Competition intense due to declining demand, high fixed costs and low-cost imports. Strong trade union bargaining power. Transport costs high. Scale economies important.	Cost efficiency through scale-efficient plants, low-cost location, rapid adjustment of capacity to output, low labour costs. In special steels, scope for differentiation through quality.
Fashion clothing	Demand fragmented by garment, style, quality, colour. Customers willing to pay price premium for fashion, exclusivity, and quality. Retailers seek reliability and speed of supply.	Low barriers to entry and exit. Low seller concentration. Few scale economies. Strong retail buying power. Price and non-price competition both strong.	Combine effective differentiation with low-cost operation. Key differentiation variables are speed of response to changing fashions, style, reputation with retailers/consumers. Low wages and overheads important.
Grocery supermarkets	Customers want low prices, convenient location and wide range of products.	Markets localized, concentration normally high. But customer price sensitivity encourages vigorous price competition. Exercise of bargaining power a key determinant of purchase price. Scale economies in operations and advertising.	Low-cost operation requires operational efficiency, scale efficient stores, large aggregate purchases to maximize buying power, low wage costs. Differentiation requires large stores to provide wide product and customer convenience facilities.

Figure 7.11 Identifying key success factors in three industries

distinctive segments, some of which are cost driven, while others are differentiation driven. This industry provides a good example of the multiplicity of available strategies.

In formulating competitive strategy, there are some important things to remember:

◆ *Resources are limited*, opportunities are infinite. The essence of strategy lies in saying 'Yes' to only some of the options and, therefore, 'No' to many others. *Trade-offs* are essential to strategy — they reflect the need for choice and they purposefully limit what a company offers.

◆ Always factor in *opportunity costs*. A dollar invested 'here' is a dollar not invested 'there', or not given back to shareholders.

◆ The essence of strategy is choosing to perform activities *differently* than rivals.

◆ In the long run, what matters is not how fast you are running, but whether you are *running faster than your competitors*.

◆ A company can only outperform rivals if it can establish a difference that it can sustain. So always test for the *sustainability* of your competitive advantage. Competitors are likely to view relieving you of your competitive advantage as their cardinal duty. Further, not all of them are likely to be stupid.

◆ The competitive value of individual activities cannot be separated from the whole. So, *fit* locks out imitators by creating a value chain that is stronger than its weakest link.

+ The long-run test of any strategy lies not in what it contributes to market share or profit margins but in what it contributes to long-term *return on investment*.

+ Strategic positions should have a *time horizon* of a decade or more, not just of a single planning cycle and/or product cycle.

7.5.1 Managing the business for value

Firms are often poor at devising practical procedures for carrying out the strategy analyses of the kind suggested in this chapter. The ideas are frequently expressed only as concepts. Data is often not collected nor organized as evidence to test out alternative possibilities. This section outlines one way of capturing the analysis of competitive advantage.

Competitive advantage is about creating value both for the customer and for the firm. The first task is to define what this means in practice. Thus, value to the customer can be defined as:

1 firm's ability to position a product better/different than competitors;

2 firm's ability to persuade customers to recognize, purchase and value the difference.

Value to the firm can be defined as

1 firm's ability to create and sustain core competences that underpin the positioning at manageable cost premiums;

2 firm's ability to run (the rest of) the business efficiently and at best practice levels.

These definitions can be operationalized according the schema shown in Figure 7.12. The four elements of value are coded as positioning, customer persuasion, capability and efficiency. Note that efficiency is not enough! Each of these requires strategic indicators by which performance can be measured. The figure suggests some starting points.

Strategic indicators		Company 1	Benchmark
Price: performance segment maps	**Positioning**		
Repeats; price premium; share	**Customer**		
Peer ratings; tech benchmarking	**Capability**		
Engineering studies cost analysis	**Efficiency**		
Financial indicators	Sales margins asset T/O RoI		

Figure 7.12 Managing the business for value

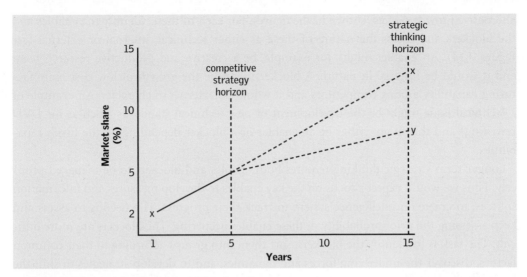

Figure 7.13 Positioning the business for growth

Then data should be collected to identify the firm's own performance on these measures and then some benchmark comparisons. To complement this strategic performance analysis financial indicators can also be shown remembering that these reflect the outcomes of previous strategies whereas the strategic indicators will presage future financial performance.

7.5.2 Positioning the business for growth

Competitive strategy will usually have a limited time scale over which assessments can be made reliably. This is usually related to the tangibility of assets and to the speed with which the product life cycle operates. As a rule of thumb firms can see to the end of the current product life cycle and are actively engaged in the planning and the next cycle. The cycle beyond that is much less clearly seen. Thus, in practice, we can expect firms to see one and a half life cycles ahead (subject to the life expectancy of their capital assets). Thus, if a car manufacturer has a product life cycle of four years, we would expect it to be able to see and forecast about six or seven years ahead. So how do we plan beyond this if the numbers are missing? Figure 7.13 shows the break in our planning horizons.

The shorter period of competitive strategy horizon (shown for example as five years) should not and does not mean that we do not do any strategic thinking beyond that. One way of dealing with this is to compare

Growth target = %			
	Technical	**Internal**	**External**
Enables			
Blockers			

Figure 7.14 Enables and blockers

alternative growth targets (shown in the figure). For each of these, identify the enables and the blockers and assess the nature of these as either technical, internal or external (*see* Figure 7.14). An enabler might, for example, be a creative and productive research team and it would be internal in nature. A blocker might be the growth of low-cost manufacturing capability among competitors and it would be external in character. An example of a technical issue might be the development of new technical standards (such as for DVD rewriting) and this might either be an enabler or a blocker depending on the firm's capabilities.

Longer-term strategic thinking requires both enables and blockers to be managed properly. Thus we would expect a focus on the key enables to develop measures and information sources, to create an intelligence system to track their progress. The need is to assess and keep assessing the prior probability of these enables occurring. The blockers are more difficult. The task is to identify the blockers, sort them into groups according to their common factors, discover the underlying forces and dynamics, and to develop strategies to shift the blocks or to get round them (note how in the reprographics industry in the 1970s Canon developed an R&D strategy to get around Xerox's network of blocking patents). For blockers we need (as for enables) to assess and track over time the prior probability of controlling the blockers and moderating their influence. This analysis should then be repeated for different growth targets. The outcomes will of course be quite qualitative and multidimensional, but Figure 7.15 suggests a way of summarizing the outputs.

The vertical axis is the prior probabilities of facilitating the enables and controlling the blockers (a joint probability of achieving a target would be one way of operationalizing this). The horizontal axis is time. The first part of this is a commitment period during which the foundations are being established (typically the first part of a J-curve), shown here for example as four years. Beyond this period we are looking for a confidence that growth can be managed – *the ring of confidence* in the figure, or not, i.e. *the undesirable region.* More generally you would expect to see a curve showing the prior probabilities rising over time. The key question is whether the probabilities are sufficiently high early enough. The bad position is when the probabilities remain low well beyond the commitment period. Conversely, happiness occurs when they rise quickly.

Approaches such as this one require considerable judgement and they often will defy the objective tests implied by quantification. However, the advantage here is of applying a systematic procedure that is rooted in the economics of the firm, in the nature of customer behaviour and that seeks to balance opportunity against risk.

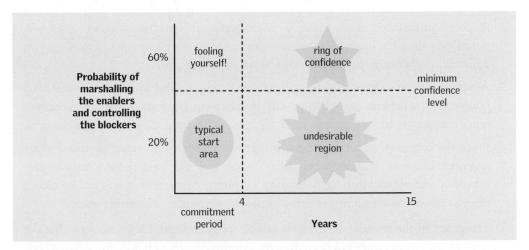

Figure 7.15 Positioning the business for growth: assessing feasibility

7.6 Summary

This chapter asserts that competitive advantage and core competence are two key intellectual constructs that together provide the foundation for understanding strategy. Competitive advantage is the basis for the market-based view, providing us with a way of assessing the positioning of the firm relative to its competitors. Core competence is one of many phrases that capture the resource-based view. The idea of *the underlying capability that is the distinguishing characteristic of the organization* and that underpins competitive advantage.

We have reviewed the various languages of the resource-based view, mentioning resources, capabilities, competences and strategic assets. However, rather than pursue semantic differences between such an array of titles, we have chosen to follow the definition of resources and capabilities as discussed by Grant (1998) and to use the term 'core competences' to cover the capabilities language of Boston Consulting Group and the strategic assets approach of Amit and Schoemaker. Further, we suggest Hamel's clarification as both practical and theoretically sound, namely:

1 A competence is a bundle of constituent skills and technologies rather than a discrete skill or technology and a core competence is the integration of a variety of individual skills.

2 A core competence is not an asset in the accounting sense of the word. A factory, a distribution channel or brand cannot be a core competence but an aptitude to manage that factory, that channel or that brand may constitute a core competence.

3   A core competence must make a disproportionate contribution to customer-perceived value. The distinction between core and non-core competence thus rests on a distinction between the relative impacts on customer value.

4   A core competence must also be competitively unique. This means either that (i) a competence is held uniquely by one firm in the competitive set or that (ii) a competence that is ubiquitous across an industry must be held at a superior level in the firm.

5   From the corporate (multi-business) perspective a core competence should provide an entrée into new markets. A particular competence may be core from the perspective of an individual business, but from a corporate perspective it will not be core if there is no way of imagining an array of new product-markets issuing from it.

The language of the resource-based view can be confusing and it is no surprise that the concept of core competence has been difficult to apply. However, it is an intellectual construct in just the same way that competitive advantage is, and it should be used to clarify thinking. It is not intended as a simple framework or tool (such as SWOT or PEST) that contains within it simple practical guidelines. The second half of the chapter is devoted to practical applications of the core competence concept. Core competence leads directly into issues of resource leverage (for value and profit). We discuss the importance of identifying intangibles. We have discussed the link to competitive advantage using the language of strategic industry factors and fey success factors. We have looked at strategic intent, strategic innovation and the role of learning. What core competence does is to focus attention on the managerial processes, information content and communications that are the intangible heart of the resource-based view. Core competences are hardly ever tangible assets – they reflect intangible, sometimes designed but sometimes informal managerial process. As intangibles it is then not surprising that firms are essentially different from one another (as opposed to the traditional view of economists who hold that firms are essentially similar in the long term). Bringing competitive advantage and core competence together as competitive strategy in practice we see how managing the business for value and managing the business for growth depends on both concepts.

In the following chapters we explore how strategy (i.e. competitive advantage plus core competence) is manifested in a number of different situations. In Chapter 8 we look at competitive strategy in a variety of different situations. Chapter 9 introduces multi-business or corporate strategy and Chapter 10 develops this into mergers and acquisitions. Chapter 11 focuses on international strategy and Chapter 12 asks how these ideas translate into the world of the 'new economy'.

Key terms

Capabilities *252*

Causal ambiguity *266*

Core competences *252*

Co-specialized assets *258*

First mover advantage *266*

Intangibles *263*

Leverage *261*

Market-based view (MBV) *252*

Path dependency *266*

Resource-based view (RBV) *251*

Rents *252*

Resources *252*

Strategic assets *252*

Strategic fit *269*

Strategic intent *268*

Strategic stretch *269*

Sustainable positional advantage *254*

Recap questions and assignments

Guide answers to these questions are given on the Online Learning Centre website.

1 Undertake a resource audit of an organization with which you are familiar, then identify which resources, if any, are unique in the sense that they are difficult to imitate. Has the organization gained competitive advantage as a result of this uniqueness?

2 Refer to Question 2 (Chapter 5). For these same two companies identify the core competences and show where they are located within their value choices.

3 Refer to Question 3 (Chapter 5). For the same organization show how its core competences are contained within the SWOT analysis. Convert your SWOT analysis into a diagram based on Figure 7.7.

Online
*Learning*Centre

When you have read this chapter, log on to the Online Learning Centre website at www.mcgraw-hill.co.uk/textbooks/mcgee to explore chapter-by-chapter test questions, further reading and more online study tools for strategy.

Case 1 How Dell keeps from stumbling: It's the supply chain, says its boss, Dick Hunter

In the high-tech universe, Dell Computer Corp. is a force of nature. In less than 20 years, company founder Michael S. Dell has amassed a personal fortune of $16 billion and built a $25 billion company, besting the likes of IBM, Hewlett-Packard, and Compaq Computer in the process. Along the way, his build-to-order model has blossomed into a new manufacturing paradigm. Impressively, the Austin (Tex.) company also has weathered the technology meltdown—at least so far. Rival Gateway Inc. just posted its second consecutive quarterly loss, and Hewlett-Packard Co. is planning to eliminate 3,000 management jobs. Outside the PC sector, things are far worse: Cisco Systems Inc. is slashing up to 8,500 jobs after writing off $2.5 billion in unsold inventory.

What insulates Dell from these troubles? Says Dick L. Hunter, the vice-president overseeing supply-chain management, the difference comes from Dell's super-efficient supply chain. 'Michael [Dell] focuses relentlessly on driving low-cost material from the supplier through the supply chain to our customers,' he says. The low-cost producer, he adds, will be the ultimate winner, and that's reflected in Dell's steadily rising market share. According to IDC in Framingham, Mass, Dell nabbed top spot in global PC sales in the first quarter, with a 13.1% share. Hunter brought 25 years of manufacturing experience to Dell. Before joining the company in 1998, he worked in operations and supply-chain management for General Electric, Texas Instruments, and Ericsson. Today, in addition to his supply-chain responsibilities, he manages Dell's largest manufacturing site, a cluster of four factories in Austin that produces most of the systems sold in the Americas. Hunter recently spoke with *Business Week* Industries Editor Adam Aston about the nuts and bolts—and chips and monitors—of Dell's supply-chain operations.

Q: How central to Dell's success is the efficiency of its supply chain?
A: It's absolutely critical. Materials costs account for about 74% of our revenues. We spent around $21 billion on materials last year. Shaving 0.1% off [that] can have a bigger impact than, say, improving manufacturing productivity by 10%.

Q: Dell is famously lean. How does that affect your performance?
A: We carry about five days' worth of inventory. Our competitors carry 30, 45, or even 90 days' worth. This is critical because in our industry, materials costs fall by about 1% per week. So if a competitor has four weeks' worth of inventory and we have one week's, right there we have 3% worth of materials cost advantage. That can mean a 2% or 3% advantage on the bottom line.

Q: Dell has been growing at double-digit rates for its entire life span. Does software play a big role in that?
A: A couple of years ago, realizing we couldn't grow to $75 billion with the tools we had in

place, we selected i2 Technologies' software. Now, 10 months later, all our global manufacturing sites are operating on the same i2 resource-planning and execution systems.

Q: And the result?

A: We now schedule every line in every factory around the world every two hours—we only bring into the factory two hours' worth of materials. With i2, we typically run a factory with about five or six hours' worth of inventory on hand, including work in progress. This increased the cycle time at our factories and reduced warehouse space. We replaced this space with more manufacturing lines.

Q: It takes a tightly knit supplier base to deliver on a schedule like that. How many suppliers do you rely on?

A: Our top 30 suppliers represent about 75% of our total costs. Throw in the next 20, and that comes to about 95%. We deal with all of those top 50 daily, many of them many times a day.

Q: How do the new systems help you manage supply crises?

A: The software tells us where we are. We monitor practically every part, every day. If we're running out of a part, it might be because demand is outstripping supply. We'd try to solve the supply problem first. We'd call the supplier to see if he can increase the next shipment. If it's a generic part—like a hard drive—we might check alternate suppliers. Once we've exhausted our supply options, we go to the sales and marketing guys to help shift the demand to something else. This happens within a few hours.

Q: But isn't demand beyond your control?

A: One of coolest things about Dell is that we talk to 10,000-plus customers every day. That gives us 10,000 opportunities to balance supply and demand. If I'm running out of a part, then I know ahead of time. I'd communicate with our sales department and we'd move demand to material that we have. For example, we can alter lead times. We might extend the lead time on a high-demand item from the standard 4 to 5 days to 10. In this case, we know statistically how much demand will move. Or we may do a promotion. If we're short on Sony 17-inch monitors, we could offer a 19-inch model at a lower price, or even at the 17-inch price. We know if we do this an awful lot of demand will move. We can alter pricing and product mixes in real time via Dell.com. Our competitors that are building to sell through retail channels can't do that.

Q: What effect does this have on excess inventory?

A: Perpetual balance of supply and demand is my main goal in life. If I'm in perpetual balance, I can always meet my customers' delivery expectations. It also helps to minimize excess and obsolete inventory. Dell writes off between 0.05% and 0.1% of total material costs in excess and obsolete inventory—that's about $21 million across our global business in a year. In other industries that figure is probably 4% to 5%. Our competitors probably have to write off 2% to 3% worth of excess and obsolete inventory. There's no way we'd end up with months of inventory someplace. If we see two or three days of softening demand for a particular product, alarm bells go off. On an end-of-life product, we'll name a number—say 50,000 more of this computer model will be built. Then that's it — we will not build a 50,001st.

Q: At this volume of transactions, and at this speed, how do you coordinate your suppliers?
A: All of the data goes back and forth on the Internet. From the long-term planning data—volume expectations over the next 4 to 12 weeks—to the two-hourly execution systems, which are making automatic requests for replenishment, every supplier can view our order information via the Web.

Q: How far has automation gone—are even your smallest suppliers wired up?
A: The issue isn't how to get the last 5% online—that's easy, everyone can see our information via the Web. The real question is: How do I get true machine-to-machine connection between me and my supplier, because today there is still manual intervention by the supplier to get the data off the Web. We're fairly automated internally at Dell. Now we want to get the suppliers connected machine-to-machine.

Q: Are you advising the suppliers on particular technologies?
A: Yes. We have a lot of leverage with our suppliers. And all of them understand our model and supply-chain management systems. We constantly ask them, 'How can you become more like Dell?' We're very loyal to these guys. I'd say just two or three of our top suppliers have changed in the past three years.

Q: So what's the next step?
A: Folks ask if five days of inventory is the best Dell can do. Heck no, we can get to two.

Q: How have Dell's operations been affected by the PC downturn?
A: We had 1,700 layoffs a couple of months ago. And our use of contract workers fluctuates depending on the cycle. As we have a downturn, we will have a smaller percentage of contract workers. As we increase production, we have a higher percent. But this recession could be a very good thing for Dell. We're able to pass on lower costs to our customers more quickly, which allows us to gain market share and put a hurt on our competitors.

Q: Some big names, such as Cisco, have been burned by excess inventory. Your thoughts?
A: Our goal is to replace inventory with information. The more information we get to our suppliers quickly, the faster we build product, the faster we receive materials from suppliers, the faster [we] alleviate a problem like Cisco is having. Cisco might have communication problems in the supply chain about what's real demand and what's real supply. It could be that they had bad high forecasting, and the suppliers never knew better.

Reprinted from *Business Week Online*, March 14, 2002 by special permission.
© 2002 by the McGraw-Hill Companies, Inc.

Case Questions

1 What resources and capabilities does Hunter identify in his answer?

2 Which of these do you think are core competences? Why?

3 How does Dell keep the inside (the firm) and the outside (the industry and the market) in balance?

Case 2 Brand extension, with jacuzzi

Should luxury-goods firms go into the hotel business?

Giorgio Armani is already one of the most diversified brands in fashion. As well as haute couture and everyday clothes, Mr Armani and his eponymous firm create scent, cosmetics, spectacles, watches and accessories. Dedicated followers of Mr Armani's minimalist aesthetics can buy furniture at Casa Armani, chocolate, other sweets, jam and even marmalade at Armani dolce and flowers at Armani fiore. There are Armani cafes and restaurants in Paris, New York, London and other cities. An Armani nightclub recently opened in Milan. Now the great Giorgio is branching out further still. On 22 February his firm announced a $1 billion hotel venture with Dubai's Emaar Properties, the Middle East's largest property developer. Mr Armani will be in charge of the design for ten new luxury hotels and four resorts, to be built in the next six-to-eight years.

Armani's is the boldest move so far by a luxury-goods company into the hotel business. But it is by no means the first. In September 2000, a hotel designed by Donatella Versace opened on Australia's Gold Coast. In February 2001, Bulgari, an Italian jeweller, announced a joint-venture with Ritz-Carlton, the luxury-hotel division of Marriott, to build six or seven hotels and one or two resorts. Bulgari and Marriott are each investing some $70m. The first Bulgari hotel, located immediately behind Milan's La Scala opera house, will (belatedly) open in May. Salvatore Ferragamo, an Italian shoemaker, has designed four hotels in Florence, his hometown. The latest Ferragamo hotel, the Continentale, opened in January last year.

Does it make sense for designers of luxury goods to go into a tricky service business? Hotels are not even a good hedge against the fickleness of the fashion world. Travel and luxury follow the same economic cycle. In the first half of last year both industries were in bad shape because of the war in Iraq, SARS and the rise of the euro. (Many luxury-goods firms are from euro-zone countries, but their revenues are mostly in dollars or yen.) In the second half of the year the two industries both started to recover, albeit timidly. Armani and Bulgari say that their hotels are managed by outside professional managers, and that they are only in charge of making the hotels beautiful. Mr Armani considers hotels a logical extension of his aim of promoting his brand in all walks of life (can Armani toilet paper be far behind?). Rita Clifton, chairman of Interbrand, a consultancy, says that this strategy can work. A strong product, strong images and a strong experience, such as staying at a fashion designer's hotel, can combine to make a super-strong brand, claims Ms Clifton.

To fit the firm's luxurious image, Bulgari says that its hotels must be as upmarket as it is possible to be. Because small is considered more exclusive, Armani and Bulgari plan to launch mostly smallish five-star hotels. Armani's Dubai hotel, due to open in 2007, will be an exception, however, with 250 rooms. Bulgari's Milan hotel will have no more than 60 rooms.

Losing control of their brand is the biggest risk for luxury firms expanding abroad or venturing into a new line of business. Over the years, Pierre Cardin, Yves St Laurent and Christian Dior have each lost their good names by doling out licences all over the world to firms that did not deliver the appropriate quality. Calvin Klein's current troubles are related to the company's loss of control of the distribution of its wares in many countries. Designers' hotels can create good publicity, as they have done for Ferragamo with its easily controllable properties in Florence. Even if Bulgari's hotels turn out not to make any money, the venture could be considered an expensive, yet effective, advertising campaign, says Antoine Colonna of Merrill Lynch in Paris. Mr Armani's hotel plans are altogether more ambitious, and the danger of brand dilution much greater. Armani says that the management company for its hotel venture will be headquartered in Milan rather than Dubai, and that Mr Armani will be fully in charge of design. So far Mr Armani has managed to control his brand tightly despite dabbling in many different businesses. Hotels, however, are a bigger challenge than flowers and marmalade.

Source: 'Brand extension, with jacuzzi', *The Economist*, 26 February 2004.
© The Economist Newspaper Limited, London (26 February 2004).

Case Questions

1 What are the core competences of the typical luxury-goods business and Armani in particular?

2 Explain why these core competences are to be transferred to other businesses such as hotels.

3 What would be the limits to this?

4 To what extent is the core competence of Armani dependent on Giorgio Armani himself? How might his family plan for life after Giorgio?

Further reading and references

Ackenhusen, M (1992) 'Canon: competing on capabilities', INSEAD case study, reprinted in B de Wit and R Meyer (1998) *Strategy: Process, Context, and Content*, 2nd edition, International Thomson Business Press, London.

Amit, R and Schoemaker, PJ (1993) 'Strategic assets and organisational rent', *The Strategy Management Journal*, **14**, pp. 33–46, reprinted in Segal-Horn, S (ed) (1998) *The Strategy Reader*, Blackwell Business.

Barnet, JB (1991) 'Firm Resources and Sustained Competitive Advantage', *Journal of Management*, **17**, pp. 99–120.

Besanko, D, Dranove, D and Shandley, M (2000) *The Economics of Strategy*, 2nd edition, John Wiley & Sons, New York.

Collis, D and Montgomery, C (1995) 'Competing on Capabilities', *Harvard Business Review*, **73**, **4**, pp. 118–28.

Fane, G, Vagheti, R, Van Deusen, C and Woods, L (2003) 'Competitive Advantage the Toyota Way', *Business Strategy Review*, **14**, **4**, Winter, pp. 51–60.

Grant, RM (1991) 'The Resource-Based Theory of Competitive Advantage: Implications for Strategy Formulation', *California Management Review*, Spring, pp. 114–35.

Grant, RM (1998) *Contemporary Strategy Analysis*, 3rd edition, Basil Blackwell, Oxford.

Hall, Richard (1992) 'The Strategic Analysis of Intangible Resources', *Strategic Management Journal*, **13**, pp. 135–44.

Hamel, G (1994) 'The Concept of Core Competence', Chapter 1 in G Hamel and A Heene (eds) *Competence Based Competition*, in the Strategic Management Series, John Wiley & Sons.

Hamel, G and Heene, A (eds) (1994) *Competence Based Competition*, the Strategic Management Series, John Wiley & Sons, Chichester.

Hamel, G and Prahalad, CK (1989) 'Strategic Intent', *Harvard Business Review*, **67**, **3**, pp. 63–76.

Hamel, G and Prahalad, CK (1993) 'Strategy as Stretch and Leverage', *Harvard Business Review*, **71**, **2**, pp. 75–84.

Lave, C and March, J (1993) *An Introduction to Models in the Social Sciences*, University Press of America, NY.

McGee, J and Segal-Horn, S (1997) 'Global Competences in Service Multinationals', in Thomas, H and O'Neal, D (eds) *Strategic Discovery: Competing in New Arenas*, the Strategic Management Series, J Wiley & Sons, Chichester, pp. 49–77.

Nelson, RR and Winter, SG (1982) *An Evolutionary Theory of Economic Change*, Harvard University Press, Boston.

Penrose, E (1995) *The Theory of the Growth of the Firm*, 3rd edition (original edition 1954), Oxford University Press.

Peteraf, MA (1993) 'The Cornerstones of Competitive Advantage; a Resource-based View', *Strategic Management Journal*, **14**, **2**, pp. 179–91.

Porter, ME (1980) *Competitive Strategy: Techniques for Analysing Industries and Competitors*, Free Press, New York.

Porter, ME (1985) *Competitive Advantage*, Free Press, New York.

Prahalad, CK and Hamel, G (1990) 'The Core Competence of the Corporation', *Harvard Business Review*, May/June, pp. 79–91, reprinted in S Segal-Horn (1998) (ed.) *The Strategy Reader*, Blackwell Business.

Schoemaker, P (1992) 'How to Link Strategic Vision to Core Capabilities', *Sloan Management Review*, Fall, pp. 67–81.

Segal-Horn, S (ed.) (1998) *The Strategy Reader*, Blackwell Business, Oxford.

Selznick, P (1957) *Leadership and Administration*, University of California Press.

Stalk, G, Evans, P and Shulman, LE (1992) 'Competing on Capabilities: the new Rules of Corporate Strategy', *Harvard Business Review*, **70**, **2**, pp. 57–69.

Chapter 8

Competitive strategy: moving from theory to practice[1]

Chapter contents

Introduction

Alfred P. Sloan once said that no company ever stops changing. Our discussion in earlier chapters has indicated that competition is a dynamic process within which firms never stop trying to pursue changing market demands. Nor do they stop trying to imitate and emulate each other. Some of this dynamism is the natural consequence of rivalry and of ambition. But some of it is due to persistent changes that take place in markets as knowledge grows and experience accumulates – the forces of technological change and economic growth. This chapter starts to move us from the basic model of competitive strategy with its notions of positioning and strategic capability to arenas where practical complexities

---

[1] This chapter is written jointly with Duncan Angwin.

are important. Later chapters explore these in terms of multi-business companies, multi-territory (international) companies, and the new economy in which knowledge and information economics prevail.

This chapter uses the **industry life cycle** model as a backdrop against which we can observe different kinds of strategies at different stages of evolution of an industry or of a firm. A general life cycle model is presented to create another generic strategy model – this one being a time-based model. But the bulk of the chapter is concerned with three practical themes. The first is the theme of start-ups and the role of entrepreneurs. The second reviews how entry strategies are conceived and deployed to overcome organized resistance and substantial entry barriers. The third theme is concerned with issues of corporate failure and turnarounds, problems that occur typically in maturity and beyond. Each of these themes enables us to reflect on the balance of forces between the need for powerful analysis of the strategic context and the personality, capability and leadership of individuals. Entrepreneurs and start-ups reflect strongly on the last point – entrepreneurs are quintessentially individualistic. Entry strategies into the complex economics of embedded firms and industries requires powerful strategizing. Turnarounds and the remedy of corporate failure require a blending of powerful leadership and operational capabilities with the need to bring the firm's economics in line with the dictates of the markets. In practice (and looking ahead to Part 4 on practice), strategies always require a blending of strategic thinking and analysis (strategizing) and personal leadership skills and capabilities. This chapter introduces these issues.

8.1 The life cycle model

Porter's famous five forces model is a static view of competition in which industry structure is seen as a stable determinant of performance of firms. In practice we know that industries evolve over time. They have a genesis and a start-up period; they have periods of rapid growth and then maturity sets in. Maturity might last a long time or the industry may pass quite quickly into decline and eventual decay. The question is whether competitive strategies have distinctive characteristics over this life cycle. Are there distinctive success factors at each stage of the cycle?

The industry life cycle model is the supply side analogue of the better-known **product life cycle.** Products are born, their sales grow, they reach maturity, and they eventually decline and maybe die. If products have life cycles then so do industries, albeit on a longer time scale. For example, the products in the computer games industry may have lives of just a few years (e.g. Sega, Sony, Nintendo) but the life of the industry continues beyond these and into successive generations of products. The life cycle is conventionally divided into four phases, as shown in Figure 8.1.

The life cycle curve has over its whole a distinctive, somewhat asymmetric bell shape. In practice we can usually observe only portions of the life cycle even though we might be

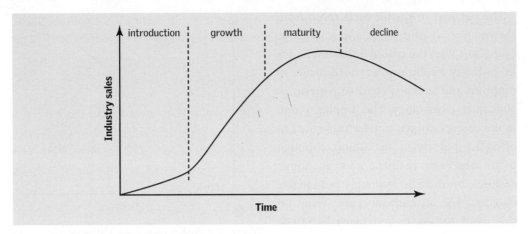

Figure 8.1 Industry life cycle model

conscious of issues of industry evolution. Robert Grant (2002) emphasizes two key factors behind industry evolution: demand growth, and patterns of knowledge creation and diffusion. Demand growth is also important for the product life cycle and can be characterized by S-shaped patterns (see Figure 8.2). In the introduction stage, the pace of growth can be slow as the new product gains acceptance and overcomes customer inertia. The growth stage is marked, if successful, by rapidly increasing sales as product formulations become more standardized and as customers become accustomed to the benefit–cost offer of the new product class. Maturity is a reflection of market saturation and sales are predominantly due to replacement demand. Finally, new technology and new knowledge cause obsolescence of the product-class and sales fall away.

The knowledge driver is more complex in its operation and much more varied in its manifestations. New knowledge is captured in the form of product innovation and rival forms of this new knowledge can result in a range of new propositions before the customer – for example, the range of videotape options, VHS, Betamax and Philips 2000, and also the different technologies behind the original automobiles: expert opinion 100 years ago favoured the steam car! In economic terms there is no dominant technology and rival designs compete for attention. The industry evolution normally evokes processes of standardization and the number of competing designs often falls to a single dominant design. This standardization reassures customers and firms are encouraged to cut costs by increasing scale and standardization. At this point the emphasis shifts to process innovations from product innovation. The most dramatic example is the automobile industry. The essential nature of the technology has barely changed for 80 years but the extent, scale and significance of process innovation has been dramatic. As Grant points out (pp. 244–5), product innovation has been incremental and not systemic, e.g. disc brakes and engine management systems whereas electric power innovation has barely made any mark at all.

The patterns of the life cycle result from the interaction of demand and knowledge (supply). Often the crucial inflection points in industry evolution can be difficult to pinpoint and much is owed to patterns of consumer psychology. The 'tipping point' in the choice between rival technologies can often be put down to fashion although many observers maintain that economic realities do underlie seemingly fashionable choices. For a contemporary view on this, read Leibowitz and Margolis (1999, pp. 119–134) on the tipping point between VHS and Betamax and see also Chapter 12.

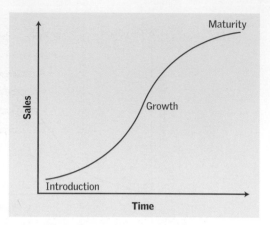

Figure 8.2 S-shaped growth patterns

The industry life cycle is a highly generic concept. It does not imply any standardization in terms of time taken at various stages. Some industries are very long-lived (e.g. railroads and automobiles). As the twentieth century progressed and as the pace and scope of technological development increased, product life cycles became progressively compressed. Many industries introduced in the last 25 years have grown very quickly (e.g. the PC industry). Some have grown and vanished (e.g. the vinyl LP record). Some started and never grew beyond the early stages (e.g. laser discs).

However, there is a standard approach to analysing life cycle effects. First, the stages of the cycle are identified, typically embryonic, growth, maturity and decline (or ageing). Second, the generic characteristics of the industry are identified. Different authors emphasize somewhat different elements but Arthur D. Little Inc. (ADL) (which pioneered and marketed much of this analysis as a consulting product in the 1970s)[2] suggest growth rate, market potential, products, number of competitors, market share stability, purchasing patterns, ease of entry, and technology. Figures 8.3a and 8.3b show how patterns of evolution can be seen in the data. From this there is arguably a general pattern over the life cycle as volumes increase, standardization increases, consumer knowledge grows and entry barriers eventually fall. Strategically the incentive to innovate and grow rests on the chances of being able to generate volumes, to protect knowledge, develop brands and have a good run at making profits before entry erodes margins and profitability. For example, a dominant position is ideal but rarely achieved. It comes about because a competitor has managed to establish a quasi-monopoly or has achieved technological dominance. Such positions have been claimed by IBM in mainframe computers, Kodak in colour film, Xerox in copying,

[2] The academic pioneers of the concept of the product life cycle were Everett R Rogers, 1962 and Theodore Levitt, 1965.

Description	Stages of the industry life cycle			
	Embryonic	**Growth**	**Mature**	**Ageing**
Growth rate				
Market potential				
Product line				
Number of competitors				
Market share stability				
Purchasing patterns				
Ease of entry				
Technology				
Overall				

Figure 8.3a Factors affecting the stages of the industry life cycle
Source: Arthur D Little Inc., 1974, 1980.

and much more recently by Microsoft and Intel in the PC industry. In the case of the first three we can see that the dominant position was eventually competed away. Mainframes were outmoded by smaller computers. Conventional colour film slowly became more competitive but digital technology has provided the real push towards obsolescence. Xerox was eventually caught by new technologies from Canon and other Japanese copier manufacturers. In each of these three cases the anti-trust authorities were sufficiently concerned about the existence and potential exploitation of dominant position to the extent of prolonged legal proceedings against all three. It is interesting to observe similar processes at work with Microsoft.

ADL was among the first to collect data on financial flows over the life cycle and Figure 8.4 shows sales following the familiar bell-shaped curve. But profits and cash flow are negative in the first two stages, significantly profitable in maturity, and appropriately declining in the ageing stage. This represents the desirable pattern in which the returns on investment have to be garnered in maturity with real profitability occurring the longer decline can be delayed. Conversely, profitability would be significantly challenged (i) if the industry fails to

Description	Stages of the industry life cycle			
	Embryonic	Growth	Mature	Ageing
Dominant	●	●	●	●
Strong	●	●	●	◐
Favourable	●	●	◐	○
Tenable	●	◐	○	○
Weak	◐	○	○	○
Non-viable	○	○	○	○

● Danger, withdraw to market niche, divert or liquidate   ◐ Cautious, selective development   ○ Wide range of strategic options

Figure 8.3b The life cycle portfolio matrix
Source: Arthur D Little Inc., 1974, 1980.

grow to large enough size, (ii) if it declines early, and (iii) if it attracts too many competitors too soon.

If Figure 8.4 indicates desirable patterns of cash flow then there are likely to be strategies that are particularly helpful at each stage. ADL calls these **natural strategic thrusts**. These are:

- *Start-up strategies* are applied in the embryonic phase to achieve high and/or defensible market position while market growth is high.

- *Growth with industry strategies* applies when the firm is content with its industry position and seeks to maintain market share: this is indicated when enjoying dominant or strong competitive position, especially in maturity.

- *Gain position gradually* is applicable when a modest share increase is necessary in order to consolidate position and defend cash flows.

- *Gain position aggressively* is an aggressive share-building strategy in an attractive industry while the growth rate is still high: it often comes in the form of pre-emptive strategies where entry-deterring capacity is built aggressively ahead of demand – this is a high-risk double-or-quits bet.

- *Defend position* applies when enjoying a dominant or strong position: the cost of defending position should be lower for industry leaders than for attackers and cash flows should be protectable,

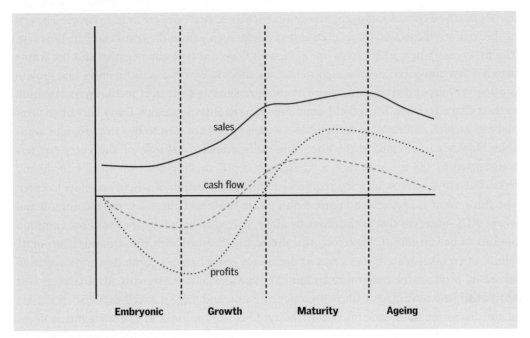

Figure 8.4 Financial flows over the industry life cycle
Source: Arthur D Little Inc., 1974, 1980.

- *Harvest* is possible at any stage. The important factor is the speed of harvest. From a strong position harvesting may be slow because the erosion of competitive position might be slow. Issues here include how strongly to defend versus harvest, given the other strategic demands for cash. Rapid harvesting may have to take place from weaker positions and may imply early closure.

The industry life cycle model needs to be used with care. Criticisms of the approach include:

1 its underlying validity and usefulness;

2 the stages vary widely in terms of time;

3 industry activity does not necessarily evolve into a well-behaved S-curve;

4 markets can be rejuvenated and maturity can turn back into growth through changes in fundamental industry conditions;

5 firms can themselves fundamentally transform life cycle positions through innovation and repositioning (see comments on industry transformation in Chapter 6);

6 the nature of competition varies greatly from industry to industry.

The life cycle is a generic model (like Porter's generic strategies) in which the general characteristics of the strategic environment can be seen in broad strategic relief unfettered by deeper practical considerations of how in practice these strategies are made to work. The rest of this chapter focuses on three 'events' that can be seen within the context of the life cycle. The first is start-ups, where costs are high, cash flows are typically negative and the young firm has few competences on which to base an effective entry; successful entry and growth is often very dependent on the nature of entrepreneurs and the next section pays attention to their characteristics. The second situation concerns entry strategies. Entry very often takes place in growth and early maturity phases where profits are seen to be attractive and available. However, such profits are often not easily available because of the entry barriers constructed by the incumbents – a strength in depth, making head-on attacks costly and risky. Therefore, successful entry requires careful consideration of where and how to enter. The third event is ageing (see Figure 8.3b), where business failures are most common and where ADL observes that withdrawal to niche, divert or liquidate are the most common options to be considered. Therefore, this theme is concerned with turnarounds. Corporate failure often takes place in the years of decline, as entry barriers come down, competition increases, products become more commodity-like and only those with advantageous cost positions retain advantage. Failure becomes common and there is a well-established activity of turning companies back into profitability. This section looks at the ways this is done. Clearly it is not correct that start-ups only occur in the early stages of the industry life cycle, nor are turnarounds only required in the maturity and decline of industries. However, both are most common in these periods and the distinctive characteristics of entrepreneurs and turnaround specialists are seen in sharp relief when placed against these portions of the industry life cycle.

8.2 **Strategy and the entrepreneur: start-ups and sustainability**

Take a moment to think of the names of a few highly successful business executives. The chances are that you have tended to pick the names of entrepreneurs such as Richard Branson, Anita Roddick, Sir Clive Sinclair, Alan Sugar and Sir James Goldsmith of the UK; Bill Gates, Steve Jobs, Donald Trump and T-Boone Pickens of the US; and Rupert Murdoch, Alan Bond and Holmes á Court of Australia.

However, such entrepreneurs are but a minority among the business leaders of the world's largest and most successful companies – and many entrepreneurs do not remain successful for reasons we shall discuss later. Why, then, do we, and the business press, give such prominence to entrepreneurs? What is it about entrepreneurs that we find compelling and what are the implications for the way our businesses, and indeed we ourselves, interpret the business world?

8.2.1 **Entrepreneurs: an overview**

Entrepreneurs are a global phenomenon. However, in Anglo-American cultures, where individualism is encouraged, they are glorified, whereas in 'collectivist' cultures they result in significant tensions. While it has been shown that entrepreneurialism declines as 'collectivism' increases, it is important to note that a balance of individualism and collectivism is important for entrepreneurship to flourish. For example, the Asian entrepreneurs in North America have sufficient autonomy to exhibit creativity and entrepreneurial behaviour, and yet their cultural background, emphasizing collectivism, helps them promote co-operation and group ownership of innovation (Li 1993). In addition, then, to perceiving entrepreneurs in purely psychological terms, focusing upon their potential as individuals, we must also recognize their positions in society at large, where social backgrounds can help to inspire and enable.

In the UK, entrepreneurs were the potent symbol of the 'Thatcher decade' and today they are once again being encouraged. They are the source of contemporary myths and legends; they are romantic, larger than life, modern buccaneers, who hold enormous wealth. They are rebels, trail-blazers and risk takers. We focus on them, for they are our 'proof' that the individual counts; that one can make a difference.

Entrepreneurs are being encouraged, with the UK Government giving substantial tax incentives and advice for the starting up and developing of businesses. There is also a more positive attitude towards entrepreneurs in society at large, as we move ever more towards an individualistic society and a 'can do' attitude. Implicit in governmental encouragement is that entrepreneurialism is good for the economy in terms of stimulating growth and encouraging innovation. Indeed, recent speeches by the UK Government aim at fostering the use of the internet, nationwide, as a major facilitator of entrepreneurial growth and, so it is hoped, economic prosperity.

This raises the questions of what entrepreneurialism is and how we would recognize it. To answer these questions, we examine:

- What an entrepreneur is
- What it takes to be an entrepreneur
- Where we find entrepreneurs
- Whether entrepreneurs have a shelf life

8.2.2 **What is an entrepreneur?**

The **entrepreneur** is often a single leader with personal charge in a highly dynamic situation, such as in a new firm, or a small one in a growing market, or sometimes within a large organization facing a crisis. This individual has a clear and distinct vision of purpose and directs an organization that is structured to be as responsive as is possible to his or her personal wishes. Such entrepreneurial vision tends to have a high potential pay-off, such as the commercial success of an idea or the turnaround of a firm in crisis.

Through 'memories of the future' (Ingvar, 1985), entrepreneurs mentally rehearse 'pathways' into the future and 'envision' a new world for their business. They seek to create the future and, to do so, they must take risks, be aggressive, proactive and innovative. Fondly, then, we think of entrepreneurs as visionary leaders. They have a profound ability with language and – often in symbolic form, as metaphor – cause others to see things from a new perspective. A good example is Edwin Land, who invented the Polaroid camera. In speaking of photography, he said, 'It's not merely the camera you are focusing: you are focusing yourself. Part of you is now permanent' (Mintzberg *et al.* 1998, p. 610).

Entrepreneurs, then, have a number of characteristics, the most widely cited of which is being visionary. However, there are many other 'traits' that are commonly associated with them. They are said to have self-confidence, the ability to bounce back, are innovative, results-oriented, professional risk takers and have total commitment (Barrow 1991). In addition, they have the ability to conceptualize and plan, manage others, manage their own time and to learn as well as adapt to change (Gaedeke and Tootelian 1985). They require technical competence, mental ability, human relations skills, high achievement drive and creativity (Hodgetts 1982).

Furthermore, a visionary leader requires integrity – a genuine feeling behind what the leader says and does. This is what makes leadership truly visionary, and what makes impossible the transition of such leadership into any formula (Mintzberg *et al.* 1998, p. 610). To take an example, when employees of Richard Branson's company Virgin are interviewed, we find this level of belief in Branson's integrity. From his idiosyncratic style and beliefs, high-profile dramatic activities (such as ballooning around the world) and high commitment, we find employees buying into and motivated by his vision. We find entrepreneurship as the 'art of turning work into play: entrepreneurial leadership creating drama' (Mintzberg *et al.* 1998).

8.2.3 What does it take to be an entrepreneur?

The interest in researching entrepreneurial traits has been driven by the question of whether entrepreneurs are born or made, as this may mean that executives can be trained to be entrepreneurial and revitalize their businesses.

It has been shown that while the 'need for achievement' is essential for the entrepreneur, it is not genetically bound. Indeed, lifetime experiences are just as important as hereditary variables. Such experiences are often externally determined by social and economic pressures, which force entrepreneurial activity as a legitimating channel or means of expression. Such groups have tended to be those groups outside or debarred from the predominant managerial or social class, such as immigrants, ethnic minorities, socially or educationally deprived groups. 'Outsiders', then, the victims of social marginalization, often have the incentive to exhibit entrepreneurial behaviour and also tend to have the support of their disadvantaged group.

At the individual level, there are three groups of factors influencing the entrepreneurial decision. The first group comprises antecedent influences, such as generic factors, family influences, educational choices and previous career experiences. The second is the incubator organization, where the geographic location may provide impetus (for example, if the entrepreneur would rather live in the country than the town), where the nature of knowledge and skills may allow transferability, where other 'co-conspirators' may be met, and where the organization may pressurize or facilitate departure. The third group consists of environmental factors, such as general economic conditions, availability of funding, other examples of entrepreneurial activity, opportunities for interim consulting and availability of supporting services (Cooper 1981).

Therefore, the choice to become an entrepreneur will be affected by the above factors and the balance between the strengths of specific competencies and self-confidence, and the restraints in terms of career, life-stage and income needs. Critical will be the presence of a trigger to prompt the entrepreneur into 'life'.

A *Wall Street Journal*/Gallup survey shows that entrepreneurs are significantly different from the senior executives of Fortune 500 firms. They take fewer holidays, are more likely to have suffered stress, have a greater need to be recognized as leaders, have made an earlier start in business, have worked for several companies, have lower socialization needs and are more likely to have been expelled or suspended from school. The 'needs' of entrepreneurs are illustrated in Figure 8.5, which shows the high level of importance of having the power and freedom to act, as well as receiving recognition, and the much lower importance of personal comfort and relationships.

Figure 8.5 Personal profiles: the 'needs' of entrepreneurs
Source: Hunt, 1981.

8.2.4 **Where do we find entrepreneurs?**

Entrepreneurs, new and small businesses

To get started, new firms, regardless of sector, seem to need personalized leadership to establish their basic direction or strategic vision. Such situations also attract strong leaders, as they can put their own stamp on things. It is not surprising, then, to find that most entrepreneurs are at the head of new and small businesses, where they have control.

By definition, entrepreneurs need to innovate, but this capacity is threatened by constraints in terms of resources and controls. It is an essential characteristic of entrepreneurs that they use more resources than they control, for they are motivated primarily by the *pursuit of opportunity*, rather than working within resource constraints.

> The entrepreneur always searches for change and responds to it, and exploits it as an opportunity. (Drucker 1985, p. 42)

Entrepreneurial firms are often young and aggressive, continually searching for new opportunities that may be perceived as too risky by large firms or, indeed, not perceived at all. There is a tendency to concentrate not on complex markets, but on niche markets, which the leader can understand. The small size of these firms, with their focused strategies, allows the organizational structure to remain simple, so that the leader can retain tight control and the firms move quickly, their flexibility out-manoeuvring the big bureaucracies. Indeed, such an intimate knowledge in one mind provides an unexcelled focus. Nothing else permits so clear and complete a vision and also allows flexibility to elaborate and rework the vision.

Firms that exhibit entrepreneurial actions are those with internal or external resource disadvantages in relation to a competitor. Such firms need to avoid competition to prevent losing in head-on battles. Their best option is to discover and seize new opportunities that rivals will not perceive or be able to easily counter. The key issue here is 'uncertainty', in that the resource-rich firm might easily duplicate the action of the firm with inferior resources, but the uncertainty surrounding the entrepreneurial action delays the response. A classic example is in the early 1980s, when Bill Gates of Microsoft played on the competitive uncertainty surrounding the development of the software industry. Clearly many larger firms could have out-competed Microsoft at the time, but Microsoft's small size and the uncertain nature of the industry meant that competitors did not pay it too much attention. The sorts of action that might be taken by entrepreneurial firms include developing new products or services, improving products or services, making geographic transfers and satisfying shortages of supply.

Entrepreneurial strategy, then, is deliberate rather than emergent. It is critically about *'seizing new opportunities early'* (Oster 1990) rather than being resource-based. Entrepreneurial strategy is characterized by creativity and first-mover advantages, which can provide industry leadership and influence the structure of competitive domains in a way that may create potentially sustainable competitive advantage.

Intrapreneurship

In the face of large declining firms in the 1980s, both the US and the UK saw entrepreneurial characteristics as a way of reinvigorating stagnating corporate behemoths. The promotion of entrepreneurial characteristics in large companies was to be a form of 'corporate renaissance', where the spirit of enterprise would be reawakened and organizational alchemy performed, to transmute smokestack industries into high-technology firms (Kanter 1983). This form of entrepreneurship gave rise to the term '**intrapreneurship**', where employees other than 'the boss' could champion some technology or strategic issue by means of an entrepreneurial role – a role in which there are not only the ideas, but also the innovation – the doing of new things. Ideas generally abound in organizations; the scarce people are the ones who have the know-how, energy, daring and staying power to implement ideas.

> *The champion is not a blue-sky dreamer, or an intellectual giant. The champion might even be an idea thief. But above all, he's the pragmatic one who grabs onto someone else's theoretical construct if necessary and bull-headedly pushes it to fruition.* (Peters and Waterman 1982, p. 207)

So, if many agree that 'champions' are pivotal to the innovation process, why not just go out and hire them? Part of the reason is that champions' working styles are at odds with the ways that most businesses are managed. In the words of Tait Elder, at 3M:

> *We expect our champions to be irrational.* (Peters and Waterman 1982, p. 202)

> *Most corporations fail to tolerate the creative fanatic who has been the driving force behind most major innovations. Innovations, being far removed from the*

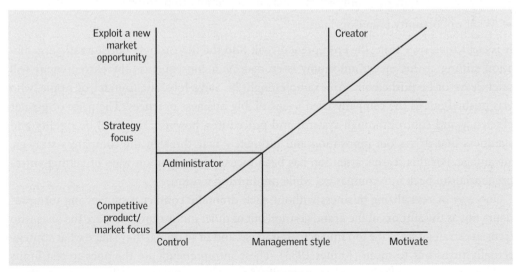

Figure 8.6 Entrepreneurial type versus administrator type
Source: Stevenson and Gumpert, 1985.

mainstream of business, show little promise in the early stages of development. Moreover, the champion is obnoxious, impatient, egotistical and perhaps a bit irrational in organizational terms. As a consequence, he is not hired. If hired, he is not promoted or rewarded. He is regarded as 'not a serious person', 'embarrassing', or 'disruptive'. (Quinn, in Peters and Waterman 1982, p. 206)

This difficulty is at the core of the debate over the place of the entrepreneur in the large firm: the debate over 'innovation versus administration'. As firms grow and become more complex, there becomes an increasing need for greater administrative control. However, such controls generally constrain innovation and so result in the loss of entrepreneurial spirit. This is illustrated by the changing importance of administrative and entrepreneurial executives (*see* Figure 8.6).

The entrepreneur asks:

- Where is the opportunity?
- How do I capitalize on it?
- What resources do I need?
- How do I gain control over them?
- What structure is best?

Whereas the administrator is characterized by asking:

- What resources do I control?
- What structure determines our organization's relationship to its market?
- How can I minimize the impact of others on my ability to perform?
- What opportunity is appropriate?

It is clear that, over time, the entrepreneur will find the increasingly bureaucratic organization stifling, as his or her autonomy is eroded. As a consequence, the entrepreneur will often leave or be pushed out. An example might be Steve Jobs, the founder of Apple, who was pushed out as the company tried to instill 'big business practices'. The price of greater efficiency and control through systems and procedures, however, may well be rigidity and staidness that drives out innovation and ultimately may threaten the company's strategic advantage. For this reason, attention has been focused heavily upon ways of getting entrepreneurialism back into companies, while minimizing tension.

One way of revitalizing business without such dramatic conflict is by viewing intrapreneurs not as the authors of the grand gesture, but of quiet innovation. They are the ones who translate strategy set at the top into actual practice, and in so doing, they shape what strategy actually turns out to mean (Kanter 1983). These intrapreneurs are the ones to test limits and create new possibilities. They generally do not start businesses, but improve them by pushing the creation of new products, leading the development of new production technology or experimenting with new humanly responsive work practices. Occasionally they may become heroes, but often by the time the achievements have found their way into company announcements, it is hard to attribute. So these 'quiet' intrapreneurs may not in themselves bring about big changes; they are, however, cumulatively, a major force for change – their micro-changes are often the first steps in major reorientations (Kanter 1983).

Internal innovation may contribute to the development of sustainable competitive advantage, but with the pace of knowledge accelerating, many, regardless of their size, cannot keep pace. Knowledge is also becoming far more specialized and often embedded within different contexts. To harness this proliferation of entrepreneurial activity, and to avoid the risks of forcing one's own organization to learn new tricks, firms are embarking more than ever before upon strategic alliances. For example, the large pharmaceutical firms are eagerly searching for opportunities to team up with biotechnology companies that can perform early-stage research, so that they can reduce their fixed costs, reduce risks and not impair their chances of discovering and marketing new blockbuster drugs.

Other methods of harnessing entrepreneurs include outright corporate acquisition, although this often leads to the types of tension mentioned above, and forms of investment whereby the large firm supplies venture capital into funds for start-ups. This allows ground-floor entry, the ability to observe and the possibility of future benefits, without the domination and stifling of the entrepreneur. However, as part of a syndicate group, returns to the large firm may be diminished.

8.2.5 **Do entrepreneurs have a shelf life?**

New organizations may grow rapidly and require specialized forms of expertise. As Greiner's (1972) five-stage model of evolutionary and revolutionary growth suggests, to cope with greater size and complexity over time, there will be an impetus towards new ways of organizing, which have important implications for the way in which the business is managed. However, these pressures can be, and very often are, in direct contradiction to the entrepreneur's instinctive need to retain power and avoid any formalization of activities that may erode his or her right 'to rule'.

In large organizations, where strong entrepreneurial leaders are used in times of crisis, such as managing a turnaround, the normal powers of existing groups are suspended, so that the leader can impose a new integrated vision. With the aversion of the crisis, the organization may revert to its traditional level of complexity and the entrepreneurial leader may then become perceived as an obstacle to the smooth running of the business.

It would seem that entrepreneurs as corporate leaders are excellent at providing vision and leadership for start-ups and in times of crisis. However, their powerful appeal is often to a specific audience at a specific time. As the business environment changes, perhaps with increasing organizational complexity as a direct consequence of their own achievements, entrepreneurs face the danger of 'the Icarus paradox':

The fabled Icarus of Greek mythology is said to have flown so high, so close to the sun, that his artificial wax wings melted and he plunged to his death in the Aegean Sea. (Miller 1992)

In other words, like Icarus, whose greatest asset led to his demise, entrepreneurs are captured by the causes of their very own successes. Success leads to specialization and exaggeration, to confidence and complacency, to dogma and ritual. We can have too much of a good thing.

Successful entrepreneurs, then, need to build an enterprise that will function without them. While they may rarely ever come to play the purely visionary role, as they will remain deeply engaged in their organizations, their roles must change for the organization to continue to flourish. They need to move from doing the work to teaching others how to do it. They will always strive for increasing impact and will aim to achieve this by focusing more on the strategy – the common purpose and organizational norms, rather than moving the product out of the door. Sir Michael Edwards – well-known for turning around high-profile businesses in the UK – always left after the firm had pulled through its crisis, rather than staying on to manage for sustained growth. He felt his management style suited a crisis situation rather than steady build. The different ways in which the role of the entrepreneur may change, as a small business evolves, is well illustrated by Churchill and Lewis's (1983) five stages of small business growth, namely, existence, survival, success, take-off and resource creativity.

In some cases, entrepreneurial CEOs cannot adjust their styles or bring themselves to leave. Especially when they were the founders of the business, it can be impossible for them to proactively manage their departure or countenance changes. They then find themselves in a dilemma: with each success they fly ever closer to the sun, blinding them to the increasing complexity and changing needs of their organizations. The heat of these tensions will melt the wings of even the most determined entrepreneur. 'Heroic' figures of the past, like those listed below, are now just names with which we struggle for association:

Alan Bond	Asil Nadir	Clive Sinclair	Holmes á Court
Cyril Lord	David Bloom	Eddie Shah	Freddie Laker
George Walker	Ivan Boesky	Jim Slater	John Ashcroft
John De Lorean	John Gunn	John Milken	Tony Berry

8.2.6 Reflections upon entrepreneurs and strategy

The topic of entrepreneurs opens many avenues in the strategy field. In terms of our view on strategy, **entrepreneurial strategy** is deliberate rather than emergent. It is top-down and directive, binding behind the entrepreneur's vision. Linked with the vision is the ability to innovate 'with 'controlled boldness' – the ideas are bold, the execution careful. Thus, there is an interesting interplay between problems and opportunities, as the entrepreneur will tend to treat problems as a crisis, which he will then turn into an opportunity. *By overselling* *the problem, he creates energy and the need for coherence.* By this means, an entrepreneur is able to achieve frame-breaking change within both the business and the industry itself. Such innovation is under-represented in traditional strategy models, where the emphasis is upon deliberate outcomes to plans to exploit unique resources, as in emphasizing lower cost or differentiation. Entrepreneurial actions are more spontaneous, based on opportunities created from market disequilibrium. Unlike the traditional approaches, which are based upon present-day or known resources, where future results should be predictable, these models understate the outcomes from entrepreneurial action, which are far more uncertain.

The powerful combination of vision and innovation in one person can give tremendous strategic punch to an organization sufficiently receptive and flexible to such autocratic power. However, increasing organizational complexity raises the issue of managerial sustainability. Traditionally, the entrepreneur would be associated with start-ups and crises, and would then be edged out, as organizational complexity increased. However, in a rapidly globalizing world experiencing a technological revolution and increasing competition, innovation is of critical importance. Those firms competing globally that invest more in innovation achieve the highest returns (Price 1996; Franko 1987). More than ever before, entrepreneurship is driving economic growth in general, and the harnessing of entrepreneurship is increasingly the secret of corporate renewal. This presents companies with significant new challenges in terms of how they should be organized, as innovators need to be woven into their very fabric and yet dysfunctional tensions must also be avoided. Within the firm, successful entrepreneurial activity and innovation require flexibility and a move away from the M-form. This is currently driving research into an N-form, which has optimistically been described as 'a new form', but in reality is a *set* of new forms of organizing. We might argue that the proliferation of strategic alliances and their many variants, the wide range of acquisition types, networks and the 'corporatization' of venture capital, are companies' attempts to organize more flexibly in order to harness innovation and yet give entrepreneurs the autonomy they need to flourish.

8.3 New entry strategies

Entrepreneurs give a very vivid picture of the strategic and operational challenges that face managers. We have used them as a device to illustrate some of the problems that typically arise at the beginning of the industry life cycle. It is worth remembering that entrepreneurs (like the turnaround specialists that we discuss later) are very real people operating in very challenging circumstances. However, the industry life cycle is simply an intellectual construct that is useful in helping us to structure and analyse problems. In this section we look a little more broadly at some of the strategic implications of the life cycle but noting as we go along that the life cycle idea is not a strategic law – there are in practice many irregularities and paradoxes as is evident in the very real world of start-ups, entry and turnarounds.

Figure 8.3a is map that displays the factors that help us define the stages of the life cycle. This leads to a view that there are four generic styles of strategy over the life cycle corresponding to the embryonic, growth, maturity and ageing phases shown in Figure 8.3a. Figures 8.3b and 8.4 show the implications in terms of strategic objectives (e.g. selective development) and financial outcomes. We need also to look at the implications for industry structure, competition and sources of competitive advantage. Figure 8.7 (taken from Grant 2002) shows demand/growth conditions and technology as drivers and other variables such as products, manufacturing and distribution, competition and key success factors as outcomes. Thus, competition changes predictably going from few firms, through multiple entries, to stabilization, then shakeout and eventual exits of many firms. The forms of

	Introduction	Growth	Maturity	Decline
Demand	Limited to early adapters: high income, avant-garde	Rapidly increasing market penetration	Mass market, replacement/repeat buying. Customers knowledgeable and price sensitive	Obsolescence
Technology	Competing technologies. Rapid product innovation	Standardization around dominant technology. Rapid process innovation	Well-diffused technical know-how: quest for technological improvements	Little or no product or process innovation
Products	Poor quality. Wide variety of features and technologies. Frequent design changes	Design and quality improve. Emergence of dominant design	Trend to commoditization. Attempts to differentiate by branding, quality and bundling	Commodities the norm: differentiation difficult and unprofitable
Manufacturing and distribution	Short production runs. High-skilled labour content. Specialized distribution channels	Capacity shortages. Mass production. Competition for access to distribution	Emergence of overcapacity. Deskilling of production. Long production runs. Distributors carry fewer lines	Chronic overcapacity. Re-emergence of specialist channels
International trade	Producers and consumers in advanced countries.	Exports from advanced countries to rest of world	Production shifts to newly industrializing countries then to developing countries	Exports from countries with lowest labour costs
Competition	Few companies.	Entry, mergers and exits	Shakeout. Price competition increases	Price wars, exits
Key success factors	Product innovation. Establishing credible image of firm and product	Design for manufacture. Access to distribution. Building strong brand. Fast product development. Process innovation	Cost efficiency through capital intensity, scale efficiency, and low input costs. High quality	Low overheads. Buyer selection. Signalling commitment. Rationalizing capacity

Figure 8.7 The evolution of industry structure and competition over the life cycle
Source: Grant, 2002, p. 311.

competitive advantage go from simple product novelty, through innovation, to differentia-tion alternatives, moves towards commoditization, and eventual commodity status. The implications for functional strategies such as marketing and manufacturing follow directly from this. Cost advantage plays a minor, even negligible role in start-up and growth, grows more important in maturity as a major contributor to profit, and eventually becomes central as the power to differentiate wanes.

The growth (and early maturity) phase attracts entry. In particular a successful pioneering of a new industry is often buttressed by significant barriers to entry, such as by patents (see the examples of Kodak in film, Xerox in photocopying, Microsoft in PC operating systems, and Intel in microprocessors). The role of the pioneers in establishing such new industries is well known. Less well known are the successful strategies of competitors striving to enter across the barriers. Table 7.4 outlines the strength of the Xerox position in 1980 behind its wall of patents and the other entry barriers that it had had time to construct. What is less well known (perhaps forgotten) is how waves of entry head on against the Xerox barriers were dashed and broken. These include many firms well known in their day but now for-gotten (such as Gestetner and Agfa) but also major players such as IBM and Kodak. However, Xerox's position was eventually undermined and broken by patterns of entry that stepped around the formidable Xerox defences and offered alternative value propositions to customers. Table 7.5 outlines how Canon rewrote the 'rules of the game'. What this means is that the old rules, the Xerox competitive advantages, were replaced by new rules, the new competitive advantages. These new rules came about through a 'sequential entry strategy' pursued by Japanese competitors, notably Ricoh and Canon. The way these new rules are put in place can be codified as **sequential entry strategy**.

A sequential entry strategy takes place gradually over time and has four main elements (McGee and Thomas 1994).

1 Gateway to entry

The process of gradual entry will lead firms to choose as gateways to entry (Yip 1982) either:

(a) a unique entry point in strategic space reflecting unmet demand-side characteristics; or

(b) a competitive positioning in the new industry based on the asset configurations of the current dominant strategic group in the industry; or

(c) a competitive positioning based on a new asset configuration representing the creation of a new strategic group.

The first represents an entry based on a new segmentation of the market where demand is currently unmet and probably unrecognized. The second is an emulation of the industry leaders and a head-on challenge to them. The third is a 'new-game' strategy where the entrant, often through new technology, intends to play the game a different way with a new and unusual mix of assets (see Steffens, 1986, for a discussion of how the PC industry was characterized by new games in its early, formative stages). Firm choice will be a function of its current strategic assets, the speed of technological change, and the costs and risks of entry which will be asymmetric between individual firms. In particular, costs will be related to differences in the height of entry barriers between market segments and risk will be related to the firm's existing asset configuration and financial resources. Typically positions (a) and (b) are not desirable or feasible. Unmet demand based on standard assets in the industry is highly unlikely and already easily captured by incumbents. Position (b) is risky given the defensive strengths of the incumbents.

2   Initial entry point

Successful entry occurs first into segments where barriers are lowest. This means that in the short run firms prefer risk minimizing as opposed to profit maximization. According to Caves and Porter (1977):

> It may be optimal to enter groups characterized by tangible asset outlays (e.g. producing for private label with no advertising outlay) first and groups requiring more risky intangible asset outlays only after a viable base in the industry is attained; the lower risk barriers are vaulted earlier.

Thus, short-term risk minimization might be a necessary prerequisite for long-term wealth creation. Therefore, on the above analysis, position (c) would be the preferred **entry point**. However, The costs of entry with a **new-game strategy** are very high and the uncertainties also high. So the temptation to go for entry points with lower costs is high even though the chances of making a successful entry might in fact be low.

3   Mode of entry

The **mode of entry** concerns the nature of the investments undertaken in order to use the particular gateway. Thus:

(a)   gateways to entry are distinguished by differences in entry costs between them;

(b)   within each gateway a range of different investments are possible given the nature of the assets required;

(c)   the nature of the entry is conditioned by the risk proclivities of firms and ways available to them for managing risks.

Different gateways require different classes and types of assets, but at each gateway there will be a variety of possible entry moves. The larger the number of strategic groups, the wider the range of possible entry strategies. The more complex an individual strategic group, the wider the range of possible strategies for entering that group. Following the example of Canon vs Xerox in Chapter 7, Canon had to construct an entirely new value chain (or business system) in order to make use of its preferred gateway. As we now know, this worked very well, but the entry cost was high and the perceived risks very high.

Dell represents a similar example. In order to get into the PC industry how do you get around the power wielded upstream by Microsoft and Intel? The answer is by appealing to buyer needs that are not addressed directly by these two orchestrators of the industry. This meant getting close to the customer and building a direct link to the customer through the telephone and through the internet. This was a different gateway and new entry point, requiring a distinct mode of entry. The rest is history and Dell is now a major force in the industry.

4 Expansion path

The **expansion path** (following Penrose's (1959) ideas about the nature of growth of the firm) concerns the subsequent strategic decisions about the path that growth should take. The subsequent entry pathway (the route for expansion) is dependent on the initial mode of entry and the firm's ability to develop firm-specific assets.

The initial entry point contains an immediate market opportunity which is assessed in the context of the systematic risk relating to the chosen gateway and the specific risks assumed by the entrant. The development of longer-term competitive advantage will require further investment in **co-specialized assets** (e.g. technology) and appropriate access to complementary assets (e.g. marketing and distribution) (Teece 1987). For example, for short-term success new entrants (innovators) may need to forge alliances with incumbents to gain access to complementary assets such as marketing and distribution. But in the longer term a different view is likely to be taken of the appropriate mix of co-specialized and complementary assets. The process of moving towards the desired mix can be thought of as the expansion path.

The idea of sequential entry can be distilled into four elements: the gateway to entry, the initial entry point, the mode of entry and the expansion path. The central concern is how to get around the existing entry barriers. Entry barriers are simply competitive advantages – the bigger the advantage, the higher the barriers. To get into an existing industry against established incumbents means being able to beat them at their own game. Where this is unlikely, a circuitous route to find a different entry point is required.[3] Entry is about the cost of imitation. This involves assessing the advantage of the incumbent and one's own capabilities.

The case box below places these themes of technology, entry and competition into a Schumpeterian '**creative destruction** context'. The example makes the claim that these processes of sequential entry are widespread in industries marked by technology discontinuities. List as many industries as you can that fit this pattern. The result may surprise you.

----

[3] This may remind some readers of Winston Churchill's strategy in the First World War to make landings in the Dardanelles against the Turks rather than waste resources taking on the Germans who were well embedded on the Western Front. This was a good strategic thought that foundered on two practical, operational points: the Allies botched the invasion and the Turks were much better prepared than had been anticipated.

Case box: **Creative destruction**

Certain themes recur throughout the history of industries such as reprographics. First, step changes in technology that are 'competence-destroying' can fundamentally change an industry's knowledge base, can lead directly to new dominant designs, and can spawn new, powerful competitors in new strategic groups. The nature of competitive rivalry changes with serious implications for the survival of incumbent firms.

Second, incumbents are affected in a number of ways. Incumbent monopolists (because of the potential erosion of profits of existing products and processes) have a smaller incentive to innovate than potential entrants (the Arrow effect, Arrow, 1962).

Third, technological change enables firms from outside the industry to capture a series of sub-markets. Entry is a complex, sequential process taking many years and involves systematic moves from a circumscribed initial entry point through a series of expansionary investments.

Fourth, sequential entry processes are important in determining the eventual competitive conditions that prevailed. Thus, the industry structure observed at any given time is the result, to a great extent, not only of exogenous technological change but also of the strategic decisions of firms.

Finally, with every step-change in technology, the market is enlarged. New product 'spaces' emerge and are filled up. Market boundaries are redefined. New ways of product differentiation and new possibilities for segmentation become available to suppliers. This creates new dimensions of competition.

These recurring patterns constitute the Schumpeterian process of creative destruction (Schumpeter, 1942). There are two steps to the argument here. The first simply states that technology can change industry structure. It can do so by changing conditions on the demand side and/or by causing adjustments on the supply side. Thus, the nature of competition changes and the nature and level of entry barriers can alter, sometimes dramatically. The second step is more fundamental to an understanding of the process and concerns the role of the firm in the way it takes advantage of technological change. The centre-piece is the idea that technology changes the asset base of the firm. The key issue for the firm concerns its ability to invest in the creation of assets that are, relative to competitors, sufficiently distinct so that it can compete in the market in ways that cannot be imitated. The distinctiveness of the assets relates to the 'uncertain imitability' of those assets by competitors and thus constitutes the basis for economic profits. The ability of the firm to create distinctiveness for itself by investing in R&D is a prime source of competitive power and taken far enough (as in the case of Xerox and plain-paper copying) is sufficient to change industry structure.

This second point underlines the possibility for firms to act so as to make technological change endogenous to the system. It is evident from this that firms will be concerned to protect their distinctive assets (which, ex post, are sunk costs) with other kinds of differentiation strategy to lock in their customers in the face of similar or newer forms of competition.

Initially the asset base is a potential entry barrier but in the course of time it might also become a prison wall inhibiting investment by the firm in new directions. In contrast, the successful firms are the ones that re-defined the industry boundaries and the relevant assets for the firm, and engaged in a continuous series of innovations.

Source: McGee and Thomas, 1994.

This section is arguing two points, one general, the other more specific. The first point is exemplified by the life cycle idea that says, as a general rule, that changes in demand growth and technology over the life cycle have implications for industry structure, competition and sources of competitive advantage. At each phase of the life cycle there are general conditions suggesting that specific competitive strategies need to evolve over the cycle and that firms should therefore plan for these changes. However, as Grant points out (2002, p. 313) generalization can be dangerous and the particulars of strategy may go beyond the simplicity of the life cycle model.

Therefore, our second point becomes relevant. Whereas the life cycle depends on a simple time line and equally simple growth extrapolation, we are concerned with more powerful theories that build on the ability of technology to create new assets, new competitive spaces, which in turn are destroyed by new rounds of technical change. The idea of sequential entry is a theory built on the interplay between these factors. All strategy development has a time line but behind the time line are powerful forces of discovery and change which Schumpeter called 'creative destruction'. The life cycle model is a useful starting point for recognizing how strategy must change over time. But we always need a more powerful model that can capture the interplay between technology, markets, costs and investment. Strategy is the taking of considered risks against the odds and against an unknown future but there are recognizable patterns for us to use.

8.4 Corporate failure and turnaround strategies

What happens when things go wrong? What are the competitive forces and managerial mindsets that lead to **corporate failure**? This chapter looks at the anatomy of failure and at the analytical and management procedures that constitute a 'turnaround' of a failing company. It covers the links between financial analysis, strategy analysis and strategic choice.

Why should we look at corporate turnarounds? They are part of the life and death of all businesses and, while the Western business culture is firmly focused on success, we should not ignore lessons that can be gleaned from when things start to go wrong. Indeed, it is worth noting that several large companies specifically ask their best managers to manage the turnaround of 'dogs' before appointing them to the main board – a trial by fire if ever there was one.

Substantial numbers of turnarounds arose after the massive wave of corporate diversifications during the 1960s–1980s. The bureaucratic inefficiencies of **diversification** resulted
in poor management of subsidiaries, and stock markets began to downgrade **conglomerates**, realizing that the sum of the parts exceeded the whole. A trend-setting bid of this
nature was Hoylake's £15 billion bid for the tobacco giant BAT industries, where the
aggressors promised to 'unbundle' the assets to realize greater value for shareholders. New
sophisticated financing methods helped corporate raiders to launch bids for even the
largest corporate, so that size was no longer a guarantee of independence. In response to
such threats, conglomerates began to recognize that continuous expansion had given rise
to the twin problems of managing the extremities as well as expansion taking its toll on the
core of business. It was the time of Tom Peter's famous homily: '*stick to the knitting*'[4].
Turnarounds of divested businesses, as well as the core, are an important feature of organizational life.

8.4.1 Issues

The Boston Box, while designed as a corporate portfolio technique for reducing financial
risk, has been widely used as a prescriptive strategic planning tool, with some disastrous consequences. This is well illustrated by 'dogs', which are characterized by business units with
low relative market share in low-growth markets. According to the Boston Box, and other
directional policy matrices of this ilk, such businesses are in decline, generate low profits,
and should be divested: they will not attract equity finance and there is greater financial risk
in this context with debt finance. However, in times of recession, some 80 per cent of UK
businesses can be described as 'dogs', and so it is dangerous to conclude that they should all
be divested. For instance, there are alternative strategies, which may lead to successful outcomes, such as recovery/rejuvenation, maturity, the end game and internationalization. All
of these strategic options offer significant potential for shaking off the negative image of
'dogs'.

We shall be concentrating in this chapter on 'turnarounds', or corporate recovery. Hofer's
(1976) classic article on turnarounds draws the distinction between operating and strategic
forms. Operating turnarounds are about 'doing things differently', so that the firm's
efficiency can be improved. This may be achieved by a fundamental change in a firm's operations, by using advanced manufacturing technology, for instance. Strategic turnarounds are
about 'doing different things'. In this instance, companies attempt to change their fortunes
by fundamental adjustments to their strategy, in terms of acquisition and divestment, for
instance.

Hofer's distinction between strategic and operating turnarounds has been challenged by
Hambrick and Schecter (1983). They argue that the difference becomes blurred as we move

---

[4] In other words, concentrate on the core business, and do not be distracted by non-core activities.

from the corporate to the business unit level. They suggest three categories: traditional asset cost surgery, product-market pruning and, their largest category, piecemeal strategies. This suggests that there is such difference between individual companies that it is difficult to establish a single turnaround framework.

Grinyer, Mayes and McKiernan (1988) have extended this discussion by carrying out a detailed examination of types of recovery employed by UK manufacturing companies, and relating these to contextual variables. In their rigorous study, they do find sufficient commonalities to suggest that turnarounds have distinct stages, even though there are different types of turnaround in existence. Their work is reviewed here, to give insight on types of turnaround and the anatomy of a turnaround.

8.4.2 Types of turnaround

In their study of 1200 of the UK's largest companies, Grinyer, Mayes and McKiernan (1988) examined the different types of corporate turnaround that had been experienced, as well as analysing the anatomy of such events. To enable them to determine between different types of turnaround they broadened their frame of reference to embrace all firms that had experienced a decline, followed by a sharp upturn in performance. It is important to note that this means that the study is also examining firms that are not facing extinction, as in the classic turnaround definition, but includes firms which, while suffering declining performance, may still be healthy. Figure 8.8 shows the different types of '**sharpbender**' identified.

- **Case A** is the firm showing *early recovery*. The firm is aware of its decline in performance and *anticipates* that on such a trend it is likely to breech its managerial-determined minimum acceptable level of performance. Although the firm is far from extinction, actions are taken in advance, the crisis averted, and a path of sustained improvement achieved.

- **Case B** is the firm taking *intermediate* action to break through its line of minimum acceptable standards. Alarm bells are ringing and actions taken to recover. However, such actions are insufficient – perhaps superficial, addressing symptoms rather than causes – and the firm returns to its decline trajectory. At this point, the firm may countenance

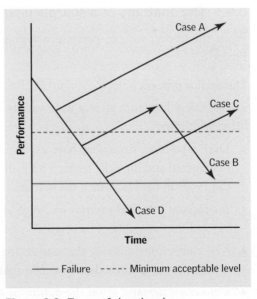

Figure 8.8 Types of sharpbender
Source: adapted from Grinyer, Mayes and McKiernan, 1988, p. 14.

more sweeping changes to restore the firm to a trajectory of sustained improvement. However, should this step not be taken, it is likely that the firm will continue to oscillate around the line of minimum acceptable standards, with successive uplifts being more difficult to achieve than previously, before ultimately failing.

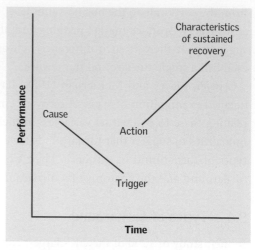

Figure 8.9 The four phases of a sharpbender
Source: Grinyer, Mayes and McKiernan, 1988.

- **Case C** is a firm which is late in reacting to the crisis. The firm has breached its managerial-determined minimum level of performance and has begun to approach the line of failure. It is the classic turnaround, as described by Slatter (1984). In this instance, the firm needed the spur of breaking its internal standards, as well as the threat of extinction, to begin to take substantial action. By so doing, sustained recovery is achieved.

- **Case D** is the firm that does not perceive the threat of extinction, despite breaking its own minimum acceptable standards, or is unable to make any changes before termination.

8.4.3 **The anatomy of a sharpbender**

From the above, we can perceive a four-phase model for a 'sharpbend', as depicted in Figure 8.9.

The decline process

The business literature gives a wide variety of reasons for corporate decline. These can be listed as follows:

- *Over-expansion*: firms that have expanded too far find that they are stretched in both managerial and financial terms. This is the classic criticism of the diversification boom of the 1960s in the UK, which led to massive under-performing conglomerates.

- *Inadequate financial controls and high costs*: these often occur when a business grows beyond the capability of its original systems, so that costs spiral out of control.

- *New competition entering the market*: the arrival of a new competitor can substantially distort the competitive dynamics of a market and damage a firm's health.

- *Unforeseen demand shifts*: the nature of the market may change dramatically. Where a firm has substantial and rigid asset configurations, this can spell disaster – the classic example being the impact on IBM of the widespread switch from mainframe to desk-top computers. The area most on people's minds at the moment is the potential impact of the internet.

◆ *Poor management*: managers may have a false sense of confidence in their own abilities. This can arise from experiencing a period of success, causing an atmosphere of infallibility, and the screening of information. Of course, poor management may also just mean poor management.

From their interviews, the sharpbender researchers concluded that primary causes of decline were in changes in total market demand, falling revenues from more intense competition and a high cost structure. In Table 8.1 we show that such variables impact differently, depending on whether the firms are staging early, intermediate or late recoveries.

How do managers react to a crisis?

Most systems within businesses, such as control systems, reporting and accounting systems, are backward-looking or historic in nature and designed for steady state environments. As a result, managers may find themselves in a situation of false security. As signals emerge, there is at first the issue of whether the managers know or accept that there is a crisis. The natural tendency is to deny that there is a crisis, on the grounds that any negative signal may well be a temporary 'blip' or extraordinary factor. The tendency is also to rationalize the signal away in terms of thinking that 'Everyone is in the same boat' and to suggest that 'We've all seen it before'. With this urge to preserve the status quo, top management will see the situation as temporary and be inclined to 'sit it out' – wait and see what happens next. This inactivity will be reinforced by a general view that knee-jerk reactions are dangerous and panic should be avoided. To maintain this stance, there may be a degree of self-delusion in terms of massaging, delaying and even hiding figures. An example of this situation might be Midland Bank's exposure to Latin American debt in the secondary banking crisis in the late 1980s. All the major banks were heavily exposed and the City waited nervously for Midland's results, as the bank had one of the largest exposures. However, instead of reporting a massive loss as

Table 8.1 Causes of decline

	Early %	Intermediate %	Late %
Market decline	25	55	75
Financial	25	55	67
Project failure	25	36	75
Strategic Problems	0	9	25
Poor marketing	75	9	8

Source: McKiernan, 1992, p. 64.

everyone anticipated, they announced a substantial profit. To achieve this, they had used an accounting sleight of hand, which was subsequently contested in court. The outcome was that the accounts had to be restated and the new results showed an even greater loss than anticipated. This extraordinary course of events shows a management team trying to preserve confidence in the bank among its stakeholders, by suggesting that the debt situation was a one-off, temporary blip, which did not impact in any substantial way upon the bank's prospects.

Stages of reactive behaviour

When the crisis is too obvious to ignore, managers tend to react in a sequential way, which may be perceived as taking the least risky actions at first, and then becoming progressively more daring if the crisis worsens and they have time to act.

Initially, managers will tighten up on existing control systems. They will go for the easy targets, which are almost invariably costs. Many investment expenditures and current experimental programmes will also be abandoned. If the crisis continues, the tendency is to tighten costs even further. To those executives who have lived through such turnarounds, it will come as no surprise the extent to which costs can be tightened. One such symbol of straitened times is the pencil trolley. Suddenly people will appear and raid everyone's desks for all writing implements. These will be carted away and a brand new pencil left behind. For the executive to qualify for a new pencil at a later stage, the stub will need to be taken to the stores to ensure that it is less than one inch in length!

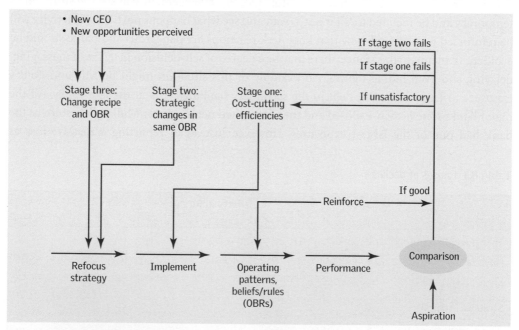

Figure 8.10 A conceptual model of the stages of reactive behaviour
Source: extended Cyert and March model (McKiernan 1992) p. 58.

If the crisis persists, then the smart executives will be preparing their own alibis and the organization will be looking for victims. Strategy may be reviewed incrementally and there may be some product market changes. If there is no improvement, the organization may descend into a state whereby no one will act unless receiving direct instructions from the top, or the prevailing modus operandi, or recipe, of the business may be challenged. This will entail a fundamental review of the organization – its purpose and logic.

These stages of reactive behaviour are well captured in Figure 8.10. Comparisons are continually drawn between reference points such as competitor performance, share performance and ambitions and aspirations for profit performance. Should this comparison be favourable then the innermost loop will be followed, with the current behaviour being reinforced. Should the comparisons prove unfavourable then the first stage will be followed.

If desirable results are not forthcoming, executives may move progressively outwards in Figure 8.10 until the third stage of a fundamental review of strategy is undertaken.

Living in crumbling palaces

Organizations build up excessive rigidity to change – as the sub-heading suggests. The difficulty with needing to change is that it is perceived to have unforeseen and frightening consequences. In addition, there are barriers to change from those executives who owe their positions to the status quo. Organizational members have to unlearn their current ways of doing things, unpackage their assumptions about how the business works and engage with a new set of parameters. This in itself can lead to a downturn in performance, and so cause despondency and sap energies. It is important to note, therefore, that change will not just happen, but requires considerable power to enforce. If left to its own devices, the likelihood is that the result will just be a series of 'cosmetic changes', rather like rearranging the chairs on the *Titanic.*

> When an organization is in this serious a state, it is rare that a turnaround can be accomplished by the incumbent senior management – the ritual sacrifice of the old leader is almost obligatory. (Grinyer, Mayes and McKiernan, 1988)

Triggers for action

While it may be clear that an organization is on a decline trajectory, it is vital that triggers are identified to bring about action. If triggers cannot be identified then it is likely that nothing will change, despite the abundance of warning signs.

The *Sharpbenders* study identifies a number of important triggers for bringing about change (see Table 8.2). It is important to note that acquisitions were specifically excluded from the study, and so we do not know how prevalent this important trigger might be. A well-known example of an acquisition as a trigger prompting a strategic change is the Hanson bid for ICI. In fighting off the bid, ICI announced the de-merger of Zeneca.

Table 8.2 Triggers

		Sharpbenders citing this factor
1	Intervention from external bodies	30%
2	Change of ownership or the threat of such a change	25%
3	New chief executive	55%
4	Recognition by management of problems	35%
5	Perception by management of new opportunities	10%

Source: Grinyer, Mayes and McKiernan, 1988, *Sharpbenders*, p. 47.

The main trigger identified is a new CEO. His or her importance is in terms of supplying a new vision and symbolizing that things need to change. Indeed, such a person has undoubtedly been appointed with a mandate for change.

In terms of early, intermediate and late stage recoveries, the broad pattern, as one might expect, is for the early stagers to have internal triggers and have a management able to perceive problems and opportunities. As we move to the late stagers, all triggers are important with an increased external emphasis.

Table 8.3 Actions taken

	____% of firms citing factor____		
	Sharp-benders	Control companies	% diff
Major changes in management	85	30	55
Stronger financial controls	80	70	10
New product market focus	80	80	0
Diversified	30	70	(40)
Entered export market vigorously	50	30	20
Improved quality and service	55	50	5
Improved marketing	75	30	45
Intensive efforts to reduce production costs	80	30	50
Acquisitions	50	80	(30)
Reduced debt	50	80	(30)
Windfalls	85	70	15
Other	25	20	5

Source: Grinyer, Mayes and McKiernan, 1988, *Sharpbenders*, p. 64.

Actions taken

If there are triggers in place then the sorts of action that might be taken to bring about a recovery are contained in Table 8.3. We are interested to know the actions that sharpbenders took and in particular those actions that are specific to them. For this reason we show the percentage of sharpbenders citing an action in column one, the percentage of other randomly selected companies citing an action in column two and the difference between the two scores in column three.

The major difference between sharpbenders and control companies in terms of action taken is management changes: 85 per cent of sharpbenders cited management changes, some 55 per cent more than the control companies. They also devoted considerable efforts to improving marketing and reducing production costs. Unlike the control companies they were very reluctant to diversify and there were markedly reduced levels of acquisition. Interestingly, they were also reluctant to reduce debt, and here there is a distinction with pure turnarounds in that the latter make considerable efforts to reduce debts. Sharpbenders are more likely to invest to improve performance.

Characteristics of sustained performance

Following the turnaround, sharpbenders needed to adopt characteristics that would enable sustained levels of performance – to refer back to Figure 8.8 organizations want cases A and C, rather than B (where the recovery achieved is only short term). The characteristics identified in the *Sharpbenders* (1988) study are contained in Table 8.4.

- Good management is seen to be critical to sustained recovery.
- Appropriate organizational structure often meant a much leaner one, with fewer layers in the hierarchy.
- Tightly controlled costs meant better controls, rather than cutting costs.

Table 8.4 Key features of sustained improved performance

		Number of characteristics cited	% of firms cited
1	Good management	4+	90
2	Appropriate organizational structure	4+	75
3	Effective financial and other controls	4+	50
4	Sound product market posture	5+	45
5	Good marketing management	2+	55
6	High quality maintained	2+	35
7	Tightly controlled costs	3+	40

Source: Grinyer, Mayes and McKiernan, 1988, *Sharpbenders*, p. 110.

Case box: **The destruction of Marconi**

Major shifts in strategic directions can work for some companies. But more often they can lead into areas that the management does not understand – with disastrous results.

General Electric Company (GEC), the UK company with no relation to America's GE, grew rapidly in the 1960s under Arnold Weinstock's domineering but effective leadership.

Like its American counterpart, GEC grew into a conglomerate with interests in such diverse businesses as white goods, defence electronics, telecoms and power systems. While there was no real logic underlying this array of businesses, Weinstock held the company together through a combination of his imposing personality and a strict system of financial controls. At its peak, GEC had sales of £11bn and a cash pile of £2bn.

Simpson's masterplan

Lord Weinstock retired in 1996 and was replaced by George Simpson, a former executive at Rover. Over the course of the next five years, Simpson and his finance director John Mayo masterminded a complete rethinking of GEC's corporate strategy.

They decided to focus the company on the fast-growing telecoms equipment industry. They bought two mid-sized US competitors (Reltec for $2.1bn and Fore for $4.5bn) for large sums of money and invested in developing a range of new products to compete with industry leaders Cisco and Nortel. To pay for this growth, most other businesses, including defence electronics, white goods and power systems, were sold off. To reflect this change in strategy, GEC was renamed Marconi.

The dénouement

Marconi's share price peaked in August 2000 at £12. Then things started to go badly wrong. The dot-com bubble burst and demand for new telecoms equipment dried up. Lucent, Cisco and Nortel all announced profit warnings. Marconi's share price dropped even though it denied that its sales had been hit. Then, when the profit warning finally came, angry investors dumped the stock.

The downturn was far more severe than anyone anticipated and with large and mounting debts Marconi was facing bankruptcy, its shares worth less than one per cent of their peak value. Simpson and Mayo were forced out. A new executive team was brought in; £37bn of market value had been destroyed in just a year and a half. In November 2003, Marconi announced half-year losses of £149m in the period to September, down from £485m a year previously.

The lesson

Marconi's story is a classic tale of an over-ambitious growth strategy and subsequent collapse. But the lesson to take away is that despite their ultimate failure, Simpson and Mayo did some important things right.

First, they correctly reasoned that if Marconi were going to become a major player in telecoms it would have to grow aggressively and it would need a strong US position. Hence its acquisitions of Fore and Reltec. This approach worked for Cisco.

Where Marconi went wrong was that it paid cash – partly because it had plenty of it, and partly because it did not have a full listing in the US (so its paper was not attractive currency).

So rule one: if you are going to overpay for an acquisition, better to overpay with your own overpaid shares. The cash drain from these acquisitions is what ultimately killed Marconi. Second, Marconi's decision to major on one business – and sell the rest – is exactly what the markets were asking for. Conglomerates were OK in the 1970s and 1980s but the trend during the 1990s was towards highly focused corporations. And, indeed, Simpson was lauded for his courage in breaking up and focusing the company he took over from Lord Weinstock.

But Marconi's failure underlines how risky this sort of refocusing can be. Simpson put all his eggs in one basket but it was a relatively untested and new basket at that. Such dramatic changes in corporate strategy can work. For example, Spirent made a successful transition from industrial conglomerate to fast-growing telecoms company during the late 1990s.

But more often than not major changes in strategy take a company into new areas that it does not really understand and the results end up being disastrous – as the shareholders of Vivendi and Enron will confirm.

Source: Julian Birkinshaw, *Business Strategy Review*, Spring 2004, Volume 15, Issue 1, pp. 74–5.
Reproduced with permission of Blackwell Publishing.

Case box: **A Rose-tinted vision**

Has Stuart Rose seen the future for M&S?

'A bit boring,' is how Stuart Rose describes some of the products sold by Marks & Spencer (M&S). Mr Rose says that he can transform M&S by going back to retailing basics – not easy in the era of Wal-Mart. M&S's relationship with its customers and suppliers was once admired worldwide. But that was when its St Michael brand of underwear could be found in the top drawer of almost every house in Britain. Retailing has since changed dramatically and traditional stores in almost every country face similar challenges. Speciality retailers, such as America's Gap in casual clothes, Victoria's Secret in underwear and Sweden's H&M in low-cost fashion, are taking business away from department stores and established chains. At the same time, supermarkets have moved aggressively into selling clothes, household goods and prepared meals (pioneered by M&S). The British firm has struggled, sacrificing its legendary high quality and employee-friendly culture to make the cost savings needed to keep profits growing through the 1990s and so meet the short-term expectations of many shareholders.

By 3 June, when Mr Green, a Monaco-based billionaire who owns the Bhs and Arcadia store chains, launched his latest attempt to buy M&S, the firm was deteriorating fast. Its efforts to transform itself had begun to stall. Its management was floundering. Rumours of Mr Green's pending bid led to a boardroom rout. Mr Rose was quickly made chief executive only days before Mr Green made his bid. That bid was rebuffed, as was his now-withdrawn later offer, which was potentially worth up to £4 a share.

The appointment of Mr Rose, aged 55 – a retail professional with an impressive reputation – was a masterstroke. Early in his career, he spent 17 years working for M&S. Selling M&S to Mr Green never seemed to be on Mr Rose's agenda. Even at £4 a share, he maintained that Mr Green's final offer undervalued the company significantly. That bid, however, has set the hurdle over which Mr Rose must climb. He believes he can deliver a company worth more than £4 a share. To sweeten shareholders he is selling M&S's financial-services business to HSBC, a big bank, in order to fund a share tender offer worth £2.3 billion, the equivalent of returning £1 per share to investors. Costs will be cut, leading to savings of some £320m in the 2006 financial year. The group's extensive property holdings have also been revalued, upwards.

Yet the really crucial thing for M&S's future is what Mr Rose describes as a return to its core. 'It doesn't need revolution,' he says, but, rather, the application of basic retailing skills in lots of areas. For a start, the business has to be made simpler. Compared with when he worked at M&S before, Mr Rose now finds each division operating like a separate company. The supply chain has become slow and overcommitted, and stores are cluttered with too many product lines. 'Do we need 23 varieties of tomato?' he asks. Mr Rose's new management team has already started to edit the products on offer, adding some new ones to plug the gaps but eliminating many more. Some 10,000 lines of clothing will be reduced to around 9,000. Its roughly 8,500 lines of home goods will be cut to 4,500. A new venture, Lifestore, specializing in homewares, has been cancelled and the unit's first giant store will be closed. Some of the company's smaller food-only stores will also be closed.

Too many sub-brands have left shoppers confused, adds Mr Rose. Some will be kept, such as Per Una, which has been a successful range of women's clothing for M&S. As part of the new strategy, he has bought this business for £125m from George Davies, the designer who developed it, in order to have control over it. Mr Rose reckons M&S's customer relationship is defined by womenswear. So, if his new team can produce appealing styles at good prices, he believes he can regain the trust of the company's most important group of shoppers.

But the transformation cannot be completed overnight; this autumn's fashion lines, for instance, are already fixed, so the new team will not have a chance to make their mark on womenswear until spring 2005. Mr Rose is adamant that he can succeed, and perhaps he can – if his shareholders have patience. Despite its troubles, M&S has much going for it: with 25m customers – around half of the adult British population – it retains a large market share, even in women's underwear (26%).

Source: 'A Rose-tinted vision', *The Economist*, 15 July 2004.
© The Economist Newspaper Limited, London (15 July 2004).

> **Questions for discussion**
>
> 1 Apply the four-phase sharpbender model to Stuart Rose's M&S recovery plan.
>
> 2 What is different about the M&S situation? Is it a conventional turnaround?
>
> 3 In what ways does the turnaround plan take sufficient account of the causes of decline? In what ways do you suspect that M&S might be a 'crumbling palace'?

8.4.4 Generic turnaround strategies

Grinyer, Mayes and McKiernan's (1988) rigorous work has suggested a time ordering of actions to achieve a turnaround. This supports a review of practitioners' work by Hoffman (1989), which suggests a three-stage process for recovery, although not all organizations need to go through all three stages. This is shown in Figure 8.11.

8.4.5 Lessons for managers

The practical lessons for managers are that:

- Financial and behavioural criteria need to be monitored for declining trends in operational or strategic performance. Strategic health requires proactive management, rather than reactive financial reporting.
- During decline, ensure that there is sufficient management talent.
- The new CEO needs to establish a reliable top team.
- Management will need a two-stage plan – an operational plan to stop the decline and generate positive cash flow and a strategic plan to reposition the organization to sustain recovery.
- It is critical to get to the root causes – there will be a temptation to address symptoms rather than causes. If one is really tackling fundamental issues then it is likely to be painful, as it will challenge the very way that executives see their roles.
- Both strategy and success are communicated effectively by and through the workforce.

We began this section with the BCG portfolio view of strategy, which perceived turnaround situations as best divested. However, turnarounds can be very successful, if well managed. By taking an anatomical view of turnarounds, we have exposed some core issues for effective management, in particular, showing the necessity for confronting basic premises upon which the organization has operated.

Turnarounds are just one example of crisis situations in corporate strategy, and readers should be aware that this has particular implications for how strategy is viewed in such circumstances. In the case of turnarounds:

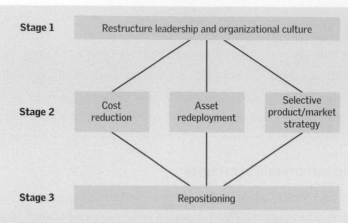

Stage 1	Restructure leadership and organizational culture		
Stage 2	Cost reduction	Asset redeployment	Selective product/market strategy
Stage 3	Repositioning		

Stage/strategy	Action	Conditions
1 Restructuring	Replace top managers Use temporary structures Alter organizational structure Alter culture	Internal causes of turnaround Need to diversify Control and communications problems Aid repositioning Culture change Structure change
2 Cost reduction Asset redeployment	Reduce expenses Institute controls Sell assets Shutdown or relocate units	Internal causes of decline Sales 60–80% of break-even Over-expansion/low capacity use Sales 30–60% of break-even Rapid technological change Rapid entry of new competitors
Selective product/ market strategy	*Defensive* Decrease marketing effort Divest products *Offensive* Increase marketing Increase prices Improve quality, service	Over-expansion External causes of turnaround High capacity use Possessing operating and strategic weaknesses
3 Repositioning	*Defensive* Niche Market penetration Decrease price Divest products *Offensive* Diversification into new products	Over-expansion (defensive) Improved short-run profitability External causes for turnaround Major decline in market share Non-diversified firms faced with external causes of decline (offensive)

Figure 8.11 Five generic strategies of recovery
Source: adapted from Hoffman (1989) Vol. 14, No 3.

- A *proactive top-down* style of management has been advocated as necessary and effective. In other areas of strategy, you will encounter a Mintzbergian bottom-up view, or indeed a middle-up-down perspective.

- *Rapid change* is critical to survival in a turnaround, although currently dominant in strategic management is the processual (Whittington 1993) view, which emphasizes the complexity and difficulty of change, so that it is perceived as a long and involved process (cf. Pettigrew 1973).

- *Structure comes before strategy* in so far as changes are made for the company's very survival before the luxury of a strategy can be considered. This is contrary to the strongly held Chandlerian view that structure follows strategy.

In an increasingly turbulent environment, businesses have to concern themselves with adjusting far more rapidly than ever before. Turnarounds and the crisis literature then, while positioned at one extreme in the strategic management literature, are a useful counterpoint to the 'incremental' 'emergent' schools of thought.

8.5 Summary

This chapter began with the industry life cycle model as a means for displaying the need for strategies to change over time. This is an unexceptional proposition but the model does have a systematic thread running through it that shows a natural progression from innovation and differentiation through to eventual commoditization. With this progression goes a series of propositions about he way in which the firm should arrange its functional strategies and how it should expect to earn profits.

This is useful for setting out a framework within which change can be seen to be taking place. But we have chosen to place against this generic model three essentially practical and difficult circumstances. One concerns entrepreneurs and how they start businesses. The second is how firms gain entry to heavily defended marketplaces. Each of these practical examples brings out its own lesson. An the third is how businesses are turned round. The entrepreneurial lesson is that the magic of start-up success is almost certainly more to do with the characteristics of entrepreneurs themselves rather than with the merits of the economic case for the start-up (otherwise we would leave everything to venture capitalists and bankers). The essence of the turnaround is the ability to reconcile the cash flows of the company with competitive exigencies. This takes operational and practical skills but it also takes a sense beyond survivability to sustainability. Entry requires much more careful consideration of the longer term, how one strategy can displace an incumbent's strategy. This requires a mix of calculation and risk taking that is different in style from either the entrepreneur or the turnaround specialist. The personal characteristics of the decision makers are less obviously important and the time scales are usually more extended.

Thus strategy over time has many faces. The underlying discipline of aceing and defeating competition is always there but the mix of personal characteristics and capabilities can vary substantially. The strategic frameworks and models that we build give us a baseline and a context against which to work. In some situations the strategic calculus (as in entry) is prominent and must be constructed with some degree of precision. In other cases the strategic context shapes the situation but is not necessarily decisive. Our concern is to recognize these different situations both as managers and as strategists so that we can operate in the right manner.

Key terms

Conglomerates *314*

Co-specialized assets *311*

Corporate failure *313*

Creative destruction *311*

Diversification *314*

Entrepreneur *299*

Entrepreneurial strategy *306*

Entry point *310*

Expansion path *311*

Industry life cycle *292*

Intrapreneurship *303*

Mode of entry *310*

Natural strategic thrusts *296*

New entry strategies *307*

New-game strategy *310*

Product life cycle *292*

Sequential entry strategy *309*

Sharpbender *315*

Sustainability *298*

Turnaround strategies *313*

Recap questions and assignments

1 Choose an entrepreneur with whom you are familiar and comment on:
   ◆ What elements are responsible for his or her success so far.
   ◆ What characterizes his or her strategic style.
   ◆ Whether he or she will continue to lead his or her business to further successes.

   You might wish to consider two issues: (i) Does your entrepreneur have a capability that is transferable to another entrepreneurial situation? (ii) Can your entrepreneur's capability apply equally as well to his or her organization as it becomes significantly larger?

2 What are the corporate arguments for and against carrying out a turnaround?

3 What are the difficulties for management in recognizing that its firm is in a turn-around situation?

4 Referring to a turnaround situation with which you are familiar, comment on the critical ingredients that contributed to its success or failure.

Online
Learning Centre

When you have read this chapter, log on to the Online Learning Centre website at www.mcgraw-hill.co.uk/textbooks/mcgee to explore chapter-by-chapter test questions, further reading and more online study tools for strategy.

Case 1　**Stelios Haji-Ioannou**

Known simply as Stelios, easyGroup's founder has become the embodiment of the business. And like one of his heroes, Richard Branson, he's already created a thriving airline business and is now parlaying that brand into ventures as diverse as buses, pizzas and hotels. But can he replicate easyJet's success, asks Richard Cree.

Stelios Haji-Ioannou hands me a bright orange business card. Under his name it says 'serial entrepreneur'. There's little doubt that this is how he views himself. Whether others agree with him is less clear. To some he is a genial buffoon who stumbled onto a good idea for a budget airline and was lucky to be in the right place, at the right time, to exploit it. His lack of entrepreneurial flair, claim his detractors, has been exposed by a series of disastrous attempts to extend the easy brand into everything from cinemas to car rental to internet cafes (with pizzas, buses, cruises and hotels all on the way). To others he is a pioneering entrepreneur and role model, with a flair for launching businesses and the courage to know when to get others to manage them.

In reality he is a little bit of both. Behind a funny man facade lurks a serious intellect with a predilection for talking about risk management and asset utilisation. It is also worth remembering that for all his recent setbacks, he is founder and majority shareholder in two highly successful businesses (easyJet and Stelmar Tankers).

For his part, Stelios admits to still finding his feet: 'I'm learning an awful lot about the job of being a serial entrepreneur,' he says, as we settle into a bland side office at easyGroup's nondescript HQ. 'I have decided to be a serial entrepreneur – I don't want to be a Plc chairman and I don't want to be a beach bum yet. I'm unemployable, I don't want a salary, and I don't want to work for anyone else. I either have to pick one business and run it, which doesn't excite me, or I have to get into the habit of creating a lot of companies and as soon as I feel confident about them, hand them over to managers.'

Never scared to contradict himself, Stelios claims this learning includes both doing more himself and getting the right people to help him with each project. 'I've discovered that what I'm best at is doing the research and deciding on the business model,' he explains. 'As soon as I've found the business model, I hire a manager to run it. But when I start a company, rather than hiring an army of people to do research, the best way is to do it all myself. If there is someone who ought to learn everything there is to know about an industry, it's me. When I decided to get into the airline industry, I didn't hire consultants. I started plane spotting at airports and talking to people. The pre start-up expense of easyJet was half a million pounds.'

The latest ventures to benefit from this hands-on approach are his planned hotel and cruise ventures, easyDorm and easyCruise, which will both use a new type of modular room. 'By accident I came across some sophisticated techniques used on cruise ships for prefabricated cabins. That is the benefit of doing the research myself. I spent a day in Finland and as a result, I've latched on to something which will allow me to develop an interior that is cheap to manufacture, easy to clean and easy to maintain.'

And with that he is off again, outlining detailed plans for a central London hotel (from £5 a night) and cruises on a 'floating hotel on the Med' (from £29 a day). Both ventures are based on the concepts of yield management and demand-based pricing, internet distribution and unbundled services that he developed at easyJet.

It's an approach Stelios says leads to better returns on invested capital. 'The Four Seasons will get an average room rate higher than my hotel, but if you calculate return on capital employed, my ratios come out ahead. With little investment and a lower price than the competition, you can still make a profit. The brand allows you to offer very little and lower expectations but people still like it.'

Which leads naturally to a discussion of easyJet the budget airline that made his name in the UK. 'My claim to fame in the airline industry is that I am the first person to sell coffee on an aircraft,' he jokes. 'Coffee had never been sold before. In 1995 this orange plane appeared and when the first passengers got on board we said "here's a coffee, that's a pound". Ryanair wasn't doing that in 1995. Some people forget that O'Leary copied more things from easyJet than the other way round. It's Ryanair that learnt from easyJet and transformed itself into a successful company, rather than them being the pioneers.'

It's the sort of comment that you expect between rivals in the airline business, an industry which attracts more than its share of characters. Mark Pilling, managing editor of *Airline Business*, says part of the attraction of the industry is the opportunity for would-be Davids to take on industry Goliaths and win, especially in the era of budget airlines. 'To want to take on the big guys you need to be the sort of character who's reaching out for a dream, someone prepared to take risks,' he says. Pilling also points out that O'Leary and Stelios both copied the ideas of Herb Kelleher at Southwest Airlines.

According to Stelios, the attraction of airlines is all to do with gravity: 'The airline industry has always attracted loonies, starting from the Wright brothers. As an industry it attracts far more attention than it deserves in terms of its size and importance. The only way to explain it is this feeling of defying gravity. There have been other monumental inventions that are not as celebrated as flight. Look what happened on the retirement of Concorde last year. This magic of flight creates media and public attention and as a result it attracts very high-profile characters, because they are the ones who survive. It's an industry where you need to outshine your competitors and those who shout the loudest get the customers.'

And so publicity stunts have become part of the marketing mix for the industry. If such stunts appear a dangerous way of raising consumer awareness, it's a risk Stelios is happy to take, and one that he hasn't left behind. Last year he made a cheeky offer to Matt Barrett, chief executive of Barclays, to give him £100,000 on an easyMoney credit card if Barrett cut up his Barclaycard, after the Barclays man admitted to a government select committee that he didn't use his Barclaycard because it was too expensive. Having been voted by *Campaign* magazine as one of the best tactical ads of last year, Stelios shows no sign of stopping. But are there risks in tying the business so closely with his personality? Laura Haynes, director of brand consultancy Appetite, thinks so. 'Heroes have feet of clay and one mistake can have a disproportionate impact across all parts of the business. Having said that, building a business around a personality rather than a product or service makes it easier to stretch into new areas. Stelios is also doing something more subtle. His personality is part of the brand, but there are other aspects to it, such as the idea of taking on the big bad guys.'

For his part Stelios is unconcerned: 'It's the only way to start a business,' he states boldly. 'By lending my name to a start-up I improve its chances of success. How do easyJet shareholders feel about that risk? I spend my own money promoting the easy brand and that creates more customers for easyJet. The rewards outweigh the risks. If *my* reputation suffered irreversibly, easyJet would survive. It has a good product at a good price and is a hell of a company to dislodge.'

Although he says he started his business in the UK because of its favourable climate for business, he admits that the start-up climate is better still in the US. He says he is happy with the way the UK media have treated him, but gives the impression that the sniping gets to him. 'Given the size of our company, small mistakes get exaggerated. By any other standards easyCinema is a respectable cinema in Milton Keynes. OK it hasn't set the world alight, but then nobody in Milton Keynes has ever set the world alight.

'The attitude to failure in the US is much better for entrepreneurship than in the UK. Whether that has to do with bankruptcy laws or whether it has to do with the attitude and education of the media, I don't know. Most American entrepreneurs take pride in having had a couple of failures in their past. In the UK people are ashamed. If you expect people to take risks, you have to allow them to fail, otherwise they become too risk-averse. I take more risks than most people, but I temper my risk-taking to levels I can afford rather than risk bankruptcy.'

But the criticism most often levelled at Stelios and easyGroup is that his failures are racking up across a wide front. Is he worried about spreading himself too thinly, stretching across too many start-ups at once? 'The danger of spreading yourself too thin is always there,' he admits. 'But learning to control things and acting as a bottleneck is a skill I have to develop. I've created this brand, been through several start-ups already and it's unlikely I will focus for the rest of my life on one company. I like the idea of a portfolio. In some ways I'm spreading risk because I'm not going to place a life threatening bet on any of those industries. I'll keep them small enough so I can manage them.'

Despite his positive outlook, he has begun to learn from recent mistakes, and change his approach to new ventures. Wherever possible, he is now getting others to share what he calls the execution risk.

'There was a shift in approach last year. I've started to think about how to manage the downside risk as well as managing the upside. I could hire people and learn to operate buses (for the soon-to-launch easyBus) but why? There are so many people who know how to do it. The best way to do it is to hire people from the industry, either licensing a company or hiring individuals, which is how easyJet started. We didn't have an airline certificate until 1998. It was flying for three years under other people's licences. It was a glorified travel agent. And that was how we wanted it.' He adds that having believed in this approach, he began to underestimate the risks involved in industries he knew nothing about. 'I'm going back to thinking that industry expertise has merit,' he says.

The two biggest companies created since easyJet – easyCar and easyInternet – have, according to Stelios, 'turned the corner'. Both have been reinvented, with new business models, new management teams ('by implication, perhaps the first management teams were not the best,' he says). In both cases he has hired an industry expert from the car rental business and from American Express's ATM business for the internet cafes. The objective means the same – getting the businesses strong enough to look after themselves. But where that used to mean flotation, Stelios is now happy to use licensing or franchise agreements. Last year he struck deals with Lloyds TSB to run the easyMoney credit card, and with Kellkoo to run the internet cost-price comparison engine easyValue. Not too familiar with the concept of modesty, Stelios explains that these moves are evidence he is following in the footsteps of his hero Richard Branson. 'It's the shape of things to come. I've built a brand and one of the ways you exploit a brand is by licensing deals.'

He has also become a big fan of franchising. 'I think franchising is an amazing tool. It's capitalism at its best. I'm using it for the internet cafes. I've made enough mistakes in that industry and I now have technology that works, I have a brand that people recognise. It's all about branding and then allowing local entrepreneurs to use the business method and name and reputation to make money. If your asset is your brand, the best thing you can do is sell it to entrepreneurs. I have a great rapport with these people. They are small versions of me and aspire to be me.'

With a delightful mix of metaphors he describes his style as 'leadership by the chin'. He repeats that he only wants to work in start-ups and will never be a manager of large groups of people or a big company. 'I wouldn't take the job of running General Electric and motivating 300,000 people I've never met,' he says. 'I think I can just about carry with me a small group of people into the unknown. I lead by example. If I expect people to work hard, I work hard. I can just about manage the 100 people I have in this room. As soon as a business is profitable and successful we kick it out.'

The problem is that he hasn't managed to 'kick out' a business since easyJet. So will the pressure to produce another success mean he loses his appetite for being a serial entrepreneur?

'I still have fun. I refuse to do anything else except have fun. As soon as chairing the board of a Plc became too claustrophobic for me or tedious I said, I'm out of here, let's hire someone else to do this job. You can never pretend to be anything other than what you really are. I like fun and humour. I'm the guy who tells the jokes at dinner parties. Having fun while doing business, poking fun at competitors through advertising, will always be my way.'

Source: taken from *The Director*, February 2004.
© Reproduced with permission of *The Director* magazine.

Further reading and references

Arthur, D Little Inc. (1974) *A system for managing diversity*, Arthur D Little, Cambridge MA.

Arthur, D Little Inc. (1980) *A management system for the 1980s*, Arthur D Little, San Francisco.

Barrow, C (1991) *The New Small Business Guide*, 3rd edition, BBC Books, London.

Bhide, A (1996) 'The Questions Every Entrepreneur Must Ask', *Harvard Business Review*, **74**, **6**, pp. 120–30.

Bull, I, Thomas, H and Willard, G (1995) *Entrepreneurship: Perspectives on Theory Building*, Pergamon Press, Oxford.

Cascio, W (1993) 'Downsizing: What do we know? What have we learnt?' *Academy of Management Executive*, **7**, **1**, pp. 95–104.

Caves, RE and Porter, ME (1977) 'From Entry Barriers to Mobility Barriers: Conjectural Decisions and Contrived Deterrence to New Competition', *Quarterly Journal of Economics*, **75**, **4**, pp. 515–43.

Churchill, NC and Lewis, VL (1983) 'The Five Stages of Small Business Growth', *Harvard Business Review*, May/June, pp. 30–50.

Cooper, AC (1981) 'Strategic Management: New Ventures and Small Businesses', *Long Range Planning*, **14**, **5**, pp. 39–45.

Drucker, PF (1985) *Innovation and entrepreneurship*, Harper & Row, London.

Franko, LG (1987) 'Global Corporate Competition: Who's winning, Who's Losing and the R&D Factor as One Reason Why', *Strategic Management Journal*, **10**, **5**, pp. 449–74.

Gaedeke, RM and Tootelian, DH (1985) *Small Business Management*, 2nd edition, Glenview, London.

Gopinath, C (1991) 'Turnaround: Recognising decline and initiating intervention', *Long Range Planning*, **24**, **6**, pp. 96–101.

Grant, RM (2002) *Contemporary Strategy Analysis*, 4th edition, Blackwell Publishing, Oxford.

Greiner, LE (1972) 'Evolution and Revolution as Organizations Grow', *Harvard Business Review*, **50**, **4**, pp. 37–46.

Grimm, CM and Smith, KG (1997) *Strategy as Action: Industry Rivalry and Co-ordination*, South-Western College Publishing, An International Thompson Publishing Company.

Grinyer, P, Mayes, D and McKiernan, P (1988) *Sharpbenders*, Basil Blackwell, Oxford.

Hambrick, DC and Schecter, SM (1983) 'Turnaround Strategies for Mature Industrial Product Business Units', *Academy of Management Journal*, **26**, **2**, pp. 231–48.

Hodgetts, RM (1982) *Effective Small Business Management*, Academic Press, London.

Hofer, CW (1976) 'Turnaround Strategies', in WF Glueck (ed.) (1980) *Business Policy and Strategic Management*, 3rd edition, McGraw-Hill, Maidenhead, pp. 427–33.

Hoffman, RC (1989) 'Strategies for Corporate Turnarounds: What Do We Know About Them', *Journal of General Management*, **14**, **3**, Spring, pp. 46–66.

Hunt, J (1981) Managing People at Work: A Manager's Guide to Behaviour in Organizations, Pan, London.

Ingvar, D (1985) 'Memories of the future, an essay on the temporal organization of conscious awareness', *Human Neurobiology*, No 4.

Jarillo, JC (1988) 'On strategic networks', *Strategic Management Journal*, **19**, **1**, pp. 31–42.

Kanter, RM (1983) *The Change Masters: Corporate Entrepreneurs at Work*, Routledge, London.

Leibowitz, SJ and Margolis, SE (1999) Winners, Losers and Microsoft: Competition and Antitrust in High Technology, Oakland: The Independent Institute.

Li, PS (1993) 'Chinese investment and business in Canada: Ethnic entrepreneurship reconsidered', *Pacific Affairs*, 66.

McGee, J and Thomas, H (1994) 'Sequential Entry Paths and Industry Evolution', in H Daems and H Thomas (eds) *Strategic Groups, Strategic Moves and Performance*, Pergamon Press, Oxford, pp. 143–54.

McKiernan, P (1992) *Strategies of Growth*, Routledge, London.

Miller, D (1992) 'The Icarus Paradox', *Business Horizons*, **35**, **1**, pp. 454–67.

Mintzberg, H, Quinn, JB and Ghoshal, S (1998) *The Strategy Process*, Revised European Edition, Prentice Hall, Englewood Cliffs, NJ.

Oster, S (1990) *Modern competitive analysis*, Oxford University Press.

Penrose, ET (1959) *The Theory of the Growth of the Firm*, Basil Blackwell, Oxford.

Peters, TJ and Waterman, RH (1982) *In Search of Excellence*, New York, Harper and Row.

Pettigrew, A (1973) *The Awakening Giant: Continuity and Change at ICI*, Blackwell, Oxford.

Price, R (1996) 'Technology and strategic advantage', *Californian Management Review*, **38**.

Segal-Horn, S (ed.) (1998) *The Strategy Reader*, Blackwell Business, Oxford.

Schumpeter, JA (1942) *Capitalism, Socialism, and Democracy*, Harper & Row, New York.

Slatter, S (1984) *Corporate Recovery*, Penguin.

Steffens, J (1986) Entry Behaviour and Competition in the Evolution of the United States' Personal Computer Industry 1975–83', PhD thesis, University of London.

Stevenson, HH and Gumpert, DE (1985) 'The heart of entrepreneurship', *Harvard Business Review*, **63**, **2**, March/April, p. 85.

Teece, DJ (1987) 'Profiting From Technological Innovation: Implications for Integration, Collaboration, Licensing and Public Policy', in DJ Teece (ed.) (1987) *The Competitive Challenge*, Ballinger, Cambridge, MA.

Whittington, R (1993) *What is Strategy and Does it Matter?* Routledge, London.

Yip, GS (1982) 'Gateways to entry', *Harvard Business Review*, Sept–Oct, pp. 85–92.

Chapter 9

Corporate strategy: adding value in multi-business firms[1]

Introduction

This chapter concerns the portfolio of businesses held within a common, 'corporate' ownership, and the organization structure and management processes required to manage such portfolios. It covers the economic analysis of portfolios using, for example, BCG and McKinsey models, the concept and practice of parenting advantage, and the role of the corporate headquarters. It also covers the elements of the organization design and structure, and methods of resource allocation and control.

The importance of the study of corporate strategy stems from the fact that large businesses are increasingly *multi-businesses* and networks between businesses (for example, strategic alliances) are becoming more

---

[1] This chapter is written jointly with Chris Smith.

common. This is true across the globe, from the *chaebols* of Korea and the *keiretsus* of Japan to the corporate sweep of America's GE and Europe's ABB. As such, it is not just ongoing competitive strategy – the long-term dynamics of serving customers better than the competition – that occupies the minds of the top managers and investors. It is also ongoing *corporate* strategy – the value gained from the mixture of businesses and how to manage those businesses to optimize that value. Corporate strategy for

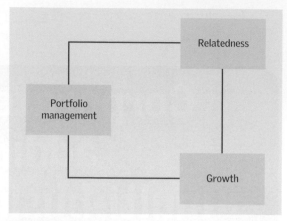

Figure 9.1 The three essential insights of corporate strategy

multi-business firms goes far beyond the traditional ideas of the choices of which industry/markets/products to be in. Figure 9.1 captures the three main ideas or insights that are fundamental to corporate strategy:

1   **Portfolio management** – the businesses that should make up the portfolio.

2   The growth idea – the way in which profitable growth is to be achieved through internal investment and/or external acquisitions.

3   **Relatedness** – the way in which the synergies between businesses are to be managed and exploited.

9.1 **The changing organizational structure**

The modern, hierarchical business enterprise arose in the 1850s in the United States and Europe, to administer the new railroad and telegraph companies. An organizational structure based on a split into functional responsibilities (the **U-form** – unitary form) was the norm at this time (*see* Figure 9.2).

Expanding size, however – particularly where expansion included diversification – compromised the effectiveness of the U-form.

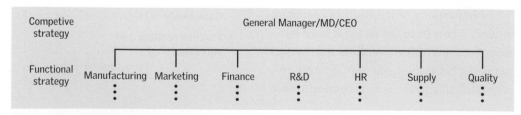

Figure 9.2 The U-form organization

> *The inherent weakness in the centralised, functionally departmentalised operating company ... became critical only when the administrative load on the senior executives increased to such an extent that they were unable to handle their entrepreneurial responsibilities efficiently. This situation arose when the operations of the enterprise became too complex and the problems of co-ordination, appraisal and policy formulation too intricate for a small number of top officers to handle both long-run, entrepreneurial, and short-run, operational administrative activities.* (Chandler, 1962, p. 299)

To overcome such problems, the large American companies Du Pont, General Motors, Jersey Standard and Sears Roebuck pioneered a movement to an innovative organizational form in the early 1920s. This innovation, which became known as the 'multidivisional' or **M-form**, divided tasks and responsibilities into semi-autonomous operating units (profit centres) organized on brand, product or regional lines (see Figure 9.3).

After slow early growth, the spread of the M-form increased dramatically following the Second World War. In 1949 less than a quarter of the Fortune 500 were divisionalized. This had risen to just over a half in 1959. By 1969 only one-fifth of companies in the top 500 were not divisionalized (Hill 1994). Similar trends have been evident in Europe and the UK and today the multidivisional form is the most prevalent organizational structure in large companies in Western economies.

> *The basic reason for its success was simply that it clearly removed the executives' responsible for the destiny of the entire enterprise from the more routine operational activities, and so gave them time, information, and even more psychological commitment for long-term planning and appraisal ... Thus the new structure left the broad strategic decisions as to the allocation of existing resources and the acquisitions of new ones in the hands of a top team of generalists. Relieved of operating duties and tactical decisions, a general executive was less likely to reflect the position of just one part of the whole.* (Chandler, 1962, pp. 309–310)

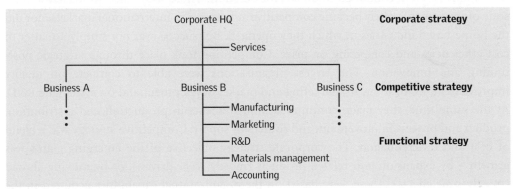

Figure 9.3 The M-form organization

The M-form has several positive attributes. It enables business managers to maximize economies of specialization, by allowing them to focus on their products and markets, while freeing corporate managers from the distractions of day-to-day operations. It makes it easy for corporate management to measure and compare the performance of business units through financial statements, and facilitates the addition (acquisition) or deletion (divestment) of businesses. On top of this, the stand-alone business ethos fits well with Western values of individualism and accountability, and encourages the development of autonomous general managers.

Alfred Chandler, the eminent business historian, chronicled the rise of the M-form organizations in the USA in his celebrated book *Strategy and Structure* (1962). He also provided a telling and powerful argument for the benefits of size in papers such as 'The Enduring Logic of Industrial Success' (1990a, 1990b). He argued that economics of scale and scope were the motive power behind large organizations. These enable large plants to produce at much lower costs than small ones (*scale*). Large plants use many of the same raw and semi-finished materials and intermediate production processes to make a variety of different products (*scope*). To capitalize on the new, larger scale of manufacturing, investment firms needed to make two further, related sets of investment. The first was to create national, then international, marketing and distribution organizations (both scale and scope effects). The second was to develop new management teams. The lower/middle levels were to co-ordinate flow of products through production and distribution. The top level was to co-ordinate and monitor current operations and to plan and allocate resources for future activities. The new levels of investment thus require an integrated and balanced economic and managerial infrastructure to ensure constant flow of product and high-capacity utilization. In simple economic terms the scale and scope driven savings in operations have to be balanced in part by higher administrative and managerial costs. But these too offer scale and scope benefits as long as volumes are maintained.

Chandler took the argument further. He observed that first movers quickly dominated their industries and continued to do so (for decades). Those who failed to make the right scale of investments rarely became competitive at home or in international markets, nor did the home-based industries in which they operated. But success was not simply a matter of cost efficiencies and competing on price. Competition took place through strategic positioning and innovation. The largest organizations were able to compete on quality improvement, innovations in marketing and market development and on systematic R&D. At the same time, they made continuous improvements in production and distribution, product and process improvement, and sources of supply. Competitive strategy was a blend of cost and differentiation. The corporate strategy objective of the emerging giants was growth – by expansion into related products (mostly *scope*-driven), or by moving abroad (mostly *scale* effects). These were based on the organizational capabilities acquired in the process of domestic oligopolistic competition. There were also some horizontal movements

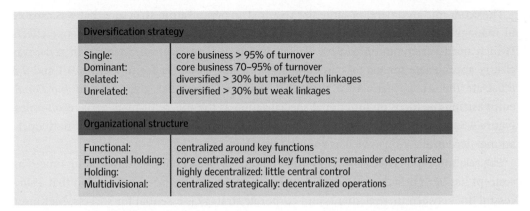

Diversification strategy	
Single:	core business > 95% of turnover
Dominant:	core business 70–95% of turnover
Related:	diversified > 30% but market/tech linkages
Unrelated:	diversified > 30% but weak linkages

Organizational structure	
Functional:	centralized around key functions
Functional holding:	core centralized around key functions; remainder decentralized
Holding:	highly decentralized: little central control
Multidivisional:	centralized strategically: decentralized operations

Figure 9.4 Strategy and structure

(acquisitions) and some vertical integration to control material supplies or distribution outlets.

This is the history of the emergence of international oligopolies, founded initially on scale and scope advantages in production and distribution but enhanced and secured by scale and scope effects in marketing, R&D, supply management and organization. However, large is not always logical. The giants can and do stagnate, with Ford Motor Co. providing the leading example in the 1920s. In its case the direct competition between two giants, Ford and GM, was to leave at least one of them injured. In post-war years, particularly the 1960s, the compulsion for growth led companies to much broader based diversification. This became known as conglomerate style diversification and was, and is, highly controversial.

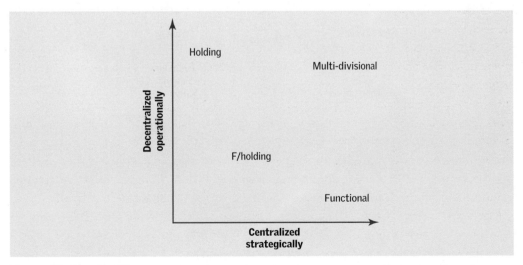

Figure 9.5 Structural types

The economic argument for large size required an organization structure that was capable of managing both scale effects (which require specialization and depth) and scope effects (which need variety and breadth). The divisionalized corporation, M-form in style, was clearly appropriate for the task in comparison to the earlier U-form. Figures 9.4 and 9.5 illustrate the strategy–structure choices. The term *U-form* has given way to *functional*, emphasizing the focus on functional specialization as the source of managerial economies. Figure 9.5 indicates the value of the divisionalized (M-form) in that it allows for both operational decentralization as well as strategic direction.

The relationship between strategy and structure has been established for a long time. The concept has been broadened to include other variables, with a further extension that a successful 'fit' between these elements and corporate strategy is essential for success. McKinsey and Company introduced the 7S Model (see Waterman (1982) and Waterman *et al.* (1980)) with seven broad areas that need to be integrated together. The seven variables are structure, systems, style, staff, skills, shared values, and strategy. Figure 9.6 shows how the McKinsey 7S model can be applied to the M-form organization, demonstrating the nature of the fit between its different components. In Chapter 10 we will show how the new network form of organization can be described by the 7S model.

However, there are also manifest drawbacks. Because corporate managers are free from operational distractions, they also tend to get out of touch with business and divisional issues and hence, are reliant on the input of their politically aware general managers. The clear structural split does not necessarily mean there is a clear split of responsibilities, and confusion often reigns as to which level is accountable for various outcomes or processes. Further complications arise due to the (rational) tendency of business units to compete

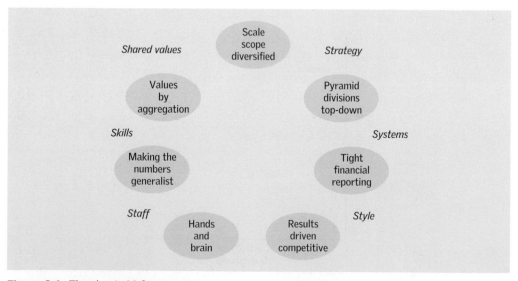

Figure 9.6 The classic M-form

rather than co-operate with each other for the limited resources available. This leads to general managers 'selling' their business needs to the corporate level, with the resultant blurring of reality that selling frequently entails. As will be discussed in more detail below, perhaps the most significant problem with the M-form is its tendency to impede the development of trans-firm competencies.

9.1.1 Issues

Given these opposing dynamics and their prevalence, the multidivisional firm has attracted the interest of academics and management authors. Two major questions have been the focus of research and writing:

1 *What is the additional value generated by such firms?*

   This is an economic question which addresses what value is inherent in having a group of potentially stand-alone businesses under one management. Writings on this question are found mainly in academic journals and focus particularly on the value of groupings of *related* businesses and the associated issue of *synergy*.

2 *How are they best managed?*

   This is an organizational/strategic question which addresses how value is optimized and, in particular, what is the role of the corporate head office in all this. This question addresses what is known as 'corporate strategy' in the strategic management literature. While 'corporate strategy' is still used by some in an all-encompassing sense, most authors now identify 'corporate strategy' with multi-business firms. Porter's (1987) view is typical:

   > *Corporate strategy,* **the overall plan for a diversified company** ... *concerns two different questions: what businesses the corporation should be in and how the corporate office should manage the array of business units.* (Porter, 1987, p. 43, emphasis added)

Thus, corporate strategy is concerned with the choice of industries to compete in, the setting of an organizational context for the operations of the component business units, and managing the relationships between those businesses.

9.2 Theory and concepts

9.2.1 The inherent value

The M-form originated as a response to the complexity of large U-form organizations. Its continued existence as the dominant structure of large companies, however, suggests that it possesses ongoing 'ecological' advantages over other organizational forms. It has been proposed that its ubiquity is driven by the status, power and material hunger of managers –

a bigger company means more benefits for the top people. The ecological argument still suggests that, even if managerial greed were a significant driver, competitive forces in free markets would select out these forms if they were sufficiently inefficient relative to other structures. (*Note*: 'Ecologists' might suggest that we should 'watch this space', as the time frame in which the M-form has existed is very short in population ecology terms.)

Writers in economics and strategic management are agreed that the *economic* logic of multi-business corporations, and hence a potential reason for their proliferation, is that the whole is worth more than the sum of its parts:

$$V_c = A_s + B_s + C_s + M_c$$

where:

V_c = the value of the corporation
A_s, B_s, C_s = the respective values of the stand-alone businesses A, B and C
M_c = the total net[2] value of corporate membership, that is, *membership benefits*

so: $V_c > A_s + B_s + C_s$ by the value of M_c

In many cases M_c has proven to be negative. When this situation prevails, the break-up of the corporation is a financially attractive strategy, as proved by the corporate raiders – asset strippers of the 1980s.

M_c has different sources. Organizational gain, derived from the splitting of strategy and operations, has a value-logic grounded in managerial efficiency and focus. This traditional rationale, allied to the benefits of size and scale, seems an adequate explanation of the *reorganization* of growing companies from (inefficient) U-form to (efficient) M-form. However, this argument does not explain why the total value of the component businesses can be higher under a corporate umbrella than if they were stand-alone. (*Note*: This is a very important issue for investors, who are free to invest directly in the stand-alone businesses without the necessity of a corporate layer.)

Theorists in the general area of what is known as **transaction cost economics** (TCE)[3] offer some of the most persuasive ideas about the potential added value of the M-form. They propose two major categories of benefit: *governance* and *scope* advantages.

[2] The idea of 'net' value acknowledges that there are a variety of 'costs' of membership. These are more than the financial overheads of corporate staff etc. Examples of other costs include business time and resource invested in corporate or inter-business activities; the potential loss of entrepreneurial drive, as market incentives are replaced by more focused, internal rewards that encourage 'satisficing' behaviour; the containment of business activities to a more narrow product, process or geographic range than might be attainable in stand-alone mode; the sustained cross-subsidizations of businesses that, in a stand-alone capacity, would be bankrupt etc.

[3] TCE breaks with neo-classical economics by dropping several of the latter's (unreal) assumptions. In particular, it concerns itself with the effects of the costs of interactions (transactions) between businesses, between businesses and customers, etc.

Governance

Under this category, the corporate office takes the role of a more informed and involved investor. Unlike arm's-length investors, it is fully knowledgeable about the businesses via direct reporting and auditing mechanisms and can pressure business managers for improved performance, while paying market-rate salaries. In a stand-alone business, a manager can take advantage of the fact that he or she controls the information flow to the investment community and can hide the true nature of any problems. In a multi-business firm, the corporate office has all the necessary information and can sanction or replace managers of underperforming units. The corporate office also has an overview that the business manager lacks, and can thus add further information and insight to his or her decisions. In stand-alone units, business managers can maximize what has been called 'on-the-job consumption', for example, making (unnecessary) spouse-accompanied weeklong, visits to desirable locations, flying first class and staying in five-star hotels. The additional corporate layer can police and prevent such dissipation of shareholders' funds. (*Note*: This 'advantage' begs the obvious question of who guards the guards. In the light of increasingly spectacular returns to directors of public companies, this is a question worth asking.)

Scope

As well as potentially dealing with the tensions between owners and managers through governance mechanisms, the multi-business organization is argued to have value-enhancing properties in that it can facilitate economies of scope. *Related* businesses (those with similar markets/technologies/processes) can share specialized physical capital, knowledge and managerial expertise. The sharing process is overseen and controlled and disputes are resolved by corporate management. With stand-alone businesses, such sharing is problematic. Potential problems include ongoing haggling, the risk of one partner exploiting the trust of the other, the risk of being let down, and the tendency for partners to try to benefit more than their input would warrant.[4] Under normal circumstances, stand-alone businesses attempt to control these problems through formal contracts and a 'trading relationship'. However, such sharing is not amenable to formal contract, particularly in the case of specialized organizational knowledge embodied in people. Tacit components, team embeddedness and the uncertainty of its value make such learning particularly difficult to trade.

It is through scope economies between related businesses that corporate *synergies* (the total being more than the sum of the parts) are hypothesized to be most attainable. A relatively recent expression of scope economies has been the popularization of the concept of *core competences* that are 'the collective learning in the organization, especially how to coordinate diverse production skills and integrate multiple streams of technology' (Prahalad and

---

[4] This is an example of the 'free-rider' problem and is familiar to students undertaking group work, when one member seems to get out of most of the duties, but shares in the overall assessment.

Hamel, 1990, p. 82). The importance of core competences for multi-business firms is that they can '*span businesses* and products within a corporation. Put differently, powerful core competencies *support several* products or *businesses.*'

Prahalad and Hamel (1990), emphasizing the importance of trans-business capabilities, assert that core competencies are the 'central subject of corporate strategy' (p. 220) and that multi-business companies should see themselves as a 'portfolio of competences' (p. 221) – as well as a portfolio of products and services, that is. Economies of scope are the nub of corporate strategy and the fundamental rationale for the M-form company.

9.3 Managing the multi-business firm

9.3.1 The strategy–structure balance

We have seen from earlier chapters that, at the level of the business, strategy has three key dimensions: competitive advantage (how to compete), the key resource allocation decisions at the business level, and the organization of the business. At the corporate level there is a parallel concern with resource allocation decisions, and with organization structure and process. But the distinguishing characteristic of the multi-business firm is that at the centre it is concerned with what businesses to be in – the portfolio question. The answer is, of course, contingent on the nature of competitive advantages, but decisions about the portfolio are taken at corporate level whereas the responsibility for securing competitive advantage is at the business level.

The economics of corporate strategy revolve around three issues (see Figure 9.1):

1 The characteristics of the portfolio expressed as its overall return and its overall risk. This allows for gains from the statistical nature of pooled variances, which means that imperfectly correlated risks of the individual businesses result in lower overall risk. This is on the basis of avoiding having all one's eggs in the same basket.[5]

2 How synergies between businesses are captured – the idea of relatedness.

3 The growth ambitions of the firm and how these are to be achieved by internal investment and/or expansion.

There are insights and traps attached to each of these. Portfolio analysis arrays the strengths and weaknesses of each business. In particular, the sources of cash and profit can be established and investment needs specified. Thus it is possible to assess for the portfolio what are its cash flow and profit characteristics in relation to its overall risk. However, if taken too literally portfolio analysis can focus excessively on eliminating unprofitable,

---

[5] We should note that the gains from diversification may mitigate against disaster but by themselves don't promote competitive advantage.

low-potential businesses and expanding high-potential businesses without attention to any underlying synergies and complementarities.

Relatedness determines whether interdependencies between businesses can create value and competitive advantage or whether each business should be treated on its own merits. The trap is that poor-performing businesses should not be maintained from 'overall strength' without strong evidence of value potential from relatedness.

Sensible growth objectives and analysis identifies how resources can be deployed to maintain a balance between investment, cash flow and profits over time. Proper analysis prevents misdirected growth that focuses on growth for its own sake, leading to inappropriate timing and falling into cash traps.

Corporate organization has to be consistent with the economics of the strategy. This too can be described in three parts:

1   Definition of division and business unit boundaries.

2   The intended lateral integration and co-ordination between business units.

3   The vertical relationships between corporate tasks and roles and line operations – the corporate–business interface.

Business unit boundaries and groupings of businesses (divisions or sectors) can be the natural and powerful way to exploit relatedness opportunities. Superior performance frequently requires that businesses be properly focused on relevant markets – that the boundaries should be drawn correctly. New boundaries should be drawn[6] when the value of increasing the focus (narrowing the scope) exceeds the cost of lost relatedness benefits, and vice versa.

The corporate–business interface sets out authority and accountability in the firm. Three particular styles are commonly observed (see the discussion below). **Strategic planning** involves corporate executives in defining and monitoring corporate and business strategies. It is most appropriate for capital-intensive operations and highly interrelated businesses. **Strategic control** involves corporate executives in influencing business-level strategies and monitoring financial results. It is a 'loose-tight' approach. **Financial control** decentralizes control of business strategy to the business and relies solely on financial control at the corporate level. It is deemed to be most appropriate for conglomerate-like strategies.

Integration mechanisms are used to balance choices made on boundaries and on the corporate–business interface. The formality of the latter two can be supplemented by less formal arrangements that can pick up on related possibilities not captured within business boundaries and neglected by the corporate level need to have strong vertical controls. Therefore, self-interested lateral co-operation has a natural place in complementing the formal organizational arrangements. More formal lateral mechanisms include centres of

---

[6]   This is often called 'reorganization'.

excellence, people transfers, transfer pricing systems, special study teams, lead business arrangements and internal consulting. Vertical mechanisms are also possible such as intermediate levels of organization and arrangements of cross-functional authority. Strategic control styles of management typically require more explicit processes for lateral integration than other forms of control.

9.3.2 Corporate strategies

Adding value through buying and selling businesses has been one form of corporate strategy. The corporate centre acts as a funds investor and seeks opportunities to buy companies that are undervalued by the market and then waits until the inherent value is recognized and sells them on at a profit. A more active role than this entails buying companies that are underperforming, and hence are available at a relatively low price, and acting to improve performance and selling price. A variant of this was undertaken by the so-called 'raiders' and 'asset strippers' of the 1980s, who bought conglomerates and then sold off the component parts for a total price far in excess of the overall purchase price. Opportunities to profit from this mode of corporate strategy are now rare, as the general market is more attuned to such opportunities, as are potential targets.[7]

Porter (1987) terms this corporate buy-and-sell approach *portfolio management*. The Ashridge researchers Goold, Campbell and Alexander (1994) call it *corporate development*, and include the reshaping of existing businesses by amalgamation or division and the creation of new businesses by internal venturing. Both sets of authors agree that this is no longer a viable value-generating corporate strategy, as the market now anticipates the potential undervaluation and reflects this in the (speculative) premium in the price paid. Such premiums ensure that profitable acquisitions must now be based on better management of the acquired business, or other forms of synergistic benefits of belonging to the new corporation.

In discussing the aspect of corporate strategy that is to do with the management of the multi-business organization, Porter (1987) identifies three organizational/process concepts of corporate strategy: *restructuring, sharing activities* and *transferring skills*:

- **Restructuring** occurs when businesses are acquired with the specific intent of achieving value by active intervention and improvement. The centre needs the capability to effect such transformation and thus it exerts strong direct influence on business performance and processes. In Porter's view, once restructuring has been successful, the business should then be sold to capture the new value, unless it benefits in some way from ongoing membership of the corporation.

---

[7] The trend for conglomerates to become focused on fewer 'core' businesses was a consequence of such threats.

- **Sharing activities** is a value activity that is based on the component businesses using the same facilities, services, processes or systems and thereby reaping utilization, learning curve (scope) scale or differentiation benefits. Management is based on interrelationships, but not necessarily interdependencies between the business units, that is, the shared facility can be a corporate-level activity.

- **Transferring skills** is managing ongoing interrelationships between the businesses. In this case, the corporate centre actively fosters the sharing of expertise or skills among the businesses, even though they might have different value chains. As with 'sharing activities', the centre is actively involved, but this time it develops and promotes linkages and interdependencies between business units.

Goold *et al.* (1994) have spent a considerable time focusing on the multi-business company and how its corporate strategy adds (or subtracts)[8] value. Consistent with the well-known 'competitive advantage', they coined the intuitively attractive term *parenting advantage* to denote the additional value that an insightful parent company can add to its component businesses through appropriate orientation and management. They suggest three requisites for parenting advantage:

1 the corporate advantage must translate into more competitive advantage in at least one business, or membership of each business in the portfolio must create extra value somewhere in the portfolio;

2 must create more value than the cost of the corporate overhead;

3 must add more value than any other possible parent otherwise the market for corporate control might eventually challenge your ownership and parenting credentials.

Goold *et al.* (1994) also identify three classes of value-adding corporate strategy: *stand-alone influence, functional and services influence* and *linkage influence*, which parallel Porter's categories. They emphasize that these are not either/or choices but can all be in operation at the same time. Figure 9.7 illustrates the range of sources of value creation.

- *Stand-alone influence* is the value created by the influence on the individual business strategy and performance. The major focus is on vertical linkages, mainly between the CEO and the MDs of the businesses. In this category, successful corporate parents have to overcome the '10% versus 100% paradox' – the idea that part-time, organizationally removed managers can enhance the performance of the business's dedicated management.

- *Functional and services influence* is again a vertical process, with the focus on adding value through the influence of a range of centrally controlled staff functions. These may replace

---

8 This is more than a technical parenthesis, as the general thrust of their findings is that value destruction is the norm in multi-business companies.

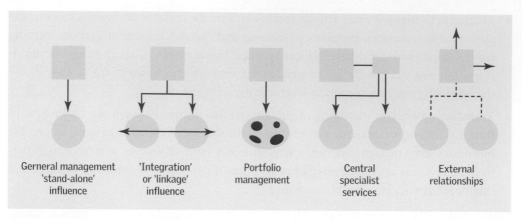

Figure 9.7 Sources of value creation

or augment those already in place in the businesses. The problem the corporate centre faces here is offering a higher value-added service than specialist outsiders – the 'beating the specialist' paradox.

♦ *Linkage influence* aims to increase value through the relationships between the businesses. The focus is on horizontal processes and incorporates both the 'shared activities' and 'transfer of skills' categories of Porter. It is difficult to explain, however, why the managers of the businesses would not do this themselves if extra value would accrue as a result, that is, the 'enlightened self-interest' paradox.

The general management influence is generally reckoned to be the key (only) justification for long-term survival of conglomerates. Linkages, portfolio effects and specialist capabilities are all part of the synergy and relatedness themes. The external relationship management theme harks back to much earlier thinking about the role of the top team and the board. This maintains that the specialist skills at the top are about understanding the external environment and finding ways to cope with it and to position against it. Modern thinking has focused very much on the internal management and dynamics of the organization, perhaps to a fault.

Case box: **Benetton: the other colours**

Diversifying from fashion into motorways and restaurants has paid off for the Benetton family

Almost 50 years ago Luciano Benetton came up with an idea that took the world of fashion by storm. His bright, casual sweaters would be dyed after they had been knitted so that stores could restock faster with the most popular colours. From artisanal origins in Ponzano Veneto, a small town about 30 kilometres (19 miles) north of Venice, the shops of the United Colors of Benetton spread across Europe and America, promoted by provocative and controversial advertising.

Benetton on the road
Edizione Holding's main businesses

	2003 sales €bn	2003 profit before tax, €m	Edizione's share*, %	Edizione's share of market cap*, €bn
Autogrill	3.143	98	56.7	1.71
Autostrade	2.570	532	31.2	2.94
Benetton Group	1.859	165	67.1	1.09

Source: Company reports: Thomson Datastream   *On August 31st 2004

But times change and colours fade. Early this year, there were whispers that the Benetton family might be in financial trouble. The figures, though, show something rather different: Edizione Holding, the Benettons' holding company, owns investments with a market value, after deducting debts, of around €6 billion ($7.3 billion). Diversifying out of the business that the Benettons knew well, the fashion industry, has worked surprisingly well for one of Italy's best-known family concerns.

The Benettons' success in clothing relied on a supply chain of outsourced production tied together with a computerised logistics system, which was well ahead of its time. But by the late 1980s, imitators and competitors were catching up. Firms such as Sweden's H&M and Spain's Zara have recently given the Italian company a tough time in high streets and shopping malls.

Rumours about financial worries, however, seem to have been prompted by the Benettons' big spending on other businesses. Not content to stick to its knitting, the family has invested heavily over the past ten years in Italian privatisations, usually as part of a consortium.

In 1994, Edizione Holding was the leading partner in a consortium that acquired Autogrill, an Italian motorway-catering business. Then came Autostrade, the largest operator of toll motorways in Italy. Stakes in municipal energy utilities, the refurbishment of railway stations, Turin's airport and Telecom Italia followed. Over two-thirds of the Benettons' wealth—they are the third-richest family in Italy—is now in Autogrill and Autostrade (see table).

Idyllic Ponzano Veneto seems a long way from the centres of power. 'We never needed to get close to politicians. I personally feel distant from politics. We like the idea of being in the countryside,' explains Mr Benetton. Yet this aversion to politicians did not hamper the family's diversification efforts much.

Edizione Holding now has a 56.7% stake in Autogrill, which became a global concern in 1999 with the acquisition of Host Marriott Services, an American catering firm. It is, says Gianni Mion, Edizione Holding's managing director, 'a nice business, well-managed and self-standing'. North America is now Autogrill's most important market; it accounted for over half of revenues in 2003. And the group's tills at airports were nearly as busy as those on the motorways.

The privatisation of Autostrade in 2000 presented another opportunity. Edizione Holding owns 60% of the consortium that obtained control of Autostrade by buying 30%. Last year, the consortium raised its stake in Autostrade to 62% with a public tender offer at €10 per share; in July it sold 10% of this at almost €16 per share, leaving it with virtually no debt.

Why have investors been so impressed? Autostrade's revenues are regulated, so tight management of costs is essential. Mr Mion says that Autostrade's spending on items such as road surfacing, guard rails and maintenance is now much lower per kilometre than was envisaged at the time of privatisation. Yet pleasing investors has proved easier than managing complaints about conflicts of interest. Autostrade grants concessions to restaurants and petrol stations on its motorways and, inevitably, Autogrill pitches for some of them. Although a firm of independent consultants handles the tendering process, there have been complaints that the process favours Autogrill. Magistrates are investigating these complaints, but Mr Mion appears unflustered, insisting that both firms have behaved correctly.

While Autogrill and Autostrade have been excellent investments, that cannot be said about all of the Benetton family's diversifications. Moves into sports equipment (Nordica ski-boots and Rollerblade skates) were a disappointment. These businesses were finally ditched in 2003. 'I like to keep the mistakes in mind,' says Mr Mion. The group did not understand the sports equipment business, he admits. More significant than the losses was the distraction for management.

There is another mistake that Mr Mion should keep in mind. In 2001, the Benettons joined forces with Marco Tronchetti Provera, the boss of Pirelli, to take over Telecom Italia through Olimpia, a highly leveraged company. That has not paid off either: Edizione Holding's 16.8% stake in Olimpia is now worth only half its cost of €1.16 billion. 'It is an investment that gives less satisfaction,' Mr Benetton remarks dryly. But at least the success of Autostrade and Autogrill means he can afford this blooper. Operating toll motorways and selling pizzas may be rather dull compared with the glitz of the fashion world, but at least they promise a steady cashflow for the next generation of Benettons.

Source: 'The other colours', *The Economist*, 9 September 2004.
© The Economist Newspaper Limited, London (9 September 2004).

Questions for discussion

1 Assess the extent to which Benetton has diversified its activities; for example, what proportion of its total revenue is taken by the core (original) business?

2 What synergies are there between these lines of business?

3 How would you judge whether these investments have been worthwhile?

9.3.3 **Corporate styles**

In an earlier study, Goold and Campbell (1987) examined high-performing corporations and concluded that the *style* of the parent is an important factor in the level of performance achieved. They examined the extent to which management styles varied along the dimensions of *planning influence* (that is, the extent to which the corporate level became involved in the strategic and operating planning of the business) and *control influence* (that is, the extent to which the businesses were held to budgetary and operational targets) (*see* Figure 9.8).

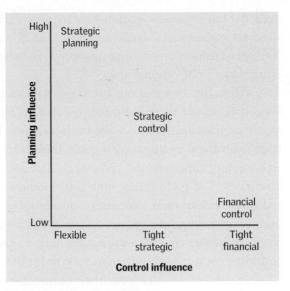

Figure 9.8 Parenting styles
Source: Goold and Campbell, 1987.

Three styles seemed to stand out. In *financial control* companies (for example, BTR), the centre allowed a high degree of strategic and operational autonomy to the businesses (low planning influence). The budget, however, was sacrosanct and any slippage from planned performance needed swift correction, if it were not to mean the curtailment of the career of the responsible GM (high control influence). At the other end of the continuum, *strategic planning* companies (for example, ICI) involved themselves on an ongoing basis in the strategic planning and management of the businesses (high planning control). They were more flexible if strategic contingencies caused operational performance to slip against budgeted targets, that is, the budget was a reflection of the strategy (low control influence). In between these two extremes were the *strategic control* companies.[9]

This work on styles is consistent with the view that optimizing corporate strategy is contingent on the appropriate organizational structures, systems, processes, etc.

> *Corporate strategies which predominantly use one or other of these three roles to realise the value inherent in their resources should, according to contingency theory, align their structure, systems and procedures according to those roles.* (Collis, 1991c, p. 7)

In accordance with this view, corporations do not need large corporate staffs if they are relying on a stand-alone influence role, whereas a co-ordinated and integrated staff is

[9] In a summary of this work in their 1994 text, the authors conclude that there is a continuing movement away from the *financial control* to the strategic *planning/control styles.*

needed if inter-business relationships are to be a major source of value. In a similar way the structure of business manager incentives should vary, with group-based incentives needed for 'inter-business'-oriented corporations and stand-alone incentives appropriate for the more 'managerial' orientations.

As well as the view that organizational structure, processes etc. should be contingent on the corporate role, there is also the view that the optimal corporate role is contingent on the degree of *relatedness* between the business units. To realize economies of scope (synergy) from relatedness, *co-operation* between businesses is required. This leads to increased centralization of functions and systems, and an increase in integrating mechanisms between businesses. The performance ambiguities inherent in sharing facilities and functions are tackled by seeking more information on a broader, less financial, range of indicators, and by business incentives based on group rather than individual performance. A value-enhancing, co-operative form may be a sustainable parenting advantage for a firm, as its unique history and social context make it idiosyncratic to the firm and, thus, more difficult to imitate.

Unrelated businesses have no opportunities for increased value from economies of scope and are argued to benefit from M-form membership due to governance benefits (Williamson 1975). Within such a framework, the corporate office of the M-form takes on the role of informed investor and runs the businesses on a *competitive* basis, as stand-alone entities that are rivals for capital which is allocated on a 'best-use' basis, consistent with external capital markets. Performance incentives are based on unambiguous, financial outputs. A summary of the proposed relationships between inherent value, basic corporate strategy and organizational factors is shown in Table 9.1.

Table 9.1 Comparing co-operative and competitive strategic orientations

	Source of inherent (economic) value	
	Economies of scope (related businesses)	**Governance (unrelated businesses)**
Basic corporate strategy:	Co-operative multidivisional	Competitive multidivisional
Operating and business-level strategic decisions:	Some centralization of critical functions	Complete decentralization
Inter-business integrating mechanisms:	Moderate to extensive	Non-existent
Business performance appraisal:	Mix of subjective and objective criteria	Primary reliance on objective financial criteria
Business incentive schemes:	Linked to corporate performance	Based on business performance only

Source: adapted from Hoskisson *et al.*, 1993, pp. 269–98.

In contrast to the optimism of multiple, coexistent corporate roles expressed by Porter (1987) and Goold *et al.* (1994), Hill (1994) points out that the 'radical differences' between these two types of M-form are such that:

it may be difficult for diversified firms to simultaneously realise economic benefits from economies of scope and efficient governance ... Competitive and co-operative organizations have different internal configurations with regard to centralisation, integration, control practices and incentive schemes. As a result **the internal management philosophies of co-operative and competitive organizations are incompatible.** (Hill, 1994, pp. 312–13, emphasis added)

This means that co-operative and competitive philosophies are different strategies with different organizational and managerial arrangements. Thus, if an M-form firm comprises a set of businesses, some of which are related and others which are not, it is faced with an economic and organizational dilemma. One resolution of this dilemma is to divest units and focus on a *core* business grouping.

Another resolution is through the creation of another organizational level – the *division*, into which all the businesses related in a particular way (for example, all those in the automotive components industry) are placed. In this sense, the division becomes an internal (quasi) corporation and the divisional-level managers can focus on optimizing the relatedness of their component businesses.

9.4 Practical frameworks and applications

The M-form seemed a boon to managers as an apparent answer to the complexities of size, growth and diversity. The intuitive value of divisionalization was further boosted during the 1960s, as diversification became a strategic imperative in its own right and acquisition and merger became a major mechanism for growth. Emboldened by shareholder approval, and armed with increasingly all-encompassing definitions of synergy[10] and faith in the transferability of general management skills, companies embarked on a diversifying buying spree.

In many cases, senior managers had no previous occupational experience of the operations and/or markets of the businesses that they bought and subsequently 'controlled'. Seemingly, however, the corporate office had no need to fully understand operational details, as this was the domain of the general managers of the business units. While demand exceeded supply, industries experienced stable growth and, hence, even relatively inefficient firms were able to prosper. By the early 1970s, a more complex and turbulent economic environment highlighted the unwieldy nature of many conglomerates. Senior managers sought different rationales and tools to manage their set of businesses. The new portfolio planning techniques and most notably, the growth-share matrix (Figure 9.9) developed by the Boston Consulting Group (BCG) seemingly met their needs. (*See* Day, 1977 for a critical review.)

[10] For example, Goold *et al.* (1994) cite the example of the British Oxygen Company (now BOC) buying a manufacturer of frozen pizza on the synergistic basis that gases were used in the freezing process.

Based on the cost-reducing effects of experience curve dynamics,[11] the **growth-share matrix** gave a cash flow rationale for business linkage, acquisition and divestment. Companies needed a balanced portfolio of investments. The 'mid-point' for relative market share was 1.0 and for market growth the mid-point was commonly the growth of the economy/GDP as a whole. The route to success implied by 'the boxes' approach was deceptively simple. (Relatively) large businesses in mature markets ('cash cows') generated free cash flow above their reinvestment needs. This cash could then be invested in the high growth (and, hence, cash-consuming) businesses, so

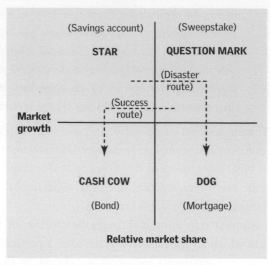

Figure 9.9 The growth-share matrix
Source: adapted from research by the Boston Consulting Group.

that the 'question marks' became 'stars', and the 'stars' maintained their strong positions, until eventually they became 'cash cows'. Relatively small businesses in low-growth industries ('dogs') were targets for divestment, or the basis for acquisition of similar businesses, to achieve the critical mass necessary to have the highest relative market share (a 'kennel of dogs'). The disaster route was equally simple to understand (*see* Figure 9.9).

When it was first used as an analytic aid with the Mead Corporation in the early 1970s, the boxes were described in neutral, investment-oriented terms – that is, 'bond', 'savings account', 'sweepstake' (lottery ticket) and 'mortgage'. The commonly known descriptors that came later are more colourful, but also more implicitly prescriptive, particularly in the case of 'dogs'. (On the way to being 'dogs', they were also known as 'pets', which, in the American context, is markedly less negative.) (*Note*: by definition, most businesses are 'dogs' and the wholesale divestment of such units by all corporations is not logically feasible. See McKiernan (1992) for a good discussion of the 'boxes' in general and the 'dog' box in particular.)

A variety of other portfolio techniques followed, with differences centred on the dimensions along the axes, such as industry attractiveness/competitive position (GE) and stage of product-market evolution/competitive position. The helicopter view offered by such techniques encouraged managers to correct past mistakes by divesting weak businesses and

---

[11] The critical *assumption* being that having a *larger market share* than competitors meant higher volumes of production, leading to swifter progress down the experience curve (each doubling of cumulative volume bringing a known percentage reduction in costs) and, hence, the advantage of lower costs.

establishing a seemingly more solid rationale for the corporate mix than some tenuous definition of synergy. By the end of the 1970s, nearly half the Fortune 500 companies were using portfolio planning in some way to deal with a collection of businesses that were often beyond the scope of senior executives to manage and control other than at arm's length. What started off as an *aid to analysis* became a strategic paradigm in its own right and one that was accepted relatively uncritically by managers.

The oversimplistic assumptions underlying such techniques became apparent with the wholesale value destruction manifest in acquisition-driven conglomerates in the 1980s and the associated success of corporate raiders, who bought (using very high debt levels) and immediately broke up and sold their acquired conglomerates at vast profits. The era of the boxes was at an end:

> In most countries the days when portfolio management was a valid concept of corporate strategy are past. (Porter, 1987, p. 51)

(*Note*: although no longer the core of corporate strategy, some of the analytic language and assumptions of portfolio management are still reflected in annual reports today; for example, the almost universally accepted idea of the need for a 'balanced' portfolio – 'balance' often being discussed in terms of three-legged stools.)

9.5 Evidence and experience

The concept of the M-form, and its associated corporate strategy, as a value-adding entity receives little support from *academic* or practical (*market*) evidence.

9.5.1 Academic

It has always been difficult to mount a successful academic defence of the pure conglomerate as a value-adding grouping. *Governance* as a justification per se assumes sufficiently endemic and material opportunism, incompetence, goal displacement and so on among managers of stand-alone businesses that the reduction of these creates corporate value, despite the added corporate overhead and lack of market incentive. It is feasible that in the relatively early days of large businesses, the development of professional management skills in formerly stand-alone units may have added value, but this offers no rationale for ongoing membership.

Academic research has tended to focus on the presumed benefits of groupings of *related* businesses. Related businesses are those where a 'common skill, market or resource applies to each' (Rumelt, 1974, p. 29) and, hence, where scope benefits are appealing as a source of potential value. Rumelt produced a landmark study of 246 US firms over the period 1949–69, which supported the performance superiority of the multidivisional form, but questioned the relative value of different forms of diversification. He confirmed the intuitive logic of academics and managers that companies that had undertaken related

Case box: **Abbey's losing portfolio**

If we don't deliver we will be hung from the lampposts. (Luqman Arnold)

A decade ago, Abbey National was a pioneer that was streets ahead of its rivals. As a leading mortgage and savings bank, it was the first building society to demutualise, the first to snap up a life insurer and the first to diversify into supposedly lucrative wholesale lending.

Now it is in crisis. The diversification strategy has gone badly wrong and Abbey has acquired the unfortunate title of Britain's most troubled bank. Few can doubt the scale of its problems after a bank statement last week revealed that Abbey will be the first British bank in a decade to slash its dividend.

The bank is facing crippling losses at its wholesale arm, a huge bill to cover write-downs on four overambitious acquisitions – such as Scottish Provident, the life insurer – and a £500m one-off accounting charge to revalue Scottish Mutual, its ailing life insurer. Overall, the cost is expected to be well over £1bn and could push Abbey to a thumping loss for 2002. The most bearish analysts believe the loss could be a massive £1.5bn, against a £1.9bn profit in 2001.

So late in 2002 Luqman Arnold, the new chief executive, and Stephen Hester, the finance director, face a daunting challenge. Arnold's plan is to reconstruct Abbey to focus on its core retail banking and personal financial businesses. Operations which are deemed to be non-core, including much of the wholesale bank, will be placed in a new Portfolio Business Unit and sold off or wound down.

Source: Abbey National and Collins Stewart estimate

What is very evident is just how badly Abbey has lost its way. Critics argue that as the bank devoted more capital to the once booming wholesale bank, which in 2000 made a huge £575m profit, the core retail bank has suffered from years of under-investment. 'What started as a small division became a core strategy to reduce the proportion of earnings from the core retail banking business,' says Arnold. 'The result was not just a loss of focus but there was an imbalance in terms of risk. We are concentrating now on rebalancing that risk.'

Hester is more blunt: 'If I had a criticism of the direction of Abbey's strategy in the past it was that in a number of cases there was not enough assessment of competitive advantage. There was too much "gosh, that is a big market that is growing fast and we should have a slice of that" but not enough asking whether we would be any good in that business.'

Source: adapted from the *Sunday Telegraph*, 1 December 2002.
© Telegraph Group Limited (2002).

diversification outperformed those that had undertaken unrelated (that is, conglomerate) diversification.

Following Rumelt's work, the relationship between the make-up of business groupings and their economic performance became a major research focus. While some authors were supportive of Rumelt's main contentions, a significant body of research was in disagreement. Factors such as industry structure and specific firm characteristics played important roles and, once these were controlled, 'relatedness' seemed to have little explanatory power. Using market-based measures of relatedness has produced equivocal evidence on the link between firm performance and the composition of the corporate business portfolio, with few *strong* findings on either side.

The problem with the demonstrated lack of relationship between relatedness and performance is argued to lie primarily with the validity of the traditional market or industry-based relatedness measures, which, while they incorporate surface characteristics of *similarity*, do not capture relatedness of *strategic importance*. The relatedness that is really valuable is that between 'strategic assets', which are important to competitive advantage and cannot be quickly or cheaply gained by non-diversified competitors. The second drawback is that traditional researchers have tended to have a narrow, static view of relatedness, which does not take into account the *dynamic* creation and accumulation of trans-business competences, so managers must specifically manage for the benefits of relatedness across the businesses, to achieve added (corporate) value.

Hamel and Prahalad (1994) are particularly scathing about the inherent structural bias of the M-form *against* the exploitation of scope economies (core competences) inherent in relatedness. They decry what they see as a dominant focus on strategic business units (SBUs) in multidivisional firms being defined in *external* terms of markets, products and competitors. The 'tyranny of the SBU', as it promotes its own autonomous functioning, does not facilitate the complex interactions and sharing that are necessary for corporate-wide development and exploitation of core competences. This ultimately results in the demise of capabilities linking the businesses and thus impairs the exploitation of potentially valuable relatedness.

9.5.2 Market

As mentioned above, value destruction became the norm for multidivisional companies throughout the late 1970s and the 1980s. So much was this the case that the value of the M-form and, in particular, the value-adding capability of its head office, became a significant focus of research and discussion. While diversified conglomerates have been seen as the main cause of value loss it has yet to be proven (see above) that corporations of *related* businesses are much better. Perhaps it is true, as some authors contend, that the future of value creation lies in huge one-business companies, although these entities will still have to deal with the complexities of size, growth, and local–global dilemmas that gave rise to the M-form in the first place. Certainly, the mid to late 1990s saw the rise of the mega-merger between businesses in the same industry, as globalization became a driver for senior executives.

(*Note*: market valuation is not a good guide to the value-creation of businesses. As Collis (1991a) points out, a *significant* loss of value is necessary before takeover-break-up-and-sell becomes a viable option. With typical transaction costs of 2% and an acquisition premium of 20%, a corporation 'can be creating only 78% of the value that could be generated . . . and yet still be immune to the threat of a change in corporate control', p. 6.)

9.5.3 Issues for the future

The past problems of optimizing the management of multi-business corporations continue to challenge managers in the modern world. However, superimposed on the 'traditional' dilemmas of centralization versus **decentralization**, business (vertical) versus pan-corporate (horizontal) focuses, and (internal) co-operation versus competition, are the local versus global issues inherent in globalization. The increasing pace of change, turbulence and complexity of the business environment continue to test the structures, systems, processes and underlying rationale reflecting and underpinning corporate strategy, as managers strive to achieve a material parenting advantage which exceeds the value-generating capability of the stand-alone units. Perhaps the biggest issue facing these managers is to be able to demonstrate to increasingly sceptical stakeholders that there are tangible benefits of corporate membership. If the whole is not demonstrably more valuable than the sum of the parts, then corporate managers will continue to battle against the inexorable economic and market forces for disintegration.

9.6 The role of headquarters: the case of ABB and Percy Barnevik

9.6.1 *The Economist* on Barnevik and ABB

By trusting in multiculturalism and decentralization, Percy Barnevik has created a world beater. Could the firm hang together without him?

If Europe has a management superstar it is Percy Barnevik, boss of ABB Asea Brown Boveri, an electrical engineering giant. A tall, bearded and fast-talking Swede who has the restless manner of a man over-endowed with energy, Mr Barnevik has won almost every honour bestowed upon his profession, from 'emerging markets CEO of the year' to (twice) boss of Europe's most respected company. His name is dropped by management theorists and by the Harvard Business Review almost as frequently as that of Jack Welch of America's General Electric. And the gap is closing fast. 'Our greatest rival is no longer GE,' confesses one Japanese competitor. 'The one we have to be most on guard against is ABB.'

For once, the hyperbole is largely warranted. There are several reasons to praise Mr Barnevik. One is that he has shown how a company can be big and small at the same time: ABB consists of 1,300 separate companies divided into 5,000 profit centres. He has also pioneered such fashionable practices as internal benchmarking, centres of excellence and corporate parenting. But perhaps his most striking idea is the 'multicultural multinational'.

Not long ago, pundits held that globalization would erase national differences and homogenize consumer tastes. Mr Barnevik's view is more nuanced. He argues that purely national companies have little chance of thriving as governments deregulate and as the cost of travel and information plummets. But he stresses that companies need to keep deep roots in local markets, because markets will continue to differ. His answer is a cosmopolitan conglomerate diverse enough to respond to local tastes but united enough to amount to more than the sum of its parts.

ABB was born with such diversity, In 1988 Mr. Barnevik fashioned the organization from two century-old companies: ASEA, the Swedish engineering group which he ran from 1980, and Brown Boveri, an equally proud Swiss competitor. Since then, the company has been involved in more than 100 acquisitions and joint ventures, expanding into Eastern Europe and Asia, and adding (after many layoffs) 18,000 workers in 40 different countries.

This makes for an impressive array of dots on the map. But how do you join them up? Remember, for instance, the recent national rivalry between different parts of Royal Dutch Shell, another multicultural multinational, over its oilrig fiasco. That is where Mr Barnevik has been particularly successful. He forces all employees to read his 'bible', a short booklet on the company's aims and values. He made English his firm's official language, although only a third of the employees speak it as their mother tongue (Mr Barnevik himself has a strong Swedish accent). He moved ABB's headquarters to Zurich so that the merger would not look like a Swedish takeover. But he keeps the headquarters staff small (currently 171 people from 19 different countries) in order to avoid the impression that ABB is now a Swiss company. In making cuts, he has made sure that the burden is spread fairly evenly. Indeed, the most common criticism is that he treats his native Sweden rather too harshly; he once needed a bodyguard there to protect him from angry former employees.

Mr Barnevik's leadership style is not risk-free. He has always relied on speed to pre-empt nationalistic passions, either within the company or in national parliaments. Merging ASEA and Brown Boveri took a mere six weeks, and Mr Barnevik has been adding companies ever since.

Some critics say that this relentless expansion has prevented ABB from putting down any deep common roots, and that it runs on nothing more substantial than the adrenalin of permanent revolution. This, remember, is a company with a small core and only a thin layer of managers to supervise myriad subsidiaries and profit centres. ABB's retort is that its identity is buttressed not only by its possession of a coordinating executive committee (with members from eight countries) but also by an elite cadre of 500 global managers, a Praetorian Guard that Mr Barnevik selects carefully, paying particular attention to the cultural sensitivity of its members, and to their spouses' willingness to move. He shifts them through a series of foreign assignments, and takes a close interest in their careers. Worth more than their weight in gold, according to Mr Barnevik, their job is to knit the organization together, to transfer expertise around the world, and to expose the company's leadership to differing perspectives.

In the end, however, a lot of ABB's corporate glue comes down to Mr Barnevik's own relentlessness. ABBers around the world speak reverently about his ability to get by on four hours' sleep a night and his familiarity with every nook and cranny of the organization. He reckons he speaks personally to 5,500 of his employees every year. He spends only a couple of days a week at headquarters (often Saturday and Sunday); much of the rest of the time he is in an airborne office in a corporate jet.

'So what?' one of ABB's many happy shareholders might ask, adding that it is difficult to imagine Mr Barnevik sitting still anywhere. But ABB's current structure – and indeed the modern management fashion which Mr Barnevik has done so much to influence – has thrust an awesome amount of responsibility to the very top of the organization. The more global it has grown, the more it has relied on a strong leader to hold it together. The bigger test of Mr Barnevik's skills may be not how *well the company performs while he is still in charge, but what happens to it after his departure.*[12]

9.6.2 *Time* magazine on Barnevik

Barnevik [is] analytical, quick, blunt and, above all, global. As chairman of ABB Asea Brown Boveri, the world's largest electrical engineering group, Barnevik, 57, presides over a $36 billion federation of more than 1,000 companies with 217,000 employees in 140 countries. Zurich-based ABB is the biggest single investor in Eastern Europe and the former Soviet Union, a Western pioneer in India and a aggressive player in East Asia and Latin America. For three years running it was voted 'Europe's most respected company' in a poll of executives by the Financial Times *newspaper. The structure Barnevik devised to run this globe-girdling behemoth 'has become the new prototype for the post-industrial-age corporation,' says Manfred Kets de Vries of the INSEAD business school outside Paris.*

The champion of globalisation started life in a provincial setting: the isolated west coast of Sweden. Educated as an economist, Barnevik left a management-consulting job to help a troubled Swedish steel company. Success there led to the CEO spot at Asea, a large electrical-engineering firm then in decline. Barnevik carried out a radical and initially painful shake-up, dubbed 'Percy's reign of terror'. He completed the ABB merger, Europe's biggest cross-border deal, in six weeks, following a key Barnevik rule: act fast, even at the risk of making mistakes. Or as the ABB 'bible' he inspired puts it, 'Not to take action is the only non-acceptable behavior.'[13]

9.6.3 Barnevik on Barnevik's management style

On his organizing principles

The only way to structure a complex, global organization is to make it as simple and local as possible. ABB is complicated from where I sit. But on the ground, where the real work gets done, all of our operations must function as closely as possible to stand-alone operations. Our managers need well-defined sets of responsibilities, clear accountability, and maximum degrees of freedom to execute.

We are fervent believers in decentralization. When we structure local operations, we always push to create separate legal entities. Separate companies allow you to create real balance sheets with real responsibility for cash flow and dividends. With real balance sheets, managers inherit results from year to year through changes in equity.

---

[12] *The Economist*, 6 January 1996.

[13] Jay Branegan, *Time*, 24 February 1997, p. 34.

ABB is a huge enterprise. But the work of most of our people is organized in small units with P&L responsibility and meaningful autonomy. Our operations are divided into nearly 1,200 companies with an average of 200 employees. These companies are divided into 4,500 profit centres with an average of 50 employees.[14]

On the organization structure

ABB is an organization with three internal contradictions. We want to be global and local, big and small, radically decentralized with centralized reporting and control. If we resolve those contradictions, we create real organizational advantage.

That's where the matrix comes in. The matrix is the framework through which we organize our activities. It allows us to optimize our business globally and maximize performance in every country in which we operate. Some people resist it. They say the matrix is too rigid, too simplistic. But what choice do you have? To say you don't like a matrix is like saying you don't like factories or you don't like breathing. It's a fact of life. If you deny the formal matrix, you wind up with an informal one – and that's much harder to reckon with. As we learn to master the matrix, we get a truly multidomestic organization.[15]

On the difficulty of managing the transition into ABB

It does require a huge mental change, especially for country managers. Remember, we've built ABB through acquisitions and restructurings. Thirty of the companies we've bought had been around for more than 100 years. Many of them were industry leaders in their countries, national monuments. Now they've got BA managers playing a big role in the direction of their operations. We have to convince country managers that they benefit by being part of this federation, that they gain more than they lose when they give up some autonomy.[16]

On creating a culture: why the 13 members of the group executive management team meet every three weeks for one day

Sitting in one room are the senior managers collectively responsible for ABB's global strategy and performance. These same managers individually monitor business segments, countries, and staff functions. So when we make a decision-snap, it's covered. The members of the executive committee communicate to their direct reports, the BA managers and the country managers, and the implementation process is under way.[17]

---

[14] William Taylor (1991) 'The logic of global business: An interview with ABB's Percy Barnevik', *Harvard Business Review*, March/April, reprint no. 91201, p. 99.

[15] ibid. pp. 95–6.

[16] ibid. p. 98.

[17] ibid. p. 100.

On diversity

We can't have managers who are 'un-French' managing in France because 95% of them are dealing every day with French customers, French colleagues, French suppliers. That's why global managers need humility. A global manager respects a formal German manager – Herr Doktor and all that – because that manager may be an outstanding performer in the German context.[18]

On building a culture of trust and exchange

Sharing expertise does not happen automatically. It takes a trust, it takes familiarity. People need to spend time together, to get to know and understand each other. People must also see a payoff for themselves. I never expect our operations to coordinate unless all sides get real benefits. We have to demonstrate that sharing pays – that contributing one idea gets you 24 in return.[19]

On selecting top managers for ABB

We sought people capable of becoming superstars – tough-skinned individuals who were fast on their feet, had good technical and commercial backgrounds, and had demonstrated the ability to lead others . . . For the merger to work it is essential that we have managers who are open, generous, and capable of thinking in group terms.[20]

On decision making

Nothing is worse than procrastination . . . When I look at ten decisions I regret, there will be nine of them where I delayed . . . Better roughly and quickly than carefully and slowly.

Take the initiative and decide – even if it turns out to be the wrong thing. The only thing we cannot accept is people who do nothing.

To emphasize the point Barnevik banned the phrase 'I think' at meetings: 'either you know or you don't.'[21]

On managers

Global managers are made, not born . . . you rotate people around the world. There is no substitute for line experience in three or four countries . . . you encourage

---

[18] ibid. p. 95.

[19] ibid. p. 97.

[20] Jules Arbose (1988) 'ABB: The new energy powerhouse', *International Management*, June.

[21] Jonathan Kapstein and Stanley Reed (1990) 'Preaching the Euro-gospel: ABB redefines multinationalism', *Business Week*, 23 July, p. 36.

people to work in mixed-nationality teams. You force *them to create personal alliances across borders ... You have to force people into these situations.*[22]

On information used by the executive committee

We look for early signs that businesses are becoming more or less healthy ... I stop to study trends that catch my eye ... [I don't] start giving orders. But I want to have informed dialogues with the appropriate executives.[23]

On communications

You don't inform, you over-inform.[24]

On the role of headquarters

We operate as lean as humanly possible. It's no accident that there are only 100 people at ABB headquarters in Zurich. The closer we get to top management, the tougher we have to be with head count. I believe you can go into any traditionally centralized corporation and cut its headquarters staff by 90% in one year. You spin off 30% of the staff into free-standing service centres that perform real work – treasury functions, legal services – and charge for it. You decentralize 30% of the staff – human resources, for example – by pushing them into the line organization. Then 30% disappears through head count reductions.[25]

Questions for discussion

1   How does ABB's organization work? What are the key roles of managers at the country level? At the Business Area (BA) level? At the front line and the business unit level?

2   What role does headquarters play in getting this organization to work? Which of the four archetypes of headquarters is most like ABB? Does ABB have its own blend of these archetypes?

---

[22] William Taylor (1991) 'The logic of global business: An interview with ABB's Percy Barnevik, *Harvard Business Review*, March/April, reprint no. 91201, p. 95.

[23] ibid. p. 100.

[24] ibid. p. 104.

[25] ibid. p. 99.

Case box: Conglomerates on trial

Conglomerates have taken a battering from management theorists. But is there something to be said for them after all?

The case against conglomerates can be summed up in two words: size and complexity. Size is said to slow down decision making; complexity to create confusion. These things make it hard even for good managers to cope with the demands of specialized markets and rapid change. Breaking companies into their constituent parts, in contrast, allows managers to focus on businesses they know something about. And investors who want to spread their risk by diversifying – once thought a good reason to invest in a conglomerate – can nowadays do so by buying shares in many different companies.

Making the case for conglomerates BCG argues[26] that the 'conglomerate discount' is little more than prejudice, and that what really determines a company's success is not the narrowness of its focus but the quality of its management. A 'premium conglomerate', as BCG likes to call the well-managed ones, manages its portfolio aggressively, setting its subsidiaries clear targets and ditching underperforming companies (Mr Welch operates on a 'fix, sell, or close' principle). But it also invests heavily in creating and transferring company-wide skills. Samsung, for instance, spends about $400m a year on training.

In addition, say the men from BCG, conglomeration can be a strength at a time when disparate businesses are tending to converge. By remaining omnivorous, Britain's Virgin Group has transferred its marketing skills from music to airlines and financial services. By contrast, British Petroleum (BP) made a conscious decision to stick to energy businesses. It has lately found, as petrol stations have become more like grocery stores, that it has had to learn more 'normal' retailing skills. Focus, argue the men from BCG, can be a straitjacket.

VEBA is a highly diversified German company. In 1991 it considered breaking up but chose instead to manage its companies more aggressively; it has since produced above-average returns. Samsung, a South Korean firm with 166 different businesses, has grown tenfold every six years since the 1960s. And how do conglomerate bashers explain away America's General Electric? This unfocused giant has given shareholders an average annual return of 20.8% (six percentage points better than the stockmarket average) since Jack Welch took over in 1979. Mr Welch wants the firm to grow bigger still: he dismisses the infatuation with focus as 'trendy'.

These are not isolated examples. Dieter Heuskel, of the Boston Consulting Group, and Timothy Plaut, of Goldman Sachs, an investment bank, reckon that between 1985 and 1995 the 40 largest American, European and Australian conglomerates generated returns for their shareholders which were virtually identical to the market average, and that the top quartile of conglomerates turned in annual returns which were almost five points above the market average.

---

[26] 'Premium Conglomerates', The Boston Consulting Group.

A verdict?

To say that a well-run conglomerate can sometimes succeed is hardly proof that conglomeration is a sound principle. BCG is frustratingly unclear about how diversified it thinks a conglomerate can be before the costs outweigh the benefits. Look behind many apparently diversified successes and you will find either or both of the following: first, some degree of focus (for instance Virgin usually concentrates on the marketing side of its admittedly varied businesses); and, second, a rare business mind, such as GE's Mr Welch or Virgin's Richard Branson, capable of holding the group together. When these rare traits are absent, as they normally are, conglomerates often lose their way.

As academics and others continue to document the failings of conglomerates, the case for them – except when they are blessed with unusually talented and disciplined bosses – remains unproven.

Adapted from *The Economist*, 3 April 1997.

You should consider the ABB experience in the light of the debate on conglomerates (see case box above). Does ABB have the management experience and talent to manage such a wide spread of businesses? Alternatively can you argue that there is a focus and a thread running through the business so that synergies can be achieved? To what extent does a management team depend on its leader? Consider again the role of Percy Barnevik. What is the nature of the management talent that can make conglomerates succeed beyond the expectations of the stock market?

9.7 Summary

This chapter has introduced a new dimension to our strategy discussion – the multibusiness portfolio. The job of designing, managing and adapting the portfolio of businesses lies generally with the corporate centre. It is concerned with the issues of competitive advantage just like individual strategic business units but it is particularly concerned to (i) make sure that SBUs do what they are supposed to do (the 'control' question) and (ii) ensure that the patterns of competitive advantage within the portfolio are mutually reinforcing (the 'synergy' question). In order to fulfil these tasks the corporate centre has to pay close attention to the structure of the organization so that patterns of specialization are created and that management responsibilities can be properly defined. Issues of organization structure and process are discussed in more detail in Part 4 and in this chapter we have gone so far as to argue that the strategy–structure fit and balance is a key task for the corporate centre.

Although the corporate centre has a distinct role to play compared with the SBUs, it still deals with the same economic issues. In particular the centre is concerned with synergy, introduced in Chapter 3 as economies of scope. This is reflected in the many practical frameworks and strategy tools that have been marketed over time. The BCG growth-share matrix is the grandfather of all these and has been succeeded by many other portfolio management frameworks. In noting these it is sensible to remember that all strategy tools and frameworks are highly contextual. They depend critically on the situation of the particular organization. Frameworks in and of themselves do not convey truth or 'good' theory: they are merely ways of presenting data and alternatives. The trick with tools is to note the exclusions or, rather, to be clever with choosing a focus on just a few elements of the strategic context.

The role of the centre is to find a way of managing the whole organization that fits its overall context. This is reflected in the range of strategies available. We discussed restructuring, activity sharing and skills transfer. These capture different ways of creating value. We also discussed how companies have different styles that also reflect the same point – how to actually create extra value.

We have also noted the academic debate. This has focused on the defensibility of the conglomerate where, in general, academics are unconvinced that this is a sustainable approach. Also, we have noted that this is an area where many big mistakes can be made. Experience suggests that these mistakes are all too common. The next chapter goes on to look at the area in which there is a high degree of controversy – mergers and acquisitions.

This chapter concludes with an extended discussion of Percy Barnevik's creation of ABB. This has been both highly celebrated and controversial. It ranks as one of the most radical and significant corporate experiments ever undertaken in Europe. It put together a wide range of businesses under a distinctive management style with a wholly new concept of a matrix structure. This exemplifies the significant role of corporate-level decisions and the high risks attached to them.

Key terms

Decentralization *360*

Financial control *347*

Growth-share matrix *356*

M-form *339*

Portfolio management *338*

Relatedness *338*

Restructuring *348*

Sharing activities *349*

Strategic control *347*

Strategic planning *347*

Transaction cost economics (TCE) *344*

Transferring skills *349*

U-form *338*

Recap questions and assignments

1   Make a critical appraisal of the importance of the centre-division relationship in the strategic direction and development of large multi-business companies. Illustrate your answer by describing the relationships that you feel would be most important to a chosen company. You may wish to choose one from the text and cases version of this book:

Diageo (in case section)

HSBC (in case section)

Rank Xerox (in case section)

2   Evaluate the nature of the additional value that is being suggested as a rationale for an ongoing merger or acquisition being reported in the current financial press. What actions need to be undertaken to realize this value? How would you classify this value in the terms used in the above chapter and how would you describe the parenting role best suited to the merged corporation?

Online
*Learning***Centre**

When you have read this chapter, log on to the Online Learning Centre website at www.mcgraw-hill.co.uk/textbooks/mcgee to explore chapter-by-chapter test questions, further reading and more online study tools for strategy.

Case 1 **Old dogs, new tricks**
Focus is no longer a minority pursuit

Shortly after Jürgen Dormann took over at Hoechst in 1994, he made a big decision. With 16 different businesses to its name, ranging from photocopiers and cosmetics to dyes and drugs, the German chemicals group was far too diversified. Its future, he figured, lay in pharmaceuticals, which at that time accounted for only a fifth of its turnover. In 1997, a restructuring plan involving the spin-off of several divisions was put before analysts, who lapped it up. But then things started going wrong. Egged on by politicians, Hoechst's unions went on the offensive. As the overhaul was taking shape, but before anyone had been fired, a group of 8,000 angry demonstrators marched on the company's headquarters to protest against the dismantling of a great industrial name. Mr Dormann held firm, but the share price wobbled, reflecting investors' belief that he would have trouble implementing his plan.

Re-engineering old-established companies in Europe is bound to be tough. As the Hoechst example illustrates, managers often find themselves caught between two powerful forces: unions backed by job-protection laws on one side, the financial markets on the other. Long-standing links between business and politics have made it hard to resist the pressure to form conglomerates. And without a strong steer from the stockmarket, as in America, managers have been able to indulge their empire-building urges. With a few notable exceptions, Europe's companies have tended to lose focus as they grow.

International investors doubt the wisdom of industrial diversification, and most studies suggest that they are right. Champions of conglomerates always point to America's highly diverse and highly successful General Electric, which hawks everything from aircraft engines to financial services. But GE is the exception that proves the rule. No European company has come close to pulling off the same trick for any length of time.

At long last, the message is sinking in. Industrial focus, until recently the mantra of a few pioneers, has become a common chant. It is notable that this chant has grown loudest in Germany, Europe's most conglomerate-stuffed economy. Since the beginning of last year, around half of Germany's top 30 companies have announced plans to sell or hive off big subsidiaries that they no longer consider part of their core business.

Fresenius, whose main activity is making medical equipment, says it plans to float all its subsidiaries on the stockmarket – so long as doing so will add value. Thyssen Krupp, a smokestack business if ever there was one, is cutting down its 23 divisions to eight, and mulling the sale of businesses worth €5 billion ($4.8 billion), including a chunk of its once-untouchable steel operations. Its cool new phrase for this is 'portfolio optimisation', which makes trade unionists' blood boil. Germany's big utilities, RWE and Veba/Viag, are undoing past, untidy diversification (into logistics, telecoms and electronics) in favour of concentrating on an area they know well: Europe's fast-deregulating electricity markets.

Why the mass conversion? For some companies, selling peripheral activities means killing two birds with one stone: it raises money for acquisitions in their main businesses, but also boosts another takeover currency, their shares, by making their operations more transparent. For others, it is simply the only option left when their excuses for doing nothing have run out. No company exemplifies this better than Siemens.

For many years Siemens was a lightning rod for criticism of the European way, and deservedly so. Its vast spread, from heavy engineering, electronics and white goods to light bulbs, mobile phones and computers, grew ever more difficult to manage from one boardroom. One problem was that its labs came before its customers. Technicians were allowed to over-engineer, and managers struggled to turn good ideas into products that sold. Moreover, the board was usually stuffed with specialists rather than general managers with a feel for strategy. Profits were often woefully thin: the old joke that Siemens would do better by selling itself and sticking the cash on deposit contained more than a grain of truth. The group was stifled by its own sense of history.

By the early 1990s, a combination of high wages, tough competition and weak management began to take its toll. Something had to be done, but the reorganizations that followed were half-hearted. Nudged by politicians, the company invested heavily in eastern Germany, but saw scant profit for its trouble. Management was spending most of its time trying to patch up holes. Some were worse than others: Heinrich von Pierer, the chairman, once described the troubled nuclear-energy division as '2% of our business and 90% of our headaches'.

Last-chance saloon

In 1998, with Siemens's share price in the doldrums, Mr von Pierer announced a grand 'ten-point plan', quickly dubbed 'von Pierer's last chance'. This time, against expectations, it has come off. The number of basic operating divisions has been slimmed from 15 to five, and businesses employing a third of the workforce have been put up for sale. Some of the assets have attracted enormous attention: the recent flotation of the recovering semiconductor business, Infineon, was 30 times oversubscribed. At long last, Siemens's share price has started to reflect its underlying technological strengths.

That is partly because the latest restructuring is about more than just sales and spin-offs. Mr von Pierer has taken a knife to the company's culture of complacency and concentrated on financial performance, installing a former investment banker as finance chief. Some 60% of top managers' pay has been linked to targets for return on capital, a radical move in a country used to predictable pay packets. Now the company's accounts are being overhauled in preparation for an American stockmarket listing next year.

None of this has been easy for Mr von Pierer, who harbours a natural distrust of financial analysts, and prefers consensus to conflict. Still, he seems a genuine convert. 'Siemens is a living organism,' he says. 'I can't promise my people that any overhaul will be the last.'

Coming from a veteran with 31 years' service in a German industrial behemoth, that is radical talk. There are still taboos, however. Mr von Pierer is clearly uncomfortable with the suggestion that the group might be worth more broken up than in one piece. That, he insists, would destroy all sorts of synergies.

Whatever it does, Siemens still has some turning around to do. After restructuring comes repositioning. Does it want to be a manufacturer or a service-provider, an engineering company or a technology specialist? It is investing heavily in its pure-technology businesses, and wants to generate a quarter of its revenue from the Internet within a year. But turning a supertanker into a flotilla of nippy motor boats will be a far greater challenge than merely throwing the unwanted lifeboats overboard. As Europe's start-up culture spreads, keeping talented employees and encouraging them to innovate in-house is becoming increasingly hard.

Several of Europe's industrial champions may be forced down the same route as Siemens, including Philips, a Dutch electronics giant that makes everything from food blenders to digital-disc players. Cor Boonstra, the first outsider to be brought in as boss, has rejigged the group's mix of businesses and cut staff numbers several times, but analysts have yet to be convinced that even after the latest overhaul, announced earlier this year, it is sufficiently nimble on its feet.

As with Siemens, the solution for Philips may be to pare its range of businesses to a more manageable number, and to do more to foster entrepreneurship in its own ranks. Were it not protected by a web of trusted shareholders, it would probably have been taken over years ago. 'Focus is especially important during times of fast technological change like this, because bigger ships take so much longer to turn,' says Mr Nilsson of Ericsson, which has just sold its century-old energy-systems business to concentrate on its mobile-phone operation.

But what happens if not just a few, but all of a company's businesses turn out to be dispensable? Europe already has several examples of companies that have thrived on getting out of everything they were in and starting afresh. In the early 1990s, Germany's Preussag was a company nobody wanted to invest in. It had mediocre managers in unexciting industries such as shipbuilding. Today, it is one of Europe's most profitable travel and tourism groups.

Preussag's transformation owed more to stealth and serendipity than to any grand restructuring plan: a well-timed asset sale here, a shrewd acquisition there, all supported by its largest shareholder, WestLB. At times like this, patient owners can be a help. When Finland's Nokia switched from rubber products to mobile telephones in the mid-1990s, its largest shareholders balked as revenues dipped and the share price halved. But they decided to stick by the chief executive, Jorma Ollila, and have since been handsomely rewarded. Had Nokia been American, he might easily have been ousted.

Not every company has the far-sightedness or the market opportunities of Preussag or Nokia, but excuses to waste money on ill-judged diversification are running out everywhere.

For one thing, political patronage is on the wane. For another, companies have acquired tools with which to manage their capital more sensibly. Buy-backs, which involve a company purchasing its own shares to reduce its capital base, became legal in France and Germany in 1998, and are starting to take off. Last year, European companies bought $25 billion-worth of their own shares, up from a mere $4 billion-worth in 1995. As buy-backs become more widely accepted, European companies should become less prone to acquire for acquisition's sake when they have more capital than they need.

Halfway there

Managers are beginning to learn that bigger is better only when supported by industrial logic. And yet much restructuring remains held up by misguided patriotism and ideology. Last autumn, Michelin, a French tyre maker, unveiled a sharp increase in profits but at the same time announced a 10% cut in its workforce. It was duly lambasted for putting profits ahead of people, even though it tried to explain that without reorganization its profitability would wane. Outraged members of parliament are still trying to introduce legislation that would give employees more say over changes in company strategy.

Nor do all the remaining barriers to change come from the outside. There are still plenty of chief executives in Europe who pay lip service to shareholders, yet pursue their own agenda. The boss of one German company explains with a chuckle that he bundles its various engineering units into a single grouping for analysts' roadshows, 'so we don't look as messy as we really are.' And not all large companies are really convinced of the importance of their share price. 'It's not our first priority', says Stefano Giussani, the investor-relations chief of Montedison, an Italian chemicals concern, to explain why he cannot recollect how his company's share price has moved over the past year.

For those managers who do embrace restructuring, the hardest part is yet to come. If laying off workers and setting financial targets were all it took, Siemens would have been a glittering stockmarket star long ago. But once a company has cut away its flab, it has to find new ways to grow profitably, which involves more fundamental change. American firms, having streamlined a decade ago, are now free to expand revenues and bring together converging industries, as in last year's merger of America Online and Time Warner. Catching them will take quite some doing.

Source: 'Old dogs, new tricks', *The Economist*, 27 April 2000.
© The Economist Newspaper Limited, London (27 April 2000).

Case Questions

1 Outline the case against conglomerates and for more closely inter-related business portfolios.

2 How would you counter the arguments often advanced by workforces and politicians that restructuring merely results in transferring jobs overseas?

3 It is often claimed that conglomerates are not able to grow profitably. Explain this argument? Is it correct?

Further reading and references

Bartlett, CA (1990) 'Matrix Management not a Structure, a Frame of Mind', *Harvard Business Review*, **68**, **4**, pp. 138–45.

Bartlett, CA and Ghoshal, S (1993) 'Beyond the M-form: Toward a New Managerial Theory of the Firm', *Strategic Management Journal*, **14**, pp. 23–46, reprinted in Segal-Horn (ed.) (1998).

Campbell, A and Goold, M (1994) 'Adding Value from Corporate Headquarters', in B De Wit and R Meyer (eds) *Strategy: Process, Content, Context*, West Publishing Company, New York.

Campbell, A, Goold, M and Alexander, M (1995) 'Corporate Strategy: The Quest for Parenting Advantage', *Harvard Business Review*, March/April, pp. 120–32.

Campbell, A and Luchs, K (1992) *Strategic Synergy*, Butterworth-Heinemann.

Chandler, AD, Jr (1962) *Strategy and Structure: Chapters in the History of the Industrial Enterprise*, MIT Press, Cambridge MA.

Chandler, AD, Jr (1994) 'The Functions of the HQ Unit in the Multibusiness Firm', in R Rumelt, D Schendel and D Teece (eds) *Fundamental Issues in Strategy*, Harvard Business School Press, Boston, MA.

Chandler, AD, Jr (1990a) 'Scale and Scope: The Dynamics of Industrial Capitalism', Cambridge, MA: Belknap.

Chandler, AD, Jr (1990b) 'The Enduring Logic of Industrial Success', *Harvard Business Review*, March/April, pp. 130–40.

Collis, D (1991a) 'Corporate Strategy: A Conceptual Framework', *Harvard Business School Case Study*, 9–391–284.

Collis, D (1991b) 'Corporate Strategy: Identifying and Exploiting Resources', *Harvard Business School Case Study*, 9–391–285.

Collis, D (1991c) 'Managing the Multibusiness Corporation' *Harvard Business School Case Study*, 9–391–286.

Collis, DJ (1996) 'Corporate Strategy in Multibusiness Firms' *Long Range Planning*, **29**, pp. 416–18.

Day, GS (1977) 'Diagnosing the Product Portfolio', *Journal of Marketing*, April, pp. 264–80.

Ghoshal, S (1987) 'Global strategy: an Organising Framework', *Strategic Management Journal*, **8**, pp. 425–40, reprinted in Segal-Horn (ed.) (1998).

Goold, M and Campbell, A (1987) *Strategies and Styles*, Blackwell, Oxford.

Goold, M, Campbell, A and Alexander, M (1994) *Corporate Level Strategy: Creating Value in the Multibusiness Company*, John Wiley & Sons Inc., New York.

Mergers,[2] acquisitions and strategic alliances are a major force for restructuring industries and companies. Barriers to such activity have been eroding rapidly during the 1990s with the opening up of new markets, deregulation of industries, increased sophistication of financing techniques and more active stakeholders.

As a consequence, one major feature of the last M&A boom has been the large increase in volume of cross-border acquisitions. Even if companies prefer organic growth to acquiring or making alliances, all must guard against the way in which these phenomena can radically redraw the competitive arena.

10.1 Acquisitions: an overview

General reading of the business press and of academic writings suggests that acquisitions, although common, are not so tractable and it is worth pausing to consider why this is so (see Tables 10.1 and 10.2). Acquisitions touch all aspects of corporate life and so can be viewed from a multiplicity of angles. From a strategic perspective, much attention has been devoted to understanding the drivers for acquisition and identifying suitable targets. The underlying assumption with this approach is that if one can correctly identify such targets then the acquisition will be successful. This exposes us to Mintzberg's criticism of

Table 10.1 Consultancy and business press evidence on acquisition failure

Consultancy	Date	Method	Failure Rate
Business International	1975	400 postal questionnaires	49%
	1978	150 postal questionnaires	48%–56%
Coopers and Lybrand	1992	Qualitative in-depth interviews with senior executives in the UK's top 100 companies	54%
Coopers and Lybrand	1996	125 companies. Low revenues, cash flow, profitability	66%
Mercer MC	1995	150 companies. Poor returns to shareholdes after three years	50%
McKinsey & Co	1995	Examined 58 acquisitions. Success was measured as financial return exceeding the cost of capital	58.6%

Source: KPMG.

[2] The terms 'merger' and 'acquisition' are often used interchangeably in the literature. There are differences in so far as mergers are generally the bringing together of businesses of equal size, paid for by the exchange of shares and with no premium. Acquisitions imply a dominant party controlling another, and often there is a premium paid. Where the distinction becomes problematic is in the post-deal phase, where 'mergers' often become 'zero premium acquisitions', and some acquisitions become rather like mergers in having a 'level playing field'.

Table 10.2 Academic evidence on failure rates

Types of academics	Conclusions	Authors	Date
Financial economists	Target shareholders benefit by c.20% whereas acquirer shareholders do not, benefiting by c.0–2%	Jensen and Ruback	1983
		Jarrell and Poulsen	1989
		Sudarsanam et al.	1993
Industrial economists			
♦ Using accounting data	♦ Bidders suffer an immediate decline in relative profitability	Hughes	1993
♦ Subsequent market share	♦ Subsequent market share showed dramatic decline	Mueller	1985
		Caves	1988
♦ Divestment	♦ 58.5% of 2,021 acquisitions (1950–1986) subsequently divested	Porter	1987

the planning school: Mintzberg questions whether successful results will inevitably follow from a good plan. Indeed, this author has often heard CEOs remark that if the acquisition failed then it was due to a poor plan! This circular argument is not helpful and, indeed, obscures the point that the causal link between plan and performance is weak at best – the relationship being substantially mediated by *implementation strategies*. As a consequence, strategy research efforts have turned to the post-acquisition phase, where 'implementation is the bridge between the islands of plan and performance'.

In focusing on implementation, a new set of strategic agenda has arisen. Implementation has opened up the black box of the 'messy' detail of organizations, which pre-acquisition planning frameworks largely overlook. This has implications for our view of strategy and the role of the HQ. Pre-acquisition frameworks tend to assume a top-down approach to strategy, whereas the latter is embedded within the organization, and is multilevel and complex. Focusing internally on the resources and capabilities of the business echoes a shift in emphasis, as noted in Chapter 5, in the field of strategy itself, from the positioning school to the resource-based school. However, rather than being an 'either/or' choice, this is really a question of emphasis, with the recognition that success in the latter is crucial to achieving the former.

10.1.1 The context

While 2002 has seen a slump in activity from the record wave experienced in the previous five years, totalling $10.84 trillion, 2003 has seen an upturn. Interestingly, mega-deals, which characterized the boom of the late 1990s, continue, as do the large-scale cross-border transactions.

not bad odds when compared with the chances of getting a new business off the ground. So they should keep looking for good targets ...

If CEOs wish to avoid some of the errors of the 1990s, they should not forget that they are subject to all the failings that flesh is heir to – and in particular the eternal tendency of business planners to be over-confident. It is a near certainty that, if asked, little short of 99% of them would describe themselves as 'above average' at making mergers and acquisitions work. Sad as it may be, that can never be true. They should also be aware that they will be powerfully influenced by the herd instinct, the feeling that it is better to be wrong in large numbers than to be right alone. In the coming months they will have to watch carefully to be sure that the competitive space into which the predator in front of them is so joyfully leaping does not lie at the edge of a cliff.

Source: Adapted from 'Spring in their steps', *The Economist*, 21 February 2004, p. 14.

10.2 Pre-acquisition planning

10.2.1 Motives for acquisition

Most texts on acquisitions will cite the following main strategic motives for making acquisitions:

- *Industry restructuring* – removing competitors in an over-saturated industry.

- *Increased market power* – the enlarged company may be able to achieve monopolistic or oligopolistic power over its customers and better control its competitors. This might also be achieved by acquiring suppliers that can allow the firm to be more competitive in the market, as well as influence the competitive balance if supplying competitors.

- *Access to new markets* – this can be an effective way of entering new countries without the difficulties of establishing new distribution systems.

- *Economies of scale and scope* – for instance, closing acquired factories and transferring production to your own factory can create economies of scale. Overhead costs can also be spread, such as with common advertising or a single head office.

- *Acquisition of new skills* – particularly in fast-developing industries, this will help the firm develop more rapidly than may be possible internally.

- *Diversification* – this may allow the firm to find opportunities for generating superior returns to those available within the sector.

All of these strategic motives are designed to achieve improved financial performance. In addition, there are also motives we might classify as purely financial:

- *Buying a bargain* – a company that is perceived to be cheap and will be sold on for a quick profit. This would also include asset stripping.

- *Tax advantages* – where companies have a significant tax liability in one country and earnings elsewhere.
- *Financing advantages* – more attractive financing means easier access to finance and/or lower cost of capital. For example:
  - a company may acquire a business in another country to gain advantages from different tax laws;
  - a private company may acquire a listed company to obtain a lower cost of capital; or
  - a company may acquire a business with a strong cash flow.

Strategists have endeavoured to identify the characteristics of a target that link with acquisition performance. These are:

- *Avoid sprat-catching* – acquisitions of less than 5 per cent of parent turnover will tend to underperform, as they are often neglected.
- *Market share* – the risk of failure increases substantially as market share decreases.
- *Avoid financially weak companies* – poor financial health will damage your wealth (unless you are a turnaround specialist).
- *Pre-acquisition experience* – only useful in so far as knowing what not to do based upon small errors in the past.

A hotly debated topic is the issue of 'relatedness', as managers believe intuitively that acquisitions should be more successful where the acquirer knows the business. However, the evidence remains contradictory on this issue and, rather like experience, the acquirer may suffer from a false sense of security.

Perhaps it is not surprising with this small list of recommendations that so many acquisitions fail – the overwhelming weight of evidence is that only some 50 per cent succeed. It is a rather sobering thought that a multi-billion-dollar merger has only a one in two chance of success!

So far, we have reviewed the 'managerial' reasons for making acquisitions that would be found in any acquisition offer document. This is not the whole picture, however, and we should not overlook:

- *Chief executive characteristics* – ego, the need for a challenge, addiction to doing deals, prestige and empire building – these will be downplayed.
- *Process issues* – the decision in a large company may be the result of many disconnected impulses, rather than a single rational decision. A top management team is likely to rationalize the process post-hoc.
- *Environmental pressures* – external pressures may force the company into action, rather than the company being proactive – for instance, the City may threaten to down-rate a company if an acquisition is not made. A top management team is unlikely to admit to not being in charge.

All of these 'drivers' for mergers and acquisitions also interact, as discussed in Angwin (2000).

10.2.2 Selecting a target

To select a target, we should consider the following:

- Resist perceiving acquisitions as one-off events, but remember that they are part of a larger strategy – how will the acquisition build on core competences and enhance competitive advantage?

- Careful analysis of industry structures to judge long-term profitability – Porter's 1980 techniques are ideally suited to this approach.

- Detailed examination of possible targets in that industry to clarify potential synergies – the value chain may be useful in identifying such synergies.

- Detailed examination to expose possible incompatibilities – the use of a cultural web (Johnson and Scholes, p. 230) will expose differences in management style and culture.

- Assessment of the target's worth and the price the company can afford – there are many ways to value a business, such as using price/earnings ratios, discounted cash flow, asset valuation (Weston *et al.* 2003). However, the final price will be the result of negotiation, rather than precise calculation.

- The acquirer must also be mindful of regulatory restrictions to prevent mergers that are against the public interest. In the US there are severe 'anti-trust' provisions. In the UK, the Monopolies and Mergers Commission is empowered to investigate any merger (combined assets greater than £30 million or combined market share of 25 per cent or more), and can recommend to the Secretary of State for Industry that the deal be prohibited. There is also a City code on takeovers and mergers, which is designed to protect shareholder interests and is administered by the City's takeover panel.

10.2.3 Doing the deal

Bidding tactics

Launching a bid is a very expensive exercise in terms of fees to professional advisers. Experts can include investment banks, commercial banks, equity houses, lawyers, accountants and PR advisers. How these experts are used depends on the nature of the bid, the expertise of the protagonists, and the national/international context (Angwin 2001). The success or failure of the bid can have very widespread ramifications for all stakeholders and directly affects adviser and management credibility (Angwin 2003).

Essentially, the bidder needs to persuade the target's shareholders that they are able to produce better performance from the target company than the current management. This gives rise to *puffing* and *knocking copy*. The bidder will embark on a vigorous campaign of propaganda designed to puff up its own management abilities and knock those of the target management team. This will involve formal presentations, circulars, and 'wining and dining' key institutional shareholders, influential analysts and financial journalists. A good example of the importance of managing the media was the acrimonious bid by Granada for Trusthouse Forte. The bid was launched on the day that the Granada group knew that Rocco Forte was on holiday, shooting game. With immediate media attention, and no one to put the Forte case, newspapers polarized the two CEOs in terms of Granada's Jerry Robinson as an industrious working-class hero, versus Forte's Rocco Forte as an aristocratic hobbyist. This unjust image of Rocco Forte did considerable damage to his defence campaign.

During the 1980s, the importance of aggressive campaigning led to a string of sensational newspaper advertisements proclaiming the virtues of each position, to the extent that there are now regulations in place to tone down such campaigns.

Defender tactics

Defence may be about trying to preserve the independence of the company or just ensuring that the best price is paid (Angwin 1996, 2004). There are numerous tactics that can be used, but countries have different restrictions upon their usage.

- **Revaluation of assets**
  Assets, especially property, can quickly become undervalued in companies' accounts; revaluing to a realistic level can force the bidder to raise its offer. Other types of asset, particularly intangibles, have been a particular focus of attention.

- **Improving profit forecasts**
  Incumbent managements will almost certainly proclaim that they are able to produce higher levels of profit than before and will issue forecasts to this effect. There are strict rules about such forecasts, and financial advisers have to be very careful in agreeing to these new estimates. Clearly, some managements may have credibility problems in this respect, although it is worth noting the unusual case of Sketchley, the dry cleaning company, which, when approached by an unwelcome bidder, decided to show that the company was a great deal worse than the bidder anticipated – the bidder withdrew.

- **Crown jewels**
  Where the bid is made for one particular asset within a business, then the sale of this asset removes the threat upon the whole business. As an example, in 1982, the American Whittaker Corporation (AWC) made a bid for the Brunswick Corporation. The latter sold its crown jewel, Sherwood Medical Industries, and AWC then withdrew.

- **Pac-man**
  Although common in the US, this is rare in the UK. Nevertheless, this strategy (named after the video game) was recently employed by two breweries in the Midlands. The idea is that the target firm launches a counter bid for the acquirer.

♦ **White knight**
As a last resort, the target may seek an alternative bidder which may offer a higher price, or retain the existing management.

Other tactics that may be considered, depending on the country, are: restrictive voting rights; dual-class stocks; employee share ownership; leveraged recapitalization; poison pill; greenmail.

10.3 Issues in post-acquisition integration

It is in the post-acquisition phase that value from the acquisition is created or destroyed. Many attempts have been made to produce diagrams that show clearly how the strategic intention behind an acquisition translates into **post-acquisition integration** actions. One such diagram is shown in Figure 10.2.

While diagrams such as Figure 10.2 indicate how the level of complexity may increase with different types of deals, it is clear that the class of acquisitions labelled 'horizontal', for instance, can give rise to almost all of the types of functional change suggested.

We are now shifting from issues of strategic fit to issues of organizational fit, from viewing companies holistically to looking at the complexities within. As Figure 10.3 shows, strategic fit offers the potential upon which organizational fit acts as a series of constraints.

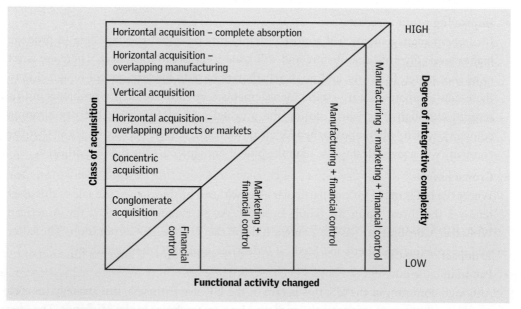

Figure 10. 2 Complexity of post-take-over integration
Source: Jones, 1982.

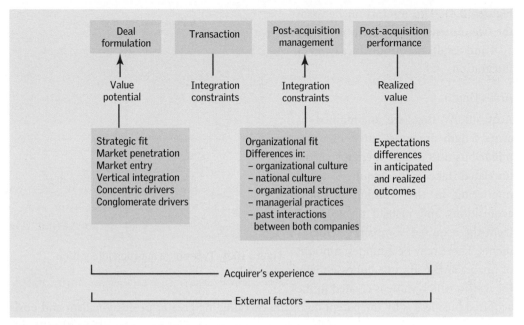

Figure 10.3 The tension between strategic and organisational fit
Source: adapted from Angwin, 2000, p. 4.

10.3.1 Organizational fit

Acquisitions are often associated with substantial redundancies. For this reason, there are numerous articles on the psychological impact of being acquired (Buono and Bowditch 1989; Mirvis and Marks 1992; Cartwright and Cooper 1996). There are many layers to culture and the number affected by acquisition will depend on the differences between the companies in terms of nationality, regionality, industry, corporate structure, history and managerial style. A further important dimension is the relative importance of employees to the organization's offering. Where employees are an integral part of the offering, for instance consultants are not separable from their advice, then cultural differences can have serious outcomes. In the words of one chief executive of a service firm, if the key employees walk out, what have you got?

10.3.2 Post-acquisition integration styles

The impact of organizational constraints, such as a culture clash, is largely a function of two factors. First, the inherent difficulties between the companies and the strategic independence of the acquired company (the need for strategic direction from the centre in Figure 10.4). Second, the extent to which value can be created from the acquisition through resource transfer or resource sharing between the two businesses (the need for resource transfer in

Figure 10.4). The interaction between the two dimensions is shown in Figure 10.4 and results in four distinct types of integration.

Figure 10.4 Types of acquisition integration approach
Source: Angwin, 2000.

Arm's length

Acquisitions that are maintained at arm's length are most often in unfamiliar business areas – perhaps classic unrelated takeovers. Acquirers avoid interfering in the running of these acquisitions and instead try to learn from the acquired company's achievements. There may be a modest amount of financial/risk sharing, but essentially the way in which value is created in the acquired business is by the parent company encouraging greater professionalism and positively influencing the ambition of the management group. The post-acquisition phase tends to be rather gentle and it can take years for real benefits to show.

Intensive care

These acquisitions are often in poor financial shape at the time of acquisition and they are usually held in isolation to avoid infecting the group. In most cases, a turnaround strategy will be employed to restore them to a healthy condition. Owing to the poor state of the acquired company, post-acquisition actions tend to occur very rapidly, with the post-acquisition phase being relatively short. As an acquisition technique, isolation acquisitions are quite risky, but, as with all turnarounds, success can be very marked.

Subjugation

Acquisitions that are subjugated rapidly lose their identity and structure and are subsumed within the parent group. Such acquisitions are often based on clear similarities between both companies, so that amalgamation will bring economies of scale and scope. The integration process is complex, potentially occurring throughout all aspects of the business. The post-acquisition phase of subjugation acquisitions tends to occur quickly and brings rapid results.

Collaboration

Acquisitions of a collaborative nature show the acquired company having considerable independence from the new parent. The acquired company has its own head, but future projects and arrangements show joint efforts for the benefit of the group. Over time, there is substantial interchange of capabilities, but this is a gradual process. Collaborative acquisitions are difficult to manage, have substantial risks, and the benefits are long term.

In theory, collaborative acquisitions offer the greatest potential for gain. However, the gains require the acquired company to retain a high degree of strategic independence, to retain the configuration of its core capabilities, while at the same time experiencing interaction of resources with the parent. This is something of a paradox, as the acquired company, in order to receive resources from the acquirer, loses some of its precious independence and has its capabilities threatened.

The Hewlett-Packard/Compaq casebox is an adaptation of a report in the *New York Times* on the way in which Hewlett-Packard is approaching the integration of Compaq into the HP business. Using the frameworks in this section, try to identify the approach that HP is taking.

Case box: Integrating Hewlett-Packard and Compaq

Three days before the deal between Hewlett-Packard and Compaq was announced in September 2001 Carleton S Fiorina, the chief executive of HP, tasked Webb McKinney to lead the team that would plan how the two companies would fit together, with what products and how the proposed company would achieve its cost savings and its revenue targets. Industry analysts were sceptical. Big mergers are always tricky. In the computer industry putting two companies together has been a recipe for trouble (for example the merger of Compaq with Digital Equipment Corporation). Typically, as the new combined company grapples with the internal turmoil created in the wake of the merger, the fast-moving technology markets move on and customers defect to competitors.

The integration team had grown to more than 1,000 employees from bit companies by March 2002. By that date they had worked an estimated 1.3 million hours on the integration planning and had studied and talked to veterans of a dozen successful large mergers.

Yet, for all the detail work, one thing was clear – the need for speed. 'We make quick decisions and get on with it,' McKinney said. 'Out of the blocks, we have to move as fast as we can,' said Barbara Braun, a senior manager on the team. To do this the team has taken as one of its operating principles the need to make tough decisions instead of 'trying to make everybody happy'. The key decisions include the product line – what products will be promoted and supported most aggressively. The top 100 customers were planned to be visited by HP representatives with bound 'play books' detailing HP's product plans and who the customers' account teams will be. A crucial element will be how convincing the corporate customers find the 'migration path' from discontinued product lines to other offerings the company will feature.

The cost of not making the difficult product decisions can be far greater in terms of wasted time and investment. A big mistake after Compaq acquired Digital Equipment in 1998 was not moving early to focus the Digital Unix business on its niche strength in technical computing rather than trying to compete broadly in the Unix market against bigger rivals such as Sun Microsystems, Hewlett-Packard and IBM.

McKinney is said to be analytic and unflappable and has the temperament suited for arbitrating the tough decisions that the team must make. He and the other senior members of the integration team will stay in place to push the merger along for 12 months after the deal is closed.

Source: adapted from the *New York Times*, 25 March 2002.

The framework in Figure 10.4 is important for making sense of different post-acquisition styles and attempting to integrate this backwards into the pre-acquisition process. There is now a growing literature on the mechanics of creating value through resource sharing and transfer. This resource-based view is based on an enhanced utilization of core competences and resources. Resource redeployment is the dominant value-creating mechanism of acquisition, primarily through capability enhancement, but also to a lesser extent through cost savings. Interesting recent research suggests the acquirer is better skilled at rationalizing its own assets and redeploying its own resources than those of the target (Capron 1999).

The case box on the DaimlerChrysler merger tells the story of the difficulties of making the new entity work. Identify the problems that have occurred in the post-merger integration. Contrast these with the benefits that were expected to flow from the merger. Then assess the probabilities and time scales associated with a successful resolution of all these problems. What does this tell you about the inherent difficulties and rewards of such large-scale mergers?

Case box: **DaimlerChrysler stalled?**

Chrysler Group Chief Executive Dieter Zetsche says, 'We have to deal with the hand we have, and turn it into a winning hand.' There's no masking the stark reality behind the biggest industrial merger in history. Five years after Daimler-Benz CEO Jürgen E. Schrempp carried out a $36 billion fusion with Chrysler Corp., his promise of creating the world's most profitable carmaker is a financial blow-out. After an unexpected $1 billion loss in the second quarter, Chrysler may end 2003 in the red, despite Schrempp's boast a year ago that the unit would earn $2 billion this year. That wipes out the gains of 2002 and follows on the heels of the $5.8 billion loss in 2001.

Chrysler is not the only thing Schrempp, 59, is worrying about these days. In July, a J.D. Power & Associates Inc. survey revealed embarrassing quality deficiencies at Mercedes itself, raising questions about whether the drain on management from Chrysler is affecting the classiest of German marques. Mitsubishi Motor Corp., another troubled imperial possession, has warned of a $683 million first-half loss and has slashed its full-year earnings forecast by

75%, as U.S. sales plunge. In July, Daimler's $30 billion truck business embarked on a sweeping reorganization to reap savings from sharing parts and pooling purchasing for its various units after losing $960 million in two years. And in August, Daimler agreed to pay $300 million to settle a lawsuit by institutional investors and still faces a $2 billion claim by shareholder Kirk Kerkorian.

Was the merger a colossal mistake? A growing chorus of voices says it was. Many experts think Chrysler, whose competitiveness Schrempp badly misjudged in 1998, might have gone bankrupt by now without its German parent. Schrempp promised a swift integration and a world-spanning company that would dominate the industry. But five years later, new products have failed to pull Chrysler out of a rut. And DaimlerChrysler dominates only where it did before – in luxury cars. It now owns or controls struggling players in both the U.S. and Asia. Analysts even speculate that DaimlerChrysler might jettison Chrysler altogether. The CEO refuses to admit defeat. 'There are one or two things we didn't do right [at Chrysler] in the beginning. But we will get it right,' a subdued Schrempp told journalists at the Frankfurt motor show. Many institutional investors and small shareholders are fed up. They want to see Schrempp replaced and the deal unwound. The market capitalization of DaimlerChrysler, at $38 billion, is well below the German auto maker's $47 billion market cap before its marriage to Chrysler. BMW, the company closest in size and market segment to Mercedes, has seen its market value rise by 27%, to $26 billion, since the end of 1998. But the most stinging criticism comes from those within the vaunted 119 year-old auto maker, who point to top management error, not market woes, for the company's dismal performance. 'The entire management board is too removed from the business. Things have being going in the wrong direction for a long period of time,' says one senior DaimlerChrysler manager.

Poor execution isn't the only problem. The logic behind Schrempp's vision of Welt AG, a world auto company with integrated parts, looks increasingly flawed. Sure, Chrysler and Mitsubishi may be able to cut their costs by sharing parts and engineering. But many auto-industry experts and top executives agree that Schrempp erred fundamentally in merging a luxury auto maker with a mass-market brand – an unnatural combination that offers limited benefits and requires twice the expertise and effort to manage. Moreover, luxury has proved a better source of growth and profits than mass-market cars.

True, when Mercedes management sets its mind to change, it can be very successful. In the early '90s when Mercedes was losing ground to the Japanese, it revamped models and invested in new market niches and factories. But the global auto market today is brutally competitive. Car sales in Asia, Europe, and the U.S. are all in a long slump, and the Japanese continue to seize market share from Chrysler. The toughest challenge may be the relentless downward pressure on prices in the U.S. Big Three rebates now average nearly $4,000 per vehicle, more than double 1998 levels. That makes it hard to earn a premium on even the newest, snazziest models. Witness Chrysler's $38,000 2004 Pacifica minivan-SUV crossover.

Consumers considered the price tag steep for a Chrysler, and it now comes with a $1,000 rebate. In August, Chrysler lost to Toyota its 53-year position as America's No. 3 carmaker. 'Chrysler could prove impossible to fix,' says Garel Rhys, professor of automotive economics at Cardiff Business School in Wales.

The Germans who are doing the driving at Mercedes and Chrysler still counsel patience. They insist that the integration of process know-how and parts sharing is just starting to kick in and that, over time, productivity gains will reduce costs while quality improvements and new models boost Chrysler. But Chrysler's problems are overwhelming the gains. The new products vital to a Chrysler rebound have been slow in coming. The first joint Chrysler-Mercedes engineering product – the sleek Chrysler Crossfire roadster – only recently hit the market. While the $35,000 car offers German engineering finesse and quality at a bargain, thanks to borrowing 40% of its components from Mercedes, the experiment is a one-of-a-kind. Future Chrysler cars will share most with Mitsubishi, not Mercedes, in order to avoid diluting the luxury German brand image.

In Stuttgart, the fear and loathing of Chrysler is palpable. 'Chrysler is the downfall of Mercedes-Benz. It is a hole for billions of euros,' says one Mercedes dealer. For the first half, DaimlerChrysler's revenues fell by 11%, to $75 billion, and net profit declined by 81%, to $773 million. For now, Jürgen Hubbert, the respected boss of Mercedes Car Group, has kept Mercedes pumping out steady profits. But there are signs that could portend an erosion of competitiveness. The C-Class compact sedan is straining under competition from BMW's older 3 Series model, while less expensive cars that were developed to spur growth, including the A-Class, are unprofitable. Worse, Mercedes recently suffered a spate of quality problems, including faulty transmissions. J.D. Power's July report on customer satisfaction flagged a number of quality problems on three Mercedes models from the year 2000: the E-Class sedan, the M-Class SUV, and the CLK coupe.

How much more bad news can Schrempp survive? His fate – and that of DaimlerChrysler – depend on Deutsche Bank, DaimlerChrysler's largest shareholder, which has seen the value of its 12% stake plunge by more than $15 billion since the merger. 'The key question is: What does Deutsche Bank think? Do you throw good money after bad, or cut your losses,' says David E. Cole, president of the Center for Automotive Studies in Ann Arbor, Mich. Deutsche Chairman Josef Ackermann says he wants to sell the bank's stake, but not at today's price. The bank is still backing Schrempp, but if Chrysler posts huge losses in the quarters ahead that push the mother company into the red, Ackermann could oust Schrempp. Dissatisfaction with the merger is growing within Daimler Benz, especially among Mercedes executives. Says one insider: 'The race is on to be [Schrempp's] successor.' The front-runners: Zetsche and Eckhard Cordes, head of commercial vehicles who edged the struggling division into the black in the second quarter, even though its margins are still way below target. Getting rid of Chrysler could be tougher than firing Schrempp. A parent company can put a subsidiary into Chapter 11 bankruptcy and shrug off its pension and health-care obligations. But that works in this case only if Chrysler's obligations aren't guaranteed by parent DaimlerChrysler. Otherwise, creditors and unions would simply take their demands to the parent.

A more likely outcome: Daimler could spin off Chrysler to its shareholders. The question is whether Chrysler's research and development, engineering, and leadership could be disentangled from Daimler's. Daimler might also sell Chrysler in pieces, as BMW did with its money-losing Rover unit. Daimler, the theory goes, could sell off Chrysler's profitable Jeep SUV and Dodge truck units for a profit and hand off the money-losing passenger-car business to diehard Chrysler loyalists for $1. That, however, would surely trigger massive political and labour reactions as thousands of car-unit jobs were destroyed, and benefits jeopardized. Short of that, DaimlerChrysler could merge Chrysler and Mitsubishi car operations into a single unit.

Deutsche Bank will probably keep Schrempp at the helm for now, barring another dramatic setback at Chrysler. But DaimlerChrysler executives concede that a real turnaround will take three to five years and billions in investment. In short: a new generation of cars built in updated plants. Zetsche and Schrempp are confident they can pull that off. But many argue that Schrempp, who quadrupled his salary after the merger and ranks in compensation reviews as Germany's top-paid CEO, with an estimated $12.1 million pay package in 2002, does not deserve a third chance. If he fails again, Chrysler's problems will overwhelm its German parent in less than five years, warns an insider. 'It will be the biggest industrial cleanup job Germany has ever seen.' Given Schrempp's chequered track record, that's a high-stakes gamble.

Source: extracted from Gail Edmondson and Kathleen Kerwin, *Business Week*, 29 September 2003, Issue 3851, p. 54.

10.4 **Managing strategic alliances**

The poor performance record of mergers and acquisitions led to corporate disenchantment with this method of expansion. Corporate indigestion meant that acquirers found the immediate advantages of acquisition to be frequently undermined by the trauma of integration. Acquirers often had difficulty in assimilating the expertise of the target company and, where the target company had considerable flexibility and innovative capacity, these characteristics were often lost in the subsequent bureaucracy. Added to this disenchantment there has also been a shortage of appropriate targets to purchase. These twin constraints led companies to search for alternative means of rapid, safer expansion, so as to improve their control over the competitive environment.

Strategic alliances appeared to overcome many of the limitations of mergers and acquisitions. They seemed to avoid culture and organizational shock and yet achieve rapid presence in specific areas for the companies concerned. However, it is worth recording that there now appears to be something of a backlash with companies recognizing problems of sustainability with strategic alliances and some feeling strongly that acquisitions would have been preferable.

10.4.1 Types of co-operative strategies

Strategic alliances are just one of two broad sub-sets of **co-operative strategies**; the other is collusive strategies. They may be defined as follows:

- **Collusive strategies**: where several firms in an industry co-operate to reduce industry output below the competitive level and raise prices above the competitive level (Scherer 1980). Such strategies are normally between firms in the same industry and may be perceived as a defensive strategy to ward off a threat by competition. Collusion may be deliberate in which case it constitutes illegal price-fixing (in most countries). It may, however, be tacit. In that case firms recognize a common interest in raising prices without explicit agreement being reached. This is not currently regarded as illegal.

- **Strategic alliances**: where several firms co-operate but industry output is not reduced (Kogut 1988). Such alliances can exist between firms in different industries and can be perceived as aimed at creating and enhancing the competitive positions of the firms involved in a very competitive environment.

The term *strategic alliance* itself covers a multitude of different arrangements and there is no agreed typology in the literature. However, it is critical to understand the different forms in existence, as they have profound implications for the way in which the alliance is to be managed. In particular, there is an important distinction on the grounds of whether or not the partner is a competitor – note that even if the partner is a competitor, this may not mean collusion.

Figure 10.5 Expansion options and types of partnership between non-competing firms
Source: Adapted from Dussauge and Garrette, 1999, p. 51.

Strategic alliances between non-competitors

The following provides a useful way of linking alliance types among competitors to options for strategic expansion. These growth options may be grouped into three categories:

◆ *International expansion*: where a company extends its activities into a new geographic market, often after having established a dominant position in their domestic market.

◆ *Vertical integration*: where a company extends its activities upstream or downstream to become its own supplier or customer.

◆ *Diversification*: where a company expands outside its industry of origin.

In Figure 10.5 the implications for these expansion options for types of strategic alliance among non-competing firms are shown. We can see there are three main types of strategic alliance among non-competing firms:

◆ **International expansion joint ventures**: these are formed by companies that originate in different countries. One company often has a product that it seeks to market in another country in which the other firm has privileged access. The mutual benefits are that the local firm gains a product to distribute, while the manufacturer gains a foothold in a new country. Often these alliances are between partners with unequal skills and resources, one coming from the developed world with technical skills and considerable resources and the other from the developing world without the ability to develop such a product on its own but having a profound understanding of the local market.

◆ **Vertical partnerships**: these bring together two companies that operate at two successive stages in the same production process. For instance, fast food chains are critical customers of soft drinks suppliers, so Coca-Cola has set up an alliance with McDonald's and Domino's Pizza.

◆ **Cross-industry agreements**: these are co-operations formed by companies from totally different industries to leverage their complementary capabilities. For instance, BMW forged an alliance with Rolls-Royce in aircraft engines in order to enter that market. Although for Rolls-Royce this meant the emergence of a new competitor, it also provided the opportunity to control their long-term development. This raises the issue of competing agendas, with the newcomer trying to close the expertise gap as rapidly as possible, while the established company attempts the reverse. Such alliances may also occur where there is technical convergence between two industries. For instance, Philips has teamed up with Du Pont de Nemours for the production of surface coatings for data storage applications.

Strategic alliances between competitors

Alliances among competitors seem rather paradoxical, but according to Morris and Hergert (1987) they account for approximately 70 per cent of all co-operation agreements. Maybe it is in recognition of this that Hamel and Prahalad's (1989) article is entitled 'Collaborate with your competitors – and win'. While some put these alliances in the collusive category, it is a question of degree, with some being more collusive than others. Through the use of cluster analysis techniques on 200 alliances, Dussauge and Garrette (1999) identified three main alliance types between competitors (*see* Figure 10.6) in terms of balance of power between the partners (degree of symmetry) and impact on competition.

The three types of alliance identified may be characterized in the following way:

♦ *Pre-competitive* or **shared supply alliance**: this may only cover one stage in the production process, so that while the final product contains inputs from both companies, these are specific to the parents and the alliance is not apparent to the market. These alliances occur when the minimum efficient size at a particular stage in the production process is much greater than for the entire product and when neither firm produces enough volume to achieve this critical size. These sorts of alliances are mainly between firms of similar size, often intra-zonal, and in areas of R&D and manufacturing. Industries with such alliances are automotive, electronics and data processing.

♦ **Quasi-concentration alliance**: this covers the entire production process and results in a common product marketed by all allies. The assets and skills brought by each partner are similar in nature and the goal is to benefit from economies of scale. Such an alliance is clearly visible to the customer, such as in the Airbus consortium or the production of the Tornado fighter aircraft. Clearly, such alliances eliminate competition between competitors, although there can be internal rivalry within the alliance. These sorts of alliances are found mostly in the aerospace and defence industries.

♦ **Complementary alliance**: when the assets contributed by the partner firms are different in nature. Most commonly, one may be a manufacturer and the other a distributor. For instance, Matra manufactures the Espace, a mini van, which is marketed in Europe

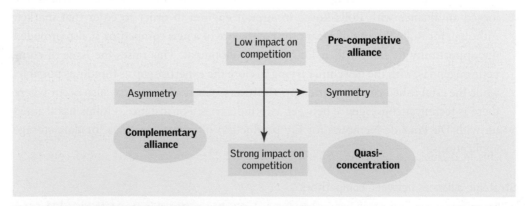

Figure 10.6 Mapping strategic alliances between competitors
Source: Dussauge and Garrette, 1999, p. 61.

by Renault. For such alliances to work, the product brought in by an ally must not compete directly with the products of the other firm. Complementary alliances are usually between two firms (unlike the other two styles) and the companies may be very different sizes. These alliances are often found in the automotive and telecommunications industries.

10.4.2 **How to manage alliances**

International expansion joint ventures

The aim of the multinational is to develop its business in the targeted country, while the local partner wishes to derive adequate profits. Both need the **joint venture** to be successful, but there are clear grounds for conflict:

◆ Profitability of the joint venture is strongly affected by the multinational partner, which controls the transfer pricing of inputs such as technology, expertise, products etc. The local partner cannot readily assess this aspect, but is totally dependent upon the profits of the joint venture.

◆ For the multinational, the joint venture is only one part of a much larger system and will manage its joint ventures to optimize the system as a whole. If profits and sales are reduced in a joint venture, the local partner suffers, as there is no other benefit.

To avoid such conflicts a management structure needs to be set up to manage day-to-day operations while respecting the views of each party.

◆ *Balance of power*. Unlike traditional shareholders, these partners[7] get involved in the day-to-day operations of the joint venture. For this reason, some partners push for a dominant equity stake. However, the link between equity distribution and performance is far from conclusive and research in developing countries suggests that there is greater chance of success as the balance of ownership moves towards the local partner (Schaan and Beamish 1988).

Equity ownership, though, is not necessarily reflected in degree of influence, which appears to have a greater impact upon performance. In Table 10.3 we can see that independent joint ventures where the general manager enjoys considerable autonomy from either parent would appear to be more successful. However, with the parents merely acting as investors and shareholders, it is difficult to see how the complementary capabilities of the partners can be leveraged.

The lower success rate of joint ventures with shared management results from problems in the balance of power, as all major decisions require consensus and, because key

---

[7] The partners (typically the multinational partner and local partner) act as both shareholders and managers, and therefore are mutually involved in the day-to-day operations of the joint venture.

Table 10.3 Balance of power and performance of international joint ventures

	JV performance*			Number of JVs terminated/ restructured
	Bad	Average	Good	
Dominant parent	23	23	54	15
Shared management	55	20	25	50
Independent JV	25	0	75	0

*Assessed by managers
Source: Killing, 1983.

areas are allocated to each partner, must be tightly controlled. While the other forms remove this endless negotiation and the problems of co-ordination, they also lose the opportunity to take advantage of the parents' complementarities.

◆ *Quality of joint venture manager.* It is vital for the manager to capture and preserve substantial autonomy compared to the parent firms (Killing 1983), establishing from the outset that leaving the manager to manage guarantees success and avoids untimely interventions from the parents. The manager must also manage each parent separately and work towards consensus without the parents confronting each other.

Vertical partnerships

It is not enough to just examine operational effectiveness for vertical partnerships. Other factors must be considered:

◆ The degree of mutual trust between partners.

◆ The commitment to invest jointly for the long term.

◆ The fit between the partners' strategies.

Commitment, then, is at least as important as technical capabilities.

Moving from subcontractor to full partner requires radical organizational change. In particular, each organization needs to be organized around projects rather than functions. This allows a greater account of people's opinions throughout the process, and so enhances overall unity, consistency and quality of product. Ways of facilitating these changes are to move people between firms for extended periods and indeed set them up in separate sites for the purpose of better understanding the partner's perspective and improving communication.

Cross-industry agreements

These can be in the form of combining complementary technologies to create a new business, or to exploit converging technologies, or to diversify into a partner's industry.

Where it is intended to combine complementary technologies, while the intention may be to blur the boundaries of existing industries, few such alliances have really achieved this, remaining a particular and limited segment of the previously existing businesses.

However, alliances between biotechnology companies and the pharmaceutical sector, for the testing, marketing and manufacture of products on a large scale, are at the very core of the biotech firm's development and the pharmaceutical firm's innovation process.

In terms of diversifying into another's industry, there may be financial benefit to the 'host'. The speed with which the entrant is capable of operating on its own in the targeted industry depends on how quickly it can acquire necessary skills and capabilities. This depends on three factors (Hamel 1991):

- *Appropriability of the incumbent's expertise* – such skills are not equally accessible, with more formalized areas being replicable upon observation, whereas more tacit knowledge is more embedded in context and far more difficult to abstract (Nonaka 1991).

- *Openness and transparency of the incumbent firm* – there may be procedures, systems and language that act as barriers to learning.

- *The ability of the entering partner to internalize new skills* – this will be affected by the similarities between the firms, the style of management and the mobility of the personnel.

Shared supply alliances

The two main areas of shared supply are in R&D and manufacturing:

- *Managing R&D alliances.* This occurs through dividing up the work between the firms' respective R&D facilities, rather than setting up a joint site that would result in technology leakage. To manage this, R&D alliances are implemented through informal structures, such as steering committees, to agree the division of work. The difficulty with this approach is that there are few incentives to make the joint work a priority over researchers' own projects, so that joint projects often drag and have disappointing outcomes. In addition, there is suspicion that when it comes to jointly applying, developed concepts to prototypes, entrusting one partner with the task becomes tantamount to subsidizing a competitor's new product development.

  The leakage of know-how is virtually unavoidable as even in scoping out projects a firm defines its areas of technical interest. A firm therefore must not rely too heavily on an alliance for developing its technological base and must maintain independent expertise alongside the project.

- *Manufacturing alliances.* Manufacturing shared supply alliances are often long-lived, but this may not be an indicator of success, as there are often barriers to dissolution. These alliances can often lack flexibility. The partner firms become captive customers of the alliance that is the 'in-house' supplier, isolated from the competitive marketplace. Contractual obligations to purchase make it difficult for the partners to carry out corrective action, which in itself is difficult, due to physical and human resource commitments. The partners also have to agree as to the way in which the alliance would be altered, which may be increasingly difficult, as their requirements of the alliance change over time.

For this reason, it is critical at formation to assess the similarity of needs between the parties, in terms of volume and technical specifications of the product, and the durability of the strategic fit, in terms of the stability of the industry and the way in which respective product lines will evolve.

Quasi-concentration alliances

These alliances aim to achieve economies of scale without merging. To achieve this, it is important that investment be minimized and economies of scale maximized. Duplications should be avoided, so that a single operator handles a specific task. Occasionally it may be necessary to pool tasks, where a separate structure is set up on behalf of the partners. If this is for the long term, such a pooling may become a business-based joint venture and is an efficient way of maximizing economies of scale.

While duplication will tend to undermine the advantages of these alliances, in many cases partners may choose to allow a certain amount of duplication, for one of the effects of the alliance may be to cause each partner to specialize to an unacceptable degree and consequently lose important skills. Although through specialization the extent and degree of rivalry will lessen, the loss of a partner can pose a serious threat to remaining partners. For this reason, in industries such as aerospace, partners allow the duplication of final assembly, as it involves a range of strategic competences; in particular, systems integration. An alternative is to rotate tasks and responsibilities.

Managing complementary alliances

In such alliances each partner contributes different and complementary assets and capabilities to the joint endeavour. However, it can be a classic case of the Trojan Horse, with each partner trying to capture the other partner's most valuable skills, to enhance its own position in the industry in general and tilt the balance of power in the alliance in particular. There is also the wish to make the other partner more dependent, so that the alliance can be influenced favourably.

Whether the alliance will remain as a win-win or degenerate into a Trojan Horse is determined by:

- The appropriability of the capabilities of the other partner.
- The value and attractiveness of those capabilities.
- The organization of the alliance – the amount of interaction will affect the amount of learning
- The 'absorptive capacity' of the firm (Cohen and Levinthal 1990) – the extent to which the firms have appropriate organizations and cultures to facilitate learning.
- The impact of a change in environment – this may affect the balance of power, as a partner's contribution may lose value.

For the alliance to prosper it is critical for the firms to continuously improve their specific capabilities and enhance the value of their contributions to the alliance, while also preparing for possible termination. Learning from the alliance is an important aspect of complementary alliances, and often leads to early termination by the partner who has captured the desired capabilities first, with the winner operating on its own and the loser having to either form a new alliance or pull out altogether. When the race to learn is over, in many cases the winner acquires the partner.

10.4.3 Evaluations and outcomes

Assessing the outcomes of alliances is no easy matter. As we have shown, there are many different types and the partners have very different reasons for pursuing them. Tables 10.4 and 10.5 show the variety of outcomes for both non-competing and competing firm alliances.

For alliances between competitors, the most frequent outcomes overall are either an extension of the alliance or premature termination – it seems it is unusual to have a natural end or be acquired. In most cases, alliances between competitors had significant strategic consequences for the partner firms, with one-way skills appropriation in particular, and such alliances tend to affect the levels of competition in the industry. However, there is considerable variation between the different types of alliance between competitors, as Table 10.5 shows.

Table 10.4 Outcomes of alliances between non-rival firms

Alliance type	Evolution of the alliance	Strategic consequences for each firm	Impact on competition
International expansion joint ventures	High mortality rate in their first years in existence, followed by stability	Stability in the partners' relative positions	Globalization
Vertical partnerships	Long-term relationship between the partners	New division of the value added within the industry	Concentration of the upstream industry and changes in the relative bargaining power of suppliers and buyers
Cross-industry agreements	Results are frequently disappointing when compared to initial expectations	Joint venture becomes independent or intensification of competition between partners	Creation of new activities and arrival of new competitors

Source: Dussauge and Garrette, 1999, p. 209.

Table 10.5 The evolutions and outcomes of strategic alliances between competitors

Alliance type	Evolution of the alliance	Strategic consequences for each firm	Impact on competition
Shared-supply	Natural end or premature termination	No consequence	No impact on the intensity of competition
Quasi-concentration	Extension	Mutual specialization	Reduced intensity of competition
Complementary	Extension or continuation by one partner	One-way skill appropriation	Increased intensity of competition

Source: Dussauge and Garrette, 1999, p. 220.

10.5 Summary

We began the chapter with a discussion of the advantages and disadvantages of mergers and acquisitions as a method of corporate renewal. Disenchantment with the method has spurred businesses to seek alternative avenues to improve their competitive advantage. A whole new set of options has arisen in the form of strategic alliances, although the chapter has pointed out that the term embodies a substantial range of different forms. However, we are now beginning to perceive something of a backlash, as managers become disenchanted with the instability of alliances, the difficulties of realizing anticipated benefits and the risks of knowledge leakage. The irony, then, is that strategic alliances, like mergers and acquisitions, also have considerable implementation difficulties that need to be fully considered before the deal is signed.

On a broader canvas, both mergers and acquisitions and strategic alliances are good examples of the difficulties strategic management as a subject has had with the planning–implementation dichotomy. Doing the deal still obscures managing the aftermath. One can only hope that the lessons that may have been learnt with managing strategic alliances may now feed back into making better acquisitions.

Key terms

Absorptive capacity *400*

Acquisition *377*

Collusive strategy *394*

Complementary alliances *396*

Co-operative strategies *394*

Cross-industry agreements *395*

International expansion joint ventures *395*

Joint ventures *397*

Merger *377*

Post-acquisition integration *386*

Quasi-concentration alliances *396*

Shared supply alliances *396*

Strategic alliances *394*

Vertical partnerships *395*

Recap questions and assignments

Choose an acquisition/merger or an alliance which has featured prominently in the business press or with which you have been involved.

1 Critically assess the motives behind the making of the deal. In answering this question, you should consider different levels of analysis and specifically address the question of how the deal contributed to the creating and/or sustaining of competitive advantage.

2 *Either* assess the outcome in terms of subsequent events, *or* comment critically upon what you perceive to be the main difficulties ahead in realizing the intentions of the deal.

3 Why do you feel that acquisitions and alliances continue to be made, when so many fail?

Online
*Learning*Centre

When you have read this chapter, log on to the Online Learning Centre website at www.mcgraw-hill.co.uk/textbooks/mcgee to explore chapter-by-chapter test questions, further reading and more online study tools for strategy.

Case 1 Disney: The battle for the Magic Kingdom

Comcast, America's biggest cable company, has launched an audacious bid for Disney. The timing is shrewd, for Michael Eisner, Disney's boss, is under attack for poor governance and disappointing results

With viciously perfect timing, Comcast, a cable-TV company, last week launched a hostile takeover bid for The Walt Disney Company, arguably America's best-known entertainment company. Comcast is taking advantage of a particularly weak point in Disney's history. Last month Disney's most important business partner, Pixar, an animation studio, abandoned it. At the end of last year, two board members, Roy Disney and Stanley Gold, resigned and started a campaign to oust Michael Eisner, Disney's boss. On the day that Comcast announced its bid, Disney's executives started an investor conference in Florida, an occasion they had counted on to boost the company and its share price. The share price did indeed jump, but this was thanks to Comcast's bid, initially worth $66 billion, rather than to any of Disney's business plans.

At its get-together with investors, the Disney high command behaved as if the Comcast bid had never happened. Indeed, the bidder's name was barely mentioned, until Mr Eisner joked that 'we're buying Comcast' when asked about possible acquisitions. The Disney boss also argued against the sort of consolidation that media distributors like Comcast have pursued. Perhaps foreshadowing the arguments that Disney's lobbyists will make in Washington, Mr Eisner said: 'Concentration of distribution usually hurts the small guy [not] the large player.'

Mr Eisner's dismissal of Comcast's approach was backed up by Disney's board, which formally rejected the hostile bid on Monday February 16th and expressed confidence in Mr Eisner's leadership. However, the board also said it would 'consider any legitimate proposal'. The problem was that Comcast's all-share bid, which by then had fallen in value to $60 billion, did not 'reflect fully Disney's intrinsic value and earnings prospects'.

Mr Eisner's rejection of merger talks was 'unfortunate', Comcast argued in a letter to him, because strategically the deal makes sense. Putting Comcast, which has 21m cable subscribers, together with Disney, wrote Brian Roberts, president and chief executive of Comcast, would unite its distribution power and technology know-how with Disney's peerless content businesses. Although the jury remains out on whether vertical integration really delivers value, other companies have already pursued such a strategy. Rupert Murdoch's News Corp, for instance, has satellite distribution plus its Fox content businesses. Time Warner unites cable with a film studio and television programming – as well as, thanks to its horribly bubbly merger with AOL in January 2000, the internet. But a merger between Comcast and Disney would create by far the biggest vertically-integrated entertainment giant of them all, with a market capitalization of over $120 billion, says Comcast, compared with Time Warner's current $78 billion. There are no obvious competition grounds for blocking the proposed deal, since Comcast and Disney mostly operate in different businesses. However, the sheer size of the proposed company has prompted regulators and politicians to insist that they will scrutinize it aggressively.

Weapons of mouse destruction

Beyond grand strategic dreams – which some observers reckon that the hard-nosed sorts who run Comcast cannot really take seriously – Disney's appeal may be that its assets are undervalued, while those of Comcast are arguably overvalued. Disney's crown jewel, for instance, is ESPN, America's most-watched sports network. Comcast is particularly keen to own ESPN, as it currently has to pay high and rapidly rising fees to carry it on its cable channels.

Under Disney's current management, the group's profits are now a third lower than they were in 1998, and its share price is at the level it was in 1997. Part of the reason for the poor performance is sheer bad luck: Disney's theme parks, which make up nearly a quarter of its revenue, suffered badly in the wake of the terrorist attacks of September 11th 2001 and because of subsequent economic weakness – they are recovering now, if slowly. A more intractable problem is the broadcast network, ABC, which Disney bought in 1995 and is still losing money. With some exceptions, Disney's movie-making has struggled for ages. It has had big hits, such as 'Finding Nemo' last year, which have propelled a significant improvement in financial performance, but these triumphs have mostly been the work of Pixar, the studio which is now divorcing Disney.

Would Comcast, a family-controlled firm with few creative credentials, be any better at managing Disney's assets? Possibly. In a sort of government-in-exile conference which ran in tandem with Disney's own efforts this week to talk to its shareholders, Comcast's management described its plans to improve profits at its target, with special focus on ABC and on the cable networks. Steve Burke, a former Disney executive who used to run ABC, and who is now Comcast Cable's president, also stressed the need to revitalize Disney's animation business, which has languished of late. In addition to improved profitability, Comcast said, cost savings could be $300m–500m a year, bringing a total cash-flow boost from the merger of as much as $1 billion annually. Wall Street, to be sure, loves the deal, with one analyst, Jessica Reif Cohen, hailing it as a 'perfect, brilliant combination'.

Comcast, which has a well-deserved reputation as a tough negotiator of deals, also has a fine record in arguably an even harder part of the merger process – execution. It bought AT&T Broadband, a company twice its size, 15 months ago, and so far the acquisition is working well – Comcast has managed to slow dramatically the number of cable subscribers being lost by AT&T Broadband. Indeed, Comcast is considered to be America's best-run cable operator. It has managed – thanks, again, to those negotiating skills – to get cheap programming without ruining relations with its content providers. In 2000, for instance, a war broke out between Time Warner and Disney over the cost of Disney's cable channels and ended up with Time Warner blocking ABC from transmission. Comcast, meanwhile, had the same fight with Disney, but carried it out in secret, winning what are believed to have been favourable terms.

Above all, Messrs Roberts and Burke appear to believe that most of Disney's long-term problems have one (easily removed) root cause: Mr Eisner, chairman and chief executive of Disney since 1984. In his first 13 years in charge he impressively raised revenues from $1.65 billion to $22 billion, and market value from $2 billion to $67 billion. But he lost his way some years ago, and the swelling crowd of influential critics of Mr Eisner has surely embold-ened Comcast to make its bid hostile.

Mr Eisner seems to have difficulty getting on with people and thereby retaining senior talent. A long list of executives, such as Paul Pressler and Steven Bornstein, have left Disney. Mr Eisner seems to have made insufficient effort to keep up good relations with Steve Jobs, chief executive of Pixar, which has been responsible for over half of Disney's studio profits in recent years. That Mr Eisner infuriated Mr Jobs, himself a fiery and short-tempered man, was confirmed recently when Mr Jobs unexpectedly ended talks to re-negotiate Pixar's co-production deal with Disney.

Mr Jobs noted that Mr Eisner told Disney's board that, after seeing an early cut of 'Finding Nemo', he didn't think the film was as good as its others – an embarrassing inci-dent since it went on to become the highest-grossing animated feature film of all time. Mr Eisner told the board that, once the film hit movie-theatres, the Pixar people would get a reality check and become easier to negotiate with. On another occasion, Mr Eisner called Mr Jobs a 'Shiite' in a Disney board meeting, according to a board member who partici-pated in it.

Losing Pixar should not immediately hurt Disney's results because the contract between the two firms obliges Pixar to deliver two more films, in 2004 and 2005. Wall Street analysts have thus been fairly upbeat about Disney's shares, even before the bid – the success of 'Finding Nemo' and a cyclical recovery in advertising and visitors to theme parks should boost profits sharply in 2004. Also, Disney has the rights to make sequels to all the films it co-financed with Pixar, a thought that Mr Jobs said makes his executives 'sick' since they will have no control over creative quality.

In the longer term, however, Disney faces a huge problem if it cannot improve the quality of its animated films: characters such as Snow White and Mickey Mouse have historically been the creative heart of the firm. Mr Jobs cruelly pointed out last week that not even Disney's marketing and brand could turn Disney's latest two home-grown animated films – 'Treasure Planet' and 'Brother Bear' – into successes: they both 'bombed at the box office'. With Comcast in charge, would Mr Jobs reconsider the divorce?

Unhappy family

The Comcast bid provides both succour and a conundrum for two of Disney's noisiest critics, who would presumably prefer the firm to stay independent: Roy Disney and

Stanley Gold, two former board members who resigned their positions in December in order to mount a public campaign against Mr Eisner. Mr Disney, the nephew of Walt, is derided by some Disney allies as a 'nut'. But the support of Mr Gold – a shrewd, tough lawyer who put Mr Eisner in his job in the first place—has been helping to create a following among some institutional investors for his 'Save Disney' internet campaign.

Whilst Messrs Disney and Gold clearly regard Comcast's bid as vindication for their campaign, they are as yet uncertain about whether to support the takeover. Perhaps they would prefer Mr Eisner simply to go, so that the firm can remain independent, or (less attractive) a 'white knight' to acquire Disney. Indeed, Comcast's offer may yet trigger either of those outcomes.

Meantime, Messrs Disney and Gold will try to persuade shareholders to oppose the election of Mr Eisner, and three other Disney directors, at Disney's annual general meeting in Philadelphia on March 3rd. So far, before Comcast bid, Mr Gold was believed to have mustered as much as 15% of Disney's shareholder vote. Messrs Disney and Gold have also attacked Disney's corporate governance and choice of directors. Investors should vote against George Mitchell, a former senator, they say, because he has been a paid consultant to Disney and because his other directorships leave him too little time for Disney. Institutional Shareholder Services, a firm which advises institutions on how to vote, has added its support to Messrs Disney and Gold by advising investors not to vote for Mr Eisner's re-election.

Whether any plausible white knight would be a more attractive partner than Comcast is debatable; indeed, it is easy to imagine blacker knights now joining the tournament to win Disney. True, Mr Murdoch has ruled out bidding for Disney. But Viacom, Liberty Media and even Microsoft may fancy the firm. Even likelier bidders are two internet firms, Yahoo and InterActiveCorp, whose respective bosses, Terry Semel and Barry Diller, hail from the entertainment world.

In theory, regulators might ride to Mr Eisner's rescue and block a merger of Disney and Comcast, but it seems unlikely. After the bid was announced, Michael Powell, chairman of the Federal Communications Commission, said that it would go through the 'finest filter'. Mike DeWine, a Republican from Ohio and the chairman of the Senate Judiciary antitrust subcommittee, said that his panel would hold hearings on the transaction. Yet Comcast says that it would make the same undertakings not to discriminate against other content firms and distribution networks that News Corp did last year when it acquired DirecTV. With luck, that should do the trick.

Mr Eisner, one of the entertainment world's great survivors, will no doubt try to fight to the death. He may offer yet more corporate governance reforms – though the easy ones are mostly done. He will point out that Comcast's opening offer, originally worth $27 a share and falling, is too low – though Comcast has surely known all along that it will have to raise its offer closer to the $35 that Lawrence Haverty of State Street Research says would tempt institutional investors. The fact is, if Disney's board really wants to keep one of the world's iconic companies independent, its best strategy may be to replace Mr Eisner forthwith. Otherwise, Comcast will soon be doing it instead.

Source: 'The battle for the Magic Kingdom', *The Economist*, 17 February 2004.
© The Economist Newspaper Limited, London (17 February 2004).

Case Questions

1 Why has Disney become an acquisition target?

2 What strategies would an acquirer pursue in order to restore profitability?

3 Do you think Comstat have the capabilities to pursue these strategies?

4 If you were a Disney shareholder, what would you wish should happen and why?

5 What conclusions do you draw from Roy Disney's (public) letter of resignation and public criticism of Eisner?

Further reading and references

Angwin, DN (1996) 'After the fall', *Management Today*, April, pp. 56–8.

Angwin, DN (2000) *Implementing Successful Post-Acquisition Management*, Pearson Education Ltd, London.

Angwin, DN (2001) 'Mergers and acquisitions across European borders: national perspectives on pre-acquisition due diligence and the use of professional advisers', *Journal of World Business*, Spring.

Angwin, DN (2003) 'Strategy as exploration and interconnection', Chapter 8 in S Cummings and D Wilson (eds) *Images of Strategy*, Blackwell Publishers, Oxford.

Angwin, DN, Stern, P and Bradley, S (2004) 'Condemned or redeemed: the target CEO in a hostile takeover', *Long Range Planning*, Vol 37, 3 June.

Angwin, DN and Saville, B (1997) 'Strategic Perspectives on European Cross-Border Acquisitions: A View from Top European Executives', *European Management Journal*, **15**, **4**, pp. 423–35.

Buono, AF and Bowditch, JL (1989) *The Human Side of Mergers and Acquisitions: Managing Collisions Between People and Organizations*, Jossey-Bass, San Francisco.

Calori, R and Lubatkin, M (1995) 'Euro-mergers 1993: Viewpoints and Predictions', in G Von Krogh, A Sinatra and H Singh (eds) *Perspectives on the Management of Acquisitions*, Macmillan.

Capron, L (1999) 'The long term performance of horizontal acquisitions', *Strategic Management Journal*, **20**, **11**, pp. 987–1018.

Cartwright, S and Cooper, C (1996) *Acquisitions – the Human Factor*, Butterworth-Heinemann

Child, J and Faulkner, D (1998) *Strategies of Co-operation: Managing Alliances, Networks, and Joint Ventures*, Oxford University Press, Oxford.

Cohen, WM and Levinthal, DA (1990) 'Absorptive Capacity: A New Perspective on Learning and Innovation', *Administrative Science Quarterly*, **3**, pp. 128–52.

Contractor, FJ and Lorange, P (eds) (1988) *Cooperative Strategies in International Business*, Lexington Books, Lexington MA.

Dussauge, P and Garrette, B (1999) *Co-operative Strategy: Competing Successfully through Strategic Alliances*, John Wiley & Sons, Chichester.

Hamel, G (1991) 'Competition for Competence and Inter-Partner Learning within International Strategic Alliances', *Strategic Management Journal*, **23**, special issue, pp. 83–103.

Hamel, G and Prahalad, CK (1989) 'Collaborate with your competitors – and win', *Harvard Business Review*, **67**, **1**, pp. 133–9.

Haspeslagh, P and Jemison, D (1991) *Managing Acquisitions*, Free Press, New York.

Johnson, G and Scholes, K (2002) *Exploring Corporate Strategy*, 6th edition, Pearson Education, Harlow.

Jones, CS (1982) *Successful Management of Acquisitions*, Derek Beattie, London.

Killing, JP (1983) *Strategies for Joint Venture Success*, London, Croom Helm, London.

Kogut, B (1988) 'Joint Ventures: Theoretical and Empirical Perspectives', *Strategic Management Journal*, **19**, **4**, pp. 319–32.

KPMG (1998) *KPMG Deal Watch*.

Mirvis, PH and Marks, ML (1992) *Managing the Merger: Making it Work*, Prentice Hall, Englewood Cliffs, NJ.

Mockler, RJ (1999) *Multinational Strategic Alliances*, Wiley, Chichester.

Morris, D and Hergert, M (1987) 'Trends in International Collaborative Agreements', *Columbia Journal of World Business*, **19**, **4**, pp. 319–32.

Nonaka, I (1991) 'The Knowledge Creating Company', *Harvard Business Review*, November/December, pp. 96–104.

Porter, ME (1987) 'From Competitive Advantage to Corporate Strategy', *Harvard Business Review*, May/June, pp. 2–21.

Porter, M (1980) *Competitive Strategy*, Free Press, New York.

Schaan, JL and Beamish, PW (1988) 'Joint Venture General Managers in LDCs', in FJ Contractor and P Lorange (eds) *Cooperative Strategies in International Business*, Lexington Books, Lexington MA.

Scherer, FM (1980) *Industrial Market Structure and Economic Performance*, Houghton Mifflin, Boston.

Sudarsanam, S (1994) *The essence of mergers and acquisitions*, Financial Times Prentice Hall

Weston, F, Chung, KS and Siu, JA (2003) *Take-overs, Restructuring and Corporate Governance*, 2nd edition, Prentice Hall, Englewood Cliffs, NJ.

Chapter 11

Global strategies and international advantage

Introduction

This chapter reviews the forces that are shaping the global economy and the responses that are being made by firms. We look at the characteristics of 'global' and 'multidomestic' strategies. We review the evolution of the multinational enterprise (MNE) and examine the contrasts between MNEs that are multidomestic, global and transnational.

> *Over the past few years the concept of global strategy has taken the world of multinational enterprises (MNEs) by storm. Scores of articles in the* Harvard Business Review, Fortune, The Economist, *and other popular journals have urged multinationals to 'go global' in their strategies. The topic has clearly*

Chapter contents

captured the attention of MNE managers. Conferences on global strategy, whether organized by the Conference Board in New York, The Financial Times in London, or Nomura Securities in Tokyo have attracted enthusiastic corporate support and sizeable audiences. Even in the relatively slow-moving world of academe the issue of globalization of industries and companies has emerged as a new bandwagon, as manifest in the large number of papers on the topic presented at recent meetings of the Academy of Management, the Academy of International Business, and the Strategic Management Society. 'Manage globally' appears to be the latest battle cry in the world of international business. (Ghoshal, 1987.)

11.1 International business: the context for international strategy

11.1.1 Definition of terms

This interaction of world, country, industry and company is inherently complex. In this section we introduce some of the terminology used in international business so that we can distinguish the concepts that we use from the words and phrases that are used in practice. The approach used here follows that of Rugman and Hodgetts' (2003) excellent introduction to **international business**.

International business is the study of transactions taking place across national borders for the purposes of satisfying the needs of individuals and organizations. These transactions consist of trade (called **world trade**), which is exporting and importing, and capital transfers – foreign direct investment. Over half of all world trade and about 80 per cent of all foreign direct investment is carried out by the 500 largest firms in the world. These companies are called **multinational enterprises** (**MNEs**). Typically they are headquartered in one country but have operations in one or more other countries. In 2000 the MNEs that earned over $100 billion annual revenue were:

Exxon (USA)

Wal-Mart (USA)

General Motors (USA)

Ford Motor (USA)

DaimlerChrysler (Germany)

Royal Dutch/Shell Group (UK/Netherlands)

British Petroleum (UK)

General Electric (USA)

Mitsubishi (Japan)

Toyota (Japan)

Mitsui (Japan)

Citigroup (USA)

Itochu (Japan)

TotalFinaElf (France)

Nippon Telegraph & Telephone (Japan)

Enron (USA)

Each of these comes from one of three geographic locales: the USA, Japan or the EU. This group is called the *triad*. Of these sixteen companies, seven are from the USA, five from Japan and four from the EU. The North American Free Trade Association (NAFTA) is a regional free trade agreement between Canada, the USA and Mexico. NAFTA is often used in place of the USA as the North American element of the triad. Also Asia can be used in place of Japan to reflect the size and growth of markets such as China, India and Indonesia etc. Table 11.1 shows the breakdown of world trade by region. World trade is the sum of all export and imports. The EU is the biggest 'trader', accounting for 35 per cent of world trade, with Asia at 25 per cent and North America at 22 per cent.

Foreign direct investment (FDI) is capital invested in other nations by MNEs through their control of their foreign subsidiaries and affiliates. Most of the world's FDI is invested both by and within the triad. This has implications for the pattern of trade and industrial activity and is a highly controversial issue (see, for example, the discussions at the Cancun meeting of the World Trade Organization about access by underdeveloped regions and countries to the rich markets of the OECD countries). The USA is an excellent example of a country that is a major target of investment as well as a major investor in other countries. In 1999 nearly $990 billion was invested in the USA and the USA itself (through its MNEs) invested over $1132 billion in all other countries. Table 11.2 shows a breakdown of US inward and outward FDI by region. This demonstrates the concentration of Europe and Asia.

Table 11.1 World trade 2000

	Imports $bn		Exports $bn		World trade $bn	
North America	1692.8	25.6%	1213.6	19.2%	2906.4	22.4%
EU	2284.9	34.6%	2283.0	35.8%	4567.9	35.2%
Asia	1563.5	23.7%	1742.6	27.4%	3306.1	25.5%
Othres	1067.5	16.2%	1129.5	17.7%	2197.0	16.9%
Total	66087.7		6368.7		12977.6	

Source: adapted from Rugman and Hodgetts, 2003, p. 6.

Table 11.2 USA: inward and outward FDI 1999

	Into USA $bn	From USA $bn
Total	987	1133
Europe	686	582
Latin America	45	223
Africa	2	15
Middle East	7	11
Asia and Pacific	168	186

Source: adapted from Rugman and Hodgetts, 2003, p. 8.

Trade and investment is subject to various rules and procedures. There are many international or supra-national bodies that help to set trading rules and resolve trade disputes. For example:

◆ *The Organization for Economic Co-operation and Development* (OECD) is a group of the 30 wealthiest countries that provides a forum for the discussion of economic, social and governance issues across the world.

◆ *The World Trade Organization* (WTO) is an international body that deals with the rules of trade among member countries. One of its most important functions is to act as a dispute-settlement mechanism.

◆ *The General Agreement on Tariffs and Trade* (GATT) is major trade organization that has been established to negotiate trade concessions among member countries.

The patterns of trade and investment are highly significant and are reflected in the nature of MNEs. The United Nations has identified over 60 000 MNEs but the largest 500 account for 80 per cent of all FDI. Of these 500, 430 are from triad countries (interpreted narrowly to mean USA, EU and Japan); 185 come from the USA, 141 from the EU and 104 from Japan. This means that the triad is a basic unit of analysis for international strategy. It also means that for MNEs the actions and policies of a few key countries are highly important for their corporate strategies. Countries are concerned to maintain and foster their own economic competitiveness. As we have seen from Chapter 12, countries have strong incentives to invest in physical infrastructure and in human capital. In doing so they hope to provide conditions under which business and trade can prosper and macroeconomic goals such as low employment, low inflation and high growth can be sustained.

11.1.2 'National' competitive advantage

Why are some firms able to innovate consistently while others are not? Michael Porter (1990) provided an intriguing answer to this question. He undertook a comprehensive study of 100 industries in 10 countries. It is not simply due to the strength of individual corporate strategies. He found that the success of nations and their individual firms is determined by four broad attributes – factor (supply) conditions, demand conditions, related and supporting industries, and market (industry) structure. He called this the **diamond of national advantage** (*see* Figure 11.1).

First, it is not just factor endowments and factor conditions that are an index of competitiveness – these are the typical concerns of government policy. Also on the supply side is the supporting, related industry infrastructure, through which various externalities come into play. Thus, an automobile assembly industry is advantaged by a domestic infrastructure of auto component suppliers, which themselves have sustainable competitive advantages. Similarly, domestic rivalry and intensity of competition are seen to have a direct effect on competitiveness.

Finally, Porter points to demand conditions as a determinant of competitiveness. The size, growth and character of demand shape the supplying industries. The sophistication of local demand will be reflected in the developing characteristics of domestic suppliers. The point to take away from Porter's diamond is that the companies are embedded in and influenced by their industries, and these industries are in turn embedded in a wider economic and social structure. However, it is not clear from this analysis, nor is it asserted in this analysis, that competitive advantage is necessarily determined by the broader economic context. It is possible to see that clusters of firms and clusters of industries might have shared benefits from a common location, at the expense of (in terms of competitive advantage) firms located elsewhere. Thus, it has been advantageous to be an auto assembler in Japan and a chemical manufacturer in Germany. It may also be the case that in these circumstances it might not pay any one local player to attempt to be different[1] from other local players.

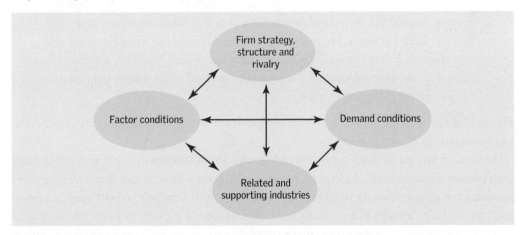

Figure 11.1 The determinants of national advantage (Porter's diamond)

[1] 'Different' in this context meaning in the strategic sense of different generic strategies or different strategic groups.

Strategically, any one firm can choose between shared local benefits ('nationality is destiny') and striving to create a unique and distinctive position.

11.1.3 The internationalization process

From this discussion we can see that the MNE has two areas of concern: its home country and its host country/countries. The linkages across these areas are in the end manifested by the cash flows across country boundaries. These are influenced by home and host government policies and by the actions of supra-national bodies in setting trade rules and regulations. Rugman and Hodgetts (2003, pp. 39–40) identify three main characteristics of MNEs:

1 MNEs have to be responsive to a number of forces across and within countries, some of which are competition related (as per the five forces) and some of which are government related (as per the diamond).

2 MNEs draw on a common pool of resources that are typically founded in the home country and which are made available throughout the MNE's affiliates.

3 MNEs link their operations through a common strategic vision and a unified international strategy.

What is **international strategy?** According to Hill and Jones (1995, p. 233):

> *Companies that pursue an international strategy try to create value by transferring valuable skills and products to foreign markets where indigenous competitors lack those skills and products. Most international companies have created value by transferring differentiated product offerings developed at home to new markets overseas. Accordingly they tend to centralise product development functions (for instance, R&D) at home. However, they also tend to establish manufacturing and marketing functions in each major country in which they do business … Ultimately, in most international companies the head office retains tight control over marketing and product strategy.*

Figure 11.2 illustrates the stages by which companies enter into foreign markets and eventually become fully blown MNEs.

Domestic firms go through a process of learning about foreign markets and minimizing the risks attached to them. Licensing, for example, gives access to the firm's standardized products for distribution by third parties in new markets. Similarly, export gains access to markets initially through independent local sales agents. If exports to particular countries become sufficiently large then there is the possibility to set up one's own sales force. This is an important stage. It marks the arrival of sales in sufficient quantities to gain efficiencies from the fixed costs of own sales activities. It also represents a stage at which direct contact with customers becomes possible with potential for customization and differentiation.

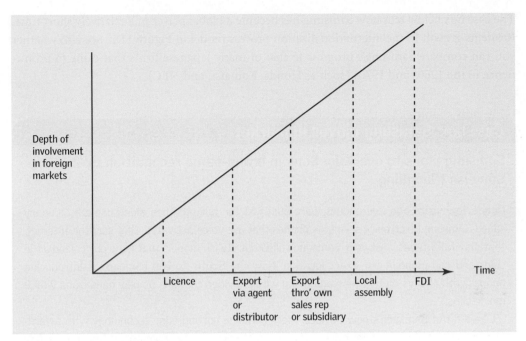

Figure 11.2 The internationalization process

It also results in familiarity at first hand with local conditions and could lead to direct investment in production and marketing and possible other value chain activities. This stage of FDI is what marks out an MNE from domestically rooted companies. At this stage there is a risk investment in a new territory and the MNE has to manifest the three characteristics shown above, namely local responsiveness, distinctive central resources and an overarching strategy.

There are many reasons why companies decide to take the plunge and take on the new, often unfamiliar, risks facing a multinational company. The usual reasons are:

1 to diversify against the risks and uncertainties of the domestic (home country) business cycle;

2 to tap into new and growing markets;

3 to 'follow' competitors;

4 to reduce costs by (i) building larger volumes and gaining scale effects, (ii) gaining access to lower factor costs, and (iii) 'internalizing' control by eliminating middlemen and other transactions costs;

5 to overcome barriers to trade; and

6 to protect intellectual property rights by undertaking value chain activities in-house rather than giving third parties access through licensing and sales agreements.

The case box below tells how Samsung has become a global player in a relatively short time. Relate its growth to the internationalization process model in Figure 11.2. See also whether you can compare Samsung's progress to that of many Japanese firms that came to prominence in the 1960s and 1970s (such as Honda, Komatsu and NEC).

Case box: Samsung moves upmarket

Samsung plans to overtake Sony in brand-name recognition by 2005 – Sony isn't laughing

Only a few years ago, cell phones were built just for talking. Then along came a company called Samsung Electronics selling us phones that are voice activated, that surf the Internet, that play MP3 tunes. Last year Samsung rolled out stylish models that keep our calendars in color and can pinpoint our exact location. Now the South Korean company is introducing phones with always-on text messaging and wireless video that lets us play games and watch movie clips.

Like a lot of Samsung's new devices, these combine cutting-edge technology with award-winning design—at premium prices. That's something new for a company that only a few years ago was known as a mass marketer of cheap TVs and VCRs. Since 1997, however, Samsung has begun rubbing shoulders with the market leaders in high-end cell phones, DVD players, elegant flat plasma TVs and a wide range of other consumer products. These gadgets are sometimes less expensive than those of Japanese or Finnish competitors—but by no means inferior.

Eric Kim, 47, Samsung's savvy Korean-American marketing chief, boldly suggests that he hopes to surpass Sony in brand recognition by 2005. Don't laugh; Sony CEO Nobuyuki Idei certainly isn't laughing. Samsung has the second most recognizable consumer-electronics brand in the world, according to Interbrand, the New York City-based consultancy. Idei has said privately that Samsung is on the verge of overtaking Sony in the consumer-products race. Graeme Bateman, head of research in Seoul for Japanese investment bank Nomura Securities, says Samsung is 'no longer making poor equivalents of Sony products. It is making things people want.'

What's more, at a time when most of the world's tech companies are still shuttering plants and trimming R & D to weather the global economic slump, Samsung is extending its reach. Bolstered by the resurgent Korean economy—which is expected to grow 3% to 6% this year after nearly collapsing during the 1997 Asian financial crisis—Samsung Electronics' worldwide revenue reached $25 billion last year.

That's not even half the revenue stream of giant Sony, but Samsung Electronics is growing fast. It is the best performer in the family-controlled conglomerate that spawned it, the Samsung Group. Investors are pouring money into the stock. Korea's consumers are spending more than ever, and they just happen to be among the most wired people on the planet, with easy access to broadband connections and new wireless local-area networks. So Samsung has an unparalleled testing platform for new gadgets right in its backyard.

Since the early 1990s, Samsung has led the global market in dram semiconductors, the memory chips that are vital to almost every digital product we use. During the current slump, as competitors like Hitachi and NEC have been backing away from the chip business, Samsung has been diving in, introducing two new lines. The company has leveraged its digital know-how to dominate the manufacturing of computer monitors and state-of-the-art flat-panel displays. In 2002 Samsung, in conjunction with Texas Instruments, introduced the world's first 50-in. TV with digital light-processing technology, now used mostly in movie theaters. Analysts who have seen the picture say it is sharper than anything on the market. And Samsung revolutionized the world of microwave ovens with a technology that senses when your food is properly cooked.

Samsung got into the U.S. phone business only in 1997, through a $600 million deal with Sprint and pledged that it would become a Top 5 phone maker within five years. It made it in two, with the clamshell-shaped 3500, which became America's top-selling cell phone in 2000. Last year, among a rush of other introductions, Samsung started selling the I300, a Palm-based PDA with a built-in wireless phone. Although there are plenty of combo PDA phones on the market, none have sold as well or enjoyed as much acclaim. 'People pull these out at meetings to show off, which makes them a walking brand advertisement,' says Peter Skarzynski, a Samsung Telecommunications America vice president. 'That's what Sony's Walkman did for them.' And that's what Samsung's products and a big advertising investment are doing for it. In 2001 its global brand recognition grew a stunning 22%.

Throughout the global slump of 2000–2, Samsung has continued to invest in new processes and research. The company refined its semiconductor and liquid-crystal-display operations so effectively that traditional competition from Tokyo was upended. 'Samsung is more cost effective, and its manufacturing technology is better than at companies like Sharp and Hitachi,' says Shiro Mikoshiba, a Nomura Securities analyst in Tokyo. 'The Japanese stopped competing two years ago.'

The next stop in Samsung's digital march is the living room. To that end, the company has worked with Microsoft to develop Home Media Center, designed to control everything from your DVD player to the PC. Last June, Texas Instruments and Samsung signed an agreement to develop ultra thin, large-screen televisions based on TI's digital light-processing technology. In 1999 TI turned down a Samsung partnership offer, thinking it would be better to work with 'established' brands. By last year it was clear that TI's initial partners were moving too slowly to get anything to market in good time. With Samsung, it took only a matter of months. The new 50-in. television made its debut in January 2002 at the Consumer Electronics Show in Las Vegas, and videophiles like Evan Powell of ProjectorCentral declared it an instant hit.

For all its technical prowess, Samsung faces big-league competition in its quest to domi-nate the digital home. Microsoft, AOL Time Warner, Apple and Sony are among the heavy hitters that are also betting that someday everything from our alarm clocks to our refrigera-tors will be linked to a constant stream of information and entertainment from the Internet. (AOL Time Warner has formed partnerships to develop digital hardware with both Samsung and Sony.) Samsung is gambling that it can move faster than its bigger rivals.

Samsung has demonstrated a century's worth of catch-up in a very short time. Now the question is whether they can fulfill the new expectations for Samsung's future.

Flat-panel monitors	DRAM chips	DVD players	Mobile handsets
1. Samsung 13.1%	1. Samsung 27.9%	1. Sony 23.3%	1. Nokia 35.6%
2. Philips 11.3%	2. Philips 20.3%	2. Samsung 11.7%	2. Motorola 15.0%
			3. Samsung 7.2%

Sources: Frank Gibney Jr, iSuppli Stanford Resources, Semico Research Corp., NPD Intellect
Source: extracted from *Time.com* March 25, 2002. © 2002 by Time, Inc. Reprinted by permission.

11.2 Globalization

There is no doubt that **globalization** and internationalization have, as ideas, fired the imagination, even though the words themselves are cumbersome and awkward. In this section we intend to give an economic meaning to the term globalization.

11.2.1 Global markets and industries

International trade incorporates many different types of competition, and across industries we can observe marked differences in the patterns of international competition. On the supply side of industries, the dimension of competition and of strategic choice in which we are interested is geographic scope, the extents to which firms' activities extend across national borders. But it is the demand side that is more important. We use the term *multido-mestic* (or *multilocal*) to describe industries where the competition in any one country is independent of competition elsewhere. We use the term *global* when competition in one country is influenced by competition elsewhere. Multidomestic is the situation where markets are different in their consumer behaviour patterns. Thus, the market for foods can be seen to be very different across the countries of the European Union and even wider across the countries of the world. By contrast, the market for Coca-Cola is broadly similar across the world, with consumers exhibiting similar if not the same utility functions and buying behaviour. **Global** markets lead to standard products, whereas **multidomestic** markets lead to product differences and diversity. Multidomestic industries are, as the name implies, a collection of domestic industries. A global industry leads directly to international rivalry. In a multidomestic industry a firm can and should manage its worldwide activities as a portfolio of independent subsidiaries in each country – this is a country-centred strategy and relatively little co-ordination is necessary or valuable. In a global industry, to have a global strategy a firm must develop and implement a strategy that integrates its activities in various countries, even though some portion of the firm's activities must take place in each individual country.

Figure 11.3 puts this approach to globalization in a broader context. 'Global' refers, broadly speaking, to an entwined web of economic forces. The world dimension indicates the extent to which there is economic interdependence between countries, as indicated by the cross-border flows of goods, services, capital and knowledge. At the country level, countries will differ in their degree of linkage between their economy and the rest of the world, using the same indicators. Our definition of global industry has thus to be seen in the context of the worldwide pattern and the role of individual countries. At the firm level, we are looking at the extent to which its revenue and asset bases are spread across borders.

11.2.2 Global companies

Table 11.3 indicates the degree of internationalization of Fortune 100 companies. Although we have a reasonably clear concept of what constitutes global at the industry level, it is much harder to distinguish a 'global' firm from any other. From Table 11.3 we can see that many firms have a high proportion of sales and production abroad. But there are deeper levels of internationalization. Table 11.3 picks out research and development, management style and membership of boards of directors as indicators of the extent to which firms can transcend national boundaries.

The nature of globalization is complex and multidimensional, even without bringing in broader issues of culture, behaviour, national tastes and so on. Accordingly, there have been

Figure 11.3 Determinants of 'globalization'

Table 11.3 Degree of internationalization of Fortune 100 companies (early 1990s)

- ◆ *c*.40 companies generate >50% of sales abroad
- ◆ <20 companies maintain >50% of production capacity abroad
- ◆ 13 companies have >10% of shareholdings abroad
- ◆ R&D remains firmly domestic
- ◆ Executive boards and management styles remain solidly national
- ◆ Almost all highly internationalized companies originate from 'small' economies:
  - – Netherlands: Philips, Royal Dutch/Shell (60% Dutch), Unilever (40% Dutch)
  - – Sweden: Volvo, Electrolux, ABB (50% Swedish)
  - – Switzerland: Nestlé, Ciba-Geigy, ABB (50% Swiss)

---

many attempts to capture the term in a single definition. The original proponent of globalization was Theodore Levitt (1983), whose concept was that of *global standardization* – a single global market with standard products and a corporate focus on gaining efficiencies through standardization. Kenichi Ohmae (1985) introduced the idea of the 'triad' – to compete effectively, firms should be present in each of the three major regions of the world. This has become known as *global localization*. Wisse Dekker, an erstwhile chairman of Philips, saw globalization as *assembly abroad* to *circumvent competition*. More recent commentators see *global niches* sitting alongside domestic redoubts. Toyota in its Annual Report in 1995 said:

> *Our global strategy used to centre on 'world cars' which we would modify slightly to accommodate demand in different markets. To-day our focus is shifting to models that we develop and manufacture for selected regional markets.*

We seem to be moving from a market-based focus on standardization (standard products and centralized production facilities) to a resource-based view of standardization. This would argue for a common approach to knowledge and learning, and resources and capabilities across the world, but with products adapted to local or regional needs from a common core competence.

Table 11.4 suggests what might be the deeper drivers. There are five forces at work. The first is a *cultural homogenization* – a 'global village' argument that we leave for you to reflect

Table 11.4 Why globalization?

- ◆ Cultural homogenization ('global village')
- ◆ Convergence of markets
- ◆ Globalization of customers
- ◆ Cost drivers
  - – economies of scale and scope
  - – increase in levels of fixed cost
- ◆ Fundamental changes in industry structure
  - – deregulation, privatization
  - – technological change

---

upon using your own experience. Two of the forces are from the demand side, *convergence of markets* and *growing similarity of customers*. Markets in this context are about the infrastructure and the processes by which markets work. This covers legislation, application of competition law, organization of selling and distribution systems, consumer protection laws, local tariffs and so on. The markets for agricultural products are vastly different between Russia and the United States. The markets for packaged groceries are different between European countries, to the extent that the laws governing price promotions and use of television advertising are different and the extent to which superstores are allowed to develop as between France and Italy, for example. One of the aims of the Single Market Acts in the EC in 1992 was to create broadly similar market conditions across Western Europe – the 'level playing field'.

The customer argument is more plainly about the degree of similarity between the utility functions of customers in different locations and the impact this has on buying behaviour. This can be exemplified by considering two buyers of auto components, one for Ford Motor Company's plants in Europe the other for General Motors. Their buying criteria are likely to be very similar and component companies are very likely to be designing and selling very similar components across Europe. It is less clear that Italian and English shoppers in supermarkets will have the same attitudes and ideas about buying food products. To the extent that these buyers are fundamentally different in their behaviour, the suppliers will be adapting their products to reflect different requirements in Italy and in England.

On the supply side of industries, the cost drivers are very important. We learned in Chapter 3 of the significance of economies of scale and experience. The costs of investment can be so high that single national markets, even those of the USA, might be too small to support them. It is difficult to see how the design and development costs of large aeroplanes can be economically supported from even the USA. The development costs of automobiles, prescription drugs, many high-technology new products, and much military hardware require a large international market. It is in the interests of companies, then, to make the offer of a standardized product across the world in competition with the more locally differentiated, but more expensive, options offered by local companies. From a cost point of view, the presence of significant scale and experience effects drives customers towards the cheaper, more standardized options. This is the basis of Levitt's approach to global standardization.

Finally, fundamental changes in industry structure can result in major changes to the underlying economics of industries (for example, through technological change). Coupled with new management teams (for example, through privatization and deregulation) this can change the terms on which companies approach their marketplaces and their opportunities to move across borders. For example, the worldwide trend to the privatization of telecommunications and utility companies has challenged the presumption that the natural market for utilities is domestic only.

Scale is commonly considered to be a major characteristic of being global. But there are other benefits:

- exposure to the world's 'best' practice;
- learning and transfer opportunities of best practice;
- access to technology;
- ability to serve new customer groups;
- ability to anticipate moves of global competitors;
- ability to defend national profit sanctuaries through counter-attack.

In looking at global industries and the firms that compete in them, you should be able to examine and test the proposition that industries do not go global by accident. They are global because of innovations in strategy. **Global strategies** can create advantage only if they:

- change the economics of the industry;
- serve local markets better than the local incumbents;
- are hard to emulate;
- are sustainable;
- are capable of further development.

As a firm gains experience in operating within a global industry, some of the original strategic innovations become embedded into the industry structure and thus, the industry economics will have characteristics such as large-scale economies – high and rising R&D costs, extensive interaction with governments, and links with changes in country infrastructures. But there are still many strategy choices open to each firm: for example, how to increase local content without sacrificing global scale, how to increase product homogeneity through design, how to shape demand, how to develop systems to make co-ordination easier. Some firms will be striving to develop local/domestic niches, others will be focusing on global segments, and others might be attempting global standardization.

11.2.3 Globalization and the value chain

The key strategic choices in globalization revolve around local differentiation versus global standardization. These might be seen as polar opposites, but more usually the question is how to secure the right blend between the two. What would this mean for how we conduct our business?

Figure 11.4 enables us to think of the implications of global choices in terms of how we manage the activities in the value chain, where we locate them, and how we co-ordinate the whole chain. The opportunity for global standardization occurs when:

- upstream value chain activities can be decoupled from downstream activities and, in particular, from buyer locations;

- these activities are a large part of total costs;
- scale effects are important in these activities.

We see that these conditions hold with automobiles. Production does not need to be close to the customer, nor even to the sales channel. Assembly is a very large part of the cost and there are very big scale economies. Conversely, multidomestic industries exist where:

- downstream activities are tied to buyer locations and market-specific entry barriers can be created;
- these activities are a large part of total costs.

These are situations where the competitive advantages reside primarily with the downstream, and the focus of strategic attention lies with managing its capacity to differentiate the product offering. This is typical of retailing, many service operations, such as investment banking, and consumer packaged goods.

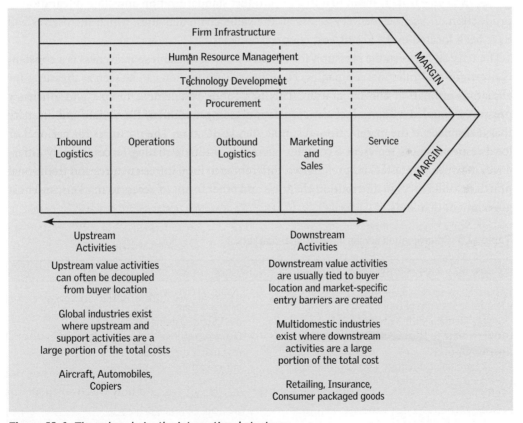

Figure 11.4 The value chain: the international strategy
Source: Adapted from Porter, 1985, p. 46. Reprinted with permission of The Free Press, a division of Simon and Schuster Adult Publishing Group. Copyright by the Free Press. All rights reserved.

The possibility for globalization usually means that the value chain has to be partitioned in some way. The key strategic dimensions of choice are:

◆ Where to perform each activity in the value chain – the *configuration* question.

◆ How to link similar activities wherever they are located.

◆ How to co-ordinate all the activities in the value chain – the *co-ordination* question.

The degree of co-ordination is in general dependent on how globally standardized the product is or, conversely, how varied the local market conditions are. Table 11.5 summarizes the kinds of high and low co-ordination patterns that might be observed. The contrast between high and low degrees of co-ordination stem from the balance between the two types of competitive pressure that are evident in global markets: pressures for cost reductions and efficiency, and pressures for local responsiveness. Typically, local differentiation requires low co-ordination, as each country operation contains much of the value chain that it needs, and those inputs it does need, such as components, will be relatively standardized. Pressures for global efficiency usually mean that there is product standardization and close integration of production and service delivery across all the value chain activities, which themselves will have been located in the lowest-cost regions/countries.

The tension between the pressures for efficiency and for local responsiveness is a constant concern for multinational companies. The efficiency dimension can be seen as pressures for global co-ordination and integration. This is a subtle restatement of cost and efficiency pressures, coupled with product standardization, taking account of the variety and diversity that takes place at the margin around simple standardization. The pressures for national or local responsiveness represent a complex aggregate of differentiating forces, namely differences in consumer tastes and preferences, differences in local infrastructures and traditional practices, differences in distribution channels and other forms of access to markets, and host government demands.

Table 11.5 Co-ordination across international markets

Reasons for high co-ordination	Reasons for low co-ordination
Share know-how and learning Reinforce brand reputation Supply identical differentiation worldwide Differentiate to local buyers by meeting their needs anywhere Seek bargaining counters with governments Respond to competitors' flexibility	Respond to diverse local conditions - product needs - marketing systems - business practices - raw material sources - infrastructure Circumvent government restrictions on flow of goods or information Avoid high co-ordination costs Acknowledge organizational difficulties of achieving co-ordination across subsidiaries

11.2.4 Sources of competitive advantage

As we have seen in Chapter 8, corporate strategy is about exploiting economies of scope across the business units of the corporation. Global strategy requires the exploitation of economies of scale, scope, knowledge and learning across national boundaries. Ghoshal (1987) provides an excellent framework (*see* Table 11.6) for understanding the sources of advantage that can spring from 'globalization' and the strategic objectives that can be pursued. As Segal-Horn puts it:

> Ghoshal creates a roadmap to guide managers of multinational companies through their choices for global strategic management. (Segal-Horn, 1998, p. 325)

Ghoshal refers to this framework as a mapping of means and ends. The means are the sources of advantage and the ends are the strategic objectives. The goals are an elegant articulation of three contrasting but complementary themes:

- *Achieving efficiency* is the dominant perspective in strategic management, where the objective is to maximize the value of the ratio between outputs and inputs. The basic strategies of cost leadership and differentiation are both maximizers in this sense, cost strategies reducing the value of inputs and differentiation strategies increasing the exchange value of the outputs.

- The notion of *managing risks* gets far too little attention in the academic and in the business literatures. Ghoshal identifies several different categories of risk:
  - macroeconomic risks
  - political or policy risks
  - competitive risks, and
  - resource risks.

- *Innovation, learning and adaptation* are an outcome of resource-based thinking. Here Ghoshal makes an interesting argument that increasing geographic scope ('globalization') is in effect an exposure to diversity and variety. The twin pressures of managing for efficiency and for local variety impose a greater need to innovate, to learn and to adapt than is faced by a purely domestic firm.

Ghoshal maintains there are three fundamental tools for building global competitive advantage:

- The first is to exploit the differences in input and output markets in different countries. This is to exploit **comparative advantage** – the economic characteristics that make national economies different.

- The second is to achieve *economies of scale*.

- The third is to exploit *economies of scope*.

Table 11.6 Global strategy: sources of competitive advantage

Strategic objectives	National differences	Scale economies	Scope economies
Achieving efficiency in current operations	Benefiting differences in factor costs – wages and cost of capital	Expanding and exploiting potential scale economies in each activity	Sharing of investments and costs across products and businesses
Managing risks	Managing different kinds of risk arising from market policy-induced changes in comparative advantages of different countries	Balancing scale with strategic and operational flexibility	Portfolio diversification and risks of options and side bets
Innovation, learning and adaptation	Learning from societal differences in organizational and managerial processes and systems	Benefiting from experience-based cost reduction and innovation	Shared across organizational components in different markets or businesses

Source: Ghoshal, 1987.

The term **national differences** refers to what economists call **factor conditions** or differences in factor costs between different countries. According to international trade theory a country will export those goods that make use of the factor conditions with which it is relatively well endowed. Thus, a country such as China is concentrating on modern assembly plants in which the low cost of Chinese labour plays a significant role in reducing costs. MNEs seek to locate their activities in regions with specific factor advantages. For example, BT along with many UK-based banks are relocating their call centres to India to take advantage of low costs but a skilful labour force. Rugman and Hodgetts (2003, p. 17) cite the example of the Netherlands as the world's leading exporter of flowers. It has maintained its position by creating research institutes in the cultivation, packaging and shipping of flowers. Therefore, any company wishing to compete in this industry has to have an operation in the Netherlands. Similarly, in Formula 1 racing the central cluster of activity is to be found in Motor Sport Valley in the South of England. Here are to be found skilled labour and craftsmen in engineering, advanced materials, software and project management. For Ferrari to become successful again in F1 racing it had to gain access to these skills by first establishing an operation in England and then finding ways to transfer this knowledge throughout their Italian home base.

From Ghoshal's framework we are able to articulate the nature of the trade-offs between alternative strategy choices. In other words, the framework is not deterministic, but it does enable discussion of the consistencies and contradictions among different moves.

In the next section we will re-visit some of the basic concepts that lie behind globalization and will return to Ghoshal's organizing framework at the end of the chapter. But before we move on, it is helpful to examine the internationalization of service industries (Segal-Horn, 1993). Service industries have traditionally been seen as domestic or local, but there have been many celebrated attempts to go global, some of which have been seen to fail (for example, Saatchi & Saatchi) and some of which are clearly successes (for example, American Express). Segal-Horn's contribution is to take Chandler's logic of internationalization (and also Ghoshal's later framework) as developed for manufacturing firms and show how the basic assumptions are now relevant for service organizations. Thus, we see that scale and scope economies – the roots of strategy analysis – are as relevant for service firms as for any others. With service firms, it is clear that the source of scope economies is rooted for the most part in the way in which knowledge and information can create scope benefits. It is worth noting also that the service element of hitherto traditional manufacturing has increased dramatically and that the role of services in the advanced economies now out-weighs that of manufacturing (Quinn 1992). Thus, the consequences of Segal-Horn's approach are significant both in terms of the economy as a whole and for the nature of inter-nationalization as a knowledge-based phenomenon.

Read the case box on US multinationals, which argues that the conventional assumption of globalization is misplaced. You should also look again at Table 11.3, which uses the same data sources. What is the criterion you would use to assess whether a company is 'global'? Also, what difference would this make to the strategies that companies should follow and the relationships that they should cultivate with their home governments and with their many host governments?

Case box: **US multinationals are regional not global**

Karl Moore and Alan Rugman argue that globalization is not what it seems

'Go global'. That's what CEOs have been hearing from gurus and academics for a while now. But how global are the US' biggest MNEs? We argue not very global at all. Each year *Fortune* magazine ranks the world's largest MNEs in its annual *Fortune 500*. The US accounts for 185 of the companies: the ERU has 141 and Japan 104. Together this 'triad' has 430 of the top 500 companies.

But, if you examine the data on the US' 25 largest multinationals it becomes clear that they are what we would call home-region based. Of the US' 25 largest MNEs 22 have more than 50% of their sales in their home region of North America. None of these US MNEs are 'global'. For example, Wal-Mart has 94.1% of its sales in the North American Free Trade Area (NAFTA); GM has 81% – and so on. Indeed, the average intra-regional sales figures for all the 185 US MNEs is 77.3%. With well over two-thirds of their sales in North America, these are home-based triad MNEs. So much for the globe-girdling US MNE.

Only IBM, ranked at number seven, is a truly 'global' firm, with over 20% of its sales in each region of the triad. Other US global firms (not in the top 25) are Intel and Coca-Cola. Indeed, only eight of the *Fortune 500* firms in the world are global – the others are Sony, Philips, Canon, Flextronics, and LVMH.

'So what?' the hard-nosed CEO may ask. Good question: what this data tells us is that US companies should focus corporate energies and push government policies to secure access to the vital regional NAFTA market. At the same time US companies should continue to increase their involvement in the two other regions of the triad economies, the EYU and the small number of critical Asian economies. That is the reality of today's global economy.

Source: extract from Karl Moore and Alan Rugman, *Business Strategy Review*, vol 14, no. 4, p. 2.
Reproduced with permission of Blackwell Publishing.

11.3 Strategic choices

11.3.1 Strategic positioning

There are four basic strategies that companies use to enter and compete in the international environment: multidomestic, international, global and transnational. These are covered in detail in Bartlett and Ghoshal (1989) and are depicted in Figure 11.5.

Multidomestic strategies are, as we described above, country centred with extensive customization for local markets and with an almost full set of value chain activities in each major market. They do transfer skills and products developed at the home base, but high degrees of local discretion are given to meet local conditions. Typically, these strategies cannot realize value from centralized, scale-effective, experience-rich production facilities. Bartlett and Ghoshal describe multidomestic companies as decentralized federations (Figure 11.5) and regard them as typically European, being conceived in days of higher transport and communication costs and higher tariffs.

International strategies create value by transferring key skills, capabilities and products to local markets. The degree of differentiation developed in the home base is advanced and the intent is that the differentiation delivered in each local market reflects this. Thus, local differentiation is complementary to that from the centre. However, the organization is usually country centred and local managers have important degrees of discretion in deciding what product portfolio to offer and how it should be presented locally. Product development and R&D tends to be centralized in the home base, but other value chain activities are usually closer to market. Head office retains close control over marketing strategy and product strategy, and also exercises close financial control. Bartlett and Ghoshal regard this as typically North American – born in the 1950s and 1960s, as US companies began to realize the benefits of the scale and technological achievement of 50 years of distinctively large, progressive markets. They see this form

Figure 11.5 International strategic environments: late 1990s
Source: Adapted from Prahalad and Doz, 1986.

as a co-ordinated federation, the degrees of co-ordination (especially in marketing and finance) being distinctive American contributions to management practice in the post-war years. Many writers are tempted to place international strategies into the bottom-left corner of Figure 11.5. This would be to deny the distinctive co-ordinating power of these companies (for example, Procter & Gamble, IBM, Kellogg, McDonald's, Merck). Moreover, with low co-ordination and low responsiveness, there would not appear to be a sustainable strategy.

Global strategies focus on increasing profitability through product standardization, and capturing the cost reductions that come from location economies (exploiting comparative advantage in Ghoshal's framework in Table 11.6), economies of scale and experience effects, and the organizational focus on procedures and processes that support low costs. Bartlett and Ghoshal see these strategies as quintessentially Japanese, having emerged in the growth years and tariff reduction years of the 1970s and 1980s. These companies are typically highly centralized, with little attempt to build local differentiation (marketing) activity. They do, however, often pursue global branding and 'quality' positioning, along with or after their initial focus on low cost (for example, Sony). Toyota was a good example of a global strategy in the 1980s – its productivity (cars per employee) was about 37 compared to 20 at Ford, which would be regarded as having an international strategy. Many industries can be seen to be global in character. Thus, the semiconductor industry has global standards with enormous worldwide demands for standardized products. Not surprisingly, the players such as Intel, Texas Instruments and Motorola pursue global strategies. Bartlett and Ghoshal describe global companies as centralized hubs, reflecting the high degree of centralization.

Transnational strategies:

> *Exploit experience-based cost economies and location economies, transfer distinctive competences within the company, and at the same time pay attention to pressures for local responsiveness.* (Bartlett and Ghoshal, 1989)

Bartlett and Ghoshal argue that the two dimensions of Figure 11.5 are an incomplete description of the strategic choices. They offer a resource-based addition, suggesting that the need for innovation and learning should be a third dimension (Figure 11.6). With this focus on capabilities, competences (Prahalad and Hamel, 1990, language) and strategic assets (Amit and Schoemaker, 1993, language), they argue that these characteristics do not simply reside in the home base. On the contrary, by careful investment, they can be developed anywhere appropriate in the company's worldwide operations. This is a locational economy (or comparative advantage), where the advantage is in the form of knowledge and capability, rather than low cost. So the flows of skills and products can be in any direction within the worldwide configuration of activities.

The role of the centre is to provide an organizational and strategic context within which the complex flows and interactions can take place. Toyota is a good example, as are other Japanese auto manufacturers such as Nissan and Honda. We saw earlier that Toyota has moved from a focus on the 'world car' to something more regional. This initially involved the development of manufacturing capabilities and sites in North America, Europe and

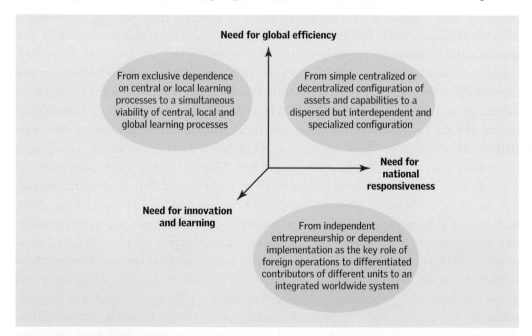

Figure 11.6 The strategic tasks
Source: based on and freely adapted from Bartlett and Ghoshal, 1989.

elsewhere in the world. Along with this goes a spreading of product development beyond Japan.

Unilever is another example. Once it was a classic multidomestic company in the European tradition. It has moved from 17 different and largely self-contained detergents operations in Europe toward a single European entity with detergents being manufactured in a handful of cost-efficient plants, and with standard packaging and advertising across Europe. Unilever's estimate of the cost savings is over $200 million per year. However, Unilever recognizes that there are major differences in distribution channels and that brand values and brand awareness vary a lot across Europe, and therefore, that local responsiveness must not be sacrificed for simple standardization benefits. In other words, Unilever have taken some steps to move from multidomestic to transnational. By contrast, Procter & Gamble have seemingly moved more in the direction of a global strategy from an international position. The transnational company is likely to need a matrix structure (see below) and is increasingly likely to move towards a network organization (Figure 11.7).

Strategic choice involves making trade-offs. It is not always clear what strategies should be followed because it is rare that one choice will dominate all other possibilities. The advantage of a pure global strategy is the ability to become a low-cost player, but the disadvantage is the lack of local responsiveness (*see* the Matsushita example in Bartlett and Ghoshal 1989).

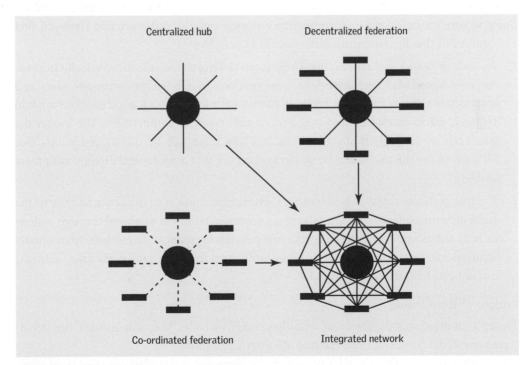

Figure 11.7 Alternative organizational solutions
Source: adapted from Bartlett and Ghoshal, 1989, Chapters 3 and 4, pp. 50–2 and 89.

The multidomestic has the opposite trade-off. It is able to differentiate to local markets and respond to local conditions, but it cannot manage itself into a distinctive low-cost position. The international company is able to transfer distinctive competences to new markets, but it can be caught between the inability to differentiate enough locally or to be sufficiently low cost. It could be a case of 'stuck in the middle' – this seems to be Procter & Gamble's own diagnosis. The transnational appears to solve all of these conventional trade-offs, but it clearly has major difficulties of implementation, because the network organization is so fundamentally different from more traditional 'command and control' organizations.

11.3.2 Country issues

The double diamond

The balancing of efficiency, responsiveness and innovation is in a sense an elaboration of Porter's classic generic strategies (cost, differentiation and focus), bringing in the dynamics of innovation to his essentially static model. Porter's later model (1990) on the diamond of national advantage and its implications for companies can also be elaborated in this context. According to the diamond model the MNE takes sustenance from its home markets and these provide the strategic asset base from which advantage can be gained.

First, here is a reminder of the four key variables in the diamond: factor conditions, demand conditions, related and supporting industries, market structure and rivalry. A first elaboration of the diamond introduces two other variables:

1   *The role of chance and uncertainty.* Unforeseen developments are paradoxically normal, viz. new knowledge and inventions, interventions of foreign governments, wars and insurrections, financial market crises, discontinuities in costs such as oil shocks, surges in demand, emergence of new competitors or new types of competition. The longer the time scale of strategic thinking, the more likely there will be unforeseen events (see Chapter 14 for the discussion on scenario planning that aims to deal directly with these problems).

2   *The role of (home country) government.* Government's task is to influence all four of the major determinants of national advantage summarized in the diamond through actions such as subsidies, education and training policies, regulation of markets (particularly financial markets), establishment of standards, its purchasing policy, tax laws, antitrust and policies towards competition.

Critique of the diamond

Figure 11.8 illustrates the diamond with these extra variables. Rugman and D'Cruz (1993) have provided a comprehensive critique of Porter's diamond.

First, they observe that the data on which the diamond is founded contains only triad-based countries and therefore refers only to firms with strong home bases. MNEs in non-triad countries would not expect such a supportive home base and these must there-fore look elsewhere for strategic assets.

Second, government is a crucial player but not all governments, even in triad regions, follow identical policies. Mistakes are possible that might, for example, result in the creation of sheltered domestic industries that cannot compete in international markets. Policy fashions might also result in misdirected investments intended to create national flagships.

Third, the diamond is uncomfortably positioned between the determinism of governments and the discretion of companies. In the end it is companies that make the strategic investments and these may often be at odds with the prevailing national orthodoxy. See, for example, the rise of Honda in spite of Japan's MITI officially disapproving of its international ambitions.

Fourth, behind Porter's model is an assumption of a life cycle of evolution of national development. This proceeds in linear fashion through factor driven (e.g. China currently), to investment driven (such as Korea's support of its chaebol), to innovation driven (such as Japan), and eventually wealth driven (such as the UK – this is Porter's rather unlikely example). Over a short period of, say, a decade this may have some merit. But over a longer period it is plainly unsatisfactory by leaving no prospect for fundamental reappraisals of national policy. Since the stage of development greatly influences the way in which a company responds, the placement of a country in the cycle is clearly critical.

Fifth, the model is peculiar in crediting only outbound FDI as a source of change and profits. But surely inbound FDI also has the same effects and thus the home country's position in the cycle can be changed. The McKinsey study (1993) of the world automobile industry is explicit in its recognition of the way in which Japanese FDI into the USA had a significant impact on Detroit.

Sixth, Porter implicitly states that factor-driven strategies will not promote international competitive advantage for MNEs from such countries. However, Canadian researchers have been quick to criticize this (Safarian, Rugman, Crookell) observing many Canadian counter-examples. In addition, the growth of Asian MNEs suggests (although the evidence is not yet conclusive) that Korean and Chinese and maybe Indian MNEs will soon be as large and as strategically well founded as their triad counterparts.

Finally, the model does not adequately address the role of the multinational in creating a distinctive position for itself. Dunning has observed:

> there is ample evidence to suggest that MNEs are influenced in their competitive-ness by the configuration of the diamond in other than their home countries, and that this in turn may impinge upon the competitiveness of home countries. (Dunning, 1983, p. 11)

Thus, Nestlé earns the vast bulk of its revenues outside its home base (Switzerland), as also do virtually all Canada's multinationals. Nearly every country outside the main triad regions and the big industrial countries within these regions has a small home diamond whereupon its MNEs overcome this problem by gaining access elsewhere. Rugman and Hodgetts conclude (2003, p. 423):

> *different diamonds need to be constructed and analysed for different countries.*

These criticisms of the original diamond model can be captured under two broad headings. First, there is the neglect of government as a major driving force. Essentially government actions create externalities that can give MNEs (or local firms) firm-specific advantages (FSAs) in terms of location decisions and the emergence and sustenance of regional clusters of economic activity. Second, the diamond has quite different implications for the big as opposed to the small MNEs. The larger the MNE, the more capability it has to take advantage of market imperfections, especially government-induced externalities. The MNEs from small home bases gain less advantage from their home locations and are impelled to seek advantages elsewhere. It is the combination of these effects that has led to the formulation of the *double diamond*. The value of this is that it gives a more realistic basis for analysing the international competitiveness of smaller MNEs. But it also captures the complex interactions (and rivalry) between the policies of governments. Figure 11.8 shows the basic figure.

In the double diamond the MNE is at the centre of the diamond but is focused on (at least) two 'home' bases. From each it gains resources and factor characteristics. From each it benefits from the nature of demand conditions. And from each it is sustained by the supporting infrastructure. However, it gains by taking a highest common factor approach, that is,

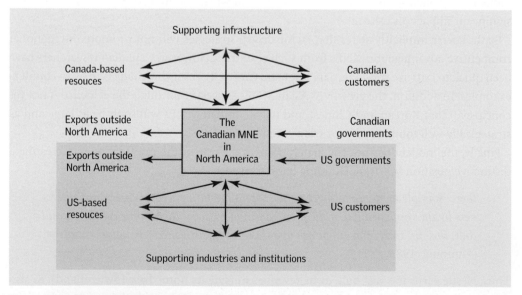

Figure 11.8 The double diamond (the Canada–US example)

it takes advantage of the best infrastructure, it locates in the lowest-cost region, it learns from the most advanced customers and so on. Rugman and D'Cruz (1993, p. 32) use the example of Canadian businesses within the North American Free Trade Area (NAFTA). Thus, Canadian plants gained economies of scale by producing for the North American market as a whole. They argue that the result of North American economic integration has been the development of a Canadian–US double diamond, which shows that, for strategy purposes in the Canadian companies, the two countries have become integrated. This suggests that the double diamond results from government policies, in this case the creation of NAFTA. However, companies themselves can take the initiative. We saw earlier that the emergence of the transnational is a deliberate attempt to be both centralized and localized and the double diamond is a facet of this. Figure 11.9 illustrates a double diamond for McDonald's, taking the USA and Europe as the two 'home' countries. We can see that any moves from the security and sanctuary of a single home base will involve the MNE with a multiple set of close interactions with its markets. For the MNE from smaller homes this enables an entry into a larger game (see, for, example, the power of Nestlé from its small Swiss base, the restored power of Philips from its Dutch home, and the growth of ABB from its Swedish-Swiss base). But multiple homes are not just the prerogative of the 'small' MNE.

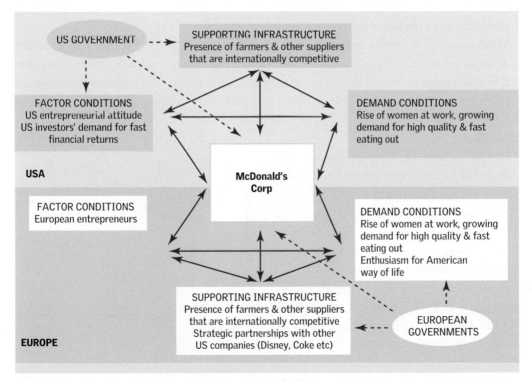

Figure 11.9 The double diamond and McDonald's Corporation
Source: case material: ENPC, Paris.

We see that companies such as Toyota and McDonald's deliberately took the transnational line and effectively work in the context of double/multiple diamonds.

The competitive advantage matrix: CSAs and FSAs

Firm-specific advantage (FSA) is a term used in the international business literature to describe the unique capabilities of an organization and is identical to the concept of *core competence* that we discussed in Chapter 7. **Country-specific advantage** (CSA) arises from the above discussion of the diamond, the double diamond, and the impact of the home base(s) on the MNE. These can be interrelated to produce a competitive advantage matrix (Figure 11.10) that provides a useful framework for discussion. Quadrant 1 firms rely on strong CSAs and are usually in mature markets that are globally oriented, commodity in style and marked by price competition. Typical CSAs would be low factor costs and low energy costs. Cost leadership would be the desired strategy. Firms in quadrant 2 display no advantages, would typically be inefficient in scale and would be candidates for exit, restructuring and/or absorption. Firms in quadrant 4 are generally differentiated firms with strengths in marketing, product development and customization. Their home base is largely irrelevant and these firms are very self-sufficient. Firms in quadrant 3 can benefit from both low cost and differentiation with major contributions from the factor costs and supporting infrastructure of the home base.

From quadrant 4 a firm can have ambitions to develop FSAs that will take into quadrant 3 with an even stronger position. However, firms in quadrant 4 are faced with exogenous CSAs and cannot in general expect to develop new CSAs unless they deliberately undertake to shift location or adopt a double diamond approach. Note, however, that firms may not be homogeneous if their portfolios are not: individual businesses may be in different quadrants and require different strategic approaches. This raises the questions posed in Chapter 8 about the nature of the portfolio and the dangers of excessive diversification. It is also worth noting that changes in the trading environment can and do affect the CSAs. The foundation of trading areas such as NAFTA have affected the positioning of Canadian companies (some companies moving from 2 to 1, and better still some moving from 4 to 3). Similarly the thinking behind European integration and the creation of the single market in 1992 was to create the conditions under which European-based MNEs might compete more effectively by enjoying stronger CSAs.

Figure 11.10 Competitive advantage matrix
Source: Rugman and Hodgetts, 2003, p. 583.

The flagship model

Much of the above discussion and indeed discussions within governments has been about the way government policy can affect the success of companies. But the theme of this discourse is more on the ability of companies to construct their own destiny and not have to be mere respondents to market and institutional change. In international business this has been evident in the ways by which successful MNEs have business networks and relationships that have the effect of creating a favourable context without being dependent on the policy whims of others. The main theme in this is the replacement of the traditional adversarial supply chain structure with co-operative supply networks. This stems from the success of Japanese companies in the 60s and 70s and in particular the Toyota production system. The Japanese recognized that creating additional value by creating close relationship with buyers/suppliers can add more to profitability than simple value extraction strategies (exemplified in the traditional explanation of the five forces). These strong co-operative relationships typically require sharing information on costs and manufacturing processes and the co-ordination of logistics to minimize inventories and waiting times. These characteristics are evident in the successful working of alliances (recall Chapter 10). The implication of this is there must be a de facto recognition of how such co-ordination takes place. In the world of value extraction this is a simple exercise in economic power. But in the world of value creation there must still be an orchestration of events by the most powerful or influential firms. This is described by Rugman and D'Cruz (2000) as the **flagship model** and is depicted in Figure 11.11.

Figure 11.11 The flagship firm
Source: Rugman and D'Cruz, 2000.

This is derived from a diamond framework but is distinctive in the way it parallels commercial relationships with network (co-operative) relationships. This extends not just to suppliers and buyers but also to competitors and the non-business infrastructure. The point about the conventional supply chain relationships is the observation that co-operation along the chain can result in better outcomes for customers. This is not always easy to prove and can easily be confounded with convenience to the players. More challenging are the emerging sets of relationships with competitors in the form of joint ventures, technology transfers and market-sharing agreements. Again there is tension between co-operation and competition and economists would argue that such co-operation is only productively possible if markets are not too concentrated with the result that co-operation would shade into monopolization. The international automobile industry provides a dramatic example of multiple linkages in a highly competitive arena. Other elements of the business infrastructure are also being pulled into co-operation. MNEs are now sharing their strategies with the unions (*see*, for example, the Detroit discussions in the summer of 2003 with the UAW in the face of intense competition). Partnerships are being effected with universities (e.g. by pharmaceutical companies). Above all, governments and MNEs are increasingly co-operating not only around issues of FDI but also about local content and other forms of local reinvestment in infrastructure. Figure 11.12 shows a picture of L'Oréal as a flagship company.

Figure 11.12 L'Oréal as a flagship firm
Source: case material: ENPC, Paris.

> ## Case box: **The first multinationals: Assyria circa 2000 BC**
>
> In an effort to fill an important gap in the history of MNEs, Karl Moore and David Lewis presented evidence suggesting that the first MNEs appeared in the old Assyrian kingdom shortly after 2000 BC. Using the eclectic paradigm as a model to analyse ancient international trade it demonstrates that the major characteristics of MNEs were a part of the Assyrian business organizations of the time. The definition of MNE accepted by the OECD and the UNCTC (the United Nations Centre for Transnational Corporations), 'an enterprise that engages in foreign direct investment (FDI) and owns or controls value-adding activities in more than one country' leads us to conclude that there were MNEs in ancient Assyria around 2000 BC. Characteristics found in modern MNEs, such as hierarchical organization, foreign employees, value-adding activities in multiple regions, common stock ownership, resource and market seeking behaviour, were present in these ancient firms. These early MNEs successfully operated considerable business empires in multiple foreign locations from their corporate headquarters in the capital of Ashur. Undoubtedly more will be learned about the commerce of the old Assyrian kingdom as records from archaeological finds continue to be translated and new finds uncovered.
>
> Were there early MNEs or proto-MNEs earlier than the Assyrian Empire? There may well have been. The records have yet to be uncovered.
>
> *Source*: extracted from Moore, K and Lewis, D (1998) 'The first multinationals: Assyria circa 2000 BC', *Management International Review*, 38, 2, pp. 95–107.
>
> *Note: The eclectic paradigm can be readily summarized by the acronym OLI which indicates ownership, location and internalization advantages. Ownership advantages are firm-specific advantages (FSAs) owned or controlled by the firm. Location advantages are country-specific advantages (CSAs) that arise from the location(s) of the MNE. Internalization advantages are those that accrue to a firm when it internalizes or brings inside the hierarchy of the firm activities which could be performed by the market (remember the discussions on make versus buy and the boundaries of the firm).*

11.4 **Managing international organizations**

The international company has always had a tendency towards complex organization structure and difficulties of management control. Stopford and Wells (1972) demonstrated how multinationals tend towards matrix structures (Figure 11.13).

Multinationals historically have moved along the route of increasing product diversity, followed by geographic expansion, or geographic expansion followed by product diversity. A multiproduct firm with limited overseas commitment will naturally organize around product divisions. A multicountry, single-product firm will naturally organize around area or country divisions. The difficulty comes with multiproduct, multicountry operations –

should it be organized around geography or around products? The pure strategies offer clear advice. A global company should operate product divisions, because of the imperative to standardize and achieve cost efficiencies. The multidomestic company should organize around countries, because the foundation of competitive advantage lies within the countries. Trade-offs have to be made in international firms and in transnational organizations.

Where there is a fine balance to be struck, there has been much experimenting with matrix structures. The **matrix** attempts to substitute formal, vertically oriented control and planning processes with more direct contact between individuals. It does this by placing line managers in situations where they have two bosses and are required to meet the needs of both. Figure 11.14 illustrates this with reference to a global chocolate company. This example is inspired by the acquisition of Rowntree by Nestlé, when the new parent argued for the continuation of its country-centred structure, and Rowntree managers argued that because the chocolate industry was global (at least it was European), there should be a product division structure. However, many managers have been very uncomfortable with matrix structures for numerous reasons, including:

- The time taken to make decisions may be too long.
- Priorities may be confused, because equal priorities are implied in the matrix.
- Responsibilities may not be clear because of dual reporting lines.
- A matrix may engender conflict because of the lack of vertical control processes.

Many MNEs use matrix structures and some seem to work quite well but, in general, they provoke much controversy. The dual line of reporting is the source of many problems and

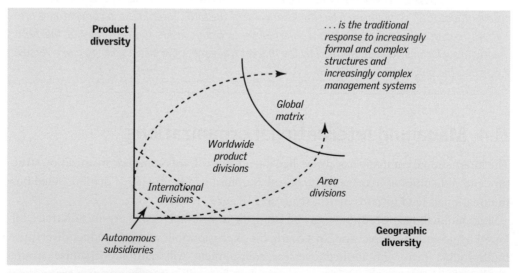

Figure 11.13 The global matrix
Source: Stopford and Wells, 1972.

requires explicit procedures that can resolve the inherent tensions. Bartlett and Ghoshal (1990) suggest three important criteria for making a matrix structure work well. These are clarity, continuity and consistency. *Clarity* refers to how well people understand what they are doing and how well they are doing it. It is built on clear corporate objectives within which relationships in the structure have to be spelt out in simple, direct terms. *Continuity* means that the company remains committed to the same values, objectives and principles of operation. This means that people know what is required and what the company stands for and how it operates. *Consistency* relates to how well all parts of the company work in relation to each other. This means that different parts of the operation should work in the same way without (too many) unnecessary variations and adaptations.

One of the difficulties with organizational design and the management processes that support each design is that they have a 'one size fits all' character. The multi-business company has more complexity than any single organization structure can accommodate. Sometimes a central policy is needed; sometimes local discretion is required; often there needs to be a debate about how something should be done. The need for innovation, learning and adaptation usually requires local discretion within a clear strategic intent (*see* ABB and Percy Barnevik for an attempt to achieve this: Taylor 1991). A useful approach is to seek to build our diagnosis of a company from the bottom up and not from the top down. Figure 11.14 implies that an overall judgement can be made about which type a company belongs to. Solid lines indicate the regulating line whereas dotted lines show information and consultation lines.

Alternatively, consider Figure 11.15. This breaks down the unit of analysis into its constituent parts (rather like a parts explosion diagram). An international-type industry

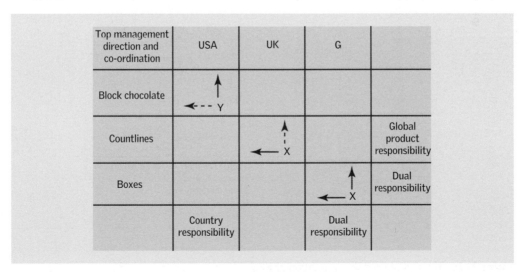

Figure 11.14 Managing the matrix, example: global chocolate company

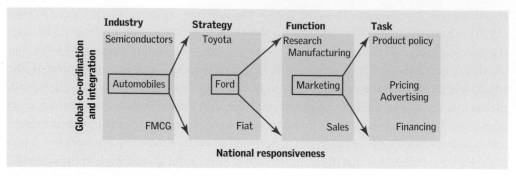

Figure 11.15 Integration and differentiation
Source: Adapted from Bartlett and Ghoshal, 1989, Ch 6.

(automobiles) is broken down into its member companies, some of which are global, some international etc. The Ford Motor Company, international in type, is broken down into its major functions. Research is seen to be global and centralized, sales are multidomestic and decentralized, and marketing is international (and it is probably difficult to decide how it should be organized).

Breaking marketing into its constituents, we see that some parts, such as product policy, should be centralized, whereas others, such as advertising, still have a complex mixture of local and central contributions. In practice, the diagnosis can be built from the bottom as well as from the top. Thus, the bottom-up approach identifies how things are done. The top-down approach can challenge this and ask how things should be done. The result might look like Figure 11.16. In this we show the integration–responsiveness trade-off diagram for KFC (Kentucky Fried Chicken, now part of Tricon Global Restaurants Inc). The company is

Figure 11.16 Integration and differentiation at KFC
Source: adapted from Bartlett and Ghoshal, 1989, Ch 6.

diagnosed in general as International in type. The vertical axis displays the tasks and functions that are to be done centrally, to gain the integration benefits. The horizontal axis displays those tasks and functions that ought to be carried out locally. Grouped around the origin of the diagram are those activities that require both central and local contributions. It is in these areas that a matrix-style structure would be relevant. Rather than adopting a one-size-fits-all structure, it would be appealing to be able to differentiate the structure according to needs.

11.5 Summary

In this chapter we have positioned international strategy as a significant extension of the logic of competitive advantage. We do not go into a full discussion of how the economics of trade interrelates with the genesis and nature of multinational firms – this is the province of international business as a subject. However, the subjects do overlap and what we do is reflect on how the eternal verities of competitive strategy (cost and differentiation) are played out on the international stage.

The chapter opened with a review of international trade and its institutional context and the significance of 'national' competitive advantage. This should be read as an extension of the discussion on macroeconomics in Chapter 4. The core of the chapter revolves around the nature of globalization and the sources of competitive advantage that flow from this. Whereas internationalization of companies (exemplified in the internationalization process) is seen as the general consequence of international trade, globalization is presented here as a particular form of this – the (debatable and controversial) trends towards international standardization.

The second key element of the chapter concerns the application of standardization strategies (crudely speaking, cost-based) versus differentiation strategies (differentiation-based). Following from this is the tantalizing debate as to whether both are possible (the transnational solution). You will recall from earlier chapters that exactly the same debate has taken place within competitive strategy about the possible simultaneity of cost- and differentiation-based strategies.

The importance of these discussions is profound because they effect the balance between country-specific advantages (CSAs) and firm-specific advantages (FSAs). These issues are discussed against the broad backdrop of Porter's diamond and the double diamond extensions popularized by Rugman. They are also discussed specifically in terms of the advent of the 'flagship firm' with its ability to manage its context and secure its position.

Just as in corporate strategy (Chapter 9) the nature of the (international) strategy has to be complemented by appropriate organization structures and processes. The logic of strategy and structure implies that complex strategies seem to require complex organizations such as the matrix form. Note that ABB, as discussed in Chapter 9, is not simply a complex corporate structure; it is also essentially an international portfolio for which Barnevik prescribed a matrix structure.

Key terms

Comparative advantage *427*

Country-specific advantage *438*

Diamond of national advantage *415*

Double diamond *434*

Factor conditions *428*

Firm-specific advantage *438*

Flagship model *439*

Foreign direct investment (FDI) *413*

Global *420*

Globalization *420*

Global markets *420*

Global matrix *442*

Global strategy *424*

International business *412*

International strategy *416*

Internationalization process *416*

Multidomestic *420*

Multinational enterprise (MNE) *412*

National differences *428*

Transnational *432*

World Trade *412*

Recap questions and assignments

1 Compare the structures of ABB, Diageo, Canon and DaimlerChrysler. To what extent do you think they are in line with current thinking on organizational structures for multinational corporations? What suggestions can you make for any changes in approach?

2 Consider the argument for global standardization as advanced originally by Ted Levitt in the *Harvard Business Review* and as popularized in the business press and in popular journalism, then:

(a) Outline the main arguments against this view.

(b) Identify an alternative to global standardization and explore its implications for multinational corporations.

When you have read this chapter, log on to the Online Learning Centre website at www.mcgraw-hill.co.uk/textbooks/mcgee to explore chapter-by-chapter test questions, further reading and more online study tools for strategy.

Case 1 **International law firms: trying to get the right balance**

London firms want to be more global; New York firms want to be more profitable. So far, the two are irreconcilable

'We're leading the way. Others will have to follow,' said the senior partner of Clifford Chance four years ago when the London lawyers merged with New York's Rogers & Wells and Germany's Pünder, Volhard, Weber & Axster. At the time, the three formed the world's biggest and most international law firm. But nobody did, in fact, follow their pioneering route, at least not on anything like the same scale.

The only proximate followers were the big accounting firms which had ambitions to build legal practices as global as their accounting businesses. 'We are aiming to be one of the top global players in legal services in the next five to ten years,' said a managing partner of Arthur Andersen, a year or so before the firm ceased to be a global player in anything.

In the late 1990s, over-confident accounting giants thought they could take the legal field by storm thanks to their extensive global networks. But they did not snap up multinational companies' big deals, nor did they lure top lawyers to their firms. Today, sobered by their experience in the intervening years, all the remaining 'Big Four' accountants are retreating from the legal arena, with KPMG the first to throw in the towel altogether.

Is it time then to abandon the idea of assembling a truly international law firm? Is commercial law such a different service to accounting, say, or advertising that it merits a very different industry structure, one characterised by small local specialists rather than big global generalists?

Non-intersecting circles

Not all firms have abandoned the attempt to become big and global. Multinational clients, they say, are clamouring for firms with a global reach. Cross-border deals are increasing, in Europe in particular where ten new countries are about to join the European Union. What's more, after the recent spate of corporate scandals, a slew of new rules on corporate governance calls for greater transnational legal expertise.

The drive for globalization of the profession has been stymied by the different nature of the business in its two biggest markets—London and New York. These two cities dominate the world of commercial law. The ten biggest firms and the ten most international are all based in one or the other (see chart 1).

Each city has a small group of highly reputable firms whose list of blue-chip clients marks them out as special. In New York, this group is seven strong and known as the 'Charmed Circle'. In London, it is known as the 'Magic Circle' and consists of five leading firms, including Clifford Chance. These two circles, however, find it peculiarly hard to intersect.

For a start, the New York firms are markedly more profitable than their London counterparts. Nine of the world's ten most profitable firms (in terms of profit per partner) are based in New York (see chart 2). While internationalisation has led to an increase in size and revenue, it has not produced an equivalent increase in profits. Of the two British firms in the 20 most profitable, one of them—Slaughter and May—has deliberately chosen not to internationalise its operations. The other, Herbert Smith, has only a quarter of its lawyers outside Britain. By contrast, Clifford Chance, Britain's leading international law firm with nearly two-thirds of its lawyers overseas, comes a poor 31st in the profit per partner league table.

At the time of its mergers it was Clifford Chance's ambition to rank among the top three firms wherever it practised. Yet its American strategy quickly ran into trouble.

Taking a chance? — Chart 1
World's most international law firms
by % of lawyers outside their home country, 2002

Rank by total number of lawyers

Firm	%	Rank
Baker & McKenzie, US		2
Clifford Chance, UK		1
Freshfields Bruckhaus Deringer, UK		3
White & Case, US		10
Lovells, UK		9
Allen & Overy, UK		4
Linklaters, UK		5
Simmons & Simmons, UK		39
Shearman & Sterling, US		17
Denton Wilde Sapte, UK		28

Source: Legal Business

Briefcase money — Chart 2
World's most profitable law firms by profit per equity partner

	2002-03 $m
Wachtell, Lipton, Rosen & Katz (New York)	2.92
Cravath, Swaine & Moore (New York)	1.96
Simpson Thatcher & Bartlett (New York)	1.85
Kirkland & Ellis (Chicago)	1.80
Milbank, Tweed, Hadley & McCloy (New York)	1.79
Davis Polk & Wardwell (New York)	1.78
Paul, Weiss, Riflkind, Wharton & Garrison (New York)	1.74
Sullivan & Cromwell (New York)	1.72
Skadden, Arps, Slate, Meagher & Flom (New York)	1.61
Cleary, Gottlieb, Steen & Hamilton (New York)	1.45

Source: Legal Business

Several of the firm's big-name New York partners defected, and morale among its junior lawyers fell. After stagnating in the 2002–03 financial year, the firm's revenue is believed to have dropped sharply in the first half of 2003–04, with profits per partner down by as much as 15% according to the *Lawyer*, a trade magazine.

Peter Cornell, Clifford Chance's global managing partner, admits that the firm's American venture has proved more difficult than anyone imagined. 'We reckoned we'd need three years to do it. Now we see it's going to take a bit more time,' he says.

The law of the asphalt jungle

The firm's biggest difficulty was its 'lock-step' system of remuneration, espoused by most English firms. Under this system, profits are shared among partners according to a sliding scale of seniority. Clifford Chance's New York arm, Rogers & Wells, however, like most American firms, used an 'eat-what-you-kill' system under which profits are shared among partners according to how much business each of them brings in.

To keep its American partners happy, Clifford Chance introduced a modified lock-step system in New York with fat bonuses for the most productive partners. But it did not do the trick. Since the merger, the firm has lost 19 of its top New York partners, including two stars. During that time, the firm points out, it has recruited twice as many new American partners. But the damage to its reputation and ability to retain top talent remains.

British firms will never succeed in America without adopting at least a modified system of 'eat-what-you-kill', says John Lynch of Latham & Watkins, a Californian firm that is expanding rapidly in Europe. A merit-based system of pay has always existed in America, but rewarding by results has become much more prevalent in the past few years. It is now beginning to undermine the traditional career path of gradual progress to the top.

Marc Bartel at Lovells, a British firm that used to harbour American ambitions, agrees that compensation is the core of the problem for British firms wanting to gain a foothold in the highly competitive American market. In the most profitable British firms, a senior partner may earn £1m ($1.87m) a year, but a top American partner can expect to earn almost twice as much. While some British firms are beginning to consider the introduction of a modified lock-step system, most are reluctant to go all the way down the American road. 'Pure eat-what-you-kill can be very ugly,' says Hugh Crisp, who takes over in April as chief executive of Freshfields Bruckhaus Deringer, another of London's Magic Circle firms.

Freshfields is the third-biggest law firm in the world (with more than 2,400 lawyers) and the third most international. It has offices in 18 countries and some two-thirds of its lawyers are based overseas. However, its presence in America is still small. 'We'd love an American merger,' admits Mr Crisp, 'but not at a risk to our culture or quality.' Linklaters and Allen & Overy, two other Magic Circle firms once in search of American brides, fared no better than Freshfields in finding a suitable transatlantic partner.

One big problem is that none of the top New York firms is interested in a merger. Relatively small and hugely profitable, they are happy to go on exploiting the biggest and richest legal market in the world on their own. Why should they bother with the risk and expense of a merger with a less-profitable foreign entity?

With the exception of Baker & McKenzie (83% of whose lawyers are abroad), White & Case (60% of whom are abroad) and Shearman & Sterling (37%), few American firms have more than a quarter of their legal staff based outside America. All London's Magic Circle firms, by contrast, have more than a quarter of their lawyers abroad. Significantly, the seven Charmed Circle firms have shown a particular resistance to moving their operations away from their own back yard.

Some British firms, such as Linklaters, seem to have abandoned the idea of a transatlantic merger in favour of organic growth in America. But with American firms offering much higher salaries, it is difficult for newcomers to attract America's brightest. Apart from Clifford Chance, no British firm has so far managed to establish a significant New York practice.

Yanks abroad

A few New York firms outside the circle have, however, been pursuing an international strategy, spurred on both by the needs of their increasingly globalised clients and by growing competition from the British. Some are convinced they would miss out on lucrative deals were it not for their presence in several different markets. Weil, Gotshal & Manges (WGM), an American firm with about 1,000 lawyers in offices in America, Europe and Asia, committed itself to an international strategy 13 years ago. In 1991 the firm did not have a single lawyer in Europe; today one quarter of its staff is there.

WGM says its international expansion was well worth the effort. 'Without our international platform, we could not have been involved in the Vivendi or the Yell deals,' says Stephen Dannhauser, chairman of the firm. In 2002, WGM advised Vivendi, a French media and utilities group, on the $1.7 billion sale of Houghton Mifflin, a publisher, to a consortium of private-equity firms. That same year, it also handled the flotation of Yell, an international-directories business, on the London Stock Exchange. In Vivendi's case the firm's Paris and New York lawyers worked together. In the Yell transaction, British and American teams co-operated.

Baker & McKenzie, one of the first American firms to pursue an international strategy actively, also believes strongly in the advantages of diversification. Baker has 12 separate practices—including antitrust, employment, tax and corporate law—each of which it runs on a global basis. This broad range of business, it says, helped it to ride out the bear market and the economic slowdown at the beginning of the decade. The firm 'could limit the pain, because it is not a big player in capital markets,' says Christine Lagarde, Baker & McKenzie's chairman.

Others also benefited from being diversified. WGM kept busy with work related to distressed deals, troubled loans and corporate restructuring, while Cravath, Swaine & Moore and Sullivan & Cromwell, members of New York's Charmed Circle (and also financial-market specialists), continued to lead charmed lives thanks to their expertise in litigation, an especially lucrative area in times of trouble.

On the other hand, several firms did not make it through the bear market, either because they decided to grow at the wrong moment or because they were over-dependent on financial deals. Altheimer & Gray, a Chicago firm, for example, and Brobeck, Phleger & Harrison, a Californian firm, both went into liquidation last year. Some of London's Magic Circle firms that specialise in financial markets were also badly hurt by the stockmarket slump.

Horses and courses

Instead of buying up other firms around the world, Slaughter and May, Britain's most prestigious and profitable firm, has built up an informal network of what it describes as non-exclusive referral relationships with the 'best of the best' firms around the world. All of them have agreed not to compete in each other's home jurisdictions, and to share documents, exchange lawyers, invest in joint developments, run joint training programmes and pool bills. All but two of America's Charmed Circle have signed up to the network. The aim, says Slaughter and May's David Frank, is to provide 'horses for courses'—the very best lawyer for any particular client in any particular jurisdiction. Mr Frank maintains that no single firm acting alone can provide this.

There is evidence to suggest that this is what multinationals really want: the best legal horse for whatever litigious course they find they have to run. For example, when Gesparal, the French holding company through which Nestlé, a big Swiss food group, and the French Bettancourt family controlled L'Oréal, a leading cosmetics firm, was dissolved earlier this month, Nestlé was advised by a French firm, an expert in its local market, despite the fact that the transaction involved both Swiss and French jurisdictions.

At the same time, there are occasions when Nestlé will seek out cross-border expertise. If it were involved in a cross-border deal within the EU, for example, it would, it says, choose an international firm as an adviser. 'In some cases we prefer international law firms, in others we go for local players,' says François Perroud, a spokesman for the company.

A growing number of legal areas are demanding cross-border expertise—the environment, shipping, aviation, antitrust, employment law, pensions, international arbitration, property rights, and so on. Small specialist firms exploiting a particular niche can benefit from this. Schulte Roth & Zabel, a small New York firm, for instance, specialises in advice for hedge funds and opened a London office when a growing number of its hedge-fund clients set up shop there. But Brad Hildebrandt, chairman of Hildebrandt International, a consultancy specialising in legal services, says that large companies and financial institutions 'are moving away from the "best firm in each location" approach to using a firm with an international capability for specific needs'.

It is becoming essential, particularly in Europe where there are EU directives as well as national laws, that one firm, or a network of close alliances, is able to pull all the threads together. 'This is increasingly difficult to do,' says Mr Hildebrandt, 'when no one firm has responsibility for the overall co-ordination and integration of the advice.' Baker & McKenzie, for instance, acts as intellectual-property enforcement counsel for Calvin Klein, a fashion designer, in countries in Europe and elsewhere. The firm fights counterfeiting and grey-market sales of jeans, underwear and sunglasses by prosecuting offenders in a number of jurisdictions.

If it ain't broke, don't mix it

British firms remain the strongest advocates of a global strategy. French law firms have stayed largely independent. Siméon et Associés, which has joined forces with Britain's Lovells, is an exception. Other top French law firms are big, diversified and predominantly French.

German law firms, on the other hand, have tended to follow the British path. In recent years they have started to merge among themselves and with British firms. Linklaters joined forces with Oppenhoff & Rädler, for instance, while Freshfields Bruckhaus Deringer is the result of a union between London's Freshfields and two top German practices.

As Americans are still giving them the cold shoulder, some British firms have started to become American, but in Britain. With 75 lawyers who have qualified in America on its payroll, Allen & Overy, a Magic Circle firm, employs more Americans in London than any American firm. Its ambition is to be 'the best non-US American law firm'. This leads to a somewhat odd segregation at the firm's offices, where Americans work almost exclusively on American business and earn considerably higher salaries than their British colleagues. Despite the resentment this can create among staff, it is the way that Allen & Overy hopes to attract and keep top American lawyers.

Michael Goldhaber, a journalist with *American Lawyer*, a trade magazine, does not think a transatlantic merger wave is imminent. At the moment, he says, mid-sized, second-tier American firms, usually not based in New York, are buying medium-size European firms. For example, in January 2002, Chicago's Mayer, Brown & Platt bought London's Rowe & Maw and created the world's 14th-largest law firm. And in the same year New York's Fried Frank, a firm with about 540 lawyers, very nearly merged with Britain's Ashurst Morris, a company with some 700 lawyers.

Rumours of a merger of Freshfields and New York's Cleary, Gottlieb, Steen & Hamilton have been denied several times by both firms in recent years. As Cleary already has a presence in Europe, the firm has little interest in joining forces with Freshfields. A merger with Freshfields might make more sense for two other Charmed Circle firms, Davis Polk & Wardwell or Sullivan & Cromwell. But they are both hugely profitable. So, since there is no urgency for top New York firms to merge, any transatlantic union is likely to be among second-tier players.

Ultimately, more big global law firms will probably emerge to provide services for the international marketplace. But the legal profession does not look as if it will go the way of accounting, with just a few firms dominating the market everywhere. Alongside any global legal giants, first-rate firms that decide to remain at home—such as Cravath, Swaine & Moore in New York and Slaughter and May in London—will probably continue to thrive as long as they can remain pre-eminent in their niches.

Despite efforts at cross-border harmonisation of certain areas of law, such as taxation, there remain big differences between legal systems. For instance, in countries with systems based on English common law the protection of investors is much stronger than in those based on French civil law. On the other hand, the recent victory in a French court of LVMH, a luxury-goods group, in a lawsuit against Morgan Stanley, an American investment bank, over allegedly tainted reports by an equity analyst probably would not have happened in an English jurisdiction.

That is why the legal profession has remained relatively parochial while its best clients have become increasingly global. Lawyers are currently catching up. But a small number of huge firms is unlikely ever to dominate the industry.

Source: 'Trying to get the right balance', *The Economist*, 26 February 2004.
© The Economist Newspaper Limited, London (26 February 2004).

Case Questions

1 Why should law firms in London and New York wish to globalize?

2 Why are these law firms reluctant to expand by acquisition – whereas other professional service firms in advertising and in property surveying have done so?

3 In what ways are the strategies of London-based and New York-based law firms different?

Further reading and references

Amit, R and Schoemaker, PJH (1993) 'Strategic Assets and Organizational Rent', *Strategic Management Journal*, **14**, pp. 33–46, reprinted in Segal-Horn, S (ed.) (1998) *The Strategy Reader*, Blackwell Business.

Bartlett, C and Ghoshal, S (1989) *Managing Across Borders: the Transnational Solution*, Harvard Business School Press, Boston MA.

Bartlett, C and Ghoshal, S (1990) 'Matrix Management: Not a Structure, a Frame of Mind', *Harvard Business Review*, July/August, pp. 138–45.

Bartlett, C and Ghoshal, S (1992) 'What is a Global Manager?' *Harvard Business Review*, **70**, **5**, pp. 124–32.

Bartlett, CA and Ghoshal, S (1993) 'Beyond the M-form: Toward a New Managerial Theory of the Firm', *Strategic Management Journal*, **14**, pp. 23–46, reprinted in S Segal-Horn (ed.) (1998) *The Strategy Reader*, Blackwell Business.

Douglas, SP and Wind, Y (1987) 'The Myth of Globalization', *Columbia Journal of World Business*, Winter, pp. 19–29.

Dunning, JH (1983) 'Internationalising Porter's Diamond', *Management International Review*, **33**, Special Issue 2, pp. 7–16.

Economist, The, 19 November 1999, pp. 27–35 and 122.

Ghoshal, S (1987) 'Global strategy: an Organizing Framework', *Strategic Management Journal*, **8**, pp. 425–40, reprinted in S Segal-Horn (ed) (1998) *The Strategy Reader*, Blackwell Business.

Ghoshal, S and Nohria, N (1993) 'Horses for Courses: Organizational Forms for Multinational Corporations', *Sloan Management Review*, Winter, pp. 23–35.

Harvard Business School (1986) *Kentucky Fried Chicken (Japan) Ltd*, Case Study 9–987–043, Harvard College, Boston, MA.

Hill, CW and Jones, GR (1995) *Strategic Management Theory: An Integrated Approach*, 3rd edition, Houghton Mifflin, Boston MA.

Jarillo, JC (1993) *Creating the Borderless Organization*, Butterworth-Heinemann.

Levitt, T (1983) 'The Globalization of Markets', *Harvard Business Review*, May/June, pp. 92–102.

McKinsey & Co. (1993) 'Manufacturing Productivity Units', *McKinsey Global Institute Report*, October 1993.

Ohmae, K (1985) *Triad Power: the Coming Shape of Global Competition*, Free Press, New York.

Porter, ME (1985) *Competitive Advantage*, Free Press, New York.

Porter, ME (1990) 'The Competitive Advantage of Nations', *Harvard Business Review*, March/April, pp. 73–93.

Prahalad, CK and Doz, YL (1986) 'The Dynamics of Global Competition', in CK Prahalad and YL Doz (eds) *The Multinational Mission: Balancing Local Demands and Global Vision*, Free Press, New York.

Prahalad, CK and Hamel, G (1990) 'The Core Competence of the Corporation', *Harvard Business Review*, May/June, pp. 79–91, reprinted in S Segal-Horn (ed) (1998) *The Strategy Reader*, Blackwell Business.

Quinn, JB (1992) *Intelligent Enterprise*, Free Press, New York.

Rugman, AM and D'Cruz, JR (1993) 'The "Double Diamond" Model of International Competitiveness: the Canadian Experience', *Management International Review*, **33**, Special Issue 2, p. 32.

Rugman, AM and D'Cruz, JR (2000) *Multinationals as Flagship Firms: Regional Business Networks*, Oxford University Press.

Rugman, AM and Hodgetts, RM (2003) *International Business*, FT Prentice Hall, London.

Segal-Horn, S (1993) 'The internationalisation of service firms', *Advances in Strategic Management*, **9**, pp. 31–55, reprinted in Segal-Horn (ed.) (1998) *The Strategy Reader*, Blackwell Business.

Segal-Horn, S (ed.) (1998) *The Strategy Reader*, Blackwell Business.

Segal-Horn, S and McGee, J (1997) 'Global Competences in Service Multinationals', in H Thomas and D O'Neal (eds) *Strategic Discovery: Competing in New Arenas*, the Strategic Management Series, J Wiley & Sons, Chichester, pp. 49–77.

Stopford, J and Wells, LT (1972) *Managing the Multinational Enterprise*, Basic Books, New York.

Taylor, W (1991) 'The Logic of Global Business: an Interview with ABB's Percy Barnevik', *Harvard Business Review*, March/April, pp. 91–104.

Yip, G (1995) *Total Global Strategy*, Prentice-Hall.

Chapter 12

Strategy in the new economy[1]

Introduction

This chapter is concerned with the 'new' world of information technology and knowledge intensity. This is a world marked by big investments in R&D, different cost structures and significantly changed demand conditions. You should read this chapter in conjunction with Chapter 19, which deals with knowledge, information and innovation. In this chapter we are concerned with how the logic of competitive advantage applies to the new conditions in which we find ourselves. To anticipate the conclusions, we will see that the strategic context has shifted a great deal. This means that fundamental demand and cost conditions have changed, resulting in different strategies

[1] This chapter is written jointly with Tanya Sammut-Bonnici.

being pursued. The new world and the new economy does mean that the old strategic logic is outmoded. Instead we see a significant change in the strategic context that results in the logic of competitive advantage being applied in different ways.

The chapter presents and contrasts the differences between the old world of scale and scope economies and the new world of **network externalities**. There is an extensive discussion of what network externalities are and how they arise but the reader should read this in the context of addition, not replacement – scale and scope have not been replaced; there is, however, another important practical phenomenon to consider. Networks are supported by many layers of infrastructure and we go into some detail to show how the technological infrastructure can be identified and analysed. There are many implications for competition which we review. Finally, we summarize the implications for strategy – although it is a new world, the logic of competitive advantage still applies.

12.1 The need for a new strategic perspective

The new information and communication technologies of the last decade are fundamentally transforming the operating methods of most manufacturing and service companies and are provoking wholesale reappraisal of the nature of support functions. These technologies have become institutionalized in the new ICT (information and communications technology) industry across the world and are now having a revolutionary effect on corporate strategy. Executives are rethinking the strategic fundamentals of business practices not just in technology and communications industries but also across the entire spectrum of industries.

Many of the component parts of this new ICT industry, such as telecommunications, the internet, computing and software, are shaping significant parts of the corporate environment into a new 'network economy'. The essence of networks is the existence of multiple nodes, the interconnectivity between them, and the co-operative (as opposed to competitive) behaviour of the nodes. As we will see, networks have increasing returns to scale characteristics. The dynamics of corporations and the new information economy will increasingly reflect these increasing returns to scale and, therefore, understanding how such networks work is the key to developing a new set of strategies in this new information-based corporate landscape (Kelly 1998).

The 'old world' was driven by economies of scale and scope, where the benefits of size are moderated by eventual diminishing returns. The 'new world', spawned by information and communications technology, is not moderated by the normally powerful influence of diminishing returns. Network effects, also known as network externalities, can result in 'winner-takes-all' phenomena (for example, the Wintel standard for PCs) and therefore result in new industry dynamics and new sets of corporate responses (for a discussion of network effects, *see* McGee and Sammut-Bonnici 2002).

The burgeoning growth and influence of the new ICT industry is making it possible for more individuals, corporations and companies to reap the benefits of the information economy. The internet has provided a free infrastructure for the rapid exchange of information and is creating new distribution opportunities in regional and global economies. The development of the 'self-organizing' web of new economy industries is affecting all elements of trade and brings commercial gains to regional and global economies. The Digital Planet 2002 report indicates the scale of this effect. At the regional level, Eastern Europe's spending grew faster in 2001 than the North America, Latin America, Middle East and Africa regions combined. Mature economies such as the US will become less dominant, as China, Poland and a host of other developing countries play an increasing role. At a more micro level, information industries are giving rise to geographic hot-spots of commercial activity, created from economic webs, corporate clusters and commercial ecosystems. California's Silicon Valley, Taiwan and Tokyo are such examples. Local concentration of ICT activity may develop spontaneously or can be created by governments and regional planners. Malaysia is developing two of the world's first Smart Cities: Putrajaya, the new seat of government providing e-government facilities, and Cyberjaya, a city for multimedia industries, R&D centres, a multimedia university and operational headquarters of multinationals wishing to direct their trading activities using information technology. The underlying feature of smart cities is the high level of ICT infrastructure, on which the whole city is developed. Another example of regional growth due to the information economy is Northern Virginia. Its economy has boomed with the explosion of internet and telecommunication companies. America Online, which set up in Northern Virginia in 1985, employs over 13 000 people, and generates over $1.5 billion in online revenues. The presence of a number of multinational companies such as AOL, UUNet and Worldcom MCI in the area attracts competitors as well as vendors through the normal multiplier effects. ICT Industries have well-documented, substantial effects on the local, regional and global economies through the **multiplier effect.**

The extent to which the ICT industry and associated network industries have proliferated in the economy is a recent phenomenon. However, network effects have been recognized for some time, since the onset of industrialization, but particularly with the advent of the first infrastructure industries (especially railroads) in Victorian times. Literature on network externalities dates back by almost a century to the works of Young (1913), Knight (1924), and Ellis and Fellner (1943). Contemporary research on networks tends to be econometric in nature (Shy 2001) and charts industry evolution over time in a series of snapshots. We adopt Shapiro and Varian's (1999) strategic perspective on network industries and develop a strategic framework that transcends ICT and non-ICT companies. We start this journey by analysing the structure of network industries and go on to look at the dynamics endemic in each level within that structure.

12.2 The emergence of a new economy

In this section we look at how the old industrial economy was characterized by economies of scale and scope, while the new information economy is driven by the economics of positive feedback in network industries. We will discuss the nature of network industries, such as railroads, telecommunications, software and hardware networks. We will see how network companies benefit from positive feedback on both the demand side and supply side. On the demand side, the more customers join a network, such as a telecommunications service, the higher the incentive for other customers to join. On the supply side, the larger a network becomes in terms of users and also in size of assets deployed, the easier it is for a company to lower costs and prices. The lower the price introduced by a network company, the more subscribers will join the network and positive feedback kicks in. The result is a self-reinforcing spiral. The importance of critical mass, competition and standards is discussed in the light of the dynamics of positive feedback.

12.2.1 The old world: economies of scale and scope

The theory of strategic management was given impetus by the realization that industrial organization as a subject could be turned around to give a perspective on the entrepreneurial profit-seeking activity of firms. This led to the notion of firms seeking market power in which rents could be protected, at least for a time, by barriers to entry. These barriers were derived from the cost functions of firms, the dominant theme being the ability of firms to sustain differential cost positions through economies of scale.[2] In the world of scale economies, where minimum efficient plant sizes are a significant fraction of the market, oligopolistic market structures prevail and are overturned principally by the growth of markets or by the advance of technology enabling the creation of new assets with more advantageous cost positions. The notion of economies of scale is therefore fundamental to strategic management because it provides a rationale for firms to be different in terms of asset configuration and in terms of performance. However, this is an insufficient argument on its own for the existence of diversified firms. Diversification requires the notion of economies of scope. These are defined as 'the cost savings realized when two different products are produced within the same organization rather than at separate organizations' (Saloner *et al.* p. 364). They arise because the products share a common input such as plant or equipment, obtaining volume discounts on purchases (exercising monopsony power), or applying

---

[2] Saloner, Shepard and Podolny (2001) identify three types of entry barriers: barriers from production or distribution technology, barriers from brand name or reputation, and legal barriers (p. 138). The first two are essentially cost barriers in that replication of the incumbent's assets is inhibited by the costs of so doing. The third type is an absolute barrier that arises from institutional characteristics that are idiosyncratic from a market point of view.

common expertise or reputation. The advantages conferred by economies of scope are not, however, inherent in the jointness of production but in the barrier to entry which protects the 'original' asset. There is nothing to prevent two firms enjoying identical economies of scope if there is free competition for the underlying asset. Thus, economies of scale convey the fundamental advantage that underpins superior profitability in single-product and multiple-product firms.

The discussions in strategic management textbooks about competitive advantage are all variations upon this same theme. The simplest articulation of the theme is the cost differential that arises in production. The more complex argument concerns knowledge assets, where the essence of the argument is about the cost to reproduce knowledge and not the possession of knowledge per se. The subtlety in strategy making resides in the variety of ways in which knowledge and expertise is acquired (which is where the cost function of knowledge acquisition is important) and then captured in products and services (the generic differentiation theme). In this almost bucolic world the supply side and the market side are linked through some form of arm's-length market exchange process. Customer desires are conveyed through the pattern of their purchasing decisions and producers respond by adjusting the nature of their offerings. Where competition is monopolistic (or imperfect) producers may attempt to shape customer preferences, and to the extent they succeed, demand functions become downward sloping in the conventional manner and producers can then price according to the nature of their marginal cost curves and the price elasticities in the market. But demand and supply are mediated through a market mechanism in which product demand is independent of other products[3] and demand is not time dependent. This latter point is crucial.

12.2.2 The new world of network industries

However, there is a class of markets and industries that do not conform to these assumptions. These are known as **network industries**.[4] According to Economides and Flyer (1997):

> *The value of nearly every good is influenced by aggregate consumption levels in its market and in the markets for related goods. In many cases, high aggregate consumption in its own market, and in the markets for complementary goods affects positively the value of a good. Traditionally such effects have been called network externalities, since they were first identified in network industries. While such effects are salient in some markets, such as for telephones, fax machines and computer operating systems, for most goods these influences are more subtle and tend to be smaller.*

---

[3] This exaggerates the point, as we will see later when we discuss product complementarity.

[4] In this discussion the terms 'industry' and 'market' are used as if interchangeable.

Network industries are not uncommon. Many physical networks have been around for a long time, e.g. railroads, telephone, electricity. So-called virtual networks have arisen largely through information technology and include facsimile machines and computer operating systems. These are 'virtual' because the key knowledge and information assets are intangible. We can distinguish intuitively between pure networks and indirect or weak networks. Pure networks exist where it is an essential characteristic of the product that it is organized through complementary nodes and links, such as a railway network or the telephone system. A key element is the notion of complementarity, thus the value of a railway station is derived from the existence of other railway stations on the network. A weaker definition relies also on complementarity between products (or nodes, in network language) but allows the links to be created *by* the customer rather than *for* the customer. Economides and Flyer (1997) have some powerful examples:

> the value of a washing machine is affected by the aggregate consumption of washing machines and the consumption level of the particular brand, since this determines the availability of parts, repairmen, detergents, fabric softeners and various other related goods and services. The value of a sporting event is influenced by the aggregate size of the audience, as this enhances the excitement level, analysis, discussion and remembrance of the event. Even a grapefruit is influenced by network externalities, since the variety of accessible complements, such as peeler, slicers, juicers, recipes, nutritional information and specialized spoons, are affected by the aggregate consumption of the fruit.

The essence of this idea is that the demand for a product is influenced by total demand for the product class or by total demand in a complementary product class. Thus, demand is conditioned by a consumer externality. Where these **consumer externalities** are powerful, the feedback effect on demand is such that there is a tendency towards a single network, or platform, or standard. The value for consumers of being on a common standard outweighs any specific differences between alternative standards. We see that the VHS standard was preferred to a 'technically better' Betamax rival to the extent that the rival standard disappeared. The Wintel standard is greatly preferred to the Apple standard although the rival does still exist as a small niche in the market. Where the externality is smaller and the intrinsic difference between standards is relatively larger then we might observe multiple competing and co-existing 'platforms'.[5] An example of a platform can be seen in the automobile industry, where a company might develop a core of components and sub-assemblies that can be used to support alternative body styling to create a product range. Such a platform can co-exist with other platforms because the scale efficiencies associated with platforms is modest in relation to market size.

---

[5] To observe multiple standards defies common sense, hence the term 'platform' which denotes an array of linked complementary products that together are compatible with other products.

12.3 **Networks**

What is the significance of networks and network externalities? To answer this we need to look first at what we mean by networks. Then we look at the implications for the demand function and the consequences for the market and the industry structure.

A network is a set of connections (links) between nodes. A two-way network allows the links to be operated in both directions, whereas a one-way network has distinct directionality. Two-way networks include railroads and telephone systems. Figure 12.1 shows a simple star network where A can communicate with B through a switch S. B can also communicate with A by reversing the direction of the link (viz. a telephone call). In Figure 12.1 we have eight nodes (A through H) linked through a switch, S. If this were a two-way network, AB and BA would be distinct products (different telephone calls, different rail journeys). The total number of products in the network is 56, i.e. $n(n-1)$ where n = the number of nodes. If there were to be a ninth member this would increase the total number of products to 72 (n is now 9), a total increase of 16 products available from the expanded network. If the value to each user of being in the network is proportional to the number of users then the value of this network has just increased by 28.5 per cent (16 as a percentage of 56) even though the size of the network has increased by only 12.5 per cent (one added to eight).[6] This is an algebraic characteristic of network economies of scale: that the value rises disproportionately higher than the increase in network size as long as prices are constant and products are independent. Intuitively we might expect that an increase in network size beyond a certain point has little value.[7] If this network were a one-way network there would be half the number of products but the value of the network would nevertheless increase at the same rate but achieving only half the value.

The analysis of complementarity is equivalent to the analysis of a one-way network. Figure 12.1 can be extended, as in Figure 12.2, to show a typical one-way network. Here we can interpret the A_i as ATMs[8] and the B_j as banks. The network runs only from A to B. The significance of the two switches S_A and S_B is that they have only one link. This means that there is compatibility between all ATMs and all banks. This maximizes the value of the network but increases the competition between banks for customers through ATMs.[9] It is this compatibility that makes the complementarity actual and the network operational. For complex

---

[6] Assuming for convenience in this example that prices are constant.

[7] Using calculus we would expect the first derivative to be positive but the second derivative to be negative. Therefore, total value increases but at a decreasing rate.

[8] Automatic teller machines

[9] Two complementary components, A and B, are compatible when they can be combined to produce a composite good. A VHS player is compatible with VHS tapes. Two substitute components A_1 and A_2 are compatible when each of them can be combined with a complementary good B to produce a composite good. Thus two VHS tapes are compatible, and two VHS players are compatible.

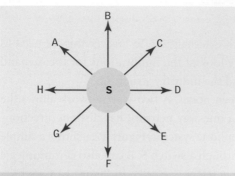

A star network has a collection of nodes clustered around some central resource. Movement of resources/products must pass through this central node, e.g. a local telephone exchange.

Figure 12.1 A simple star network

products actual complementarity has to be achieved through adherence to specific technical standards. Other complementary products can be visualized in terms of

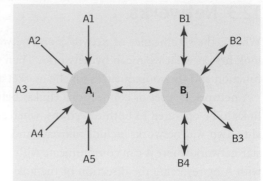

Occurs when the central resouces are distributed among connected star networks. In a normal star network, movement can occur from any point on the network to any other point. Movement from one star to another will involve both central connections (hubs). Movement within one star will require only one – e.g. long-distance telephone network

Figure 12.2 A crystal 'one-way' network

Figure 12.2. VHS tapes could be the A_i and VHS players could be the B_j. Think also of copier paper and copiers, or printer paper and printers, or car accessories and cars, or local and long-distance telephone networks.

Case box: **Real and virtual networks**

The concept of network can be segmented into real and virtual networks (Shapiro and Varian 1999). Real networks are found in industries such as telephony and railways where a physical network is present. Virtual networks are typified by computer and software platforms where the interconnection between users is intangible. The two types of networks are discussed below.

In real networks the interconnection between users is tangible. Examples are cable networks for telephone users and radio transmissions in mobile phones. Electricity grids, telecommunications networks encompassing telephones, fax machines, online services and the internet are typical examples of products or services within real networks. There are one-way networks, such as broadcast television, where information flows in one direction only. In two-way networks, such as railroads and telephone systems, links are operated in both directions. Any network may be viewed as a set of connections (links) between nodes. A two-way network allows the links to be operated in both directions whereas a one-way network has specific direction. Two-way networks include railroads and telephone systems.

In virtual networks the interconnections between users are intangible, but users remain interdependent. Computer systems are typical of virtual networks. For example, Mac users are part of the Mac network, with Apple as the sponsor of the network. Mac users are locked into a network determined by the technology standard of this platform. They can only use software that is compatible to the system and will exchange files with users within the system. Operating systems such as Windows and Unix are other examples of virtual networks. Virtual network dynamics also operate in the entertainment industry for Sony PlayStation, Microsoft Xbox and Nintendo's Gamecube networks.

Network size is still important in virtual networks in that a large consumer base makes production viable and usage possible. In addition, the value of a product increases as the number of, or the variety of, the complementary goods or services increases. Indirect network effects in the computer industry are referred to as the hardware–software paradigm. The success of an operating system for personal computers depends on the variety of software applications available in the market. Value may depend more critically on software applications.

12.3.1 Network externalities: the new economic force

Earlier in this chapter we looked at the traditional economic model for the 'old world', which was driven by economies of scale and scope. The 'new world', characterized by information and communications technology, is governed by a different dynamic. Network externalities are the new drivers of the network economy. It is important to recognize that economies of scale/scope and network externalities represent the extreme ends of a spectrum of effects, and that the presence of one does not imply the exclusion of the other. Companies may experience the effects of both to varying degrees, with a tendency for network externalities to have more strategic relevance in the new network economy.

The concept of network externalities has attracted the attention of academics and practitioners alike. The extent to which network industries have proliferated in the economy is a recent phenomenon. The effects of network externalities, however, have been recognized for some time with the development of the older network companies such as the railroads and the electricity systems. In 1804 Trevithick constructed the first practical locomotive in England. In 1882 the Edison Electric Lighting Company completed the first commercial generating station at Holborn Viaduct in London. The first commercial telephone line was installed in Boston, Massachusetts, in 1877.

Network externalities are defined as the increasing utility that a user derives from consumption of a product as the number of other users who consume the same product increases (Katz and Shapiro 1985). For example, the more people there are in a telephone network, the more users can be reached on the network, thereby increasing its usability. Fax machines, broadcast industry services, credit card networks, and computer hardware and software are examples of products exhibiting network externalities.

Networks were originally analysed on the assumption that each network was owned by a single firm and research concentrated on the efficient use of the network structure and on the appropriate allocation of costs (Economides 1996; Sharkey 1993). With the anti-trust cases against AT&T and its later break-up, attention shifted towards economies of scope, the efficiency gains from joint operation of complementary components of networks (Baumol *et al.* 1982). This led to issues of interconnection and compatibility in parallel with the reduced role of IBM in the 1980s and 1990s in the setting of technical standards in computer hardware and software. As technology has advanced, there have been significant reductions in telecommunications costs and a shift towards fragmented ownership of telecommunications networks. Market structure has shifted from natural monopoly to oligopoly. Similar trends are evident in other IT-intensive industries. Thus, the focus of interest in network economics has shifted from the analysis of natural monopoly towards issues of interconnection, compatibility, interoperability and co-ordination of quality.

12.3.2 Network externalities and the battle for critical mass

For normal goods, the demand curve slopes downwards. As price decreases, more of the product is demanded. Other elements in the demand function, such as income or advertising, serve as 'demand shifters' that elevate demand to a higher level. Figure 12.3 illustrates the traditional role of a demand shifter. Higher levels of consumption are derived from higher incomes (positive income elasticities) or from lower prices (negative price elasticities).

This fundamental relationship is greatly distorted in the presence of network externalities. In the presence of network externalities, we specify that sales rise as accumulated sales (the

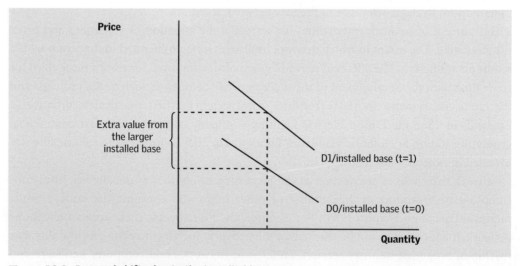

Figure 12.3 Demand shifts due to the installed base

installed base) rise and there arises a chicken and egg problem. Customers may not be interested in purchasing because the installed base is small and/or not expected to grow. For example, imagine the purchase of complex software without internet support, help lines and user groups. Alternatively, there may be confident expectations that the installed base will grow substantially and therefore consumers will confidently make purchases. The paradox is that consumers will not buy if the installed base is too low. However, the installed base is too low because customers will not buy. The crux of the paradox lies in the management of expectations. In markets for normal goods, equilibrium is explained in terms of a balance between costs and demand, between marginal costs and marginal utility. In network markets, there is also equilibrium to be struck between actual demand and expectations of total demand.

This gives rise to an economic paradox. Almost the first law of economics is that value comes from scarcity. However, in the new economy value comes from plenty: the more something is demanded and the more it is expected to be demanded then the more valuable it becomes. Expectations are so important in driving demand that a point exists where the momentum is so overwhelming that success becomes a runaway event and we observe a 'winner takes all' phenomenon (see Figure 12.4).

The **'tipping point'** is when the installed base (or size of network) tips expectations sharply towards one player (or one network) and away from its rival. We have experienced this effect when the market moved towards Windows as the prevailing computer operating system, rather than OS2. Another example of tipping would be IBM-compatibles versus Apple, as shown in Figure 12.5. The tipping point comes somewhere in 1984–5 when IBM-system sales overtake those of Apple.

The exception to the winner takes all phenomenon would be a regulated network market with strong interconnections between competing platforms. The mobile telephone

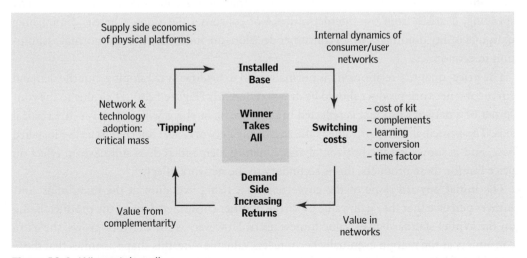

Figure 12.4 Winner takes all

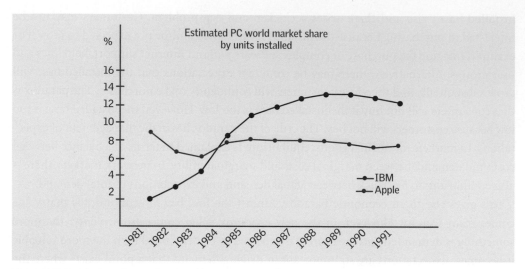

Figure 12.5 Market share of IBM and Apple

industry is a classic example. The standards are harmonized across the network providers, at least by continental region. The platforms are interlinked and the sales curves of the regulated network providers follow the pattern of the overall subscription curve for the industry.

Traditional economic thinking is based on **negative feedback systems** in which the strong get weaker at the margin and the weak get stronger, thus providing a drive towards a competitive equilibrium. This is captured in economics by the concept of diminishing marginal utility as consumption grows. In the new world of networks, feedback rules. In this world the valuation of a product increases the more that others consume the product. Strictly speaking, it arises from the interdependence of consumer decisions, whereas diminishing marginal utility dominates when consumer decisions are independent – the normal assumption in economics.

The price–quantity relationship is normally held to be downward sloping, but the demand curve for a network product should be drawn differently (Figure 12.6). The value to the consumer of a network product is reflected in the price he or she is willing to pay – the vertical axis. The principal driver of value is the size of the network, also referred to as the installed base, and is shown on the horizontal axis. Quantity demanded does still have an effect on price but for these products, this is secondary to the network effect.

The initial upward slope of the curve reflects a rising valuation at the margin, as consumers perceive that they gain value by virtue of other consumers having the product. Being on the Wintel standard gives value to new users. However, as the network grows, the extra consumers at the margin eventually become less valuable – i.e. this shape assumes that those users with higher potential valuation of the network will join first. As the network gets very

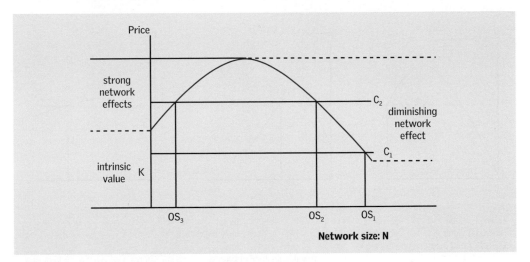

Figure 12.6 The network demand curve: the idea of optimal size

large, further growth has less value for future customers.[10] The intercept on the vertical axis represents the value the network product has as a stand-alone product. Thus a Wintel computer has some stand-alone value, but a telephone has no value on its own and is a **pure network good**.

There is a notion of an optimal size of a network. This can be seen from the interaction of demand and cost so that as less and less valuable customers join the network there may come a time when the costs of acquiring and servicing new customers begins to exceed the price those customers are willing to pay. This determines the optimal size and has significant implications for competition.

The three configurations shown in Figure 12.7 indicate the range of possibilities. The first is a pure network good, such as a telephone system, in which the optimal size of network is a very high proportion of the available market. This implies there is little or no room for rival networks. The second is a product with a significant intrinsic value that attracts a modest size group of users. For example, this could be a corporate software package (e.g. enterprise solutions) that attracts dedicated user support from the supplier through the web. Alternative networks could co-exist. The third case is one of very high intrinsic demand but extensive consumer interactions (small in size but very many in number) provide a substantial total network value. The obvious example is word processing software where the value from standardizing on MS Word is very high, with the result that alternative standards (such as WordPerfect) are being frozen out of the market even though the intrinsic value of any word processing package is high.

---

[10] In the language of demand curves, this is an average revenue curve.

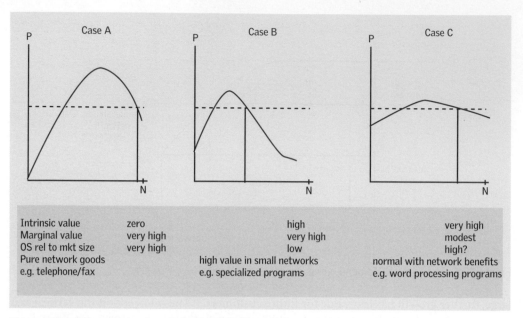

Figure 12.7 Alternative network demand configurations

12.4 **The technological infrastructure of network industries**

Much of the popular discussion of technology and its effects makes powerful but general claims for the effect of technology but is less than clear about the underlying mechanisms. We observe four nested levels of infrastructure within network industries. Each of these levels has its own economic dynamics and each makes a contribution to the overall network (increasing returns characteristic). These levels are (i) technology standards, (ii) the supply chain driven by such standards, (iii) the physical platforms that are the output of the supply chains and are the basis from which the company delivers its product (e.g. the digital TV, the decoder, the satellite system, and the telephone lines that are the platform from which Sky TV delivers its programmes), and (iv) the consumer network (Figure 12.8). The economic characteristics of the first three levels are the prevalence of fixed costs and joint products coupled with economies of scale. Networks of interacting and interdependent customers provide the increasing returns characteristic of networks. Then the whole can have such powerful positive feedback characteristics that the winner might be able to take all.

Each level displays distinctive economic characteristics of significance. Technology standards can be achieved either by rule or by emergence and in the latter case early mover advantages are important. The economics of modularity and the specialization of knowledge shape the structure of supply chains. Physical platforms are a melding of standards and components in which modularity and the economics of substitution also play a

	Language of networks	Wintel	WWW	Mobile phones	Satellite TV
Network externalities, consumer lock-in, market equilibrium and tipping	Consumer network	PC producers, retailers, offices and homes	PC producers, retailers, offices and homes	Individual corporations	Households
Economies of scale, critical mass, positive feedback, externalities, path dependence	Physical platform	PC producers, retailers, offices and homes	Global net of millions of computers, ISPs, online services, software	Mobile phones, transmitters, land lines, BT phones	Satellite transponder, decoder, TV shopping signal via phone
Supply-side economics, economics of substitution, versioning, switching costs	Technology standards	Win95 runs on x86 only. WinNT runs on non-x86 chips. Linux runs on x86	HTML IP, TCP/IP, VoIP	3G, 2.5G, GSM, GPRS, UMTS	Proprietary decoder vs CPSI
Technical capabilities ahead of markets: R&D races, JVs and alliances	R&D supply chain	New 'itanium' chip is being held back to preserve current version	Integration of internet with cable TV: Microsoft Mobile Internet	I-mode technology by DoCoMo	IoS – Internet over Satellite Currently for ISPs

Figure 12.8 Strategic levels of network industries

significant role. Consumer networks, of course, require positive feedback effects for their full power to be gained. We use the mobile telecommunications business as a running example to show how these technological dimensions and strategy interact.

12.4.1 Technology and standards

The significance of the economics of information is attributed to two key factors: the continuing reduction in cost of information technology hardware products and the scale effect of global standards. Gordon Moore, founder of Intel Corporation, created a corporate empire on his eponymous Moore's Law, which states that every year and a half processing power doubles while costs hold constant. Moore's foresight proved prophetic and 'Moore's Law' is expected to remain valid for the foreseeable future (but *see* Leyden 1997). Computer memory, storage capacity and telecommunications bandwidth are all going through a similar pattern of cost reduction. This makes it very affordable for individuals and small businesses to be equipped with the electronic means to conduct commerce and transfer information as fast and freely as large corporations can. Hence, the demand for the products of the ICT industries continues to grow.[11]

----

[11] In spite of the feast and famine evident in the telecommunications industry reminiscent of the fragility of corporate structures during the railway boom of the 1840s.

However, the rapid growth of products from the ICT economy depends on operating technology standards as well as on production costs. For example, automated teller machines across the world must work on an agreed standard to ensure customers can use one card in different countries. A technology standard is the important enabler to create wide reach and to capture a wide network of subscribers. With the globalization of commerce, national and regional boundaries blur and the need for international standards is more urgent and critical.

A new **standard** can be registered with organizations such as the British Standards Institute, the American National Standards Institute or the International Standards Organization. But the process to determine the prevailing standard does not stop there. The path to achieving a de facto standard stems from three modes of selection process: market-based selection, negotiated selection and a hybrid selection process where both market competition and negotiation operate jointly.

Market-based selection is reflected in standards wars such as that between VHS and Betamax, where consumers decided on the dominance of the VHS standard. The marketing strategies of firms are key to which firm and standard is most likely to win. VHS gained a decisive advantage from a strategy of wider distribution channels and a range of complementary products (Hollywood films) as well as longer recording time than Betamax, in spite of other more advanced features available only on Betamax.

Negotiated standardization is becoming more widespread. Organizations that determine prevailing standards are emerging to reduce the cost and the uncertainty associated with adopting new standards. Negotiated standard setting guarantees the smooth interchange of information, technical components and services along different networks. The telecommunications industry was able to keep up with the speed of technological development by opening up the negotiation process to market players (David and Steinmueller 1994; David and Shurmer 1996). Groupe Speciale Mobile (GSM), the current mobile technology in Europe, is an association of 600 network operators and suppliers of the mobile phone industry. The UMTS Forum is a similar association, developed to speed convergence between telecommunications, IT, media and content suppliers for the 3G industry. As with GSM the name of the UMTS association is synonymous with the name for the industry technology standard.

The internet has a different history of standardization to telecommunications. Standards were completely open and established within the research communities of universities. As the internet has become a commodity for the domestic and the commercial communities, other players are increasingly influencing its evolution.

Hybrid standard setting emerges as private firms adopt strategies to undercut collaborative decisions taken in negotiated standardization. They introduce new products, which initiate unprecedented developments but also create incompatibilities, lock-in effects, and pockets of market power. Internet telephony is a typical example, where companies, standards organizations and governments create a hybrid standard setting environment (Vercoulen and Wegberg 1998).

Case box: **Standards versioning**

Standards organizations are playing an increasingly important role in the process of upgrading standards (called 'versioning'). The GSM Association is guiding the evolution of the mobile industry through a family of wireless technology standards from today's standard through to GPRS, EDGE and 3GSM. Each subsequent standard offers a higher level of service. GPRS provides open internet. EDGE facilitates faster data streaming, and 3GSM will provide video streaming. The network of companies supporting the technologies will go through grades of service levels in order to phase out older standards and introduce new ones (Figure 12.9). At the end of the life span of a standard the technology platform is decommissioned, with the exception of equipment and software that is forward compatible with the next generation of standards.

Software standards follow a similar versioning strategy. Microsoft publishes the *Windows Desktop Product Lifecycle Guidelines* to provide advanced notice of changes in product availability and support. Microsoft makes Windows licenses available for purchase for a minimum of five years and provides assisted support for a further four years. The guidelines are important so that companies can plan their investment through software upgrades of Windows 98, NT, 2000, ME, and the latest version of Windows XP.

Switching costs are minimized when standards are designed to evolve from one another. The introduction of revolutionary standards, however, is costly. The pay-off is superior performance against the high cost of switching standards. The telling example is the price paid by mobile telephone operators to switch to third-generation technology. Mobile spectrum auctions earned European Governments £200 billion with Britain and Germany raising £22.5 and £60 billion respectively. The mobile operators had to bid – to renounce third-generation spectrum was to opt out of the future (but did they have to pay so much?). The outcome of these auctions left mobile operators with increased debt, depleted cash flow, and delay in third-generation launches, all of which became the more significant as the stock market faltered and then stopped dead.

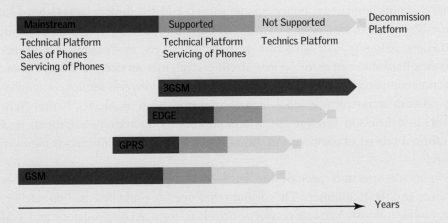

Figure 12.9 Standards versioning in the mobile telecommunications industry

12.4.2 Supply chain

In the last twenty years, the structure of the information economy has evolved through the interaction of three factors: the increase in computational capacity for data mining; the growth of telecommunication networks both fixed and mobile; and the explosion of information sharing via the internet.

These new, powerful characteristics of information have created opportunities for all industries, including network industries, to take advantage of new ways of managing supply chains. How to integrate company functions became the key concern and enterprise resource planning (ERP) systems provided the solution. Integration of the elements of the supply chain was seen as a move to dilute the boundaries of the rigid corporate departmental structures that were restricting business growth. The ERP era was the first wave of change in supply chain management. Deconstruction policies soon followed. Based on the example set by the automotive industry, many companies split their business processes and pushed some of them out to suppliers. Companies would retain the processes they liked and outsource the remainder. The elements of the supply chain would then be controlled through proprietary resources, which are difficult to replicate, such as a strong brand identity. MMO2, the UK mobile network provider that has recently faced upheaval is deconstructing its value chain as a means of strengthening its position (Pesola 2002). The company will move all its IT systems, including such functions as customer care, e-payments and billing to IBM. The outsourcing agreement covers ten years and is worth £50m in its first year. MMO2's tactics are an interesting pointer of how the European mobile industry is changing its operating model in order to emulate the US model.

With the outsourcing of functions and the need for specialist knowledge in handling electronic transactions, the number of organizations involved in the supply chain is increasing. As a result of integration and deconstruction, suppliers are developing modular structures with Lego-like snap-together interconnectivity. The complexity of the new supply chain structure is becoming akin to a business ecosystem of networked co-operation, rather than the traditional chain of competing suppliers, manufacturers and distributors (*see* Mathews 2002).

Figure 12.10 depicts the modular structure of the ICT industries, which constitute the new information economy. The structure is built on layers of communication network companies, hardware and software manufacturers, internet service providers, e-commerce transaction companies, media and content companies, and myriad service companies.

The network infrastructure suppliers are companies such as Alcatel, Nortel Networks, Motorola and Ericsson that provide communications networking equipment. Intel and 3Com form a sub-set of companies in this category, which supply interfacing hardware and software.

The network operators provide the basis of the exchange of information between companies and their customers. The medium they operate could be based on satellite, telephone, mobile, television or area networks. British Telecom, AT&T, Vodafone and T-Mobile

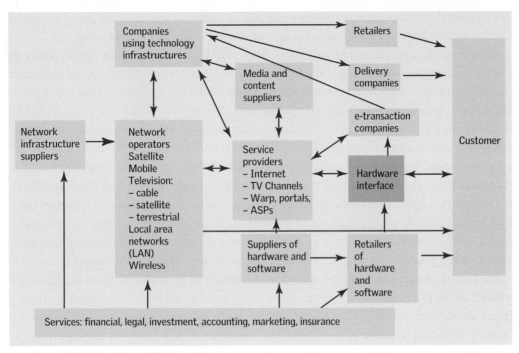

Figure 12.10 The modular infrastructure of the ICT economy

offer landline and mobile telecommunications networks. The operation of these companies is interconnected with other companies. For example, Vodafone uses BT's network. Credit card companies use Vodafone's mobile network for off-site credit verification. Vodafone has sold fixed-line telephone services from Energis and Racal Telecom networks. The interoperability of different telecom networks has become a complex business operation. British Telecom set up BT to develop and manage such relationships. BT Wholesale sells its fixed network product to independent service providers: businesses that wish to provide telecom services to end consumers without owning their own networks. The independent SP purchases the network facility from BT and other network operators, adding their own value and service brand.

Satellite networks provide the infrastructure for long-distance television, telephony and data interchange transmission. SES GLOBAL, Gilat Satellite Networks and Alcatel Space/SkyBridge have formed a €200 million joint venture to provide two-way satellite broadband services in corporate and home office markets across Europe. The new company plans to cater for the growing demand for broadband communications services in Europe via advanced VSAT satellite technology.

Digital television networks operate on a host of platforms such as satellite, copper or optic fibre cable. Interactive television has opened a host of business opportunities for retailing. The use of two-way cable networks, or a return medium via a normal telephone line, is changing the way consumers use and respond to television content. The business model for this service implies a new form of supply chain, for a new form of retailing.

Internet service providers are part of a complex web that provides the supply chain of information to the internet user. ISPs such as AOL and Fastnet convey internet content over the infrastructure of the telecommunication companies. At the back-end of the supply web, ISPs receive web pages from various organizations. The owners of the web pages would be the media and content suppliers, or, in many cases, they may have purchased the services of the media and content suppliers to create their web presence. At the front-end, where the supply web touches the customer, ISPs have to collaborate or conform to consumer interface manufacturers, which in the internet scenario would be computer suppliers. The supply web for the internet is due for another major revolution with third-generation (3G) mobile communication, which carries high-speed internet and video streaming. The 3G telephone, which will become the new customer interface, could dictate a change in internet transmission management and the nature of media content all the way down the supply chain.

The supply chain in the information economy shown in Figure 12.10 takes the form of a weblike network where each member may have to collaborate with many other members. Intercollaboration is possible because of software and hardware compatibility, and necessary because of the high degree of knowledge specialization at each point on the supply chain. An example of this weblike structure is the relationship between e-transaction companies, ISPs and media content providers and the companies that own the web pages. The four types of organization have to ensure the compatibility of their services across the supply network.

The infrastructure of the information economy does not look like a normal, traditional and competitive supply chain in the 'old' industrial economy. Telephony and the internet have made it possible for corporations to have commercial partnerships with many more companies. The notion of 'information is power' is turned on its head. As more companies have access to more information through communication, power is dissipated to more members in the supply chain. This increase in information exchange has become the overriding equalizer of power throughout the supply networks.

The basis of this new economy is the increase in connectivity among the various players in the chain. The connectivity level itself is rapidly evolving as communication and computational technologies become faster. The whole supply network is in a state of flux. Flexibility and adaptability have become essential strategic stances. Faster connectivity within the supply chain not only implies more interconnections between companies, but it also creates more volatile and replaceable interrelationships.

The concept of replaceable interrelationships has come about because companies are becoming 'isomorphic' or similar in nature. DiMaggio and Powell (1983, p. 149), drawing from Hawley (1968), define isomorphism as 'a constraining process that forces one unit in a population to resemble other units that face the same set of environmental conditions'. With the standardization of technology, products are becoming more similar in design and quality. With the standardization of internal operations, through materials resource planning (MRP), enterprise resource planning (ERP) and electronic customer relationship management (eCRM), the service levels of competing companies are becoming similar in content and in construction. The implication is that suppliers are easily replaced with similar companies that have similar products and similar delivery attributes.

The information economy is creating a web of companies that have lower barriers of entry but fewer safety nets for retaining business. The older, hierarchical value chains of the industrial economy reinforced exclusivity, while the information economy is more inclusive.

Case box: The rise of co-evolution and co-operation

The new weblike value chain gives rise to a 'self-organizing' system. In nature, flocking is a form of self-organization. The formation of flocking birds is a self-organizing form of collaboration, with simple goals of direction and velocity. Similarly, companies organize and adapt their relationships with vendors and distributors. They select and substitute their partners in the value chain according to changes in the consumer market. Vendors and distributors in turn adapt to new market scenarios. For example, a wave of collaborative buying (when competitors join forces for purchasing) is counteracted by a wave of collaborative vending from vendors. The system eventually normalizes the balance of power.

The 'self-organizing' aspect in the information economy leads to the concept of 'co-evolution' (see Kelly, 1994, for an overview of the implications of adaptive behaviour). Evolving to meet the needs of other members in the value chain is becoming a more effective strategy than satisfying the company's own needs. Adapting to meet other companies' need leads to more business. Riding the new wave of co-evolution, companies are avoiding costly races against each other in favour of a strategy to join forces to gain more customers. We are observing this effect in NEC and Siemens, which have joined forces to supply the networks for Hutchison 3G, a key network provider of third-generation telecommunications in Europe.

Co-evolution and collaboration are even more relevant in industries where network externalities are a vital part of corporate success. The more customers join a network, such as a telecommunications service, the higher is the incentive for other customers to join. This effect is causing companies to collaborate on issues of compatibility. With 3G mobile phones on the horizon for Europe and the US, the standards war for a mobile internet operating system has begun. Microsoft, Linux, Symbian and Openwave are in the race to establish a widely accepted standard. This is an example of old-style competition, but it has caused a wave of co-evolution in another layer of competitors. The issue of standards has motivated Nokia and Siemens, Europe's largest manufacturers of mobile phones, to collaborate. They have teamed up to accelerate the introduction of third-generation mobile services. The collaboration of two companies will guarantee that Nokia and Siemens handsets can communicate with each other seamlessly. In this way the two companies, which have a combined global market share of 45 per cent, will benefit from network externalities and the positive feedback generated from providing a larger compatible technology network. Nokia and Siemens anticipate that other equipment vendors will link up with them to minimize industry fragmentation.

12.4.3 Physical platforms

A **physical platform** is the tangible infrastructure (such as computers, telephones, satellites, digital TV and local area networks) that delivers a service to consumers. A simple example of a platform is the PC on your desk. This comprises a set of hardware and software items joined together to provide a computing service. The component items are built according to to explicit technology standards and are delivered through separate but parallel supply chains to the PC assembler. Similarly, to obtain Sky's pay-TV service one needs a physical platform consisting of digital TV receiver, set-top decoder, telephone landlines, satellites and ground stations. The physical platform is an assembly of items, each constructed to specific standards and integrated to deliver service to the customer.

Case box: **Globalstar**

Globalstar is another example of a physical platform. Globalstar provides mobile telecommunications using Low Earth Orbiting (LEO) satellites. Its telephones look like mobile or fixed phones but the difference is that they can operate in areas outside normal reach. The satellite platform picks up signals from the Earth's surface, and relays them to the terrestrial gateway. Gateways distribute the calls to existing fixed and mobile networks. Terrestrial gateways are vital to integrate the company's services with existing local telephony networks.

The size of a physical network does not guarantee success. Iridium had a larger physical platform of satellites than Globalstar, but faced marketing-related difficulties at start-up. When it launched in 1998 it targeted the consumer users, who rejected the service because of its cost and bulky first-generation phones. Iridium filed for bankruptcy in 2001 and planned to decommission its satellite platform. It was purchased by a consortium, which paid $25 million for the inactive satellite system, which cost $5 billion when it was built in 1998. Iridium has recuperated most of its losses by changing its marketing segmentation strategy. Its current major user is the US Department of Defence, which is in line with its sales strategy to service large industrial users in remote locations (Weiss 2001).

Physical platforms have evolved from the simple structures, such as the older regional railway system, to a complex structure of interconnected sub-platforms. For this reason, the joints between the sub-networks become the strength of the whole structure, or, conversely, it could be its Achilles heel. It is therefore vital to define standards for joints. The standards that govern how a system and its modules interact is called the network's architecture (Morris and Ferguson 1993).

Henderson and Clark (1990) review two kinds of dynamic processes in modular systems: **modular innovation** and **architectural innovation**. The former type retains the architecture of the network, including its joints, but modifies the modules. By preserving the basic architecture of a system, network providers offer users enough compatibility to shift from one product generation to the next. The changes occur in the innovations and improvements of the modular components. They are be fitted into the system when required, and will be removed when obsolete. The result is a hybrid dynamic of change that preserved the platform's architecture while creating innovations within the module structure. A series of minor incremental modular changes can lead to an overall network platform that is radically new (Vercoulen and Wegberg 1998).

In architectural innovation, the modules are largely unchanged, but the architecture that connects them (the jointing system) is changed (Henderson and Clark 1990). The speed of innovation can be fast, as a key part of the system, the modular structure, is retained. New joints between these modules are installed. In some cases, adopting new standards and installing some new modules that embody these standards create an architectural innovation. The development of the internet in the late 1990s is an example of an architectural innovation in a network platform. The main proponents of the internet evolution are standard-setting bodies such as the World Wide Web Consortium and the Internet Engineering Task Force (Vercoulen and Wegberg 1998).

Case box: **Managing interoperability**

Physical platforms in the telecommunications industry are typically open platforms (like Wintel is for PCs) that provide interconnectivity with other telecom networks to add value and create network externalities. Open platforms have stipulated protocols, which are implemented by a large user base, as in the case of IBM clones. Closed platforms or proprietary platforms make it difficult for others to interact properly with those systems. Microsoft software and Apple computers are examples of closed platforms.

Open networks require interconnections and compatibility with surrounding networks. Telecommunications platforms have had to cope with the complexity of interoperability among different systems, as well as the agility required to shift rapidly to newer standards. The dynamics of complexity and agility used to be opposing forces (Vercoulen and Wegberg 1998). A complex interconnected physical platform tends to develop slowly. Railway systems and the telecom networks in many countries show this inertia. Communications and technology firms progressively created a solution to these opposing dynamics of development. As in the supply chain case discussed earlier, companies divided their platform structure into separate modules, each with some degree of autonomy (Langlois and Robertson 1992; Garud, Kumaraswamy and Prabhu 1995). Each module is designed with the flexibility for rapid change, such as the shift from ETACS to GSM. The complexity feature is retained because each module is interoperable with other modules to form a weblike complex system. The modules are therefore interdependent through the nodes, or joints between the modules. Interoperability between modules creates value for the user, as we observe in the ability to call overseas on a mobile telephone. Roaming of mobile telephones from country to country is another example. Interoperability exists between platforms of different network providers in the same country, or different platforms in different countries.

Building alliances

The reach of a technical platform determines the size of the consumer base. For this reason, companies are building alliances to gain the rewards of positive feedback. Apple and Microsoft have collaborated to create a version of Office that operates on an Apple computer. The effect is to allow the Apple computer platform to overlap with the Microsoft Office platform. In the mobile industry, competing telephone manufacturers are clamouring to create a communications platform with a common operating system. Ericsson and Nokia use the Symbian operating system on their third-generation mobile phones. Panasonic and Motorola are planning to introduce telephones with the software platform. Symbian will receive a total of $17.95 million in funding from Nokia Corp., Motorola Inc., Panasonic, Sony Ericsson and Psion to support its development (Evers 2002).

The Ethernet is an earlier example of alliance formation intended to increase the size of a physical platform. In 1973 Metcalfe and Boggs invented the Ethernet, the local area networking (LAN) technology that acts as a means to send vast amounts of data at high speed to the laser printers that Xerox was designing. Interestingly, the Ethernet came before the PC, yet it was to create a breakthrough in computer networking that would eventually tie together over 50 million PCs worldwide. The Ethernet quickly attracted Digital and Intel's interest to adopt the communication platform. Metcalfe had moved on to form 3Com but remained the key player in the discussions between Xerox, Digital and Intel. The DI3X group was formed, named after the first letter of the company names. The alliance lobbied for Ethernet to become a standard approved by the IEEE. Xerox agreed to license Ethernet to all users at a nominal fee of $1000. It realized that it would have to provide an open standard to get computer manufacturers to take on Ethernet as an interface to their printers. The strength of Ethernet was that it allowed PCs and workstations from different manufacturers to communicate by using an agreed standard, hence increasing the size of its physical platform and therefore its reach.

12.4.4 Consumer networks

A **consumer network** requires interdependencies between consumers. In a consumer market there are two levels of value attached to a product. 'Autarky' value (Liebowitz and Margolis 1999) refers to the value associated with a product irrespective of the number of other users. In marketing terms, this would be the 'core' value of a product. In economics this is the normal assumption and the theory of the firm is based on assumptions about the independence of individual consumer preferences. 'Synchronization' value is the augmented value derived from being able to interact with other consumers. The latter fuels the dynamics of the network effect discussed earlier in this chapter and in McGee and Sammut-Bonnici (2002). For example, the relative abilities of Microsoft, Symbian or other companies to capture synchronization value will determine who will gain critical mass first and win the race to establish the new operating system for third-generation mobile telephones. Customers will buy the 3G phones with the operating system they expect to be the most popular in the future. In this way they will be able to communicate and exchange video clips and photos with the widest possible set of users. The success of the winning operating system might depend on the psychology of consumer choice, or it could depend on technology characteristics from supply chain strategies and technology standards. For example, Microsoft and Intel co-operated to make Windows 95 exclusively compatible with Intel x86 microprocessor architectures and vice versa. The media coined the effect the 'Wintel Advantage'. In the case of mobile operating systems, Symbian and Microsoft are rallying their respective set of supporters to establish separate supply networks.

Lock-in and switching costs

The Wintel case led to a situation of **lock-in** for Windows users. The Wintel operating system quickly gained critical mass through rapid adoption and it became the most popular system throughout the world. On top of this, Windows users then invested in complementary software such as the Microsoft Office suite. Lock-in arises whenever users invest in the multiple complementary and durable assets of a physical platform and then find the costs of switching to an alternative to be prohibitive. Lock-in can occur on an individual level, company level and even a societal level. Thus, individuals may face switching costs in adopting a rival to Microsoft software, but so also do companies in having to provide systematic retraining costs, and so might whole communities in having to move from one software product to another. The key is that it would usually be necessary to switch from one dominant product to retain the interdependencies and complementarities between consumers. Private users were locked into the long-playing record technology because records could not be used on CD players (but were persuaded to switch when the benefit–cost ratio of the new products became sufficiently large). Note that the benefits of tape recording were never large enough to persuade customers to make a wholesale switch from LPs but the extra benefits of tapes (ability to record) were sufficient to persuade customers to invest in parallel systems. Companies became locked into Lotus 1-2-3 spreadsheets because their employees were trained in using the program command structure but later were persuaded to switch to Excel within Microsoft Office because of the extra complementarities. On a societal level, millions of users throughout the world are locked into using Microsoft's Windows desktop operating environment, as it has become the standard software in offices around the world.

Case box: **Lock-in and switching costs in mobile communications**

Telecommunication systems providers have chosen to offer new, superior technologies despite high switching costs. The industry has undergone three generations of technologies – TACS, ETACS, and GSM – and is now in the early days of introduction of 3G, incurring significant investment costs. Their calculation is made on the basis that the new systems will provide backward compatibility plus the expected benefits of new services.

Switching costs and lock-in at the consumer level can be deliberately used to inhibit or prevent consumers from adopting newer technologies or moving to alternative networks. In mobile communications, users may switch to another network provider with the same technology but with a different price structure. They may choose to switch to another technology when they replace their handsets with higher-level models. The strategies of the mobile telecommunication companies have focused on manipulating the tangible and intangible consumer costs when switching networks. In the introductory phase customers were contractually bound to a network for a year. They had to pay a release fee to end the contract and a connection charge to go to the next network. In the later 1990s switching networks became easier with the introduction of pay-as-you-go cards. But the hidden, intangible costs of switching remains, irrespective of payment structures and Oftel's recent pressure to minimize switching cost in the industry. Customers are deterred from switching by the investment in the time required to get used to a new product and are further inhibited by the uncertainty about the quality of untested products. The influence of brand loyalty is also significant. To the consumer, another very relevant switching cost is the loss of the mobile number when moving to another network (this was also a very big issue in the development of the telephone system in the USA over a century ago). Subscribers' reluctance to give up their familiar numbers resulted in the introduction of subsidized phones and more competitive tariffs. The power of switching costs can be observed in the entry strategies against powerful incumbents. Vodafone and Cellnet started to operate in 1984 and had a captive customer base by the time Orange and One2One entered the market in 1993 and 1994 respectively. The new entrants had to generate new customer-winning strategies with stronger branding and lower costs.

On a societal level economists observe that the practice of using lock-in strategies can have negative welfare effects as new superior technologies are suppressed. Liebowitz and Margolis (1990) discuss the fascinating example of typewriter keyboard layouts. In the 1870s the QWERTY configuration was selected by the creators of the TypeWriter brand in order to slow down typists in order to reduce jamming of the keys. The Dvorak layout patented in the 1932 is a more efficient layout and allows faster typing. This would suggest that QWERTY should then give way to the more efficient keyboard layout. The phenomenon of sticking to the slower QWERTY system is explained in terms of switching costs.

The collective switching costs are far higher than the individual switching costs because the co-ordination for mass switching to Dvorak is so difficult. With the advent of electric type-writers if the 1950s and then computer keyboards the expectation is even stronger but QWERTY still remains.

12.5 Networks, standards and competition

According to Economides and Flyer (1997):

> Firms that compete in markets where network externalities are present face unique trade-offs regarding the choice of a technical standard. Adhering to a leading compatibility standard allows a firm's product to capture the value added by a large network. However, simultaneously the firm loses direct control over the market supply of the good and faces (direct) intra-platform competition. Alternatively, adhering to a unique standard allows the firm to face less or no intra-platform competition, but it sacrifices the added value associated with a large network.

This trade-off is a key strategic decision that depends in part on the control that firms have in making their output compatible with competitors' outputs and complementary products. The ability to conform to a common standard opens the opportunity to make this trade-off. Where standards are proprietary, the decision rests with the owner of the standard. The owner's trade-off is the pay-off associated with developing the existing network and its spillovers versus the introduction of more intra-platform competition. Essentially the trade-off is the same: to adhere to a common standard or to seek uniqueness. This can be expressed as a sequential game: at the outset, one chooses the appropriate technical standard (and, therefore, the network to join), and later one chooses how to compete. Normal markets do not have this choice of network and there are consequences for market structure and competition in the presence of network externalities. The mathematical model in Economides and Flyer (1997) defines networks as coalition structures and analyses the stability of coalitions under different standards regimes and varying levels of network externalities. There are a number of implications for market structure in the presence of network externalities.

First, it is intuitively clear that industry output will be higher when there are network externalities and when standards are open. Firms are free to choose which standard to adopt and are deterred only by the costs of adoption. Second, when standards are incompatible and the owners of standards can exercise proprietary control, incumbents are more strongly protected against the consequences of new entrants. Moreover, there will usually be considerable asymmetries between firms in terms of outputs, prices and profits. (Under incompatibility regimes, firms are equivalent to platforms and constitute one-firm networks.) For pure network goods the asymmetries are particularly marked.

In general, with total incompatibility of standards market concentration, output inequality and price and profit inequality increase with the extent of the network externality. This is an important result because it explains why one or two firms so often dominate network industries. The mechanism is straightforward. The leading network establishes its critical mass, leaving the second network to establish a critical mass across the remaining untapped market coverage. The third network follows in the same fashion and so on. It follows that there will be a tendency to provide large incentives to organize customers into few platforms so as to maximize the added value from the available networks. Firms will be keen to abandon their own weak standards in favour of the higher value obtainable from a leading network.

There is a third implication. Where there are proprietary standards and strong network effects, there is no natural equilibrium in terms of network offerings. There are always incentives for at least one firm to move to a stronger network and the consequence of any one move is to shift the incentives for all other firms. However, equilibrium can be reinforced by the refusal of firms to make their proprietary standards available. Again, the mechanism is straightforward. Under strong externalities, the owner of a standard has a considerable incentive to exploit the standard by itself and to exclude other firms with weaker standards. Conversely, where the externality is weak, the owner will find a stronger incentive to admit other firms to its proprietary standard in order to grow the network through collective effort and thus generate more added value.

In summary, strong network externalities suggest the following conclusions:

1 Larger industry output.

2 Very large asymmetries between firms/platforms.

3 Likelihood of market dominance.

4 Enhancement and protection of proprietary standards.

5 Equilibrium market structures that are the reverse of the world without network externalities.

12.6 Implications for strategy

This chapter argues that there are major differences between the economic and strategic characteristics of the **new economy** compared to the old industrial order. These major differences can be summarized as follows:

1 The information economy depends on connectivity. Without connectivity, consumer interdependence is indirect. Positive feedback gives an economic law of plenty – more gives more.

2 Upfront costs are very large and revenues can be substantially delayed and are

significantly at risk. As a result, the nature of business models is different, with higher degrees of risk embedded in them.

3 It is also a world of immense uncertainty where even the range of potential outcomes is not known, but also where there is a significant probability that future technological change might undermine an apparently winning position.

4 The competition between rival networks/standards can be hard to call in advance.

5 'Tippy markets' substantially raise the level of risk.

In this new world there is much more uncertainty and companies need to take bigger risks in order just to survive. The prospect of entrepreneurial profits is enticingly large but there are probably greater probabilities of failure. The list of failures and near failures in the last decade by large companies is very long. There are some new strategic 'rules' for competing in the new economy. While these are quite generic in nature they illustrate that companies need to come to these markets with a different mindset about how to compete:

1 **Expectations management** is central to the way in which marketing strategy is conceived (see the case box below).

2 **Open standards** are the key to volume. Protected standards are only viable as small high-priced niche markets. The old preoccupation with protection of intellectual property is giving way to a sharing and co-operating approach.

3 There is a law of inverse pricing. The best (i.e. the most valuable in the future) products are given away, such as web browsers, in order to create a consumer standard, and sheer volume causes both marginal costs and prices to fall over time as the product becomes more valuable. The cash flow machine consists of modest (even small) margins multiplied by gigantic volumes to defray massive investments. The machine is volume driven and protected by very large switching costs.

4 The first strategic choice is which network to join (which standard to adopt). The second, and a long way behind, is how to compete within the network of choice.

5 Networked complementarities and co-operative strategies are replacing the old order of hierarchical business organization and competition.

6 In a world of uncertainty, customers are also uncertain about which standards, technologies and products will prevail. This will increase the power of brands and place upon marketing the need to manage customer expectations so as to speed adoption rates towards tipping points in the market.

The economic characteristics of network industries are dependent in large part on the interconnectivity that is characteristic of the technologies of information goods. Interconnectivity allows customers to view, use and link products, giving rise to virtual networks of customers. In these networks, powerful demand-side increasing returns can operate. Where consumer-based externalities are powerful there are strong pressures towards 'winner takes all' phenomena (e.g. Wintel globally, and Sky TV in the UK). In these circumstances conventional economic laws are challenged. De facto monopoly can emerge: but uncertainty is high and markets may be intrinsically unstable. Successive waves of technology may outmode old monopolies and serve as the basis for new monopolies.

The rate of growth and now the sheer size of the ICT industry has been the progenitor of major changes in the economy. We have seen major effects on other industries through the new value possibilities that information technology offers and through the substantial fixed costs and minimum scales required for effective deployment of these technologies. When linked to networks of interdependent customers we see the potential emergence of 'winner takes all' strategies and the emergence of new monopolies.

We have decomposed the ICT industry into its component parts in order to see who the players are and how they interact with one another. In doing this we argue that we are beginning to see a new type of industrial order – one marked by networked complementarities and co-operation in place of the traditional model of hierarchy and competition. We have also decomposed the industry into four horizontal levels – technology, supply chain, platform, and network – to show that these have different economic characteristics and therefore that corporate strategies have different dynamics. The examples quoted indicate the range and extent of the possibilities inherent in the new technologies and for the nature of rivalry in the form of pre-emptive strikes and technology races. We note particularly the pervasive changes that are taking place in supply chains generally. The increasing importance of connectivity and modularity is forcing a shift from competitive mode towards co-operative mode. This raises thoughts of self-organizing systems and the notion of co-evolution, rather a long way from the search for and exercise of crude bargaining power. The sheer size and cost of physical platforms also create new dynamics. The pervasive use of alliances is an obvious example. Less obvious is how the need for interoperability requires new attitudes towards complexity and requirements for agility.

A new set of strategies is emerging to offset the risks and pressures exerted by these rules. This is visible in the setting up of global standards and their ensuing platforms. For example, Group Speciale Mobile, commonly known as GSM, is an association of 600 network operators and suppliers of the mobile phone industry. Their primary objective is to set a common standard for mobile communications in order to create a homogeneous industry where equipment, software and networks can seamlessly talk to each other. Strategies of standardization are stabilizing the markets and charting the course for research and development policies.

Finally, we remark on the significance of interdependence between consumers. This effect at its strongest completely shifts our thinking from the prevalence of oligopolistic competition (size matters but so do diminishing returns) to the possibility of winner takes all and the monopoly (size matters – full stop). Clearly such network effects are not always going to be so extreme but there is a real possibility that the combination of high fixed costs, significant economies of scale, and high degrees of knowledge specialization will, when taken together with consumer bandwagons, create massive new corporate structures to which the major (and perhaps only) discipline will be further developments in technology. However, the analysis of consumer lock-in suggests the real possibility that switching costs might inhibit the adoption of valuable new technologies.

Case box: **Expectations management**

When consumers choose products in network markets, their expectations play a crucial role on sales of the products or their network components, since consumer utility depends on the number of other consumers purchasing the same products. Rival firms in the network industry influence consumers' expectations in order to maximize their profits. The process is facilitated by consumers' imperfect information about the size of the installed base in the market. Sales figures are often exaggerated to impress consumers about leadership in the installed base over rivals. The competition between OS/2 and Microsoft Windows in 1992 is an example of firms' intentions of influencing consumer expectation. IBM and Microsoft both announced wider adoption of their operating systems than actual. Later on, each company disputed the estimated numbers of sales of the other (Bensen and Farrell 1994).

Figure 12.11 Adoption processes: networks and technologies

Expectation manage-
ment is a strategic device
that goes beyond the
inflation of penetration
figures and moves into
the realms of brand and
corporate image building.
In competing to become
market leaders in the
mobile communications
industry, or at least to
achieve critical mass,
consumer expectations

Market to create momentum:
    create the belief that this technology will be the standard
Leverage reputation:
    brands and reputation matter
Commit to 'open' standards:
    open standards can give access to volume
    proprietary standards can result in small niches
Win over an influential buyer
    e.g. supermarkets and UPCs (barcodes)
Advance sign ups:
    prior commitments create confidence
Wink at piracy:
    adoption at zero price is better than no adoption
Pricing:
    leasing, long-term contracts, give-aways, penetration pricing

Figure 12.12 Managing the adoption process

were significant. The mobile company that was expected to grow the fastest would gain most market share. Self-fulfilling expectations are one manifestation of positive feedback economics and bandwagon effects. The mobile industry has made consistent use of semiotics in expectations management through its media campaigns. Images, music themes and slogans are used to imply magnitude and leadership.

The model in Figure 12.11 illustrates the adoption process. Adoption typically follows an S-shaped pattern around the long-term trend growth rate. The early adopters ('anoraks') rush in. There is then a pause while the prospective early adopters make up their minds – marketing is focused on persuading them to move quickly and decisively so as to create a rapid growth that will become self-sustaining (through point B in the diagram). Following this, the push to sustain the market through attracting late adopters is the next marketing focus. This suggests some rules for marketing – these are summarized in Figure 12.12. Marketing is about creating momentum so as to minimize the risks that are endemic in this new world. Brands and reputation are, if anything, even more important. The emphasis is on volume, so open standards are attractive and low, penetration-style pricing will be common.

Vodafone's corporate image campaign in its early days included images of the Thames Barrier and the cliffs of Dover. Symbols of national interest were used to give the subliminal message that Vodafone will succeed throughout the UK. The musical theme in the Thames Barrier campaign was from *Close Encounters*, implying universal reach. The cliffs of Dover campaign involved the draping of a large section of the cliffs with material, by a contemporary artist. The message could have been directed at conquering 'coverage' issues of radio transmission. Orange has had one of the most famous slogans in UK media history: 'The future is bright, the future is Orange'. One2One has had equally expansionist media campaigns, particularly with its award-winning 'Welcome to Our World'. All these campaigns imply market leadership and a sense of network growth.

The effects in Figure 12.11 can be seen in research by Huberman (1988), which shows how consumers' expectations are being linked to the critical mass. The stronger the consumers' expectation that a new network will be widely adopted in the future, the faster the market reaches critical mass. Once a critical number of users is achieved, the rate of increase of new users increases exponentially, up to the limit of the user population (or to some other natural limit; *see* Figure 12.11). The implication for strategists it that the time required to achieve critical mass can be reduced in proportion to the degree of optimism of people's expectations.

Hence, strategic action aimed at increasing consumers' expectations of the success of a new product would have a double effect of inducing more new users, who in turn influence even more users. This effect can be powerful – Huberman's simulations demonstrate that even if there is only a small group of individuals with double the propensity for innovation in relation to the group average, the critical mass can be reached very rapidly. This has been evident in the mobile telecommunications industry. Once the phones were affordable and accessible to the youth market (the early adopters), sales boomed for this particular segment. As a result even more users from other segments were attracted to the market.

12.7 Summary

Thus, the brave new world has a sting in the tail. The pervasive development of the ICT industries has promoted, and continues to promote, very substantial consequential changes throughout the economy. In doing so, industry economics and dynamics do change and significant adaptations have to take place in order to avoid getting run down by the juggernaut. Changes are needed in the nature of the corporate strategies and in the mindsets required. Where the conjunction of certain technological and consumer circumstances takes place, the strategy game becomes a very direct race to establish dominant position. Even where such games fail to achieve their objectives, the cost of unproductive investment could be enormous. Where they in fact succeed, many will nevertheless have failed, and we would also face the difficulties in managing the consequences of de facto monopoly. The data available does not suggest that winner takes all is likely to be a frequent phenomenon. However, all the other indications suggest that various forms of scale-intensive, pre-emptive strategies will become much more common (see, for example, the telecommunications boom and bust). But as a counter-point we can also see that there are very considerable forces promoting more co-operation and stronger incentives towards a much more subtle blending of co-operative and competitive modes of practice within industries.

Key terms

Architectural innovation *478*
Consumer externalities *462*
Consumer network *480*
Critical mass *466*
Expectations management *485*
Installed base *467*
Interoperability *479*
Isomorphism *476*
Lock-in *481*
Modular innovation *478*
Multiplier effect *459*
Negative feedback systems *468*

Network externalities *458*
Network industries *461*
New economy *484*
Open standards *485*
Physical platforms *478*
Pure network good *469*
Real and virtual networks *464*
Standards *472*
Standards versioning *473*
Switching costs *473*
Technical platform *473*
Tipping point *467*

Recap questions and assignments

1 Explain how network externalities might (or might not) occur in the following situations, paying particular attention to the way in which critical mass is reached:

(a) The Apple–IBM PC battle in the PC industry;

(b) The mobile telecommunications industry;

(c) BSkyB and the satellite TV market.

2 For the situations in question 1, give examples of co-evolution and/or cooperation. In which case is co-operative behaviour most marked? Why?

3 For any internet-based business with which you are familiar, explain its business model and compare it to any one of the business models discussed in Chapter 6.

Online LearningCentre

When you have read this chapter, log on to the Online Learning Centre website at www.mcgraw-hill.co.uk/textbooks/mcgee to explore chapter-by-chapter test questions, further reading and more online study tools for strategy.

Case 1 **How good is Google?**

If the ultimate measure of impact is to have one's name become a new verb in the world's main languages, Google has reason to be proud. When they founded the company five years ago, Sergey Brin and Larry Page, friends at Stanford University, chose a word play on 'googol' – the number 1 followed by 100 zeros – because their ambition was to organize the information overload of the internet in a transparent and superior way. These days, singles 'google' suitors before agreeing to a date, housewives 'google' recipes before cooking, and patients 'google' their ailments before visiting doctors. Dave Gorman, a comedian, even has a popular show, the 'Googlewhack Adventure' – a Googlewhack being what happens when two words are entered into Google and it comes back with exactly one match.

As search engines go, in other words, Google has clearly been a runaway success. Not only is its own site the most popular for search on the web, but it also powers the search engines of major portals, such as Yahoo! and AOL. All told, 75% of referrals to websites now originate from Google's algorithms. That is power. For some time now, Google's board (which includes two of Silicon Valley's best-known venture capitalists, John Doerr of Kleiner Perkins Caufield & Byers and Michael Moritz of Sequoia Capital) has been deliberating how to translate that power into money. They appear to have decided to bring Google to the stockmarket next spring. Bankers have been overheard estimating Google's value at $15 billion or more. That could make Google Silicon Valley's first hot IPO since the dotcom bust, and perhaps its biggest ever. That alone is enough to have some sceptics whispering 'Netscape'. Now that the worst of the dotcom hangover is clearing, they wonder, will Google become one of the few valuable internet survivors, joining Amazon and above all eBay? Or will it simply be the next over-hyped share sale to make its founders rich only to wither away miserably, either for lack of a sustainably profitable business model, or, like Netscape, because it finds itself in the path of that mighty wrecker, Microsoft?

The search for profits

Google, naturally, is determined to avoid Netscape's fate at all costs. This was why it made Eric Schmidt its chief executive in 2001. Mr Schmidt was 46 at the time – Messrs Brin and Page were in their twenties – and was the boss of Novell, a software firm decimated by Microsoft but given another lease of life under his leadership. He seemed suitably 'adult' to turn Google into a money-making machine.

Mr Schmidt understood that the key to monetising all those customer searches (now 200m a day) was to place small, unobtrusive and highly relevant text advertisements alongside Google's search results. Advertisers like this system because they pay only if web surfers actually click on their links. And consumers either do not mind, or even learn to love these commercial links for their relevance, just as they appreciate the Yellow Pages.

Google did not pioneer this 'paid search' advertising. That honour falls to Overture, a Californian firm bought this year by Yahoo! which still has about half of the $2 billion-or-so market. Nor did Google's founders readily embrace the concept. Mr Page was once heard to say at a trade show that commercial exploitation was 'bastardising' the search industry. Mr Schmidt made the concept uncontroversial at Google, thereby helping paid search to become the fastest growing part of the advertising industry today.

The next step is to take this approach to advertising from the results pages of search engines and on to other web pages. Increasingly, web publishers – from hobby bloggers to small businesses – allow firms such as Google to crawl through the content of their pages and place relevant text advertisements in the right margin. Once page visitors click on the links, the webmasters share the revenues with Google. At a stroke, this so-called 'contextual advertising' makes much of web publishing self-financing. This may result in better web content by making hitherto unprofitable online activities economically viable.

Meta Group, a consultancy, reckons that the market for paid search and other contextual advertising will grow to $5 billion by 2006. This is Google's main market opportunity (although it also gets some revenues from licensing its search technology). Currently, Google is thought to make annual profits of about $150m. To be worth the rumoured $15 billion for longer than it takes a bubble to burst, it will need to raise its profitability substantially. That means matching such internet stars as eBay (market capitalisation $37 billion), but without the natural-monopoly advantages that have made eBay so dominant – the classic network effect of buyers and sellers knowing they do best by all trading in one place. For Google to stay permanently ahead of other search-engine technologies is almost impossible, since it takes so little – only a bright idea by another set of geeks – to lose the lead. In contrast to a portal such as Yahoo!, which also offers customers free e-mail and other services, a pure search engine is always but a click away from losing users.

The arrival of competitors

Yahoo!, in fact, will probably be the first to attack. It now owns rival search technologies including AltaVista, AlltheWeb and Inktomi. With the contextual-advertising technology of Overture, Yahoo! now has under its own roof all the elements of the business model that made Google such a success. It cannot be long before Yahoo! turns from a lucrative customer of Google's into a powerful rival.

Even more frightening (especially to those who remember Netscape's fate in the browser wars), Microsoft smells blood. It is currently working on its own search algorithm, which it hopes to make public early next year, around the probable time of Google's share listing. Historically, Microsoft has been good at letting others (Apple, Netscape, Real) pioneer a technology before taking over, exploiting its dominance in desktop operating systems.

Google the new-age advertising agency makes money, but it is Google the search engine that builds the consumer brand which makes the ad agency powerful. Whenever users click on advertisements on Google's own site, Google gets all the revenues. Whenever users stray to other search engines, even ones where Google has placed sponsored links, Google has to share the revenues with the site owner. As the competition between Google, Overture and others heats up, Google's profit margins will fall.

This may already be happening. Craig Pisaris-Henderson, the chief executive of FindWhat.com, a smaller rival to Overture and Google in contextual advertising, reckons that Google's operating margins on sites other than its own must be much worse than FindWhat.com's (23%) or Overture's (12%) because it has been wooing advertisers away from Overture by being more generous to webmasters.

One thing that might help against Microsoft, says Danny Sullivan, the editor of SearchEngineWatch.com, an online consumer guide to the industry, is Google's image of 'niceness' – at least by implicit comparison with the forces of darkness in Redmond. Scott Banister, a pioneer of paid-search technology (and now a founder of IronPort, an e-mail infrastructure firm), thinks that Google has already built sufficiently deep networks with advertisers to mount an effective resistance to Microsoft's impending assault.

Even so, Google is no sure thing – as those who hope to sell its shares are no doubt aware. John Doerr and Michael Moritz, for instance, between them also brought Netscape and Yahoo! to market, and may remember their lessons. With luck, Google's owners will remember to work out a viable strategy for Google beyond the point at which they cash out.

Source: The Economist, 11 January 2003, Vol. 369, Issue 8348, p. 57.

Case Questions

1 Describe Google's strategy and explain how its business model works.

2 What are the risks facing Google and how can it defend itself against them?

3 What characteristics of the 'new economy' are present in this case? To what extent do these characteristics make the analysis of Google's competitive position and its future strategic choices unique or unusual?

Case 2 **Browser wars, part two**

Remember the browser wars, when Netscape and Microsoft fought for dominance of the web? For a while, each rushed out ever more complex browsers in the software equivalent of an arms race. In the end, Microsoft prevailed by bundling its browser with its Windows operating system.

That fight may, however, prove to have been just a warm-up. Now a new browser war is under way, as software firms compete to provide the browsers for 'information appliances' such as set-top boxes, handheld computers and smart phones. Such devices are still in their infancy, but they are widely expected eventually to outnumber PCs. So the stakes in this new browser war are high. And this time round, the battlefield looks very different.

For a start, Microsoft is almost nowhere to be seen. Its strongest weapon in the desktop browser wars – the ability to include new software as part of Windows, and thus ensure its installation on millions of PCs – no longer works. Microsoft's cut-down version of Windows for appliances has been a flop, and the firm's strategy of tying its browser to its operating system is no help if that system is not dominant. But Netscape, which is now part of AOL, is still very much in the running, alongside dozens of rivals including Opera, OpenTV, Lineo, QNX and Pixo.

Another difference is that the appliance makers and service providers (such as cable-TV and mobile-phone companies) will decide which browser comes installed on a particular device. On a PC, a new browser can be downloaded and installed with a few clicks. Not so with appliances, whose users will have no choice in the matter. Rival browser makers are thus courting appliance makers and service providers, rather than trying to woo users. To maximise its chances in this beauty contest, a browser must be fast and work with many different kinds of hardware.

With so many firms in the race, it seems unlikely that any browser will win a dominant share. The resulting diversity will mean that, for everything to work properly, it will be vital that web pages and the browsers that display them conform to the technical standards laid down by the World Wide Web Consortium (W3C). So browser makers are rushing to show how well-behaved their software is. Contrast this with the old Microsoft-Netscape battle, when both firms added proprietary extensions to existing web standards in an attempt to lock in users.

Netscape claims that its software, called Gecko, is the most standards-compliant browser around. Jon Stephenson von Tetzchner, Opera's boss, makes a similar claim about his firm. The problem, he says, is that only 5% of web pages comply with W3C standards. Most are designed to look good on Netscape's or Microsoft's old browsers, rather than playing by the rules. On December 6th, Opera said it will offer the Windows version of its browser free. The idea, says Mr von Tetzchner, is to increase Opera's market share and to encourage web designers to look beyond the 'big two' browsers to a more diverse future.

This is just one of the many subtle links between the old and new browser wars. Netscape's new strategy is similarly informed by its bruising previous encounter with Microsoft. By making Gecko freely available, and encouraging its use with the free Linux operating system, it hopes to allow appliance makers to avoid 'vendor lock-in'. Netscape does not benefit directly from this strategy, but the result is to make it hard for any single firm (i.e., Microsoft) to establish a stranglehold on the market. Although the new browser wars are very different from the old, in some respects little has changed.

Source: 'Browser wars, part two', *The Economist* 14 December 2000.
© The Economist Newspaper Limited, London (14 December 2000).

Case Questions

1 What was Microsoft's strategy in the first browser wars? How important were network externalities in its thinking?

2 Why is the new generation of browser wars different? Does Microsoft now have a competitive disadvantage?

Further reading and references

Arthur, B (1996) 'Increasing Returns and the New World of Business', *Harvard Business Review*, July/Aug.

Arthur, WB (1989) 'Competing technologies, increasing returns, and lock-in by historical events', *Economic Journal*, **99**, pp. 116–31.

Arthur, WB (1990) 'Positive feedback in the economy', *Scientific American*, **262**, pp. 92–9.

Baumol, W, Panzar, J and Willig, R (1982) 'Contestable markets and the theory of industry', *American Economic Review*, 72.

Bensen, SM and Farrell, J (1994) 'Choosing How to Compete: Strategies and Tactics Standardization', *Journal of Economic Perspectives*, Spring.

David, PA and Shurmer, M (1996) 'Formal standards-setting for global telecommunications and information services: towards an institutional regime transformation', *Telecommunications Policy*, 20, 10.

David, PA and Steinmueller, WE (1994) 'Economics of Compatibility Standards and Competition in Telecommunication Networks', *Information Economics and Policy*, 6.

Digital Planet (2002) *The Global Information Economy*, Data by International Data Corporation, World Information Technology and Services Alliance, USA.

DiMaggio, PJ and Powell, WW (1983) 'The iron cage revisited: institutional isomorphism and collective rationality in organizational fields', *American Sociological Review*, **48**, April, pp. 147–60.

Dumont, B (2000) Book Review of Carl Shapiro and Hal R. Varian, Information Rules: A Strategic Guide to the Network Economy, *Journal of Network Industries*, **1**, **1**, pp. 101–7.

Economides, N (1996) 'The economics of networks', *International Journal of Industrial Organization*, **14**, **2**, pp. 675–99.

Economides, N and Flyer, F (1997) 'Compatibility and Market Structure for Network Goods', Discussion Paper EC–98–02.

Ellis, HS and Fellner, W (1943) 'External economies and diseconomies', *American Economic Review*, 33.

Evans, P and Wurster, TS (2000) *Blown to Bits*, Harvard Business School Press, Boston, MA.

Evers, J (2002) 'Siemens joins Symbian Consortium', IDG News Service, Amsterdam Bureau, ITworld.com 4/23.

Garud, R, Kumaraswamy, A and Prabhu, A (1995) 'Networking for Success in Cyberspace', *IEEE Proceedings of the International Conference on Multimedia Computing and Systems*, pp. 335–40.

Henderson, RM and Clark, KB (1990) 'Architectural Innovation: The Reconfiguration of Existing Product Technologies and the Failure of Established Firms', *Administrative Science Quarterly*, 35.

Huberman, BA (1988) *The Ecology of Computation*, Elsevier Science Publishers, Amsterdam.

Katz, M and Shapiro, C (1985) 'Network externalities, competition and compatibility', *American Economic Review*, **75**, **3**, pp. 424–40.

Kelly, K (1994) *Out of Control – The New Biology of Machines*, Addison Wesley.

Kelly, K (1998) 'New Rules for the New Economy: 10 ways the network economy is changing everything', Fourth Estate.

Knight, FH (1924) 'Some fallacies in the interpretation of social cost', *Quarterly Journal of Economics*, 38.

Langlois, RN and Robertson, PL (1992) 'Networks and Innovation in a Modular System: Lessons from the Microcomputer and Stereo Component Industries', *Research Policy*, **21**, **4**, pp. 297–313.

Leyden, P (1997) 'Moore's Law Repealed, Sort of', *Wired*, Issue 5.05, May.

Liebowitz, SJ and Margolis, SE (1990) 'The Fable of the Keys', *Journal of Law and Economics*, Vol. XXXIII, April.

Liebowitz, SJ and Margolis, SE (1999) *Winners, Losers & Microsoft*, The Independent Institute, Oakland.

Mathews, JA (2002) 'Strategizing vs Economizing: Theorizing dynamic competitive behaviour in disequilibrium', unpublished paper, November.

McGee, J and Sammut-Bonnici, T (2002) 'Network Industries in the New Economy: the Effect of Knowledge and the Power of Positive Feedback', *European Business Journal*, September, **14**, **3**, pp. 116–32.

Morris, CR and Ferguson, CH (1993) 'How Architecture Wins Technology Wars', *Harvard Business Review*, **71**, **2**, pp. 86–96.

Pesola, M (2002) *Financial Times*, 11th April.

Saloner, G, Shepard, A and Podolny, J (2001) *Strategic Management*, Wiley, New York.

Sammut-Bonnici, T and McGee, J (2002) 'Network Strategies for the New Economy: Emerging Strategies for New Industry Structures', *European Business Journal*, December, **14**, **4**, pp. 174–85.

Shapiro, C and Varian, H (1999) *Information Rules: A Strategic Guide to the Network Economy*, Harvard Business School Press, Boston, MA.

Sharkey, NE and Sharkey, AJC (1993) 'Adaptive generalisation and the transfer of knowledge', *Artificial Intelligence Review*, Special Issue on Connectionism, 7, pp. 313–28.

Shy, O (2001) *The Economics of Network Industries*, Cambridge University Press, Cambridge, UK.

Vercoulen, F and Wegberg, M (1998) 'Standard Selection Modes in Dynamic, Complex Industries: Creating Hybrids between Market Selection and Negotiated Selection of Standards', NIBOR Working Paper, nib98006, Maastricht.

Weiss, T (2001) *Computer World*, April 2.

Young, AA (1913) 'Pigou's Wealth and Welfare', *Quarterly Journal of Economics*, 27.

Part 4

Strategy and practice

Introduction

This section moves on from the micro and macroeconomic analyses of strategy and focuses on more *process-based* analyses to help our understanding of what happens in the strategy formulation and implementation phases. A briefer description of the section would be that it investigates 'what happens when strategy meets organization'.

The objectives of this section are to introduce the reader to the more process-orientated perspectives on strategy. Part 2 began with the economic analysis of strategic decision making, while this part opens with a *process* analysis for strategic decision making. This sets the scene for the following chapters. The logic for this section is that we neglect the influence of organizations, interest groups (stakeholders) and individuals on strategy at our peril.

The interactions of external context, organizational context, behaviours and strategy are complex, yet they colour what happens in practice. There can be 'many a slip between cup and lip' in the strategy process. It is only by taking the perspectives outlined in this part that we can fully appreciate how these factors may interact to shape, block, change or radically modify strategy.

Chapter 13 characterizes the strategic decision making process. First, it deals with the concept of choice. How do strategists make choices between competing avenues for action? Three important techniques are introduced: game theory, sensitivity analysis and options theory. Each of these helps decision makers choose between alternative courses of actions. However, the chapter shows that choice is only one aspects of understanding decision processes. The chapter goes on to show how we can identify different processes that are more associated with the characteristics of the decision (how complex and how politically contested between stakeholders) than with the topic itself (e.g. a new product or a reorganization) or the choice process between alternatives. All decisions have to be put into practice, so the chapter also shows how characteristics of implementation can relate to performance. In particular, two factors stand out as being important, the *knowledge base* of the organization and the *receptivity* of the organizational infrastructure to the strategic decision.

Chapter 14 builds naturally on the decision making perspective by introducing the concepts and practicalities of risk and uncertainty. The chapter first of all distinguishes between risk and uncertainty and provides some working definitions of each. The chapter then identifies the sources and types of risks typically faced by decision makers. It depicts ways risk may be both assessed and handled as a natural part of the decision making process. The chapter outlines models for risk analysis. These include models based on expected utilities and introduces techniques such as net present value, internal rate of return and the use of decision trees to reduce both uncertainty and risk. The chapter concludes by looking at scenario building, a way of reducing risk and uncertainty by looking forwards to plausible futures. The chapter outlines a method for conducting scenario analysis and reflecting this back on the firm so that scenario building can help inform the strategy process.

Chapter 15 takes on board the fact that the implementation of any strategic decision will involve both individuals and organizations in often substantial degrees of change. This chapter examines the organizational and individual aspects of managing these changes. The chapter outlines the many different approaches that have been taken to understanding change in relation to strategies and it covers a number of levels of analysis ranging from the contextual to the individual. This chapter argues that looking at strategy without also looking at questions of organizational change exposes strategies to increased risks and, in the worst case, problems with organizational and individual change can prevent strategic decisions from being implemented altogether.

Chapter 16 deals with how organizations ensure survival and continuity by not simply adapting to their operating environment, but also by learning. Organizational learning is a much debated and contested concept and the chapter takes the reader through the main debates, showing how foresight, insight and learning are key to long-term development and growth for the organization and its individuals. The chapter emphasizes the dynamics between learning and strategy, showing how the process can be viewed as recursive. The one informs the other. Without strategy, there can be little learning. Learning from doing is necessary, but not sufficient. Organizations and individuals must also create, sustain and feed learning back into the strategy process so that new decisions can be made, based on the new knowledge created by learning. The chapter examines the benefits and the pitfalls in this theoretically virtuous circle between learning and strategy.

Chapter 17 looks at the most senior echelons of organization, the board or the top policy making team. In particular, the chapter examines the processes of governance and assesses what we know about more effective and less effective boards. Drawing on a wide range of literature and research the chapter outlines the role of the board as the top strategic team of the organization and emphasizes its pivotal role in shaping both the strategy process and the fortunes of the organization overall. The chapter provides details of recent changes in regulations and recommended guidelines for effective governance. The bulk of these guidelines have been formulated in the UK and apply directly to UK companies. However, as the chapter emphasizes, other countries are struggling with very similar problems of trying to ensure effective governance. So the chapter should not be read as solely a UK-specific chapter, but as one which shows how different governance characteristics can impede or enhance the strategy process.

The chapters cover the areas depicted in the strategy resources concepts map and the strategy process concepts map (introduced in Chapters 1 and 2 of this book). The shaded boxes represent the primary focuses of this part of the book. The non-shaded boxes are covered in other parts of this book. The degree of shading in the boxes represents the degree to which these topics are covered here and also indicates the interconnections explored in each chapter. These maps also appear overleaf.

Clearly this part deals in far more detail with the process concepts but there are also key references to the resource concepts, in particular the interrelationships between internal and external environments (context), actions and outcomes.

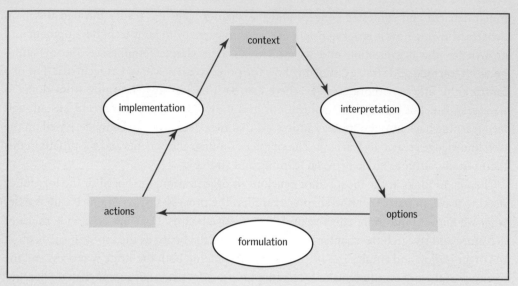

Based on Figure 2.2
Strategy process concepts map

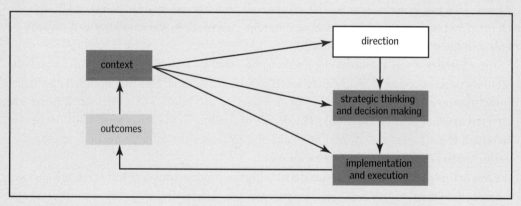

Based on Figure 1.6.
Strategy resources concepts map

Chapter 13

Process analyses for strategic decision making

Introduction

At the heart of strategy lies decision making. Having analysed the environment, assessed organizational capabilities and investigated technological shifts, managers have to take preferred courses of action. They have to examine possible alternatives and choose among them. As Coyne and Subramaniam (1996) observe, strategic decisions are the handful of decisions that drive or shape most of an organization's actions, are not easily changed once made and have the greatest impact on organizational perform-ance. Strategy may be a grand concept, but it is the individual strategic decisions that matter.

At its simplest, decision making may be considered an instantaneous action, a choice between two or more known alterna-tives, made by individuals or groups.

However, this 'point of decision' approach is unable to capture the richness and complexity of the processes that lead up to the point of decision, the influences on putting the decision into action and the ultimate performance of that decision. It also assumes that managers have full agency and control over decisions. Sometimes they may have very limited discretion to make decisions or choose among alternatives. This could be the case, for example, where strategic decisions in organizations are heavily constrained by interventionist government policies (such as privatization or deregulation) where all strategic decisions are framed and shaped by this wider **context**. Nevertheless, managers still have some degree of **strategic choice** (Child 1972) even if the wider context (e.g. privatization) is firmly set in place. Managers can still make strategic decisions, concerning for example, such key topics as organizational design, choice of suppliers, choice and sophistication of information systems and general product or service portfolios.

Of course, most people are aware that much of decision making is not a simple process that happens in a linear sequence a period of thinking followed by a period of acting. Decision making and the development of alternative courses of action are fashioned in their doing. Therefore, factors such as previous experience or whether things 'feel' right are likely to have as much influence over strategic choices (and what follows) as analysis and planning. Yet, these decisions are what will influence the fortunes or otherwise of any organization (from a sports club to a multinational enterprise) and understanding strategic decision making processes therefore represents a key aspect of examining how strategies are put into practice. A great deal of what has been discussed in Part 3 of this book has enabled us to see how strategy, as an overall direction an organization might take, can be achieved by analytical and rational thinking. Strategy is a positioning process by which organizations chart their ways through the seas of competition, internationalization and changing markets and technologies. Positioning alone, however, leaves open the question of how particular choices are made among a set of alternatives however incomplete those alternatives might be. In short, to understand strategy fully we need to understand the processes of strategic decision making.

13.1 Different perspectives on the nature of decision making

Like many theories of how we organize, plan and act, decision making has multiple lenses through which we might try to understand its complexity. We examine some of these perspectives in this section. For example, Mintzberg, Quinn and Ghoshal (1998) identify five different (and sometimes mutually exclusive) perspectives on strategic decision making:

- ◆ Decision making as a *plan*: the decision is a consciously intended course of action. In the same way that you might intend to catch an aeroplane to a specific destination at a particular time, decision making is a process that is carried out in advance of the action that follows and is developed with a clear purpose.

- Decision making as a *ploy*: a decision from this perspective is a set of actions designed to outwit the competition and may not necessarily be the 'obvious' content of the decision. For example, a decision to construct a new building in order to expand may not be the overt strategy, but is more concerned with increasing barriers to entry for potential competitors. There are obvious connections here with game theory (Van Neumann and Morgenstern 1944), which examines the choices players make in every possible situation. Forcing one's opponent to move (to achieve a short-term win), so that this puts them at a longer-term disadvantage, is an example of such a ploy. Equally, there are connections with strategy as conceived in its military roots, where the plans of campaigns may have similar intentions to the game analogy (Von Clausewitz 1976).

- Decision making as a *pattern*: decisions are not necessarily taken with a planned purpose and decision makers do not always have access to the range of knowledge required to plan wholly in advance. What happens is that multiple decisions taken over time form a pattern. It is this pattern of resulting (emergent) behaviour that we call the strategy of the firm. Strategy is therefore characterized as a pattern that emerges from a stream of decisions.

- Decision making as a *position*: decisions are less about the dynamics of planning or gamesmanship and more about trying to achieve a match between the organization and its environment (Hofer and Schendel 1978). This position can be one of alignment, so that the organization matches its environment (for example, highly decentralized structures to match a turbulent and unpredictable environment) or one of trying to secure competitive advantage (where the organization achieves a unique position in the market for some time). Positions, of course, can be planned, emerge or be a combination of both emergent and planned processes.

- Decision making as a *perspective*: decisions here are characterized as a reflection of how strategists in an organization see and perceive the world and their organization. For example, the strategic perspective of Nokia is one of continuous and sometimes radical change (Nokia began as a paper and pulp company); IBM favours a dominant marketing perspective, while Hewlett-Packard favours an engineering excellence perspective. This perspective, if pervasive enough, can influence the kinds of decision taken, in respect of their content and their processes. We can see the effects of this embedded view of decision making by observing that organizations in similar industries often choose similar strategic decisions. They become institutionalized. Universities tend to follow broadly similar strategies as do large retailers or service organizations.

Whittington (1996) reminds us that not only can we identify different perspectives on decision making, but the past forty or fifty years has also seen radical changes in the ways in which links between strategic decisions and corporate strategy have been established. For example, the 1950s/1960s saw an emphasis on the planning approach to decision making.

The focus was on tools and techniques to help managers make informed decisions about future business directions. Such tools included industry structure analyses and portfolio matrices (for example, the Ansoff matrix or the Boston Box, see Part 3 of this book). Decision making was mostly about planning. The 1970s onwards saw a changed emphasis. Decisions were now supposed to emphasize the pay-offs to organizations that may accrue if they pursued different strategic directions. Typical **options** were diversification decisions, but this was also the era of innovation (R&D), acquisition, joint venture and internationalization decisions.

The 1980s saw a move away from examining the content of strategic decisions (that is, what they were about) to examining them more as processes. The question now became whether we could map the progress of a strategic decision and make any inferences about why such processes might occur. Hickson *et al.* (1986) characterized such processes as sporadic (discontinuous), fluid (continuous and smooth) or constricted (restricted to a small group of stakeholders). Mintzberg *et al.* (1976) had also identified a number of specific process types in a similar vein. Pettigrew (1986) underscored the importance of such processes since they underpinned the recognition among managers for strategic change. Here Pettigrew established a clear link between strategic decision making and change (a theme which will be described in greater detail in Chapter 15). The 1990s onwards have seen a continuing interest in unfolding the characteristics of decision processes, but the emphasis has changed to focus on whether or not there are any links between decision making activity and performance (did the decision succeed or fail?). We examine this aspect of decision performance later in this chapter.

13.2 Choice selection and strategic decision making

The question of how individuals make decisions is deceptively simple. Deeper analysis reveals that trying to explain the *how* of decision making, even if limited to trying to explain how managers make decisions in organizations (rather than, say, the cognitive processes of individuals generally), is still very complex indeed. One of the enduring features of complex organizations is that they operationalize and codify the knowledge and experience of individuals. As managers take decisions, the rules of thumb they may use become standardized as procedures and activities for *planning* and *evaluating*. This allows a degree of *strategic programming* to take place (*see* Figure 1.1). Resource allocation, schedules and priorities can be planned, evaluated and assessed by such metrics and they become embodied in the formal planning system of the organization.

The links between planning and forecasting metrics and strategy vary, depending on how strategy is viewed. If the classic Chandler (1962: 13) perspective is taken – strategy is 'the determination of the long-term goals of an enterprise' then tools such as **scenario planning** and **macroeconomic forecasting** are appropriate metrics. These help assess complex environments often over long time horizons (25 years is not unusual in scenario analysis, for example) from the perspective of the organization–environment interaction. We describe these techniques in more detail in Chapter 14. Alternatively, if we define strategy as the sum of its parts – a pattern among a handful of decisions – then we need metrics that are finer grained. Once the level of analysis becomes the decision itself, managers need more specific tools and techniques to help them in option selection from a range of alternatives. Table 13.1 summarizes some typical planning and forecasting techniques.

13.2.1 Game theories

Game theories help decision makers to make sense of (and react to) the actions of others. By posing choice among alternatives in the form of different games, decision makers can judge to what extent their assumptions about others' rationality are valid. Typically portrayed as a matrix between two 'players', **game theory** examines what is likely to happen when two players make choices and what are the best outcomes or pay-offs. Powell (2003: 392) gives an example, using two firms facing investment opportunities in an existing market. Each firm can invest in process, quality or can make no investment. Investment in process should reduce price, and investment in quality should improve differentiation. Table 13.2 shows the pay-offs.

Table 13.1 Planning and forecasting techniques and strategy

Strategy is viewed as ...	The remit of strategists	Typical techniques
The long-term alignment of an organization with its economic, social and political environment	Long-term, wide span control of organizational affairs	◆ Scenario building ◆ Macroeconomic analysis and forecasting
The handful of strategic decisions that drive and shape the fortunes of an organization and which characterize its strategy	The management of shorter-term decisions that involve the disposition of limited resources	◆ Game theory ◆ Sensitivity analysis ◆ Options

Table 13.2 A simple example of game theory

Company B	Company A		
	Invest in process	Invest in quality	Make no investment
Invest in process	50 : 50	30 : 70	85 : 15
Invest in quality	60 : 40	45 : 55	80 : 20
Make no investment	25 : 75	20 : 80	30 : 30

Source: adapted from Powell, 2003.

The rules of the simple game depicted in Table 13.2 are that Company A chooses first which column to play. In the cells of the table are the pay-offs in percentages to Company B and Company A (in that order). The pay-offs are not symmetrical since each company has different capabilities. If both companies choose not to invest then it will be easier for new entrants to come into the market, hence both Company A and B will only receive 60 per cent.

Company A logically chooses the least worse case. This is a decision to invest in quality where, whatever the choice of Company B, Company A will receive at least 55 per cent pay-off. Company B would also reason similarly. The least worse choice is to invest in quality where Company B would receive at least 45 per cent. The game assumes that these decisions are made at the same time, although even if they were made in sequence, the inbuilt time lags in the market would reduce immediate effects of the investment.

If the game is played deliberately in sequence, making the assumption that Company B moves first and immediately sees the choices of Company A, then Company B has the following decision choices. Investing in process would be likely to make A choose quality (this would yield a pay-off of 70 per cent). Investing in quality would persuade A to choose quality as well since the pay-off will be larger for them (55 per cent) than B. If B were to choose not to invest then A would invest in quality to gain an 80 per cent return. The best case is, therefore, for B to invest in quality and gain 45 per cent, with A gaining 55 per cent.

There are many variants of this simple game. The most well known is perhaps the prisoner's dilemma where two criminals are in separate cells and have to decide whether or not to betray each other (having agreed not to betray in advance of the game). The greatest pay-offs come from both prisoners sticking to their agreement, but most betray each other and the pay-offs are significantly reduced.

From a decision making perspective, these type of game may vary depending on whether the game is played more than once with the same 'players'. If both parties know that they will be playing the same game again, under the same rules, then the evidence suggests that they will be more predisposed to co-operate and trust each other than if the game were only played once.

Of course, these simple heuristics make some heroic assumptions. For example, players are assumed to be perfectly rational in their behaviours and choices. They are also assumed to have perfect knowledge of the rules (shared equally between them) and will always want to maximize their returns. Nevertheless, they do show clearly some of the choices and returns which may happen, should managers make best use of the resources and knowledge at their disposal.

13.2.2 Sensitivity analysis

In many respects, this heuristic is akin to scenario planning but **sensitivity analysis** operates at a much more operational level. It is a technique for investigating what happens if the assumptions underlying a strategic decision are questioned and changed. For example, a strategic decision may be taken to launch a new product with a five-year horizon over product price (no increase for two years and a small increase after that). However, even small changes in price might yield large changes in volumes sold; therefore, managers need to know what will happen if they make even slight changes to product price. This technique requires that a portfolio of variables are entered on to a spreadsheet and can then be subjected to simulation on the computer.

Again, this technique makes an array of assumptions which decision makers need to take into account, but the exercise of 'mapping' the decision trajectory under different pricing structures (for example) can be very useful in revealing the multi-variate interaction of key variables in the process, such as demand, cost and levels of competition.

13.2.3 **Options**

This technique helps managers make key decisions about future activities when current strategic decisions seem to be failing or not working as well as they might. This is often called **strategic decay** (Williamson 1999). Decay indicates the urgent need to take strategic decisions in order to try to reverse the process of decline. There are a number of measures of decline, but the most evident are:

+ Reaching limits to profit generation: diminishing returns.

+ Revenue grows faster than profits year after year (efforts are to run a growing organization harder, but with a diminishing contribution to profit).

+ The firm records high profits but share prices fall (confidence in the sustainability of returns is low).

+ **Core competences** (strategic assets) begin to depreciate in the amount of profit they generate. These include, for example, patents, long-term contracts which are nearing their end and intellectual capital which other firms can now recruit or train.

+ Industry convergence: over time major competitors begin to adopt similar strategies. Products and service are hard to differentiate; the only firms which survive over the long term are low cost and highly competitive. Profits of all survivors are squeezed.

All of the above can contribute individually or together to create decline. Perhaps the least self-evident cause of decline is where the organization is earning good profits but the share price collapses since confidence in maintaining profits over the long term erodes. For example, in the retail industry Tesco managed to increase its return on capital employed by some 35 per cent (1995–2002). British Airways was not far behind with a return of 23 per cent. Yet the share prices of each organization differ markedly. British Airways has seen an almost static price/earnings ratio for the last ten years while Tesco has seen its p/e ratio rise by over 40 per cent (*The Economist* 2003). Confidence in British Airways is significantly less.

In order to maintain profits they have had to make savage cuts in the organization, laying off large numbers of staff as well as cutting back on the range and type of routes offered to customers. Other airlines are creating stiff competition, especially low-cost providers. Tesco, on the other hand, has engendered confidence and has managed to stay well ahead of the competition without having to savage the fixed costs of its organization. On this basis, British Airways is in urgent need of strategic decisions that will help stem the decline and that will help create value in the near future. Once identified, these decision choices are known as options.

The formal analysis of options can help inform an organization and its decision makers about likely ways forward. From a decision making perspective, the word options can be misleading in that it can be taken to refer to the micro-detail of operations (costs, sales volumes and so on) so that forecasts can be 'exact'. In fact, options techniques are relatively macro in their focus. They rely on two related dimensions: the identification of additional or alternative organizational capabilities that might be needed to meet product or service needs in the future; and the identification of potential future markets and/or new customer behaviours. In order to assemble an accurate set of options, decision makers need to assess both of these dimensions. For example, in the mobile telephony industry, customer needs might be predicted to change towards using the mobile telephone as the major way of accessing internet and telephony needs. Thus the mobile telephone becomes the key focus in terms of an organization's capabilities to deliver such technologies. Bandwidth and voiceover internet protocols will all be capabilities that will have to be developed and honed in order to meet market demands. Figure 13.1 illustrates how the need both to address capabilities and to develop a knowledge of new potential markets is important for decision makers.

Figure 13.1 simply outlines the options available to organizations which fall into the various cells of the matrix. While this is a useful analysis, it tells decision makers little about actions or the types of action they may take. For example, decision makers may have

Figure 13.1 Strategic options in decision making

identified two or three options but then chosen to retain these as ideas which might be explored sometime in the future. Just holding these options as ideas is fairly cost free, but is obviously low on action. Decisions between options and **implementation** require often significant analysis and investment. Choosing between options is necessary since pursuing all identified options would be prohibitively expensive. Then decisions have to be made over how to implement the chosen option or options. We explore these processes of strategic decision making in the following sections.

13.3 The processes of strategic decision making

The processes of making decisions can appear deceptively simple. Actions are formulated towards the solution of a particular problem. The problem with this approach is that there may be discernible actions and there may be observable outcomes, but they need not necessarily be wholly related to one another. Problems may be solved by factors other than strategic decisions and, sometimes, taking a strategic decision can create a whole new set of problems (without solving the initial problem the decision was supposed to address).

These polar views can be represented by the *planning* versus the *chaotic* processes of strategic decision making. They are extremes and, although most decisions lie somewhere between the planned and the chaotic, both perspectives are useful for understanding the processes of strategic decision making. Viewing processes as basically a set of planning tools allows *actions, procedures* and *measurement* to be explicitly addressed (*see* Figure 1.6) Planning facilitates decision makers in analysing and codifying what appear initially as complex problems. Planning simplifies complexity and helps reduce uncertainty. Because of this, planning can also help decision makers examine current planning practices in their organization and assess their utility in the light of current problems. From a behavioural perspective, planning can ensure that others in the organization are involved and are communicated with as fully as possible. Note that although involvement and communication can be explicit parts of the plan, this may not endow those participants with any influence over the process or its eventual outcome. Finally, planning processes help decision makers identify key performance indicators by which progress of the decision can be monitored and judged.

Chaotic processes (Cohen *et al.* 1972; Stacey 1993) argue that organizations can be viewed as an 'anarchy' or as a system with chaotic tendencies. Hence decision makers can neither understand fully nor control decision processes. Means and ends are unlikely to be coupled (Weick 1976), which implies that actions do not lead to expected outcomes and are swayed one way or another by other decisions, other actions and unforeseen circumstances. The main components of a strategic decision making process (problems, solutions, participants and choice situations) interact in an apparently haphazard way, a stream of demands for the fluid attention and energies of managers. Participants move in and out of the decision making process (every entrance is an exit elsewhere) and this can create discontinuity. At other times, participants fight for the right to become involved and then never exercise any influence they may have.

Viewing decision making processes as chaotic also has some advantages for decision makers. Unlike the planning approach, the chaos perspective does not seek to simplify and to reduce uncertainty. It avoids any oversimplification of the process and allows decision makers to appreciate and expect the role of politics and influence to be a natural part of the decision making process. In theory, the chaos perspective should encourage decision makers to think creatively around complex problems and help them to avoid thinking solely in linear sequences. Creativity and innovation may be enhanced by decision makers being encouraged to take actions which seem unrelated to the decision under consideration. On the other hand, we should bear in mind that the distinction between creativity and madness is a rather fine line (March 1999)! From a decision making perspective, this means that no one will know whether the tangential explorations were useful or folly until a long way down the track of the decision process. Figure 13.2 summarizes four polar types of **decision process characteristics** which can arise from counterposing planned versus chaotic and political versus planned perspectives.

13.4 **The architecture of strategic decision making**

Trying to put together the above perspectives is a complicated task but is one that decision makers are required to understand. This is because strategic decision makers need to understand how such perspectives may predominate and hence characterize their organization and how decisions might flow through its structures. If you know how decisions might be configured in your organization, you stand a greater chance of being able to predict and perhaps influence what is going on.

	Problem solving	Political process
Chaos/ anarchy	**Uncoupled** strategic decision making (means unrelated to ends)	**Uncontrolled,** random strategic decision making
Planning/ coherence	**Intended** strategic decision making (means related to ends)	**Incremental** strategic decision making (step by step, mutual adjustment to stakeholders)

Figure 13.2 A typology of decision processes
Source: adapted from Cummings and Wilson, 2003.

Any attempt to configure the architecture of strategic decision making will necessitate some degree of integration of at least three aspects. These are:

- Decision-specific characteristics.
- The organizational context.
- The influence of the wider environment.

This chapter will look at decision-specific characteristics and the organizational context. The wider environment is covered in detail in Part 3 and Chapter 14.

13.4.1 Decision-specific characteristics

We can categorize decision-specific characteristics into two broad areas:

- The interpretation of a problem or problems by decision makers.
- The characteristics of the decision or problem to be solved.

Research into decision making cognition and labelling suggests that the same internal or external stimulus may be interpreted differently by managers across different organizations, or sometimes even within the same organization. Therefore, relying on the stimulus itself is unlikely to tell us much about what follows in terms of strategic decision making.

It has also been shown that the ways in which managers categorize decisions strongly influences the ways in which subsequent processes happen. For example, decisions may be perceived as an opportunity or as a crisis. Where managers perceive decisions to be more of a crisis than an opportunity, the process is characterized by the overarching threat of the crisis. The search for alternatives becomes wider and the collection of information and intelligence relevant to the decision becomes greater. Overall, the decision making activity becomes more comprehensive in scale and scope (since it tends to involve more participants).

The characteristics of the problem to be solved have been shown to have links with the strategic decision making process and to influence its trajectory through an organization. For example, problems have been characterized as 'wicked' or 'tame' (de Wit and Meyer 1999). Wicked problems are not evil, but are complex. They are permeated with uncertainty caused by either the technical nature of the decision or by the politics and intrigue it engenders among decision participants. Hickson *et al.* (1986) characterized these 'wicked' decisions as complex, political or both. Complex decisions are those that are unprecedented, carry high levels of uncertainty and may have fundamental precedent-setting consequences for subsequent decisions. They may also require information of a different type and from a different source to be gathered and interpreted. Political decisions are those that draw in a specific set of stakeholders (inside and outside the organization). The more interests that are represented in the decision (multiple and conflicting voices), the more political is the strategic decision.

Complex and/or political decisions share some or all of the following characteristics:

- They are difficult to define precisely (the nature of the problem is elusive).
- Understanding the problem is also part of understanding the solution.
- There is rarely one best solution, but a series of possible solutions.
- Each solution is associated with different trade-offs and priorities.
- They are difficult to assess in terms of performance since they tend to continue through the organization without a clear, final end point against which performance can be judged.
- They are highly inter-connected with other problems in the organization.
- They have high levels of uncertainty associated with them.
- They require strategists to accept fairly high degrees of risk in making decisions.
- Once made, they are difficult to reverse.
- They are likely to be discontinuous and political, with different competing interests trying to influence the outcome in line with their preferences.

Simple (or tame) decisions reflect the opposite characteristics to those listed.

13.4.2 The organizational context

There are many ways of defining the organizational context, but the major descriptors are:

- Systems
- Structure
- Ownership and control
- Organizational culture

Internal *systems*, such as information or formal planning processes, both influence the flow of information across the organization and, to some extent, determine the nature and context of human interaction. It is not surprising, then, that they have a strong influence over strategic decision making and its practice. Control systems and measurement and reward systems also prescribe what is given priority and therefore what decision makers focus most of their attention upon. In decision making, such systems will set parameters around trade-offs and what levels of risk are tolerable, for example:

- The more regulated the formal systems, the more strategic decision making tends to be routine and predictable and the more it will have to accommodate a large number of specialist functions.
- The more complex the systems, the more decision making becomes reliant on knowledge experts, and information gathering and synthesis.

◆ The more automated systems become, the more flexibility and space there is for strategic decision making that relies on expertise (or the intellectual capital of the organization). The obsession with control tends to be reduced, since controlled systems do not require watching over. (When they go wrong, however, they can cause havoc!)

◆ The greater the scope of the system, the greater the reliance on expertise and intellectual capital. This is true of e-commerce and e-business, for example, where the scope of information goes beyond the single organizational unit.

The *structure* of an organization also has an impact on strategic decision making. The most obvious example of the interrelationship between strategy and structure is the debate (which still rages) about whether structure follows strategy or vice versa. In this book we take the view that strategy and structure are like two legs. You need both to walk, but whether you lead with the left or the right leg is fairly arbitrary. One may be said to follow or to lead the other. No matter, you are still walking. Decisions both *create* structures and are also *influenced* by them.

That there are a set of relationships between strategic decision making and structure can be identified in a number of aspects of management. In relation to strategic decision making, some of the key influences are listed below:

◆ Formalized structures are associated mainly with older organizations. Decision making becomes formalized and has a tendency to become more predictable. This is especially so in the 'seen it all before' attitudes that may prevail, and repeating what was done in the past as solutions to today's problems.

◆ Larger organizations formalize processes more, even if they are structured into smaller business units. Strategic decision making becomes more about rule-following than rule-bending (or breaking) practice.

◆ Decentralized structures may appear to avoid the above, but decision making can become dominated by trying to ensure co-ordination and communication across the decentralized organization (rather than producing new products and service for example). Decentralized structures often require more, rather than less, hands-on management before they can become effective and efficient.

Organizational structures reflect the age of the industry from its founding date. Industries which pre-date the Industrial Revolution (for example, the Church or the military) are characterized by centralized and formal structures (whatever the age of the organization in the industry). It seems that industry age is a better predictor of the organizational structure, even of a new entrant into the industry.

In terms of organizational size, the main effect on strategic decision making appears to be formalization rather than size itself. Hickson *et al.* (1986) found no differences in strategic decision making processes which could be attributed to organizational size. So large organizations that manage to retain less formal structures may not necessarily exhibit the rule following strategic decision making processes of their more formalized counterparts.

Ownership and control exert separate influences over strategic decision making. In family-owned firms, for example, the overlap between the two social systems of the family and the firm create decision processes in which personal stakes are high and delegation may be rare, since decision making authority and the strategic direction of the firm are controlled by the owners. Interestingly, there is strong evidence to show that public versus private ownership seems to make little difference to the ways in which strategic decision making occurs (at least in the UK).

According to Hickson *et al.* (1986), public sector organizations:

- Take no longer than privately owned organizations to make strategic decision.

- Do not have more committees involved in the decision making process.

- Do not have more stakeholders than private sector organizations (but the type of stakeholder may differ, with government agencies such as the Treasury prevailing).

It is still debatable whether national ownership exerts much influence on strategic decision making. There is some evidence to show that patterns of national cultural stereotypes permeate the practice of decision making. For example, North American organizations decide quicker than UK firms and both are significantly faster than Swedish organizations. But the results are far from conclusive.

The *culture* of an organization can be described as:

> *the underlying assumptions, beliefs and values in an organization which inform, influence and shape strategic decision making.*

The influence of organizational culture on decision making reveals what is often taken for granted in decision making processes. The impact of organizational culture often goes unnoticed by members of an organization. Culture is continually reinforced by symbols, stories and routines, as well as by organizational structures and the power plays of

Basic assumptions	Value-led decision making	Artefacts
e.g. Taken-for-granted beliefs	e.g. Goals and strategies	e.g. Organization structures
Perceptual habits (ways of thinking)	Answers to the question 'why?'	Technologies
Basic attitudes	Vision and mission	Jargon and dress code

Figure 13.3 Artefacts and assumptions in strategic decision making
Source: adapted from Schein, 1992.

various interests. Culture tends to be self-reinforcing. In addition, culture provides a set of values which are reflected in choice behaviours and processes. Schein (1992) shows how decision making is influenced both by artefacts and basic assumptions held by individuals in organizations, as illustrated in Figure 13.3.

Organizational culture, therefore, colours decision making from a palette that can include such things as ritual and language alongside the influence of technology and organizational structure. These factors all intermingle to colour decisions that we would be tempted otherwise to view as rational choices. The cultural perspective shows how values are added to the decision process. Sometimes such values are overt. They can be seen in mission statements such as Yamaha's 'Kill Honda', Federal Express's 'Absolutely on Time', or 3M's 'To solve unsolved problems innovatively'. At other times, values can be shaped by taken-for-granted behaviours, jargon or dress codes (for example, we all wear business suits in sober colours). These are more covert influences.

Simpler versions of how strategic decisions are influenced by the context or culture of organizations can be found in the work of Collins and Porras (1996). They argued that successful companies were those where the core decisions were influenced by timeless guiding principles which require no external justification. This cherished core ideology represents the key values of the organization and is the cultural glue that holds it together in the face of other changes. So long as key decisions were taken in line with these cherished principles, outstanding performance over a sustained period was the result.

However, organizations can also become trapped by their coherent cultures into routines which impair the development of new and different strategies. The practice of strategic decision making, therefore, becomes constrained rather than enhanced by the organizational culture. Decision makers can only think along the rigid lines demarcated by the strong culture. Innovation and creative thinking are precluded and invoking learning into the organization becomes very difficult, since the culture resists new ideas.

Decision makers, therefore, have to be very clear whether the culture of the organization is working for its success, or is actually constraining choice activities. Spotting the difference can be very difficult since the choice-enhancing factors identified by Collins and Porras (1996) very closely resemble the 'mindguards' that can detract from innovative thinking.

13.5 Strategic decision making and performance

What are the relationships between decision processes and their outcomes? Does it matter what managers do in the strategic decision making process? What difference, if any, do managerial actions make to both processes and outcomes?

For nearly thirty years, practitioners and scholars alike have argued about what brings success. So complex have some of these arguments become that there is virtually a whole industry of analysts devoted to arguing whether planned or emergent strategies (for example) capture the essence of strategy, and whether the effective positioning of the organization in its industry and value chain leads to greater or lesser performance. Sub-industries also sprung up, including, for example, focusing on whether organizations could learn from failures and successes and whether key technological advancements (for example, killer applications) rendered any form of strategic planning redundant. Other analysts focused on the levels of uncertainty facing decision makers, arguing that when faced with extreme uncertainties, success was more probable if managers took action (leaps of faith in the dark) than if they took no action at all. Of course, this rich analysis has not only provided a large number of industry overviews and industry shake-outs (for example, in the telecommunications industry) but has also provided many case studies and war stories for others to pick over and make sense of.

Focusing on strategic decisions rather than sectors (for example) allows us to examine the many slips that can occur 'between cup and lip' (that is, between decisions processes and outcomes). Spotting decision 'failures' is easy after the event. They can take the organization into decline or, in extreme cases, can seal the demise of the organization. Typical decision failure characteristics include such features as:

◆   Failure to address the original (or the real) problem.

◆   The decision made the problem worse rather than better.

◆   The decision becomes irreversible when things begin to go wrong and decision makers get deeper and deeper into crisis.

So where do things go wrong in this process view of decision making? If we knew in advance that decision pathways were going to result in failure then we would not waste our time on them and would choose other alternatives. However, such is the level of uncertainty surrounding strategic decisions that this predictive dimension is almost impossible to identify, especially at the early stages of decision making. For example, it can be in the implementation stages of decision making that things can go wrong, despite what may have seemed like good ideas during formulation. Of course, there is a critical temporal element here. Before implementation, it is extremely difficult to differentiate what will be an effective strategy from one which ultimately fails. Despite all the attempts to assess the degree of future risk (through techniques such as risk analysis), strategic decisions seemingly succeed or fail independently of such criteria.

Research is beginning to identify patterns of implementation which indicate key factors associated with higher-achieving decisions (Hickson *et al.* 2003; Miller *et al.* 2004). These factors are a combination of organizational features, such as structures and the receptiveness of organizational culture to the decision; features of what actions managers take during the process, such as how far they can specify what must be done in advance or whether the required expertise can be accessed inside the organization; and features of the decision process itself, such as its **duration**. We look at duration in the next section.

13.5.1 Duration and decision success

Hickson *et al.* (1986) produced an empirical classification of strategic decision processes up to the point of authorization. One aspect of process was duration. They found that from first mention to the point of authorization, the bulk of decisions take between 4 and 24 months to process. The mean for 150 cases was 12.4 months. Implementation, however, covers a far greater range of time, with some decisions only taking a few months to put into practice and others taking many years.

Implementation is defined here as the time taken from the point of authorization to when the decision is put into practice (for example, the new building is constructed or the reorganization is put in place). Duration of implementation is not associated directly with success. It seems that the time taken to implement strategic decisions matters little in terms of decision performance. Long-drawn-out implementation processes can be associated with very successful decisions, while faster implementation times are no guarantee of success. The following two vignettes show examples of these temporal extremes, one decision taking four years, the other nine months.

Case box: Long implementation time (successful)

Organization: Glass manufacturer
Strategic decision: Build a new manufacturing plant
Implementation time: 4 years
Achievement: Highly successful

This organization has always enjoyed a worldwide reputation for technical excellence in process and product innovation, especially in the revolutionary float glass process it pioneered. However, first mover advantage in float glass was soon eroded, and market share reduced considerably, as competitors moved to float glass technology. Benchmarking revealed that the glass division in general was becoming increasingly inefficient compared to competitors producing similar products with similar technology. Competition was hotting up, especially after the expiry of its manufacturing process licences.

The senior planning team assessed the situation and set up a lengthy process of working parties and committees to consider whether to increase dramatically the production of float glass by building a new plant. The decision was made even more dramatic since it would signal this organization's possibly complete move into float glass technology. Parallel production processes of other types of glass might have to be abandoned.

Fortunately, the necessary technical expertise was in-house. A very strong R&D team provided up-to-the minute technical information to the planning team, assisted by very strong design information from the engineering department. The decision was by no means clear to the planning team and a further two years were spent deliberating the costs and benefits associated with the investment. During this time, the business environment was becoming increasingly competitive, but the planning team chose to consult widely across the organization, so that managers and workers could absorb the need for change and could become its supporters once the decision had been put into practice.

The new site was built following this two-year deliberation and consultation period. It subsequently became the most successful plant of its type worldwide and became a role model for change within the organization, spreading out to other divisions such as insulation and opthalmics.

Case box: **Short implementation time (unsuccessful)**

Organization:	Paint and model manufacturer
Strategic decision:	Expand capacity
Implementation time:	9 months
Achievement:	Unsuccessful

This highly successful international organization had developed a very profitable business, manufacturing and supplying plastic model kits of planes, cars, ships and so forth. They also had a successful business manufacturing and selling the specialized paints model builders needed to decorate their plastic models. All was going well in the market and a possible joint venture with a French company was being considered. Such a move would make this the largest plastic model manufacturer in the world.

The operations manager, who was associated with a number of successes in the plastic kit business, had been looking at alternative materials for model kit-building. In this case he was assessing the potential for balsa wood kits as an alternative to plastic construction. Margin on balsa wood kits was, however, not attractive, since the supply of balsa wood around the world was virtually a price monopoly. However, the managing director located another supplier in Chile who was prepared to undercut the balsa monopoly. A hastily convened meeting between the managing director and the operations director ended with the realization that if they were to enter the balsa kit market on any scale, they would have to invest in a new production line in a new factory to accommodate it.

Coincidentally, a new site for the new factory became available. A government grant was available with the only proviso that an extra 20 people were employed. Neither manager thought this to be a problem and the investment was made. Almost immediately, the first shipment of balsa wood became a problem. It was full of dead insects and other debris, which made it unsuitable for building model kits. While trying to negotiate with the balsa wood suppliers, the joint venture with the French plastic kit manufacturer was abandoned (the French company pulled out of negotiations). It now became even more crucial to get good-quality supplies of balsa wood.

The French company introduced a range of innovative plastic kits which were an immediate success. Demand for balsa wood kits plummeted worldwide. The organization was left with a supply contract for material they did not now need, a factory with rent to pay and a workforce to lay off. It took five years to recover financially from this strategic decision.

From the boxed examples it can be seen that success and the speed at which implementation occurs seem to be unrelated. So which factors seem to be associated with success? We explore these in the next section.

13.5.2 Factors of success

Curiously, there have been relatively few studies at the level of strategic decisions that focus on the performance of the decision. Recent research (Hickson *et al.* 2003; Miller *et al.* 2004) has summarized this work, relating characteristics of how a strategic decision was made to how successful the decision was in practice.

Using achievement as a surrogate measure of performance (to what extent did the decision achieve stated objectives?), two key factors emerge:

♦ The knowledge base of managers.

♦ The receptivity of the organizational context to the strategic decision being implemented.

The knowledge base of managers

The key factors which emerge as related to performance are how *familiar* managers are with the problem to be addressed. Where managers are clear about the parameters of the problems and what information is needed to address it, they can begin to take action toward implementation. Two other processes are associated with this knowledge base. They are the *ability to plan* and *to resource* strategic decisions. Knowledge facilitates planning and argues a good case for resourcing. Strategic decisions do not succeed on knowledge alone; they need resources to back them up.

The receptivity of the organizational context

The key factor here is how ready the organization is to adopt the changes incurred by the strategic decision. The greater the readiness in the organization's culture to undertake the change, the easier it is for managers to take action and to begin to prioritize their various strategic decisions.

However, even a high state of cultural readiness can be blocked by organizational structures that are overly formal or bureaucratic. Hence, both organizational culture and structure have to be co-aligned if higher levels of performance are to be expected from the strategic decision making process.

13.6 Summary

To look at strategy through the lens of decision making is a complex activity. Decisions can focus on choices made or on how managers make decisions. The focus can also concentrate on the characteristics of the decision process itself and recent work has begun to establish some relationships between these process characteristics and decision performance.

Key features of these decision making processes are knowledge, planning, resourcing and specifying. Stakeholders must also be broadly aligned to be supportive of the decision. Organizational culture should be open to the changes the decision will bring about, and organizational structure should not impede the process of implementation by being too formal or cumbersome.

Key terms

Chaotic processes *511*

Context (and decision making) *504*

Core competences *509*

Decision process characteristics *512*

Duration (of strategic decisions) *518*

Game theory *507*

Implementation (of strategies) *511*

Macroeconomic forecasting *506*

Options *506*

Scenario planning *506*

Sensitivity analysis *508*

Strategic choice *504*

Strategic decay *509*

Recap questions and assignments

1 Pick a strategic decision with which you are familiar, or in which you were a participant. How would you describe its key process features?

2 Using the same example (or you can choose another strategic decision), describe what was done and by whom during the process.

3 What, in your view, were the major influences on the decision and its final outcome?

When you have read this chapter, log on to the Online Learning Centre website at www.mcgraw-hill.co.uk/textbooks/mcgee to explore chapter-by-chapter test questions, further reading and more online study tools for strategy.

Case 1 **Freud, finance and folly**

Human intuition is a bad guide to handling risk

People make barmy decisions about the future. The evidence is all around, from their investments in the stockmarkets to the way their run their businesses. In fact, people are consistently bad at dealing with uncertainty, underestimating some kinds of risk and overestimating others. Surely there must be a better way than using intuition?

In the 1950s and 60s, a group of researchers at American universities set out to find a more scientific method. They created a discipline called 'decision science' which aimed to take the human element out of risk analysis. It would offer a way of making soundly based decisions for a future fraught with uncertainties. This would involve using computer models for forecasting, estimating the probabilities of possible outcomes and determining the best course of action, thus avoiding the various biases that humans brought to decision-making. Such models, the researchers thought, would provide rational answers to questions such as whether to build a factory, how to combat disease and how to manage investments.

Business schools soon adopted their teachings, and even some policymakers were persuaded. Decision science's heyday may have been the Vietnam war when Robert McNamara, then America's defence secretary, used such techniques to forecast the outcome of the conflict (though, as it turned out, without much success). But mostly the approach did not quite catch on. Decision-makers, whether in business or politics, were loath to hand over their power to a computer. They preferred to go with their gut instincts.

Think like a machine

Daniel Kahneman, now a professor at Princeton, noticed as a young research psychologist in the 1960s that the logic of decision science was hard for people to accept. That launched him on a career to show just how irrationally people behave in practice. When Mr Kahneman and his colleagues first started work, the idea of applying psychological insights to economics and business decisions was considered quirky. But in the past decade the fields of behavioural finance and behavioural economics have blossomed, and in 2002 Mr Kahneman shared a Nobel prize in economics for his work.

Today he is in demand by organisations such as McKinsey and PartnerRe, and by Wall Street traders. But, he says, there are plenty of others that still show little interest in understanding the roots of their poor decisions. The lesson from the analyst's couch is that, far from being random, these mistakes are systematic and predictable:

- **Over-optimism**. Ask most people about the future, and they will see too much blue sky ahead, even if past experience suggests otherwise. Surveys have shown that people's forecasts of future stockmarket movements are far more optimistic than past long-term returns would justify. The same goes for their hopes of ever-rising prices for their homes or doing well in games of chance. In a recent study of Dutch game-show contestants, people's estimates of their odds on winning were around 25% too high. Americans are perhaps the most optimistic: according to one poll, around 40% of them think they will end up among the top 1% of earners.

Such optimism can be useful for managers or football players, and sometimes turns into a self-fulfilling prophecy. But most of the time it results in wasted effort and dashed hopes. Mr Kahneman's work points to three types of over-confidence. First, people tend to exaggerate their own skill and prowess; in polls, far fewer than half the respondents admit to having below-average skills in, say, love-making or driving. Second, they over-estimate the amount of control they have over the future, forgetting about luck and chalking up success solely to skill. And third, in competitive pursuits such as betting on shares, they forget that they have to judge their skills against those of the competition.

♦ **The anchor effect**. First encounters tend to be decisive not only in judging the character of a new acquaintance but also in negotiations over money. Once a figure has been mentioned, it takes a strange hold over the human mind. The asking price quoted in a house sale, for example, tends to become accepted by all parties as the 'anchor' around which negotiations take place, according to one study of property brokers. Much the same goes for salary negotiations or mergers and acquisitions. If nobody has much information to go on, a figure can provide comfort—even though it may lead to a terrible mistake.

♦ **Stubbornness**. No one likes to abandon a cherished belief, and the earlier a decision has been taken, the harder it is to give up. In one classic experiment, two groups of students were shown slides of an object, say a fire hydrant or a pair of spectacles. The slides started out of focus and were gradually made clearer until the students could identify the object. Those who started with a very blurry image tried to decide early and then found it difficult to identify it correctly until quite late in the process, whereas those who started less out of focus kept a more open mind and cottoned on more quickly.

The same sort of thing happens in boardrooms or in politics. Drug companies must decide early to cancel a failing research project to avoid wasting money, but find it difficult to admit they have made a mistake. Bosses who have hired unproductive employees are reluctant to fire them. Mr Kahneman cites the example of Israel's failure to spot growing threats in the lead-up to its 1973 war with its Arab neighbours. Part of the explanation was that the same people who had been watching the change in political climate had to decide on Israel's response. Similar problems have arisen in recent counter-terrorism work in America. In both cases, analysts may have become wedded early to a single explanation that coloured their perception. A fresh eye always helps.

♦ **Getting too close**. People put a lot of emphasis on things they have seen and experienced themselves, which may not be the best guide to decision-making. For example, many companies took action to guard against the risk of terrorist attack only after September 11th, even though it was present long before then. Or somebody may buy an overvalued share because a relative has made thousands on it, only to get his fingers burned.

In finance, too much emphasis on information close at hand helps to explain the so-called 'home bias', a tendency by most investors to invest only within the country they live in. Even though they know that diversification is good for their portfolio, a large majority of both Americans and Europeans invest far too heavily in the shares of their home countries. They would be much better off spreading their risks more widely.

♦ **Winning and losing**. Fear of failure is a strong human characteristic, which may be why people are much more concerned about losses than about gains. Consider the following bet: with the flip of a coin, you could win $1,500 if the coin turns up heads, or lose $1,000 on the tails. Now describe it in another way: with heads, you keep all the money you had before the bet, plus $1,500; with tails, you also keep everything, except $1,000. The two bets are identical, and each one, on average, will make you richer by $250 (although that average will be little consolation to the punter who has just lost $1,000). Even so, people will usually prefer the second bet.

Behavioural economists say that is because the prospect of losses seems far more daunting in isolation, rather than in the context of looking at your entire wealth, even if the average outcome is the same. This sort of myopia in the face of losses explains much of the irrationality people display in the stockmarket.

♦ **Misplaced priorities**. More information is helpful in making any decision but, says Mr Kahneman, people spend proportionally too much time on small decisions and not enough on big ones. They need to adjust the balance. During the boom years, some companies put as much effort into planning their Christmas party as into considering strategic mergers.

♦ **Counterproductive regret**. Crying over spilled milk is not just a waste of time; it also often colours people's perceptions of the future. Some stockmarket investors trade far too frequently because they are chasing the returns on shares they wish they had bought earlier.

Mr Kahneman reckons that some types of businesses are much better than others at dealing with risk. Pharmaceutical companies, which are accustomed to many failures and a few big successes in their drug-discovery programmes, are fairly rational about their risk-taking. But banks, he says, have a long way to go. They may take big risks on a few huge loans, but are extremely cautious about their much more numerous loans to small businesses, many of which may be less risky than the big ones.

But at least when businesses try to assess their risks, they have to worry only about making money. Governments, on the other hand, face a whole range of sometimes conflicting political pressures. This makes them even more likely to take irrational decisions.

Source: 'Freud, finance and folly', *The Economist*, 22 January 2004.
© The Economist Newspaper Limited, London (22 January 2004).

Case Questions

1 Why do you think individuals find it difficult to accept and utilize the tools and techniques of decision science?

2 Taking each of Kahneman's roots of poor decisions (over-optimism to counterproductive regret) suggest ways in which organizations and decision might be designed to alleviate some or all of them.

3 To what extent do you think Kahneman's roots of poor decisions are generalizable across different nations and different types of organizations (e.g. public, private, nonprofit). What differences (if any) would you expect to encounter? Why or why not?

Further reading and references

Chandler, AE Jr (1962) *Strategy and Structure: Chapters in the History of the American Industrial Enterprise*, MIT Press, Cambridge, MA.

Child, J (1972) 'Organizational Structure, Environment and Performance: The Role of Strategic Choice', *Sociology*, **6**, pp. 1–22.

Cohen, M, March, J and Olsen, J (1972) 'A Garbage Can Model of Organizational Choice', *Administrative Science Quarterly*, **17**, pp. 1–25.

Collins, JC and Porras, JL (1996) *Built to Last*, Century Books, New York.

Coyne, K and Subramaniam, S (1996) 'Bringing Discipline to Strategy', *The McKinsey Quarterly*, pp. 14–25.

Cummings, S and Wilson, DC (eds) (2003) *Images of Strategy*, Blackwell, Oxford.

De Wit, B and Meyer, R (1999) *A Strategy Synthesis*, International Thomson Press, London.

Hickson, D, Butler, R, Cray, D, Mallory, G and Wilson, D (1986) *Top Decisions: Strategic Decision Making in Organizations*, Jossey-Bass and Blackwell, California and Oxford.

Hickson, D, Miller, S and Wilson, D (2003) 'Planned or Prioritized? Two options in managing the implementation of strategic decisions', *Journal of Management Studies*, **40**, 7, pp. 1803–36.

Hofer, CW and Schendel, D (1978) *Strategy Formulation: Analytical Concepts*, West, New York.

March, JG (1999) *The Pursuit of Organizational Intelligence*, Blackwell, Oxford.

Miller, S, Wilson, D and Hickson, D (2004) 'Beyond planning: strategies for successfully implementing strategic decisions', *Long Range Planning*, **37**, 3, pp. 201–18.

Mintzberg, H, Raisinghani, D and Theoret, A (1976) 'The structure of "unstructured" decision processes', *Administrative Science Quarterly*, **21**, pp. 246–75.

Mintzberg, H, Quinn, JB and Ghoshal, S (1998) *The Strategy Process*, Prentice Hall, New York.

Pettigrew, A (1986) *The Awakening Giant: Continuity and change in ICI*, Blackwell, Oxford.

Powell, JH (2003) 'Game theory in strategy', in D Faulkner and A Campbell (eds) *The Oxford Handbook of Strategy*, Oxford University Press, Oxford.

Schein, E (1992) *Organizational Culture and Leadership*, Jossey-Bass, San Francisco.

Stacey, R (1993) *Strategic Management and Organizational Dynamics*, Pitman, London.

Van Neumann, J and Morgenstern, O (1944) *Theory of Games and Economic Behaviour*, Princeton University Press, Princeton.

Von Clausewitz, C (1976) *On War* (translated by M Howard and P Paret), Princeton University Press, Princeton.

Weick, K (1976) *The Social Psychology of Organizing*, Wiley, New York.

Whittington, R (1996) 'Strategy as practice', *Long Range Planning*, **29**, **5**, pp. 731–5.

Williamson, PJ (1999) 'Strategy as options on the future', *Sloan Management Review*, **40**, **3**, pp. 117–26.

Chapter 14

Risk, uncertainty and strategy

Introduction

All strategic decisions are taken in the context of both uncertainty and risk. Decisions are about future states of affairs and are based on incomplete information. They also commit resources which could otherwise be used elsewhere in organizations, hence there is a large degree of opportunity cost. Putting resources into one project therefore carries with it varying degrees of risk. It might be a poor choice and jeopardize the chances of taking an alternative course of action which may have yielded better results. On the other hand, the decision itself may turn out to be poor, yielding poor results or, in the extreme, financial disaster for the organization, for example.

The concepts of risk and uncertainty are, however, difficult to define precisely. This is made even more difficult because many authors define one aspect (risk) in terms of the other (uncertainty). For example, Hertz and Thomas (1983: 9) note that many authors define risk as 'degrees of variability or uncertainty'. This does not help distinguish the key elements of risk and uncertainty. To do this, we need to add more precision to the definitions of each concept. Uncertainty is relatively easier to define. In this chapter, we take **uncertainty** to mean:

> the limits to the precision and the extent of knowledge about a subject or an event.

For decision makers, phrases they associate with uncertainty include 'it is likely' or 'the chances are' or, in the case of little uncertainty, decision makers may say 'it is quite certain that'. All of these phrases, while in themselves imprecise, cluster around the notion of probabilities. Another way of defining uncertainty, therefore, is to describe uncertainty as:

> the subjective interpretations of probability by decision makers and analysts of problems in organizations.

Risk is harder to define. Dictionaries typically describe risk in terms of the possibility of destruction, loss or damage. In business organizations, however, risk also takes on other characteristics. For example, insurance companies categorize risk into at least two distinct types 'pure' risk and 'speculative' risk. An example of a pure risk is the likelihood of damage to assets and liabilities through fraud or criminal acts. It either will happen or it will not. However, speculative risks are characterized by the likelihood of gains *and* losses from which decision makers hope profit will eventually accrue (Hertz and Thomas 1983). Risk and reward are the essence of business. Investment in marketing, production and financial underpinning for a project are all risks undertaken by decision makers – and are risks from which they eventually hope to make some profit. Knight (1921) argues:

> The only 'risk' which leads to a profit is a unique uncertainty . . . profits arise out of the inherent, absolute unpredictability of things.

This takes us nearer to defining risk. It is about the *degree and type of unpredictability* (rather than the notion that unpredictability exists, which is closer to describing uncertainty). We may say, then, that risk can be defined generically as:

> The assessment, severity, amount and nature of losses which an action may incur, whether such actions are generated within an organization (such as a decision,) or are imposed upon it (such as a natural disaster). Risk is the measurable consequence of uncertainty for an organization.

Taking risks appears endemic to human behaviour in social groups. In the 1960s social psychologists such as Stoner (1968) showed that individuals will accept higher levels of risk when taking decisions in groups. He found that there was tendency for groups to go for risky and high pay-off decisions, while individuals favour relatively safe decisions with moderate pay-offs. Groups do not represent the 'average' risk of their members. Stoner referred to this tendency for higher risk taking in groups as 'risky shift' decision making.

Since organizations comprise many groups, the likelihood of many examples of risky shift decision making increases. In addition, degrees of uncertainty will vary from sector to sector and from decision to decision. We explore these aspects of uncertainty and risk in the next sections. First, we need to explore the many different images and origins of risk.

14.1 Different images of risk

From one perspective, risks faced by organizations can be viewed (and defined) as a set of wholly exogenous influences or shocks which they have to face. These could include changes in the natural environment or macroeconomic stability. Natural disasters such as hurricanes, earthquakes or tornados would fall into this category, as would disruptive technological changes which force decision makers to make choices not of their own making (technologies may be invented outside the organization, forcing decision makers in the organization to respond reactively). However, few analysts of risk maintain that uncertainties due to these exogenous shocks are wholly key to understanding how organizations both create and deal with risk. A noticeable movement has taken place over the last twenty or so years toward viewing risk as 'man-made' (Turner, 1978) or manufactured (Beck 1992). Both these authors argue that these organizationally created risks influence the social and natural environments. Furthermore, they may also influence national and global economic systems. The number of completely exogenous shocks to organizations is very small indeed, according to these theorists.

Events which seem to be 'natural' are argued to have an organizational origin. For example, the risks posed by earthquakes have been argued to have an organizational component, namely poor or disregarded building regulations. However, the possible occurrence of the earthquake itself is undeniably an exogenous risk. Technological failures, such as the Bhopal disaster, or the *Challenger* space shuttle, are argued to be rooted deeply in organizational processes. Perrow (1984) argued that one common factor in disasters that places people at risk is the mismatch between organizational structure and its technology in use. The explosion in the Union Carbide plant in Bhopal, India, was argued to be a result of the firm growing in size but not adapting to new technologies. When a fault occurred in the plant, it was not immediately noticed since the specialization of roles together with the remoteness of the manufacturing process (relying on arm's-length safety checks) did not accommodate inter-role communication, which would have been needed to avert disaster. When a switch was thrown (accidentally), giving a false 'all systems OK' message, role specialization meant there was no possibility of checking this, despite it being obvious that something was wrong. By the time the problem was recognized it was too late. No individual had the capacity to stop the inevitable explosion which caused long-term damage to human and plant life.

Alexander (1996) accounts for the bursting of a gas pipeline in New Jersey in March 1994 as being attributable to the structure of the Texas Eastern Transmission Company, which was traditional, centralized and inflexible, unable to cope with the demands of gas transmission. Greening and Johnson (1996) argue that highly interactive, tightly coupled and high-risk technologies can spell high risk in an organizational structure which is bureaucratic and inflexible. They argued that one of the problems of such organizations is the inability of top-level managers to cope with (or to prevent) disasters. This was seemingly prophetic, given the economic disasters which were to follow as a result of top-level failures (such as Enron; *see* Chapter 17). The events of 11 September 2001 and the subsequent invasion of Iraq have also been blamed on organizational failures, in this case the paucity of information exchange between security agencies worldwide. Therefore, we can view risk as being something organizations create, as well as have to manage when external events (such as natural disasters) are imposed directly upon them.

Table 14.1 Categories of risks facing organizations

Risk category	Examples	Endogenous/exogenous to the organization
STRATEGY	Changing patterns of demand	Mostly exogenous
	Competitor actions	Mostly exogenous
	Changing markets	Mostly exogenous
	Business/government relationships	Endogenous and exogenous
	New disruptive technologies introduced	Exogenous
OPERATIONS	Manufacturing/process systems	Endogenous
	Financial/accounting controls	Endogenous
	Regulators	Exogenous
ECONOMIC	Poor cash flow	Mostly exogenous
	Changes in interest rates	Exogenous
	Currency exchange	Exogenous
	Poor credit	Exogenous and endogenous
HAZARDS	Natural disasters such as earthquakes or volcanoes	Exogenous
	Terrorist attacks	Exogenous
	Criminal activity	Exogenous and endogenous
	IT failure	Exogenous

To try to bring some order to understanding risk in an organizational context, it is useful to break down risk into subcategories that correspond to organizational activities. This allows decision makers to assess risks which are internal to the organization and those which are external to it. Table 14.1 gives some examples of how this might be done.

Table 14.1 is not intended to be exhaustive. There are many more risks than those illustrated here, but breaking down risks into these (or similar) categories allows decision makers to assess what would happen in the worst case if one or more of these were to occur. In that way, decision makers can rate each risk for severity and potential loss. In total, such a rating can produce an overall risk assessment score for an organization.

It is difficult for many of these risks to label them either as endogenous or as exogenous. In the majority of cases, they are a combination of both. For example, new technologies and scientific developments (such as genetic engineering or gene therapy) have been described as the 'new' risks by a number of commentators (Jorian 2000). Mostly these are seen as exogenous risks to organizations (and to individuals in society). Nuclear power and biotechnology are developed 'out there' and provide sources of cheap energy or improved crop production for organizations. But they are considered risky since the 'downsides' of each are well known. Yet, decision makers inside organizations can actually increase (or multiply) these risks. For example, decision makers in Monsanto ignored public anxieties about the testing of gene technologies and it incurred heavy financial losses as a result. What began as an external risk was badly managed internally and resulted in Monsanto facing even greater levels of risk.

However, even narrowing down risk to categories and origin (endogenous or exogenous) is not without its problems. Several strands of research have emphasized different attributes of and meanings to risk. The main difficulties stem from the difficulties in disentangling *organizational* risk from *managerial* risk. We explore this difficulty in the next section.

14.1.1 Organizational risk and managerial risk

Many authors have grappled with the many different definitions and descriptions of risk. Baird and Thomas (1990) argue that risk is multidimensional and that it is important to distinguish between *managerial* and *organizational* risk. **Managerial risk** taking is where managers make choices associated with uncertain outcomes. **Organizational risk** is where organizations face volatile income streams which are associated with turbulent and unpredictable environments. It is important not to confuse the two. If, for example, we use organizational risk as a substitute term for managerial risk, we make the unwarranted assumption that managerial risk taking leads to variations in organizational performance. This may not be the case. There is little empirical evidence on the relationships (if any) between organizational and managerial risk. Miller and Bromiley (1990) found that risk loaded on three separate factors (managerial, firm performance, market performance) but their study concluded little about the possible interrelationship of these factors.

Table 14.2 Organizational and managerial risks

Organizational risk factors	Characteristics
COMPLEX–SIMPLE ENVIRONMENTS	The more complex the environment, the greater the degree of organizational risk. Complexity corresponds to industry size as well as the number and heterogeneity of competitors. Simple environments, such as oligopolies, have institutional rules of behaviour. Complexity is likely to lead to blind spots, making it difficult for organizations to calculate risk or prepare for the responses of rivals since not all are understood or even known.
SCARCITY–MUNIFICENCE	Munificence refers to the abundance of resources, which include human, financial and capital. Abundance provides a context in which greater risk can be tolerated more easily. For example, mergers are tolerated to a greater extent in periods of growth rather than periods of economic closure. The reverse is true of scarcity, when firms face less risk as they all look inward to tighten controls and to reduce costs.
DYNAMISM	Dynamism refers to the stochastic characteristics of the environment. These include, for example, discontinuities caused by the introduction of new technologies or novel products from competitor organizations.
Managerial risk	**Characteristics**
ASPIRATIONS AND EXPECTATIONS	Aspirations are used to judge the quality of actual performance. Expectations indicate the level of anticipated future performance. Higher aspirations induce higher risks. Higher expectations mean better performance is more likely and this will induce lower levels of risk taking. The framing of a situation as either a gain or a loss may also influence propensity to take risk. For example, when managers/decision makers are faced with the likelihood of failing to meet their objectives, they are likely to accept greater levels of risk in order to try to reach their objectives and to avoid losses. When managers/decision makers are faced with the likelihood that they will achieve objectives, they are likely to favour safer options and avoid risk.
TOP-TEAM CHARACTER-ISTICS	High levels of heterogeneity in top teams are likely to promote greater risk taking. Managers with varied backgrounds (educational, international, other companies) will bring different perspectives and interpretive schema to bear upon decisions. Such groups are more likely to consider and take action on more risky, uncertain and non-routine decisions. High levels of homogeneity will induce a greater tendency to preserve the status quo and only take action on less risky decisions.
OWNERSHIP	Managers/decision makers who do not hold an equity stake in their organizations are less likely to take risky decisions than managers/decision makers who do hold a stake. Equity ownership prompts owner-managers to make decisions which are in line with shareholder goals through carefully calculated risk taking. Other things being equal, equity ownership mitigates the risk aversion of managers who hold risk-neutral preferences held by diversified shareholders. Non-owner-managers may feel that taking risks puts their employment at risk, because gambles which do not succeed can result in them being fired or, in the extreme, firm bankruptcy. They also have a less strong interest in the outcomes of successful risky decisions.

Table 14.2 continued

Managerial risk	Characteristics
SLACK	Slack means an organization has spare resources which can buffer it against fluctuations in environmental conditions. It acts to absorb shocks which could otherwise harm performance. Slack allows managers/decision makers to avoid risky decisions and major strategic changes. Low levels of slack induce more risky decisions. This 'hunger-driven' view of risk taking is shared by some authors and not by others. For example, Wiseman and Bromiley (1996) provide evidence that supports the argument. On the other hand, Singh (1986) found a positive relationship between slack and risk taking by managers. Firms do not necessarily have to be hungry for managers to take risks in this perspective. Palmer and Wiseman (1999), however, found evidence in favour of the hunger-driven view of risk taking, showing that organizations which have greater levels of slack take fewer risks.

Source: adapted from Palmer and Wiseman, 1999.

Despite the relative lack of empirical evidence and the theoretical confusion, Palmer and Wiseman (1999) provide some clear and concise definitions of risk at the managerial and organizational levels. These are summarized in Table 14.2.

Differentiating between these two levels of analysis (organizational and managerial) allows decision makers a clearer evaluation of both the location and source of risks. Hazards that are clearly identified as being at the organizational level help decision makers focus on (say) environmental characteristics and help avoid needless and perhaps pointless examination of managerial processes (such as the composition of top teams). Clarity, not only over the source of risk (Table 14.1,) but also its levels of analysis (Table 14.2), helps decision makers begin the process of **assessing risk**.

However, the interrelationships (if any) between organizational risk and managerial risk are much more in dispute. Some authors (for example, Fiegenbaum and Thomas 1988) assume managerial risk taking to be congruent with organizational risk. The one and the other are essentially the same. Others (for example, Palmer and Wiseman 1999) argue that decisions which have high levels of uncertainty (such as R&D investments) provide only a partial explanation of organizational risk. There is presently too little empirical evidence to support one view or the other. It is clear that there are some interrelationships between managerial and organizational risk, but the extent of that relationship is, as yet, unknown.

14.1.2 Prospect theory and risk

Fiegenbaum and Thomas (1988) utilize 'prospect theory' to reach their conclusions. Prospect theory is a modification of expected utility theory. It helps explain choice behaviours which do not fit with expected **utility theory**. For example, decision makers can be observed to persist in committing resources to risky and uncertain projects in an attempt to try to recover prior sunk costs which were invested earlier in the decision process. This behaviour considers *sunk costs to be relevant* to future decision trajectories, but it is in violation of the assumptions of expected utility theory which argue that *sunk costs should be ignored* in risky decision making. **Prospect theory** holds that decision makers make choices between risky alternatives influenced by both the magnitude and the probabilities of outcomes. Outcomes are evaluated as gains or losses (positive or negative deviations) from a neutral reference point. Gains and losses are evaluated using an S-shaped value function which illustrates that (say) the disappointment at losing a lot of money is greater than the pleasure associated with winning the same amount. It also implies that decision makers will tend to prefer a sure gain over a probable gain of expected equal value. This means that a sure chance of winning 20 000 euros is preferred to a 50 per cent chance of winning 40 000 euros, but a 50 per cent chance of losing 40 000 euros is preferred to a sure chance of losing 20 000 euros.

One critical aspect of prospect theory is that gains and losses are assessed relative to a neutral (or reference) point. However, this point is not really neutral. Options can be framed or presented in a highly positive way, thus affecting the placement of the supposedly neutral point (Kahneman and Tversky, 1973). A set of prospects presented as likely losses will induce risk taking, whereas a set of prospects presented in terms of gains will induce less risky decision making.

However, prospect theory appears to explain many decisions one can observe in organizations. Organizations with returns which are above target level are characterized by having managers who are risk-averse. Organizations which have returns below target levels are characterized by managers who are risk-seeking in their decision making. Prospect theory also helps explain what may seem, at first sight, to be odd behaviour. This is because individual managers are likely to set different levels of aspiration. For example, one manager may have set his or her aspirations very high (say for a new product). These may be aspirations about brand strength for example. The new product may indeed reach the aspirations of one manager in terms of brand strength, but may actually perform less well in the market. Few people buy the new product. A second manager whose aspirations centred around sales would likely argue against further investment and take the sunk costs as something to write off. The first manager, however, is much more likely to commit more money to advertising and promotion of this product which (by another's criteria) is failing. So prospect theory helps us untangle the relativism which pervades individual choice processes. Gains or losses are subjectively constructed and a so-called neutral point from which potential gains and losses are calculated is rarely neutral. Finally, this begs the question of whether the reference point is individually or organizationally constructed. Organizations, as well as individuals, have goals and objectives. Organizational goals can mask what appear to be behaviours at solely managerial levels and vice versa.

14.2 **Uncertainty**

Uncertainty is the principle that there is a limit to the precision and the extent of knowledge about a subject or an event. Uncertainty creates risk for strategic decision makers. Uncertainty arises because we cannot know everything:

> *We do not perceive the present as it is, and in its totality, nor do we infer the future from the present with any high degree of dependability, nor yet do we accurately know the consequences of our actions. In addition ... we do not execute our actions in the precise form in which they are imagined and willed.* (Knight 1921: 203)

Such uncertainties vary in themselves, with some strategies being taking in response to a relatively predictable future, while others are taken in the face of highly unpredictable and sometimes unknowable futures. This may be seen as a scale of uncertainty, ranging from *predictable uncertainty* at one end to *uncertain uncertainty* at the other (Luhmann 1993). An example of a relatively predicable uncertainty would be world demographics. An uncertain uncertainty might be trying to predict technologies which have not yet been invented or developed.

As far as demographics are concerned, we already know, for example, that the worldwide population is estimated to grow by 29 per cent by 2021 (a rise of 1.79 billion people). In the UK, estimates are for a 4 per cent population increase in the same period (2.5 million people). The number of 16–34-year-olds will decline by 15 per cent (1995–2021) and the number of 55–64-year-olds will have increased 40 per cent in the same time period (source: Office of National Statistics). The question for the strategic decision maker is what effects will such knowable futures have on business and what strategic decisions might be taken now in anticipation of these changes? Table 14.3 lists some of the factors a clothes retailer might take into consideration to inform future strategies in relation to the relatively predictable uncertainties of demographics.

Uncertainties also stem from not being able to anticipate changes in the macro or competitive context or not being able to predict the consequences these might have for the firm. Uncertainties also stem from the nature of the business you are in. An example of this can be seen in the film industry (*see* case box).

Table 14.3 Some typical effects of demographic changes on clothing retailers

- Larger market for clothers in the late-middle-aged group of the population
- More opportunities for design and style in this market (feeding the 'Jeans Generation' which comprises this segment of the population).
- A declining number of high-spending fashion-conscious 15–24-year-olds (and 25–34-year-olds)
- A greater number of more affluent 'grannies' (who may spend more money on clothes for the fewer babies that will be around)

Case box: **The film business and uncertainty**

The film business is one of the most unpredictable (and costly) in the world. It occupies a space which is at the nexus of art and commerce and is one where directors, actors and producers want to make a lot of money and get noticed for doing it. Yet it is notoriously difficult to tell what is going to be a successful film at the outset of the decision process. Many seemingly good ideas crash badly at the box office. Some films become the disaster stories they seek to portray. For example, *Cutthroat Island*, a pirate-thriller, made a splash for all the wrong reasons on its release in 1995. The film cost $100 million to produce, promote and distribute, but made only $11 million at the box office. As well as walking the plank commercially, the film was heavily criticized. The *Washington Post* remarked, 'Cutthroat's lame cliff-hangers are enough to make you a cliff jumper.' This film destroyed Carolco, a studio known for big-budget sci-fi films such as *Terminator 2, Judgement Day* and *Total Recall*. At the time of its making, *Cutthroat* was judged by the studio likely to be a sure-fire success.

Yet, a film argued at its inception to be a stupid idea (everyone knows the ending before they see the film) became the biggest-grossing film to date. *Titanic* (Paramount) became the first film to ever take US$1 billion at the international box office. The film set included a replica of the ill-fated luxury liner, a model only 10 per cent smaller than the actual vessel and an enormous 7-acre tank that could hold 77 million litres (17 million gallons of water). Computer-generated effects helped to recreate the world's worst single peacetime maritime disaster, as well as sink the biggest film budget. It cost over US$200 million to make, when the industry average was around US$30 million (today it is US$ 60 million – still significantly under Titanic's budget). Director James Cameron persuaded Fox and Paramount executives to accept budget overruns, arguing that there was an urgent need for a film which could blow the market away. He gained commitment from executives for reasons which, at the outset, were little different from those used to support *Cutthroat Island*. *Titanic*, however, was the success, with the most number of Oscars awarded to a single film: 11 accolades including Best Picture, Best Director, Best Actress and Best Visual Effects.

Source: interviews by the author with *Entertainment Data International* (EDI) and *Prescience Film Finances*, July 2004.

Uncertainties in the film industry lie in the intractable problems of prediction of success. They also lie in making decisions to continue, even though the film is going over-budget and over-time. Such decisions are, of course, key, since the question becomes: if we continue, what might happen? Or do we just stop and take as losses expenditure to date? Since there are no data which can reliably inform these decisions, gut feel, persuasion and ego can be the factors which drive continuation in this uncertain industry.

Yet decision makers are always surrounded by uncertainties. What techniques have they developed over time to cope with and to reduce uncertainty and risk?

Table 14.4 Macro and micro-level influences

Environmental uncertainties	Industry uncertainties	Firm uncertainties
Political War Revolution Coup d'état Other political turmoil Raw materials shortages	**Input market** Quality uncertainty Shifts in market supply Changes in quantity used	**Operating** Labour uncertainties Labour unrest Employee safety Input supply
Governmental policy Fiscal and monetary Price controls Trade restrictions Nationalization Trade restrictions Government regulation Barriers to earnings Inadequate provision of public services Repatriation	**Product/market** Quality changes Changes in consumer tastes Spare parts restrictions Availability of substitutes Production uncertainties Scarcity of complementary goods Machine failure	
Macroeconomic Inflation Changes in relative price Exchange rates Foreign exchange rates Interest rates	**Competitive** Rivalry among competition New entrants Technological uncertainty Innovation	**Liability** Product liability Emission of pollutants
R&D Terms of trade Uncertain results of R&D	**Credit** Problems with collectibles	
Social Social unrest Riots Changing social concerns Demonstrations Small-scale terrorist movements		
Natural uncertainties Variations in rainfall Hurricanes Earthquakes Other natural disasters		

Source: adapted from Miller, 1992.

One well-known tool for this assessment is the PEST analysis. This will be familiar to many readers (it was also introduced in Chapter 1 of this book) and includes:

- **Political/Legal**: legislation (e.g. monopolies), environmental protection, taxation and foreign trade regulations, employment law, government stability.
- **Economic**: business cycles, interest rates, inflation, income and GNP trends, market share and price/volume relationships.
- **Socio-cultural**: demographics, income distribution, lifestyle changes, levels of education, attitudes to work and leisure and social mobility.
- **Technological**: levels of research spend (government and industry), rates of obsolescence and innovation, speed of technology transfer, e-commerce and the impact of digital technologies more broadly.

However, such macro-changes also need to be assessed alongside the more micro-changes which organizations face (such as industry structure, the influence of suppliers, competitors and customers). Although complex, Miller (1992) provides an example of combining macro and micro influences. These are shown in Table 14.4.

Some factors (such as product/market) in Table 14.4 span both industry- and firm-level uncertainties. Hence they can appear 'between columns'. Complicated though Miller's list is, it nevertheless allows the strategist to consider simultaneously both macro- and micro-level factors. It also presents the strategist with the problem of both measuring and analysing these factors. Many of them are difficult to measure with any level of precision or probability. We examine techniques to assess probabilities in the next sections of this chapter.

14.3 **Risk analysis and assessment techniques**

A variety of methods have been proposed to assess the level of risk associated with pursuing a particular strategy in the face of uncertainty. These range in complexity from observation (taking action and seeing what happens) through to quantification via Delphi techniques and multivariate analyses such as econometric and computer models.

Risk analysis provides a set of techniques for assessing the effects of uncertainty on decision making, especially capital investment decisions (Hertz and Thomas 1983). There are a number of variations in a set of different techniques, but they tend to be variations on a theme. The theme is that:

> the assessment of whether or not the decision is 'worth' making is achieved by taking into account the varying degrees of uncertainty surrounding the input variables to a decision.

There are a number of commonly used measures of worth, such as **net present value** (NPV) and **internal rate of return** (IRR). The decision maker first has to define the input variables to a decision and then has to make subjective assessments of the probabilities of each. Typically, the uncertain variables are costs, prices and economic factors, and these can be identified and quantified.

For example, decision makers may be considering an investment decision in a research and development (R&D) project. In a totally certain world, decision makers would know the cash flow pattern that would occur over the life cycle of the project and a definite value could be calculated for NPV. Uncertainty, however, means that there will be unpredictability in the various factors which comprise the cash flow pattern for the project. Risk analysis provides a technique whereby the decision maker can assess and characterize the impact of these uncertainties on NPV. The probability of the NPV distribution is derived from the input variables and the expected value of NPV can be mapped out and evaluated. The basic steps in such a risk analysis comprise:

- Identify the main factors of the decision which are uncertain (e.g. raw material costs, selling price of final product, likely level of sales).

- Estimate the range of values within which each variable is expected to fall and assess the likelihood of occurrence. For example, raw material costs may be expected to lie within a range of 20–45 euros per tonne. Decision makers, however, might assign a probability of 0.5 that the cost will be 40 euros and 0.1 that it will be 20 euros. Each variable in the decision can thus be assessed. However, some variables may be interdependent (raw material costs will influence selling price) and the decision maker must estimate the strength of the correlations between them. This can be done by a series of probability distributions in a specified range of values.

- Select at random from the distribution of values for each factor one particular value. Then, combine the values for all the factors and compute the rate of return (NPV) from that combination. For example, the lowest in the range of prices might be combined with the highest in the range of growth rate.

- Conduct the previous stage many times to define and evaluate the odds of occurrence of each possible rate of return (NPV). There are, of course, potentially many thousands of possible combinations of values. Therefore, we need to work out the likelihood that various specific returns on the investment will occur. This whole procedure has been referred to as the simulation method or the Monte Carlo method. The distribution of NPVs thus obtained can be used to calculate its mean and variability, ranging from a loss (if the factors go against the decision) to whatever maximum gain is possible (if all factors support the decision).

Obtaining this distribution has been likened by Hertz and Thomas (1983) to tossing two die and assessing how many times we may expect the total of seven to be thrown. A total of seven can be achieved by more than one combination of die values (e.g. by throwing a three and a four; a six and a one; a five and a two). The greater the number of combinations for a given value, the higher are the chances of achieving it. The average expectation is the average of the values of all outcomes weighted by the chances of each occurring. The variability of outcome values from the average also needs to be calculated since it is preferable to have a lower variability for the same NPV if given the choice.

Figure 14.1 shows some possible shapes for NPV distributions derived from the risk analysis. Faced with these data, decision makers would want to know:

◆ What is the probability of making a loss? (NPV < neutral)

◆ What is the average NPV?

◆ What is the probability of making a gain greater than some pre-specified level?

◆ How risky is the project? Is the variability or spread of the NPV distribution large in relation to the mean?

With reference to Figure 14.1, we can see that project C has about a 50:50 chance of an NPV exceeding zero. Project B has about a 75 per cent chance of an NPV below zero. Project C is highly risky (it has a large spread in relation to the mean) and project B is unlikely to yield a positive NPV. Project A always yields a positive NPV and this is low risk. Based on this analysis, decision makers would choose project A.

Knowing the shapes of possible NPV distributions helps decision makers assess the expected NPV. Of course, the shape of the distribution depends for its validity on the degree of accuracy with which subjective probabilities of the key variables in the decision or project are assessed. In addition, the decision eventually arrived at by using this technique does not take into account later decisions which may be dependent on the original decision. Risk analysis only considers the levels of risk of one decision at a time. Decision makers, however,

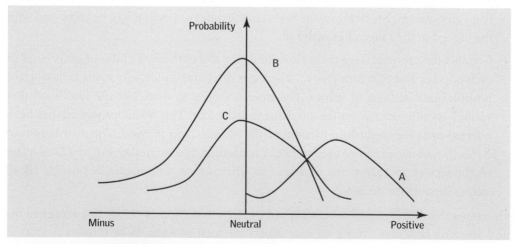

Figure 14.1 Three possible NPV distributions for three projects
Source: adapted from Moore and Thomas, 1976.

want more than just knowing the level of risk as assessed by probabilities; they also want to make choices. In making choices, decision makers build up multiple and interrelated patterns of decisions. They rarely just make one stand-alone decision (*see* Chapter 13). To consider risk in multiple related decisions, we need to combine risk analysis with techniques such as **decision trees**.

14.3.1 Decision trees and risk analysis

Hespos and Strassmann (1965) developed the stochastic decision tree method as a way of representing and analysing a series of decisions over time. It puts together classic decision tree analysis (where individual decisions are built up over time) with risk analysis techniques such as those described in the previous section. This technique is designed to handle situations of sequential investment decision making (e.g. new product launches, downsizing or internationalization) and assess risk across a series of related decisions.

According to Hespos and Strassman (1965), such stochastic decision trees assume that:

◆ All quantities and factors, including chance events, can be represented by continuous, empirical probability distributions.

◆ The information about the results from any, or all, possible combinations of decisions made at sequential points in time can be obtained in a probabilistic form.

◆ The probability distribution of possible results from any particular combination of decisions can be analysed using the concepts of utility and risk.

Hertz and Thomas (1983) give an example of structuring an investment decision using this technique. First the decision team identifies the range of alternative options and assesses the chance events which might occur along the way. They also examine potential ways of measuring performance and outcomes. Then they can begin to structure the decision tree, as in Figure 14.2.

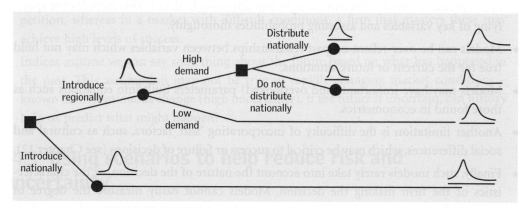

Figure 14.2 Stochastic decision tree for the launch of a new product
Source: adapted from Hertz and Thomas, 1983.

According to Bain & Co. (website):

> *Scenario planning is not about predicting the future. Rather it attempts to describe what is possible. The result of a scenario analysis is a group of distinct futures, all of which are plausible. The challenge then is how to deal with each of the possible scenarios.*

In Shell's words (website)

> *Scenarios are carefully crafted stories about the future embodying a wide range of ideas and integrating them in a way that is communicable and useful. They help us link the uncertainties we hold about the future to the decisions we make today. When we reflect on situations, we see the world through our own frames of reference. The purpose of scenario work is to uncover what these frames are, respecting differences rather than aiming for a consensus that puts them to one side.*

These definitions remains broadly unchallenged. More recent approaches use language such as 'visualizing alternative futures' so that we can design 'flexible options for strategy' to cope with the 'diversity within these futures'.

In practice, scenarios are:

- Attempts to look into the future by bundling together plausible and logically consistent factors.

- Together, these factors help tell a story about the future influences in an organization and give it key characteristics (no matter how apparently wild these seem today).

- Such characteristics are key to helping strategists plan and effect changes to meet the anticipated futures.

14.5.1 Which organizations should use scenarios?

- In theory, all organizations can use scenarios, but it is clearly important for large, capital intensive firms (such as oil companies) to get the future context as right as possible. Sunk costs and opportunity costs are very high in these industries and getting it wrong can have disastrous consequences. Equally pharmaceutical firms have very high R&D levels and manufacturing costs. Getting the future wrong can be a disastrous problem in such industries.

- Scenarios can be projections of up to (and beyond) ten years into the future. The advantage of this that strategies for change can be formulated which are relatively independent of business and economic cycles.

- Organizations which need to use scenarios are especially those which are unable to react quickly and effectively to changing events as they occur.

- Organizations which can react quickly and maintain high levels of flexibility have the option of pursuing a 'trading' strategy involving rapid changes and quick fixes. So long as this capability lasts, such organizations need not necessarily concern themselves with longer-term scenarios.

14.5.2 Scenarios and scenario thinking

In Chapter 6 we considered the difficulties of planning over time scales that fall beyond the limits of competitive strategy. In particular we noted that most companies have difficulty in quantifying any factors beyond two product life cycles. Yet strategic thinking cannot be neglected. It was Alvin Toffler who said;

> *There is a slightly odd notion in business today that things are moving so fast that strategy becomes an obsolete idea. That all you need is to be flexible or adaptable or, as the current vocabulary puts it, 'agile'. This is a mistake. You cannot substitute agility for strategy. If you do not develop a strategy of your own you become a part of someone else's strategy. You, in fact, become reactive to external circumstances. The absence of strategy is fine, if you don't care where you're going.* (Source: Bain & Co. website)

We suggested in Chapter 6 an adaptation of competitive advantage thinking that would in a qualitative way enable strategic thinking to be taken beyond two product life cycles. In this section we look at scenario planning, a method of longer-run thinking that has become very well known and adopted in a great many diverse situations. A search on the internet through Google reveals over 50 pages of sites whose prime descriptor is scenario planning. It is said to have its roots in military strategy studies and notably through Herman Kahn, who was famous for his work related to the possible scenarios associated with thermonuclear war ('thinking the unthinkable'). It was transformed into a business tool in the late 1960s and early 1970s at Royal Dutch Shell, firstly through Pierre Wack, Kees van der Haydn and Peter Schwartz. At a time of very low oil prices Shell's use of scenario planning enabled it to be better prepared for the oil shocks of the 1970s, the oil crisis followed by the oil glut. Indeed the subsequent success of the method owes much to Shell's success in predicting the first oil price shock in 1973. High-profile users in the USA include the White House, the Pentagon and the Economic Planning Agency.

14.5.3 How useful are scenarios?

A scenario is useful in assessing the long-term ramifications of a firm's overall strategy. Analysis of multiple scenarios enables the assessment of the implications of different futures for alternative strategies and the uncertainties and risks associated with them. According to Shell (again, from their website):

> *Scenarios are particularly useful in situations where there is a desire to put challenges on the agenda proactively (for example when there are leadership changes*

and major impending decisions) and where changes in the global business environ-
ment are recognised but not well understood (such as major political changes and
emerging technologies).

A well-constructed scenario enables the ordering of one's perceptions about alternative
future environments in one of which it is likely that one's decisions might be played out.

Therefore, there are two key characteristics of a good 'story'. The first is that it results from
the subjective assessments of a wide range of informed individuals or groups. A valid story
has to be built on facts and assumptions that can be validated and supported in a reasonably
objective way. This requires that the process of scenario development should be objective
and replicable and not rest simply on guesswork, however inspired. Second, it recognizes
that decision makers have some influence on future development. The simple assumption is
that decision makers are in position to react to the dimensions of the story as it unfolds. The
stronger view is that the unfolding story allows for the dynamic interaction of the decision
makers with the environment.

14.5.4 **Writing a scenario**

A scenario starts with the focal issue or decision. A generic worry about, for example, the
implications of new technologies will lead in myriad directions. The issue for the firm must
revolve around key dilemmas or challenges that are on the horizon (or just over) but for
which there is little early guidance. The purpose of the scenario is to provide a frame within
which some guidance for major commitments can be developed. Nevertheless, the focal
issue can be described in quite broad terms (e.g. what will be the future for technology in
banking?). Or they could be quite specific (what are the implications of new technologies for
traditional banking organizations?). The longer the time frame, the broader will be the focal
issue. The shorter the time frame, the easier it is to collapse scenario thinking into detailed
forecasting and planning.

The second stage is to identify the primary driving forces of the future. This is usually
based on the PEST analysis that we introduced in this chapter and Chapter 6. Because the
scope of PEST includes politics, economics, technology and social dynamics, this encompasses most of the forces that are likely to be relevant.

You are now ready to construct your story of the future (Schoemaker 2002).

A structured view of the **scenario planning** process might look as follows:

1 Identify the focal issue(s).

2 Specify the scope of the planning and its time frame.

3 Establish the broad background that includes the organization within its 'deep' structure (PEST characteristics).

4 Identify the driving forces that link the focal issues with the long-term future: these are
events that are predetermined and virtually certain to occur.

5   Identify the critical uncertainties in the environment. At this point macroeconometric forecasting will be useful.

6   Combine the driving forces with the uncertainties to create alternative futures (the scenarios).

7   Validate the alternative futures (e.g. by Delphi-style processes or by qualitatively assessing their likelihood of occurrence). The latter can easily be assessed on a probability scale ranging from 0 (little likelihood of occurrence) to 1 (high likelihood of occurrence).

8   Analyse the scenarios for similarities, differences and sources of difference, mutual dependence.

9   Quantify the effect of each scenario on the firm and formulate appropriate strategies. Again the impact on the firm can be assessed on a 0 to 1 scale where 0 equals little impact and 1 equals high impact.

10   Develop strategy options and criteria for future choices and paths.

Although some of the above may seem similar to the probabilities and assessments made in risk analyses described earlier in this chapter, there are two main differences with respect to scenarios. First, the time horizon considered is significantly longer. Scenarios typically look ten or fifteen years into the future. Second, the specificity of the analysis is far broader and, of necessity, less precise.

The processes around points 3, 4, 5, 6, 7 and 8 may take place typically in workshop settings where executives, technical experts and policy analysts bring together a wide range of experience and expertise in order both to identify and to validate the key assumptions about the driving forces and the uncertainties, and how they interact to create the basic scenarios. Figure 14.3 shows the basic drivers of two scenarios distilled into three sets of variables, some common to both scenarios and some exclusive to one or the other.

The analysis methods at points 8 and 9 involve testing each scenario in two ways. The first is a cross-impact analysis to establish the extent to which scenarios have common drivers and different drivers. And the second is to relate each scenario to a short list of the key variables to test for sensitivity/robustness.

Figure 14.4 shows the early stages of the analysis in which the PEST environment is determined and the competitive strategy horizon for the firm (see Chapter 6) is established,

	Common variables	Variable one	Variable two
Scenario one	Yes	Yes	No
Scenario two	Yes	No	Yes

Figure 14.3 Distinguishing the drivers of scenarios

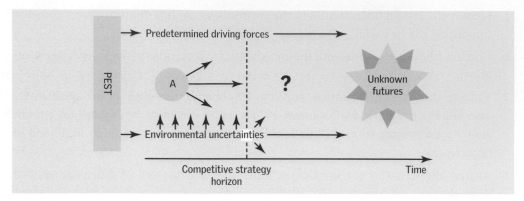

Figure 14.4 Setting out the assumptions

leading to a specification of the focal issues. The futures are unknown and even the points of arrival on the competitive strategy horizon are uncertain.

Figure 14.5 shows the establishment of the basic stories, here characterized as 'optimistic' and 'pessimistic'. They depend on the specification of the assumptions from the first figure and the way in which the drivers and the uncertainties interact. A difficult part of this is initially to keep the stories distinct it is all too easy to end up with minor variants on a common theme. The second problem is to restrict the number of stories to a manageable number, typically two or three. Here the need is to sacrifice complexity for the tractability of analysis. This is why at this stage it is important to restrict the key drivers and uncertainties to only the most important. Hence you can appreciate the need to consult opinion from far and wide so as to avoid our normal perceptual filters.

Figure 14.6 articulates the strategies, the options, and the paths. The paths illustrate the potential complexities. First, the starting point at the competitive strategy horizon may not be clear, points a, b and c are possible, but are broadly similar. However, point d is

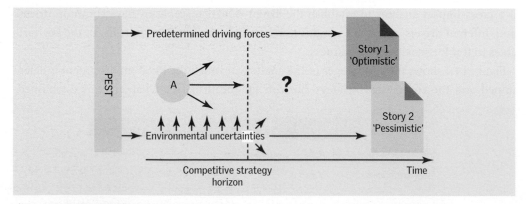

Figure 14.5 Establishing the stories

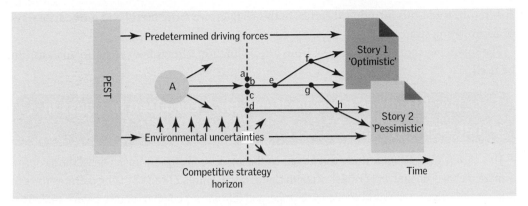

Figure 14.6 Figuring out the strategy options and paths

quite different (i.e. the current competitive strategy has failed to deliver). Second, common paths are possible and choices might be deferred until the situation becomes clearer. Thus, points e, f and g represent choices to be made along the top path. Point f leads unambiguously (as far as we can see now) towards the 'optimistic' story with the possibility of two paths onward, one being more optimistic than the other. Point g represents a more difficult choice where either story is possible but a commitment must be made. Point h is a point along the low path to the 'pessimistic' story, the main question being how pessimistic?

The process of scenario planning seeks to achieve a set of options with assessments of potential pay-offs and risks that can be unfolded over time, taking account of events as they emerge, correcting errors and acknowledging expert opinion as it changes (which it will do). Scenarios are not intended or expected to be 'right' in the sense that forecasts are intended to anticipate the correct outcome. They are intended to:

1 explore the long term beyond conventional planning horizons;

2 build on a wide set of assumptions;

3 explore a wide range of outcomes;

4 meld assumption-outcome sets to derive ranges of possible futures;

5 explore paths required to move from the present to these futures.

In doing this we need to keep our mindset very strategic. Look for common paths. Watch out for forks in the road divergences. Identify the key risks. Find common paths where possible. Do not commit too early avoid the avoidable commitments. But, in the end, the commitments have to be made against the risk. If scenario planning achieves anything (and it is not a panacea) it helps to *assess risk* over the longer term and identify strategic options for the organization. It should be emphasized that organizations are unlikely to survive by scenarios alone. In the short and medium terms, decision and risk analysis alongside the risk/return trade-offs introduced earlier in this chapter, are more useful and immediate ways of formulating strategies.

The following short case example, from a real situation, shows how scenario analysis can be used.

Case box: **Strategic considerations for a European business in a global economy**

This case is taken from a study conducted on the implications for European-based firms of a more global economy and greater economic integration within Europe. It demonstrates three levels of analysis, the world economy, Europe, and (European) companies (see Figure 14.7). It also shows the distinctive variables established at each level of analysis. These then were taken to be distinctive factors that shaped each level, although recognizing that there were other actors common across the levels.

World economy
- Rate of growth
- Trade/GATT
- Russia/E. Europe
- China
- Security

Europe
- Protectionism
- Factor costs
- Reinvestment
- Political and social development
- Single voice?

Companies
- Convergence of markets
- Country vs global view
- Capacity to innovate
- Capacity to be complex
- Corporate government

Figure 14.7 Establishing the assumptions

Two scenarios were established – 'pessimistic' and 'optimistic'. For the world economy this elicited the following comparison:

Pessimistic	Optimistic
Low growth	Sustained growth
Inability of LDCs to grow	LDC and ex-communist growth
Protracted difficulties in China and Russia	Islam and Christian rapprochement
Inability to balance budgets: welfare costs and macro policy problems	Welfare reforms
The 1990s bubble remains burst	Radical Right makes a breakthrough?
	New surge of innovation

For Europe, there is a similar dichotomy:

Pessimistic	Optimistic
Regulation and protection increases	Political voice
Divergence from rest of world	Major trading bloc
Politically inchoate	Thrives on variety and innovation
High cost	Good home base for global companies
Low innovation	Transformation of labour markets

In staying with a dichotomy the distinction is probably too sharp and a third possibility should be explored but a simple middle of the road. The dichotomy for companies is also sharp:

Pessimistic	Optimistic
Country managers remain	Strong global market growth
Global view restrained	New federal organizations
MNEs do not evolve into more complex federal forms	Innovation becomes central to profitability
Efficiency concerns outweigh innovation challenges	Service and financial companies have v. high growth
Country company difficulties	Emergence of new breed of MNEs from China, Russia and East Asia

The simple interaction between the pessimistic columns produces the overall 'pessimistic' scenario, and likewise for the 'optimistic' columns.

Pessimistic scenario

1 Failure to resolve the current set of dilemmas against background of stagnation, insecurity (anarchy?) and weakening of political control and influence. There is continued failure of macroeconomic policy to resolve excessive government spending. Consumer pessimism continues to hold back aggregate demand.
2 Growth will be around 'polar' points rather than uniformly spread. World increasingly has different speeds.
3 Companies seek national or regional patronage from host countries. Trade becomes politicized politico-economic trade-offs become the norm; trade fortresses re-emerge.
4 Power of existing MNEs is likely to be reinforced because of lack of effective competition.

Optimistic scenario

1 Marked by prosperity and high growth across the world. Multiplier effect of major investments enhanced by rapid learning in newer economies. Emergence of major new markets plus increased innovation and opportunity for development of large, new corporations.

> **2** Corporate environment is competitive but highly dynamic. Political influence focused primarily on investing and opening up rather than on protection.
>
> **3** Companies are able to change through growth. They are able to develop transnational and federal character but against a background of increasing segmentation, thus not dominated by the largest players. Look for emergence of Chinese and Russian MNEs.

The scenarios in the case box lead to the development of two possible strategies for an organization. Companies either seek to become expert at politico-economic trade-offs, or they seek to grow transnationally and become expert on innovation and segmentation and seek to establish new organizational structures to support the federal approach. So far, so good. But as Schoemaker (2002) points out, strategy formulation is only one (important) part of the story. Should the firm pursue such strategies, there will need to be a careful assessment of the extent to which the organization is capable and able to implement these chosen strategies

14.6 Back to the organization: identifying gaps

The above examples (and the use of scenarios in general) show that it can be easy to treat scenarios as ends in themselves. That is, the question of whether or not the organization *is capable* of implementing the future strategies informed by the scenario is either not addressed or is overlooked. Scenarios are simply tools which help reduce uncertainty and risk. They also help identify one or two future strategic directions which the organization might take, but they cannot help determine to what extent such strategies are capable of being implemented, or what changes would need to occur to make such strategies a realistic proposition for the organization concerned. The same holds true for strategies identified by risk and decision analyses. Our mythical firm in Figure 14.2 may decide to market the new product nationally rather than regionally. But the key question is, to what extent it can do this effectively?

Fahey and Randall (1998) suggest that, following the identification of future strategies, decision makers should:

- Reflect the formulated strategy back against the organization. What gaps are there (if any) in key factors such as capabilities, capacities, competences and structures?

- Identify what changes may need to be made to the organization in the light of the above 'gap' analysis.

- Identify and select key indicators and signposts which will help monitor and assess the implementation and the performance of the chosen strategies. This will involve careful selection and imaginative choice as well. Using current performance indicators may not be appropriate.

There are a number of ways of doing the above, but most revolve around some form of **gap analysis**. This is where core competences of the organization are assessed against future strategies that have been crafted following the scenario analysis.

Table 14.7 shows a typical gap analysis. This is based on defining an organization's core competences and then assessing to what extent each competence contributes towards (supports) the chosen strategy. This can be done simply by using plus, minus or neutral signs. Plus signs indicate where a **core competence** supports the strategy. Neutral is where the core competence provides little or no support and minus signs indicate where a current competence actually detracts from a future strategy. Core competences are difficult to define as we have seen earlier in this book, but they can be thought of as distinctive capabilities of the organization which:

- create value in terms of economic rent;
- are difficult to imitate (why can't competitors do that?);
- are 'implicit' as part of an organization's history, routines and social capital.

In our mythical example organization in Table 14.7, we can see that two future strategies had been crafted, each based on a particular scenario. One strategy (based on an optimistic scenario that there will still be demand for these types of products) is to retain the existing technology base, but to compete on the strength of expanding the existing product range. A second strategy (based on a pessimistic scenario that new products will be needed as well as new technologies to produce them) is to develop an entirely new product range and to invest in new or emerging technologies. The table also records the firm's current strategy.

Table 14.5 Gap analysis: future strategies and core competences: an example

Core competences (examples)	Current strategy	Future strategy one (e.g. expand product range incrementally; retain existing technologies)	Future strategy two (e.g. adopt new technologies and develop new product ranges to meet anticipated future)
Product advantages (lighter, smaller, cheaper)	+	+	0
Time to market (faster)	+	+	0
Ability to innovate (high)	0	0	+
Proprietary knowledge	+	0	+
Flexible structures	0	0	+

Key terms

Assessing risk 535	Organizational risk 533
Core competence 555	Prospect theory 536
Decision trees 543	Risk 530
Gap analysis 555	Risk indices 545
Internal rate of return 540	Scenario planning 548
Managerial risk 533	Uncertainty 530
Net present value 540	Utility theory 535

Recap questions and assignments

1 Build three scenarios for an organization with which you are familiar. Name them and provide a thumbnail sketch of their key characteristics.

2 Choose the scenario you consider to be most likely and assess the impact of this on organizational factors such as customer demand, costs, levels of competition, changes in technology etc.

3 From the story told in (2) above, suggest one or two strategies the organization might adopt now to prepare for the future you have outlined.

4 Assess the organization's capabilities in implementing your identified strategies. What additional core competencies will be needed (if any) and which current competences may become redundant?

Online
Learning Centre

When you have read this chapter, log on to the Online Learning Centre website at www.mcgraw-hill.co.uk/textbooks/mcgee to explore chapter-by-chapter test questions, further reading and more online study tools for strategy.

Case 1 **Decisions, risk and uncertainty and the use of game theoretic models**

The examples of Intel Polaroid vs Kodak and the breakfast cereals industry

When the environment is predictable and only a few decision variables are involved, all the assumptions for a game theory approach are present. In particular, it is possible to identify all the possible moves of each of the players and the financial consequences of these moves. This allows decision-makers to identify the optimal strategic move(s) for each of the players. We illustrate this approach using three examples.

Intel's dilemma: a prisoner's dilemma game

The rivalry between Intel and Advanced Micro Devices Inc. (AMD) (Business Week, 1999b) has some similarities with the classic game of prisoner's dilemma (Luce and Raiffa, 1957; Rappaport and Chammah, 1965). In this game, two players are suspected of a hypothetical major crime, such as murder. They are imprisoned and held incommunicado, so each must decide whether to cooperate or to defect, without knowing what the other will do. The authorities possess evidence to secure conviction on only a minor charge, such as illegal possession of weapons. If neither prisoner squeals, both will draw a light sentence on the minor charge – this state is called a mutual cooperation (MC) pay-off. If one prisoner squeals and the other stonewalls, the squealer will go free (unilateral defection, UD), and the stonewaller, or 'sucker,' will draw a very heavy sentence (unilateral cooperation, UC). If both squeal, both will draw a moderate sentence (mutual defection, MD).

Each prisoner's preference ordering is UD > MC > MD > UC. Each prisoner will be better off squealing than stonewalling, no matter what his partner chooses to do, because UD > MC (the temptation of cheating) and MD > UC (the fear of being cheated upon). But if both defect, both do worse than if both had cooperated (MC > MD). Hence the dilemma (Parkhe, 1993, pp. 796–7).

Figure 1 Pay-off matrix for the prisoner's dilemma

Figure 1 shows the pay-off matrix of the prisoner's dilemma.

Intel's situation in 1999 was as follows:

> Intel's aggressive marketing and price cuts have delivered big share gains, but the impact on its rivals has been so severe that some are now struggling to survive. For anti-trust enforcers who continue to watch over Intel's practices since it settled a Federal Trade Commission (FTC) suit in March 1999, the failure of one of its competitors would set off alarm bells. At the end of 1998, Intel had 75 per cent of the PC processor market, down from 86 per cent the year before, as a result of gains by rivals Advanced Micro Devices Inc. (AMD) and National Semiconductor Corp. (National), whose low-cost knockoffs of Intel's Pentium chip were getting a huge chunk of the hot sub-$1000 PC business. Although Intel still dominated the chip market and had a lock on the upper-end of the business, that wasn't enough. Intel responded by cutting the price of its low-end Celeron chips in half and courting PC makers with discounted packages of PC parts. Since February 1999, US retail sales of sub-$1000 Celeron PCs have surged 50 per cent. Rivals, meanwhile, are reeling. On May 5, National dropped out of the PC processor business, saying it couldn't make a profit in it. AMD has lost 10 points of market share in cheap PCs. Intel can be super aggressive on price in Celerons because it generates big profits on other lines. Nearly all of Intel's expected $7.7 billion profit this year will come from processors used in computers costing $1200 or more. What Intel is doing is perfectly legal. But antitrust experts say Intel could run foul of regulators if they found that its actions were meant to protect a monopoly through predatory pricing. If for no other reason than to keep the FTC at bay, Intel needs AMD and other rivals to stick around. If AMD collapsed, the FTC would surely react. (Business Week, 1996b).

For Intel, the dilemma is the following: it can pursue its aggressive marketing and price cuts to gain market share (that is a UD situation), but if AMD leaves the market, the FTC will punish Intel for antitrust practices (a MD situation). Therefore, Intel would be better to try to keep AMD in the market even if its market share would suffer (an MC situation). Figure 2 shows the pay-off matrix for Intel and AMD.

Figure 2 Pay-off matrix for the Intel and AMD

Polaroid–Kodak

Another example of the prisoner's dilemma is the competition between Polaroid and Eastman Kodak in instant photography in 1976 and 1977. Prior to 1976 Polaroid had faced no serious competition in instant photography. In 1974 Kodak for the first time revealed that it was working on its own system of instant film and cameras. On April 20, 1976, Kodak announced that it would challenge Polaroid's 28-year monopoly of the instant photographic field (HBS Case 376–266, 1984; Bettis and Weeks, 1987). At that time, the competitive environment was characterized by a limited number of competitors and innovation was incremental and regular in nature thus making the environment quite predictable. The number of decision variables was also limited: Kodak could either enter the instant camera market (fight) or not (détente). Then, Polaroid could either cut its prices (fight) or not (détente) and Kodak could either choose to follow Polaroid (fight) or not (détente). This is clearly a situation where game theoretic models apply. The decision tree presented in Figure 3 shows the different alternatives for Kodak and Polaroid.

In this situation, a sequential model with repeated moves could have helped Kodak to anticipate what Polaroid would do and then, based on this information, determine an optimal decision path. The main rule of competitive strategy in a situation of sequential moves has been described by Dixit and Nalebuff (1991) and can be summarized as follows: *look ahead and reason back.* Kodak had to think about the possible reactions of Polaroid to its entry into the instant camera market and how to react. Kodak could have predicted the fact that Polaroid would cut its prices to maintain its market share and highlight the necessity of Kodak's own subsequent price cuts. It was another example of a prisoner's

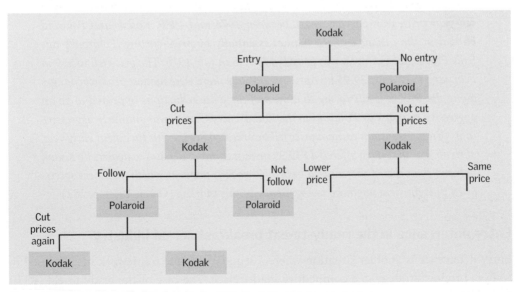

Figure 3 Decision tree for Kodak's entry into the instant camera market

dilemma is presented in Figure 4. All the elements of a price war existed. At that time, Kodak clearly dominated the US conventional photographic market with market shares of 90 per cent for film and 85 per cent for cameras. Protected by its patents, Polaroid earned monopoly profits in the instant camera market. By April 1976, its Colorpack

Figure 4 Pay-off matrix for Polaroid and Kodak

system contributed at least 95 per cent to Polaroid's earnings; therefore, Kodak's entry into the instant camera market was clearly a threat for Polaroid's market share and profitability. Therefore, it was predictable that Polaroid would react aggressively to protect its market share.

If Kodak had used a game theoretic model to analyze the situation, it is likely that it would not have entered the instant camera market and the subsequent price war would have been avoided. The following quote presents Polaroid and Kodak's moves after Kodak's entry.

> 'On April 20, 1976, Eastman Kodak Company announced that it would challenge Polaroid Corporation's 28-year monopoly of the instant photographic field' (HBS Case 376–266, 1984). The entry of Kodak into the instant camera market starts a ten-year price war. For ten years, between 1976 and 1986, Kodak and Polaroid battled in the instant camera market essentially by price-cutting. Polaroid's no-frills Pronto, for example, was priced at $79.95 in July 1976. The price fell to $59 in February 1977 and $39.95 by April 1977. While there were modest product changes along the way, it is fair to say that most of the price reductions appeared to be an aggressive response by Polaroid to the Kodak entry. Kodak was similarly aggressive in its prices. Its instant camera price fell by over $20 during this turbulent early year of rivalry, so that it too offered a $39.95 instant camera. Rebates to dealers by Kodak reduced the price of the camera even further to a point at which outsiders speculated that the firm might be losing money in this market. (Oster, 1999, p. 282)

Entry deterrence in the ready-to-eat breakfast cereal industry

Entry deterrence is another situation where a sequential-game framework may be used to analyze product strategy in a competitive marketplace. The case of the ready-to-eat (RTE) breakfast cereal industry (Schmalensee, 1978; HBS Case 9–795–191, 1997; HBS Case

9–796–122, 1997) is a good example of such a game, because the environment is quite predictable and the number of decision variables is limited.

In this situation, entry into a market normally occurs one or two firms at a time. As a new firm enters, it will position itself by looking at its costs, at consumer preferences, and at the position of other firms already in the market. It may also be important for firms to take into account the likely future product behaviour of current and potential rivals in market. Firms will wish to pursue product positions that are least destabilizing to the existing industry and most defensible against entry threats in the future by filling the gaps in the product space (Schmalensee, 1978; Gruca and Sudharshan, 1995). In sum, a firm will take into consideration what it believes will be the final shape of the market in making its own product-line choices.

In the RTE breakfast cereal industry in the USA, between 1950 and 1972, the six leading producers introduced over 80 brands (Schmalensee, 1978). During the same period of time, there was no significant firm entry into the market. The product strategy of the leading producers in the RTE breakfast cereal industry may be described by a competitive game in which each firm positions its brands in market space so that new launches by insiders cannot erode its profits, and therefore, entry by price-matching outsiders is deterred. More formally, the game may be described as follows: RTE cereals provide different attributes relevant to consumers (sweetness, protein content, shape, grain base, vitamin content, fibre content, and crunchiness, for instance). These different attributes define a multi-dimensional space in which cereal brands are positioned. The strategy of the existing firms in the RTE cereal industry is to continually launch new brands to occupy all the cells of the space. There are only two rules for the choice of the position of a new brand: (i) The new brand should be positioned as far away as possible from the position of any other existing brands to avoid price competition and cannibalization of the existing brands of the firm; (ii) The new brand should also be positioned to maximize the space occupied by the brands of the same firm. The brand launches stop when all the cells are occupied by one and only one brand. For simplification, the product map of Figure 5 uses only two dimensions: Sweetness and Fibre content and shows an example of the possible first few launches for two competitive firms A and B.

Moreover, a pattern of rivalry focusing solely on advertising, launching new brands and avoiding price competition seems likely to be self-reinforcing once established. The logic of the pattern follows. The more effectively the established brands are differentiated, the less incentive any seller would have to engage in price competition. The less the price competition among established sellers, the greater the typical price-cost margin, and the greater the

Figure 5 Product map for ready-to-eat-cereals

incentive to advertise. To the extent that advertising outlays resemble fixed costs, increased advertising intensity increases the asymmetry between the positions of potential entrants and established sellers. The latter's brands will be kept on the market as long as variable costs are covered, while an entrant will only launch if it can expect to cover total costs. The greater the difference between variable and total cost, the less attractive aggressive price-cutting entry appears to the new firm (Schmalensee, 1978).

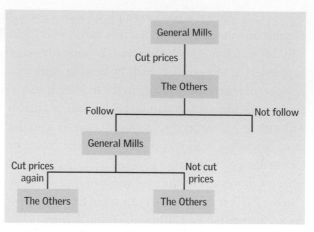

Figure 6 Decision tree for ready-to-eat cereals

This game was profitable for the players, as long as all followed the same rules. However, in April 1994 after a drop in its stock price, General Mills decided to change the rules of the game and announced that it planned to cut $175 million out of its trade promotions and couponing budget, and simultaneously to reduce price. This created a new game similar to the one between Polaroid and Kodak in which players either had to follow the General Mills strategy and reduce prices to maintain market share or continue with the old strategy of brand proliferation. If they decided to cut prices, a destructive price competition may develop like that described earlier (cf. Figure 6) and 'private-label' producers may be forced to exit the industry.

These examples show that game theoretic modelling may be applied to various competitive situations, such as market entry, product positioning and pricing strategy. However, such models are limited to situations where the environment is predictable and where the number of decision variables is limited. When the environment becomes less predictable, other models such as simulation, scenarios or systems are more appropriate.

Source: abstracted from Furrer, O and Thomas, H (2000) 'The rivalry matrix: Understanding rivalry and competitive dynamics', *European Management Journal*, 18, 6, pp. 619–37.

Case Questions

1   Given the analysis of Intel in the prisoner's dilemma matrix, what would you advise Intel to do next? Why?

2   Using Polaroid and Kodak as examples, what are the limitations of using game theoretic models in assessing risk and deciding future strategies? What would you suggest could reduce such limitations?

3   Are scenarios of any more utility than game theoretic models? Assess with reference to Intel, Kodak and the cereal industry.

Further reading and references

Scenarios and scenario-based planning

Peter Schwartz (1991) *The Art of the Long View – Planning for the Future in an Uncertain World* Doubleday 258pp; ISBN 0-385-26731-2, paperback 1996; ISBN 0-385-26732-0)
This is one of the best starting books describing the fundamentals of scenario planning. Peter Schwartz is a futurist and a founder of the *Global Business Network* (GBN) but has also worked at Stanford Research Institute (SRI) and Shell.

Kees van der Heijden (1996) *Scenarios – The Art of Strategic Conversation*, Wiley, 305pp; ISBN 0-471-96639-8)
An excellent book about scenario planning in a business context because it connects to strategy and its practice in a strategic context. The author Kees van der Heijden is one of the founders of GBN and has also a history as head of the Scenario Planning group at Shell.

Gill Ringland (1998) *Scenario Planning – Managing for the Future*, Wiley; 401pp, ISBN 0-471-97790-X
This is mainly focused on providing experiences from a number of scenario planning projects in different companies. Gill Ringland works for ICL and the book reflects scenario projects within ICL, but there are also examples from a number of other projects in other contexts.

Liam Fahey and Robert M. Randall (1998) *Learning from the Future*, Wiley 1998; 446pp; ISBN 0-471-30352-6
This contains a number of articles focusing on different application areas or aspects of scenario planning.

Art Kleiner (1996) *The Age of Heretics*, Doubleday, 414pp; ISBN 0-385-41576-1
This book relates stories about the heretics who challenged the prevailing views at companies like Royal Dutch/Shell. By using scenario planning they saw possible future events which management didn't see at all. Art Kleiner, among other interests, teaches a scenario class focusing on the future for telecommunication infrastructure at New York University.

Wilkinson, Lawrence (1996) 'How to Build Scenarios', *Scenarios: Special Wired Edition*, January, pp. 74–81.

Useful websites

www.library.nijenrode.nl/library/publications/nijrep/1997-01/1997-01.html
Scenarios, strategy and the strategy process
Interesting paper by Kees van der Heijden, a strategic planning veteran from Shell who is also a member of GBN. Scenario planning is treated as a strategic tool that can be used to develop business idea by testing it in several futures and getting a more powerful and more robust strategy.

www2.shell.com
Current Royal Dutch/Shell scenarios and introductory texts
Shell provides both introductory information about scenario planning as well as several downloadable scenarios.

www.innovation.gov.uk/projects/converging_techn/summary/html
Converging Technologies – consequences for the new knowledge-driven economy
A UK government initiative on innovation has produced a number of scenarios on the effects of technology on an economy.

References

Alexander, CB (1996) 'Planning for disaster', *American Gas*, **78**, **2**, 24–7.

Baird, IS and Thomas, H (1990) 'What is risk anyway? Using and measuring risk in strategic management' in Bettis, RA and Thomas, H (eds) *Risk, Strategy and Management*, JAI Press, Greenwich CT, pp. 21–52.

Beck, U (1992) *Risk Society: Towards a New Modernity*, Sage, London.

Fahey, L and Randall, R (1998) *Learning from the Future: Competitive Foresight Scenarios*, West.

Fiegenbaum, A and Thomas, H (1988) 'Attitudes toward risk and the risk-return paradox: prospect theory explanations', *Academy of Management Journal*, **31**, pp. 85–106.

Goodnow, JD and Hansz, JE (1972) 'Environmental Determinants of Overseas Entry Strategies', *Journal of International Business Studies*, **3**, pp. 33–50.

Greening, DW and Johnson, RA (1996) 'Do Managers and strategies matter? A study in crisis', *Journal of Management Studies*, **33**, **1**, pp. 25–51.

Hertz, D and Thomas, H (1983) *Risk Analysis and its Applications*, Wiley, New York.

Hespos, RF and Strassmann, PA (1965) 'Stochastic decision trees for the analysis of investment decisions', *Management Science*, **11**, **10**, pp. 244–59.

Jorian, P (2000) 'Value, risk and control: the call for integration', *The Financial Times*, 16 May.

Kahneman, D and Tversky, A (1973) 'Judgement Under Uncertainty', in Kaufman, GM and Thomas, H (eds) *Modern Decision Analysis*, Penguin: Harmondsworth.

Knight, FH (1921) *Risk, Uncertainty and Profit*, University of Chicago Press, Chicago.

Litvak, IA and Banting, PM (1968) 'A Conceptual Framework for International Business Arrangements', in RL King (ed.) *Marketing and the New Science of Planning*, AMA Fall Conference Proceedings.

Luhmann, N (1993) *Risk: a Sociological Theory*, Aldine de Gruyter, Berlin.

March, JG (1999) *The Pursuit of Organizational Intelligence*, Blackwell, Oxford.

March, JG and Shapira, Z (1999) 'Variable risk preferences and the focus of attention', in JG March (ed.) *The Pursuit of Organizational Intelligence*, Blackwell, Oxford.

Miller, KD (1992) 'Framework for Integrated Risk Management', *Journal of International Business*, Summer, pp. 311–31.

Miller, KD and Bromiley, P (1990) 'Strategic risk and corporate performance: an analysis of alternative risk measures', *Academy of Management Journal*, **39**, pp. 91–122.

Moore, PG and Thomas, H (1976) *The Anatomy of Decisions*, Penguin, Harmondsworth.

Palmer, TB and Wiseman, RM (1999) 'Decoupling risk from income stream uncertainty: a holistic model of risk', *Strategic Management Journal*, **20**, pp. 1037–62.

Perrow, C (1984) *Normal Accidents: Living with High Risk Technologies*, Basic Books, New York.

Schmalansee, R. 1978. '*Entry Deterrence in the Ready to Eat Breakfast Cereal Industry*', *The Rand Journal of Economics*, **9**, pp. 305–327.

Schoemaker, PJH (2002) *Profiting From Uncertainty: Strategies for Succeeding no Matter What the Future Brings*, Free Press, New York.

Singh, JV (1986) 'Performance risk and slack taking in organizational decision making', *Academy of Management Journal*, **29**, pp. 562–85.

Stoner, J (1968) 'Risky and cautious shifts in group decision: the influence of widely held values', *Journal of Experimental Social Psychology*, **4**, pp. 442–59.

Turner, B (1978) *Man-Made Disasters*, Wykeham, London.

Wiseman, RM and Bromiley, P (1996) 'Toward a model of risk in declining organizations: an empirical examination of risk, performance and decline', *Organizational Science*, **7**, pp. 524–43.

15.3 Strategic change and organization

The basic question which surrounds **change and organization** is in the tension between continuity and discontinuity and the size, scale and scope of the change (Greiner 1972; Gersick 1991). **Continuous change** assumes a gradual evolution of changes which emanate out of the current state of affairs in the organization. Change is thus incremental, taken in small steps and each change effort continuously builds upon the previous phase of change activity. Strategy implementation is therefore concerned with ensuring that current strategies 'fit' with existing practice by either not deviating too far from the existing script, or adding incrementally to what is already in place. Key examples of this approach can be found in the process improvement approaches in manufacturing industries.

Case box: **Process innovation: continuous change in Airbus UK**

Process innovation is a way of stealing a march on rivals by firms getting better at what they do and the way they do things – their practices and processes. Beginning in Japan in the 1950s, these process improvements have a lot of empirical evidence to back them up. Continuous improvements in the ways organisations manufacture products (or provide services) pay off in terms of competitive advantage. For example, in 2004, Airbus UK boosted productivity in wing assembly by 25% and increased product quality by 40% in six months. All this was achieved by looking at the assembly process and continually refining it over a period of months. It became obvious that there had to be a shift from a mass production mindset (and technologies) to a lean production mindset and technologies. Employees take a much bigger role in production and assembly – for which they need different mental as well as physical equipment. Managers are required to stop managing at one remove and engage with the shop floor or the design team, wherever the issues appear. The series of changes which have led to this shift of emphasis from machinery to people has been smooth and continuous, including revision of pay and administrative systems. Continuous change seems to have paid off at least in the case of Airbus UK.

Source: S. Caulkin, 'Lean times for innovation', *The Observer*, 23 May 2004.

We deal in more depth with process and quality issues later in this book (Part 5) but the Airbus example is a typical one of continuous and incremental change to production methods which, in turn, have led to quite significant changes in organizational design and practices. This model of continuous change embraces a business model which goes far beyond manufacturing improvements. Its philosophy is that only by ensuring continuity in strategic changes will organizations be able to realize their strategies. As de Wit and Meyer (1999: 144) point out, the tortoise of Aesop's fable keeps moving slowly, but surely and continuously. It wins the race. The hare, on the other hand, shows off its ability to sprint and take great leaps forward, but eventually loses the race. Diligent tortoises, it seems, win the day. Endurance, persistence and small, but significant, improvements to the ways in which we organize help ensure survival and growth for firms.

Advocates of continuous change cluster around three basic principles:

- Continuous improvement
- Continuous learning
- Constant adaptation to changing conditions

Continuous improvement means that all individuals in an organization should always be driven to change, which is rooted in their dissatisfaction with the status quo. This attitude needs to be constructive so that changes can be suggested, designed and put in place. The overall philosophy is that things can always be done better (Stacey 1993).

Continuous learning means that all individuals in an organization should continually update or increase their knowledge base. This means acquiring new knowledge and techniques as well as acquiring knowledge sufficient for decision makers to say 'no' to what might seem reasonable proposals at first sight and to be able to challenge taken-for-granted behaviours and attitudes in the organization. Crises need to be avoided as far as possible since they inhibit longer-term thinking and promote short-term reactions and decisions (Senge 1990).

Constant adaptation to changing conditions means that organizational design must be such that it avoids becoming inflexible and hence a barrier to further change. Flexible structures and systems, coupled with open and change-receptive cultures, provide sufficient motivation, security and curiosity for individuals to tolerate the inevitable uncertainty and insecurity associated with change (Kagono *et al.* 1985).

On the other hand, many scholars and practitioners argue that continuous change is a false friend in terms of trying to plan change (intention) and in terms of accurately describing what happens in practice. This is the argument for understanding change as a *discontinuous* process. The basic principles of discontinuity derive from the maxim that both organizations and individuals resist change. This is not resistance for its own sake but is a function of the organizing process whereby most organizations develop routines over time (accepted and settled ways of working) and individuals feel comfortable in such rather predictable structures. Indeed, this is one of the ways that can bring about the demise of many organizations (Miller 1990). Success can breed the seeds of its own destruction since it further embeds and reinforces routines and practices in organizations which run deep and are resistant to change.

Organizations are very effective at creating stabilities which act as strong barriers to change. These stabilities can be found in formal and informal systems, standard operating procedures, the distribution of power and the strong ties of organizational culture. They can also be found in factors such as long-term contracts and commitments, fixed investments and inflexible financial and accounting procedures (Arthur 1996; Ghemawat 1991).

So, long terms of stability occur in organizations, held together by these multi-ingredients of the corporate glue. If significant change is to happen then crises (real or constructed) need to be created. The organization becomes jolted into action. This kick-start effect is known as the punctuated equilibrium view of change (Gersick 1991). Change happens in bursts of activity (followed by further periods of consolidation). These discontinuities can be analysed at different levels of analysis. At the individual level, reluctance to change and settled ways of doing things makes individuals predisposed to maintain the status quo and only embark upon change when things become too tough to remain as they are. Groups (social or work) will also exhibit the same behaviours. Organizations will have structural and cultural – institutional – arrangements which act as barriers to change unless significant and threatening events spur action. Industries, too, will exhibit inertia until a crisis point means the equilibrium is punctured and radical change occurs. The airline industry is a good example of **discontinuous change** at this level of analysis.

Case box: **Airlines in crisis: forcing the pace of change**

Of the top eight US airlines, only two are making profits and the remaining six are making sizeable losses (at least two are under bankruptcy protection from their creditors). Things are going to have to change radically in the industry. The two profitable airlines (JetBlue and Southwest) are low-cost carriers just like many of the internet-based airlines which service European destinations (e.g. easyJet, Ryanair and Thompson). The challenge of low-cost carriers and greater price transparency via the internet has created a crisis among full-cost airlines.

Frederick Reid, President of Delta Airlines, suggests that this environmental shock to the

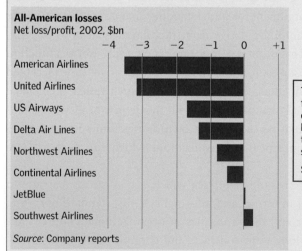

All-American losses
Net loss/profit, 2002, $bn

American Airlines
United Airlines
US Airways
Delta Air Lines
Northwest Airlines
Continental Airlines
JetBlue
Southwest Airlines

Source: Company reports

These huge losses act as 'crisis' trigger, points for strategic change in the mainstream carrier industry. These organizations will have to change both their business model the ways in which they organize their systems, structure, processes and people.

Source of data: OECD.

industry is like the meteor which struck Earth and created a winter which the planet's then rulers (the dinosaurs) could not survive. He paints a picture of full-cost airlines getting fat on the high returns they could extract from business travellers, especially those who were looking for last-minute and flexible tickets. Those days have gone forever. The metaphorical meteor has struck this industry in the form of travellers being able to surf the net for cheap unsold seats. The only ways for mainstream airlines to survive are to cut costs and to raise productivity to a level where they can compete with the profitable low-cost carriers.

This is true discontinuous change. For the first time, mainstream airlines have been forced into making major changes (the 1980s shakeout in the industry which saw the demise of PanAm, TWA and Eastern Airlines was just that a shakeout which did not significantly see a change in the structure of the industry or the firms in it). Some of the changes now required may prove to be a little too difficult to achieve. For example, most need to reduce costs by over 50 per cent per seat. And they need to cut their workforce, but a strongly unionized organization (especially in the USA) could make this very difficult. For example, American Airlines is losing around $5 million per day which is covered by borrowing. At the same time, it needs to cut costs by $4 billion. It has already introduced leaner flight operations and ticketing has been streamlined. Simplifying the fleet (from 12 types of aircraft to 5 types) and using fewer gates has brought some benefits but these are a drop in the ocean in comparison to what is needed for this airline (and the other mainstream carriers) to survive.

Now the airlines need to cut labour costs. This means renegotiating labour contracts to try to save at least $1.8 billion off the wage bill in the short term. Unions will resist if past form is anything to go by. If many mainstream airlines fail to persuade staff to take a pay cut in order to keep their jobs, bankruptcy looks the only option.

Discontinuous change can also occur as a result of perhaps risky, rash or ill-informed decisions which can trigger a series of unplanned and unanticipated events (see also Chapter 13). These strategic decisions can lead the organization into a series of bad moves which, in the worst case, can seal the demise of the firm. Another example from the airline industry (European) illustrates this process clearly (*see* the Sabena case box).

Case box: **Bankruptcy at Sabena**

This Belgian airline Sabena became bankrupt in 2001. There were many explanations for the bankruptcy, but a report to the Belgian government in 2003 has revealed that the organization undertook a series of key strategic decisions which together led to Sabena's demise. The final of these 'fateful' decisions was made when McKinsey were called in to advise Sabena on future strategy. Just as they had with Swissair (which controlled Sabena), McKinsey recommended the airline embark upon a high-risk growth strategy. Swissair went bankrupt trying to follow the same strategy in 2001.

McKinsey's strategy for growth, however, was based on some flimsy foundations in the airline. In 1996, Sabena's then Swiss boss, Paul Reutlinger, took a series of strategic decisions which embarked Sabena upon a era of deal making with Virgin Express (part of the Branson airlines). The first of these was a one-year deal on Sabena's London–Brussels route. Virgin's planes and crew flew the route using Sabena's Heathrow slots. Sabena payed Virgin Express for 85 seats whether or not they were filled. This decision was quite normal in the airline industry and was a way of reducing competition. However, Reutlinger followed up this decision with another two similar deals signed later the same day (29 October 1996). These were eight-year deals with Virgin for flights to Rome and Barcelona. During these decisions, the London–Brussels deal was also extended from one to eight years. These deals became a huge cash drain in Sabena, costing over 30 million euros a year. Virgin were kept well afloat financially by these deals while Sabena haemorrhaged. Moreover, over 80 per cent of passenger complaints to Sabena originated in these Virgin flights. In March 1997, Reutlinger sold Sabena's slots at Heathrow for $8 million to Virgin Atlantic Airways. The report to the Belgian government alleges that these decisions were taken without full consultation and ratification by the Sabena board. When McKinsey was called in and recommended a strategy of growth, the strategy was in effect built upon a financial house of cards. It failed and the airline went bankrupt.

The Sabena example vividly illustrates discontinuous changes which were prompted by the strategic decisions of one individual (or a small groups of individuals) and the perhaps misplaced external advice from McKinsey to embark upon a high-risk growth strategy, which proved fatal to both Swissair and Sabena.

In addition to examining the continuity or discontinuity of change processes, the size, scale and scope of change relates both to organization and to the likelihood of success in implementing the change. There is relatively little empirical work in these areas, but work by Hannan, Polos and Carroll (2003) uncovered some revealing (if mathematically complex) relationships. Using the collapse of Barings Brothers (a British Bank) in 1995 as an example, these authors argue that reorganization in the bank had created an infrastructure (organizational architecture) which allowed Nicholas Leeson (the so-called 'rogue trader') to operate in a way which sealed the demise of the bank. Without letting Leeson off the hook for rogue trading activities, these authors explain that the organizational conditions under which these activities took place allowed his actions to go undetected. In a different firm with a different architecture, Leeson would have been identified early on in the process and prevented from trading.

In brief, the context of Barings allowed a number of activities to take place which amounted to significant changes in its size, scale, scope and eventual disaster for the organization. According to Hannan, Polos and Carroll (2003: 428):

- The structure of the organization was porous with no clear lines of responsibility and accountability. This allowed Leeson to operate undetected for at least two years.

- Confusion of the reporting lines in the organization could be traced to the recent reorganization of the bank.

- The matrix structure which resulted from the reorganization failed to work in practice. It was never clear who Leeson's product managers were (a common problem of ambiguous responsibility in matrix structures) and they had little knowledge of his trading activities.

- Leeson was in charge of both the front and back office functions of the bank and was therefore in a position to override any internal controls.

- The organizational sub-units (departments) which dealt with Leeson's activities were very poor at communicating with one another and this allowed Leeson to trade in the now infamous account 88888, of which senior managers of the Baring Group claimed they had no knowledge.

The conclusion drawn from the above example is that changes can go badly wrong when organizations change their architectures. The new design of the organization can allow large changes to sweep through the organization, with often few or no controls to keep them in check. These authors derive two concepts from their mathematical model. These are:

- **Opacity:** low opacity occurs when there is limited foresight about how different units in the organization are interconnected and work together. The lower the opacity, the higher the likelihood of changes becoming out of control and beyond the capacity of the organization to deal with them when things go wrong.

- **Asperity:** high asperity indicates an organizational culture (see Chapter 2) which will not readily accept changes and which will cling to the 'old' ways of working. The higher the asperity, the greater the likelihood that changes will fail.

Key explanations for failure lie in the scale and scope aspects of change processes. For example, high opacity leads to individuals underestimating the time a reorganization will take as well as the associated costs of change, thereby prompting them to undertake changes with adverse consequences. Put simply, complex, opaque organizations which have a high level of cultural asperity will tend to get themselves into trouble by implementing changes that cost far more than was foreseen. In the worst cases, these can be costs that cannot be covered by whatever new organizational form or circumstances the change has brought about. Like Barings, the organization may well go bankrupt.

The Barings and the Sabena examples also illustrate the impact one person, or a small group, can have on the fortunes of an organization and the speed with which change (mostly discontinuous) can occur. We examine these aspects of change in the next section.

15.4 Change, individuals and strategic leadership

Popular literature (both management and non-management) is replete with the contribution that individuals can make to the success (or otherwise) of the processes and outcomes of change. Much of the literature focuses on the contribution of individuals through the process of leadership, although a sizeable proportion of work also examines the contribution of, for example, creative or innovative individuals to drive change in organizations. To cover the field of leadership is beyond the scope of this chapter. Instead, we focus on what has become termed 'strategic leadership' (Senge 1990). This term describes how individuals may lead changes in ways which are non-individualistic and are not necessarily related to the charisma or power of the individual concerned. Strategic leadership is concerned with teaching, learning, stewardship and the ability to challenge prevailing modes of thought in the organization.

Whatever their position in the organizational hierarchy, strategic leaders are strongly associated with the strategic changes which occur in their organizations. In some cases this may mean that other individuals (who may be more senior in the hierarchy) defer to these strategic leaders since their abilities or their reputation ensures they have credibility and support. In other cases, strategic leadership may be more systemically rooted. For example, the founders of a family firm or the owners of a small business will almost certainly assume a strategic leadership role since they are the 'owners' of the business idea as well as the business philosophy. Another way in which strategic leadership may be systemically rooted is through organizational history. For example, an individual chief executive may have implemented very successful strategies in the past, or may have saved the company from decline. Such a history endows this individual with a position of strategic leadership since they embody, or personify, the organization, its development and its success.

Some organizations which rely on individual leaders to drive strategic changes have difficulty in sustaining this process through time. In particular, family firms seem to suffer from this lack of continuity. The Motorola example below gives an illustration of this problem (*see* case box).

Case box: **Strategic change and leadership at Motorola**

In September 2003, Christopher Galvin, the grandson of Robert Galvin, founder of Motorola, resigned as Chair of Motorola, Christopher Galvin had been Chair since 1997. Investors and the City were relieved at his resignation. He had failed to implement much needed changes in the organization, which had been making losses in its mobile phone business.

The problems started with Robert Galvin, who invested very heavily in the ill-fated Iridium satellite mobile phone. Motorola also missed the technology shift from analogue to digital with Nokia leading the competitive charge. A radical change was needed, but Christopher Galvin did not provide it. Instead, he continued with business as usual. Motorola's share of the mobile phone market (40 per cent of its revenue) continued to fall. Galvin laid off 56,000 employees. He also closed a number of plants. Revenue continued to fall.

For almost four years the firm continued to fail, with a share price fall to match (a high of $60 in 2000 and an all-time low of $8 in 2003). In 2000, things began to change. The board, previously filled with Galvin family acolytes, was restocked with outsiders. These were influential individuals from successful companies. They included Indra Nooyi (from Pepsico), Douglas Warner (JP Morgan Chase) and John Pepper (Procter & Gamble). These directors had none of the family affiliation which Galvin embodied. They are able to seek a new successor for Christopher Galvin as well as make decisions which a family member would have found difficult if not impossible to make. For example, a likely strategy is to sell off some of Motorola's businesses (such as wireless infrastructure and semiconductors). One of the first suggestions of the new directors was to talk to Siemens about the possibility of exchanging the wireless business for Siemens' mobile phone business, but Galvin still at the helm prevented this deal progressing. Now he has gone, the board can explore new and perhaps radical directions for Motorola.

As the Motorola example illustrates, some powerful individuals can both drive change and act as effective barriers to further change. The offspring of founding fathers are prime examples of individual leadership that can prevent an organization thinking and acting strategically and effecting change.

Just as there are polarized views on whether or not strategy is planned or emerges as a pattern in a stream of decisions, strategic leadership can be viewed from the same, mutually exclusive perspectives. Assuming that strategic leadership is planned means that we view leaders as:

◆ Predominantly people who plan a path forward by thinking analytically.

◆ Predominantly people who bring past experience to bear on the present situation (the change worked successfully last time, so it should work again in the new situation).

◆ Appointable chiefly through their demonstrable analytical ability and foresight and their ability to think systematically through a problem and come up with an implementation plan.

On the other hand, we may take the position that strategic leadership emerges in organizations rather than it being planned. This perspective means we would view strategic leadership as:

◆ Less associated with individuals in key positions, but something which emerges from new and sometimes competing ideas from all parts of the organization. Capturing such ideas is a key activity and it may be that this is the key role of individual leaders.

◆ A role in which highly intuitive individuals who have demonstrable vision should be favoured in any appointment process. These individuals can see what others cannot and are happy to embrace new ways of seeing the organization or undertake new ways of working.

The small amount of empirical evidence so far produced on this topic suggests that both approaches can bring performance benefits and can enhance change processes. Peters and Waterman (1982) argued that strategic leadership was about an individual being able to take a highly abstract and perhaps intuitive view as well as being able to handle the operational detail involved in change implementation. Leavy and Wilson (1994) demonstrated how these abilities may be time dependent. In some circumstances, change requires hands-on detail; in others, change requires abstract and perhaps lateral thinking, leaving the processes of implementation to others in the organization. Debates as to whether any of the above approaches are connected to the personality of individual leaders are many, but inconclusive. We just do not know whether or not personality makes a key difference to a leader's ability to handle or manage change (*see* Farkas and Wetlaufer 1996).

15.4.1 Creative individuals and change

Once we shift our focus from key 'leadership' positions in an organization, we may see that individuals who can see beyond the self-evident, and often in quite creative ways, can be the drivers of organizational change wherever they are in the organizational hierarchy. For example, writers and artists (such as Baudelaire or Picasso) challenged established beliefs with new ideas, which in turn transformed our understanding and appreciation of art and literature. Political leaders (such as Gandhi or Luther) were individuals who were also able to effect such transformations. In business organizations, people such as Sloan, Carnegie, Packard and Barnevik (ABB) are commonly cited as those who questioned received wisdom about organizational designs and manufacturing procedures. They said the unsayable and thought the unthinkable.

In change strategies, the temptation is to seek individuals who have this special insight and foresight. However, they are remarkably rare. As March (1999: 226) reminds us:

most current leaders seem to be competent and analytical rather than imaginative and visionary ... they seek to refine the establishment rather than challenge or transform it.

This may be a product of modern times and organization, or it may simply be that we have learned to distrust creativity alone as a guide for strategic change.

The difference between visionary genius and delusional madness is much clearer in history books than in experience.

The problem lies in identifying which novel ideas will turn out to be successful and which will turn out to be little more than crackpot visions. The ratio of successful creative ideas (in practice) to ones which turn out unsuccessful is not good. Most new ideas will not pay-off, so we usually retreat into what is knowable, familiar and do-able. The paradox here is that without a heavy reliance on conventional thinking, highly creative leadership is in more danger of failing than it is in succeeding.

At the same time, organizations need to have stimuli which prevent ossification and encourage new ideas and new ways of thinking and acting strategically. Such leadership (which can come from any part of the organization, not just senior executives) is commonly termed 'transformational' in the management literature. Such leadership seems to centre upon:

- Successfully coping with and developing the intellectual challenge of new ideas (for example, a new or unique competitive position in an evolving environment). Many 'dot.com' companies are founded on such expertise and yet many fail because individuals cannot successfully continue to differentiate their companies from other dot.coms.
- Meeting the social and political challenges of keeping dialogue and communication going when different stakeholders view the same world through very different lenses.
- Having a design in mind which will align the activities, structures and processes in organizations with the strategic intentions. This involves being able to synthesize a great many ideas which may come from all parts of the organization.
- Being able to live with the results of the change in terms of both ethics and performance.

Such a list of factors is a tall order. Individuals are notoriously poor at achieving even one of the above factors, never mind all of them. In relation to strategic management, we can identify a number of reasons why this is so.

Managing change by individual foresight is only possible if environmental signals are seen clearly and in time to act. This is a conundrum which has beset organizations from the very beginning. As Arie de Geus, strategy analyst with Shell, pointed out:

You cannot see what your mind has not experienced before.

Case box: Mind traps: locked in our own worlds of experience

We are all familiar with the example of explorers who stumble upon a tribe of natives isolated from the outside world. Their chief is highly intelligent and has a rich and deep understanding of the world from the tribe's perspective. The explorers begin to explain the modern world. They take the chief to a large city and show him what is going on. He is exposed to thousands of signals from a new environment. However, when the explorers ask him what he has learned, he mentions only one thing. He has seen a market trader pushing a cart full of vegetables, more vegetables than he has ever seen before. This is what he wants to bring back to the tribe from his experiences, more vegetables. All other signals had been discarded as irrelevant to the chief's needs!

Individuals with different backgrounds pick up different signals. Yet even long-standing and highly experienced companies miss important and relevant signals. Why?

One explanation lies in the ways in which individuals relate to knowledge and the future independently of their prior experience. We are all familiar with the adage that experienced managers utilize more knowledge from the past than the present and future. The path, looking backward, is relatively clear. Looking forward, the path is full of uncertainty and ambiguity. However, even in looking forward, strategists can become locked into what de Geus terms the 'memory of the future'.

He argues that managers are constantly looking at potential futures and making plans and programmes for these futures. These plans become organized in an almost sequential way so that they create time paths into the future. The variable nature of this activity lies only in how many alternative paths are created (de Geus argues that this is dependent upon how healthy is the brain, with more healthy brains seeing more alternative time paths). However, all brains store and code these alternative future paths and commit them to memory. Paradoxically, therefore, strategists can create a memory of the future! The implication of this way of thinking is that individuals will tend to pick up only those signals which are relevant to a future they have already worked out. The rest are likely to be missed.

15.4.2 Subjectivity: emotion and organizational change

An emerging perspective on individuals, organizations and change is that strategic change is a complicated and highly emotional psycho-social drama (O'Donnell 2000). The ability to trust your own and others' emotions is argued to be at least as important as viewing intelligence or creativity as a set of cognitive attributes which a person 'has'. The ability to be aware of one's own mental processes lies at the heart of understanding change as an emotional activity. It is key to understanding change as a *subjective* phenomenon (Sparrow 2000). This ability has become known as **emotional intelligence**. It is argued that managers who display emotional intelligence are able to use meta-abilities or meta-cognitions to understand both how they act and how their actions are interpreted by others, and they are able to develop better information networks, generate higher levels of trust and have greater levels influence in implementing change. Although much work on emotional intelligence has been conducted outside formal work organizations, its attributes can easily be seen. According to Sparrow (2000: 26), emotional intelligence:

♦ Emphasizes pre-conscious thought and shares many common neurological processes with creativity and intuition.

♦ Is a strong source of energy (feelings and personal drive) which can sustain individuals through a change process and can guide individuals to see unexpected or previously unseen possibilities.

♦ Helps individuals cope with change since it emphasizes self-awareness, empathy, personal style and communications.

A key difficulty is one of assessing or measuring emotional intelligence. Many of its reflections (such as high levels of trust or effective communication and empathy with opposing viewpoints) are best assessed through the eyes of others (Steiner 1997). Dulewicz and Herbert (1998) assessed emotional intelligence as:

♦ Sensitivity

♦ Resilience

♦ Influence and adaptability

♦ Decisiveness and adaptability

♦ Energy and leadership

They found that managerial advancement was positively related to the 'possession' of emotional intelligence (36 per cent of managerial advancements could be traced to emotional intelligence). This finding should be put in the context of other findings from the same study: 27 per cent of promotions could be traced to rational and intellectual analysis (such as judgement, planning and organizing) and only 16 per cent to management process effectiveness (such as business sense, initiative and independence). Although we are not yet at a stage where we can clearly demarcate emotional intelligence as a valid construct with a set of valid measures, it nevertheless seems to have a beneficial influence both on smoothing change processes and on advancing the careers of managers who display higher levels of it.

Emotional intelligence would also seem to be vital to underpinning Beer and Eisenstat's (1996) principles of the relatively more successful implementation of strategic change:

♦ Change should be systemic: the focus of the change should accommodate and recognize the complex system that is the organization. Such factors include strategy, structure, behaviours, analysis and emotions.

◆ Change should allow the discussion of barriers: people cannot develop realistic and implementable plans for change unless all impediments are taken into account.

◆ Change should involve a partnership between all stakeholders in the process.

Argyris (1992) suggests that individuals mostly operate on the basis of what he terms 'defensive routines' and hence never engage with the emotional desiderata listed above. He suggests individuals:

1 Bypass embarrassment or threat wherever possible.

2 Act as if they were not bypassing them.

3 Refuse to discuss bypassing behaviour or actions as above.

4 Don't discuss the undiscussability of the undiscussable.

It remains to be seen whether or not emotional intelligence develops into a valid construct and stops being potentially perceived of as a yet another management fad and fashion. Nevertheless, Argyris's four principles, above, apply to virtually all change processes and can act as significant barriers to the implementation of strategic change.

15.4.3 Using outsiders to implement change

The 'external' aspects of change are rather less well covered in the literature than the 'internal' features of structures, cultures and individuals. Outsiders can take a number of forms. They can include, for example, bringing in a new chief executive from a related industry where he or she has had demonstrable success. Or, a significant influx of new managers to an organization (especially over a short time period) can also help break down high asperity cultures (strong cultures which are change resistant). The old guard can be swept away effectively by these newcomers. Taking a stakeholder perspective, there are likely to be a large number of strong influences from outside the organization which have an impact on the change process. These can include suppliers, customers, investors and government agencies.

By far the most obvious of external **change agents**, however, are management consultants. The role of the vast majority of consultants (both individual consultants and consultancy firms) is that of providing expert advice. It is hardly surprising, therefore, that the majority of large consulting firms (e.g. McKinsey, PricewaterhouseCoopers) become involved with the execution of strategic changes in organizations. These processes are complex, take time and (perhaps cynically) can create the opportunity for new or continuing relationships between consultant and organization.

Different consulting firms become involved in different phases of the change process. For example, McKinsey have a reputation as being excellent at the analytical and planning phases of strategic change, but are rather less well involved in the implementation phases (putting idea into practice). KPMG are the reverse. These consultancies, offshoots of audit practice, are centrally involved in the performance aspects of implementation (such as standardized solutions for cost reduction, or the application of programmatic 'solutions' to change such as business process re-engineering). Technical and functional expertise (for example, human resource management) can be found in consulting firms such as Hay or PA Consulting. Given the longevity of change as an organizational problem, some consulting firms (such as Cap Gemini) have specialized in producing customized change models (such as the 'transformation' model of Gemini) and these have become major products in their own right. The Gemini model is described briefly in the case box below.

Case box: **The Gemini model of corporate transformation**

The high failure rate of business process re-engineering (BPR) projects has led to the development of a more subtle approach which has been called a biological model of corporate transformation, identifying the corporation as essentially an organic evolving entity. The model consists of four broad categories of activity leading to transformation and, as developed by Gemini Consulting, corporate transformation is defined as 'the orchestrated redesign of the genetic architecture of the corporation, achieved by working simultaneously – although at different speeds – along the four dimensions of Reframing, Restructuring, Revitalisation and Renewal'. These four dimensions are seen as a biological process as follows:

- *Reframing* is seen as shifting the company's perception of what it is and what it can achieve and is designed to open the corporation's mindset and allow it to refocus.
- *Restructuring* deals with the body of the corporation and addresses competitive fitness. This activity is most akin to the BPR approach and involves similar techniques.
- *Revitalization* endeavours to link the revised corporate body to its environment, and is considered to be the factor which most clearly differentiates transformation from the harshness perceived of re-engineering. The intention is not to obliterate activities but, rather, to change them positively to encourage revitalized performance.
- *Renewal* is concerned with the 'people' side of transformation and with the spirit of the company. It is concerned with investment in skills and purpose to allow the company to self-regenerate with new confidence and enthusiasm rather than the often morale-sapping impact of re-engineering projects, which are a major cause of failure. This activity is perhaps the most difficult to achieve, and is seen by many critics of re-engineering change to be the point at which many consultants, brought in as change agents, leave their clients.

Gemini believes that 12 corporate 'chromosomes' comprise the biocorporate genome, three for each of the four Rs. While each chromosome can be considered independently they are all integrated into a total system. The chief executive officer and the executive leadership are seen as the genetic architects of the corporation and are thus not expected to be involved in operational detail.

The reframing chromosomes

1 *Achieve mobilization*. This activity is the process of bringing together the mental energy required to initiate the transformation process, and involves moving motivation and commitment from the individual to the team and ultimately to the total corporation.

2 *Create the vision*. The development of a corporate vision is essential to provide a shared mental framework which stretches the future dimensions of the corporation and in human terms provides a common sense of purpose which people can identify with. The role of the CEO in establishing such a vision is crucial.

3 *Building a measurement system*. Once the corporation is mobilized and provided with a vision, new measurement systems which allow management to monitor progress towards the future will usually be required. While often quantified, such measures will usually emphasize the strategic progress rather than the financial history. In human terms, the system should also create an identifiable sense of commitment; *see* balanced scorecard.

The restructuring chromosomes

4 *Construct an economic model*. This involves the systematic top-down disaggregation of a corporation in financial terms from shareholder value-based planning to activity-based costing and service level assessment. It provides a detailed view of how and where value is created or cost allowed in the bio-analogy of the cardiovascular system for resources to be deployed where they are needed, and redistributed from where they are not needed.

5 *Align the physical infrastructure*. This element is analogous to the corporate skeletal system and consists of the appropriate alignment of the resources of the corporation's assets, such as plants, warehouses, transportation, equipment and the like. While these are relatively fixed, there is also a need for continuous monitoring and, on occasion, change as when a bone is fractured, to allow for strategic healing.

6 *Redesign the work architecture*. The work of the corporation is achieved via a complex network of processes which is identified as the work architecture. These need to be correctly configured and aligned and this process can be linked to re-engineering.

The revitalization systems

7 *Achieve a market focus*. To Gemini, revitalization implies growth. To achieve this, customer focus provides the starting point, as developing new and perhaps undiscovered benefits that the corporation can offer to its customers leads to business growth. For the corporation, market focus provides the senses in the biological analogy.

8 *Invent new business*. Growth can also occur as the result of the development of new businesses. These can emerge from the cross-fertilization of capabilities from within the corporation or by the introduction of activities from outside via mergers and acquisitions,

strategic alliances, joint ventures and the like. The biological analogy of this concept can be seen as the reproductive system.

9 *Change the rules through information technology.* The strategic use of information technology can produce new ways to compete by redefining the rules of the game in many traditional industries. Biologically, the use of such technology is analogous to the nervous system.

The renewal systems

10 *Create a reward structure.* An appropriate reward structure is seen as a major motivating force on human behaviour. When the motivation system is wrongly aligned with desired behaviour it can also act as a serious demotivator and encourage undesired behaviour.

11 *Build individual learning.* Corporate transformation can only successfully take place when the skills and learning of many individuals are also transformed. Individual learning promotes self-actualization of the people who constitute the corporation.

12 *Develop the Organization.* Corporations are seen as needing to organize for continuous learning, enabling them to constantly adapt to an ever-changing environment in which the pace of change is often accelerating. Organizational development thus allows the corporation to evolve and fosters a sense of community among individuals.

Conclusion

The corporate transformation process has been applied in many corporations around the world. Such transformations often involve modifying the behaviour of many thousands of people, often on a global basis. Such transformations take time, often involving a number of years, but the end result is expected to produce transformed corporations capable of continuous adaptation to permit successful evolution.

Source: McGee, J and Channon, D (eds) (forthcoming 2005) *Encyclopedic Dictionary of Strategic Management*, 2nd edition, Blackwell, Oxford.

Whether or not consulting firms help or hinder organizational change processes (or are relatively neutral in their influence) is an open question for which there is insufficient evidence to present any firm conclusions. On the positive side, there are arguments that consultants learn from academics and from their client organizations. In these ways, consultants both codify often abstruse and complex academic thinking (mostly form business schools) and also develop their own knowledge base from clients so that effective knowledge can progress from one client to another ideally from leaders to laggards (Abrahamson 1991).

On the more negative side, some authors argue that consultants 'borrow your watch to tell you the time' (they are simply symbolic agents, often engaged to fulfil a political motive of driving a change through an organization which would have been more difficult if solely an internal process) or they overgeneralize their solutions so that one size fits all (Alvesson 1993).

15.5 **Creative organizational contexts**

If creative foresight and heretical, off-the-wall ideas are so elusive (and likely to be just as dangerous as they are useful), then how can organizations be designed and arranged to encourage strategic thinking to enable the strategic change process? This is an approach to strategic change which relies less on the creativity of individuals and more upon designing the creative organizational contexts in which strategies for change can be crafted.

Kanter (1999) argues that such creative contexts are formed and sustained by three major elements:

- *Concepts*: These are ideas and technologies which are driven by innovative thinking and the innovations produced by other organizations.

- *Competences*: These are the repertoires of skills and abilities of individuals in the organization. They also involve the ability to use such skills in the organization. Many individuals who work in organizations have useful skills which they only use in hobbies (for example) away from the workplace. The trick is to engage these competences in the workplace.

- *Connections*: These are the important strategic relationships which individuals, teams and organizations create (such as networks). They are nurtured by collaboration rather than competition and can be extended and reconfigured as new ideas emerge.

Chapter 16 picks up some of these organizational themes in more detail in the context of assessing how organizations might remain innovative and how they might continue to learn.

15.6 **Summary**

This chapter has examined the issues of, and widely differing approaches to, strategic change. Since the implementation of virtually any strategy will involve an organization and its members in a degree of change, understanding its processes and its problems can be an advantage.

The chapter has highlighted variation in both the degree of change (radical to incremental) and the extent to which change is discontinuous or is smoother and more continuous. It has also shown how we can examine change from a multitude of levels of analysis.

There are important links in this chapter to the themes and debates of other chapters in this book. In particular, readers should work through this chapter in conjunction with the material in Chapters 2, 13 and 16.

Key terms

Asperity *579*   Emotional intelligence *584*

Change agents *586*   Mind traps *584*

Change and organization *574*   Opacity *579*

Continuous change *574*   Process innovation *574*

Discontinuous change *576*   Strategic tensions *571*

Recap questions and assignments

1   Identify an *unsuccessful* strategic change with which you are familiar. You may wish to choose an example from the business press, a case example you have studied, or you may draw on experience of a strategic change in which you were involved in an organization. What were the key characteristics which contributed to this being an unsuccessful change process?

2   Identify a *successful* strategic change and identify its key characteristics as above.

3   What aspects would you introduce in your organization to improve the implementation of strategic change and why?

When you have read this chapter, log on to the Online Learning Centre website at www.mcgraw-hill.co.uk/textbooks/mcgee to explore chapter-by-chapter test questions, further reading and more online study tools for strategy.

Case 1 **How to manage a dream factory**

Harder times are reminding the industry of the critical importance of creating good content. But that means managing the tensions between artists and suits

One by one, the men of extravagant vision and exaggerated showmanship have been toppled from the upper ranks of the world's media giants. The departure of Steve Case from AOL Time Warner and of Tommy Mottola from Sony Music are only the latest in a lengthening line-up that includes Bertelsmann's Thomas Middelhoff, AOL Time Warner's Jerry Levin and Bob Pittman, Vivendi's Jean-Marie Messier, Canal Plus's Pierre Lescure and EMI's Ken Berry. Into their places has stepped a parade of dull men in suits, such as Andrew Lack, new head of Sony Music, who has never worked in the record industry, Jean-René Fourtou, an ex-pharmaceuticals boss, at Vivendi or, at Bertelsmann, Gunter Thielen, ex-head of the group's printing and industrial operations.

This trooping of grey faces into the unruly media world marks a distinct change of mood. Talk of 'vision', 'synergy' or 'new paradigms' is out; the daily grind of evaluating and improving operating performance is paramount. Gone are the days when moguls such as Mr Messier posed jauntily for *Paris Match*, a French celebrity magazine, while skating in Central Park. Except for the two wise old birds of media – News Corporation's Rupert Murdoch and Viacom's Sumner Redstone – today's rising media stars, such as Tony Ball at BSkyB, Britain's leading pay-TV operator, or Jeff Bewkes, co-deputy head of AOL Time Warner, go largely unrecognised on the streets and unquoted in the press.

The need to return to the basics of the business was summed up recently by Peter Chernin, Mr Murdoch's right-hand man at News Corp. 'What the hell were we thinking?' he asked. 'Where did [the industry] get our grandiose ideas the media business was on the way to complete and utter re-invention?' His point was that during the boom, the industry was distracted by gadgets, mergers and convergence theories; now it is time to relearn old lessons about fostering creativity and manufacturing entertainment that people are willing to pay for.

The rediscovered importance of content is encapsulated at perhaps the most troubled media giant, AOL Time Warner. Recent news of the departure of Steve Case as chairman, under heavy pressure, marks the end of an era when new media held any sway at all. Mr Case, the founder of AOL, masterminded the merger with Time Warner three years ago (and pocketed a handsome profit). None of the architects of that deal remains in charge. Yet another battered division, CNN, saw its head, Walter Isaacson, quit in 2003. Today, it is the success of such traditional old-media assets as 'The Lord of the Rings' and 'Harry Potter' films that keeps the group afloat.

But how to get content right? Why is it that Walt Disney, once a finely tuned Hollywood dream factory, has lost its touch in animation? Its latest offering, 'Treasure Planet', which cost $140m to make, flopped at the pre-Christmas box office and forced the company to revise its 2002 results to reflect a $74m write-down. How can Home Box Office (HBO), by contrast, consistently turn out genre-busting television dramas, from its hit comedy 'Sex and the City' to such dark series as 'The Sopranos' and 'Six Feet Under', which are at once critical and commercial successes?

Oiling the dream machine

The answer is not simply the burden of scale, as some observers suggest. HBO is, after all, yet another part of the AOL Time Warner empire. It comes down to a less tangible factor. As Viacom's Mr Redstone puts it: 'Size is not the barrier to creativity, it's bad management.'

Pinning down the elusive quality of good management is particularly hard in entertainment because it is such an odd industry, in two ways. First, it is hugely hit-driven. Most films flop, most records lose money, most TV series fail. A single hit – 'American Idol', say, for the FOX network – can transform profits. The fizzling out of a hit – as Disney's ABC found when viewers tired of the over-exposed 'Who Wants to be a Millionaire?' – can drag down an entire division.

Entertainment bosses therefore need certain qualities: a readiness to take big risks, laser-quick reactions to fickle changes of taste, and a supreme confidence in their own gut instincts – all virtues, as Michael Wolf puts it in his book 'The Entertainment Economy', that reinforce the mogul model of leadership. But the best moguls trust their managers to take decisions too. 'Show business doesn't attract leaders who know how to listen properly or leave people alone,' comments Roger Fransecky, head of the Apogee Group, which advises many media bosses. 'But when you manage creative people, you must intrude carefully.'

Resisting the temptation to interfere, but at the same time enforcing operational control, makes for a delicate balance. With their unpredictable, autocratic management styles, Messrs Murdoch and Redstone might look like ruthless meddlers. Yet in fact each gives his trusted division heads and right-hand men – respectively, Mr Chernin at News Corp and Mel Karmazin at Viacom – the freedom to get on with their jobs.

The second oddity of entertainment is that managers have to be able to handle talent, or at least to handle the handlers of talent. Manufacturing content is not like manufacturing furniture. Armchairs do not get in a strop, go into rehab or become hospitalised for 'exhaustion' – as Mariah Carey, a singer who had just signed an $80m contract with EMI's Virgin Records, did shortly before releasing a new album in 2001. Six months later, EMI sacked her, at a cost of $28m.

Because of the allure of fame, the entertainment industry attracts an unusual mix of aspirant managers, from the star-struck to the ice-cool. 'Most people in the creative world think that they are artists themselves,' comments Alain Levy, head of EMI Recorded Music. Up to a point, this is necessary. Simply navigating the star system, with its shifting alliances of publicists, agents, record labels and studios, requires unnatural quantities of ego. But managing creative types, and imposing some order on their whims, is tricky.

'What is really hard is managing the interface between the creative thinking and the corporate profit-centre,' says Peter Kreisky, a media consultant who is writing a book about the management of creatively driven industries. The two cultures – of the ponytail and the suit – are a world apart, and combustible together. Few managers combine both creative credibility and commercial discipline. But the best entertainment companies manage to impose operational control without squashing artistic freedom.

Three companies illustrate how, or how not, to go about this. In each case, success – or failure – hinges on getting the balance between creative and operational leadership right. The first, HBO, shows that it is possible even for a vast corporation to retain an edgy creative outfit that achieves both critical and commercial success. HBO's series were nominated for twice as many Golden Globe awards this year as those of any of the broadcast networks. Insiders suggest that profits at HBO for 2002 could be up by 17% from the previous year, to $850m, on revenues of about $2.8 billion, or 8% ahead of 2001.

The second company is EMI, the world's biggest independent record company. It is busy trying to bring an end to an era of creative extravagance and financial excess, and to refashion itself as a tightly controlled music company that invests for long-term creative return. The improvement is beginning to show. In the six months to September 2002, EMI made a post-tax profit of £138.4m ($208m), after a loss of £54.4m in the same period of 2001.

The third company, Disney, a media conglomerate built from an animated-film studio, offers a lesson in how creative supremacy can be lost – even during the reign of a single boss. Michael Eisner, in charge since 1984, was once widely admired for transforming a faltering film studio into a slick entertainment empire. Today, the company's creative touch has faded, and Mr Eisner is battling to keep his job.

It's not TV

To the untrained eye, HBO might look like just another bit of the sprawling AOL Time Warner empire. But it is fiercely independent, and has carved out a distinct identity. Employing only 1,770 people, less than 2% of the group total, HBO is physically and operationally removed from even the group's other TV activities, notably Warner Brothers in Los Angeles. That nobody ever suggests merging New York-based HBO into the other TV studios points to its strength as an autonomous operation. The secret has been twofold: the creation of a small boutique-like identity within a huge corporate institution; and the granting of creative independence within a tightly controlled operation.

On the first count, people working at HBO have a clear sense of what they are trying to achieve. As the company's slogan puts it: 'It's not TV. It's HBO'. HBO prides itself on making difficult original drama that would not ordinarily find a place on the ratings-driven broadcast schedules. 'We all know what we're looking for, we know how to smell it,' explains one HBO executive. This sense of purpose has been entrenched by stable management in an industry notorious for high turnover. Mr Bewkes, its former boss, was at HBO for 23 years until last year; Chris Albrecht, today's head, has been there for 17 years.

By itself, a boutique-like identity is no guarantor of creative strength. What drives HBO's success in original drama is its determination to grant writers artistic freedom – always to a commercial end. Talk to screenwriters in Hollywood and they enthuse about HBO. 'It's an amazing place to work,' gushes one. 'Once they have hired the right people, they give you the liberty to do what you want.'

Part of this luxury stems from the business model. HBO's revenues come from subscriptions, not advertising, so it does not need to chase ratings and can afford to be daring. But there has also been a deliberate effort by Messrs Bewkes and Albrecht to liberate creative people in order to keep pushing at the edges of television drama.

Unlike such media bosses as Harvey Weinstein at Miramax, who notoriously meddles with scripts and edits, HBO bosses let the creatives off the leash. When Alan Ball, who won an Oscar for his screenplay for 'American Beauty', began to discuss 'Six Feet Under,' he was hardly pushing what looked like a commercial hit: a dark series set in a family-run funeral parlour and starring a repressed gay funeral director. The reaction from Carolyn Strauss, the commissioning executive at HBO? Make it weirder. Today, it is often the directors and writers who come knocking at HBO's door, not the other way round.

Escapology

Across the Atlantic, in its oddly cramped headquarters – by record-industry standards – in London's West End, EMI has been grappling with a similar effort to invest in artistic freedom while mopping up after an era of excess. When Eric Nicoli, EMI's chairman, hired Alain Levy, a music-industry veteran and former head of Polygram, as his head of recorded music in 2001, the Frenchman inherited a company that had turned profligacy into an art form – notably at Virgin Records in America. In an industry already troubled by piracy and illegal online file-sharing, the company did itself no favours by letting spending on marketing, salaries, parties and first-class travel spin out of control.

Mr Levy purged the place. He changed more than 30 heads of record labels; he trimmed the headcount by about 20%; he pruned the roster of artists by nearly 400, or about a quarter (all 49 artists in Finland got the chop). Out went Ken Berry, along with his wife, Nancy, vice-chairman of Virgin Music Group, whose reputation for partying and jetting about with stars was legendary. In came a two-headed structure that Mr Levy refers to as 'my creative head and his Mr No'. At Virgin Records, he installed a new duo: Matt Serletic, a young creative type in charge of sniffing out new talent, and Roy Lott, whose job is to keep him from financial excess.

Mr Levy, who mixes a business-school background (MBA from Wharton) with a creative's uniform (shock of curly salt-and-pepper hair, charcoal polo sweaters), does not pretend to second-guess musical taste. 'My people just laugh at my French accent and remind me of my age [56].' But he does keep a tight watch on the profitability of his operations. He meets monthly with the financial head of each of the American record labels to go through the numbers; and every three months with the creative heads, to discuss artist development.

This is not meant to squash creative freedom. On the contrary, it is an attempt to put the right people in charge of signing and managing artists, but under tighter financial control. Mr Levy argues that the industry has lost sight of the need to invest in artists for the long term, and become mesmerised by overnight, overpackaged success. 'Nobody is going to be successful if they don't have number ones,' he concedes. 'But it all depends on how you get them.' TV talent shows may create instant hits and help grab market share, but will not develop lasting acts that build up a back catalogue for the future. This is the reasoning behind EMI's apparently extravagant new contract with Robbie Williams, which gives the music company a greater share in all his future revenues, not just those from record sales.

Nobody pretends that the record industry is an easy business to be in right now. But there are signs that EMI's new approach might help, not only from the company's financial improvement. Upcoming or new EMI acts, from Coldplay to Norah Jones, are doing well in America, EMI's traditional weak spot. *Billboard*, the American record-industry bible, named Coldplay's new album the best of 2002. Norah Jones's debut album hit number one in the American charts this week.

Over on the west coast, meanwhile, Disney's troubles throw light on how easily such creative feel can be lost. In his early years, Mr Eisner transformed a faltering company whose film studio had only a 4% share of the American box office into a global entertainment empire. By the early 1990s, Disney was a polished creative machine, turning out a stream of well-crafted animated films, such as 'Beauty and the Beast' (1991) and 'The Lion King' (1994). It was a commercial success too, pioneering the concept of generating branded characters that could be pumped out profitably as TV series, theme parks, fluffy toys, lunch-boxes and so on. Between 1984 and 1993, net profits at Disney shot up nearly sevenfold; by 1993, its box-office share was 16%.

In recent years, however, the Disney machine has sputtered. The most cutting-edge animated output it has distributed – 'Toy Story', 'Monsters Inc' – has not been made in-house, but by Pixar, Steve Job's computer-animation studio. There are now only two more films left in its partnership deal with Pixar. And Disney's home-grown animated output tends to be charmless. In the year to September 2002, Disney's operating profits dropped by 33% from 2001, to $2.8 billion. The group has just replaced its head of animation.

What went wrong? There are various competing theories, including Mr Eisner's decision in 1995 to buy the ABC TV network, now the group's biggest single headache. But the two most persuasive explanations turn on the problem of balancing creative freedom with operational restraint. The first is that Disney has never recaptured the fine balance that existed when Mr Eisner's creative strengths were tempered by the operational sense of Frank Wells, his chief operating officer, who was killed in an accident in 1994. Since then, Mr Eisner's instinct for meddling, along with his increasingly centralised and controlling management style, has gone largely unchecked. Managers feel second-guessed; artists fear surrendering creative freedom. 'Disney's problem isn't management,' says one Disney executive, 'it's over-management.'

The second reason is Mr Eisner's inability to retain his top talent. The loss in 1994 of Jeffrey Katzenberg, whom he recruited to revamp the film studios, was searing. Frustrated at Disney, Mr Katzenberg went on to found, with Steven Spielberg and David Geffen, DreamWorks SKG, which has since released such superb animated films as 'Shrek'. More recent defectors range from Joe Roth, who quit as the studio head in 2000 to found Revolution Studios, to Paul Pressler, who threw in his job last year running theme-parks to join Gap, the clothing chain. That there is now no credible successor to Mr Eisner within Disney's own ranks, in contrast to the smooth transition at HBO after Mr Bewkes's departure, only emphasises this failing.

Dedicated followers of fashion

On paper, the recipe for successfully managing an entertainment company appears simple: carve out small creative units within big companies to give them their own identity; grant them creative freedom from meddling bureaucracies; but do not do either recklessly. Yet striking the right balance between the artists and the suits remains remarkably hard.

Over the years, entertainment companies have often failed, and have instead swung, alternately, from being too strongly in favour of letting creative types rule, towards being too much in hock to the bean-counters. EMI has lurched from periods when the suits were in charge, notably under Jim Fifield's stewardship from 1988 until his sacking in 1998, to times of financial excess, when the creatives went untamed, as happened with the rise of Mr Berry in the late 1990s until his eviction in 2001. The firing of Mr Mottola from the loss-making Sony Music represents yet another attempt to bring an end to an era of creative and financial extravagance: Mr Mottola was so close to the talent that he ended up marrying – and later divorcing – one of the artists he had once signed in her pre-EMI days, Ms Carey.

If the pendulum theory of managing the creative industries is right, today's gallery of grey faces may last only as long as the downturn. Boom times tend, after all, to unleash profligacy – and not just in the entertainment business. The best companies are likely to be those that avoid swinging too wildly in favour of either ponytails or suits: both have their place.

Source: 'How to manage a dream factory', *The Economist*, 16 January 2003.
© The Economist Newspaper Limited, London (16 January 2003).

Case Questions

1 What are the key issues in managing 'creatives' as opposed to managing 'suits' in strategic change? What lessons can be learned from HBO?

2 Taking Disney as your example, what would you advise them to do next? What difficulties are they likely to encounter as they embark upon your suggested change route? Can you suggest ways in which such difficulties might be minimized or alleviated?

3 To what extent do you think strategic change is more or less difficult to achieve and manage in different organizations (e.g. creative organizations, media firms).

Further reading and references

Abrahamson, E (1991) 'Managerial fads and fashions: the diffusion and rejection of innovations', *Academy of Management Review*, **16**, pp. 586–612.

Alvesson, M. (1993) 'Organizations as rhetoric: knowledge intensive firms and the struggle with ambiguity', *Journal of Management Studies*, **30**, **6**, pp. 997–1015.

Argyris, C (1992) *Organizational Learning*, Blackwell, Oxford.

Arthur, WB (1996) 'Increasing returns and the new world of business', *Harvard Business Review*, July/August pp. 100–9.

Beer, M and Eisenstat, RA (1996) 'Developing an organization capable of implementing strategy and learing', *Human Relations*, **48**, **2**, pp. 97–126.

De Wit, B and Meyer, R (1999) *Strategy Synthesis: Resolving Strategy Paradoxes to Create Competitive Advantage*, International Thomson Press, London.

Dulewicz, V and Herbert, PJ (1998) 'Predicting advancement to senior management from competencies and personality data: a seven year follow-up study', *British Journal of Management*, **10**, **1**, pp. 13–23.

Farkas, CM, and Wetlaufer, S (1996) 'The ways chief executive officers lead', *Harvard Business Review*, May–June, pp. 110–12.

Gersick, CJG (1991) 'Revolutionary Change Theories: A Multi level Exploration of the Punctuated Equilibrium Paradigm', *Academy of Management Review*, **6**, pp. 10–36.

Ghemawat, P (1991) *Commitment: the Dynamics of Strategy*, Free Press, New York.

Greiner, LE (1972) 'Evolution and Revolution as Organizations Grow', *Harvard Business Review*, July/August, pp. 37–46.

Hannan, M, Polos, L and Carroll, GR (2003) 'Fog of Change' *Administrative Science Quarterly*, **48**, **3**, pp. 399–432.

Kagono, T, Nonaka, I, Sakakibara, K and Okumara, A (1985) *Strategic versus Evolutionary Management: A US-Japan Comparison of Strategy and Organization*, North Holland Press, Amsterdam.

Kanter, RM (1999) 'Change in Everyone's Job: Managing the Extended Enterprise in a Globally Extended World', *Organizational Dynamics*, Vol 28, No 1, pp. 7–23.

Leavy, B and Wilson, DC (1994) *Strategy and Leadership*, Routledge, London.

March, JG (1999) *The Pursuit of Organizational Intelligence*, Blackwell, Oxford.

Miller, D (1990) *The Icarus Paradox: How Excellent Companies Bring about Their Own Downfall*, Harper Business, New York.

Nutt P, Backoff, R and Hogan, M (2000) 'Managing the Paradoxes of Strategic Change', *Journal of Applied Management Studies*, **9**, No 1, pp. 5–31.

O'Donnell, D (2000) 'The Emotional World of Strategy Implementation', in P. Flood, T. Dromgoole, S Carroll and L Gorman (eds) *Managing Strategy Implementation*, Blackwell, Oxford.

Peters, T and Waterman, R (1982) *In Search of Excellence: Lessons from America's Best Run Companies*, Harper & Row: New York.

Pettigrew, A and Whipp, R (1991) *Managing Change for Competitive Success*, Blackwell, Oxford.

Senge, P (1990) 'The Leader's New Work: Building Learning Organizations', *Sloan Management Review*, Fall, pp. 7–23.

Sparrow, P (2000) 'A World Turned Upside Down', in P. Flood, T. Dromgoole, S. Carroll and L. Gorman (eds) *Managing Strategy Implementation*, Blackwell, Oxford.

Stacey, R (1993) 'Strategy as Order Emerging from Chaos', *Long Range Planning*, **26**, **1**, pp. 10–17.

Steiner, C (1997) *Achieving Emotional Illiteracy*, Bloomsbury Publishing: London.

Wenger, E and Snyder, W (2000) 'Communities of Practice: The Organizational Frontier', *Harvard Business Review*, January–February, pp. 139–45.

Wilson, D (1999) *A Strategy of Change: Concepts and Controversies in the Management of Change*, International Thomson Press, London.

or consistent (Vera and Crossan 2003) and finding work which builds cumulatively is very difficult indeed. Different authors use different concepts or different terminologies to describe learning. The following section attempts to outline the key authors and approaches in the field and concludes by presenting an overall framework by which we might interpret and understand organizational learning.

16.1 **What is learning?**

Garvin (1993) defines a learning organization as one able to create, acquire and transfer knowledge and to change its behaviour to reflect new knowledge. Organizational learning involves experimentation, creative moments, learning from experience as well as best practice and transferring knowledge quickly and efficiently throughout the organization.

However, as Senge (1990: 285) argues:

> *Human beings are designed for learning ... children come fully equipped with an insatiable drive to explore and experiment. Unfortunately, the primary institutions of our society are oriented predominantly toward controlling rather than learning, rewarding individuals for performing for others rather than for cultivating their natural curiosity and impulse to learn.*

Here, Senge is pointing out two important aspects of learning:

- Learning can be viewed from different levels of analysis, ranging from individual learning to organizational learning.

- Organizations appear rather less adept at learning than individuals.

We will examine these different levels of analysis later in this chapter. For the moment, it is necessary first of all to examine the generic features of the processes of learning. Only then can we sensibly examine learning across different levels of analysis.

Senge (1990) suggests that learning is both an *adaptive* process and a *generative* process. **Adaptive learning** describes the processes whereby an organization can adapt to its environment and to accelerating or decelerating rates of change. Adaptive learning can thus best be described as the processes organizations engage in to cope with changing external conditions. But the learning process is much deeper than a desire to respond and adapt to external changes. Such responses may render an organization more efficient or effective in the short term, but cannot generate increased or new capabilities – the bedrock of innovation and creativity. Only **generative learning** can provide this. Generative learning requires new ways of looking at the world, whether this involves making sense of the external environment or in understanding how to manage internal business processes better. Such learning is important for the visionary aspects of strategy formulation. To achieve new ideas, an organization needs to develop its capacity for strategic thinking, which is the generative (or creative) learning to which Senge refers. However, in order to understand an organization's capacity to implement strategy as well as to formulate it (thinking and acting strategically), it is necessary to engage and develop both adaptive and generative learning.

These two types of learning originate from what Argyris and Schon (1987) termed single and double-loop learning. This has been variously referred to in the literature as first and second order learning, exploitation and exploration, or convergence and reorientation (see Table 16.1). When learning enables the organization to carry out its present activities and goals without disturbing existing cultural values and norms, it is termed **single-loop learning**. Single-loop learning is important for increasing effectiveness in implementing strategy because it ensures that the organization is becoming better at undertaking its existing strategies. In the terminology of Peters and Waterman (1982) this form of learning helps an organization to 'stick to the knitting'. Single-loop learning is embodied in the experience curve of an organization. The more experience a firm has of an activity, the greater its efficiency and effectiveness become *in that activity*.

However, single-loop learning does not expose an organization to new activities or new ways of conceptualizing old activities. When learning involves modification of an organization's underlying cultural values, assumptions and norms, it is termed **double-loop learning**. In terms of complexity, single-loop learning is relatively simple to achieve while double-loop learning is far more complex. This is because individuals are constrained by their mental models to identify familiar patterns for solving problems. As existing patterns are within the managerial 'comfort zone' of tacit knowledge and experience, this occurs even when the problem is significantly different and requires new solutions. The longer an organization has been using an existing set of practices, the harder it is to conceptualize new ways of doing things. Thus, paradoxically, single-loop learning, which involves existing mental models, is necessary for improving efficiency and effectiveness in existing strategic practices, but poses a barrier to developing new ways of learning.

Double-loop learning may occur when a change in strategy is so difficult to implement that it exposes the problems in existing practices, causing fundamental changes in the way the organization approaches strategic problems. Senge (1990) provides a classic example of this at Shell. Realizing 'that they had failed to change behaviour in much of the Shell organization', Group Planning set about altering the mental models of managers. They developed tools, such as scenario planning, to encourage managers to envision alternative futures. In this way, managers learned flexibility in their current practices. Using scenarios, they could work backwards from a series of anticipated futures to change the practices in the current organization. The capacity to learn enabled Shell to be more responsive than its competitors to changes in the political environment, such as the development of OPEC.

However, for many organizations, the gap between efficient current practices, which involve single-loop learning, and the capacity to double-loop learn, that is to create viable futures, is only exposed during a performance downturn. An organization needs to engage needs no emphasis. In the old economy, organizations sought advantage through market imperfections that were brought about by the unequal distribution of economic assets. Organizations sought to out-do each other in terms of a competitive strategy. In the new economy, organizations increasingly have to out-know each other, putting emphasis on innovation, creativity and foresight. These are the new tools of competition.

This raises two important questions:

◆ How does learning take place across levels of analysis?

◆ How does **knowledge transfer** take place in organizations?

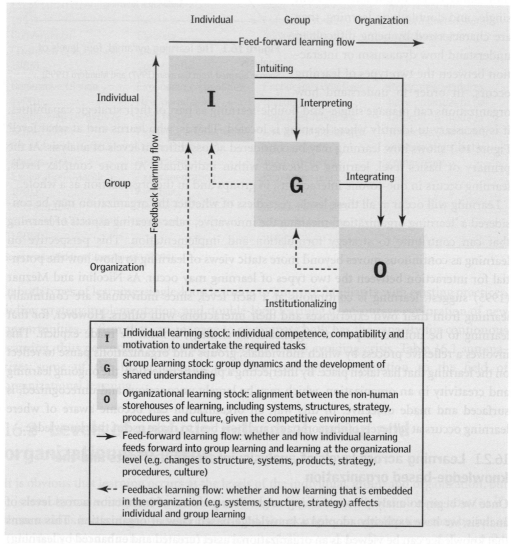

Figure 16.2 Interrelationships between levels of analysis in learning: 4I framework of organizational learning
Source: adapted from Crossan *et al.* (1999: 532).

In addressing the first question, the 4I framework captures the key processes that need to be enacted before learning can take place across levels of analysis. This framework is shown in Figure 16.2.

The three levels (individual, group and organizational) are linked together in a learning process that rests on four social and psychological processes. These processes are described by Crossan *et al.* (1999) as *intuiting, interpreting, integrating* and *institutionalizing*. Within these processes, behaviours (what people do) influence cognition (what people think). We do not know to what extent this is a linear process since cognition also influences behaviours, but these are the key processes that underpin the 4I model and facilitate learning across levels of analysis. Note that Crossan *et al.* have subsumed one-to-one learning (see Figure 16.1) as part of group learning; hence they deal with three (and not four) levels of analysis.

As Vera and Crossan (2004) explain, *intuiting* represents two important elements in learning. First, it is the start of learning. It occurs at the level of the individual. Second, intuiting can only occur in an individual's mind since this is largely a subconscious process. Nevertheless, this represents a stock of knowledge that resides at the individual level in organizations. In order to extract the conscious elements of this intuition, *interpretation* allows this knowledge to be articulated and shared at group level. Individuals thus inform groups and help increase the stock of knowledge at group level. *Integration* is the process by which group learning and the group stock of knowledge is collectively identified (from many groups for example) and is translated into understanding at the organizational level. Finally, *institutionalizing* is the process by which learning is incorporated in the organization by embedding this stock of knowledge in organizational structures, systems, practices and routines.

Vera and Crossan (2004) emphasize the importance of recognizing stocks and flows of knowledge within an organization. Stocks of knowledge can be found at each level of analysis. They underpin the inputs and the outputs of the learning process. Flows of learning are where knowledge passes from one level to another, feeding forward from individual to group and organization and feeding backward from the organization to the individual and group. As Vera and Crossan (2004: 226) explain:

> *The tension between the feed-forward and the feedback flows of learning represents the tension between exploration and exploitation (March 1991). The feed-forward process allows the firm to innovate and renew. The feedback process reinforces what the firm has already learned and ensures that organizational level repositories of knowledge (such as culture, structures, systems, procedures and strategy) guide individual and group learning.*

Vera and Crossan's work demonstrates graphically how information flows and resides in organizations at various levels. These knowledge assets become part of the

Of course, these stories continue and the news that Viagra has been cited as a major cause in marital breakdowns is something that Pfizer may want to consider! But serendipities such as the discovery of Viagra are not uncommon. Most of us will know the story of the development of the Post-it note (a 3M product), which was born out of the company producing an adhesive which failed all the tests for effective glues. It would not stick anything together, but the knowledge that it would adhere to paper and could be removed on many occasions without damaging the paper to which it had been attached was soon communicated around the organization and the Post-it note was born.

British Telecom is another organization which takes knowledge stocks and flows seriously. To facilitate this the knowledge management division have concentrated on trying to transform a company whose sole strategic ambition was to become a cost-effective utility, to an entrepreneurial culture which values and acts upon originality and creativity.

Case box: Utilizing knowledge to increase organizational learning at BT

Only a short time ago, executives at BT were expected to communicate only with one layer up or one layer down the extensive hierarchy which characterized BT's organizational structure. Today, BT UK is structured into nearly 40 business units and is organized into a network structure where communication across many levels is via email and the group's intranet. The top executives have their own websites which detail their priorities and their strategies. Anyone can ask a question of anyone else via email or online discussions. The result is that anyone is approachable with an idea and responses are usually fairly rapid. The company has an organization-wide directory which lists the contact details of everyone in the organization, together with their whereabouts and a hot link to their personal and their departmental websites. Around 80 000 staff use the intranet every day. BT is careful to ensure that knowledge flows and that learning occurs as a result. To do this, BT assesses how well knowledge flows and how well people collaborate. The focus is on four areas: the economic case for sharing knowledge more effectively; the level of sophistication of the unit's knowledge management technology; the cultural environment and a leadership commitment to a new way of working. The results of the assessment are fed back to the management team so that they can identify knowledge problems, barriers to learning or opportunities in each unit. Then the unit can begin to formulate an action plan, reduce the unnecessary or the irrelevant and emphasize what are identified as key competences for the development of future plans. Learning to value what people know is the hardest task of all, but the BT approach seems to be successful in revealing this hidden (tacit) aspect of knowledge and learning.

16.2.3 An alternative perspective on organizational learning models: neo-institutionalism

One of the key questions which surrounds both Nonaka's and Vera and Crossan's models of learning is that they, perhaps, naively assume the dominant flow of learning to be from the individual to the organization and that, in turn, the organization codifies and reinforces such learning back to groups and individuals. The alternative view is that organizations are effective systems for ensuring that all learning at both the group and individual levels of analysis is institutionally bounded. That is, organizational systems, procedures and dominant coalitions predominantly decide who is recruited, how they behave, which ideas are taken forward and which are discarded. In terms of Crossan *et al.*'s model (Figure 16.2) the bold arrows and the dotted arrows should change places. The *organization* is where the dominant logic of operations and learning resides. Everything else (individuals and groups) have to fit into place and their behaviour as well as their learning is bounded by the organization. Groups and individuals are recipients of organizational constraints and the dominant flow of knowledge is from the organization to groups and individuals.

This institutional view of organizational learning has strong support among a number of scholars. Organizations are, as Morgan (1986) argued, self-producing systems of learning. The institutionalised system of interactions, systems and forms in the organization drive both strategy and learning (or, arguably the lack of learning at the organizational levels of analysis). The Arthur Andersen example illustrates this process.

Case box: **Arthur Andersen**

Prior to the collapse of Enron, Arthur Andersen was a highly successful professional service organization. In such firms, differentiation is via the collective ability of its professionals the intellectual capital of the organization – and this becomes embodied in the brand. Andersen was one of the top five employers of choice of graduates; it selected its graduates from top universities and provided glittering salary packages. In return, entrants were socialized into a workaholic lifestyle in which responsiveness to the client was the priority at all times. To further their stock of intellectual capital Andersen invested heavily in an MBA for their staff. This was designed to serve three major objectives central to what, at first sight, appeared to be a model of a learning organization. First, the MBA was designed to retain middle rank professionals (retention being a key aspects of keeping the knowledge within the firm). Second, it represented an investment in their intellectual capital, developing the idea of a one-stop shop for their clients, cross-selling high-value consultancy to a client base that had been developed on the basis of a now maturing auditing service. The MBA was considered useful in broadening and developing the perspectives and knowledge base of specialist processionals. Third, the MBA signalled to the client the significant levels of investment the firm was making in learning and developing individual and organizational competences.

> However, on closer inspection, Andersen turned out to be a firm which had a structure and a culture that precluded organizational learning. Although, formally, Andersen declared itself to aspire to becoming a learning organization, there was little evidence of this happening. The partnership structure and the culture of individualism (you became a senior partner on the basis of your client base) prevented intuitive knowledge ever being shared with peers and thus developing into interpretive knowledge. Individuals did not network. They rarely, if ever, shared their MBA assignments with others (even with peers taking the same MBA). Knowledge was seen as private and an asset from which the individual, rather than the organization, could benefit. Knowledge was shared, but outside the organization – with clients. It could be used to impress clients through better (or better packaged) advice. Client acquisition and retention were key to securing a senior partnership.
>
> *Source*: adapted from Legge, Sullivan-Taylor and Wilson, 2004.

In the Andersen case, the explanation of why individual learning took place, but organizational learning did not, can be found in institutional theories of organization (*see* for example, Greenwood and Hinings 1996). Although the stocks of knowledge are significant at the level of the individual, these stocks are rarely transferred, shared or embedded in the organization. More precisely, this barrier to learning can be seen as a facet of **neo-institutionalism** (Powell and DiMaggio 1991). Old institutionalism argued that the influence of key managers, dominant coalitions of interests groups and the general exercise of power were the barriers to organizational development, change and learning. In other words, organizations were precluded from learning because powerful people within the firm prevented the process from happening. It was in their interest to block learning and this helped sustain and maintain their power base.

Neo-institutionalism, on the other hand, is the effect we see in the Andersen example. Here, it is much less the power of elites which is the barrier to learning and much more the embeddedness of routines, legitimacy and taken-for-granted behaviours in the organization which preclude learning. Neo-institutionalism explains stability and similarity of organizational arrangements within and between organizations (it is likely that Andersen is very similar to other professional service firms in these respects). This phenomenon is called 'isomorphism', which is a powerful force against organizational learning.

The links between isomorphism and strategy are obvious. If organizations do not learn, they are unable to adapt to (or to anticipate) change. Stability on learning translates into stability and ossification in strategy. Isomorphism is a powerful force against both innovation and learning (*see* Chapter 15 on organizational change).

Bringing the concept of isomorphism into the world of practice reveals that one of its key effects is to produce what is known as 'dominant logic' among managers who formulate and participate in strategy.

16.3 **Learning traps: dominant logic**

Dominant logic is 'the way in which managers conceptualize the business and make critical resource allocation decisions' (Prahalad and Bettis 1986). Based on their experience, managers evolve mental models that influence their selection and retention of relevant information about the business and the business environment. These mental models or cognitive maps, arising from top management's existing knowledge banks, affect the selection of strategic choices for the firm. Thus, the breadth and depth of the experience base of the top management team influences firm strategy. A team with a lower degree of diversity in its experience base will have less capacity to envision diversity in its strategic portfolio.

Furthermore, when a team has had long experience in a particular type of business environment, it will build up a strong managerial logic that constrains any capacity to select new environments. The degree of cohesion in the dominant logic has varying influences on the strategic portfolio depending on the different phases of strategic decision-making. High diversity is important in the early phases for conceptualizing a broad business domain and conducting a wide search and evaluation of potential businesses. Lower diversity and high top team consensus are necessary, however, in order for strategic actions to be implemented.

Therefore, while wide diversity, associated with a broadly defined but also potentially diluted dominant logic, is important in the early phases of strategic decision-making, a narrower, more cohesive dominant logic is instrumental in implementing strategic decisions (Ginsberg 1990). As dominant logic aids strategy implementation, the managerial challenge is to create a unitary dominant logic by achieving a similar strategic understanding across all levels of the organization (Von Krogh and Roos 1996). From this perspective, dominant logic is a form of corporate glue, providing a cohesive set of core beliefs that guide consistency in strategic action across divisions (Lampel and Shamsie 2000).

When dominant logic is cohesive across the organization, it becomes embedded within the routine tasks and processes by which strategy is put into practice. The relationship between the way that managers think and how organizations act strategically may be understood through the notion of procedural memory. Procedural memory is the skill-base associated with thinking. This is the familiar routinized actions, developed from experience, which managers undertake without conscious thought (Cohen and Bacdayan 1994). They simply 'know' how to approach certain strategic tasks, such as strategy formulation, resource allocation and performance monitoring.

Managerial mental models for conducting strategic action readily transmit to the organization through the formal administrative processes and the informal, tacit, locally understood methods of acting. These routines and processes make up the knowledge infrastructure of the firm. This knowledge base provides learning about, response to, and understanding of problems in the organization. Over time, such knowledge becomes a key component of the firm's dominant logic, reinforcing existing patterns and procedures for acting strategically. The dominant logic forms the basis of decision-making and action whenever a problem is perceived. However, a strongly cohesive dominant logic results in a tendency to interpret and solve all problems in essentially familiar ways, even where the business environment may have changed, requiring new ways of thinking and solving problems.

Thus, managerial thinking and the administrative processes and organizational knowledge arising from it tend to become static over time, predisposing an organization to single-loop learning. Organizations with a very cohesive dominant logic will not be receptive to creative ideas that may be arising at the peripheries. They will lack the methods for surfacing learning (as discussed above). Rather, employees will rapidly socialize to the unitary dominant logic and understand that rewards and incentives are tied into the existing practices and procedures. As dominant logic is such a self-reinforcing process, adapted to the existing procedures, interpretations and strategies, it is likely to remain largely unchanged until declining performance reaches a level of crisis where new learning is imperative for survival (Bettis and Prahalad 1995; Cote *et al.* 1999).

16.3.1 The counter argument: groups help organizations learn and combat dominant logic

The role of communities of practice

In spite of pressures for isomorphism, learning in organizations is argued to occur continuously in individuals and in the groups in which those individuals interact. Such groups are called **communities of practice** because they involve people participating in the actual practices of work (Brown and Duguid 1991). The practice of work may not mirror the formally documented rules and regulations by which work is supposed to occur. In practice, people innovate and experiment with ways of getting the job done more easily or more efficiently, or may improvise because the existing rules (organizationally codified procedures) fail to provide them with sufficient information to get the task done. The immediate work community provides a learning context because people tell each other stories about work and they share information and concepts through the social processes of the group.

Such learning is occurring at the peripheries of the organization all the time and may be extremely valuable to the firm. However, its value and its occurrence can easily be overlooked in the wider organizational context (and by neo-institutionalists) for two reasons. First, it occurs at the margins or peripheries where the specific task is located, therefore, it is not within the 'mainstream' of organizational activities. Second, since such practices do not always mirror the formal descriptions of how to act, they may be suppressed in discussion with supervisors or senior managers. Indeed, the community may not see itself as a valuable learning resource, simply regarding itself as a group of people who help each other.

However, as senior management and organizations generally have begun to understand the value-creating properties of knowledge, they have become more interested in ways of tapping into the existing knowledge and learning potential of their companies. Wenger and Snyder (2000) suggest that communities of practice are a means of doing this. Communities of practice help to drive the emergent properties of strategy and help to surface organizational innovation. Furthermore, they provide an important learning forum for the various forms of knowledge creation proposed by Nonaka (1994).

Members of a community learn through participation in tasks together, transferring practices, ideas and concepts about the work process. As they do so, the individuals in the group increase their own knowledge and skill base, creating a virtuous circle of enlarging knowledge at the individual and group level. Such communities provide particular benefit where they bring together individuals with different skills and backgrounds. As communities are spontaneous, informal and free forming, they are difficult to manage, particularly since much of the work such communities do does not look like work in any traditional sense.

However, as Wenger and Snyder (2000) note, while communities of practice cannot be organized, they can be cultivated by providing a fertile environment. They suggest that managers can:

- Identify potential communities of practice that will enhance the company's strategic capabilities.
- Provide the infrastructure that will support such communities and enable them to apply their expertise effectively.
- Use non-traditional methods to assess the value of a community of practice.

In most organizations informal networks of people already exist and may be considered part of the core competences. The manager's task is to identify such groups and encourage them to come together. Shell has a structured method of encouraging communities of practice. If a person wants to develop a community, he or she teams up with a consultant to determine the problems and challenges that different units have in common, which might serve as the basis for a community. People are then interviewed for their views on how a community might support them and their capacity to advance the company's strategic agenda. This flags up the idea of a community of practice, provides information on what the community would value, and generates enthusiasm and interest in joining such a community. This is one of the ways in which Shell has built upon its early success with scenario planning in order to develop itself as a learning organization.

In order to bring the work of communities from the periphery into the mainstream of organizational information flows, they need to be given legitimacy. Communities need to be given resources, such as IT support and reward structures that create incentives for collaboration, if they are to be recognized as important to the strategic development of the company. American Management Systems (AMS) has managed this through a formalized system of sponsoring communities. Recognizing that they were losing their capacity to leverage knowledge due to their rapid growth during a period of global development, AMS encouraged business units to nominate 'thought leaders'. The company paid for up to three weeks of the leaders' time each year to be devoted to developing communities of practice in strategic areas. Community membership is seen as a privilege for people recognized as experts by their business units. The communities are actively involved in developing knowledge-creating projects for which they are funded. An annual conference brings together all the communities of practice once a year to share knowledge across the organiz-ation. In this way, communities of practice are recognized, given resources and perceived as prestigious because their work is important to the company. Many companies do not have such formal processes for developing and recognizing communities, but they may, nonethe-less, provide senior management support for informal groups that arise.

While it is generally accepted that developing the capabilities of individuals should help to develop firm capabilities, the process of transfer from individual to firm capabilities is poorly understood (see Figure 16.2). As such, it is difficult to assess the value of a com-munity of practice in terms of wider value of the organization. First, the outcome of a community of practice may not occur in a measurable way within the community itself, but in the work of the business units that surround the community. Second, since communities have informal processes, it is difficult to know whether innovative ideas are a result of the community or whether they may have occurred anyway. It is complex to evaluate the moti-vational, knowledge-sharing opportunities and outcomes that communities provide. Wenger and Snyder (2000) suggest that senior managers need to listen to the *stories* arising from communities of practice to understand how such communities provide value. They note that AMS, which has formal processes for developing and recognizing communities, conducts an annual 'audit' of such stories. An analysis of a sample of stories revealed that the communities had saved the company between $2 million and $5 million and increased revenue by more than $13 million in one year. Other companies, such as Shell, recognize the value of communities' stories as learning resources for the wider organization, publishing them in internal newsletters and reports. We explore the value of stories in developing organizational learning through stories in the next section.

16.4 Using storytelling to develop organizational learning

Shaw *et al.* (1998) note that **storytelling** plays an important role in strategic learning. In a discussion of strategic planning as storytelling, they show how stories have, for example, helped 3M to become a learning organization, as illustrated in the case box.

> ### Case box: **Organizational learning in the 3M Corporation through storytelling**
>
> Through stories, managers and scientists at 3M are able to discuss organizational failures as well as strokes of genius and intuition. Such stories allow employees at 3M to explore reasons for failures in a non-threatening way, enabling learning from mistakes. Equally importantly, successes arising from creative thinking can be disseminated, serving as examples of what is important and valued at 3M. They allow ideas to be shared throughout the company. Storytelling has become so important to the culture at 3M that it has replaced traditional forms of strategic planning. Gordon Shaw, the executive director of planning at 3M, realized that traditional strategic plans were too 'thin' to inspire commitment or generate learning. Traditional plans could articulate goals and provide extensive lists of what the organization should do in each of its divisions. However, they could not build links between divisions to illustrate the complex relationships involved in putting the strategic plans into practice. Neither could they encourage participants to internalize company goals. Stories, on the other hand, were able to provide these links and enable individuals to understand the complexity of strategy implementation.

The 3M example is a good illustration of what happens when traditional strategic planning methods and approaches are converted into stories. There were several advantages:

- Strategic stories enable learning by increasing the capacity to think through issues. When strategic plans are told as stories, it is necessary to envision the steps involved in a particular action, building a rich picture of what such an action may involve.

- During this process ideas emerge as part of the construction of the story. Thus, stories increase the creativity involved in planning.

- Because stories are visual, involving characters and situations, they capture the imagination. A strategic story can inspire commitment to the firm's goals and the processes for achieving them.

- Stories build identity and image. Identity is the internal representation of the company; what members believe the firm is. Image is how people would like their organization to be perceived in the outside world. Stories can be used to build a strong picture of what the company's identity currently is and how it relates to what the company would like to become. Stories then show how current realities can be translated into future images. Thus, storytelling can be used to build commitment to the strategic goals of the company.

- As stories are rich in detail, they explain complex relationships between divisions and actions. They can be used to paint a picture of how a strategy will happen and the role that each part of the organization will play in bringing that strategy to fruition. Such richness is inclusive, creating a sense of ownership over organizational goals.

♦ Storytelling also allows assumptions that underlie the organizational strategy to be brought to the surface. Thus, implicit or tacit beliefs about the future of the market, organizational capabilities, products, probable areas of growth and the relationships between them can be made explicit and better evaluated.

Stories are a means of creating a strategic dialogue within an organization. Shaw *et al.* (1998) propose some general guidelines for developing strategic stories that can replace traditional strategic plans. Good stories:

♦ use analysis to set the stage and paint in the background to the current situation;

♦ introduce dramatic conflict by showing what has to be done and why it is important; in this way, a sense of urgency and excitement is developed; and

♦ reach a resolution by explaining what can be done and how it should be put into action.

Essentially, storytelling increases communication and allows strategic planning to assume a reality for the organizational participants. They can envision the strategy being enacted and see how their role contributes to the whole. This builds a sense of inclusion, excitement and confidence about achieving strategic goals. Clearly, such commitment and participation is an important feature of organizational learning. Storytelling creates a sense of community in the wider organization. It is a method of putting Nonaka's (1994) models of knowledge creation into practice.

16.5 Enhancing organizational learning

16.5.1 Risk taking

In order to counteract the tendency for dominant logic to become overly unitary, managers need to encourage diversity, creative conflict and dissonance in organizations. Such conflict, well managed, provides an opportunity for debate and discussion, enabling new ideas to be surfaced. This is difficult since organizational cultures frequently suppress innovation because of an underlying fear of risk taking. In a learning organization it is necessary for managers to avoid a culture of blame, to be open to risks where these are well considered, and to accept the occasional failure. As the chief executive at 3M notes:

> *The freedom to persist implies the freedom to do things wrong and to fail. We accept that ... but at the same time, we expect mistakes to have originality. We can afford almost any mistake once.* (Easterby-Smith, 1991: 26)

In this way, risk-taking can occur within a supportive culture with the expectation that, where ideas fail, this experience is used to generate further learning.

16.5.2 Devil's advocacy and dialectic inquiry

Some techniques can help to generate and surface ideas and manage the creative tension arising from multiple points of view. Devil's advocacy (DA) and dialectic inquiry (DI) are decision making techniques designed to improve the quality of decision-making (Schwenk 1984). DA involves appointing a member of the group to act as devil's advocate for a particular decision. This member's role is to pose all the reasons why a decision should not be implemented. The group must then work through the countervailing views, encouraging them to debate the decision and surface underlying assumptions. DI is another technique designed to improve the levels of debate and creative tension surrounding decision-making. In DI, multiple options are put forward for major strategic decisions. These possible choices, even where they appear inappropriate, must be debated, creating a wider pool of thought and discussion surrounding the decision. Such techniques deliberately impose tension and conflict into the decision-making arena in order to enhance decision quality.

16.5.3 Leadership

While learning is not a top-down initiative, the behaviour of senior management is very important in developing an appropriate context for organizational learning. Senge (1990) suggests that leaders are responsible for building shared vision, surfacing and challenging mental models, and engaging in systems thinking, meaning helping employees to see the big picture and their role in it. He outlines three leadership roles. First, the leader is a designer, building a foundation of purpose and core values within the organization. Second, the leader is a teacher who facilitates the surfacing of tacit knowledge and underlying assumptions within the organization. Finally, the leader is the steward responsible for the sense of ownership and commitment of employees, as well as having a personal commitment to furthering the mission and goals of the organization. Such participative and supportive leadership is consistent with Nonaka's (1994) advocacy of middle-up-down management to stimulate knowledge creation in organizations. Nonaka is critical of top-down management as it presumes that knowledge creation and learning are the province of senior management. However, he notes that bottom-up management is unlikely to be feasible in large corporations because it is time consuming and difficult to co-ordinate:

> The middle-up-down model takes all members as important actors who work together horizontally and vertically. A major characteristic of the model regarding knowledge creation is the wide scope of cooperative relationships between top, middle and lower managers. No one major department or group of experts has the exclusive responsibility for creating new knowledge. (Nonaka, 1994: 30)

In middle-up-down management, senior management are seen as the sponsors and catalysts for creating knowledge. They build the goals, set the deadlines and develop a supportive and receptive context in which learning can occur. Middle managers provide the bridge between lower-level experience in the daily operations of the company and top-level visions. They translate both viewpoints into reality, allowing visions and experience to be combined in the actual practices and strategic actions of the organization. Organizations that embrace middle-up-down management are characterized by self-organising teams, intrapreneurship, diversity, and shared tacit and explicit knowledge. The benefits for both strategy formulation and implementation the practice of strategy would seem to be substantial.

16.6 Summary

This chapter has explored the relationships between organizational learning and organizational strategy. In particular, it has focused on the practice of strategy and how this relates to the ways in which knowledge and learning are arranged and designed in organizations.

It should be clear from reading this chapter that there is no single standardized agreement about what constitutes organizational learning. There are many conflicting theories and many of them have been covered in the chapter. However, the prevailing message seems to be clear. The practice of strategy depends on both knowledge and learning. The ability of an organization and individuals to learn and to communicate and share that knowledge is vital for innovation and strategic renewal.

Even authors who subscribe to the dominant logic or isomorphism schools of thought subscribe to the above view that learning, knowledge and knowledge flows are a vital trio of competences that can help inform and shape strategy.

Key terms

Adaptive learning *602*

Communities of practice *614*

Double-loop learning *603*

Dominant logic *613*

Generative learning *602*

Isomorphism *612*

Knowledge-based view *605*

Knowledge creation *608*

Knowledge transfer *606*

Neo-institutionalism *612*

Single-loop learning *603*

Storytelling *616*

Recap questions and assignments

1   What would you describe as being the key features of a learning organization?

2   Pick an organization with which you are familiar (or is in the public domain) and assess to what extent it is a learning organization, or to what extent it is an organization trapped by routines, stories and dominant logic.

3   If you were asked by an senior manager to help improve learning in his or her organization, which features would you analyse first?

4   Lex Donaldson has criticized much of the 'learning and knowledge' aspects of strategy, saying that the links between knowledge, learning and organizational performance have not been demonstrated at all. What is your view on this statement? Do you agree or disagree? Why?

Online
*Learning*Centre

When you have read this chapter, log on to the Online Learning Centre website at www.mcgraw-hill.co.uk/textbooks/mcgee to explore chapter-by-chapter test questions, further reading and more online study tools for strategy.

Case 1 **Future learning: Discovering internal contradictions in a strategy**

In his well-known book on the art and practice of the learning organisation, *The Fifth Discipline*, Peter Senge introduced the idea of the *Microworld*.[1] It is a common observation that human beings learn through firsthand experience – 'learning by doing'. The repertoires of children's play (dolls, building blocks, swings and other playground equipment) create learning by doing through experimentation with transitional objects (the dolls etc.) in small self-contained worlds (microworlds). Adults create microworlds in which complex phenomena can be examined. Senge mentions wind tunnels (aeronautical engineers) and wave tanks (naval designers). Managers use role playing exercises for supervisory training and outdoor exercises for team building. But Senge observes that there are few microworlds available to managers for creating and testing new ideas and new insights. In particular:

> *few existing microworlds develop individual or team capacities to deal productively with complexity. Few capture the dynamic complexity that confronts the management team when it seeks to craft new strategies, design new structures and operating policies, or plan significant organisational change.* (Senge 1993, p. 315)

Senge's new world of microworlds is built on the use of computer simulation models that enable complex team interactions to be integrated with complex business interactions. The framework of the simulation model (the new microworld) allows groups to test out their mental models of how their business operates, knowing that the essential real world characteristics of the business are captured in the logic of the simulation model. This is, then, a microworld that is essentially a 'practice field'[2] where teams can learn how to learn together while engaging their most important business issues. This is captured in the old adage 'practice makes perfect'. This is readily achieved in performance activities such as sports and theatre where the polished performance seen by the customer is the result of many, many hours on the practice field. But the manager has fewer mechanisms for practice and microworlds are one attempt to remedy this situation.

The case that follows constructs one microworld in which a management team discovers internal contradictions in a strategy that is being put into place.

Lying behind all strategies are assumptions, which often remain implicit and untested. Frequently, these assumptions have internal contradictions. When they do, the strategy also has internal contradictions, which will prove to make it difficult or impossible to implement. One benefit of microworlds is bringing these assumptions into the open and discovering these inconsistencies.

---

[1] Senge (1993) pp. 313–16.

[2] Senge's term.

One such case occurred at a highly successful manufacturer of microcomputers (here called the 'Index Computer Company').[3] The top management team had introduced a microworld as a part of a two-day planning retreat. They had taken on a strategic goal four months earlier: to reach $2 billion in sales in four years. They were all committed to the goal, from Index's President Tom Jamison on down. And everyone seemed happy with the progress so far.

That's why the vice-president of sales, James Sawyer, felt so uneasy. It was difficult enough to keep and train his present sales force – how did they expect him to double it? He had shared his qualms with other top managers, but they had only responded with platitudes: 'You'll work it out. After all, you'll have the budget for it.' Now he was in a bind. He didn't want his fellow executives to think he lacked their commitment to that magic $2 billion figure. He didn't want to get the reputation of a 'nay sayer'. And he certainly didn't want to let on that he thought he might not rise to the occasion, especially since he had a reputation as a 'fixer' who could solve any problem. But every time he thought about the future, an 'involuntary shudder of pain' ran through his stomach.

Soon the executives split into three-person microworld teams to explore the consequences of the sales plan. Their first task was to construct an explicit model on the computer of the assumptions behind the plan.[4] The plan called for a 20 per cent annual sales growth, a continuation of the growth rate of the past ten years. And it also called for 20 per cent more salespeople each year. As they looked at sales figures for the next four years, it didn't take them long to recognize that the official plan implicitly assumed that the productivity of salespeople would hold steady as the sales force expanded. Hire 20 per cent more salespeople, you make 20 per cent more sales.

Making the assumption explicit prompted Sawyer to say, 'Well, wait a minute. Not all salespeople are equal. There is so much they have to learn – about office automation, software, training, accounting, engineering, consulting, and manufacturing – before they can place a single system. Much of our historic growth,' he continued, 'came from hiring experienced salespeople whom we lured away from our competitors. We could do that as long as we were small. But now the numbers of new hires we need to sustain our 20 per cent are getting much larger. We will not be able to get this many people by hiring away from our competitors. We'll be hiring many more inexperienced salespeople in the future.'

Sawyer's comment sparked a lively debate about the differences between experienced and inexperienced salespeople. All agreed that it was necessary to distinguish new,

---

[3] The name and the company are changed, but the insights are based on a real case involving Barry Richmond, of Dartmouth College and High Performance Systems.

[4] The teams were using a software package called STELLA with which simulation models can be built at a screen of a personal computer with advanced graphics capabilities. STELLA is available from High Performance Systems, Inc., Lyme, N.H.

inexperienced salespeople from veterans. When they split back into teams, each team modified their models to make more realistic assumptions. Sawyer's team, for instance, assumed that veterans would be four times as productive as rookies. Some groups assumed less, some groups assumed more, but everyone assumed that training and developing an experienced salesperson required two to four years.

Now, however, none of the models reached that $2 billion sales goal. Sawyer's model projected sales under $1.5 billion.

The problem came from the average productivity of the growing sales force. As the computer simulated the consequences of the projected hiring, it showed more and more rookies, because the rate of new hires exceeded the rate at which rookies became veterans. Although they hired enough total salespeople to meet their plan, the mix of inexperienced and veteran salespeople shifted progressively toward the inexperienced, pulling down average productivity.

The different work teams tried furiously to find a set of assumptions they could believe which would produce $2 billion in sales in four years. No one could do it. To see just how extreme the situation might become, one group asked the question, 'How many salespeople would we have to hire if we simply kept hiring until our sales targets were met?' They found that 'We'd end up almost doubling the sales force in the fourth year alone, if we doggedly kept adding bodies until our sales target was reached.' All knew that this magnitude of personnel growth would wreak havoc on the sales organization, not to mention the overall personnel budget.

After an hour, the president stood up and asked, 'Is there anyone here who still believes that our strategic plan is internally consistent?' No one responded.

The managers had known both halves of the contradiction: that novices are less productive salespeople, and that the new sales goals would require them to hire more novices. But the assumptions came together only when they were put into a microworld that simulated their interaction over time. Now that everyone could see the internal inconsistency, Sawyer found himself able to articulate, for the first time, his general reservations.

'I've felt for some time that executing the new strategic plan will cause problems,' he told the group. 'And the problems might be even worse than even these simulations suggest. We have a tradition of not revising our business goals once we've announced them publicly. So, not only would we be likely to hire a lot more new salespeople than our official plan projects, but there will be a lot more pressure on our veterans. Couple that with the distractions and frustrations for our veterans who have to help all these new people get up to speed and I wouldn't be surprised if we end up with more veterans leaving and lower productivity from those who stay. We could get into a really vicious cycle. Many of our veterans came to us in the first place to escape this kind of situation somewhere else.'

The other managers sensed that Sawyer's fears might well materialize. 'Perhaps,' said the president, 'it's time to step back and consider some of the challenges we face.' He had hardly finished his sentence before Susan Willis, the vice-president of human resources, had motioned for the floor.

'This is crucial,' said Willis. 'Our people have some problems with the sales managers that I'd like to get on to the table.' Willis talked about the strained relationship between human resources and sales. The sales managers, she said, especially resisted any call to invest their time in training and developing new salespeople. Why, she asked Sawyer, were they so reluctant?

'Well we grew our sales organization by attracting the most aggressive people, the kind of people who spend all their time out in the field,' said Sawyer. 'They don't want to mentor any new hires. They thrive on closing a sale. That's not just where they get their kicks, it's where they make their money. Thanks to our strong incentives, the sales managers with high quotas are among the best-paid people at Index. There are no comparable incentives for helping newcomers; our organization is a lot stronger at rewarding individual accomplishment.'

Sawyer added that the new strategic plan would simply reinforce this problem. 'You must keep in mind that our whole sales organization is geared to meet aggressive targets,' he said. 'Give them a tougher target, and they'll respond by selling harder. I'll have a tough time getting them to think about taking time in developing new hires. I understand Susan's problems. I have the same problems.'

The microworld had brought to the surface a set of frustrations which had been brewing for some time. Moreover, it focused those frustrations on critical changes which needed to occur if the organization hoped to sustain past success. Most important, the declining sales productivity had failed to galvanize action to date, because *it had not yet taken place in the real world*. The microworld gave them a unique window on the future.

As their strategy retreat continued, the management team saw the core issue as either lowering their growth targets or transforming their sales organization. They concluded that the growth target was realizable *if* new salespeople could be trained much more quickly. This presented a significant challenge, because it meant that veteran salespeople would need to be more committed to mentoring inexperienced colleagues. There would need to be new rewards for sales managers to develop their staffs. More support to help senior salespeople in mentoring and training would be needed. And they'd need to look more carefully for new hires who wanted to work in a collaborative team environment, where people helped one another become more effective. The changes were significant but achievable.

One tool for change would be another microworld – this one designed for sales managers, in which they could learn to balance, week by week, their time allocation between direct sales efforts, recruitment, training and management. The salespeople could then discover the long-term benefits of allocating time to personnel development rather than to direct sales efforts.

Predictions such as those achieved at Index are different from normal business forecasts. As former Shell planner Pierre Wack observed: 'Suppose heavy monsoon rains hit the upper part of the Ganges River basin. With little doubt you know that something extraordinary will happen within two days at Rishikesh at the foothills of the Himalayas; in Allahabad, three or four days later; Benares, two days after that.'[5] This is a prediction, not a forecast. It is something you can say with confidence about the future because it depends not on projecting historical data into the future but on understanding the dynamics of an underlying system. By analogy, some of the most interesting learnings that come out of microworlds come from discovering implications for the future, when decisions play out in what had been unrecognized organizational systems.

Source: adapted from Peter Senge (1993) *The Fifth Discipline: the art and practice of the learning organisation*, Doubleday, London, pp. 316–20.

Case Questions

1 What are the key lessons you can learn from the Index Computer Company's use of microworld methodology?

2 What do you consider to be the major weaknesses of microworld thinking in strategy formulation?

3 Can microworld thinking (and similar techniques) enhance both individual and organizational learning? How?

5 Pierre Wack, 'Scenarios: Uncharted Waters Ahead,' *Harvard Business Review*, September/October 1985.

Further reading and references

Argyris, C and Schon, DA (1987) *Organizational Learning: A Theory of Action Perspective*, Addison-Wesley Publishing Company, Reading MA.

Bettis, RA and Prahalad, CK (1995) 'The Dominant Logic: Retrospective and Extension', *Strategic Management Journal*, Vol 16, pp. 5–14.

Brown, JS and Duguid, P (1991)'Organizational Learning and Communities of Practice: Toward a Unified View of Working Learning and Innovation', *Organization Science*, **2**, **1**, pp. 40–57.

Cohen, MD and Bacdayan, P (1994) 'Organizational Routines are Stored as Procedural Memory: Evidence from a Laboratory Study', *Organization Science*, **5**, **4**, pp. 554–68.

Cote, L, Langley, A and Pasquero, J (1999) 'Acquisition Strategy and Dominant Logic in an Engineering Firm', *Journal of Management Studies*, **36**, **7**, pp. 919–52.

Crossan, M, Lane, H and White, R (1999) 'An organizational learning framework: from intuition to institution', *Academy of Management Review*, **24**, pp. 522–38.

De Geus, A (1988) 'Planning as learning', *Harvard Business Review*, **66**, **2**, pp. 70–4.

Easterby-Smith, M (1991) 'Creating a Learning Organization', *Personnel Review*, **19**, **5**, pp 24–8.

Garavan, T (1997) 'The Learning Organization: A Review and Evaluation', *The Learning Organization*, **4**, **1**, pp. 18–29.

Garvin, DA (1993) 'Building a learning organization', *Harvard Business Review*, (July–August) pp. 78–91.

Ginsberg, A (1990) 'Connecting Diversification to Performance: A Socio-cognitive Approach', *Academy of Management Review*, **17**, **3**, pp. 514–35.

Greenwood, R and Hinings, CR (1996) Understanding Radical Organizational Change: bringing together the old and the new institutionalism', *Academy of Management Review*, **21**, **4**, pp. 1022–54.

Huber, GP (1991) 'Organizational Learning: The Contributing Processes and the Literatures', *Organization Science*, **2**, **1**, pp. 88–117.

Jarzabowski, P (2004) 'Recursiveness and adaptive strategic practices in use', *Organization Studies*, **25**, **5**, pp. 412–25.

Lampel, J and Shamsie, J (2000) 'Probing the Unobtrusive Link: Dominant Logic and the Design of Joint Ventures at General Electric', *Strategic Management Journal*, **21**, **5**, pp. 593–602.

Lant, TK and Mezias, SJ (1992) 'An Organizational Learning Model of Convergence and Reorientation', *Organization Science*, **3**, **1**, pp. 47–71.

Legge, K, Sullivan-Taylor, B and Wilson, DC (2004) Organizational Learning and Corporate MBAs, paper presented at the EGOS Colloquium, Ljubljana, Slovenia, July.

March, JG (1991) 'Exploration and Exploitation in Organizational Learning', *Organization Science*, **2**, **1**, pp. 71–87.

Mason, B (1998) 'Switchboard: Exchange Culture', *People Management*, **4**, **21**, pp. 46–9.

Morgan, G (1986) *Images of Organization*, Sage, London.

Mumford, A (1995) 'The Learning Organization in Review', *Industrial and Commercial Training*, **27**, **1**, pp. 9–16.

Nicolini, D and Meznar, MB (1995) 'The Social Construction of Organizational Learning: Conceptual and Practical Issues in the Field', *Human Relations*, **48**, pp. 727–46.

Nonaka, I (1994) 'A Dynamic Theory of Organizational Knowledge Creation', *Organization Science*, **5**, pp. 14–37.

Peters, T and Waterman, R (1982) *In Search of Excellence*, Harper Row, London.

Powell, W and DiMaggio, P (1991) (eds) *The New Institutionalism in Organizational Analysis*, University of Chicago Press, Chicago.

Prahalad, CK and Bettis, RA (1986) 'The Dominant Logic: A New Linkage between Diversity and Performance', *Strategic Management Journal*, **7**, pp. 485–501.

Schwenk, CR (1984) 'Devil's Advocacy in Managerial Decision-Making', *Journal of Management Studies*, **21**, pp. 173–88.

Senge, P (1990) 'The Leader's New Work: Building Learning Organizations', *Sloan Management Review*, Fall.

Shaw, G, Brown, R and Bromiley, P (1998) 'Strategic Stories: How 3M is Rewriting Business Planning', *Harvard Business Review*, May–June pp. 41–50.

Tushman, ML and Romanelli, E (1985) 'Organizational Evolution: A Metamorphosis Model of Convergence and Reorientation', in *Research in Organizational Behaviour*, LL Cummings, and BM Staw (eds) (7th edition), Greenwich, CT, JAI Press, pp. 171–222.

Vera, D and Crossan, M (2003) 'Organizational Learning and Knowledge Management: Towards an Integrative Framework', in M. Easterby-Smith and M. Lyles (eds) *Handbook of Organizational Learning*, Blackwell, Oxford.

Vera, D and Crossan, M (2004) 'Strategic leadership and organizational learning', *Academy of Management Review*, **29**, **2**, pp. 222–40.

Von Krogh, G and Roos, J (1996) 'A Tale of the Unfinished' *Strategic Management Journal*, **17**, pp. 729–37.

Wenger, EC and Snyder, WM (2000) 'Communities of Practice: The Organizational Frontier', *Harvard Business Review*, Jan/Feb, pp. 139–45.

Chapter 17

Strategy and corporate governance[1]

Chapter contents

Introduction

In recent years the importance of **governance** has become of prime concern in the strategic management of organizations of all kinds. Effective, honest, accountable and transparent modes of governance are now sought of organizations by stakeholders of all varieties.

There is no single model of good governance. However the OECD (2004) has identified corporate governance as one of the key elements in improving economics efficiency and growth as well as enhancing investor confidence. The OECD (2004) describes corporate governance as:

> … *involving a set of relationships between a company's management, its board, its*

---

[1] Contributions to this chapter were made by Derek Condon, Warwick Business School.

shareholders and other stakeholders. Corporate governance also provides the structure through which the objectives of the company are set, and the means of attaining those objectives and monitoring performance are determined. Good corporate governance should provide proper incentives for the board and management to pursue objectives that are in the interests of the company and its shareholders and should facilitate effective monitoring.

The OECD's *Principles of Corporate Governance* go on to say that:

Corporate governance is only part of the larger economic context in which firms operate that includes, for example, macroeconomic policies and the degree of competition in product and factor markets. The corporate governance framework also depends on the legal, regulatory and institutional environment. In addition, factors such as business ethics and corporate awareness of the environment and societal interests of the communities in which a company operates can also have an impact on its reputation and its long-term success.

There have been a number of recent scandals and exposés of alleged poor governance ranging from Enron, through Parmalat to Shell. These failures expose some of the key principles and the importance of governance structures, processes and accountabilities. We outline the case of Enron below.

Case box: **The Enron collapse**

On 2 December 2001, Enron filed for bankruptcy. On the same day, Irwin Steltzer writing in the Business News of the *Sunday Times* praised Kenneth Lay (Enron's Chairman) for 'converting this American Industry into a lean, mean and internationally competitive machine'. Houston-based Enron went bankrupt amid revelations of hidden debt, inflated profits, questionable accounting and governance. Thousands of workers lost their jobs and millions of investors who hadn't already bolted watched their shares become worthless. Dozens of people, including Enron founder and former Chairman Kenneth Lay, former Chief Executive Jeffrey Skilling and former finance chief Andrew Fastow, have been charged with crimes in the Justice Department's continuing investigation of what caused the collapse. Mr Fastow is among 10 former executives who have pleaded guilty, while Messrs Lay and Skilling are among the 20 who have pleaded innocent and are facing trial. The ventures that once defined Enron as a leader in energy and other markets, such as trading and broadband, are long gone. Unsecured debts in the UK alone reached over £600 million involving Barclays, the Royal Bank of Scotland and Abbey.

Since the collapse of Enron, a key focus has been on how organizations are governed and how boards of directors in particular can let such events happen – and how they might prevent them happening again. The Enron story reveals a board which effectively turned a blind eye to events which should have sounded alarm bells. In brief, the story goes: Enron forged a close relationship with the then Secretary of State for Energy (John Wakeham) in 1990. Wakeham gave Enron permission to build a large gas-fired power station on Teesside. John Wakeham was an accountant by training and was trusted and largely left alone by his two Prime Ministers (Margaret Thatcher and John Major) to secure the deal. In 1994, John Wakeham left the government and joined the main board of Enron. The Tories' policy of energy privatization was vigorously opposed by Labour (especially by its spokesman on industrial affairs, Tony Blair). Once appointed Prime Minister in 1994, Blair began to change policy and secured close relationships with private energy companies and with John Wakeham (now Lord Wakeham, a Tory peer). Enron made small donations to both US political parties, including $10,000 to support the Florida recount in the Presidential elections. Kenneth Lay subsequently secured a seat on a key advisory committee on energy policy (a post previously unavailable to anyone outside government). Enron also lobbied New Labour in the UK.

In 1998, Peter Mandelson (then Trade and Industry Secretary) gave permission for Enron to purchase Wessex Water without referring this decision to anywhere else in the Government. Wessex Water became the core of Enron's new water unit, Azurix. In 1999, Azurix went public and Enron began commercial operation of its nationwide fibre network for high bandwidth uses. Also in 1999, Helen Liddell (Industry Minister) gave Enron permission to build a gas-fired power station on the Isle of Grain, Kent, also without referring the decision elsewhere. By 1999 the Labour government had reversed their energy policies and were strongly backing gas-fired power stations. Labour ministers insisted that the regulation of privatized industries would ensure fair play and healthy business practices.

The response of the Enron board was to recruit the regulators. In October 2000, Claire Spottiswoode, the Gas regulator joined the board of Asturix (the new title of Wessex Water) and in August 2001, Stephen Littlechild, the electricity regulator, was appointed to the board of Teeside Water (a subsidiary of Enron). Following this, the Enron board turned a blind eye to several deals carried out by executives and sanctioned their actions.

These deals put large dents in Enron's funds but were not recorded on the balance sheets. Billions of pounds were used to support these initiatives. In February 2001, a group of Andersen partners met to discuss Enron's accounting and disclosures, but decided to retain the company as a client. Kenneth Lay discussed energy policy with Dick Cheney, US Vice-President, and Cheney's energy task force included some recommendations favourable to Enron. During a public appearance in June 2001, Skilling was hit by a cream pie thrown in protest for Enron allegedly profiteering from California's energy crisis which had begun in May 2000. In August 2001, Skilling resigned as President and CO and Kenneth Lay returned to the position of CEO. In October 2001, the *Wall Street Journal* revealed that Fastow made at least $7 million from running LJM partnerships in order to hedge investment in an internet company. In October 2001, Andersen began shredding Enron-related documents despite knowing of an SEC inquiry.

Enron replaced Fastow as CEO with Jeffrey McMahon from the industrial markets division and the SEC elevated its inquiry into Enron's financial dealings to a formal status. Enron restated its earnings for 1997 to 2001, reducing net income over that time by $586 million and boosting debts by $2.6 billion. By November 2001, major credit rating agencies had downgraded Enron's bonds to junk status at 61 cents per share. The bankruptcy file (for Chapter 11 protection) in December was the biggest in the US at the time ($62 billion in assets).

In 2002 Enron's trading operations were sold to UBS Warburg. Enron received no money but did secure the promise of one-third profits. Enron's board fired Andersen as auditors. Andersen claimed the relationship ended when Enron went into bankruptcy. On 23 January 2002, Kenneth Lay resigned as Chairman and CEO, replaced by Stephen Cooper as acting CEO. The Powers Report, commissioned to investigate blame, spreads the reason for Enron's collapse among Lay, Skilling, Fastow and Andersen, among many others.

Stephen Cooper revealed reorganization plans in May 2002 and one month later a jury found Andersen guilty of obstruction of justice in the investigation of Enron, sealing the demise of the accounting firm in the process. Between October 1998 and November 2001, Lay sold shares with gross proceeds of $184 million; Skilling $71 million; Fastow $34 million and Rebecca Mark $83 million.

By July 2004, the US Government had launched 31 Enron-related prosecutions including the criminal case which brought down Andersen in 2002. It has also set up criminal investigations into around 20 former Enron employees including Lay, Skilling and Fastow. So far, 11 have resulted in convictions or guilty pleas.

Source: authors' own data.

In New York in July 2004, US bankruptcy judge Arthur Gonzalez signed off Enron's plan to exit Chapter 11 bankruptcy protection with no notable adjustments. The reorganization plan aims to pay most of the more than 20,000 creditors about $12 billion of the approximate $63 billion they are owed in cash and stock in one of three new companies created from Enron's remains. Sales are pending for two of those companies – CrossCountry Energy Corp., which comprises Enron's whole or part interest in three domestic natural-gas pipelines, and Portland General Electric, its Pacific Northwest utility. The third is Prisma Energy International Inc., a smattering of pipeline and power assets in 14 countries, mostly in Latin America.

If the sales of CrossCountry and Portland General close later this year as expected, the $11 billion will be distributed to creditors with 92 per cent in cash and 8 per cent in Prisma stock. If one or both of the sales crumble, creditors will receive less cash and more stock in the multiple companies. The Enron name will disappear.

CrossCountry has so far attracted two buyers. In May the first bidder, Texas billionaire and Coastal Corp. founder Oscar Wyatt Jr, offered $2.2 billion. Then, a joint venture of Southern

Union Co. and GE Commercial Finance a unit of General Electric, offered $2.3 billion. Both offers include $430 million in assumed debt. Judge Gonzalez is to consider those and any other bids at a 1 September auction, and he is to approve the winning bid by 9 September.

CrossCountry's holdings include the 2600-mile Transwestern pipeline, which transports natural gas from west Texas, Oklahoma, eastern New Mexico, the San Juan Basin in north-western New Mexico and southern Colorado to California, Arizona and Texas markets; half-ownership with El Paso Corp. of Citrus Corp., a holding company that owns the 5000-mile Florida Gas Transmission pipeline from southeast Texas to Florida; and a less than 2 per cent interest in Northern Border Partners, which transports natural gas from Canada to the Midwest.

Last year Enron announced plans to sell Portland General to an investment group backed by Texas Pacific Group for $1.25 billion in cash and $1.1 billion in assumed debt.

Stephen F. Cooper, Enron's acting CEO and chief restructuring officer, said in a news release:

> *Undoubtedly, this was an extremely complex bankruptcy. Today's court approval acknowledges not only the tremendous amount of work that has been accomplished during the last two and a half years, but also the overwhelming support of our economic constituents.*

The Enron debacle was seen as a serious failure of strategists at board level. It heralded a new era of reviews and prescriptions for board behaviours and regulation, which will be discussed later in this chapter. A new era, since the first code of good governance originated in the USA in 1978. There were, of course, other high-profile failures in the US WorldCom, Global Crossing and Tyco. In Asia the economic crisis of 1997 was laid firmly at the door of poor governance by the Asian Development Bank. And, in Europe, Parmalat and Shell Oil have also been blamed for poor governance. Clearly not just a problem in US companies; nevertheless, the US Business Roundtable issued a report concerning the roles and composition of boards of directors of large publicly owned companies. Monks and Minnow (1992) argued that the origin of this code was in response to increasingly criminal corporate behaviour and included guidelines to quell the occurrence of hostile takeovers. This focus on board behaviours and processes was essentially about the structure, composition and conduct of boards. The main points identified the chairman's main duties as:

- Overseeing board members' selection and succession.
- Reviewing the organization's performance and allocating its funds.
- Overseeing **corporate social responsibility**.
- Adherence to the law.

It was not until 1989 that the next **code of governance** was issued, this time in Hong Kong by the Hong Kong Stock Exchange and this was rapidly followed in 1991 by a best practice set of guidelines issued by the Irish Association of Investment Managers (Aguilera and Cuervo-Cazurra 2004). After this date, the Cadbury Committee Report in the UK (1992) heralded the authorship of many codes of good conduct with Aguilera and Cuervo-Cazurra (2004: 419) concluding that there were 72 codes of good governance by the end of 1999 spread across 24 industrialized and developing countries. Table 17.1 summarizes the position.

The codes produced under different **legal systems** have often been customized to particular national settings and this has reinforced the governance differences identified by Charkham (1999). However, institutions such as the World Bank and OECD are calling for

Table 17.1 Numbers of codes of governance worldwide (to end 1999)

Country	Total number of codes
English-origin legal system:	
Australia	4
Canada	4
Hong Kong	4
India	2
Ireland	2
Malaysia	1
Singapore	1
South Africa	1
Thailand	1
UK	11
USA	17
French-origin legal system:	
Belgium	4
Brazil	1
France	4
Greece	1
Italy	2
Mexico	1
Netherlands	2
Portugal	1
Spain	2
German-origin legal system:	
Germany	1
Japan	2
Korea	1
Scandinavian-origin legal system:	
Sweden	2
Total countries 24	**Total codes** 72

Source: adapted from Aguilera and Cuervo-Cazurra, 2004, p. 423.

common principles and common governance structures and processes, at least to a minimum level. *Exogenous* forces are influencing the adoption of reasonably common codes. As organizations become more a part of the global economy for example, the transmission of common practices becomes easier and, some would say, necessary. Government liberalization and the increasing influence of foreign institutional investors also force the pace for common codes and standards. In this way, exogenous pressures force countries to show that their codes of corporate governance are 'legitimate' in the global economy.

17.1 **The context of corporate governance**

As early as the 1930s, Berle and Means (1932) drew attention to the growing separation of power between the executive management of major public companies and their increasingly diverse and remote shareholders. This view focused on the problem of control. The central question was to what extent could boards control executive management and thereby maintain the rights and influence of the shareholders as owners of the organization? This question has been addressed in terms of **agency theory**, in particular in economics. In this theory, the *agents* are corporate management, and the *principals* are the shareholders. In agency theory, the board is viewed as an alternative monitoring device which helps to control the agents to further the interests of the principals. It is assumed in agency theory that effective boards will identify with shareholder interests and use their experience in decision making and control to exert leverage over any self-interested tendencies of corporate management – the agents. For boards to exercise their vigilant role over the chief executive officer (CEO), the board needs power (Keasey, Thompson and Wright 1997). For the CEO to engage in self-interested activities there must presumably be a power imbalance between the CEO and the board.

Cadbury (2000) and Cassidy (2000) offer accounts of the rise and rise of corporate governance as an issue in the USA and Europe since the 1980s. Central to their argument about why this issue has risen so far up the policy agenda have been:

- a succession of corporate scandals;
- performance weaknesses of many firms which could be attributed at least in part to poor governance and leadership;
- disjunctures between the compensation of CEOs and executive directors and the financial performance of the companies they are managing (Conyon and Murphy 2000).

Despite these varying accounts, it is clear that there are a common set of *endogenous* pressures and questions which revolve around the purposes, responsibilities, control, leadership and power of boards. These questions include:

- How is oversight to be exercised over those delegated to the executive management of the firm?

- How are owners' interests to be protected?

- How are the interests of the other stakeholders such as consumers, employees and local communities to be protected?

- Who sets the purpose and direction of the organization and ensures its accountability?

- How is power over the organization legitimized and to whom is an organization accountable and responsible?

17.2 **Corporate governance in the UK**

Modern UK corporate governance regulations began with the Cadbury Report (1992), which reviewed the financial aspects of corporate governance and led to the publication of the Code of Best Practice. This was followed by the Greenbury Committee (1995), which reviewed directors' remuneration, while the Hampel Committee on corporate governance (established in 1995 and reporting in 1998) had a broader remit that built on Cadbury and Greenbury, essentially picking up new issues that had arisen from both reports. Following the report of the Hampel Committee, the first edition of the **Combined Code** was published by the London Stock Exchange (LSE) Committee on Corporate Governance and was added as an appendix to the LSE Listing Rules. The code superseded all previous codes for UK-listed companies and was derived from Cadbury, Greenbury, Hampel and the LSE's Listing Rules. The principles behind the code were those of market and self-regulation. The code was not legally enforceable, but a company was required to explain how the principles of the code had been followed and to disclose when and why they did not follow the code. If these reasons were not deemed acceptable by the stock market, it would be reflected in the company's stock price.

Since the publication of the first edition of the Combined Code, three other important reports have been published to date. These are the Turnbull Report, which provides guidelines for directors on how to meet the code's provisions on internal control; the Smith Report, which relates to the provisions on audit committees and auditors; and the Higgs Report, which was a review of the role and effectiveness of **non-executive directors**. The findings of these reports have been incorporated into the latest edition of the Combined Code (Higgs 2003). It represents something of a 'capstone' on the previous reports and it has had a significant impact on the structures and processes of boards in the UK. Like all previous codes, the Combined Code seeks to influence board structure and conduct by means of codes of practice and not through legislation. Boards are expected to *comply or explain* why they have not complied in their reporting mechanisms. The key requirements of the Combined Code are summarized in Table 17.2.

The reasons for not choosing a legal requirement for disclosure and relying on codes of practice lie, on the one hand, in the less than adequate provision of the legal structure in the

Table 17.2 Key elements of the Combined Code

> ***The main disclosures required are***:
> - A statement of how the board operates and which types of decision are taken by the board and which are delegated to management.
> - Number of meetings of the board and its committees including a list of annual attendance by directors.
> - A description of how performance evaluation of the board, its committees and its directors is conducted.
> - What steps have been taken to ensure that members of the board, especially non-executive directors, understand the views of major shareholders about their organization.
> - A description of how the nomination committee works and why open advertising or an external search agency have not been used in either the appointments of a chairman or a non-executive director.
> - A description of the processes and activities of the remuneration and audit committees.
>
> ***The main principles of the code are***:
> - Every company should be headed by an effective board which is collectively responsible for the success of the organization.
> - A clear division of responsibilities. The roles of chairman and chief executive should not be exercised by the same individual and no one individual should have unfettered powers of decision. It is worth noting here that almost 10 per cent of UK-listed companies have a joint chairman/chief executive (Hemscott 2003).
> - The board should include a balance of executive and independent non-executive directors.
> - Transparency of all procedures.
> - The board should undertake a formal and rigorous evaluation of its own performance and that of its committees and individual directors.
> - All directors should be submitted for re-election at regular intervals subject to continued satisfactory performance. Refreshing the board with new members should be planned and implemented.
> - Levels of remuneration should be sufficient to attract, retain and motivate directors but this should not include paying more than is necessary for this purpose. There should be a transparent policy on remuneration.
> - Financial reporting should be understandable and transparent and subject to strict internal controls.

UK to ensure good practice and, on the other, to encourage the spirit of self-regulation. For example, UK law rests on the principle that the owners (shareholders) appoint agents (directors) to run the business, and the directors report annually on their stewardship. In practice, in public limited companies (of which there are around 2,000 in the UK), there is a two-link chain of accountability. Management is accountable to directors, and directors are accountable to shareholders. PLCs registered after 1 November 1929 are legally required to have at least two directors. There is no distinction between classes of directors; for instance, between executive (inside or full-time) directors and non-executive (outside and part-time) directors. The law refers only obscurely to chairmen and barely mentions boards. This legal minimalism leads Charkham (1999) to conclude that

> *the superstructure as we know it: boards, board committees, chairmen, non-executive directors are pragmatic adaptations. In law none is essential; to this day ICI could legally be run by two directors, like the consulate of the Roman Republic.*

Many UK boards divide the chairman and chief executive officer (CEO) roles, and the position of chairman is often part time. Chairmen have major responsibilities in determining the size, balance, composition and agenda of the board. They can also play a significant part in handling external relationships with key stakeholders such as government, institutional investors, regulators and banks. Chairmen are normally appointed by non-executive directors. Non-executive directors play an increasingly important role in influencing board processes, heading up important committees of the board such as the audit or remuneration committees. Audit and remuneration committees comprise only non-executive directors and nomination committees are headed by a non-executive director or the chairman, who must meet the independence criteria laid out in the Combined Code.

17.2.1 Compliance with codes of governance in the UK

Conyon (1995) reveals a clear pattern of company adherence to the Cadbury recommendations. There is no statutory requirement for a company to reveal its board committee structure, so the failure of a company to reveal the existence of a committee does not necessarily mean it does not exist. (Since Cadbury, however, it is in companies' interests to be as transparent as possible in reporting non-controversial matters about board structures.) Tables 17.3, 17.4 and 17.5 summarize the main patterns in the data from the Conyon study and is reported in Pettigrew (2004).

Table 17.3 Board composition and size in the UK

	Average size of board	Average number of non-executive directors	Average number of executive directors
FT-SE top 100 Companies	12.30	6.15	6.16
FT-SE mid 250 Companies	8.89	4.57	4.32
FT-SE top 350 companies	9.87	5.02	4.85

Source: Conyon, 1995.

By 2003, these data had hardly changed. On average, a UK-listed board has around 7 directors. FTSE 100 boards are still larger, with an average of 11.5 directors (Hemscott 2003).

Table 17.4 Remuneration committee structures in UK companies, 1994

	Number of companies with remuneration committee	Average size of remuneration committee	Average number of non-executive directors on remuneration committee	Number of non-executive-only remuneration committees
FT-SE top 100 companies	100	4.61	4.28	73
FT-SE mid 250 companies	233	4.07	3.63	161
FT-SE top 350 companies	333	4.23	3.82	234

Source: Conyon, 1995.

Table 17.5 Audit committee structures in UK companies, 1994

	Number of companies with audit committee	Average size of audit committee	Average number of non-executive directors on audit committee	Number of non-executive-only audit committees
FT-SE top 100 companies	100	4.24	4.05	92
FT-SE mid 250 companies	246	3.94	3.59	208
FT-SE top 350 companies	346	4.03	3.73	300

Source: Conyon, 1995.

Again, the Hemscott (2003) survey of boards reveals very few changes in the above data from the Conyon study.

Key points from the Conyon study are:

- The overall average board size for the FTSE 350 companies is 9.87. The ratio of non-executive directors to executive directors for large UK companies is approximately equal. The average of 5.02 non-executive directors per company considerably exceeds the Cadbury minimum recommendation of three.

    In a 1993 postal survey of 400 of the *Times* 1000 top UK companies between 1988 and 1993, Conyon (1994) found the average proportion of non-executives on the main board in 1993 to be 44 per cent, up from 38 per cent in 1988. There is possibly a rising trend in the use of non-executive directors in large UK plcs.

- Table 17.4 indicates close adherence to the Cadbury and institutional shareholders' committee recommendations on the creation and composition of remuneration committees. Almost all the FTSE 350 companies have remuneration committees that set top pay. Table 17.4 also shows the minimal presence of executive directors on such committees. Even so, among the 1994 FTSE 100 companies, there were still 33 executive directors who sat on their company's remuneration committee. According to Conyon's 1993 study, in contrast, only 54 per cent of companies sampled had had remuneration committees in 1988.

◆ The Cadbury Report states that 'all listed companies should establish an audit committee' (1992, 4.35, p. 28) in order to help safeguard shareholder interests. Table 17.5 shows that by 1994, 98.9 per cent of the FTSE 350 companies had audit committees and that non-executive directors were a dominant feature of the audit committee. This high disclosure of the existence of audit committees again shows considerable change from the disclosure rate in 1988, when a Bank of England (1988) company survey found that only 56 per cent of the *Times* 1000 top 250 companies reported the existence of audit committees.

The picture that emerges from the Conyon studies (1994 and 1995) is one of substantial change in the prevalence of remuneration and audit committees between 1988 and 1994. Bostock (1995), however, has shown a lesser rate of adoption of board-nominating committees. Nominating committees, when available, may be able to bring a more objective approach to the selection of executive and non-executive board members. Using publicly available data disclosed in company annual reports, Bostock (1995) showed that 53 per cent of the top 100 UK companies by market capitalization did not have a nominating committee. The incidence of nominating committees trebled between 1998 and 1993, yet Conyon (1994) found that only approximately 40 per cent of UK quoted companies had them in 1993, despite the Cadbury code of practice.

The Cadbury code of practice does not recommend companies to split the roles of chairman and chief executive. It does, however, recommend that where the roles are not

Table 17.6 Number of companies with women on the board for 1995

	Number with at least one woman non-executive director	Number with at least one woman executive director	Number with at least one woman board member (exec or non-exec)
FT-SE top 100 companies	34	7	40
FT-SE mid 250 companies	29	7	33
FT-SE top 350 companies	63	14	73

Source: Conyon and Mallin, 1997.

Table 17.7 Percentage of females on the board in 1995

	Percentage of female non-executive directors on main board	Percentage of female executive directors on main board	Percentage of all female directors on main board
FT-SE top 100 companies	3.08	0.56	3.65
FT-SE mid 250 companies	1.44	0.40	1.84
FT-SE top 350 companies	2.02	0.46	2.49

Source: Conyon and Mallin, 1997.

split, there should be a strong independent element, with a recognized senior member, on the board. The Cadbury Committee's own research on compliance (CADS, 1995) shows that by 1994 the roles of chairman and chief executive were split in 82 per cent of UK firms in the top 500 by market capitalization. Conyon's (1994) postal survey of 400 firms in the *Times* 1000 found that, in 1993, 77 per cent of quoted companies had split the two roles, compared with 57 per cent in 1988.

In a slightly later study, Conyon and Mallin (1997) report on women's participation rates in the UK boardrooms. Tables 17.6 and 17.7 report respectively on the number of companies with women on the board, and the percentage of females on the board of UK plcs in 1995.

These data reveal the very limited participation of women in the main boardrooms of the UKs top plcs. IN 1995, there were just 73 companies with at least one female director on the main board and very few of those were executive directors. In 1995 there was only one company in the FTSE 100 with a female CEO. In 2000, this figure had doubled to two. Only 2.49 per cent of the directors were female and females are more likely to be non-executive than executive directors. By 2003, just over one in ten FTSE non-executive posts were held by females and one in forty FTSE executive posts were held by women (Hemscott 2003). Things do not seem to be changing in terms of the gender imbalances in the boardroom. Most strategists are male.

Although the above data show the extent which UK organizations comply with the various codes, the data should not be taken to imply anything about the effectiveness of these boards. Ticking the boxes of compliance and working effectively are two very different processes. In the next sections, we look at **board effectiveness** generally (i.e. in companies worldwide) and in the UK, referring to a recent empirical study of UK boards by McNulty and Pettigrew (1999).

17.3 **Board effectiveness**

Conger *et al.* (2001), Ward (2000) and the OECD (2004) all offer principles against which board effectiveness might be judged. In particular, these authors emphasize that the board should be able to exercise judgement in decision making and corporate affairs generally, independently of other influences, particularly the voices of management. Since boards should appoint non-executive directors to exercise independent judgements over key areas such as financial reporting, nomination and remuneration, the board ought to be able to exercise independent and informed judgements away from the day-to-day managerial concerns of the organization. In addition, these authors emphasize the importance of boards being able to access and be supplied with accurate, timely and relevant information in order to carry out their strategic decision making roles effectively. Finally, the role of accountability is emphasized, not only compliance with the law and acting on good faith, but also in the interests of all shareholders and the social responsibilities of the organization. These issues are summarized in the next sections.

17.3.1 **The board as a team**

Surprisingly, the board as an organizational team has been relatively neglected in empirical study. While there are plenty of studies on teams (and top teams) in organizations (see Katzenbach and Smith 1992; Hambrick *et al.* 1998), there are very few studies of boards using the key variables identified from these team studies. Applying the empirical knowledge of team processes and performance to boards would emphasize a number of key aspects.

First, boards should ensure they focus on the correct issues during their meetings and avoid much of the side-tracking which can take place in groups. For example, this would mean being able to focus on and distinguish between long- and short-term factors with full discussions at board meetings before any strategic decisions are taken. As with all organizational groups, size is important. Extrapolating from the team-based literatures, boards should restrict their size as far as possible to around six or eight members for a small organization to ten or twelve members for a larger organization. All members should feel that they can contribute freely and effectively to meetings and be well prepared in advance of the meeting. Regular meetings with high levels of attendance would also be beneficial in terms of effective decision making.

Second, the board needs to build in maintenance and learning functions to its operations and processes. The board's role as the key strategic decision making body calls for a high level of commitment of all members as well as the ability of those members to learn from experience and apply that learning to decisions and judgements they are required to take. Training and development (e.g. perhaps an induction programme for newly appointed directors) should also be beneficial as should specific training in the key areas of decision making (see Chapter 13) such as strategy, risk and evaluating performance. Like all groups in organizations, some assessment of their own performance as a team and as individuals in that team should ensure greater effectiveness.

17.4 The board and strategic decision making

As the key group in strategic decision making processes, the board needs both to understand how decisions are made (on what basis and with what stated objectives for example) and how they go about decision making as a team. This is another aspect of the interface between organization and strategy (see Chapter 2). In making strategic decisions, the board stamps its mark on the organization and, in turn, the organization becomes a distinctive entity with

Table 17.8 Levels of non-executive board member involvement in strategy

	Taking strategic decisions	Shaping strategic decisions	Shaping the content, context and conduct of strategy
Definition	Influence is exerted inside the boardroom at the end of the capital investment decision process	Influence occurs early in the decision process as part-time board members shape the preparation of capital investment proposals by executives	Influence is continuous and not confined to decision episodes
Board behaviour	Inside the boardroom, boards take decisions to accept, reject or refer capital investment proposals	Consultation with part-time board members by the executive, either formally or informally, while a capital investment proposal is being prepared enables board members to test ideas, raise issues, question assumptions, advise caution, and offer encouragement. *Executives 'sieve' capital investment proposals in anticipation of the need for board approval*	The board develops the context for strategic debate, establishes a methodology for strategy development, monitors strategy content and alters the conduct of the executive in relation to strategy
Board involvement	All boards take strategic decisions	Some boards shape strategic decisions	A minority of boards shape the context, content and conduct of strategy

Source: adapted from McNulty and Pettigrew, 1999.

its own structure, culture and philosophy. A resource-based view of the organization would imply that a key role of the board is to ensure precisely what is the core business or purpose of the organization and to ensure that organizational competences and resources are in place to support that core purpose. This is akin to creating and preserving that 'cherished core ideology' that Collins and Porras (2000) argue is the vital constant of successful organizations when all else around them is subject to change. In essence, the board represents and needs to preserve the glue which holds the organization together and which symbolizes the guiding principles by which key decisions are made.

The board also has the responsibility of overseeing not only its own internal processes in this respect, but also of ensuring that this 'strategy with values' is disseminated effectively throughout the organization and that processes, rewards and organizational structures are aligned with the strategy. Opinions differ about the level of involvement that is both possible and desirable for boards in the strategy process. Some argue that boards should have a proactive or initiating role of shaping strategy. Others contend the board should challenge, question and eventually approve strategic ideas and decisions formulated below the board in the executive team. McNulty and Pettigrew (1999) have examined the contribution to strategy by chairmen and non-executive directors of large UK companies. The collective label of part-time board member was used to refer to individuals performing these two roles (although a limited number of chairmen in the UK have executive and virtually full-time positions). Table 17.8 summarizes the forms of strategic involvement of boards in strategic decision making.

Most non-executives claimed they were much more influential in stopping initiatives than in starting them (McNulty and Pettigrew 1999). The executives interviewed claimed that around 80 per cent of the strategic decisions they took to the boardroom were approved or confirmed by the whole board.

Shaping strategic decisions entails a higher degree of non-executive board member influence. Here the non-executives are consulted and involved earlier in the strategy process and thereby can shape the assumptions, alternatives and actual choices in the process. Shaping also occurs when executives restrict the range of their own proposals (knowing that certain alternatives will not be accepted at board level).

The ultimate way for a board to shape strategy is to fire the CEO and other executive directors. This is happening with increasing frequency in UK boardrooms. The new generation of CEOs entering UK boardrooms are likely to be younger, to have had experience in more than one company and industry, and to have a shorter tenure in post than their predecessors of the 1980s and early 1990s.

17.4.1 The board and performance

Like any process, it is vital that boards have some way of agreeing what the key drivers of performance are. These can include a variety of measures such as financial results, corporate reputation or customer satisfaction, or can be a holistic grouping of such measures. An example of such a broad-based performance measurement system is Kaplan and Norton's (1992) balanced scorecard approach to using multiple measures for assessing performance. These include financial and non-financial measures of performance with a view to assessing future potential as well as assessing current performance.

A broad-based performance measure means boards must be clear about:

◆ How do our customers see us.

◆ What we must excel at.

◆ How we can continue to improve and create value.

◆ How good our financial performance is.

Each of these measures can be sub-divided into two component parts. These are outcomes, which *measure* the results of actions in the past, and performance drivers (*goals*), which predict future success. This allows future strategies to be reflected in today's goals and targets. Figure 17.1 shows the multi-dimensional nature of the balanced scorecard.

Measures can be metrics such as return on capital employed or return on net assets. They can also include factors such as employee attitudes, extent of customer satisfaction or core competences. *Goals* are future desired states which predict future success.

Of course, such a broad-based performance tool requires boards to be effective at both *prioritizing* strategic decisions (see Chapter 13) and assessing *risk*. The task of the board is to manage risk effectively rather than try to eliminate risk altogether. Bernstein (1996) reminds us that risk is a choice rather than a fate. The degree of risk taken by boards is really an expression of the amount of action (in an uncertain world) they dare to take. In this sense, risk is also an integral part of strategic decision making alongside prioritization. It is also

Figure 17.1 The balanced scorecard
Source: adapted from Kaplan and Norton, 1992.

management's responsibility (as well as that of the board) to monitor and assess risk as well as to keep the board informed of future risk-related projects or developments.

Handling risks (and setting the appetite for risk in an organization) are the responsibility both of the board and management. Effective risk management means there must also be good patterns of communication and understanding between the board and the management of an organization. Risks can arise from virtually all organizational activities. Some boards establish risk committees to look explicitly at some of the risk factors outlined in Table 17.9.

The main challenge to boards is to incorporate risk assessments into their own processes and to be able to prioritize significant or key risks (which may range from ethical issues to health and safety). Many practitioners advise that the board should make a detailed risk analysis every time they make (or ratify) a strategic decision. The Turnbull Report recommended a risk-based approach to designing, operating and maintaining a sound system of internal governance. Kirkbride and Letza (2003) note that Turnbull is the first official UK corporate governance document where the role of risk in corporate governance practice has been explicitly included and articulated.

Table 17.9 Some risks facing boards

Source of risk	Examples
Corporate strategy	◆ Strategy and organizational capabilities not aligned ◆ Unsuccessful acquisition ◆ Major change programme goes wrong
Financial	◆ Major accounting irregularities ◆ Fraud ◆ Cash flow problems
Legal	◆ Health and safety risks ◆ Breach of regulatory laws ◆ Failure to protect intellectual property
Supply chain and alliances	◆ Strategic alliances and joint ventures do not work ◆ Supply chain problems (e.g. suppliers) ◆ Overdependence on outsourced services
The operating environment	◆ Not responding to market trends ◆ Failure to innovate ◆ Overdependence on a few customers/suppliers
Human resources	◆ Loss of key people ◆ Poor motivation and communication among staff ◆ Leadership unable to take the organization forward (unable to formulate/implement strategies)
Social responsibility	◆ Stakeholder concerns about ethics of organization ◆ Dealing with unethical suppliers or contractors ◆ Human rights violations

The board is responsible for the company's system of internal control and it is the role of management to implement board policies on risk and control. Reports to the board should provide a balanced assessment of the significant risks and the effectiveness of the internal control mechanisms to handle those risks.

Other risks identified in the Turnbull Report include the following.

Strategic risk

- Changing conditions in the regional, national or world economy having an effect on the company's business
- Becoming a takeover target
- The risk of obsolescent technology
- Being in an industry in decline

Financial risk

- Shortage of cash (liquidity risk)
- Trying to expand the business too quickly
- Having unrecorded liabilities (e.g. guarantees about which senior management is unaware)
- Taking decisions with incomplete or inaccurate financial information.

Compliance risk

- Breaching financial regulations
- Litigation risks
- Breaching the requirements of the Companies Act (or its legal equivalent)
- Incurring tax penalties

Operational risk

- Vulnerability of IT systems to unauthorized access (e.g. hackers)
- Loss of key people
- Succession problems
- Reputation damage or loss

17.5 Boards and corporate social responsibility

A question of increasing importance to all organizations is to what extent the board has ensured that strategic decisions incorporate ethical, socially responsible and sustainable factors. It is the duty of a diligent board to assess and to take into consideration issues of a sustainable environment. In many respects, corporate social responsibility (CSR) is not a separate issue but is one which permeates all board activities (in particular decision making and risk assessment).

An organization which operates in a manner contrary to CSR faces the risk of poor market ratings and adverse publicity. Those which face large ethical concerns also face the results of poor and adverse publicity. A well-known example of this is the case of BP-Amoco which suffered greatly as a result of its exploration activities in Colombia. Eventually accused of working for a corrupt government, BP Amoco suffered bad publicity, a drop in market value and a drastic drop in reputation. Few boards would want to ignore CSR. They would do so at their peril.

Two aspects of formalizing CSR have now become the remit of boards worldwide. The first is known as the 'triple bottom line'. This means that, alongside financial and other hard measures of performance, a measure of CSR (the third measure) should be included as an equal arbiter of performance. The second is known as the 'global compact', resulting from a meeting of the World Economic Forum in 1999. The then UN Secretary General, Kofi Annan, set out nine principles on human rights, labour and the environment that organizations need to address (and be judged against). Table 17.10 summarizes the nine core principles of the global compact.

A study by Contardo and Wilson (2001) revealed a patchy take up of these nine principles by the boards of twenty organizations. These twenty organizations were drawn from ten different nations in order to see if country of origin had any significant impact on the implementation of the nine principles. The results revealed that country of origin had no

Table 17.10 The nine principles of the global compact

Human rights	Businesses should: ◆ Support and respect the protection of international human rights within their sphere of influence ◆ Ensure their own corporations are not involved in human rights abuses (implicitly or explicitly)
Labour	◆ Recognize the right of labour to collective bargaining and freedom of association ◆ Eliminate forced and compulsory labour ◆ Abolish child labour ◆ Eliminate discrimination in terms of employment and occupation
Environment	◆ Take a precautionary approach to environmental challenges ◆ Promote greater environmental responsibility ◆ Encourage the development and diffusion of environmentally friendly technologies

impact at all. The data from this study revealed that boards were experiencing some difficulties in implementing the nine principles, especially in older organizations. Boards in older organizations experienced difficulties in assessing the relative priority of these principles in relation to other externally determined standards (such as International Standards or Health and Safety). In general, the boards of older organizations were making progress in networking with stakeholders in order to try to establish partnerships and had often set up new functions in the organization to deal with CSR issues. For example, Unilever had created a special department addressing CSR issues and had engaged with many stakeholders (including strong critics of the organization) in order to weave environmental consciousness throughout their business. Shell Brazil has introduced a clause in its contracts with distillers forbidding the use of child labour. Shell Brazil was awarded the title 'Child Friendly Company' for its work in discouraging the use of child labour in the production of sugar cane alcohol, which it is legally obliged to sell on its forecourts and include in its gasoline. BASF has established a sustainability council at board level to try to make sustainability a part of everyday processes in the company. Overall, however, the data from Contardo and Wilson (2001) point to a very patchy worldwide take up of the nine principles by a wide range of organizations, with boards in particular finding it difficult to add these responsibilities to their existing portfolio of activities.

17.6 **What is an effective board?**

There are many autobiographical accounts by practitioners of board effectiveness but few independently conducted analyses of board conduct and performance. Recently a study conducted by Pettigrew and McNulty has generated first-hand data on board conduct, power relationships and strategy processes (Pettigrew and McNulty 1995 and 1998; McNulty and Pettigrew 1999). This study used a multi-method approach combining a survey of the chairmen, CEOs and non-executive directors of the top 500 plcs, with personal interviews with 65 part-time and 43 full-time board members and the analysis of publicly available documentary material.

Most of the board members we interviewed acknowledged that it was somewhat easier to identify the characteristics of an ineffective board than to catalogue the features of an effective one. Indicators of ineffectiveness included:

- Poor chairing of the board
- Over-dominance by the chair
- Marginalization of the non-executives
- Cliques and politicking between and inside board meetings
- Failure to reveal critical information to board members
- Failure to encourage open discussions and allow issue spotting

- A board focused on a narrow set of issues and fixated by historical reporting and operational matters

- A closed process of recruitment to the board

Looking more broadly at board effectiveness, there are some important conceptual distinctions. These include considering effectiveness both against a set of agreed board purposes and against a trinity of design choices (inputs, processes and outputs); recognizing that effectiveness has to be customized to local circumstances; and being clear that performance in the boardroom is a dynamic issue and may require continuous performance assessment, learning and change. McNulty and Pettigrew (1999) characterized effective boards as 'maximalist' and less effective boards as 'minimalist'. Table 17.11 summarizes their characteristics.

The maximalist board does not have the extreme power asymmetrics to be found in the minimalist board. With greater sharing of power and information, and more clearly defined purposes and roles, better relationships and communication flows are apparent in the maximalist board. In time, with greater trust and better shared understandings between the chair and CEO, the board culture changes. With greater trust, more challenge and dissent becomes

Table 17.11 Characteristics of maximalist (successful) and minimalist (less successful) boards

Characteristics of minimalist boards	Characteristics of maximalist boards
Run by individuals and small factions	Trigger for change often a performance crisis
Big power asymmetries between chair or chair/CEO and rest of board and executive	Top-level change: new personalities and purpose and processes
Non-execs have low legitimacy; selected to maintain power asymmetries; starved of information; confined to the boardroom; isolated from the strategic process	Attempts to distinguish roles more clearly
	Recruitment of new non-executive directors: given greater legitimacy
Board agenda is stylized and predictable in its historical reporting	Board agenda and process opened up
	Space for issue spotting and resolutions
No space to spot issues, even less for dealing with them	Non-execs allowed into strategic process
	Non-execs allowed to roam outside boardroom
Little or no conflict, challenge or dissent	Roaming enhances perspective, judgement, confidence and trust
	Greater trust and openness allows greater challenge and dissent and more informal working and better relationships
	Often tensions about power. Non-execs are prepared to use it, and executives have felt it
	Checks and balances and fluidity of information and relationships allow control and leadership purposes to be realized

possible and more fundamental strategic issues are opened up for discussion and possible resolution. Although there is a more comfortable dynamic balance of power on maximalist boards, there may still be an appropriate tension about power. This tension may be a left-over from the company performance crisis, when the non-executives were prepared to use power and when the executives felt the use of power. Without this tension about power there would be no checks and balances, and without these the apparently contradictory board purposes of control and strategic leadership would be less likely to be realized.

17.7 Summary

This chapter has examined some key aspects of boards and their role in strategic decision making. Board have a strategic and public responsibility to provide direct returns for shareholders and employees, suppliers and have a responsibility towards the communities in which they operate. In the wake of recent corporate scandals and collapses, governments worldwide have been reviewing the role and the processes of governance.

Because the board is in place to lead and control the organization, it should have a clearly defined set of responsibilities and codes of operation. This chapter has outlined the main features of those responsibilities and it has outlined some of the major features of the emerging guidelines.

Although board structures differ from country to country, most countries have a common set of principles of governance, namely that no individual director has unrestrained power to control and direct the organization and that there should be a countervailing influence (on insiders on the board) from outside directors who act as the guardians of board conduct and decision making processes

Key terms

Agency theory *635*

Board effectiveness *641*

Code of governance *633*

Combined Code *636*

Corporate social responsibility *633*

Governance *629*

Legal systems *634*

Non-executive directors *636*

When you have read this chapter, log on to the Online Learning Centre website at www.mcgraw-hill.co.uk/textbooks/mcgee to explore chapter-by-chapter test questions, further reading and more online study tools for strategy.

Recap questions and assignments

1 Why are governance processes and structures important to our understanding of strategy?

2 With regard to an organization you know well (or is in the pubic domain) what would you assess as its good and less good features in terms of governance structures and processes?

3 What do you see as the key changes and challenges for the future for corporate governance

Case 1 **Walt Disney Company: 'The case against Michael Eisner'**

Timeline

1984 Following a long period of relative decline, reflected in both its stock price and profits, corporate raider Saul Steinberg launches a takeover bid for Disney. Although unsuccessful it leads to a power struggle that is eventually won by a group of shareholders led by directors Roy E. Disney (nephew of Walt Disney and son of Roy O. Disney the co-founders of Walt Disney Productions) and Stanley Gold (Disney's close friend, attorney and financial advisor). The existing management – Raymond Watson (Chairman) and Ron Miller (CEO), Walt Disney's son-in-law – is replaced by Michael Eisner (Chairman and CEO), the President of Paramount Pictures (a division of Gulf & Western), and Frank Wells (President), a former CEO of Warner Bros (a division of Warner Communications). Both were equals in the sense that they reported directly to the board, with Eisner seen as the 'creative talent' and Wells the 'businessman', an arrangement similar to that found in the original Walt Disney Productions where Walt Disney (creative) was Chairman and CEO and Roy O. Disney (businessman) was President.

Roy E. Disney (who had previously resigned his executive position at the company while remaining on the board of directors) returns as Head of Animation.

Jeffery Katzenberg joins as Head of the Film Division.

1984–94 Over the next 10 years as the stock price rises 6000%, the company opens EuroDisney, makes numerous successful films and TV shows targeting all types of audiences, expands Disney World, buys TV stations and the Anaheim Mighty Ducks ice hockey team. Eisner is lauded as one of the great CEOs of the 1980s and 1990s.

1994 (April) Frank Wells is killed in a helicopter crash.

1994 (July) Katzenberg (seen by many commentator's as Eisner's eventual successor) leaves after a clash with Eisner. Only one month after *The Lion King*, overseen by Katzenberg, becomes the most successful animated film ever.

1994 (July) Eisner undergoes quadruple bypass surgery.

1994 Prince Alwaleed invests in the failing EuroDisney preventing the collapse of the project which is renamed Disneyland Paris.

1995 (Oct)	'Super-agent' Michael Ovitz, frequently described as the 'most powerful man in Hollywood', leaves Creative Artists Agency (CAA) to become Disney President. He is seen as a potential successor to Eisner by many industry insiders and institutional investors.
1995	George Mitchell joins the board.
1996 (Feb)	Disney purchases Capital Cities/ABC for $19 billion. It is the largest media takeover to date and the second largest acquisition of a US firm.
1996	Disney purchases the Anaheim Angels baseball franchise.
1997 (Jan)	Ovitz leaves the company after a public clash with Eisner with a $140 million severance package.
1997	*Business Week* names the Disney board the worst board in America (for the first time).
1999	Disney's lawsuit with Katzenberg, regarding future profit participation, is settled when he accepts a $275 million payout.
2000	Roy E. Disney and Stanley Gold begin their campaign to force the board to develop a programme to identify Eisner's eventual successor and become more independent. The board of directors includes Eisner's friends such as actor Sidney Poitier, architect Robert A.M. Stern, who has designed many Disney properties, and former Sen. George Mitchell, who consults for Disney. The board's judgement is particularly questionable with regard to the compensation packages awarded to Eisner. In the spring of 2001, *Forbes* concluded that in the previous five years, Eisner made $737 million. This was in a period when the company's profits fell and in which the company's stock performed poorly.
2001 (Oct)	Disney acquires the Fox Family Channel for $5.3 billion, a price that is seen by many as far too high.
2002 (Aug)	During the previous five years, Disney performed worse than all but three of the 30 Dow stocks. Eisner's failures are becoming increasingly commonplace, they include the poor performance of the ABC network, the leading network, possessing an envied news organization and cutting-edge original programming such as *NYPD Blue* when it was purchased seven years earlier; a botched plan to build an American history theme park; the loss of millions of dollars on an expensive new California Adventure attraction at Disneyland, which failed to draw significant crowds; and a loss of more than $1 billion in an attempt to replicate Yahoo!'s portal with the go.com network.

2003	The Securities and Exchange Commission began investigating whether Disney failed adequately to disclose payments made by the company to directors and their family members in 2001.
2003 (April)	Disney sells Anaheim Angels baseball franchise.
2003 (May)	Disney announces plans to sell its badly performing Disney Stores.
2003 (Nov)	Roy E. Disney learns he will not be entered on the slate of directors for the next election (March 2004).
2003 (Nov)	Roy E. Disney resigns from the board and publishes his letter of resignation in which he claims that some of his associates have been required to report his conversations and activities back to Eisner, the company has lost its creative direction, Eisner is guilty of micro-management and has refused to establish a clear succession plan. He concludes by saying '... it is my sincere belief that it is you who should be leaving not me. Accordingly, I once again call for your resignation or retirement.'
2003 (Dec)	Stanley Gold resigns from the board and publishes his letter of resignation in which he criticizes the board for 'not actively engaging in serious discussions regarding the Company's flawed plans and management's unmet projections and unfilled promises'. He also questions the board's adoption of its Corporate Governance Guidelines which he describes as 'another example of this Board's commitment to image over substance'.
2004 (Jan)	Pixar, the company behind blockbusters such as *Finding Nemo* and *Monsters Inc*, ends its distribution deal with Disney following the failure of the two parties to negotiate a new distribution deal. The five movies created by Pixar for Disney have grossed more than $2.5 billion at the box office.
2004 (Feb)	Comcast announces a hostile bid for Disney ($54 billion in stock). The bid is rejected.
2004 (Feb)	Institutional Shareholder Services (Proxy Advisor) recommends shareholders to withhold their vote on the re-election of Michael Eisner.
2004 (Feb)	Glass Lewis & Co. (Proxy Advisor) recommends shareholders to withhold their vote on the re-election of Michael Eisner and George Mitchell.
2004 (March)	A five and half hour annual shareholder meeting sees 43% of shareholders withhold their vote for Eisner and 24% for Mitchell (final results including proxy voting show 45.37% and 25.69% respectively). Later in the day it is announced that Eisner will be replaced as Chairman of the Board by Mitchell.

2004 (April)   *Forbes* magazine names Eisner as one of the five worst CEOs in America (based on annualized total return of minus 5% and average compensation over the six year period of $121 170 940).

2004 (April)   Comcast drops bid for Disney (now worth $48 billion).

2004 (Sept)   Eisner announces that he will retire when his contract expires in September 2006. The two-year period of transition to a new CEO is heavily criticized for being too long, increasing uncertainty, handicapping the development of corporate strategy and creating a 'lame duck' CEO. The search for Eisner's successor will be led by Chairman George Mitchell, who will also be leaving the board in September 2006, who announced the company's intention to name the new CEO in June 2005, leading to uncertainty as to whether Eisner would leave the company earlier than planned. Mitchell also announced Robert Iger (a long-time executive at Capital Cities/ABC before its sale to Disney, who became Disney's President in 2000). This was Eisner's personal choice as his successor and the only internal candidate for the post.

Following initial suggestions that he would not rule out continuing to serve on the board and reclaiming the Chairmanship if asked to by the board after his 'retirement', Eisner said in a *Fortune* magazine interview that his assumption is that he would not continue on the board or as Chairman. Mitchell added that 'as far as the Board is concerned that is the end of it.'

The California Public Employees' Retirement System (one of the US's largest investors and a leading advocate for improved corporate governance) called for Eisner's resignation, saying in a press release that Eisner's 'continued presence on the board would prevent the company from the clean break that is needed to restore investor confidence.'

Upcoming   A lawsuit filed by shareholders against Disney is expected to be tried in Delaware's Court of Chancery in October 2004. The suit is challenging Ovitz's $140 million severance package. Eisner, and the directors of the company will defend against allegations that their mishandling of Mr Ovitz's hiring and termination cost shareholders millions.

The defendants will have to face claims they breached their duty to Disney in 1995 when Mr Ovitz negotiated the terms of his employment deal, and in 1996, when he was allowed to leave the company under a 'no-fault' clause.

Attorneys for shareholders argue that Mr Ovitz's performance was so poor in the president's slot that the company should have fired him for cause, a move that would have meant a much smaller severance package. Mr Ovitz's attorneys say the evidence will prove otherwise.

In a pre-trial hearing, the judge ruled that instead of resigning or being fired, Disney's president may have colluded with Mr Eisner to engineer a no-fault departure. In court papers, Mr Ovitz's attorneys have said the $140 million no-fault payment was justified and a bargain, compared with the $320 million in damages that Ovitz could have won had Disney fired him unfairly for cause. If shareholder allegations that Mr Ovitz lied and alienated Disney executives prove to be true, the judge may find that the no-fault termination was unjustified and that Disney's board is to blame for not firing him.

The Disney directors are already in a difficult position as the board never met to approve Ovitz's departure or the payment of his severance package and it is unclear whether the payment ever was properly authorized.

Upcoming Disney and Gold have promised to run an alternate slate of potential Disney directors if the board does not remove Eisner by the March 2005 annual meeting.

The above case covers many of the key issues in the present debate on corporate governance:

1 CEO rewards

2 Chairman/CEO split

3 Succession planning

4 Board independence

5 Effectiveness of the board

6 Communication among and to board members

7 Responsibilities of directors

8 Payments to directors' companies and family members

9 Ceremonial adoption of corporate governance guidelines

10 The role of financial institutions

The letter from Stanley Gold is below:

[Letterhead of Stanley P. Gold]

December 1, 2003

To the Board of Directors of the Walt Disney Company:

It is with regret that I resign effective immediately from the Board of Directors of the Walt Disney Company and second Roy Disney's call for the removal of Michael Eisner as Chairman and C.E.O. I am proud of my more than 15 years of service and my role in reshaping the Company in 1984 by bringing Frank Wells and Michael Eisner to the Company. I do, however, lament that my efforts over the past three years to implement needed changes has only succeeded in creating an insular Board of Directors serving as a bulwark to shield management from criticism and accountability. At this time, I believe there is little that I can achieve by working from within to refocus the Company. I hope that my resignation will serve as a catalyst for change at Disney.

The most recent evidence of the drive for insularity is reflected in the Governance Committee's determination that Roy Disney should no longer serve on the Board, ostensibly because Roy had surpassed the expected retirement age established by the Board's Corporate Governance Guidelines. In fact, these very rules regarding age, by their terms, only apply to non-management directors, not to Roy, who, as the Committee knows, has been deemed a management director. The Committee's decision and George Mitchell's defense of it yesterday are clearly disingenuous. The real reason for the Committee's action is that Roy has become more pointed and vocal in his criticism of Michael Eisner and this Board. This is yet another attempt by this Board to squelch dissent by hiding behind the veil of 'good governance.' What a curious result.

Roy has devoted a lifetime to Disney as both an employee and Director. He has served with renewed vigor during these times of malaise, disappointment and instability at the Company, trying to maintain the morale of employees, focusing on the magic that makes Disney special and attacking bonuses to the CEO and increased compensation for Board members while the Company falters and shareholder value erodes. He and his family have a very large financial stake in the Company. Unlike Messrs. Watson and Murphy who have asked to be replaced, Roy has sought even more involvement only to be told that his input in animation will continue to be minimized and that his role as a Director is no longer welcome. This Board has become an enabler to entrenched management and, in so doing, is not effectively discharging its duties to the shareholders. This conduct has resulted in yet another valuable human asset of the Company slipping away. Within the last year this Board will have managed to cull from its ranks Andrea Van de Kamp and now Roy, two of the staunchest critics of Michael Eisner and the Company's poor performance. I cannot sit idly by as this Board continues to ignore and disenfranchise those who raise questions about the performance of management.

As this Board knows, during my tenure I have tried to be an active, engaged Director. I believe a board should not merely rubber stamp decisions of senior management. I decided in August of 2002 that it was not enough just to express my views in the limited time set aside for our infrequent Board meetings. I therefore began a series of written communications to the Board regarding the Company, its management and the Board. I wrote to express my disagreement and growing concern with management, its policies and the effectiveness of the Board. I focused on the failed initiatives of the Company over the past five or six years and admonished the Board for not actively engaging in serious discussions regarding the Company's flawed plans and management's unmet projections and unfulfilled promises. In particular, I have urged the Board to concentrate on the Company's 'poor performance, lack of credibility and accountability and poor capital allocation.' In an effort to get Directors to seriously assess management's 5-year strategic plan (a plan that is only discussed with this Board, but not submitted for Board approval), I wrote to the Board to detail the Company's unsatisfactory financial performance for the past several years and to suggest a process, a so-called Diagnostic Review, designed to give the non-management directors the tools necessary to evaluate performance and establish a comprehensive framework and baseline from which the Board could be active partners in developing plans to maximize the value of Disney's existing assets and businesses. That approach was opposed by management and then, not surprisingly, rejected by the Board. The Board and its Chairman even criticized me for putting on paper these serious questions about fundamental matters.

I believe the Board's adoption of its Corporate Governance Guidelines was yet another example of this Board's commitment to image over substance. Among other things, those Guidelines were carefully crafted to stifle dissent while allowing those supportive of senior management to continue business as usual. This was apparent when the Board applied its Guidelines to conclude that I was not 'independent' despite the fact that I frequently challenged management at Board meetings and criticized both the Board's and the Company's performance. That decision was initially based on my daughter's employment in a non-executive position at Disney and, then, after that reason became insufficient under the new NYSE Governance Guidelines, because of my association with Roy. This resulted in my further isolation as I was no longer permitted to serve on the Governance and Nominating Committee or the Compensation Committee. On the other hand, John Bryson was deemed 'independent' and appointed Chairman of the Nominating and Governance Committee despite the fact that his wife is an executive officer at Lifetime Entertainment Television, a 50% owned subsidiary of Disney, where she earned in excess of $1 million in total compensation in fiscal 2001. In addition, Senator Mitchell was appointed Presiding Director, despite having been recently employed as a Company consultant and notwithstanding that the law firm of which he was chairman received in excess of $1 million for legal services on behalf of the Company in fiscal 2001.

At the time the Company's new Corporate Governance Guidelines were being considered, I also urged the Board to separate the positions of Chairman of the Board and CEO. This separation would empower the Board and help establish its independence and oversight role. Not only did the Board reject that initiative, the Board failed to give the newly established Presiding Director any real substantive powers.

Continuing through March of this year I wrote to express my concerns regarding the financial performance of the Company and the repeated failures of management to achieve its forecasts. I urged this Board to feel a sense of urgency in dealing with the issues of leadership, performance, operations and accountability. Those efforts failed. Instead, Mr. Eisner was awarded a bonus of $5 million in Disney shares by the Compensation Committee despite objections by Roy and me. I believe that bonuses for senior management must be tied to performance; by that measure, no bonus was warranted.

In a similar vein, I recently wrote to express my objection to the Compensation and Governance Committee's joint recommendations that fees paid to Disney Directors be increased dramatically, that stock grants to Directors be substituted for options (and thereby render meaningless the requirement that Directors own $100,000 in Disney shares) and that greater compensation be paid to the Presiding Director. Raises for the Disney Directors at this time are inappropriate based on my assessment of the Company's performance. I objected to the increase for the Presiding Director on the grounds that it did not reflect a reasonable payment for the only slightly increased duties. Finally, I could not make sense of a share ownership requirement for Directors that would be satisfied by a direct issuance from the Company at the same time Directors' cash compensation was being increased.

It is clear to me that this Board is unwilling to tackle the difficult issues I believe this Company continues to face – management failures and accountability for those failures, operational deficiencies, imprudent capital allocations, the cannibalization of certain Company icons for short-term gain, the enormous loss of creative talent over the last years, the absence of succession planning and the lack of strategic focus. Instead, the Board seems determined to devote its time and energies to adopting policies that focus not on substance, but on process and, in reality, only serve to muzzle and isolate those Directors who recognize that their role is to be active participants in shaping the Company and planning for executive succession. Further, this Board isolates those Directors who believe that Michael Eisner (when measured by the dismal results over the last 7 years) is not up to the challenge. Perhaps acting independently, from outside the Boardroom, not hamstrung by a recently enacted Board policy barring Board members from communicating with shareholders and the media, I can have greater success in shaping the policies, practices and operations of Disney than I had as a member of the Board.

In accordance with Item 6 of Form 8-K and Item 7 of Schedule 14A, I request that you disclose this letter and that you file a copy of this letter as an exhibit to a Company Form 8-K.

Very truly yours,

(Signed) Stanley P. Gold

The letter from Roy Edward Disney is as follows:

Letterhead of Roy Edward Disney

November 30, 2003

Dear Michael,

It is with deep sadness and regret that I send you this letter of resignation from the Walt Disney Company, both as Chairman of the Feature Animation Division and as Vice Chairman of the Board of Directors.

You well know that you and I have had serious differences of opinion about the direction and style of management in the Company in recent years, for whatever reason, you have driven a wedge between me and those I work with even to the extent of requiring some of your associates to report my conversations and activities back to you. I find this intolerable.

Finally, you discussed with the Nominating Committee of the Board of Directors its decision to leave my name off the slate of directors to be elected in the coming years, effectively muzzling my voice on the Board – much as you did with Andrea Van de Kamp last year.

Michael, I believe your conduct has resulted from my clear and unambiguous statements to you and to the Board of Directors that after 19 years at the helm you are no longer the best person to run the Walt Disney Company. You have a very successful first 10 plus years at the Company in partnership with Frank Wells, for which I salute you. But, since Frank's untimely death in 1994, the Company has lost its focus, its creative energy, and its heritage.

As I have said, and as Stanley Gold has documented in letters to you and other members of the Board, this Company, under your leadership, has failed during the last seven years in many ways:

1 The failure to bring back ABC Prime Time from the ratings abyss it has been in for years and your inability to program successfully the ABC Family Channel. Both of these failures have had, and I believe will continue to have, significant adverse impact on shareholder value.

2 Your considered micro-management of everyone around you with the resulting loss of morale throughout this Company.

3 The timidity of your investments in our theme park business. At Disney's California Adventure, Paris, and now in Hong Kong, you have tried to build parks 'on the cheap' and they show it and the attendance figures reflect it.

4 The perception by all our stakeholders – consumers, investors, employees, distributors and suppliers – that the Company is rapacious, soul-less, and always looking for the 'quick buck' rather than long-term value which is leading to a loss of public trust.

5 The creative brain drain of the last several years, which is real and continuing, and damages our Company with the loss of every talented employee.

6 Your failure to establish and build constructive relationships with creative partners, especially Pixar, Miramax, and cable companies distributing our products.

7 Your consistent refusal to establish a clear succession plan.

In conclusion, Michael, it is my sincere belief that it is you who should be leaving and not me. Accordingly, I once again call for your resignation or retirement. The Walt Disney Company deserve fresh, energetic leadership at this challenging time in its history just as it did in 1984 when I headed a restructuring that resulted in your recruitment to the company.

I have and will always have an enormous allegiance and respect for this Company, founded by my uncle Walt, and father, Roy, and to our faithful employees and loyal stockholders.

I don't know if you and other directors can comprehend how painful it is for me and the extended Disney family to arrive at this decision.

In accordance with Item 6 of Form 8-K and Item 7 of Schedule 14A, I request that you disclose this letter and that you file a copy of this letter as an exhibit to a Company Form 8-K.

With sincere regret,

(Signed) Roy Edward Disney

cc. Board of Directors

Case Questions

1 What went wrong on the Disney Board? Suggest ways you might avoid or alleviate these factors.

2 To what extent do you think any of the regulatory and advisory codes of conduct for Boards would have been useful in addressing Disney's problems of governance? Why would they have been useful (or why not)?

3 Examine the letters from Stanley Gold and Roy Disney. What do they reveal about board structures, processes and ethos?

4 What are the implications of poor governance (such as in the Disney case) for strategic thinking and acting in organizations?

Further reading and references

Aguilera, RV and Cuervo-Cazurra, A (2004) Codes of good governance worldwide: what is the trigger? *Organization Studies*, **25**, **3**, pp. 415–43.

Bank of England (1998) 'Composition of Company Boards', *Bank of England Quarterly Bulletin*, May, pp. 242–5.

Berle, AA and Means, GC (1932) *The Modern Corporation and Private Property*, Macmillan, New York.

Bernstein, PL (1996) *Against the Gods: The Remarkable Story of Risk*, Wiley, New York.

Bostock, R (1995) 'Company Responses to Cadbury', *Corporate Governance: An International Review*, **3**, **2**, April, pp. 72–7.

Cadbury Report (1992) *Committee on the Financial Aspects of Corporate Governance*, Moorgate, London.

Cadbury, A (2000) 'The Corporate Governance Agenda', *Corporate Governance: An International Review*, **8**, **1**, pp. 7–15.

CADS (1995) *The Financial Aspects of Corporate Governance: Compliance with the Code of Best Practice*, May, Stock Exchange, London.

Cassidy, DP (2000) 'Wither Corporate Governance in the 21st Century', *Corporate Governance: An International Review*, **8**, **4**, pp. 297–302.

Charkham, JP (1999) *Keeping Good Company: A Study of Corporate Governance in Five Countries* (2nd edition), Oxford University Press, Oxford.

Collins, JC and Porras, JI (2000) *Built to Last: Successful Habits of Visionary Companies*, Random House, New York.

Condon, D (2003) 'The Role of the Turnbull Guidelines and the Management and Identification of Risk in UK Multi-National Companies', PhD in progress Warwick Business School, UK.

Conger, JA, Lawler, EE and Finegold, DL (2001) *Corporate Boards: Strategy for Adding Value at the Top*, Jossey-Bass Pfeiffer, San Francisco and Wiley, Chichester.

Contardo, I and Wilson, DC (2001) 'The United Nations' Global Compact: A Report on Case Study Evidence', Research Paper, Warwick Business School, UK.

Conyon, MJ (1994) 'Corporate Governance Changes in UK Companies between 1988 and 1993', *Corporate Governance: An International Review*, **2**, **2**, pp. 97–109.

Conyon, MJ (1995) *Cadbury in the Boardroom*, in Arthur Anderson Corporate Register, Hemmington Scott, London.

Conyon, MJ and Mallin, C (1997) 'Women in the Boardroom: Evidence from Large UK Companies', *Corporate Governance: An International Review*, **5**, **3**, pp. 112–17.

Conyon, MJ and Murphy, KJ (2000) 'The Prince and the Pauper? CEO Pay in the US and UK', *The Economic Journal*, **110**, F640–F671.

Greenbury, R (1995) *Directors' Remuneration: Report of a Study Group Chaired by Sir Richard Greenbury*, Gee Publishing, London.

Hambrick, DC, Nadler, DA and Tushman, ML (1998) (eds) *Navigating Change: How CEOs, Top Teams and Boards Steer Transformation*, Harvard University Press, Boston, MA.

Hampel, R (1998) *Committee on Corporate Governance: Final Report*, Gee Publishing, London.

Hemscott (2003) 'The current population of non-executive directors', Hemscott Group Limited, London

Higgs, D (2003) Review of the Role and Effectiveness of Non-Executive Directors, Department of Trade and Industry, London. Printed in the United Kingdom by The Stationery Office 19585 809438 01/03.

Hutton, W (1996) *The State We're In*, Vintage Press, London.

Institute of Chartered Accountants (1999) 'Internal Control: Guidance for Directors on the Combined Code', ICA, London.

Institute of Chartered Accountants (1999) 'Implementing Turnbull: A Boardroom Brief', ICA Centre for Business Performance, London.

Kaplan, RS and Norton, DP (1992) The Balanced Scorcard: Measures that Drive Performance, *Harvard Business Review*, Jan/Feb.

Katzenbach, JR and Smith, DK (1992) *The Wisdom of Teams: Creating the High Performance Organization*, Harvard Business School Press, Boston, MA.

Keasey, K, Thompson, S and Wright, M (eds) (1997) *Corporate Governance: Economic Management and Financial Issues*, Oxford University Press, Oxford.

Kirkbride, J and Letza, S (2003) 'Establishing the boundaries of regulation in coporate governance: Is the UK moving toward a process of collibration?', *Business and Society Review*, **108**, **4**, pp. 463–85.

McNulty, T and Pettigrew, AM (1999) 'Strategists on the Board', *Organization Studies*, **20**, **1**, pp. 47–74.

Monks, RAG and Minnow, N (1992) *Power and Accountability: Restoring Balance of Power Between Corporations, Owners and Societies*, Harper Business, New York.

OECD (2004) *Principles of Corporate Governance* (available at www.OECD.org).

Pettigrew, AM (2004) 'Corporate Governance', *Distance Learning MBA Notes for Strategy and Practice*, Warwick Business School.

Pettigrew, AM and McNulty, T (1995) 'Power and Influence in and Around the Boardroom', *Human Relations*, **48**, **8**, pp. 845–73.

Pettigrew, AM and McNulty, T (1998) 'Sources and Uses of Power in the Boardroom', *European Journal of Work and Organizational Psychology*, **7**, **2**, pp. 197–214.

Ward, RD (2000) *The Boardroom Insider Guidebook*, New York, Wiley.

Part 5

Strategy and the future

Part contents

In this part you will find the following chapters:

Introduction

In Parts 2 and 3 we introduced the language of competitive advantage. Coupled with industry analysis (five forces analysis) and the value chain concept, this provided the kickstart for the modern theory of strategy and was the genesis of an entire academic and consulting industry devoted to the production of analysis-based concepts, frameworks and tools. The idea of strategy as the design of firm-specific market imperfections in the pursuit of profit gave rise to the language of *value*, for example value creation, value capture, value-based management, shareholder value, economic value added and so on. The term value encompasses multiple stakeholders: distinctive value for customers (remember we used the idea on consumer surplus in Chapter 6), superior profits for firms (we used the term rents in Chapter 5), and returns to the labour force in terms of higher rewards for higher productivity. If value is created by skilful strategic management then that value filters through to all the stakeholders and beyond (e.g. through taxes and through larger business volumes).

In Part 4 the focus shifted from the strategic positioning of the firm in relation to its competitors and its customers to those internal arrangements from which an external value-creating position derives. From this perspective we see the roots of value lie within the organization, through its structure, through its management processes and decision rules, through its governance arrangements, and by virtue of its ability to adapt, to change itself, and sometimes to transform itself. All these internal foundation stones rest on the ability of its people to manage strategically so as to achieve long-term objectives. In this part we also created an important counterbalance to the simple idea of value in the earlier sections. Here we looked at risk and uncertainty leading us to the idea of risk-return trade-offs – a concept central to strategy and especially the evaluation of alternative strategies. Along with this we used the idea of scenario planning as a way of creating and understanding strategic options that can then be evaluated in a risk-return way.

From the building blocks in these earlier parts we can see the idea of value and value-based management taking a central role in strategic thinking. In Part 5 we extend our strategy discourse into a more holistic view of how value creation and capture takes place. There is an entire literature on the topic of value-based management and its many variants. The purpose of this discussion is to give this literature a foundation in strategic management thinking. One variant is the idea of *value disciplines* (Treacy and Wiersema 1994).[1] These disciplines are operational excellence, product leadership and customer intimacy. Some prestigious public awards for management excellence focus more on internal management processes. The Baldridge Award, which is highly respected in the USA, is a good example. This identifies seven arenas of management activity that are used to assess the management system and its capability for excellence. These arenas are leadership; strategic planning; customer and market focus; measurement, analysis and knowledge management; human resource focus; process management; and business results. These approaches underline the point that excellence and value creation are a joint product of external positioning and internal management processes. Management is the process, and positioning is the external manifestation of it.

In this part we take up three of these arenas as themes because they are particularly close to the core of strategic management thinking. These are (i) performance assessment; (ii) organizational knowledge, learning and value innovation; and (iii) total quality management and customer value. The assessment of *strategic* performance is central to any strategy discussion. Innovation and learning has been the dynamic behind economic growth and the

---

[1]   Treacy, M. and Wiersema, F. (1994) *Discipline of Market Leaders*, Addison Wesley.

stock market value of companies. Total quality management has been the major innovation that has transformed the thinking of companies since the traumas of the 1970s.

Chapter 18 is concerned with analysing and measuring strategic performance. This is not a replay of the financial calculus of shareholder value of the accounting detail of return on investment. Nor is it a wider review of the social responsibility of companies, their corporate citizenship or their ethical standards. Both of these are dealt with in other textbooks. This chapter is about how to distinguish *strategic* performance from conventionally measured financial performance. To do this we use the balanced scorecard approach and we build on the business model approach that was introduced in Chapter 6.

Chapter 19 is about the nature of innovation and technological change. We introduced the idea of creative destruction back in Chapter 8. This chapter builds on that and discusses the effects of disruptive technologies and the dilemmas that face innovators (should we or should we not cannibalize our existing business?). The chapter develops a knowledge-based view of strategy that enables us to discuss ways of fostering organizational commitment to innovation and how to structure organizations so as achieve growth through innovation.

Chapter 20 builds on the writings on operational excellence, much of which is in the operations management area. Much of this literature is about the pursuit of excellence in every corner of the firm's operations. But a strong element of it is concerned with the nature of *quality* and *quality management*. We focus here on the implications of quality for the process of strategic management and the way this is driven by customer perceptions of value. We see from the examples how the rethinking of supply chain and value chain concepts from a total quality perspective actually enables firms to compete differently and often to out-compete those with conventional approaches.

Chapter 18

Analysing and measuring strategic performance

While the principle that the fundamental objective of the business corporation is to increase the value of its shareholders' investment is widely accepted, there is substantially less agreement about how this is accomplished. (Rappaport, 1986, p.1)

Introduction

The concept of strategic performance and its measurement is a central issue in the field of strategic management. In earlier sections of this book, performance constructs such as a 'business model' (Chapter 6), managing a business for value (Chapter 7) and the **balanced scorecard** (Chapters 5 and 17) illustrate the fundamental importance of analysing the performance and health of

Chapter contents

the firm. And, our organizing framework – the systemic model (*see* Figure 1.6) – shows that performance feedback provides the framework within which organizational renewal and strategic reorientation take place.

In this chapter, we note that firms have a range of targets or goals with profit maximization or shareholder value maximization often stated as one of the key strategic objectives. We will also discuss the following issues about performance metrics:

- The idea of multiple measures of performances, e.g. accounting-based, market-based, etc.

- The concepts of economic value and, in particular, 'shareholder value' and 'economic value added'.

- An examination of the 'value-based' management approach.

- An analysis of the 'balanced scorecard' approach to performance measurement, with its focus on key performance indicators to address the multiple goals and foci of the business (e.g. financial, marketing, internal process and learning goals).

In summary, organizations and managers must link their choice of performance measures and key performance indicators with the overall strategy and any likely re-evaluation of strategic priorities. Appropriate and robust performance metrics allow managers to evaluate strategic success and 'fine tune' the **business model** to achieve corporate goals and targets.

18.1 **The domain of business performance**

Venkatraman and Ramanujam (1986) present a very useful conceptualization to explain the domain of business performance. This is shown in Figure 18.1. We shall use this as an organizing structure for this chapter.

In this diagram, three perspectives of performance are offered, namely, financial performance, operations performance and organizational effectiveness. We will discuss each briefly in turn.

Financial measures of performance

The narrowest view of performance (represented by the inner circle) focuses on *financial performance* and argues that well-crafted strategy pursues primarily profitability goals, well examined in the accounting literature, such as return on investment, return on equity or earnings per share. This approach assumes the dominance of financial goals and associated measures, whether they are accounting based or financial-market based.

Operational measures of performance

Operational performance indicators (the middle ring of the diagram) examine a range of internal performance factors which might lead to success for the company and its set of

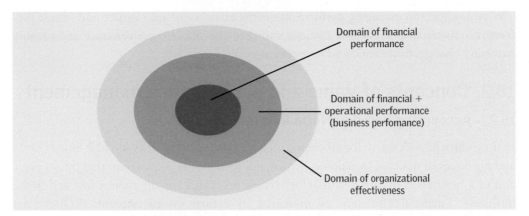

Figure 18.1 Domain of business performance
Source: Venkatraman and Ramanujam, 1986, p. 803.

businesses. These include market position indicators such as the absolute level or growth rate of sales, market share (as a percentage of sales) and the rate of new product introductions. Other measures might involve a focus on efficiency and include value added in manufacturing, product quality and other indicators of technological efficiency (e.g. potential economies of scale and scope).

Measures of organizational effectiveness

Beyond economic and operational performance fundamentals, the selection of performance factors that should be monitored and benchmarked must respond to the strategic goals of the entire firm (the outer ring of the figure), and their often multiple and conflicting nature (Cameron and Whetten 1983). Management's challenge, therefore, is to build systemic relationships with all stakeholders and constituents of the firm from shareholders, suppliers and employees through to consumers, in order to build value throughout the organization. For example, they might measure such human-resource indicators as employee job satisfaction and labour turnover and examine supply-chain relationships in order to build and create long-term strategic knowledge and value for the organization.

In summary, value creation in performance terms is clearly the central task and purpose of senior management. It means that managing performance outputs rather than resource inputs is an imperative and requires a perspective that encompasses a systemic and dynamic understanding of performance. In other words, if performance is sound then it can be assumed that there is a clear 'fit' between the elements of strategy (e.g. competition, capabilities, etc.) and organizational success. If, on the other hand, there is evidence of performance weaknesses, these may indicate that there are problems in the strategic framework, involving perhaps a weak competitive strategy or a shortfall in organizational core competences and capabilities.

What is critical in managing performance is the existence of appropriate and robust performance metrics, which enable managers to predict economic performance and identify necessary changes in strategic and operational positioning.

18.2 Concepts of value and performance management

18.2.1 Accounting-based performance metrics

In the industrial era's search for efficiency, managerial thinkers such as Alfred P. Sloan (1963) and his financial director, Donaldson Brown, put forward the proposition that the strategic aim of a business is to earn a satisfactory return on capital (or the money invested in the business). Financial efficiency as measured by **return on investment** (ROI = net income/capital investment) became perhaps the most commonly used of the measures of financial position alongside **return on equity** (ROE = net income/shareholders' equity), **return on sales** (ROS = net income/sales revenue) and **return on assets** (ROA = net income/assets employed in business). The financial press and corporate analysts' reports also placed great emphasis on measures of **earnings per share** (EPS = net income/number of shares outstanding) and **price/earnings ratios** (P/E = ratio of stock price/net income) as a scorecard of corporate performances.

Managers and analysts use accounting earnings and accounting profits as a benchmark because financial accounts are readily available and the measures themselves are easy to calculate. Yet, according to Doyle (2000, pp. 26–7), the measurement of accounting earnings can be arbitrary and subjective and easily manipulated by management (*see* also Smith 1992). Accounting profits also exclude investments, ignore the time value of money (*see* Rappaport 1986) and produce a focus on short-term results. Indeed, many of these criticisms stress the fact that managers may uncritically focus on accounting numbers without recognizing the judgements, conventions and realities involved in the construction of those numbers.

Writers, such as Rappaport (1986) in particular, demonstrate the detailed shortcomings of accounting numbers and advance the concept of shareholder value creation as the new standard for business performance. Indeed, Rappaport points out that research confirms that satisfactory earnings growth (for example, growth in EPS) does not necessarily lead to a concomitant increase in the market value of the company's shares.

Hayes and Abernathy (1980) also point out the shortcomings of management who wrongly assume that by improving ROI, ROE, etc., consequent improvements in share price must necessarily follow. Indeed, they criticize ROI for helping to hasten the process of 'managing our way to economic decline'. They point out that ROE, with its short-term emphasis, can lead to a decline in investments of a long-term character such as those in innovations, which provide the growth paths and long-term strategic direction for many organizations.

Quite apart from the accounting judgements necessary to measure accounting earnings, there are a similar set of problems in measuring assets. Typically, financial accounts recognize and measure physical assets but ignore the intangible assets increasingly developed by knowledge-based companies, e.g. patents, R&D, new technologies, brands and customer loyalty. With the wide growth of knowledge-based companies in IT, biotechnology, pharmaceuticals etc., measures of ROA will be over-recorded with such companies, since knowledge assets will be under-recorded. There will also probably be similar over-recording for mature manufacturing companies that have gradually depreciated their assets over time, making the book value of the assets quite small in the denominator of the ROA measure. Such anomalies in the measurement of ROA, therefore, suggest that comparing the financial performance of companies in the FTSE (*Financial Times* Share Exchange), for example, using ROA would provide a very questionable measure of comparative performance. Indeed, there may be an inverse relationship between ROA performance and improvements in share price performance.

In summary, writers such as Rappaport and others hastened the value creation trend in measures of financial performance.

18.2.2 Economic value added (EVA) and financial performance

Consultants such as Stern Stewart (1996) promoted the movement from a focus on accounting profit to economic profit, or economic rent as exemplified in our earlier discussion of the resource-based view (RBV), (*see* Chapter 7). Indeed, Kay (1993) defines added value as the difference between the value of a firm's output and the cost of the firm's inputs. Stern Stewart define an essentially similar concept, which they call **economic value added** (EVA). They define EVA as net operating profit after tax minus the weighted average cost of capital. The resulting value of EVA can then be interpreted as a measure of the strategic value of the business and a useful metric for judging ongoing performance. In consequence, the EVA approach argues that a firm and its set of businesses are creating value when they earn returns in excess of the firm's weighted average cost of capital – a position which is consistent with an objective of maximizing shareholder value. However, EVA links value creation to current operating performance, i.e. it is a single-period measure of value creation, developed from balance sheet measures, and provides a tight financial discipline for a company to address whether it is adding value for shareholders.

It is important to recognize that measures such as 'economic profit' or EVA help firms identify the value for the business. However, the main problem with the 'economic profit' metrics is that they do not help to address the issues associated with future investments such as new product development, whose time period, future earnings and capital requirements are somewhat uncertain and unpredictable. In this situation, the **shareholder value approach** (SVA), with the emphasis on discounted cash flow, and the shareholder value principle popularized by Rappaport (1986) is the more appropriate methodology. This is discussed in more detail in the next section.

Case box: **Freeserve's business model**

Freeserve described their mission in their flotation prospectus as being: 'to become the UK's preferred internet portal by delivering both free internet access and an integrated offering of UK focussed content, e-commerce and community'.[1]

Freeserve believed when they launched that they could improve on the fundamental Internet business model with their 'free access' approach. In their presentation to investors at the time of flotation they describe the traditional business model with the diagram below:

The Traditional Internet Business Model[2]

They recognized income as being gained either as an ISP through subscriptions or as a portal through advertising, sponsorship and commission from commerce.

They positioned themselves to provide their customers with both of these services:

♦ a dial-up mechanism to access the internet, in which they compete with other ISPs such as AOL and BT; and

♦ an internet portal which offers content,

Freeserve's 'improved' Business Model

[1] Freeserve. The Freeserve Solution. Freeserve Mini Prospectus (12/7/99), p. 4.

[2] Freeserve. Freeserve Investor Presentation (1999) URL: http://www.aboutfreeserve.com/investor/presentations/index.html

tailored web services and a virtual marketplace for consumers to buy and sell products or services, in which they compete with the likes of AOL, Yahoo!, Microsoft, Lycos, etc.

They proposed to change the business model described above profoundly by not charging users for connect time to their ISP. They went on, in the same presentation to investors, to describe their improved business model with the diagram on p. 676.

Their belief was that by offering free access to the internet they would corner the market in people dialing-up to get online. Some income would be generated by agreements with the telephone companies to split the revenue from the telephone call charges, but more importantly, those people would, by default, come to the Freeserve portal first. If the Freeserve portal was good enough, offering sufficient flexibility and a wide range of niche areas, the user would stay with Freeserve, access the internet through its pages and its search engine, read its adverts and buy goods through its sponsors. In that way, the free ISP would be a loss leader to get people into the portal, which would generate the income.

Questions for discussion

1   Examine the Freeserve business model using the Yip framework in Figure 18.2. What, if anything, is missing from Freeserve's model?

2   Can you describe how Freeserve proposes to generate cash flows and profits?

3   What risks does its business model identify?

18.2.3 The shareholder value approach (SVA)

The clear operating principle underlying the SVA is that the company's dominant strategic goal is to maximize its shareholder wealth. In essence, this means that corporate and business strategies should focus on the economic gains they produce for shareholders, i.e. in terms of maximizing the value of their shares through dividend policies and share price rises.

Rappaport (1986) then addresses the issues of how to value the company's shares and advances the view that share prices should be calculated by evaluating expectations of the cash flows that will arise from the company's corporate and business strategies over time. SVA, then, measures the total value of the corporate strategy by discounting these cash flow predictions to allow for the time value of money and risk. Any introductory textbook (e.g. Brealey and Myers (2002)) explains clearly the discounted cash flow (DCF) approach and it has been widely used for many years in practice, for example, to evaluate the worth of alternative capital projects or capital investments (*see* also Chapter 14 in this book). However, it is only over the last fifteen years or so, through Rappaport's influence, that the focus of DCF has switched to shareholder value and the evaluation of strategic planning and management strategies. Ultimately, the SVA calculates an NPV (**net present value**) for each alternative strategy option available to the company, using the company's weighted average cost of capital as the discount rate. That strategy that has the highest NPV of all the options is generally selected as the preferred alternative.

It is important to stress that SVA is not simply a financial approach or a financial technique. It requires all of the corporate knowledge, core capabilities and strategy development processes that have been discussed in this book for the senior managers to outline a viable series of strategic options before putting them under the 'financial' microscope of the SVA.

Case box: Punch Taverns

Punch Taverns is a public limited company which owns about 7400 pubs across the UK. The company has agreements with retailers, who are self-employed and operate a retail business within our pub. The company does not directly manage the retail business in the pubs.

The agreements are generally leases (10 to 25-year agreements assignable after two years and with full repairing liability), or tenancies (non-assignable non-repairing agreements of up to 6 years). Lease agreements generally apply in bigger outlets. The primary lease offer currently is the Punch Growth Lease (PGL). Other short-term agreements exist for temporary situations (notably the tenancy at will – TAW). We also have a legacy of older agreements.

Under all agreements the retailer pays a rent based on a share of the estimated fair maintainable profitability of the pub. The rent is usually index-linked and subject to upward-only rent reviews (after 5 years in leased pubs).

The retailer is also required to buy certain products from the company ('the tie'). In general the tie covers all beer and lager products (sometimes with the exception of one guest ale). Depending on the agreement it may also cover cider, soft drinks, and flavoured alcoholic beverages.

The gross price charged for products is the brewer's or manufacturer's national wholesale price. Discounts are offered off invoice in the Growth Lease. In certain other agreements we offer a retrospective volume target based discount incentive scheme.

In some agreements the company agrees to manage the machine income opportunity in the pub and shares the net income, usually 50:50, with the retailer. The company also receives a rebate from machine suppliers where their machines are sited in our pubs.

The agreements provide a low cost entry into running a business with professional support. We expect adherence to the terms of the agreement, but we are prepared to consider special situations.

The key operational output is business planning, with the objective of helping the retailer to build a better business. The main activities that drive success are:

◆ Recruiting and training the right retailer.

- Agreeing the right business lease, and ensuring adherence to this lease.
- Developing the pub to give the right consumer offer, often using shared investment with the retailer.

Fundamentally, the two key company objectives are to maximize the profitability of each pub, and to optimize the company's share of that profit.

The company has organized support functions to assist the retailer to build his business. Support activities range from essential processes (order taking, debt collection), through care and maintenance (business manager support, customer administration) to development (estate management and investment). In addition the company maintains an infrastructure covering finance, systems, purchasing, HR etc.

A third key company objective is to expand the estate by acquiring more pubs. This can be successful as the company is able to add value to a pub through its purchasing power and support services, thereby earning a good return on investment.

The profitability of the company is driven by two main income streams of beer margin and rent. Machine income and non-beer margin are important growth areas, but of smaller scale. Overhead costs are relatively low and with fairly stable income streams the company has very low operational gearing risk, and is very cash generative.

The company is financed by debt and equity, having floated on the London Stock Exchange in May 2002, and ranked within the UK FTSE 250. Debt comprises some 70% of enterprise value, relatively high but secure due to the nature of the income model. The main debt is securitized in two pub groupings, known as security nets, with further debt capacity for new acquisitions. The business is asset rich, with pub values being comparable to the enterprise value of the company.

Questions for discussion

1 Rewrite the Punch Tavern's business model using the Yip framework in Figure 18.2. What, if anything, is missing from the Punch model?

2 Can you describe how Punch Taverns proposes to generate cash flows? Profits?

3 What risks does its business model identify?

4 Compare the Freeserve and Punch Tavern's approaches to describing and presenting their business models. Which do you prefer? Why?

First and foremost, therefore, the senior managers must develop their own *business model* (*see* the discussion in Chapter 6 and particularly Yip 2004), which is essentially a 'theory' about how their particular business system (i.e. the total corporate set of businesses) operates. Such a model is a set of assumptions about the processes and structures necessary for the business to achieve competitive success. It involves a clear outline of how the whole business system will work and provides full details about the economic and business relationships that must be in place for the corporate strategy to work in the competitive marketplace. As such, it will include many of the strategic system features (*see* Figure 1.6) already discussed in this book: an environmental and competitive model; a capability (core competence) framework; a marketing/consumer model; an operations model and an overall organizational structure and systems model which links people, incentive systems, vision, leadership etc. with the economic relationships necessary for effective strategy implementation. In practice[1] a business model can be articulated in terms of detailed plans and budgets that provide guidance to managers relating to their operational responsibilities. The logic that drives plans and budgets lies within the business model. The business model itself is the mechanism through which a business intends to generate revenue and profits.

Yip (2004, p. 20) identifies the following elements in his conceptualization of a 'business model', as shown in Figure 18.2:

- Value proposition (i.e. the strategic concept)
- Nature of inputs
- How to transform inputs (including technology)
- Nature of outputs
- Vertical scope
- Horizontal scope
- Geographic scope
- Nature of customers
- How to organize

What Yip's business model does is to articulate the logic of the intended strategy in terms of the key strategic choices and the specific operations that have to take place. With this detailed plan the consequences for cash flows can be determined and the link between (intended) strategy and (expected) performance can be established. In many ways this is simply a restyled value chain – an activity map on to which can be placed assets, and revenues and costs. The value chain reflects the firm's strategic choices – the business model goes one step further in making the link to cash flows.

Yip demonstrates the application of his business model using a range of examples including easyGroup's core value proposition of bringing cheap and efficient services (airlines, rent-a-car, etc.) to the mass market. Chapter 6 shows two examples, the 2G (mobile telephony) model (Figure 6.27), and a model of a leasing business at a London-based bank (Figure 6.28).

---

[1] See Chapters 2 and 6 for further discussion.

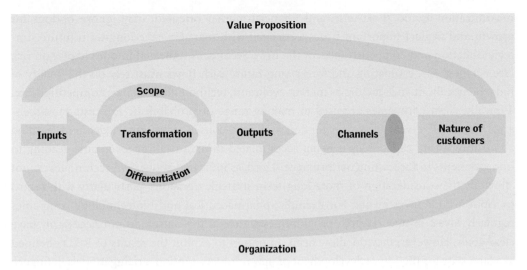

Figure 18.2 Elements of a business model
Source: Yip, 2004.

Assuming, then, that a sound 'business model' is developed, the elements and steps involved in the SVA for valuing strategies are:

1   Clear identification of the 'business model', including the organization value drivers (e.g. capabilities), operational drivers (including supply chain management), marketing drivers (including brands, image, loyalty, etc.) and financial drivers (including cash flows, financial strength, risk profile, etc.).

2   Derivation from the 'business model' of the set of viable strategic options for the company in the competitive marketplace.

3   Evaluation and estimation of the cash flow profiles associated with each strategic option.

4   Estimation of the company's cost of capital (weighted average cost of capital) in view of the company's current and future projected investments (e.g. debt and loan structure implications).

5   Discounting the cash flow profiles for each strategic option (using the weighted average cost of capital) and calculating a net present value for each option.

6   Choosing the strategic option/alternative with the highest net present value.

In summary, therefore, the highest NPV strategy ensures that the option chosen maximizes firm value from the perspective of shareholders and provides the positive net cash flow to satisfy the claims of other stakeholders/constituents in the business system.

However, as with all such 'financially oriented' approaches, there are limitations and issues involved in its application. First, an objective of shareholder value maximization is not always understood by employees and senior managers who feel that the objective of share maximization is too short-term and financial-market oriented, may ignore options for growth and neglect important issues associated with managing the long-term future strategic direction and competitiveness of the firm. Second, as indicated in our chapter on risk (*see* Chapter 14), estimating and forecasting future cash flows must rely on the quality of judgements about such factors as market evolution, technological change, competition, etc. Typically, most companies are used to making range or probabilistic forecasts (and scenarios) over a five-year planning horizon and, as a consequence, knowledge and learning about forecasting capabilities is being accumulated in organizations over time, leading to improvements in forecasting performance. Third, as indicated above, SVA techniques do not allow for the consideration of more long-term strategic decisions, particularly with regard to 'option-type' investments. For example, pharmaceutical and biotechnology companies regularly invest in new research programmes which, at the outset, do not necessarily have clear goals. However, they do allow firms an option to exploit the results of R&D obtained at a later date for the future development of new products. Option-pricing models in finance such as the Black-Scholes model (see Brealey and Myers, 2002) provide a basis for attacking this problem and writers in the strategy field such as Bowman and Hurry (1993) have suggested adaptations to strategy valuation processes using option-type models.

Overall, therefore, the evolution of performance measurement techniques based on 'economic profit' such as EVA and more systemic 'value-based' management techniques as SVA have usefully linked strategy to the finance literature and have provided vehicles for companies to both understand the 'business models' and drivers underlying shareholder value and develop the capability to identify further strategic options and alternatives to create value for the business.

The 'balanced scorecard' approach is a logical development of EVA and SVA techniques, and provides a broader perspective and framework for managers to use in determining which key performance indicators should be used to monitor and, subsequently, drive organizational strategy.

18.2.4 The balanced scorecard concept: managing for value

We introduced the idea of the balanced scorecard in Chapter 5 and showed an example in Figure 5.12. The context for this in Chapter 5 was to show how progress against objectives might be assessed and how the scorecard approach enables managers to relate progress to the concepts of competitive strategy and to the content of a strategic plan.

The balanced scorecard concept developed by Kaplan and Norton (1992) is a clear example of how **value-based management** approaches have become much more than a toolkit of financial techniques to apply to critical business issues. The scorecard concept provides insight into the linkages between the *strategic value drivers* (e.g. operational efficiency at Toyota, high-quality production engineering and engine design at Honda) and *strategic outcomes*, and forces senior managers to question both the soundness of the overall corporate strategy and the potential need to reorient the strategy towards an alternative set of strategic priorities.

Case box: The National Model Agency

Sales Memorandum

Confidentially offered for sale

The National Model Agency
Profits available to the owners
Exceed £176,000 per annum
Asking Price
£800,000
Business profile

This model and promotional agency provides more services for clients and models than either the high profile London based agencies, which act for a limited number of big name professional models or the provincial agents who serve small local communities. The difference being that none of these traditional agencies have the number of models or geographical coverage that this successful national agency has to offer, by way of choice and a full United Kingdom wide promotion campaign.

The National agency represents professional and amateur models regardless of race, gender, ethnic or national origins, marital status, sexuality, education, age, physical impairment, religion or belief, language, appearance or class. The agency offers access to the world of fashion, film, television and photography.

Several thousand prospective models approach the agency each month.

Online use of the unique bespoke software enables their national database of more than eighteen thousand contracted models to be searched precisely and accurately for clients' requirements producing for them comprehensive data including instant photographic images.

Clients who employ the agency can call for a choice of models at very short notice, for various work fields including advertising, promotions, television, film, fashion, photographic, catalogue, and media and see a national selection immediately downloaded from their PC.

Commercial photographic shoots, television commercials, and magazine layouts that are being shot every day used to expect expensive, time-consuming postal portfolios to be sent by small inefficient agencies. Now these same clients, casting directors, and magazine editors can look at the models portfolio on the web from the computer on their desk and find the model they require in minutes, versus several days or weeks!

The agency avoids so-called glamour work.

The length of management contract between each model and this agency is one to three years.

Ancillary services to models include photographic shoots, training courses, videos, books and merchandise together with access to over 400 professional United Kingdom Master photographers.

As a 'Client focused' agency the agency has achieved excellence in understanding and responding to the demands of new and existing clients, thus generating maximum satisfaction and profitability.

This agency has a strong ability to identify trends and establish itself in new markets thereby exploiting the most profitable opportunities. This has led to heavy investment in a sophisticated computer structure and an increasing focus in establishing a significant Internet presence.

The ten thousand quarterly newsletter and merchandising range provide a potentially strong marketing platform.

The agency is now poised for global development with a licensed franchised system ability to encompass European and Intercontinental business.

Types of Clients

Clients represent a wide variety of organizations:

- Retailers
- Restaurants
- Hospitals
- Religious organizations
- Universities
- Manufacturing firms
- Film & Video producers
- Television Companies
- Racecourses
- Motor Racing Groups
- Luxury Hotel Groups
- Hairdressers
- Drinks Companies
- Dairy Companies
- Newspapers
- Car Rental
- Theatres
- Publishing Houses
- Car Manufacturers
- Building Societies
- Hospital
- Brewers
- City Councils
- ... and others.

Financial information

The business and property are being offered for sale on a going concern basis.

All financial discussions will take place directly between the vendors and interested party.

Market and competitors

There is no known direct national competitor.

Management and staff

The operation is fully managed with guidance provided by the principals.

Future prospects

The media requirement for the human image for advertising and promotion remains almost insatiable.

> The business model could grow to a worldwide operation should the new owners have the drive and ability to manage an operation of this size.
>
> **Reason for sale**
>
> The owners feel the business is reaching the optimum size for their management ability.
>
>
> ## Questions for discussion
>
> The above is a notice advertising the sale of the National Model Agency.
>
> 1 From the content of this notice for sale, identify the business model that is in place.
>
> 2 Also how would you assess the performance of the National Model Agency from this data?
>
> 3 If you were selling a company of this kind, how much information would you give about the underlying business model and the historic performance of the company?

The balanced scorecard allows managers to examine each business and the overall corporate vision and strategy through four perspectives or lenses: financial, customer, internal, and innovation and learning. Figure 18.3 shows the logic of the approach.

What the basic concept of a balanced scorecard provides is a disciplined framework through which to impose a series of questions (Kaplan and Norton, 1992, p. 22) that should be addressed by the company and its senior managers:

♦ *How do we look to shareholders?* (The financial lens): Metrics in this area encompass the SVA and the EVA approach, as well as accounting-based measures of performance.

♦ *How do customers see us?* (The customer lens): Metrics in this area include market share, brand image and customer satisfaction.

♦ *What must we excel at?* (The internal lens): The issues in this area involve the internal business processes necessary to develop a successful strategy. Metrics would include supply-chain processes, quality etc.

♦ *How can we continue to improve and create value?* (The innovation and learning lens): Metrics in this area address the firm's ability to innovate and develop new capabilities through new product growth and development and improved R&D processes.

Doyle (2000, pp. 152–4) provides a basic and more extended checklist of potential measures or **key performance indicators** (KPIs) for each of these lenses. Broadly, these comprise:

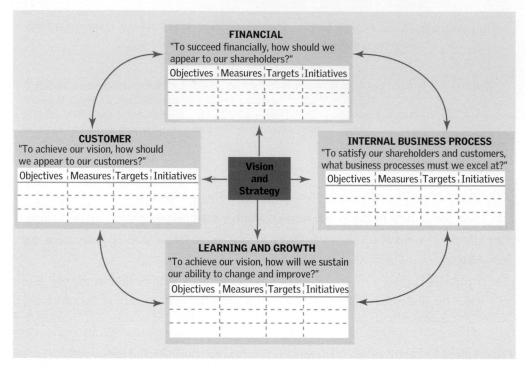

Figure 18.3 Translating vision and strategy: four perspectives
Source: Kaplan, RS and Norton, DP (1996) 'Linking the balanced scorecard to strategy', *California Management Review*, Fall, 39, 1, p. 54.

- **Financial lens measures**
  - Return on capital employed
  - Operating margins
  - Economic value added
  - Cash flow
  - Sales growth

- **Consumer lens measures**
  - Market share
  - Brand image and awareness
  - Customer satisfaction
  - Customer relations
  - Customer acquisition

- **Internal lens measures**
  - Percentage of sales from new products
  - Manufacturing cost
  - Manufacturing cycle time

- ◆ Inventory management
- ◆ Quality indices
- ◆ Supply chain management processes
- ◆ **Innovation and learning lens measures**
  - ◆ New product development capabilities
  - ◆ R&D core competences
  - ◆ Technological capabilities
  - ◆ Human resource development and capabilities
  - ◆ Improved manufacturing and business processes
  - ◆ Improved sales methods and techniques

Checklists of measures, however, beg the question of what the best set of measures or key performance indicators (KPIs) are for any company. Fundamentally, we argue that important KPIs must link to the company's strategy and vision and track/monitor the key elements of that strategy. They must also take account of any changes in the broader economic and technological environment the company faces. In essence, the KPIs chosen should be regarded as a future-oriented set of metrics that will allow the company to benchmark and monitor the economic and competitive outcomes and examine the stability of the firm's strategy (the long-term perspective) and operations (the short-term perspective).

These KPIs relate back to the discussions in earlier chapters. Whereas KPIs are a manifestation of performance that we seek to measure, the drivers of KPIs are deep within the firm and within the logic of the strategy analysis in Part 3 and within the process analysis of Part 4. Performance analysis and the analysis of progress against strategic milestones was introduced in Chapter 5. The idea of rents and 'superprofits' as goals for strategy making stems for the economic analysis of markets that was introduced in Chapter 3. These discussions provide essential background for the very financially oriented KPIs in the financial lens measures. The trade-off between long- and short-term profits (the time horizon problem) is unresolved by any of these measures. The correct way to account for long-lived assets is captured to some degree by EVA measures.

The customer lens relates to the ideas that were germinated in Chapters 5 and 6 and discussed explicitly in Chapter 7. **Key success factors** (KSFs) and KPIs can be confused. KSFs are often portrayed as intuitive in their conception but Chapter 7 shows how they derive from what customers want (analysis of demand; see Chapter 3 for a close discussion of this) and from how to beat competitors (analysis of competition). Thus, KSFs are manifestations of strategic choice and should reflect the intended competitive advantages. They should therefore be drivers of KPIs and high scores on KPIs would be an indication that the KSFs are in place as intended. Furthermore, Chapter 7 shows a framework for analysing value (*see* Figure 7.12). This captures elements of customer value and shows some examples of KPIs of customer value. It also captures elements of costs and efficiency inherent in the strategy (the internal lens measures). Chapter 20 goes further into the internal process characteristics of the firm in terms of total quality management and supply chain management and these also contribute to the internal lens.

The innovation and learning lens presents many complexities, largely because the issues involved are process-sensitive and are both subtle and complex. The usual KPIs are relatively crude and often do not do justice to the underlying strategic choices. Chapter 16 introduced learning as an organizational phenomenon. Here the idea of the learning pyramid and its four levels of activity (from individual, to one-to-one, to group, to organization) in Figure 16.1 and the framework for organizational learning in Figure 16.2 provide important perspectives that allow general managers and strategists to 'unpack' the KPIs shown in this lens. Chapter 19 takes further the discussion on knowledge and learning. This is driven from the resource-based view (Chapter 7) and provides a strong, albeit subjective, framework for generating useful KPIs for the innovation and learning lens.

The strength of the balanced scorecard approach is its inclusivity of the range of strategy concepts and the way of linking them together in a single map (Figure 18.4). There is strength also in the way in which measurable KPIs are used to ground the map in reality and to make it an operational tool for managers. But this is also its weakness. Not all elements of competitive strategy are easy to measure, although many firms have strategic planning

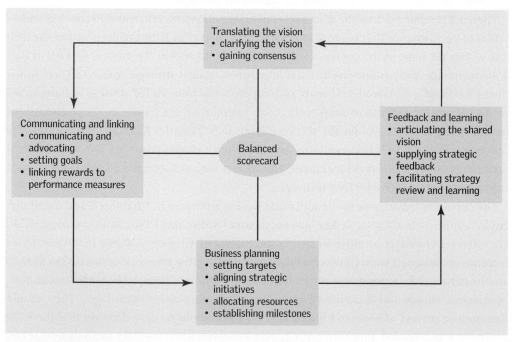

Figure 18.4 The balanced scorecard as a strategic management system
Source: Kaplan, RS and Norton, DP (1996) 'Using the balanced scorecard as a strategic management system', *Harvard Business Review*, Jan/Feb.

processes that make a heroic attempt to do this. More difficult is the area of management process which, as we have seen in Part 4, provides an essential grounding for strategy analysis decisions. Without good or appropriate process, good decisions cannot be made – decisions do not make themselves. The balanced scorecard is relatively silent on matters of process. The balanced scorecard should really be seen as a designed set of KPIs that provide early warning indicators rather than as a diagnostic system that indicates the nature of problems and the sources of them. This is a controversial area that will benefit from progress on two fronts: (i) better conception and measurement of KPIs, and (ii) better linkage of strategy process elements to strategic decisions. The management process issues have been the subject of much attention and are discussed below.

As Kaplan and Norton note (1996, p. 75), the earlier version of the balanced scorecard as a balanced multi-perspective performance measurement system has evolved to a new strategic management system, linking long-term strategic objectives with short-term actions (*see* Figure 18.4), following the usage and experience gained from applying the original scorecard concept in a wide range of 100 or so organizations. Each of those organizations found that the balanced scorecard approach supplied a structure and a framework for such critical management processes as goal setting, business planning, capital allocations, strategic initiatives, and feedback and learning that facilitated strategic thinking and stimulated the analysis of alternative policy options for the organization.

The new strategic management system involves a set of four management processes that interact to enable the management of the strategic balance between short-term productivity objectives and long-term growth perspectives. The first of these processes is that involved in the *translation of the vision and strategy statements* using the model shown in Figure 18.3, so that they form a clear and well-understood set of objectives and measures that are agreed and endorsed by all senior managers.

This vision/strategy facilitates the framing of the strategy map and identification of the long-term drivers, whether marketing, organizational or financial, that will determine the long-term success of the company. Ultimately, a well-structured vision and strategy statement builds organizational commitment.

The second of these processes – *communicating and linking* – requires managers to discuss and communicate their strategy as the corporate vision throughout the company and link that strategy to departmental and individual objectives. Thus, the scorecard provides a vehicle for debate and undertakes a strategic role in ensuring that the organizational strategy is understood by all organizational levels and, more importantly, that both departmental and individual objectives are linked and closely aligned to the strategy.

The third of these processes – *business planning* – provides a basis for the integration of business and financial plans. Since the balanced scorecard links strategy to performance measures (KPIs), managers can use the scorecard measures and associated goals to allocate resources and set priorities to achieve long-term strategic objectives at the business unit level. In other words, business unit scorecards are designed to link with the corporate scorecards.

The fourth of these processes – *feedback and learning* – allows the company to use feedback from the balanced scorecard and benchmarking processes to provide an insight into, and evaluation of, existing strategy at business unit and corporate levels. Thus, strategies can be changed, or reoriented, to take account of the real-time learning and feedback achieved by the company and its employees. Thus, corporate and business unit scorecards can be reviewed and updated. As Kaplan and Norton point out (1996, p. 77), the balanced scorecard in this context can be viewed as a systems dynamics model that provides a comprehensive, quantified model of a business's value creation process and enables the corporate strategy and vision to be continually refined and reviewed.

Kaplan and Norton also argue that the strategic plan should ultimately describe how the company intends to maximize shareholder value and continually create and sustain that shareholder value over time. By focusing on value, the strategic scorecard approach breaks the organizational effectiveness value equation into at least three main elements, namely, operational effectiveness (improving the efficiency of core business processes), customer management (understanding and leveraging customer relationships better) and product innovation (developing new products, markets and relationships to sustain future growth). Operational effectiveness strategies have a relatively short-term focus; customer management strategies have a more medium-term focus; and product innovation strategies are much longer-term in orientation. In each case, management must set 'stretch' objectives/targets for each of the KPIs and benchmark them on a regular basis. It is important to note that corporate strategy may be modified as economic and other conditions change (for example, in recessionary environments) with, in some cases, shorter-term productivity and operational strategies taking precedence over more innovative, longer-term product strategies.

18.3 How does the strategic management system work in practice?

The vision and strategy element of the balanced scorecard process in Figure 18.3 is the core process owned by the senior management team. It leads to a strategy map such as that shown in Figure 18.5.

This strategy map unfolds the four lenses of the balanced scorecard (the core process) and builds them systematically from workforce and operational issues to a customer value proposition that leads to improved shareholder value. The important KPIs are outlined in the diagram.

Once the vision and strategy has been identified through the strategy map, different senior managers must take responsibility for managing the four strategy processes shown in Figure 18.4, with the balanced scorecard activity as the 'hub' and organizing framework of the

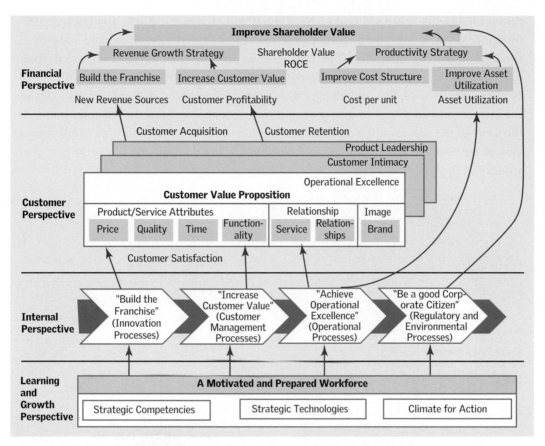

Figure 18.5 Describing the strategy: the balanced scorecard strategy map.
Source: Kaplan, RS and Norton, DP (2001) *The Strategy-focused Organisation*, HBS Press, Boston, MA, p. 96.

process. It is likely that the director of strategic planning or a very senior executive officer will manage the strategic planning process to clarify and translate the vision and strategy exemplified in the strategy map. Normally, the CFO (chief financial officer) has responsibility for annual planning and budgeting and can be assigned the management of the business planning process, including target setting and resource allocation. The process of strategic feedback and learning may be given to a chief information officer, or a strategic planning director. He or she would have clear responsibility for competitive intelligence benchmarking and the management of strategic databases/management information systems. The important role of communicating and linking should probably be the function of the director of human resources, who would manage the goal-setting, incentive and reward systems in the organization.

A number of points are of critical importance in implementing the scorecard as a strategic management system. First, it is critical that the CEO and the senior management team responsible for the scorecard system should meet and exchange dialogue about system performance on a regular basis. Second, the role of managerial intuition and judgement throughout the organization will be important in drawing conclusions from system feedback and the wide range of KPIs offered by the scorecard (often 25 or so in Kaplan and Norton's framework). The underlying logic of how to interpret this data relies critically on the creativity, openness and rapport among members of the senior management team. At the heart of the process is the capability to translate KPIs into a 'bottom-line' performance view of the business and the willingness to continually amend, craft and evolve the emergent strategy of the business.

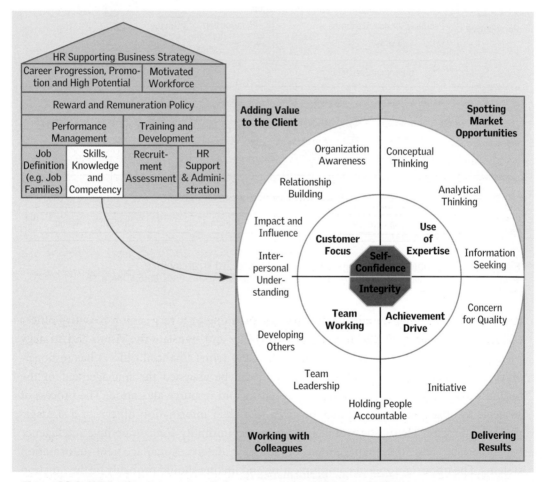

Figure 18.6 Winterthur International's human resource management process
Source: Kaplan, RS and Norton, DP (2001) The Strategy-focused Organisation, HBS Press, Boston, MA, p. 243.

18.3.1 An example of the scorecard in practice: integration with the human resource process

Kaplan and Norton (1996, p. 81) ask the following question: 'Should compensation systems be linked to the balanced scorecard measures?' Clearly, the attractiveness of linking financial compensation rewards to performance is a powerful motivator discussed at length in the literature of strategic human resource management (e.g. Tichy, Fombrun and Devanna 1982).

The main potential pitfalls are whether the performance reward process involves too many risks in implementation. For example, are the right measures on the scorecard? Are valid and reliable data available for each of the selected measures? Other questions could clearly be posed here. To illustrate the dilemma, we offer an example from Kaplan and Norton (2001, pp. 242–3) based on the experience of Winterthur International, a major insurance company, which tried to link the balanced scorecard to a performance management model for the HR function. The diagram shown in Figure 18.6 presents a new HR management structure that Winterthur executives designed and which specifies job families and defines KPIs, skills and knowledge/competences associated with each job family.

The company's experience was that many of the skills and competences were difficult to measure, e.g. conceptual thinking, relationship building, etc. However, the exercise of proposing the measures and identifying the organization's strategic themes made clear to many employees how they could contribute to achieving the strategic objectives of the organization. This alone made them more motivated employees. It should be noted from this evidence that the eventual goal may be to spend more time on the HR processes of translating organizational and business scorecards and associated KPIs into personal development scorecards, which employees can use with HR personnel to review and monitor performance. This may, in turn, lead to subsequent design of rewards/incentive systems as a longer-term goal.

18.4 Summary

The underlying theme of this chapter has been that the performance feedback loop is critical in terms of both assessing and making strategic choices. Taking purely a planning approach to strategy (for example) is rather a one-eyed perspective, since it ignores the value of the feedback from actual (or expected) performance. Curiously, much of the field of strategic management has paid relatively scant attention to analysing and measuring performance as it relates to the strategy process. This chapter has attempted to fill that gap. The importance of the performance feedback loop cannot be overstressed. It enables strategists to assess strategic decisions, of course, but, more importantly, it facilitates the generation of new ideas, allows human resource managers to assess appropriate rewards, and underpins organizational as well as individual learning.

In this chapter we have discussed the evolution of concepts of performance measurement and their linkage to the strategy process. Given a goal of shareholder value maximization, we have presented a range of performance measures, including accounting-based measures of performance, economic value added (EVA) metrics, based on concepts of 'economic profit', and shareholder value approaches (SVAs), based on discounted cash flow concepts from finance. We concluded with a discussion of a set of more holistic value-based management techniques known as the balanced scorecard approach. We believe that this approach has considerable value as a strategic management tool, particularly in its linkage to strategy and a range of KPIs. We continue to develop this theme in the next chapter, when we focus on managing innovation/knowledge and the development of the future strategic path for the organization.

Key terms

Balanced scorecard *671*

Business model *672*

Earnings per share (EPS) *674*

Economic value added (EVA) *675*

Key performance indicators (KPIs) *685*

Key success factors (KSFs) *687*

Net present value *677*

Price/earnings ratio (P/E) *674*

Return on assets (ROA) *674*

Return on equity (ROE) *674*

Return on investment (ROI) *674*

Return on sales (ROS) *674*

Shareholder value approach (SVA) *675*

Value-based management *682*

Recap questions and assignments

1   Based on your analyses of the business models used by Freeserve, Punch Taverns and the National Model Agency, identify (i) the principal use and value of business models, and (ii) the practical difficulties in using business models.

2   What is the difference between a business model and a balanced scorecard process?

3   Does the existence of a performance feedback loop invalidate the idea of top-down planning? How much of a deviation from planned performance can an organization tolerate before abandoning a planning approach?

Online
Learning **Centre**

When you have read this chapter, log on to the Online Learning Centre website at www.mcgraw-hill.co.uk/textbooks/mcgee to explore chapter-by-chapter test questions, further reading and more online study tools for strategy.

Case 1 **The Continental Household Mortgage Company**

The Continental Household Mortgage Company (known internally simply as 'the Company') is a US-based financial services company specializing traditionally in household mortgages and latterly in personal savings products. Tom Howlett is a newly appointed strategic planner with a remit to review the planning and performance assessment processes.

The Company's strategic planning process uses a balanced scorecard approach for assessing progress against its objectives and for assessing the relevance and the sense of its competitive strategy.

It describes its strategy as follows:

1 Scale is central to all products and services.

2 All business units are required to make accounting profits.

3 Customer relationships are central to business retention and development of new products.

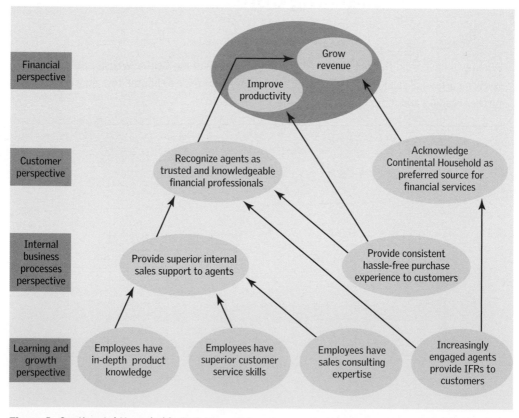

Figure 1 Continental Household: strategy map

4   Product development relies on the core product (mortgage services) being able to attract customers and then to generate interest in other products.

Its approach to assessing its strategy is captured in the strategy map (Figure 1). In this the four lenses of the balanced scorecard are used to identify the key management processes that will 'deliver' the strategy. For example, the learning and growth lens identifies the need for in-depth product knowledge and customer service skills (and other elements as well). From a customer perspective there is a need for the company's agents to be 'trusted'. The strategy map provides a linkage between key processes and financial measures relating to sales growth and productivity.

Behind the strategy map is another document that provides a strategy perspective (Figure 2). This shows how the four lenses of the balanced scorecard are reflected in 'vision' statements. The financial vision is about profitability. The customer vision is about access to professional advice. The internal perspective concerns the nature of the customer contact experience. Finally, the learning and growth vision is about how these customer relationships will evolve and be developed in the future.

Purpose
To help people manage the risks of everyday life, recover from the unexpected, and realize their dreams. By offering a comprehensive portfolio of financial products to help customers secure their financial future, agents can deepen their existing customer relationships and strengthen the long-term retention of customers

Financial perspective
Each business unit will become self-sustaining and profitable, contributing to top-line revenue growth and bottom-line results

Customer perspective
Every client will have access to a knowledgeable, friendly professional who is able to conduct a personalized financial review (IFR) and offer a range of financial products that help clients achieve their financial goals

Internal perspective
Agents and customers will have a consistent, friendly, responsive and hassle-free experience across all contact points. Integrated back-office operations will focus on providing superior service so that agents and customers, want to do business with us

Learning and growth perspective
Agents will move to a relationship-oriented approach to customers. Agents will establish a new pattern of interaction with customers by focusing on proactively understanding customers' financial goals and needs, and marketing an expanded set of products. Employees will focus on helping the agent have successful client relationships by providing timely assistance, friendly support, and knowledgeable guidance

Figure 2 Continental Household strategy perspective

Strategic position
To become the provider of choice for customers who want help securing their financial future, we must offer financial products that are perceived by customers as better value than those offered by our competitors. At the same time, our offering has to be matched by a cost structure that is capable of delivering an acceptable rate of return on investment

Customer perspective
The Company's reputation and brand will extend to all financial services so that our existing customer base readily acknowledges the Company as a preferred source for quality financial products. In addition, more customers than ever will recognize their agent as a knowledgeable and trusted financial professional capable of delivering personalized, high-quality service and meeting their needs with a full line of financial products

Financial perspective
At least three of our four business units will be profitable. Regardless of profitability, all business units will contribute significantly to top-line revenue growth and meet expense management targets

Learning and growth perspective
More than half of our agents will be increasingly engaged in marketing and selling products that meet the broad financial goals of our customers by providing a personalized financial review (IFR) to interested customers. These engaged agents, with the support of their staff, will be achieving sales success that meets or exceeds scorecard levels of production. While employees in every business unit will be providing superior customer service to agents and customers, those employees in support roles will also possess in-depth product knowledge and sales consulting skills so that they can help agents build deeper relationships with clients

Internal perspective
The application process for core, high-volume financial services will be integrated and simplified so that our customers' purchase experience is consistent and hassle-free. Agents will be receiving superior internal sales support for core financial products from an integrated contact and support system

Figure 3 Continental Household strategy objectives

This perspective is supplemented by a strategy objective statement that identifies specific business objectives so as to make measurable progress towards company goals. These are expressed through each lens of the balanced scorecard (*see* Figure 3).

The strategy is then elaborated in terms of products scope, market scope, market segmentation and key target markets, capped by a clear value proposition. This is phrased in terms of quality products, simple transactions, skilled and friendly staff, convenient and consistent customer service, and a professional approach to sales.

In the strategic plan there are entries for each of the balanced scorecard lenses. Each of them contains the following headings: business goal and its measure, action plan, and major initiative. The principal measures are as shown in the following table.

Balanced scorecard lens	Business goal	Measures (KPIs)
Financial	1 Increase sales revenue	1 Percentage revenue growth (12% pa 2004–6)
	2 Improve productivity	2 Expense ratio (21% falling to 16% 2004–6)
Customer	1 Wide recognition by customers of Company products	1 Percentage households with a company product (20% to 25% 2004–6) and number of Company products per Company customer (1.8 to 2.25 2004–6)
	2 Customer recognition of sales agent as financial professional	2 Percentage Company agents fully participating in the product line
Internal	1 Customer-facing business processes integrated and simplified	1 Percentage agents satisfied with the application process (increase over 2003 of 0% in 04, and 10% by 06)
	2 Company agents receive superior sales support from integrated contact and support system	2 Percentage agents satisfied with internal support (increase over 2003 baseline of 5% in 04, 10% in 05 and 15% in 06
Learning and growth	1 More agents providing a personal financial review to actual and potential customers	1 Percentage agents fully participating in marketing Company product-line
	2 Employees in internal sales support possess in-depth product knowledge, sales consulting expertise, and superior customer service skills	2a Percentage agents very satisfied with employee product knowledge (increase over 2003 of 5% in each yr to 06)
		2b ditto with customer service
		2c ditto with sales consulting skills

Note that sales agents are self-employed and typically marketing financial services products from a range of providers.

Tom Howlett is worried about a number of things.

Case Questions

1 Is the strategy described properly?
2 What are the key success factors?
3 Do these relate to the key performance indicators?
4 What initial steps should the company take to improve the process?

individuals to improve strategies and to organizational members to facilitate organizational learning. New areas of strategy and organizational science such as knowledge management (Nonaka 1994), organizational learning (de Geus 1997) and the knowledge-based view of strategy (Grant 1996; Spender 1996) have mushroomed and have, in turn, posed critical questions about processes of **innovation** and the meaning of knowledge.

In this chapter we discuss the literature on innovation and technological change and introduce a number of competing concepts including 'disruptive innovations and the innovator's dilemma' (Christensen 1997), 'innovation as revolution' (Hamel 2000), and 'value innovation' (Kim and Mauborgne 1999). We try to define key terms such as knowledge, technology, innovation and core competences as a basis for examining four different perspectives on knowledge: knowledge as assets, knowledge through innovation, knowledge embedded in routines, and knowledge through learning. We then try to present the elements of the knowledge-based view of strategy and provide insights about how to foster organizational commitment to innovation and to structure the organization to achieve growth through innovation.

19.1 Concepts of knowledge and innovation

In their path-breaking book *The Knowledge-creating Company* (1995), Professors Nonaka and Takeuchi have stressed clearly the proposition that the *systemic knowledge* ingrained in the firm, its processes and its people is the single most important resource for the firm. This systemic knowledge is slowly developed, is distinctive and unique to the firm, is not easily transferable to others and may be protected by intellectual property regulations or other competitive barriers. The ease with which the knowledge is capitalized by the firm depends in part on how the knowledge is managed internally in the firm and transferred and replicated easily throughout the organization. Wal-Mart's inventory management and replenishment systems and McDonald's knowledge transfer of restaurant technology throughout its restaurant system are prime examples of good knowledge management and transfer in successful organizations. We define knowledge management as follows:

> The process of identifying, extracting and managing the information, intellectual property and accumulated knowledge that exists within a company and the minds of its employees.

Strategists such as Cooper and Schendel (1976) point out the nature of strategic responses to technological threats and indicate that incremental technological changes (competence-enhancing changes) reinforce the competitive positions of established firms in the industry, whereas more radical technological innovations (competence-destroying changes) may pressure existing incumbent firms to develop new competences, skills and capabilities. Dussauge, Hart and Ramanantsoa (1996, p. 14) emphasize the distinction

Table 19.1 Product innovators and winners

Product	Innovator	Product winner (follower)
Jet plane	British Aerospace: Comet	Boeing (707)
CT scanner	EMI	GE
Video-cassette recorder	Ampex	Sony/Matsushita
Video games	Atari	Nintendo/Sega
Photocopier	Xerox	Canon
Office P/C	Xerox	IBM

Source: D.J. Teece, 1987; P Anderson and M. Tushman, 1990.

between 'incremental' innovations (refining and improving existing products or processes) and 'radical' innovations (introducing totally new concepts). Innovation may involve the development of new technologies, such as bio-engineering and genetic engineering which define new industries, or the application of existing technologies to create new products, such as PCs, or to enhance existing products, such as digital cameras versus 35mm cameras. Generally, new products such as the CT scanner or the PC are new product configurations which link existing technologies and components in a new way. In these cases of new innovations (arising from *inventions* that create new products from new knowledge or distinctive combinations of existing knowledge) the product innovator is often not the eventual product winner. For example, Table 19.1 shows a range of innovative products for which the innovator is not the product winner. From a British viewpoint Sir Geoffrey Household of EMI won the Nobel Prize for the CT scanner yet the innovation was capitalized by GE. As a counter example, however, Pilkington Glass of the UK was the innovator for float glass and also the winner in the marketplace despite US competition from Corning.

19.1.1 Disruptive technologies

Christensen (1997) focuses very closely on what he calls the innovators' dilemma in confronting different innovation types. He distinguishes between **sustaining technologies**, which foster improved product performance among existing firms and **disruptive technologies**, which result in worse near-term product performance and which precipitate the leading firm's failure. The dilemma for incumbent leading firms is that any adoption of disruptive breakthrough technologies requires cannibalization of purchases of existing products by current mainstream customers. This loss of revenue can lead these firms to go slow on implementing breakthrough technologies. Their mainstream customer focus, and associated market research, can then prevent leading firms from new product development, new markets and new customers in the future. This strategic weakness can allow entrepreneurial firms to exploit the new product pathway left open by the incumbent, leading firms.

Table 19.2 shows a list of the impacts of such disruptive innovations on the economic performance of leading incumbent firms.

19.1.2 Value innovation

Writers such as Kim and Mauborgne (1999) extend the concept of technological innovation to **value innovation**. They point out that while an innovator such as Ampex failed to capture the rents from inventing the VCR, their inventions nevertheless benefited the economy because later value innovators such as Sony and Matsushita made a success of the Ampex innovation. Value innovation places emphasis on the buyer as the centre of strategic thinking. To *value innovate*, companies must ask two questions:

1 Are we offering customers radically superior value?

Table 19.2 Examples of disruptive technologies (innovations)

Company	Disruptive innovation	Firms disrupted	Prior industry leader
DEC (Digital Equipment Corporation)	Mini computer	Mainframe computer manufacturers	IBM
HMOs e.g. Kaiser Permanente	Health maintenance organizations	Conventional health insurance	Blue Cross/Blue Shield
Compaq	Personal computer CPC	Mini-computer manufacturers	IBM, DEC
Dell	Direct order, customized PCs	Retail stores	Compaq
Charles Schwab	Discount trading/ broking	Investment banks	Merrill Lynch
Ford	Model T	Specialized car makers	Many
Toyota	Small cars and lean manufacturing	Large-volume car manufacturers	GM, Ford
Canon	Desk top photocopiers	High-speed photo-copying manufactuers (IBM, Kodak, Xerox)	Xerox
Wal-Mart	Discount retailing	Department stores	Macy's
Sony	Portable radios, TVs	Vacuum tube-based electronic products	RCA, Zenith

Source: Christensen, 1997.

2 Is our price level accessible to the mass of buyers in our target market?

As a consequence, the major inputs for value innovation are knowledge and ideas, new product concepts etc., which reject competitive strategies based on imitation but do not necessarily require new technology in order to succeed.

Table 19.3 shows a range of examples of value innovation given by Kim and Mauborgne (1999). It is instructive to note that in virtually all the cases given, the innovation shown is generally not a new 'technology' of a technical kind, but really a new product concept or a new way of framing a business opportunity using existing technologies and knowledge.

19.1.3 Revolutionary innovators

In his book *Leading the Revolution* (2000), Gary Hamel also stresses the importance of innovation as the engine to sustain corporate growth. Like Kim and Mauborgne, he believes that imitative strategies based on competitive strategy analysis have no basis in today's marketplace. He believes that the time has passed for strategies based on efficiency models (e.g. productive efficiency or benchmarking 'best practices' in competitors or the

Table 19.3 Example of value innovation

Company	Innovation
Callaway Golf – 'Big Bertha'	– made playing golf less difficult and more fun
SWATCH	– a price-competitive watch as a fashion accessory
Starbucks	– good coffee in a 'coffee bar'
Wal-Mart	– discount retailing
Charles Schwab	– investment and brokerage account management
CNN	– innovation in news broadcasting (24-hour news)
IKEA	– fashion home products and furniture retailing
SAP	– business applications software
Barnes & Noble	– book retailing
Southwest Airlines	– short-haul
Body Shop	– organic cosmetic retailing
Home Depot (B&Q)	– home improvement retail
Virgin Atlantic	– 'Upper class' – first-class service at a business-class price

Note: In virtually all these cases, with perhaps the exception of SAP, the concept is not a patentable innovation i.e. a scientifically excludable innovation.
Source: Kim and Mauborgne, 1999.

best-run companies). Senior managers must recognize the clear differences between innovation and imitation. Imitative approaches to the market mean that companies act reactively and try to emulate existing competitive strategies. In so doing, they misunderstand the customer demands and buyer needs in emerging mass markets.

Table 19.4 gives a few examples of companies seen as revolutionary innovators by Hamel.

Again, many of the ideas here rely on creative ideas and product concepts, and creative reconfigurations of existing technologies. New economy strategies are different and are discussed in Chapter 12.

The chapter now takes us systematically through four perspectives on knowledge which encompass economic concepts discussed earlier (for example, the resource-based view of the firm), alternative definitions of innovation (for example, radical, incremental, disruptive or value-based) and organizational approaches based on organizational evolution, routines and organization learning.

The traditional economic approach treats knowledge as an entity which affects the nature of the economic equilibrium, like so many other variables, but does not feature as a central player with regularity of effects on the competitive outcome. As we move towards placing knowledge at the centre of strategy theory we argue that there are four distinct approaches of how knowledge works. The first is the resource-based view (RBV) that provides us with the 'knowledge as asset' metaphor. A second view is Schumpeterian (Schumpeter 1934) in origin, picturing knowledge as innovation and as an essential element in the general theme of creative destruction of existing technological/knowledge bases. Third, evolutionary economics[1] moves away from a decision orientation towards a focus on the internal organization

Table 19.4 Hamel's revolutionary innovators (Hamel, 2000)

Company	Innovatory idea
SWATCH	Small objects of desire – combines Swiss watch making with Lego plastics
easyJet/Ryanair	Reinvented basic economics of airline business – real value to customers
Dell	Reinvented product cycle and cost structure of PCs
Nokia	Understood youth culture and its linkage to mobile phones

Source: Hamel, 2000.

---

[1]   Nelson and Winter (1982) are most commonly identified with evolutionary economics. But the roots run deeper: *see* Veblen, 1898, on cumulative change; Marshall, 1920, on 'economic biology' and his well-known appreciation of dynamic analysis, and Alchian, 1950, 1953, on the implications of selection for the economic system.

of the firm and the role of organizational routines. The use of a Darwinian natural selection process coupled with adaptive feedback mechanisms explains the nature of organizational routines in large organizations. Such routines and their adaptation over time require embedded knowledge, acquisition of knowledge and transfer and integration of knowledge within organizations. Finally, the Teece, Pisano and Shuen (1997) approach to dynamic capabilities adds the elements of learning and other dynamics to the RBV and suggest paths by which both RBV and evolutionary approaches can take place in practice. The writers of these approaches did not place knowledge per se at the centre of their writing so, to a large degree, what follows is a reinterpretation of existing theory in terms of our view of knowledge and the role of knowledge in the processes of competitive strategy formulation and strategy development.

Case box: **What do we know about the knowledge economy?**

Pundits and politicians are forever proclaiming that we live in a knowledge economy, where success depends increasingly on brains not brawn. Yet little is actually known about the knowledge economy. An OECD study in 1999 made a start at filling in the picture – and debunks some myths.

For starters, Germany, not America, tops the OECD's knowledge-economy table. Knowledge-based industries accounted for 58.6% of German business output in 1996, compared with 55.3% in second-placed America (see chart). Japan is third, with Britain and France close behind, and Italy a notable laggard. In the OECD as a whole, knowledge-based industries accounted for over half of rich-country business output in the mid-1990s, up from around 45% in 1985.

The OECD's definition of the knowledge economy is pretty broad. As well as high-technology industries, such as computing and telecoms, the Paris-based think-tank counts sectors with a highly skilled workforce, such as finance and education. One reason that Germany is ahead of America is because of its big car, chemicals and machinery industries. Yet even in high-tech industries, where America is widely thought to be streets ahead, the United States comes behind Japan and Britain. High-tech industries produce 3.7% of Japan's business output and 3.3% of Britain's, but only 3% of America's. The United States is level-pegging with France, and only a bit ahead of Germany.

Growth in knowledge-based industries requires investment in knowledge as well as in physical capital. Such intangible investment is pretty hard to measure. By adding together spending on research and development (R&D), investment in software and public spending on education, the OECD puts it at 8% of rich-country GDP. Throwing in incomplete data on private education spending brings the total up to 10% of GDP, compared with physical investment in plant and machinery of 20% of GDP.

Sweden is the keenest investor in knowledge. Its investment in intangibles came to 10.6% of GDP in 1995; it spends far more of its national output on R&D than other countries.

France ranks second, thanks to its generously financed public-education system. America lags behind, because its government spends so little on schools. Japan, which spends a whopping 28.5% of GDP on physical investment, invests a puny 6.6% in intangibles.

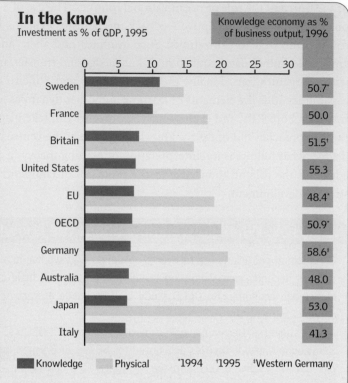

In the know
Investment as % of GDP, 1995

Knowledge economy as % of business output, 1996

Sweden		50.7*
France		50.0
Britain		51.5†
United States		55.3
EU		48.4*
OECD		50.9*
Germany		58.6‡
Australia		48.0
Japan		53.0
Italy		41.3

■ Knowledge   ■ Physical   *1994   †1995   ‡Western Germany

Another myth that the new study pokes holes in is that the service sector, unlike manufacturing, does not innovate. Admittedly, R&D spending in services has traditionally been low. But in most countries it is now rising faster in services than in manufacturing. In 1980 services accounted for only 4.1% of business R&D in America; by 1996 its share had risen to 19.5%.

Moreover, spending on R&D is only a fraction of total business spending on innovation. According to new evidence from business surveys compiled by the OECD, service industries spend far more on innovation than previously thought. Indeed, in Britain, spending on innovation in services is higher, at 4.02% of business sales in 1996, than in manufacturing, at 3.16%.

There are inevitably many gaps and flaws in the OECD's study. Its definition of the knowledge economy is far from perfect. It lumps together investment banking, a high-tech and pretty high-skill business, with estate agents, where knaves with badly written brochures still prosper. Another problem is that it includes many unskilled workers who work in knowledge industries. So, for example, hospital cleaners are counted as knowledge workers. But despite these shortcomings, the new report sheds new light on the knowledge economy.

Source: 'Knowledge gap', *The Economist*, 14 October 1999.
© The Economist Newspaper Limited, London (14 October 1999).

Questions for discussion

1 How would you define the 'knowledge economy'?

2 What are 'knowledge workers' and how are they different from other workers?

3 How do you expect the knowledge economy to develop over the next 10 years? 20 years? What implications does your answer have?

19.2 **Knowledge as assets**

Figure 19.1 portrays the market-based view commonly found in economic models in resource-based terms. The internals of the firm are here fleshed out in terms of resources and capabilities, the conventional description that permits discrimination between assets based on knowing and skills based on experience and actions. We do not summarize the key elements of the resource-based view here. They are familiar enough (see Wernerfelt 1984, Barney 1991; Grant (1991) and presented in depth in Chapter 7. Instead we suggest some conclusions in the language of *core competences.*

First, core competences can have a very significant impact by their effect on firm scope (boundaries), and by the (long) time scales over which they exist and change. They arise typically through collective learning – very much in the economics tradition of **objectified knowledge** (Spender 1996). Also, their impact is to create a framework through which we can view competition. This view is about contests for the acquisition of distinctive skills, in which competition in product markets is a 'superficial expression' of the more fundamental competition over competences. Therefore, the dynamics of the strategic theory of the firm focus on the process of core competence acquisition and collective learning because it occurs logically prior to product market evolution.

Figure 19.2 is a simple expansion of the range and nature of asset positions that are implied in Figure 19.1.[2] The broad categories give some idea of the differing demands on internal processes and on the challenge for integration of these different positions through some form of *corporate glue*, which integrates and binds these diverse asset positions for corporate value maximization. Many authors have provided classifications and explanations of the language of resources, assets, capabilities and competences. Grant (1991), for example, distinguishes between resources and capabilities, viewing resources as inputs and capabilities as those intermediate processes derived within the production function that are

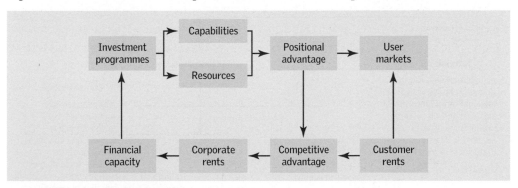

Figure 19.1 Resource-based view

---

[2] See the teaching notes in De Wit and Meyer (1994) for a practical illustration. Also see Barney (1991) and Grant (1991) for similar deconstructions of resources.

the main source of competitive advantage (refer back to the discussion in Chapter 7). Both are hard to define objectively and indeed Grant goes as far as to say that capabilities are organizational routines. Amit and Schoemaker (1993) (first discussed in Chapter 7) also deploy the language of resources and capabilities but seek to draw links with the industry analysis framework. Resources for them are intermediate goods (in contrast to Grant), and capabilities are *'based on developing, caring and exchanging information through the firm's human capital'*. They are built by combining physical, human and technological resources at the corporate level. The link with industry (or product market) arises when certain resources and capabilities become the prime determinant of economic rents and value. This can only occur if these resources and capabilities are subject to market failure and their possessions can therefore be firm-specific. Amit and Schoemaker refer to these as 'strategic assets'. This enables a distinction to be drawn between those resources and capabilities that are generally attainable and those that are asymmetrically distributed between firms, and difficult to trade and imitate.

Prahalad and Hamel (1990) (also first introduced in Chapter 7) have made famous the language of core competence and avoid using the language of resources and capabilities. For them, *'core competences are the collective learning in the organization, especially how to co-ordinate diverse production skills and integrate multiple streams of technologies'*.

Just as Amit and Schoemaker extend their notion of strategic assets towards product markets with a concept of strategic industry factors, so also do Prahalad and Hamel in making core competences the foundation for core products. For them the insight is not what is a core competence and how to build one, but a view of the strategic architecture

Figure 19.2 Resource positions (expanded)

of the firm, by which they mean '*a road map of the future that identifies which core compe-tences to build and their constituent technologies*'. For these and other authors writing in the same vein, the common characteristic is the appeal to economic reasoning in the form of asymmetric distribution of assets to support economic rents and value. But the mainspring of firm-specific resources can lie anywhere between inputs and outputs with alternative scenarios about the contributory roles of organization structure and process, and mana-gerial culture.

Our own approach in Figure 19.2 is more modest in intent. We seek only to distinguish between some categories or resources and capabilities so that we can see more clearly the dif-ferent roles that knowledge can play. The distinction between tangible and intangible assets occurs prior to any distinction between resources and capabilities. We divide intangibles into three parts. The first companies those assets that are relational in character and involve the relationship of the organization with the outside world. The second is more explicitly concerned with knowledge and know-how. Although some entries under this heading suggest explicit knowledge (such as patents) they are surrounded by or produced by know-how that is essentially tacit. In the third part, our term competences can be used interchangeably with capabilities without any loss of meaning. There are, following Grant, intermediate processes, some of which are explicit in their design but many are likely to display characteristics of organizational routines.

19.3 **Knowledge as innovation**

The resource-based view provides a theory of protection and sustainability of competitive advantage. For an understanding of the genesis of advantage we have to turn elsewhere. The Schumpeterian approach (Schumpeter 1937) offers innovation as the medium through which creative destruction of existing technologies and knowledge bases takes place (see Box 1, Chapter 8). The element of destruction depicts intuitively and vividly but also convincingly how the old is replaced by the new. But it also sets these mechanisms in waves and floods of change, suggesting that a calculation of the benefits of change and innovation is overwhelmed by the magnitude of the opportunities on offer. Thus, Schumpeter suggested there were pat-terns of change and ferment (radical innovation) interspersed with stability (incremental innovation). In this way Schumpeter emphasized dynamic efficiency above static efficiency. Some recent writings clearly have their origins in Schumpeter. See, for example, d'Aveni's (1994) approach to hypercompetition, where he argues that the sources of competitive advan-tage are being created and destroyed at an increasingly rapid rate. Hamel and Prahalad (1993) use the language of dominance to assert a doctrine of strategic intent and define the gap between ambition and resources as strategic stretch. But the Schumpeterian world of enor-mous opportunity is not the only context for innovation. Firms may wish to create their own shocks or, more modestly, may seek to calculate finer pieces of sustainable advantage.

19.3.1 **Innovation competition**

But who innovates? Economists such as Kenneth Arrow have formulated models to explain whether new entrants have advantages over incumbents, whether monopoly can innovate more readily than competitive markets, and whether potential entrants can outwit monopolists. Of course, the answers depend on the situation but there is good reason for thinking that incomers often provide the wellspring of innovation – eventually. The behaviour to be explained is not that of the innovator who rationally examines the balance between costs and revenues in the light of prevailing competition and makes innovations when the return–risk ratio looks promising. The more difficult behaviour to explain is the reluctance of incumbents to refrain from innovating in the light of expected innovation from new entrants (*see* also Christensen 1997). The two rational economic reasons for this are the **sunk cost effect** and the **replacement effect**. The former arises when the incumbent assesses his existing technology by comparing its contribution margin to no new costs of investment beyond that of simple replacement. By contrast a new technology has a stiffer hurdle because the contribution margin (assuming for simplicity the same revenue stream from both technologies) has to cover new investment as well (*see* Besanko *et al.* 2000, pp. 488–9). The replacement effect was first formulated by Arrow (1962) in considering who has the greater propensity to invest, the monopolist or the new entrant. The incentive for the monopolist to invest in a radical new technology requires a comparison of the new stream of monopoly profits with the existing stream. However, for the new entrant who, if successful, will become the new monopolist, the incentive is simply the new stream of monopoly profits.

Through innovation an entrant can replace a monopolist but a monopolist can only replace itself, hence this is called the replacement effect. Thus, established firms under this thinking are less willing to stretch themselves to innovate. However, where the monopolist anticipates that new entry is likely then the incentives reverse to favour the monopolist. The incentive for the monopolist to innovate in the teeth of potential competitive intrusion is that of retaining monopoly profits from successful innovation versus sharing the market with a new entrant as a duopoly within which prices will be lower due to competition. This is greater than that of the new entrant who, expecting the monopolist to defend by innovation, can only anticipate the profit streams from sharing a competitive duopoly. Arrow called this the **efficiency effect.** The balance between these three effects depends on the probability of successful innovation by potential entrants. Where this is low, the sunk cost and replacement cost effects will dominate and the monopolists will prefer to maintain their existing cash flows. Where the probability is high then the efficiency motives will dominate and monopolists will seek to maintain their market position even if it is less favourable in absolute terms.

Case box: **Outsource your innovations**

When Frito-Lay added a little curl to its snacks, the company's sales improved. Of such seemingly modest innovations are great fortunes made. Next month Gillette will launch the successor to its sensationally successful Mach3 razor. Much as the company would like it to be as revolutionary as the Mach3 was in its day, the battery-operated vibrating beard-remover is unlikely to be more than evolutionary. That may not, however, prevent it from making a sizeable contribution to Gillette's profits.

Big firms still aspire to make truly great breakthrough inventions – products that will underwrite their profits for at least a decade. They are, however, coming up with such inventions less and less often, even though many industries, notably pharmaceuticals, continue to spend vast sums trying. Indeed, for most of industrial history, small firms have been responsible for the bulk of breakthrough products. America's Small Business Administration claims that the pacemaker, the personal computer, the Polaroid camera and pre-stressed concrete all emerged from small entrepreneurial outfits, and those are taken only from the list of items beginning with the letter P.

Big firms are better at less eye-catching forms of innovation – for example, Frito-Lay adding a little curl to its snacks, the clever twist allowing consumers to scoop up their guacamole or salsa dip and place relatively more of it in their mouths and less on their rugs, and generally improving the ways in which products invented elsewhere are manufactured, marketed and continually enhanced. Henry Ford did not invent the automobile. He 'merely' invented a far superior way to manufacture it – namely, the mass-production assembly line. And on that was built an industrial empire that has thrived for almost a century. Likewise, in the past few decades most of the companies that have created truly extraordinary amounts of wealth have done so by inventing great processes, not great products. Dell, Toyota and Wal-Mart, for example, have risen to the top of their respective industries by coming up with amazingly efficient ways of getting quite ordinary products into the hands of consumers more cheaply than their rivals.

Does this mean that big firms should sack all their scientists and leave inventing to others? In practice, more and more are doing just that. For some time, the computer industry has, in effect, relied for much of its research and development on small firms backed by venture capital, and the telecoms industry is outsourcing more and more research to smaller firms in India and elsewhere. Without their own in-house labs, however, big firms fear that they will be taken by surprise by what a Harvard professor, Clayton Christensen, famously described as a 'disruptive technology', an innovation so revolutionary that it will enable an upstart outsider to crush them, much as the PC did to the mainframe-computer business.

But, as history has shown time and time again, a bevy of in-house scientists gives no guarantee that their output will protect their employer from technological change. Xerox, AT&T and IBM spent billions on research but all failed to exploit much of what came out of their labs, and all ended up being caught out by new technologies. It is far better if big firms' managers keep their binoculars well trained on the outside world and their minds open to any new ideas they spot there. They can then buy them and do what they do best: find innovative ways to bring them to market.

Source: 'Less glamour, more profit', *The Economist*, 22 April 2004.
© The Economist Newspaper Limited, London (22 April 2004).

Questions for discussion

1 If in-house R&D is so risky, what are the arguments for doing it?
2 What are the arguments for outsourcing R&D?

19.3.2 Technology races

This analysis of innovation competition focuses on the pay-offs to innovation. There is also a literature on choosing the right levels of R&D under market uncertainty and under uncertainty about the response of rivals. The analysis of first mover advantage is well known. It asserts that the first mover gains advantage by establishing explicit knowledge protected by patents and trademarks and goes on to build advantages of scale, experience and scope so that later movers can never erode the early advantage (*see* the discussion in Chapter 6 of Ghemawat's 1997 analysis of Du Pont in titanium dioxide). There is also an interesting empirical literature on technology races and patent races (Gottinger 2003). These races describe the battles between firms to complete a successful R&D programme and to be the first to market with an innovation with all the benefits of first mover advantage. A race is an interactive pattern of competition characterized by firms constantly trying to get ahead of their rivals, or trying not to fall too far behind. Like the **dominant design** literature,[3] racing behaviour is also a dynamic story of how technology unfolds in an industry recognizing the fundamental importance of strategic interactions between competing firms. A simple race between two firms might involve the following. The leader may consider further investment to outdistance its rival and get to the winning post first. But it is aware of the diminishing marginal productivity of research for itself and the uncertainty of innovation for its rival. It therefore has to balance the risks and expenditures associated with pressing on with the benefits of delay in terms of consolidating its own knowledge and the difficulty for its rival of catching up. By contrast the follower is faced with the need to catch up, but has the same concerns about the productivity of research offset to some degree by at least some knowledge about the successful path followed by its rival. The leader has considerable incentives

---

[3] Dominant design can be defined as 'after a technological innovation and a subsequent era of ferment in an industry, a basic architecture of product or process that becomes the accepted market standard', from Abernathy and Utterback 1978, cited by Anderson and Tushman 1990. Dominant designs may not be better than alternatives, nor innovative. They have the benchmark features to which subsequent designs are compared. Examples include the IBM 360 computer series and Ford's Model T automobile, and the IBM PC.

to be cautious, whereas the follower might be more inclined to plunge ahead. Clearly the variables are many and imponderable given the uncertainty of success in R&D and the difficulty of predicting the responses of rivals. Gottinger summarizes the implications:

> At one level, racing behaviour has implications for understanding technology strategy at the level of the individual firm and for understanding the impact of policies that aim to spur technological innovation. At another level, racing behaviour embodies both traditions that previous writings have attempted to synthesize: the 'demand-pull' side emphasized by economic theorists and the 'technology-push' emphasized by the autonomous technological innovation school. (Gottinger 2003, pp. 37–8)

Gottinger observes from his research on telecommunications and computer industries the apparent inability of technology-oriented companies to maintain leadership in fields that they pioneered (op. cit. p. 51). These failures might be due to agency problems or other suboptimal managerial behaviour. But of more interest to our thesis here is the existence of market asymmetries that affect racing behaviour: (i) risk-driven and (ii) resource-driven asymmetries. The latter are clearly linked to the replacement effect (above). All this literature (Abramowitz 1986; Gottinger 1998 and 2001; Lerner 1997; and Scherer 1991) carries implications for knowledge in terms of its creation, how it is accessed, transferred and integrated, and who has the incentives for these activities.

Case box: **Does IT matter?**

Nicholas Carr has foisted an existentialist debate on the mighty information-technology industry

His argument is simple, powerful and yet also subtle. He is not, in fact, denying that IT has the potential to transform entire societies and economies. On the contrary, his argument is based on the assumption that IT resembles the steam engine, the railway, the electricity grid, the telegraph, the telephone, the highway system and other technologies that proved revolutionary in the past. For commerce as a whole, Mr Carr is insistent, IT matters very much indeed.

But this often has highly ironic implications for individual companies, thinks Mr Carr. Electricity, for instance, became revolutionary for society only when it ceased to be a proprietary technology, owned or used by one or two factories here and there, and instead became an infrastructure – ubiquitous, and shared by all. Only in the early days, and only for the few firms that found proprietary uses for it, was electricity a source of strategic – i.e., more or less lasting – advantage. Once it became available to all firms, however, it became a commodity, a factor of production just like office supplies or raw materials, a cost to be managed rather than an edge over rivals, a risk (during black-outs) rather than an opportunity.

Computer hardware and software, Mr Carr argues, have been following the same progression from proprietary technology to infrastructure. In the past, American Airlines, for example, gained a strategic advantage for a decade or two after it rolled out a proprietary computerised reservation system in 1962, called Sabre. In time, however, its rivals replicated the system, or even leap-frogged to better ones. Today, the edge that a computer system can give a firm is fleeting at best. IT, in other words, has now joined history's other revolutionary technologies by becoming an infrastructure, not a differentiator. In that sense, and from the point of view of individual firms, 'IT no longer matters.'

And what's IT all about?

Surely though, Mr Carr's critics counter, IT is different from electricity or steam engines. Even if hardware tends to become a commodity over time, software seems, like music or poetry, to have infinite potential for innovation and malleability. True, it may have, answers Mr Carr, but what matters is not whether a nifty programmer can still come up with new and cool code, but how quickly any such program can be replicated by rival companies. Besides, today's reality in the software industry has nothing to do with poetry or music. Many companies are furious about the bug-ridden, pricey and over-engineered systems that they bought during the bubble era and are doing their best to switch to simple, off-the-shelf software, offered in 'enterprise-resource planning' packages and the like. If there is any customisation at all, it tends to be done by outside consultants, who are likely to share their favours with other clients.

But surely Mr Carr does not appreciate the impressive pipeline of new technologies that is about to hit the market – the wireless gadgets, the billions of tiny radio-frequency identity tags that will turn Aspirin bottles, shirt collars, refrigerator doors and almost everything else into smart machines, and so on? Those are impressive indeed, says Mr Carr. But again, the issue is whether they will be proprietary technologies or open infrastructures. And everything points to the latter.

This is not a debate for the ivory tower. Since IT can no longer be a source of strategic advantage, Mr Carr urges CIOs to spend less on their data-centres, to opt for cheaper commodity equipment wherever possible, to follow their rivals rather than trying to outdo them with fancy new systems, and to focus more on IT's vulnerabilities, from viruses to data theft, than on its opportunities. As it happens, CIOs have been taking exactly this approach for the past three years, and their bosses like it that way.

Source: 'Does IT matter?', *The Economist*, 1 April 2004.
© The Economist Newspaper limited, London (1 April 2004).

Questions for discussion

1 If all innovations are destined to become commodities, what is the incentive to innovate?

2 What is it about knowledge that makes it 'strategic' for the economy and for society but a mere commodity for firms?

3 How might a firm resist the move towards commoditization of its intellectual property?

19.4 **Knowledge embedded in routines**[4]

Recently the strategy literature has paid attention to the organizational processes that form the basis for the development of the firm's strategy (Teece *et al.* 1997; Eisenhardt and Martin 2000). These scholars, along with others, focus on the routines, competences and capabilities of the firm that shape its development in the long run. This approach shifts the focus of attention from the market-positioning view (described earlier) to a more micro-analytic approach that aims to go even deeper than the resource-based view, aiming to understand the way in which competitive advantage is actually developed (Johnson and Bowman 1999). Our interest here is in the routinized elements of strategy making. This is well grounded in the literature (March and Simon 1958; Nelson and Winter 1982; Cyert and March 1963; and Teece *et al.* 1997).

Less well known and certainly less commonly cited alongside the above scholars is the long-standing preoccupation of economists with evolution.[5] Veblen (1898, p. 397) talks about *the process of cumulative change.* Marshall used the term *economic biology* and argued that the '*the key-note is that of dynamics rather than statics*' (Marshall 1920, p. xiv). These represent early arguments about economic evolution. Although economists have spent considerable time developing the neoclassical theory of the firm (a misnomer for a theory of markets), the notion of *evolutionary economics* has gained considerable momentum. Some of the impetus for this derived from the long controversies about *marginalism.*[6] This led to the breaking open of the black box that was the firm in traditional microeconomics and the onset of the new theory of the firm. The essence of this is to throw light on the internal organization of the firm. Whereas the traditional theory is concerned with prices and output, the new theory is interested in how transactions are organized. The intellectual progress of this strand of economics is marked by Coase's (1937, 1988) path-breaking paper on the nature of the firm, new approaches to understanding the nature of ownership bringing in property rights (Alchian and Demsetz 1972) and agency costs (Jensen and Meckling 1976), and Williamson's transaction cost economics (1985, 1987). Coase anticipated all of this in pointing out that the essential differentiating feature of intrafirm transactions, as opposed to interfirm transactions, is authority and hierarchy. This stream of thinking does reinforce the idea of 'efficiency management' – Williamson expressed it as the strategy of *economizing* (1981), and this has strong resonance with the idea of cost minimization from neoclassical theory. But, more important than this, it opens the door to ideas about the evolution of efficient organizational forms. Vronen (1995, p. 2) maintains that evolutionary economics is inspired by the new institutional economics. This examines

---

[4] The approach adopted in this section owes much to Menuhin (2001) and Menuhin and McGee (2003).

[5] This is described and analysed in great detail by Vronen (1995).

[6] See, for example, the anti-marginalist critique exemplified by the Oxford Research Group in the 1930s, especially Hall and Hitch (1939) and the American economist Lester (1946).

processes through which institutions evolve (Langlois 1986). Similarly, the sociologist Granovetter (1985, p. 488) argues that:

> *social institutions and arrangements previously thought to be the adventitious result of legal, historical, social or political forces are better viewed as the efficient solution to certain economic problems.*

The central part of evolutionary theory is the selection proposition that argues that competitive markets select for the most efficient organizational forms. Although there are considerable debates about the precise forms and implications of this process, the selection argument is the hard core of evolutionary theory. Evolution is a form of organizational ecology where firms engage in behaviour that is routine rather than purposive. Adaptation takes place by mimicking the survivors which are accidentally well adapted. Managers get little credit in this view. Scholars such as James Brian Quinn have argued for processes that are typically fragmented, evolutionary and intuitive. He describes this as *logical incrementalism* (Quinn, 1978) in which minor changes in strategy take place as a response to changes in the external environment in an evolutionary and adaptive manner.

Nelson and Winter's (1982) approach (drawing heavily on Winter, 1964) is a sustained argument that selection is not an ad hoc or involuntary response, but is systematic and purposeful firm behaviour. They – famously – argued for collections of routines based on **tacit knowledge** supplemented by organized search behaviour for modifications or substitutes. This allowed, in our view, for the evolution of economic thinking (over many decades) to map on to the newer thinking from management theorists attempting to understand and map organizational processes. The essential link is the purposive behaviour of managers and we shall argue that this is characterized by asset and knowledge accumulation and by learning processes that allow knowledge to be transformed from a tacit to an explicit form (a distinction also offered by Nonaka and Takeuchi 1995). Thus we see Burgelman (1983) arguing that the intellectual basis for activist and explicit roles for top managers is based on complex organizations that are subject to both evolutionary and planned processes.

Nelson and Winter introduced us to evolutionary economics but much is owed to Simon (1955, 1959) with his seminal concepts of *satisficing* and *bounded rationality* and Penrose's (1959) theory of the growth of the firm. Although Nelson and Winter's tone is somewhat hostile to traditional economics, their approach can be seen as a rehabilitation of the theory of the firm by providing (far more) realistic assumptions. They shift attention away from an overarching organizational decision calculus (how can one continually make these complex trade-offs about everything?) to internal organization where organizational routines regularly and automatically make 'decisions' based on the knowledge and best practice embedded in those routines. The argument for routines that make 'good decisions' is based on two points: one, a Darwinian natural selection process at an organizational level that ensures that only the 'best' routines are kept in operation and, two, on an adaptive feedback mechanism at the individual level that permits new knowledge to be accessed and then diffused through the organization to be eventually embedded in routines. Routines are thus embodiments of organizational memory – better called organizational genetics.

The evolutionary approach is saved from ecological sterility by the learning process (based on Simon). Through this we can see the essential elements and characteristics of a **knowledge-based view** (KBV) starting to take shape: tacit versus explicit knowledge; relative roles of individuals, groups and organizations; sourcing and accessing of knowledge, transfer and integration of knowledge (note the classic formulation by Nonaka and Takeuchi 1995).

19.5 **Knowledge as learning**

Nelson and Winter's second set of routines are those that determine the long-run changes in the firm's stock of capital – hence they are called *strategizing routines*. Attention has been paid to the contribution of planning and budgeting processes to the accumulation of fixed assets over time. But more central to our argument are the product and technology development processes. For example, Henderson and Clark (1990) developed the concept of *architectural knowledge* explaining how the dominant organizational design '*incorporates a range of choices about the design that are not revisited in every subsequent design*' (1990, p. 15). They go on to link this architectural knowledge to the development of innovation processes.

Strategizing routines contribute to strategy and strategy making as they store the firm's experience in such a way that it can be used in a new context (for example, consultants such as McKinsey and Bain discuss how they develop experience libraries of problems and problem solutions through their ongoing consulting activities). They channel the structure of decision-making processes into the type of behaviour that has brought success in the past. But such routines have a negative side. Over time, as the environment changes, new forms of organization become appropriate and gaps emerge between environmental requirements and existing capabilities. These gaps cause routines to become dysfunctional (Teece *et al.* 1997; Leonard-Barton 1992) and inhibit future development of the firm (Levitt and March 1988; Henderson and Clark 1990; Leonard-Barton 1992; Teece *et al.* 1997). This leads to the processes of organizational learning by which routines are modified over time.

The literature makes many references to types of organizational learning. Cyert and March's (1963) view of organizations as complex adaptive systems suggest *modes of learning*. Levitt and March (1988) refer to change processes at several *nested levels*. Cohen and Baclayan (1994) illustrate the role of *experimental learning*. Bettis and Prahalad (1995) suggest that firms *unlearn* ineffective routines. Hedberg (1981, p. 18) suggests that unlearning is 'a process through which *learners discard knowledge*'. All of these notions build on the idea that routines flow from history and serve as the organizational memory in which knowledge about best practice is stored. The propositions about learning fall into two camps. The cognitivists (e.g. Porac, Thomas, and Baden Fuller 1989; Porac and

Thomas 2002) focus on learning at the individual level and on individual mental maps. Structuralists suggest that learning is an organizational phenomenon based on the firm's routines and that these routines are subject to formal change processes. Nonaka and Takeuchi (1995) combine these two views into their knowledge-creation spiral. This begins with a distinction between tacit and explicit knowledge and maps how tacit knowledge starts with the individual and proceeds through socialization and integration processes so that knowledge becomes a key ingredient in the organization's capital stock (see Figure 19.5 which is shown later in this chapter). More generally, such learning can be described as a *sense-making process* (Weick 1979, 1995) through which the members of an organization construct a *common reality* that influences the way they seek to achieve an *objective economic reality.*

Teece, Pisano and Shuen (1997) in their well-known paper on dynamic capabilities may have intended to add primarily to the RBV but they also provide a sense of the internal mechanisms by which learning and adaptation may actually take place. Their definition of dynamic capabilities is '*the sub-set of the competences and capabilities which allow the firm to create new products and processes and respond to changing market circumstances*' (1997, p. 270). In some ways this is a restatement of Nelson and Winter's strategizing routines but inherent in their discussion is recognition of learning. They identify three characteristics that permit learning. The first is the nature of the internal processes: co-ordination/integration (a static notion), learning (dynamic), and reconfiguration (a renewal or transformational concept). Second, they are specific about the variety of resource positions that might need to be addressed. Finally, they pay attention to the paths by which developments can take place. It has to be said that these concepts can be very slippery. Path dependency, for example, is celebrated only as an idea. However, they are on more firm

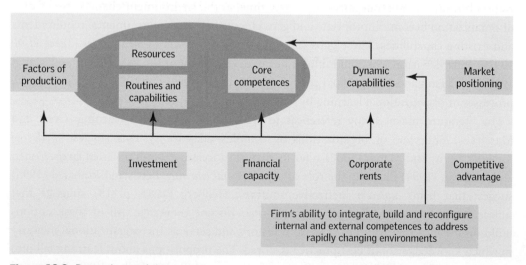

Figure 19.3 Dynamic capabilities view

ground in outlining the ways in which technological opportunity can shape the future. The hints they provide on the nature of increasing returns are suggested here.

We revisit our schematic again in the form of Figure 19.3. This time the resource side is further elaborated by the inclusion of learning and dynamics (feedback loops). Note, however, that the resource (knowledge) element defies construction in linear form – we begin here to see it as an interconnected whole (via the multiple arrows). Learning, moreover, creates multiple feedback effects.

19.6 **Towards a knowledge-based view**

We have reviewed four different perspectives on knowledge in strategy and in strategy making: knowledge as assets for protection, knowledge through innovation, knowledge embedded in routines, and knowledge through learning. In doing this we have touched on a wide variety of themes in strategic management, competitive advantage, the resource-based view, strategy making, and strategizing routines. We have also commented on developments in economic thinking ranging from neoclassical theory, through Schumpeter to evolutionary economics, with a hint also of institutional economics. Thus we have progressed from market positioning and the firm as a black box to serious consideration of internal organization and those processes that underpin competitive advantage. Knowledge makes its entry as an asset, albeit largely invisible, that protects competitive position. But we have moved to a more subtle position where knowledge is embedded in individuals and by complex processes is socialized and reintegrated into the organization at large. Do these various perspectives on knowledge enable us to articulate a *knowledge-based view of strategy* whose implications allow us to draw inferences about strategy and strategy making that are either absent from other theories or in contradiction to them? What are the essential ingredients of the knowledge-based view?

19.6.1 **Organizational knowledge**

Grant and Spender in a Special issue of the *Strategic Management Journal* in 1996 have two much quoted papers that step outside conventional economic approaches. Grant sees the firm as an institution for integrating knowledge, where knowledge is individually held and is typically tacit. The organization's role is to access, transfer and integrate that tacit knowledge within and throughout the organization. His approach is very similar to that of Nonaka and Takeuchi (see below). In Grant's view, the firm is a co-ordinating mechanism with implications for organizational design and for the nature of organizational process. Spender sees knowledge as too contentious a concept to easily bear the weight of a theory. The biggest problem, he sees, is the multitude of types and definitions. He therefore argues (as Grant does implicitly) for a pluralistic viewpoint and advances the idea of interplay between explicit and tacit knowledge, and between different units within the organization (from individuals through to collectives). This leads to a set of ideal types (see Figure 19.4). He moves from this to knowledge as activity and argues eventually for a Penrosian view – a historical, path-dependent process in which the individual rather than organizational machine bureaucracies are the important strategists. It is useful to start with Spender's view that our concepts of knowledge are highly varied and in many ways inconsistent or incapable of being interrelated:

> *Knowledge is a highly contentious concept, far too problematic to bear the weight of a useful theory of the firm without a clear statement of the epistemology which gives it meaning* (Spender 1996, p. 48).

He then proceeds by making three points.

1 Knowledge is interplay between the *tacit/implicit* and the *explicit*, the vertical dimension in Figure 19.4.

2 This distinction allows for several different *adaptation mechanisms* – for example, Nelson and Winter's own use of adaptive feedback mechanisms where the interplay between tacit and explicit takes place through individual choices that are eventually embedded in organizational routines ('organizational genetics').

3 Many theorists, starting with Polanyi (1966) and famously in Nonaka and Takeuchi (1995), see the origin of all knowledge in individual intuition. So the third element is the transformation and communication of what is known tacitly by individuals into collective or social knowledge. Hence the second, horizontal dimension in Figure 19.4.

Therefore, Spender advances four ideal types connected by an adaptation mechanism. He observes that the organizational intent is to transform tacit, individual knowledge into collectively owned, objectifiable knowledge – this is the world of standards, procedures, practices, patents, science, training, but still recognizably a world that remains dependent on the knowledge held by individuals although, in this diagram, the adaptation mechanisms of transformation and conversion process operate in silence. Given different types of knowledge, are there different types of knowledge-based theory, Spender asks. A theory of *conscious* knowledge would have to solve agency problems – how can inventors be persuaded to pass on their codified knowledge to an organization? A theory based on *automatic* knowledge also has agency problems where the brilliant man must be persuaded to stay with the firm (cf work-out clauses for entrepreneurs when they sell their businesses).

	Individual	Social
Explicit	Conscious	Objectified
Implicit	Automatic	Collective

Figure 19.4 Different types of organizational knowledge
Source: Spender, 1996.

A theory of *objectified* knowledge raises problems of imitability in a world where knowledge is explicit. A theory based on inherently immobile *collective* knowledge (this is where Nonaka and Takeuchi would wish to take us and where Nelson and Winter go with their extra-rational learning processes) leads to a conclusion that this is the most secure and strategically significant kind of organizational knowledge.

Nonaka and Takeuchi's knowledge spiral (Figure 19.5) predates Spender by some three years. Their arena (matrix) has become a standard framework of its kind. Their focus is on a *knowledge spiral*, an adaptation mechanism through which knowledge is converted and then transferred between the tacit and the explicit (it can go either way) and among individuals, groups and the whole organization. *Socialization* is the sharing of experiences so that tacit knowledge is shared between individuals, from individuals to the organization through the development of culture and shared mental models, and from the organization to individuals. *Externalization* is the conversion of tacit into explicit knowledge through its articulation and systematization within the organization. *Combination* involves the conversion of explicit knowledge held by individuals and groups into explicit knowledge at the organizational level, and subsequent conversion of organizational knowledge back to the individual in different form. This is the key role of information systems within the firm. *Internalization* is conversion of explicit knowledge back into tacit knowledge in the form of individual know-how and organizational routines. The *knowledge spiral* is the dynamic process by which knowledge is translated through separate but related stages, through socialization to combination and externalization, and back to internalization.

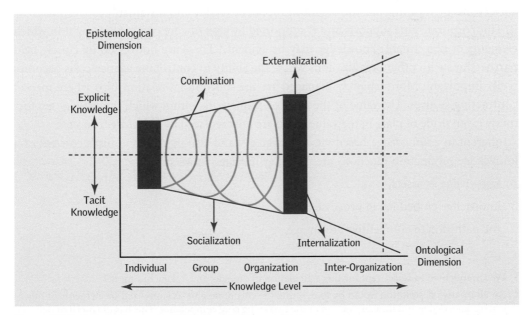

Figure 19.5 Spiral of organizational knowledge creation
Source: I Nonaka 'On a knowledge creating organization', Paper presented at AIF National Congress, Posma, October 1993.

Thus, individual creativity can be linked to the growth of collective knowledge.[7] Spender's contribution relates to the different types of organizational knowledge whereas Takeuchi and Nonaka use the same intellectual space to portray the adaptation mechanisms that organizations can use to convert and transfer various kinds of knowledge to inimitable and therefore rent-earning organizational knowledge.

19.6.2 From value chain to value web

The value chain, popular for its simple and robust character, can be restated firstly in the language of core competences and the RBV but more fundamentally in this language of knowledge. This characterization restates the linear chain of activities as a similar chain of core competences. The activities of the value chain might be dispersed across different owners but in any event they are controlled in economic terms through the operation of core competences. Thus economic power is operated through the conjunction and interaction of core competences. However, the linearity of the chain metaphor is uncomfortable where the empirical record suggests knowledge is multifaceted and capable of being attached to other pieces of knowledge in a variety of expected and unexpected ways, particularly as interface standards are developed and 'knowledge as Lego' becomes more and more possible.

The notion of a web is intuitively appealing (Figure 19.6). At the centre is the *corporate glue* (McGee 2003), that is, the organizationally held tacit knowledge that cannot readily be imitated – the *collective knowledge* according to Spender, and the *knowledge architecture* according to Henderson and Clark. This is characteristically a collective concept but also a tacit and sticky concept, meaning that the organization can be readily and sustainably differentiated by it. This corporate glue supports and is supported by a set of core competences within which elements of objectifiable knowledge may be evident.[8] These are buttressed by closely held partnerships with other organizations where the ability to control the agency costs becomes really important. More remotely managed are the subcontract relationships where market contracting suffices. The value of the web is a framework within which the *activity sets* formerly given pride of place in the value chain are now replaced by *knowledge concepts*.

Inherent in a knowledge-based view of strategy (and also in an economist's concept of a knowledge production function) are three key linkages between:

1   knowledge as assets;

2   knowledge embedded in processes; and

3   the pathways to competitive advantage.

---

[7]   We are indebted to Rob Grant for this articulation of Nonaka and Takeuchi's model.

[8]   An alternative description would be to describe the corporate glue as supported by elements of objectifiable knowledge and the conjunction of the two being core competence. This has the merit of defining core competence explicitly in terms of knowledge concepts.

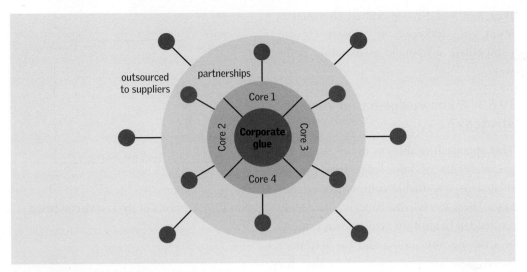

Figure 19.6 The knowledge web
Source: McGee, 2003.

According to the Teece *et al.* (1997) discussion of dynamic capabilities, there are four knowledge processes:

1 entrepreneurial (creative);

2 coordinative and integrative (static);

3 learning (dynamic); and

4 reconfigurational (transformational).

In asset or resource terms we see knowledge as embedded in many different classes of assets such as technology, complementary, financial, reputational, structural, institutional, and market structure. For example, Amit and Schoemaker (1993) provide an excellent description (see Chapter 7) of strategic assets and their linkage to organizational rent (competitive advantage). Following but not replicating Teece *et al.* (1997), we express the linkages to competitive advantage in terms of *dynamic pathways*. Whereas Amit and Schoemaker (1993) and Peteraf (1993) only assert that assets create profit possibilities, in this approach the dynamic pathways are defined in terms of path dependency (which allows us to call on an evolutionary perspective) and technological opportunities (which allows for returns to scale,[9] first/early mover advantage, and oligopolistic gaming). The strength of this approach lies in its organizational inclusivity, ranging from internal process to asset positions, linked over time through management of the pathways. Empirical evidence here is patchy but attracting research interest as we speak. In summary, this approach includes entrepreneurial (creative)

---

[9] Especially network externalities where 'winner takes all' strategies are possible; McGee and Sammut-Bonnici (2002, 2003), summarized in Chapter 12.

processes and a more explicit characterization of linkages of knowledge to
competitive advantage as dynamic pathways.

19.6.3 A knowledge-based view of strategy?

This approach enables us to see that there
are elements of knowledge that can be
related to sustainable competitive advantage. These knowledge concepts lie deeply
embedded behind the well-known notions
of strategic positioning and the resource-
based view and are powerful in that they, in a
fundamental sense, are the drivers behind core
competences and competitive advantage. So, is it
possible to draw this thinking together into a perspective that we might call the knowledge-based
view of strategy? Our approach is to suggest three
categories (Figure 19.7) called specific knowledge,
organizational knowledge, and the **knowledge
web**.[10]

Specific knowledge (Figure 19.8) relates to the
knowledge production function and draws links
between knowledge, production, access to knowledge, knowledge diffusion, connections between
elements of knowledge, and knowledge renewal
(including the discarding of knowledge). The

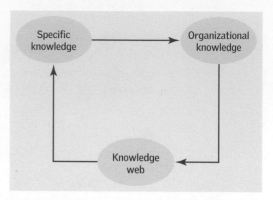

Figure 19.7 Elements of the knowledge-based view

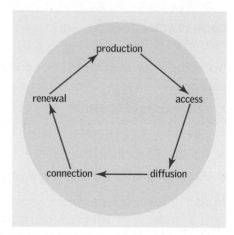

Figure 19.8 Elements of specific knowledge

foundations of this are highly dispersed throughout the academic literature. There is a considerable economic literature on innovation competition and on R&D. There is a
considerable scientific and social science literature on innovation processes. There is also
some considerable mystery about creativity, usually captured under the heading of
serendipity.

Organizational knowledge (Figure 19.9) is the process by which various elements of specific
knowledge are taken into the organization, transformed into social/collective knowledge
and, through dynamic pathways, linked into other organizational activities. The key
elements are characterized as types of organization knowledge, the knowledge creation

---

[10] Alternatively knowledge in action.

process, and dynamic pathways. The inheritance from such writers as Spender, Takeuchi and Nonaka, and Teece *et al.* is self-evident.

The knowledge web (*see* Figure 19.6) represents the way in which specific knowledge and organizational knowledge is captured into value-creating activities within the firm (discussed above) (*see* also Winter 1987 for an earlier exposition of this point). Both specific and organizational knowledge feed into the knowledge web. The notion of corporate glue or knowledge architecture stems

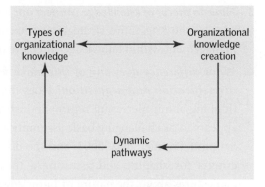

Figure 19.9 Organizational knowledge

directly from the conjunction of tacit and social knowledge. But specific knowledge is also evident from its role within core competences and within the core competences of strategic partners. The knowledge web is also dynamic in that incentives to innovate and to create new linkages between knowledge components are created here and therefore provide the link back to the knowledge production function that is captured within the category of specific knowledge.

This approach allows us to connect three strands. The first concerns the ways in which knowledge is produced, accessed, diffused, renewed and discarded. The second concerns the notion of organizational knowledge as an essentially invisible asset fostered and conditioned by visible and defined organizational routines and ad hoc processes. The third is a strategic theory of the firm in which positioning and resource-based approaches are recast in the form of knowledge.[11] Again, knowledge is the invisible asset but captured here in the form of specific activities on which management focuses attention. This does not answer all the questions but perhaps does allow us to define the arena of interesting questions and permit the formation of some conjectures. We suggest the following list.

1 *How is knowledge produced and accessed?* This includes the imponderable of 'knowledge creation' as well as 'knowledge conversion' (a word used by Grant (1996) and by Nonaka (1994) and has a parallel to the economists' idea of a production function). We know more about the processes of innovation and we also know quite a lot about the economic analysis of new technology decisions.

2 *How does knowledge fit into supply chain and value chain thinking* – in other words, how does it link and co-ordinate with the other activities of the firm to produce competitive advantage? The knowledge web is a useful framework but much needs to be done to identify the specifics in actual cases and applications.

[11] A link here could be made with Rumelt (1984) by developing the argument that our use of knowledge as corporate glue is directly analogous to his use of isolating mechanisms.

3   *How do pieces of knowledge connect up?* How do they change the nature of the corporate 'glue' – the integrative strategic architecture? The burgeoning function of knowledge management within knowledge-intensive organizations reflects these considerations.

4   *What difference does any of this make for the analysis of strategic decisions such as diversification and acquisition?* Does this have anything to contribute to economists' thinking about increasing returns industries – another arena where the 'new economy' appears to be challenging basic assumptions behind traditional thinking (*see* McGee and Sammut-Bonnici 2002, 2003, and the discussion in Chapter 12)? These are not simply criteria for shaping and assessing a theory but they are also conjectures. They are conjectures about the nature of knowledge itself, whether such a multi-faceted concept can be marshalled into the constraints inherent in a normative, organizationally focused theory.

Case box: Patient money at Corning Glass

Some companies prosper by making continuous improvements to their business practices. Others grow by using their market clout to acquire rivals for the skills and markets they covet. A few thrive by making patient investments in far-sighted ideas of their own that can take decades to pay off. Rarely does any company attempt to do all three things at once.

Corning, a glass maker that was founded 150 years ago, is one of those rare manufacturing enterprises that has managed to cling to its innovative roots. Apart from the upheaval of the 1970s and 1980s, which affected many American companies that had grown fat in the decades after the second world war, Corning has been remarkably consistent in giving full rein to the ingenuity of its researchers while pursuing total mastery over its process technologies.

Its reputation for continuous innovation over a century and a half is unrivalled anywhere. Without Corning's ribbon machine, electric light bulbs, vacuum flasks and cathode ray tubes would have been far costlier and more fragile affairs. Without its patented borosilicate glasses, there would have been no Pyrex ovenware. The glass ceramics called Pyroceram, which the company developed originally for missile nose cones, has not quite made Corning a household name. By contrast, its Corelle line became one of the world's most popular brands of tableware.

The firm's successful casting of the 200-inch (five-metre) mirror for the Hale telescope on Mount Palomar in 1934, a feat that even the mighty General Electric had attempted but failed to achieve, reinforced the company's reputation in the scientific world. Its patented vacuum-deposition processes, secretly used for years in the optics aboard American spy satellites, have made Corning the mirror maker of choice for optical astronomers everywhere since the end of the cold war. Corning's invention of ceramic substrates for catalytic converters made the firm the darling of Detroit. And then there was the optical waveguide – the invention, better known as optical fibre, that has transformed telecommunications the world over.

'Patient money' was the principle that guided the Houghton family when it first invested in a small glass company in Somerville, Massachusetts, in 1851. (The firm moved to the city of Corning, New York in 1868.) And the Houghton dynasty has influenced the company according to that principle ever since. Lacking access to the cheap immigrant labour, raw materials and exploding markets that rival glass makers enjoyed across the Alleghenies in the Ohio valley, to the west, the Houghtons also insisted that their fledgling corporation should focus exclusively on the specialist end of the business and use inventiveness as its principal competitive weapon. Producing me-too products was out of the question, so Corning's only choice was to be endlessly unorthodox – and so, for the most part, it has remained.

Central to Corning's success in turning unorthodoxy into a winning way has been the management's profound understanding of the value of the company's intellectual property, and its willingness to protect that at any cost. This has meant investing in research and development at a rate almost double that of the rest of the industry. It has also meant refusing to blink when bigger companies with deeper pockets infringed Corning's patents and sought to out-spend it in the law courts, as when, one by one, wealthy corporations tried to muscle their way into Corning's optical fibre business. Even giants such as ITT in America and Sumitomo in Japan found to their cost that the feisty little glass maker from upstate New York refused to roll over and play dead. Today, Corning has 40% of the market for optical fibre – nearly three times more than its nearest rival. But it took Corning 15 years of patient investment in optical-fibre technology to make a profit.

Only once has Corning stumbled badly. The 20-odd acquisitions the company made building its MetPath business into the largest medical-testing organization in the world smacked of impatient money. Yet in the end, this helped the company rediscover its innovative roots. Once again, the Houghtons, still around and still influential, were there to help nudge Corning back to its 150-year-old formula for patient innovation.

Source: 'Patient money', *The Economist*, 5 July 2001.
© The Economist Newspaper Limited, London (5 July 2001).

Questions for discussion

1 Why should Corning Glass have succeeded in its close control of intellectual property when so many others (see the case box on the knowledge economy) have outsourced their R&D?

2 What risks did Corning take and how did it manage them?

3 Use the 'knowledge spiral' (Nonaka and Takeuchi) to describe and classify Corning's approach to intellectual property.

19.7 Summary

Having taken a reasonably broad view of the writings in and around knowledge and strategy we have made a number of observations about current thinking:

1 Whereas knowledge is only implicit in the market-based view it is a central element of the resource-based view.

2 Dynamic theories of the firm cannot operate without some clear and operational concepts of knowledge. For example: (i) tacit and explicit and (ii) a knowledge production function incorporating innovating, accessing, transferring, integrating, and codifying.

3 However, we sympathize with assertions that knowledge is a highly contentious concept. For example: know-how vs know-what; explicit vs. implicit; individual vs collective; knowledge as knowing, as learning, as activity etc.

4 Nevertheless, our conjectures about the applicability of knowledge as a significant explanatory variable may be supported empirically; for example, see the wide range of citations in Eisenhardt and Santos (2001).

5 The writing on organizational knowledge has shown it as the lynchpin between internal organizational structures and processes and the capture of economic rents.

6 More controversially, there is a case for an evolutionary theory incorporating dynamic pathways as the external manifestation of organizational knowledge.

Our own approach to this has not been to attempt to provide 'a unified theory of absolutely everything'.[12] Rather, we have attempted to find a way of incorporating knowledge variables into the explanation of the long-run performance of firms, their long-run sustainable competitive advantages. To do this we offer a simple categorization that links three types of literature: on specific knowledge (a very dispersed literature), on organizational knowledge (which made considerable progress in the 1990s), and on the strategic theory of the firm. These strands we suggest are mutually reinforcing and interconnected. In particular, from a managerial perspective we can see how knowledge issues have a very direct economic content via the knowledge production/diffusion function, and a very organizational and individual element through analysis of organizational knowledge. These do not stand, however, as separable issues although elements of the problem can be treated in isolation. Rather, the system-wide characteristics of knowledge are evident particularly in the knowledge web through which value creation activities are composed.

We would also offer the final organizational observation that the knowledge web is a framework that allows firms to monitor threats. It should allow managers to question

---

[12] See the debates that have taken place in theoretical physics on just this issue.

the adequacy of existing business models and to analyse the unconventional responses that new entrants and innovators may be 'cooking up' to attack the entrenched positions of leading firms. In fact we believe that many leading firms fail to innovate because they act like hierarchies, not markets. They allocate resources for bureaucratic, political but not economic reasons. Too few of them make their organizational processes and routines receptive to idea and value innovation. Unfortunately they do not see innovation, learning and knowledge acquisition as key elements of the corporate DNA.

Key terms

Disruptive technologies *703*

Dominant design *714*

Efficiency effect *712*

Innovation *702*

Knowledge-based view *719*

Knowledge web *726*

Objectified knowledge *709*

Replacement effect *712*

Sunk cost effect *712*

Sustaining technologies *703*

Tacit knowledge *718*

Value innovation *704*

Recap questions and assignments

1 Compare the discussion of the knowledge economy in this chapter with the discussion of the new economy in Chapter 12. Identify the common elements and their effect on strategic discussions.

2 Consider also the discussion of risk in Chapter 14. What does a knowledge-based view of strategy imply for strategic risk and strategic decision-making?

3 Compare the action of disruptive technologies in this chapter with Schumpeter's 'Creative destruction' explained in Chapter 8. What role does tacit knowledge play in these ideas?

When you have read this chapter, log on to the Online Learning Centre website at www.mcgraw-hill.co.uk/textbooks/mcgee to explore chapter-by-chapter test questions, further reading and more online study tools for strategy.

Case 1 **Procter & Gamble: Jager's gamble**

Durk Jager, Procter & Gamble's new chief executive, wants to turn it into an innovative company. Easier said than done

A few years back, scientists at Procter & Gamble hit upon a big idea. Combining know-how in absorbent paper with a new 'dry-weave' polyethylene mesh, they came up with a thin, highly absorbent sanitary towel, the first breakthrough in feminine hygiene in 50 years. Today, P&G's 'Always' pads, now jazzed up with wings and even thinner, are sold in 80 countries, and are the mainstay of a product family that generates around $1.6 billion in annual sales.

This is just the kind of innovation that Durk Jager, who took over at P&G in January, sees as essential to rekindling growth at the world's largest consumer-products group. As its latest move, P&G announced on October 26th that it is prepared to give away or license any of its 25,000 patents, including those used in established brands. Chuck Hong, the firm's director of R&D for corporate innovations, thinks this will 'force us to continually invent'.

But why must P&G be forced to invent? Surely a firm with $38 billion in sales, more than 300 brands and 110,000 employees in 70 countries, with patents spanning fats and oils, plant fibres, surfactants and calcium, with vast marketing and financial resources, ought to be churning out exciting new products all the time? The trouble is, the new sanitary towel, which Mr Jager himself admits was the company's last big innovation, was launched away back in 1983. The story at P&G is not so much 'Always' as 'almost never'.

Mr Jager blames the consumer-product industry's problems on its failure to innovate. It has, he told this month's annual meeting in Cincinnati, 'led to commodity products and pricing pressure'. P&G has done worse than most. It has lost some 10% of its global market share in the past five years. Volumes this year will grow by 2% at best.

Turning a marketer into an innovator requires money, ideas and a nimble culture. P&G's problem has never been a lack of money or even ideas. Last year it was America's 21st-largest investor in research and development, spending $1.7 billion. Its R&D budget has grown from 2.9% to 4.5% of net sales over the past decade – still well below the 15% typical in the pharmaceuticals industry, but double that of Gillette. That spending has, however, yielded little. Less than 10% of P&G's thousands of patents are used in its hundreds of brands.

The fault lies with the culture. The firm has stifled innovation and prevented new ideas from getting to market quickly. Years after P&G developed its tissue-towel products, they have only just started to be rolled out globally. 'We're slower than my great-grandma,' says one executive.

Mr Jager is trying to change all that. In June he announced a big internal shake-up, sacking 13% of the workforce to streamline management and speed up decision-making. He is tying strategy and global profit targets to the performance of brands, rather than countries, and handing responsibility for new ideas to new business managers, not ones steeped in existing businesses. He has set up innovation teams to shoot promising ideas rapidly around the company and rush the best to market. And P&G plans to take more risks, cutting pre-market laboratory testing and putting products on sale earlier.

Spiffy Swiffer

P&G has had some success with the recent launch of products, including Swiffer, a dry mop that traps dust, Febreze spray to eliminate smells in fabric and Dryel, a home dry-cleaning kit, all of which he says are 'new-to-the-world' products, not just variants of old ones. Febreze, which was introduced in June last year, is already America's fifth-most successful new packaged product, with sales of $230m in its first year. And whereas Febreze took forever to be launched, Mr Jager boasts that Swiffer went from test marketing to global roll-out in a record 18 months.

P&G has even started looking outside for new ideas. To develop 'NutriDelight', a fortified orange powdered drink unveiled at the annual meeting, P&G worked with Unicef and licensed in the technology that lets iron exist with iodine and vitamin A in a stable form, helping undernourished children put on weight. And the group recently bought Iams Petfoods, admired for a scientific approach to pet health that includes low-calcium nosh for big dogs prone to overgrown bones, and oil and mineral formulas for 'senior' pets with bad joints.

Mr Jager is getting on the Internet, too. In November P&G will launch its majority-owned venture, reflect.com, an Internet-only range of 50,000 beauty products sold direct to consumers. Nathan Estruth, who helps run reflect.com, calls the venture 'heresy' for a mass-market company that has always sold through retailers.

Yet turning a marketing giant into a nippy innovator will be hard. P&G's line managers and country chiefs are trained to squeeze the last drop of sales out of existing products, not back risky new ones. Sam Stern, a professor at Oregon State University who has written a book on creativity in consumer-goods companies, points out that new ideas threaten the status quo.

However esoteric they sound, most consumer-goods technologies are unlikely to fend off imitators for long. A drug's effect is tied closely to its complex technology. Having gone through rigorous approval and lengthy clinical trials, patent challenges on drugs are rare. By contrast, Gillette's patent on a new toothbrush may specify with utmost precision how bristles are laid out; but there are lots of different 'technologies' that can clean teeth just as well. Lynn Dornblaser, director of the Global New Products Database, estimates that only 10% of the 55,000 brand new products that were launched globally last year are really innovative.

Even when consumer-products companies do come up with something novel, competitors catch up fast. 'Always' went unchallenged for ten years. Now, only one year after the launch of Febreze, Johnson & Johnson, Clorox and others have launched their own improved versions – mainly because Febreze was in pre-market testing for two years.

Similarly, Gillette took ten years and spent $1 billion developing its Mach3 triple-blade razor, launched last year. Within a few months, Asda, a British supermarket, rushed in with its own product, Tri-Flex, claiming that it was just as good and 40% cheaper.

What is more, packaged-goods companies not only have to develop the product, but also try to get jaded consumers to think they need it. That sometimes works. Upbeat marketing turned a very ordinary orange drink, Sunny Delight, into one of P&G's best brands.

But few new products are so successful. Information Resources, which researches packaged goods in America, finds that less than 1% of products launched in 1998 achieved $100m of sales in their first year. More than two-thirds flop in their first year. Hence, many managers in consumer-goods firms associate innovation with failure. Mr Jager has to persuade them that it is a condition for success.

Source: 'Jager's gamble', *The Economist*, 28 October 1999.
© The Economist Newspaper Limited, London (28 October 1999).

Case Questions

1 Why must P&G 'be forced to invent'? (p. 733)
2 Describe the incentives to innovate and the rewards and risks of innovation in terms of this P&G experience.

Further reading and references

Abramowitz, M (1986) 'Catching up, forging ahead, and falling behind', *Journal of Economic History,* **66**, pp. 385–406.

Alchian, AA (1950) 'Uncertainty, Evolution and Economic Theory', *Journal of Political Economy,* **58**, pp. 211–21.

Alchian, AA (1953) 'Biological Analogues in the Theory of the Firm: Comment', *American Economic Review,* **43**, pp. 600–3.

Alchian, AA and Demsetz, H (1972) 'Production, information costs, and economic organisation', *American Economic Review,* **62**, pp. 777–95.

Amit, R and Schoemaker, PJ (1993) 'Strategic assets and organisational rent', *Strategic Management Journal,* **14**, pp. 33–46.

Anderson, P and Tushman, ML (1990) 'Technological Discontinuities and Dominant Designs', *Administrative Science Quarterly,* **35**, pp. 604–33.

Argyris, C and Schon, D (1978) *Organisational Learning: A Theory in Action Perspective,* Addison-Wesley, Reading, MA.

Arrow, K (1962) 'Economic Welfare and the Allocation of Resources for Inventions,' in RR Nelson (ed.) *The Rate and Direction of Economic Activity,* Princeton University Press, Princeton, NJ.

Barney, J (1991) 'Firm resources and sustained competitive advantage', *Journal of Management,* **17**, pp. 99–120.

Besanko, D, Dranove, D and Shanley, M (2000) *Economics of Strategy,* 2nd edition, John Wiley & Sons, New York.

Bettis, RA and Prahalad, CK (1995) 'The dominant logic: retrospective and extension', *Strategic Management Journal,* **16**, **1**, pp. 5–15.

Brandenburger, AM and Nalebuff, BJ (1995) *Co-opetition,* Doubleday, New York.

Brown, JS and Duguid, P (1991) 'Organisational learning and communities of practice: Toward a unified view of working, learning and innovation', *Organization Science,* **2**, pp. 40–57.

Burgelman, RA (1983) 'A model of the interaction of strategic behaviour, corporate context, and the concept of strategy', *The Academy of Management Review,* **8**, **1**, pp. 61–70.

Chandler, AD Jr (1990) *Scale and Scope: The Economics of Industrial Competition,* Harvard University Press, Cambridge, MA.

Christensen, CM (1997) *The Innovator's Dilemma,* HBS Press, Boston, MA.

Coase, R (1937) 'The nature of the firm', *Economica,* **4**, pp. 386–405.

Coase, R (1988) 'Lecture on the nature of the firm, III', *Journal of Law, Economics and Organisation,* **4**, pp. 33–47.

Cohen, MD and Baclayan, P (1994) 'Organisational routines are stored as procedural memory: evidence from a laboratory study', *Organisation Science*, **5**, **4**, pp. 554–68.

Cooper, AC and Schendel, DE (1976) 'Strategic Response to Technological Threats', *Business Horizons*, **19**.

Cyert, RM and March, JG (1963) *A Behavioral Theory of the Firm*, Prentice-Hall, Englewood Cliffs, NJ.

D'Aveni, RA (1994) *Hypercompetition: Managing the Dynamics of Strategic Manoeuvring*, Free Press, New York.

De Geus, A (1976) *The Living Company*, HBS Press, Boston, MA.

De Wit, R and Meyer, R (1994) *Strategy: Process, Context, and Content*, West, St Paul, MN.

Dussage, P, Hart, S and Ramanantsoa (1996) *Strategic Technology Management*, Wiley, New York.

Eisenhardt, KM and Martin, JA (2000) 'Dynamic capabilities: what are they?' *Strategic Management Journal*, Special issue, pp. 1105–21.

Eisenhardt, KM and Santos, FM (2002) 'Knowledge-based view: a new theory of strategy?' in AM Pettigrew, H Thomas, and R Whittington (eds) *The Handbook of Strategy and Management*, Sage Publications, London.

Evans, P and Wurster, T (1997) 'Strategy and the New Economics of Information', *Harvard Business Review*, Sept/Oct, **75**, **5**, pp. 70–82.

Evans, P and Wurster, T (1999) *Blown to Bits: How the New Economics of Information Transforms Strategy*, Harvard Business School Press.

Ghemawat, P (1984) 'Capacity expansion in the titanium dioxide industry', *Journal of Industrial Economics*, **32**, pp. 145–63.

Ghemawat, P (1991) *Commitment: The Dynamics of Strategy*, Free Press, New York.

Ghemawat, P (1997) *Strategy and the Business Landscape*, Addison-Wesley, Reading MA.

Gottinger, H-W (1998) 'Technological races', *Annual Review of Economics* (Japan), **38**, 1–9.

Gottinger, H-W (2001) 'Stochastic innovation races', *Technological Forecasting and Social Change*, **68**, pp. 1–18.

Gottinger, H-W (2003) *Economics of Network Industries*, Routledge, London.

Granovetter, M (1985) 'Economic action and social structures', *American Journal of Sociology*, **91**, pp. 481–510.

Grant, RM (1991) 'The resource based theory of competitive advantage: implications for strategy formulation', *California Management Review*, Spring, pp. 119–45.

Grant, RM (1996) 'Toward a knowledge-based theory of the firm', *Strategic Management Journal*, 17 (Winter Special Issue), pp. 109–22.

Hall, RL and Hitch, CJ (1939) 'Price theory and business behaviour', *Oxford Economic*

Papers, 2, reprinted in T Wilson and PWS Andrews (eds) (1951) *Oxford Studies in the Price Mechanism*, Clarendon Press, Oxford.

Hamel, G (2000) *Leading the Revolution*, HBS Press, Boston, MA.

Hamel, G and Prahalad, CK (1993) 'Strategy as stretch and leverage', *Harvard Business Review*, March/April.

Hedberg, BLT (1981) 'How organisations learn and unlearn', in PC Nystrom and WH Starbuck (eds) *Handbook of Organisational Design*, Volume 1, pp. 2–27, Oxford University Press, New York.

Henderson, RM and Clark, KB (1990) 'Architectural innovation: the reconfiguration of existing technologies and the failure of established firms', *Administrative Science Quarterly*, **35, 1**, pp. 9–30.

Huff, AS (1994) 'Mapping strategic thought', in AS Huff (ed.) *Mapping Strategic Thought*, 2nd edition, pp. 11–52, John Wiley & Sons, Chichester.

Jensen, MC and Meckling, W (1976) 'Theory of the firm: managerial behaviour, agency costs, and ownership structure', *Journal of Financial Economics*, **3**, pp. 305–60.

Johnson, G and Huff, AS (1998) 'Everyday innovation/everyday strategy', in G Hamel, CK Prahalad and H Thomas (eds) *Strategic Flexibility: Managing in a Turbulent Economy*, John Wiley & Sons, Chichester.

Johnson, G and Bowman, C (1999) 'Strategy and everyday reality: the case for study of micro-strategy', working paper, 15th EGOS Colloquium.

Kim, W Chan and Mauborgne, R (1999) 'Strategy, Value Innovation and the Knowledge Economy', *Sloan Management Review*, **40, 3**, Spring, pp. 41–54.

Kogut, B and Zander, U (1992) 'Knowledge of the firm, combinative capabilities, and the replication of technology', *Organisation Science*, **3**, pp. 383–97.

Langlois, RN (1986) 'Rationality, institutions, and explanation', in RN Langlois (ed.) *Economics as a Process: Essays in the New Institutional Economics*: Cambridge University Press Cambridge, pp. 225–55.

Leonard-Barton, D (1992) 'Core capabilities and core rigidities: a paradox in managing new product development', *Strategic Management Journal*, **13** (Special Issue), pp. 111–26.

Lerner, J (1997) 'An empirical exploration of a technology race', *The Rand Journal of Economics*, **28, 2**, pp. 228–34.

Lester, RA (1946) 'Shortcomings of marginal analysis for wage-employment problems', *American Economic Review*, **36**, pp. 63–82.

Levitt, B and March, JG (1988) 'Organisational learning', *Annual Review of Sociology*, **14**, pp. 319–40

March, JG and Simon, HA (1958) *Organisations*, John Wiley, New York.

Marshall, A (1920) *Principles of Economics*, 8th edition, Macmillan Press, London.

McGee, J (2003) 'Strategy as Orchestrating Knowledge', in D Wilson and S Cummings (eds) *Images of Strategy*, Basil Blackwell, Oxford.

McGee, J and Sammut-Bonnici, T (2002) 'Network Industries in the New Economy', *European Business Journal*, **14**, **3**, September, pp. 116–32.

McGee, J and Sammut-Bonnici, T (2002) 'Network Strategies for the New Economy: Emerging Strategies for New Industry Structures', *European Business Journal*, **14**, **4**, December, pp. 174–85.

Menuhin, J (2001) *Strategising Routines: The Emergence of Strategic Initiatives,* unpublished PhD thesis, University of Warwick.

Menuhin, J and McGee, J (2003) 'Strategising routines in HSBC (UK), unpublished working paper, University of Warwick, Warwick Business School.

Nelson, RR and Winter, SG (1982) *An Evolutionary Theory of Economic Change,* Belknap Press, Cambridge, MA.

Nonaka, I and Takeuchi, H (1995) *The Knowledge-creating Company: How Japanese Companies Create the Dynamics of Innovation,* Oxford University Press, New York.

Nonaka, I (1994) 'A dynamic theory of knowledge creation', *Organization Science*, **5**, pp. 14–37.

Penrose, KT (1959) *The Theory of the Growth of the Firm,* Basil Blackwell, Oxford.

Peteraf, MA (1993) 'The cornerstones of competitive advantage: a resource-based view', *Strategic Management Journal*, **14**, **3**, pp. 179–91.

Porac, JF, Thomas, H and Baden Fuller, C (1989) 'Competitive groups as cognitive communities: the case of the Scottish knitwear manufacturers', *Journal of Management Studies*, **26**, pp. 397–416.

Porac, JF and Thomas, H (2002) 'Managing Cognition and Strategy: Issues, Trends and Future Directions', in AM Pettigrew, H Thomas and R Whittington (eds) *Handbook of Strategy and Management*, Sage Publications, London.

Polanyi, M (1966) *The Tacit Dimension,* Anchor Day Books, New York.

Porter, ME (1980) *Competitive Strategy,* Free Press, New York.

Porter, ME (1982) *Competitive Advantage,* Free Press, New York.

Prahalad, CK and Hamel, G (1990) 'The core competence of the corporation', *Harvard Business Review,* May/June, pp. 79–81.

Quinn, JB (1978) 'Strategic Change: Logical Incrementalism', *Sloan Management Review*, (Fall).

Rumelt, RP (1984) 'Towards a Strategic Theory of the Firm', in Robert Boyden Lamb (ed.) *Competitive Strategic Management,* Prentice-Hall, Englewood Cliffs, NJ.

Scherer, F (1991) 'International R&D races: theory and evidence', in L-G Mattsson and B Stymme (eds) *Corporate and Industry Strategies for Europe,* Elsevier Science Publishers, New York.

Schumpeter, J (1934) *The Theory of Economic Development,* Harvard University Press, Cambridge, MA (first published in 1911, republished 1968).

Simon, HA (1955) 'A behavioural model of rational choice', *Quarterly Journal of Economics,* **69,** pp. 99–118.

Simon, HA (1959) 'Theories of decision-making in economics and behavioural science', *American Economic Review,* **49,** pp. 253–83.

Spender, J-C (1996) 'Making knowledge the basis of a dynamic theory of the firm', *Strategic Management Journal,* 17 (Winter Special Issue), pp. 45–62.

Teece, DJ (1980) 'Economics of scope and the scope of the enterprise', *Journal of Economic Behaviour and Organisation,* **1,** pp. 223–47.

Teece, DJ (ed.) (1987) *The Competitive Challenge: Strategies for Industrial Innovation and Renewal,* Ballinger, Cambridge, MA.

Teece, DJ, Pisano, G and Shuen, A (1997) 'Dynamic capabilities and strategic management', *Strategic Management Journal,* **18, 7,** pp. 509–33.

Tsoukas, H (1996) 'The firm as a distributed knowledge system: a constructionist approach', *Strategic Management Journal,* **17,** Winter Special Issue, pp. 11–25.

Veblen, T (1898) 'Why economics is evolutionary science', *Quarterly Journal of Economics,* **12,** pp. 373–97.

Vronen, J (1995) *Economic Evolution,* Routledge, London.

Weick, KE (1979) *The Social Psychology of Organising,* McGraw-Hill, New York.

Weick, KE (1995) *Sense making in Organisations,* Sage, Thousand Oaks, CA.

Wernerfelt, B (1984) 'A resource-based view of the firm', *Strategic Management Journal,* **5, 2,** pp. 171–80.

Williamson, OE (1981) 'Strategizing, economizing, and economic organization', *Strategic Management Journal,* **12,** Winter Special Issue, pp. 75–94.

Williamson, OE (1985) *The Economic Institutions of Capitalism,* Free Press, New York.

Williamson, OE (1987) 'Transactions costs economics', *Journal of Economic Behaviour and Organisation* **8,** pp. 617–25.

Winter, SG (1964) 'Economic "natural selection" and the theory of the firm', *Yale Economic Essays,* **4,** pp. 225–72.

Winter, SG (1987) 'Knowledge and competence as strategic assets', in DJ Teece (ed.) *Competitive Challenge – Strategies for Industrial Innovation and Renewal,* Ballinger, Cambridge, MA.

Chapter 20

Total quality, customer value and process impacts

Introduction

Almost any business studies student now has a compulsory course (or courses) in the areas of operations management and strategy as part of their degree. The subject is considered an essential element of a manager's toolkit. Indeed, Slack and Lewis (2002, p. 3) in their recent text, on operations strategy, pose the question, 'How can "operations", which is generally concerned with the day-to-day creation and delivery of goods and services be considered strategic?' They argue that operations is a key part of a firm's strategic system and define operations strategy as the strategic reconciliation between the requirements of the markets in which the firm operates with the capabilities of its operational resources – i.e. what they can and cannot do. In other words, a continual and critical element of strategic process design, feedback and renewal is the analysis of how to achieve 'fit' between the company's resources and processes (i.e. capacity, supply network, process technology and organization) on the one hand and the requirements of its market positioning (i.e. customer segmentation, product differentiation, branding etc.) on the other hand.

From a strategic systems perspective two elements of this 'fit' process are particularly important and are considered thoroughly in this chapter. The first is the concept of quality (and the associated phrase **total quality management**) as a value driver for customer satisfaction and coherence across internal **business operations processes**. The second is the feedback impact of understanding **customer value** on the strategic redesign of the company's processes and market positioning.

Therefore, we examine in this chapter:

- Concepts of quality and their linkage to strategy.

- Examples of quality processes in practice explaining the Kaizen process (i.e. step-by-step improvements) and continuous improvement processes.

- Linkages between quality concepts and customer perceptions of value.

- The close linkage between operations management and strategy.

- The relationship between value and operations in creating value and achieving value innovation.

20.1 **Quality concepts**

> *When everything would seem to be matter of price, there lies still at the root of great business success the very much more important factor of quality ... After that, and a long way after, comes cost.* (Carnegie 1920)

The principles, practices and tools that comprise quality management have become a major focus of managerial attention in the West recently, in part because Japanese firms have used them with great commercial success in areas such as product quality, sales growth and profitability. Nonetheless, it seems to us that there is still a lack of clarity about the implications of quality for the process of strategic management in particular. Too many managers still think of quality as essentially an operations' problem: a functional issue of importance only to marketing or to production. On the other hand, many managers have been subjected over the last decade to innumerable siren calls urging them to view quality as the centrepiece of business activity. However, despite the significant attention paid to quality in recent years, strategic management practice and research remain a key area for extension of the quality concept (Godfrey 1993). In this discussion, we briefly review some perspectives on quality, offer an integrative strategic-level definition, and raise a series of issues that we believe are central to understanding the relationship between quality concepts and strategy.

20.1.1 What is quality anyway?

Goodness

Often, people will describe quality as meaning that something is outstanding in an indefinable way: 'even though Quality cannot be defined, you know what it is' (Pirsig 1974, p. 213). This common perspective can be found even in organizations which already seem quality-orientated. For example, one of the authors recently conducted a series of workshops at a large public-sector pension system well-known for productivity, innovation, and excellent client service and relations. However, despite the organization's reputation for high quality, not a single employee, form senior manager to clerk, could provide a specific operational definition of quality that the organization used to guide its work. Indeed, Pegels (1995 p. 4) notes that quality definitions have broadened to include quality processes and quality products, e.g. a definition of total quality management (TQM) is *'providing the customer with quality products at the right time and the right place'.*

A valuable product

Economists tend to view quality in a way familiar to many managers and consumers – as something valuable contained in a product, and hence a basis for price differences. Leffler (1982) suggests that quality is not the entire good but the amounts of an unpriced desired attribute contained in each unit of a priced attribute. For example, the cost of down comforters (duvets) depends mostly on the quantity of down, but most buyers are probably seeking a warm comforter, not a heavy one per se. In other words, what people want when they buy a good or a service is not necessarily the product itself but what it does for them. Marketing experts address this problem by disaggregating product quality into generic dimensions or attributes from the user's point of view. Figure 20.1 summarizes some of these marketing views of quality.

Physical Goods		Services	
Garvin (1987)	Moen, Nolan and Provost (1991)	Parasuraman, Zeithaml, and Berry (1985)	Zeithaml, Parasuraman and Berry (1990)
Performance	Time	Tangibles	Tangibles
Features	Consistency	Reliabilty	Reliabilty
Reliability	Uniformity	Responsiveness	Responsiveness
Conformance	Harmlessness	Access	Assurance
Durability	**Personal interface** ⟶	Courtesy	Empathy
Serviceability		Communication	
Aesthetics		Credibility	
Perceived quality ⟶⟶⟶⟶⟶		Security	
		Knowing customer	

Figure 20.1 Customer-based dimensions of quality

Analytical tools	Practices
Pareto charts (frequency of occurrence	Quality circles
Ishikawa (fishbone) diagrams	Team-based organization with specialized roles
Run charts	Benchmarking
Histograms	Design for manufacturability
Control charts	Vendor certification
Scatter diagrams	Customer certification
Flowcharts	Mistake-proofing (poka-yoke)
Forcefield analysis	Predictive maintenance
Process capability analysis	Design of experiments
Taguchi loss function	
Quality function deployment (house of quality)	
Failure and effects analyses	

Figure 20.3 Some quality management tools and practices

The process improvement view of quality is grounded in work on process control. Anchored in Shewhart's (1930) theory of variation and process improvement, it emphasizes the use of data analysis (Ishikawa 1982; 1985) and other managerial tools and practices to support a focus on data-driven, process-centred decision making (Crosby 1979; Deming 1986; Juran 1978; Juran and Gyrna 1988). This view has, however, moved far beyond considering just the production process. Quality is as much about design as it is about process (e.g. Susman 1992; Taguchi 1986). Organizational links to suppliers and customers, and the use of integrative planning techniques, are efforts to build quality into product design, production, delivery and service. A key in this perspective is the development and use of tools to guide decision making (Figure 20.3)

Case box: **Deming's 14 points of management**

The fourteen points of management of Dr W. Edward Deming represent for many people the essence of total quality management (TQM). Deming's fourteen points are:

1 Create constancy of purpose for improvement of product and service (organizations must allocate resources for long-term planning, research and education, and for the constant improvement of the design of their products and services)

2 Adopt the new philosophy (government regulations representing obstacles must be removed, transformation of companies is needed)

3 Cease dependence on mass inspections (quality must be designed and built into the processes, preventing defects rather than attempting to detect and fix them after they have occurred)

4 End the practice of awarding business on the basis of price tags alone (organizations should establish long-term relationships with [single] suppliers)

5 Improve constantly and forever the system of production and service (management and employees must search continuously for ways to improve quality and productivity)

6 Institute training (training at all levels is a necessity, not optional)

7 Adopt and institute leadership (managers should lead, not supervise)

8 Drive out fear (make employees feel secure enough to express ideas and ask questions)

9 Break down barriers between staff areas (working in teams will solve many problems and will improve quality and productivity)

10 Eliminate slogans, exhortations, and targets for the workforce (problems with quality and productivity are caused by the system, not by individuals. Posters and slogans generate frustration and resentment)

11 Eliminate numerical quotas for the workforce and numerical goals for people in management (in order to meet quotas, people will produce defective products and reports)

12 Remove barriers that rob people of pride of workmanship (individual performance reviews are a great barrier to pride of achievement)

13 Encourage education and self-improvement for everyone (continuous learning for everyone)

14 Take action to accomplish the transformation (commitment on the part of both [top] management and employees is required)

Strategy-based definition

Strategic management raises several issues central to any integrative definition of quality. First, the very notion of strategic management suggests the significance of the firm's environment. Some of the significant external forces that affect a firm include the actions of other firms. Technological change, customer needs and preferences and governmental and social influences; each of these may be relevant to quality. Other firms provide both areas and competitive standards for quality. Change drives and is driven by quality. The evolution of customers' expectations presents a moving target for firms, but what customers expect is partly a function of how firms choose to manage quality. Further, government and society look to business for guidance, yet they also mold firms' approaches. For example, the proliferation of government-sponsored quality awards has substantially raised firms' awareness of the significance and complexity of quality issues.

Second, strategy means little without a clearly-defined purpose (mission). Leadership and the importance of defining purpose are common themes in quality literature.

Third, if strategy is about finding better ways to pursue the mission, the methods of managing seem relevant to strategy. Since much of quality management research and practice is indeed centred on the basic structure and approach to work, there clearly is potential for substantial bonds between quality management and strategic management.

Perspective	Core message	Element of systems perspective
Quality as goodness	Quality permeates the whole of a thing	Quality is greater than the sum of the parts
Production	The processes to accomplish purposes can be improved	Quality can be pursued through broad methodical improvement
Marketing	Quality is in the eye of the beholder and can be defined	Quality is the purpose of serving others well
Strategy	Purposeful actions are needed in an uncertain world	Organizations 'do' and 'change' subject to a system of supplier-organization-user links, an environment, and guiding purpose

Figure 20.4 Summary of themes

Last, although strategy places a primary focus on the firm, it implicitly recognizes that the firm is but one element in the value-chain system leading from raw physical and human inputs to the delivery of goods and services to final customers. Since any one firm is only part of a larger process, the micro-level concepts and techniques used to manage for quality within a firm's operations also may be useful at the corporate and industry levels. These four elements – the environment, leadership, method, and a systems view – are the contributions that a strategic management view can make to an integrative concept of quality management.

The themes discussed thus far can be integrated. Clearly, quality includes notions of the goodness and value of a product or service as experienced by the user, as well as some notion of the relative merits of the process which produced it. The process view suggests that superior, less-costly quality is possible through improvement mechanisms. Both the process and marketing perspectives provide specific tools and practices to pursue quality. Finally, the strategy perspective suggests that the firm must seek beneficial change including the effects of technological change in order to cope with changing environments, that planning matters, and that a firm is only part of a larger system. Figure 20.4 summarizes these themes.

20.2 Quality and strategy

Quality is a strategic firm-level concept which has become a competitive necessity. However, it also highlights the significance of the larger system of which the firm is a part, including suppliers and customers. Suppliers and customers have much in common in a systems perspective. Each provides needs, capabilities, and resources to the rest of the system. Finally, each can benefit from, and contribute to, the strengthening and integration of the overall system's efforts, purposes and understanding. The quality-focused firm adopts the role of partial 'co-ordinator' for the system. The firm's involvement and influence may decrease further up or down the demand–supply chain of which it is a part, but it can nonetheless foster self-aware-ness and co-operation into the system. This concept of systemic improvement is potentially a strategic issue of central relevance to a firm's senior management: the firm is not simply a narrow independent unit competing with suppliers, customers, and 'direct competitors'.

Thus, a strategic construct of quality which incorporates the perspectives we have raised is as follows: the strategic management of quality means that the firm using quality, co-operation and long-term viability as interrelated guiding themes works to inform, educate and motivate itself, and those with which it interacts, in order to continually improve and strengthen the human and processual inputs, interactions, dependencies, relations and outputs which constitute the firm and the system to which it belongs. In other words, quality is the continuing pursuit of system optimization (Deming 1986, 1993).

Quality-driven changes can be characterized on a least two dimensions, *locus* and *type*, as shown in Figure 20.5. In terms of *locus*, firms initiate changes internal to the firm or in interactions with its environment. For clarity Figure 20.5 considers only environmental interactions with upstream suppliers and downstream customers (key elements of the **value chain**).

In terms of *type*, since the techniques that managers employ depend in part on assumptions underlying their approach to management, the philosophical changes required by the quality approach must at least partly precede the technical ones. Quality 'problems' can be traced to either lack of information/knowledge or lack of motivation, both of which are problems of management, not of quality (Crosby 1979). A predominant theme in quality management literature is that the only members of a system who can intentionally and fundamentally change its philosophical underpinnings are those who manage it (Deming 1986; Hayes and Abernathy 1980; Ishikawa 1985; Taylor 1911). Of course, the dynamics between and within type and locus are more interactive than Figure 20.5 suggests.

Figure 20.6 provides another way of understanding this systemic impact on productivity. On the upstream or input side, the firm which pursues system improvement may enjoy lower negotiating costs for inputs, less cumbersome relations, better inputs and, in some cases, lower direct input costs. Inside the firm, outputs may improve and direct costs decline due to reductions in system waste and reworked or discarded output. Note that the

Type	Locus		
	Upstream interactions (suppliers)	**Internal to 'firm'**	**Downstream interactions (customers)**
Philosophical	Less cost-bidding Move toward sole-sourcing. Focus on improving supplier fit, quality, capability Acknowledge shared destiny	Systems, not people, as source of problems. Acceptance of human variation Systems optimisation Primacy of purpose	Commitment to customer delight Customer retention based on value, not price Acknowledge shared destiny
Technical	Shared planning and strategic information Suppliers linked with internal demand and development Training	Institutionalised mechanisms for systems analysis and change Management by fact Functional integration Training	Mechanisms to know customer Education of customer

Figure 20.5 Representative changes suggested by the quality paradigm

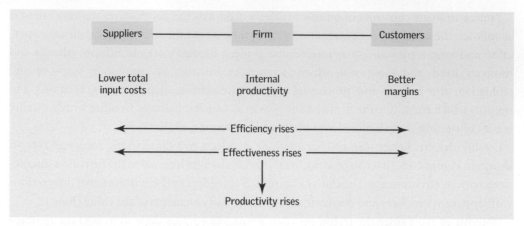

Figure 20.6 Effects of the quality paradigm

concept of productivity improvement includes elements that, although hard to assess, are known to have substantial impact on a firm's productivity – morale, absenteeism and turnover, decision processes, planning and so on. On the downstream or output side, stronger ties with buyers improve the firm's ability to satisfy them, may allow higher prices, and reduce total selling costs (including costs of poor quality such as reputation cost, lost customers and warranty support).

Further, as quality performance improves, the types of problems change (Garvin 1986). By identifying increasingly subtle problems and opportunities, technological changes, and systemic and environmental changes (which in turn lead to new problems and opportunities) the firm shifts its productivity horizon, as illustrated in Figure 20.7.

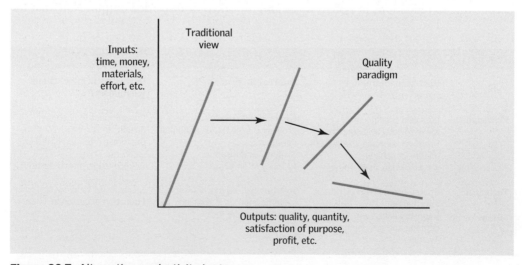

Figure 20.7 Alternative productivity horizons

Adding value is the salient feature of Figure 20.7. Widening the gap between quality (expressed as a broad set of desirable outputs) and cost (expressed as a broad set of inputs) means adding value. Although higher quality may mean lower cost, investments in quality are not entirely free. There may be significant direct and indirect expenses associated with change, and the most important ones may be the ones that cannot be quantified (Deming 1986).

Case box: Illustrative examples of the impact of TQM and value principles on competitive advantage

The automobile industry: Toyota v Ford v GM

The battle for dominance in the automobile industry is an important demonstration of the break between the old industrial order (an efficiency focus) and the new order (a focus on TQM and knowledge specialization).

In the first instance, Henry Ford's dream of the Model T Ford ('you can have it in any colour as long as it is black') in the early 1900s led to the principles of economies of scale and highly specialized mass production. His 'value innovation' was the assembly line focused on a single model (Model T) whose necessary components were carefully analysed and standardized to achieve cost efficiency and economies of scale. Ford's mass production strategy was, in turn, matched by an organizational structure which was highly functional and centralized – it was essentially a pyramid-shaped organization with Henry Ford at the apex, issuing orders and maintaining quality through efficiency management and application of the Taylorist principles of scientific management. In fact, by the 1920s Ford had a very significant cost advantage over the competition.

Competitors realized that they couldn't compete with Ford simply on a focused 'low cost' leader strategy. General Motors, formed in the early 1900s by William Durant through acquisition of a number of car assemblers and suppliers, realized that it needed to differentiate itself from Ford. Alfred P. Sloan (see *My Years with General Motors*) suggested that GM, with its range of brands, could offer 'a car for every purse and purpose'. Sloan's strategy for GM was, therefore, to understand the customer, offer the customer added value in each segment and cater for customer needs through product variety. However, the problem in implementing this differentiation strategy is how to offer such product variety at an affordable cost of production for GM. This problem was solved by Sloan by his invention of the multidivisional corporate structure. In essence, as noted by Alfred D. Chandler, the eminent Harvard business historian, this organization structure exploited economies of scale in production and design and economies of scope and focus in marketing and sales across the product range. Over time, in order to reduce costs further, GM decided to become vertically integrated and, for example, bought Fisher car body works to guarantee a supply of car bodies for its production schedules. Extending the organization structure in this fashion along the value chain offered two main advantages, namely, the guarantee of raw material sources and lower costs through better co-ordination across the value chain.

The preoccupation with scale and scope economies, vertical integration and hierarchical multidivisional structures lasted until the early 1970s and the oil crisis. Toyota had been a minion in the car industry since the 1950s, unable to exploit the principles of economies of scale and vertical integration. Indeed, Toyota relied on outside suppliers for parts and components such as gear transmissions and braking systems. In addition, because of the physical space limitations imposed by the geography of Japan and its lack of working capital, it could not afford to hold inventory and 'buffer' stocks to create slack in the production process.

As a consequence Toyota developed the now well documented system of lean production (Womack, Jones and Roos, 1990) and *just-in-time* inventory. Toyota demonstrated clearly that a supply chain (involving a range of suppliers) could be managed effectively without tying up capital in ownership of elements of the supply chain. It also pointed out that flexible, lean production meant that the production process allowed workers to stop production when problems occur, thus addressing the basic causes of poor quality. Toyota's system of continuous improvement, in essence, meant that through the mechanism of quality circles, problem solving in the production process was the preserve of the assembly line workers. They all participated in decision making and, as a result, Toyota developed a wide range of tools and techniques known as TQM (total quality management) to improve the quality of manufacturing and organizational processes. Not surprisingly, product quality also improved at a very rapid rate. Clearly Toyota has generated a sustainable competitive advantage based on cost and quality arising from its organizational practice, its 'value innovation' in supply-chain management and its continuous improvement (Kaizen) philosophy.

Lessons learned from the Toyota experience

In summary, the Toyota experience has a number of key characteristics:

- Auto firms were originally assemblers of components sourced from a supply network. **Vertical integration** (VI) plus scale gives high profits due to standardization, mass production and mass marketing. The market thus becomes concentrated where the key success factors are uncontroversially seen as VI with in-house assembly supported by hierarchical management structures.

- The Japanese came to this industry with a different set of initial conditions (and therefore assumptions). Japan was resource-poor, leading to high import content and the need to trade. They had technical capability but underdeveloped financial markets and a hostile labour force (post-war conditions). The Japanese observation of the US business model was high waste and low flexibility in production. Thus, initial assumptions were that (i) the work environment needed to be changed (hence life-time employment), and (ii) less waste was essential.

◆ At this point we see a gradual transition from the industrial age to the information age. With a reliance on a different intellectual capital model they created (i) a continuous improvement model of manufacturing processes, and (ii) new ways of working. The new intellectual capital was more intangible in nature – intellectual property (patents, copyright, trademark, trade secrets), concepts, information, etc.

◆ The Toyota production system has two key features: (i) outsourcing and just-in-time inventory to give reduced investment in working capital and space, and (ii) a human dimension in which labour is seen as an asset requiring constant on-the-job training, job rotation, skills and techniques programmes for production line workers and operations training for middle managers.

◆ The industrial age requires specialized capital, high task specialization, and separation of planning and management functions from actual production efforts (mental from physical). The information age requires team production with consensus and co-operation, flexible production with multi-purpose equipment and cross-trained workers running their own environments. This results in a new demarcation of responsibilities between managers and front-line workers (see Table 20.1).

Note that the Toyota model is an example of 'value innovation' through creative destruction – a Schumpeterian approach – i.e. the upgrade and move to more sophisticated types of production assets. The industrial age focuses on refining capital assets and on the tangibility of knowledge and its incorporation into assets. The information age maintains the shift towards capital-intensity but has a parallel deployment of capital – intensive tangible assets with capital-intensive intangibles.

◆ The horizontal structures typical of the information age have a number of interesting characteristics: (i) team production (flexible work teams, quality circles, job rotation); (ii) cross-training labour for multi-task performance; (iii) empowering workers to participate in continuous process improvement and to control their immediate work environment. These are the **Kaizen**. Also the **Keiretsu** – the creation of close networks of supply linkage – and the **Kanban** – co-ordination among related units. The management of this depends on a particular form of intellectual capital (which can be contrasted with the industrial age's need for intellectual capital to manage vertically controlled organizations). This capital-induced expansion increases the marginal product of labour

Table 20.1 Staff responsibilities in the information age

	Technical and functional activities	Administrative and operations planning	Strategy, conceptual and entrepreneurial
Senior	10%	20%	7%
Middle	30%	50%	20%
Front line	75%	20%	5%

automatically and the benefits are shared between firms, shareholders, labour, and consumers (lower prices thus fuelling further growth . . .).

The innovation is in new methods of production, new forms of organization, new sources and organization of supply, and new trade routes to markets (a completely different *business model*). Overall, the Toyota production system is a combination of lean production and new organization, more specifically:

- Flexible batch production (complete with cross-trained workers etc.)
- JIT (just-in-time inventory) invented
- Waste elimination
- Minimum use of capital equipment
- Higher labour productivity
- Continuous product and process improvement
- Line workers identifying and controlling problems
- Supplier organization

Case box: **General Electric**

General Electric, as can be seen from the extensive range of Harvard Business School cases and Jack Welch's exploits as CEO for 20 years from the 1980s, has been a leader in strategic management and one of the most closely examined of modern corporations. Since the Second World War, it has had relatively few CEOs and its structure has mirrored the changes outlined by Alfred D. Chandler in his seminal work on the structure and scope of US corporations – Borch, the CEO in the 50s, stressed functional, Vertical Integration (VI)-type structures; Cordiner, the CEO in the 60s, stressed departmental, divisionalized structures; Jones, the CEO in the 70s, advanced the concept of GE as a portfolio of strategic business units (SBUs) whereas Jack Welch in the 1980s and the 1990s moved the company through several phases marked by simple messages and themes. Indeed, Gordon Walker (2003, p. 225) summarizes the various corporate mandates and leadership themes (in chronological order) which Welch devised to create a flexible, quick and adaptable organization:

- Reduce bureaucratic behaviour
- Define markets globally
- Develop managers as leaders
- Promote sharing across business units
- Set very aggressive goals
- Build service businesses
- Implement six-sigma quality programmes

- Identify and remove managers who are underperforming compared to their peers
- Force all business units to implement e-commerce strategies

It can be seen that these range from Welch's earlier mandates to be 'number 1 or number 2 in any market or else get out' to an increasing focus on organizational learning, sharing promising practices and moving planning to the business unit level (with short five-year plans). In the middle 1990s for example, Jack Welch began his TQM approach based on the six-sigma principles advocated by quality theorists such as Deming and Juan. However, Welch took a very strong systems approach to the quality process and focused very closely on the customer and the customer value proposition (*see* also Doyle 2000). GE asked customers to state exactly what they value about a specific product or service and, in essence, define the value he or she wants. These are the customer value drivers, the value innovations/proposition, that are the critical quality elements for the specific GE product or service. GE then manages its organizational and strategic processes from a systemic, customer value viewpoint so that every process element along the value chain, from product design through manufacturing operations to the selling and distribution chain, is geared to provide the maximum value and delight to the eventual customer. When quality levels are below the six-sigma requirements managers must analyse and address the fundamental causes of poor quality and provide quick, workable solutions. For example, in one exercise GE found that customers had a very low tolerance for late deliveries of electrical appliances, leading GE to examine the service offered regularly by its dealers.

Table 20.2 Quality matrix

	Goals (organizationally determined)			
	A	B	C	D
KEY FACTORS				
Quality leadership				
Supplier management				
Process control and improvement				
Quality management and processes				
People commitment				
Customer value programme				
New product innovations				
Change capabilities				

Note: Rating scale to table (within matrix): 1 = No Activity; 2 = Ongoing efforts; 3 = Competent; 4 = Best practice; 5 = Leader
Source: adapted from Walker, 2003.

It is clear that Jack Welch, in developing each of his strategic themes, was adamant that employers must be encouraged to follow common goals. In the six-sigma (TQM) quality situation, GE developed tools such as the **quality matrix** (Walker 2003, p. 227) shown in Table 20.2 (p. 755) to ensure that each business unit and product category continually assessed and monitored its progress towards the production of the highest quality products.

In summary, GE's experience of TQM shows that when a company has a 'value innovation' focus, and a value proposition espousing customer value, it looks at its products closely from the outside-in perspective (as Robert Burns, the Scottish poet, said, 'try to see ourselves as others see us'). This allows the firm to focus on providing innovative products of high quality which address customer needs and wants – not simply producing products from the inside perspective without recourse to the customer. For example, when GE realized that locomotive customers did not want bigger and more powerful trains but more reliable, productive and easily scheduled vehicles, it addressed those needs and this, in turn, opened a whole new lucrative market in providing service, back-up and other services for operators of railroads and railroad operators.

Case box: Processes of improvement: how to survive in difficult times

One thing that helps companies survive in recession and in the teeth of fierce competition is having good business processes, and improving them all the time. The best Japanese companies, for example, are extremely good at logistics, both in their global operations and at home. Honda has a network of factories around the world, all hooked into the same supply chain. Each operates in the same way, so each is able to make any vehicle in the product range according to demand. This gives the company tremendous flexibility, thanks as much to slick logistics as to excellence in manufacturing.

Honda pays meticulous attention to detail to help ensure that its products are made on time. It has special data systems installed in each of its factories to monitor weather forecasts. These allow factory managers to talk in advance to parts suppliers about bad weather and how it might affect deliveries. They can decide what and when to stock up.

One of the best Japanese companies at logistics is Seven-Eleven, the largest convenience-store chain in the country. It is a rare example of a company whose business is largely domestic that is doing well despite Japan's deflationary environment. Its biggest strength is its custom-built information system that compiles extensive sales data (collected three times a day and analysed in 20 minutes). The system helps improve **quality control** and assists the company in pricing, product development and inventory management.

In the Japanese economy, any excess inventory can quickly translate into losses for firms that become too anxious to shift stock. For this reason, Kao has been working hard to improve its supply-chain management. Just as Toyota and other carmakers gained competitive advantage from honing their 'just-in-time' delivery systems in the 1980s, so Kao has been steadily improving its inventory management – to the extent that it has saved around ¥10 billion ($85m) a year for the past 15 years. Companies such as Canon, Takeda Chemicals and Yamato Transport, the biggest parcel-delivery company in the country, are also strong in logistics and supply-chain management.

In many cases, these process improvements have gone against the grain. Japan is remarkably backward in its use of information technology. Its spending on IT jumped to 4.4% of GDP in 2001, from 3.9%. But the comparable figure for Europe was 5.2%, and for America, 5.3%. There is no shortage of computers on Japanese workers' desks, but many are still connected to old mainframes and run outdated software. Access to the internet is often available only via the one or two PCs around the office that are wired to the web.

Many of the firms that seem to have made the biggest productivity gains from IT are big exporters – car manufacturers and electronics firms. They are the ones with the global strategies that enable them to see what the rest of the world is up to.

Source: 'Rising above the sludge', *The Economist*, 3 April 2003.
© The Economist Newspaper Limited, London (3 April 2003).

Questions for discussion

1 How can process improvement lead to a sustainable competitive advantage?

2 Explain how process improvement is more than just engineering management.

3 Is process improvement objectified, explicit knowledge (in terms of Figure 19.4) or is it collective, implicit knowledge? What is the significance of your answer?

20.3 Implications for strategic management

European and American attempts, beginning in the early 1970s to explore the ill-understood quality paradigm emerging from Japan had a fairly narrow emphasis on tools and techniques. Although understanding in many firms has moved beyond this narrow view, as is clear from the GM, Ford, Toyota and GE examples, we believe that there still are strategic issues which merit increased attention, from both senior management and strategy researchers.

20.3.1 How strong is self-interest?

A variety of traditional management practices and concepts rest on the subtle assumption that human behaviour is dominated by self-interest and that people (and firms) will often cheat if conditions permit.

Transaction costs and agency theories are often seen in strategy research and are used to provide insight into basic strategic issues faced by firms. **Transaction cost theory** is concerned with the efficiency of organizational forms – given alternative ways to structure economic activity, what is the most efficient way to do so? It is applied most often to the traditional 'make-or-buy' question (Williamson 1985). **Agency theory** asks how non-owners (agents) charged with managing resources will treat those resources and their outputs, and how owners (principals) can select, motivate and control agents to get the most productive, equitable resource employment (Eisenhardt 1985, 1989). Both of these perspectives emphasize that a firm risks being cheated by people and other firms.

The quality paradigm does not argue against self-interest. It does, however, argue that opportunistic (unfair) behaviour may be largely an outcome, the *result* of a system of beliefs and practices, not a dominant genetic element in human behaviour. In other words, many people and firms cheat when taught to cheat and when they do not perceive themselves as part of an interdependent system. The potential problem with efforts to control cheating is that the systems devised to prevent problems may also have a substantial, adverse impact on non-cheaters. Just as surveillance cameras breed mistrust, so too can adversarial, control-oriented management practices. The American retailer Wal-Mart had a reputation of subjecting suppliers to a particularly difficult bargaining process. However, in order to fully exploit the potential of the tightly integrated distribution system it was building, Wal-Mart discovered that its semi-adversarial, 'arm's-length' relations with suppliers could not provide the co-operation and commitment it needed.

On the other hand, consider the popularity of vendor certification programmes. In the certification process, a firm's probing and participation may extend deep into suppliers' fundamental planning and management practices. Even relying on third-party certification such as ISO 9000 means that a firm cares how its suppliers conduct their operations. On the downstream side, if a firm's marketing efforts include managing inventory for its customers, then the firm must become tightly linked with the customer's production system. Such activities internalize upstream and downstream elements beyond the formal boundaries of the firm, and help to overcome the failure for co-operative learning which can be found in a more competitive supplier–buyer market relationship. In other words, 'arm's-length' business relationships make it more difficult for firms to learn together.

Open co-operation is a matter of degree, of course, but firms are becoming increasingly focused on the benefit of building knowledge ties with suppliers and customers and with other firms, rather than focusing on the possibility that 'outsiders' will exploit their openness. For example, although winners of the American Baldridge Award for quality are *required* to share their experiences, many well-known firms have pursued the award. Further, the increasingly popular practice of benchmarking cannot take place without an attitude of openness regarding information and knowledge. (Interestingly, some of these knowledge-sharing ties, in the United States at least, could be interpreted as anti-trust violations.

The inability of anti-trust law to cope with co-operative learning systems may pose a growing problem as more firms move towards the quality paradigm.)

Motorola, for example, is famous for its efforts to educate not only employees but also suppliers, customers, and interested firms and parties. Motorola actively seeks to improve the generation, processing and dissemination of knowledge both within and beyond the firm's formal boundaries. The sharing of ideas and data is seen as the key to creativity and prosperity, as opposed to the presumption that knowledge is to be hoarded and kept secret from others in the pursuit of competitive advantage. Motorola considers the relevant members and beneficiaries of the firm's creative efforts and concern to extend far beyond the firm itself. It is a strong voice for the sharing of knowledge across firms and industries, and pushes strongly for quality-oriented changes in the content, method and assumptions of management education. Motorola's efforts extend to unusual places – a limousine driver, working for Motorola's headquarters, recently explained to one of the authors how his limousine business had become a sole supplier, and what Motorola's six-sigma quality focus had to do with livery service.

20.3.2 Is management the crucial resource and competence?

Two other common strategy perspectives, the *resource-based view* of the firm and *core competence*, highlight the importance of inputs and specialized skills. The resource-based view describes firms as bundles of resources and suggest that the most crucial resources may also be the most difficult to develop, acquire or change (Barney 1986; Dierickx and Cook 1989; Ghemawat 1991; Mahoney and Pandian 1992; Wernerfelt 1984).

Often, however, a firm may recognize a valuable resource only in hindsight, for example after it has gained valuable experience in a particular skill or area. Resources matter, but perhaps the key to business success is not resources per se, but the firm's ability to manage systems. After all, merely identifying resources may give little clue about how to use them. An overemphasis on resources obscures the critical issue of a firm's basic managerial approach and systems. Resources are not much use without a system which makes good use of them. How a firm mobilizes its resources determines what activities it becomes good at. Moreover, the capacity to achieve high quality is difficult to develop, hard to buy and provides a substantial benefit, which sounds much like the definition of a valuable resource. Clearly, a management system which manages for quality is an abstract form of a resource.

Core competence, a variation on the resource theme, suggests that a firm may be particularly good at some fundamental activity which can be leveraged in pursuit of success (Prahalad and Hamel 1990). Again, however, it seems to us that, from a strategic perspective, fundamental competence may lie not in the type of functional activity (such as engineering, marketing or research) but in *how* the activity is carried out. This is the distinction between competence building and competence leveraging. For example, possessing skilled mechanical engineers as does Mercedes-Benz, or chemical expertise as does ICI, does not lead to competence per se. Competence arises from the managerial assumptions and practices which provide the structure for productive activity. Superior assumptions and practices are those which integrate a firm's activities and leverage the firm's value equation.

20.3.3 Does competition hinder systemic improvement?

One controversial thought is the idea that some aspects of competition may be quite destructive. Kohn (1986), for example, argues that logic and evidence do not support the widespread belief that competition between individuals is beneficial. Deming (1986, 1993) believes that such competition conflicts with human psychology and hinders a systemic perspective.

Business competition takes many forms, including the following:

* With suppliers: holding bidding wars, arbitrary price reduction targets, multiple sourcing.

* Internally: competitive resource allocation processes, meritocracies, profit centres.

* With customers: 'shaving' product quality or quantity, price increases to customers with no alternative supply, withholding needed information.

* With other firms and governments: opportunism within consortia and cartels, industrial espionage, tax fraud, shedding of costly consequences of strategic and operating decisions.

A firm can never be fully independent of other parties (including suppliers, customers and direct competitors) in the productive system, but it can choose win-win or win-lose approaches to the interdependencies it must manage (the age-old issue of the individual versus the group). The quality paradigm does not deny the existence of conflicting interests, but suggests that conflict and competition are partly the result of a failure to think on a system level. Indeed, a glaring shortcoming of traditional microeconomic and strategic thought is that they primarily offer theories in which firms are independent competitors attempting to maximize their share of economic wealth. Both microeconomics and strategy have been relatively silent on the issue of interdependent firms co-operating to enlarge the aggregate economic wealth. Figure 20.8 illustrates the interdependence between members of productive chains, and between the chains themselves. As firms strengthen relations in their respective chains, competition is narrowed to some, but not all, facets of the inter-system level.

As a simple example, the 'Big Three' US automakers – General Motors, Ford and Chrysler – once were highly financially vertically integrated, particularly GM. Having de-integrated to some extend (particularly Chrysler and Ford), they now have worked in various ways to strengthen ties with suppliers and customers. The three firms do compete vigorously in the retail markets, but they also share suppliers and produce parts for each other they also share suppliers and produce parts for each other; they are highly interdependent. For example, if GM were to close all of its in-house suppliers tomorrow, automobile production at Ford and Chrysler would be substantially disrupted, at least temporarily. Another perspective on close interaction can be found in the contrast between the tight supply links in the relatively healthy Japanese auto industry (Cusumano and Takeishi 1991) and the more arm's-length links in the fairly troubled British one (Turnbull, Oliver and Wilkinson 1992).

The competition–co-operation issue also sheds light on the question of vertical integration. From a system level, the question of the formal boundaries of a firm appears relatively trivial in comparison to how the broader productive system is managed. In other words, downsizing and outsourcing in integrated firms, and acquisition in the opposite case, are not solutions to the need for a productive way to operationally manage interdependence between steps in the value chain which leads from raw materials to final customers. Whether owned or not, productive activities are interdependent and their links must be managed. Figure 20.8 illustrates linkages and the interdependencies created within and between them.

The standard view is that markets will mesh demand with supply. However, it can be difficult to integrate demand with supply in a competitive environment, since the capacity for co-operation is quite limited. This limited co-operation also hinders the firm's ability to change and learn. Indeed, in some cases fiercely competitive markets create market failures for co-operative learning and system improvement.

For example, Homescape is a regional real estate development company in the US which finances, plans and builds residential subdivisions. In a pattern typical for the industry, the firm has only two employees on direct payroll. They co-ordinate numerous independent contractors including engineers, roadwork firms, realtors, and a builder. The builder then co-ordinates the numerous subcontractors who build a house – masons, carpenters, etc. Homescape explains the tradition of independent contractors as the result of the cyclical nature of housing demand. When demand is strong, construction occurs at a frenzied pace, with multiple developers competing for contractors and subcontractors. Developers and builders have been known to walk on to competitors' job sites and offer contractors cash to leave for another project. Homescape possesses more sophisticated management and much greater capital than most of its competitors.

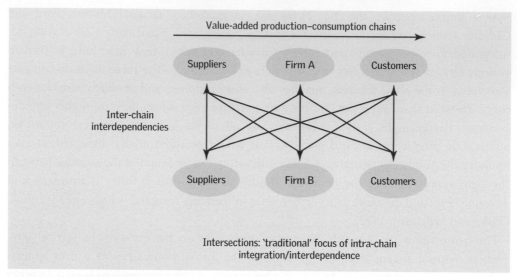

Figure 20.8 Interdependencies

Many developers are not particularly wealthy and, with high debt loads, tend to avoid integrating forward into the activities of their contractor network because they fear high fixed personnel costs and carrying costs for unsold properties which could occur in times of low demand. Although informal relationships certainly continue, low demand typically leads to the laying off of contractors. It is interesting to consider, however, that this response to market cyclicality also makes the cycle *worse*. Rising demand for houses tends to lead to overbuilding, and falling demand often leads to a wave of deferred projects. Given the substantial lead-time in project development, these responses simply widen the market swings. Further, despite the importance of technical skills in construction, developers typically do not invest in training for contractors and subcontractors, since many of the relationships are fairly arm's-length and short term. Contrast this with Motorola, which requires forty hours per year of formal training for each of its employees (Bales 1992).

20.4 Does organization get in the way?

Strategy may get in the way of quality and may serve to reduce it. So, too, may organizational factors (*see* Part 4). Wilson (1999, p. 101) observed that many organizational characteristics served to confound or potentially reverse systemic attempts at quality improvement. Some examples are:

- *Sectional interests*: Quality programmes can intensify local rationalities. Those who support the programme will be its (often) fanatical supporters while others may view it with less enthusiasm. The potential systemic effects of quality improvement are thus lost as sectional interests fight among themselves.

- *The sponge effect*: Because quality programmes are systemic in their scope, they can easily become all-embracing processes into which all organizational problems are put. Quite reasonably, the programmes have little hope of solving these problems (such as labour disputes or key decisions such as a reorganization) and so is judged to have failed. Systemic quality programmes are open to soaking up more problems than they can realistically handle.

- *Recreating the rigid organization:* Because programmes are organization-wide, they demand absolute commitment from all parts of the organization. The outcomes of a successful programme can, as a result, simply recreate another level of status quo from which further change becomes difficult. Organization can drive out the intended continuous characteristics of quality change.

- *Distinctions between means and ends become blurred*: Quality programmes can easily slip into becoming ends in themselves rather than means to an end (e.g. creating organizational change to increase levels of customer loyalty or satisfaction). This is particularly true of incremental, step-wise quality programmes where achieving the steps becomes the end in itself rather than the means to systemic organizational change.

Wilson (1999, p. 102) also points out other organizational phenomena which relate to systemic quality programmes. They can, paradoxically, make things worse rather than better. This can occur, for example, where the organization is in a state of decline. Scarce resources mean that allocating key resources to quality could seal the demise of an already declining organization. Finally, much of the evidence from quality programmes is collected from manufacturing organizations with a lesser degree of evidence from service firms. It is unclear to what extent there can be direct translation from manufacturing contexts to service or non-profit organizations and more empirical research is needed before we can answer such questions.

20.4.1 The complexity of performance

Financial profit is often stressed as the central goal of firms, but a systemic view of quality suggests a more complex set of purposes, acknowledging customer satisfaction, the interests of employees, the system capacity for continued existence, and benefits to others contributing to the organization (including, certainly, profit for the owners of capital). This is basically the stakeholder argument (e.g. Freeman 1984) with a dynamic emphasis on system improvement. It echoes changes in accounting research and practice, such as activity-based costings (Kaplan 1990) and the balanced scorecard approach to top management reporting practices (Kaplan and Norton 1993).

20.4.2 The operations basis of strategy

Despite longstanding calls (Skinner 1969), an understanding of production and systems views is still infrequent in the strategic planning of many firms, particularly those in which finance or marketing have been the traditional path into senior management. Recall the truck equipment maker Trucko. Top management clearly felt driven by marketing and financial concerns, and manufacturing issues literally took the back seat. An under-appreciation of the complexities of production also seems to be lacking in some management researchers. For instance, a recent academic seminar discussed a study of changes in workforce management practices due to advanced manufacturing technologies. The audience, consisting mostly of organizational change researchers, seemed fundamentally surprised to learn that many firms in the study fully recognized the importance of changing employees' attitudes and skills to remain in step with new technology. The 'dark Satanic mills' stereotype of manufacturing still has true believers, even among management scholars.

Quality management includes the use of very specific tools developed mostly in the production arena, but this does not limit it to only a narrow functional relevance. For instance, quality and finance both have many tools and methods, but most firms do not keep finance isolated – they train and expect a variety of managers to understand relevant financial concepts (Juran 1981). It seems difficult to develop or study strategy without an elementary understanding of what a firm actually does, and how it does it. This requires basic knowledge of production and operations management issues and concepts.

For example, Porter's (1980) three generic strategies – cost reduction, differentiation and focus – are popular themes for firms. However, in a systems view of quality they are not strategies but mutually reinforcing *elements* of strategy. This suggests that a firm can simultaneously reduce costs by improving processes and relations with suppliers *and* focus on improving service to a well-understood customer set and differentiate itself through both perceived and actual quality. Researchers have demonstrated that these elements can move together (Cho and Lee 1993). The success of a firm such as Toyota suggests the value of using quality as a strategic concept is that it can help integrate specific production (cost-reduction) and marketing (differentiation) skills developed over time.

There is a very substantial body of strategy literature typified by the Porter generic strategies. However, it is worth noting that this literature often seems associated with a particular view of production, one in which long, standardized runs in dedicated, inflexible production systems lead to efficiency and in which high quality is a high-cost craftsman approach. That perspective (*see* Abernathy 1978) is increasingly outmoded by technological changes and new thinking about management.

20.5 Summary

The central theme of this chapter, which stresses an integrative, strategic-level view of quality, is also to raise issues that merit scrutiny. Organizations actually foster problems while trying to solve them:

- A focus on a balance between competition and cooperation creates a market for learning.
- Firms do better to develop strategies that seek improved performance for the value-chain as a whole, rather than pursing success alone.
- A greater appreciation of operations and production improves the way we conceive of and implement the strategy systems process.

It is paradoxical that both strategies and organizational characteristics have the capability to reduce rather than increase quality. Hence the importance of including quality in the strategic portfolio of any organization.

Key terms

Agency theory *758*

Business operations processes *742*

Customer value *742*

Kaizen *753*

Kanban *753*

Keiretsu *753*

Quality control *756*

Quality matrix *756*

Six-sigma concept *755*

Total quality management (TQM) *742*

Transaction cost theory *758*

Value chain *749*

Vertical integration *752*

Recap questions and assignments

1 Use the Deming philosophy in Figure 20.2 to draw a comparison between Toyota and Ford (or GM).

2 In what sense is 'quality' a strategic rather than an operational issue?

3 Was General Electric under Jack Welch (pp. 754–5) different from Ford and GM in the way in which it used Total Quality Management?

Online
*Learning***Centre**

When you have read this chapter, log on to the Online Learning Centre website at www.mcgraw-hill.co.uk/textbooks/mcgee to explore chapter-by-chapter test questions, further reading and more online study tools for strategy.

Case 1 **Wasting disease**

A tale of poor quality and inefficiency

'OUR attempts to deliver today's technologies with today's medical production capabilities are the medical equivalent of manufacturing microprocessors in a vacuum-tube factory. The costs of waste, poor quality and inefficiency are enormous. If the current delivery system is unable to utilise today's technologies effectively, it will be even less able to carry the weight of tomorrow's technologies and an ageing population, raising the spectre of even more variability in quality, more errors, less responsiveness and greater costs associated with waste and poor quality.'

This indictment of America's health-care system comes not from an angry blogger but from the prestigious Institute of Medicine in a landmark report, 'Crossing the Quality Chasm'. The result of years of work by a committee of experts, it is scathing about the poor standards and wastefulness that it found.

One manifest sign of poor quality is the number of people who die because of medical errors. In an earlier report, the institute estimated that such errors in American hospitals were responsible for at least 44,000 deaths a year, and perhaps more than twice that. Medication errors alone, such as incorrect dosages, accounted for 7,000 deaths. According to the institute, health care was 'a decade or more behind other high-risk industries in its attention to ensuring basic safety'.

Not only can medical errors result in human tragedies, they also waste money because of compensation claims and the additional spending needed to try to put things right. Another kind of waste stems from the inappropriate use of medical procedures on patients for whom the risks outweigh potential benefits. This happens on a worryingly large scale; for example, 14% of bypass surgeries in America have been assessed as inappropriate.

The picture in other countries is much the same. Recent studies in Canada and Denmark have documented a high incidence of medical errors in hospitals. Thomas Schioler of the Danish National Board of Health says that in many countries a large number of patients are injured because of medical treatment and not because of their underlying disease. Over-use of medical procedures is also common. In Sweden and Britain, for example, 10% and 16% respectively of bypass surgeries have been found to be inappropriate.

Yet another form of waste is under-use of appropriate medical care. A report from the National Committee for Quality Assurance, an independent watchdog of American health care, estimated in 2003 that over 57,000 American deaths a year could be attributed to a failure to deliver best-practice care. The NCQA calculated that this failure generated an annual bill of $1.6 billion in avoidable hospital costs.

According to a recent survey from the RAND think-tank, American adults receive little more than half the medical care recommended. Reviewing a subsequent comparison of the quality of care in five countries – Australia, Canada, New Zealand, Britain and America –

Elizabeth McGlynn, who led the RAND study, recently wrote in *Health Affairs* that other countries were doing no better than America. Ms McGlynn believes that if the RAND survey were repeated in the other four countries, 'we would find very similar levels of performance to those found in the United States overall.'

Getting it together

Medical systems are inefficient, too. As the Institute of Medicine's report says: 'Surgeons know that operations rarely start on time; doctors and nurses wait 'on hold' as they try to track down vital information, and delays and barriers involved in referrals eat up the time and energy of both referring doctors and consulting specialists.' In Britain's NHS, many operating theatres stand idle unnecessarily, even though there is huge pressure to cut the numbers waiting for operations. Auditors have calculated that operating rooms are used on average 24 hours a week instead of an intended 40.

One of the biggest failings of modern health-care systems is that they so seldom provide integrated medical care. In emergencies, patients head for the local hospital; for minor illnesses they consult their family doctor. But for chronic conditions such as diabetes and cardiovascular diseases, which are becoming increasingly prevalent, they require care and advice both from their primary physician and from the hospital. Effective co-ordination of this care results in better and cheaper treatment, yet too often it does not happen. According to the OECD, 'health-care organizations, hospitals and physicians typically operate as separate "silos", acting without the benefit of complete information about the patient's condition, medical history, services provided in other settings, or medications prescribed by other clinicians.'

Inefficiency also stems from poor allocation of resources across different parts of the health-care system. Too much is done in high-cost hospital

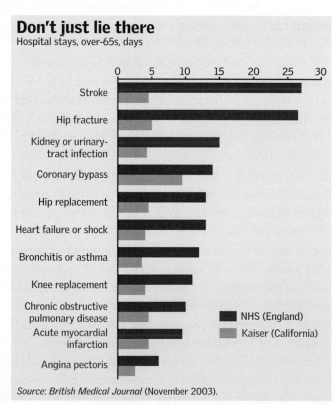

Don't just lie there
Hospital stays, over-65s, days

- NHS (England)
- Kaiser (California)

Source: *British Medical Journal* (November 2003).

settings, and too little in lower-cost primary settings. Traditionally, physicians in primary practice have worked as independents from small offices. Given the demands of patients for round-the-clock access and the increasing complexity of medicine, this structure no longer works well. But it has left a legacy of under-capitalised primary care, even though many treatments are now better carried out away from hospitals.

Germany's medical-delivery system has long been organised in a particularly inefficient way. With only a few exceptions, hospitals have been confined to in-patient care, and hospital specialists have not been able to provide their services in cheaper out-patient clinics. This restriction, which dates back to 1931, has created an opportunity for independent specialists, but half of them work on their own rather than in well-capitalised group clinics. This strict separation of care has prevented effective integration of services between primary-care physicians and hospitals – for example, for cancer patients, says Reinhard Busse of Berlin's Technical University. Not before time, reforms have now been launched to get rid of these restrictive practices.

But Germany is only an extreme example of medical-delivery systems organised to serve the interests of doctors rather than patients. One exception to the rule is Kaiser Permanente, a health-maintenance organization (HMO) that provides care to 8.2m Americans insured with it. Established in 1945, Kaiser has a distinctive model of health care. It owns most of the hospitals and medical facilities that it uses. Its physicians, who are salaried rather than paid on a fee-for-service basis, work together in group practices which they manage themselves. This structure has enabled it to develop a genuinely integrated form of medical care.

Richard Feachem, executive director of the Global Fund to Fight AIDS, Tuberculosis and Malaria, based in Geneva, is impressed: 'There is no perfect system in the world, every one has serious flaws and makes serious mistakes which people suffer from, but Kaiser comes closer to an ideal than any system I know.' Shortly before starting his present job, he led a controversial comparison of Kaiser's operations in California and Britain's NHS, which suggested that Kaiser achieved a better performance overall with roughly the same resources per head as the NHS. But how? Mr Feachem puts it down mainly to better integration. 'Without question Kaiser has achieved a greater degree of integration than the NHS – integration between prevention and cure, out-patient and in-patient services and between primary-care physicians and hospitals,' he says.

This allows Kaiser to treat patients at the most cost-effective level of care, economising in particular on expensive time in hospital. A subsequent comparison of the two systems, led by Chris Ham, director of the strategy unit at the Department of Health in London, dealt with some of the methodological objections to the original study by looking at acute care for those aged 65 and over. Across a range of 11 common clinical conditions, it found that admission rates were mostly higher in the NHS than in Kaiser. Once admitted, NHS patients spent much longer in hospital than

Kaiser patients. The disparity was highest for strokes and hip fractures, where NHS stays were five to six times higher than those in Kaiser hospitals. Kaiser pays a great deal of attention to the patient's journey through hospital, explains Mr Feachem: when a patient enters the hospital, staff are already planning his discharge. This strategy has the 'full backing of physicians, not just managers, because it is good medicine'. A systematic approach to the patient journey is crucial, because 'if you cumulate a small number of delays, you can lose 48 hours'. The patients like it too, he adds, because they feel that staff are on the case.

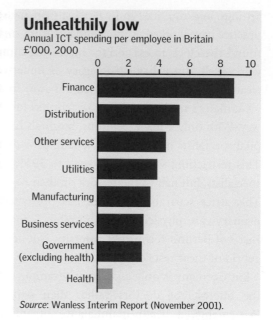

Unhealthily low

Annual ICT spending per employee in Britain £'000, 2000

Source: Wanless Interim Report (November 2001).

The NHS is taking a leaf out of Kaiser's book. Managers from several hospitals and primary-care organizations have spent time in California observing its methods, and are now trying to implement them in various parts of Britain. It will not be easy. Replicating the Kaiser model has proved tricky even in America.

Deus ex machina

But there is another, more universally applicable way to achieve better, more integrated medical care. Information technology provides a means to avoid many medication errors: computerised systems, including electronic patient cards, would allow checks on the accuracy of doses and improve patient safety by telling doctors about other drugs that patients may be taking. Electronic patient records also make it easier to integrate medical services between physicians in primary care and hospitals in the secondary sector.

Health-care systems are now scrambling to make more use of IT. Germany is investing 1.8 billion to develop electronic patient cards by the start of 2006. In France, Philippe Douste-Blazy, the health minister, has announced a plan to computerise health records, partly to control the excessive use of doctors by the country's notoriously demanding patients.

In America, Medicare will insist on doctors using electronic methods for prescribing drugs to elderly Americans after the government starts bearing part of the cost. 'The question is when, not whether,' says Mark McClellan, administrator of the Centres for Medicare and Medicaid Services (CMS). He also expects IT to play a big role in new chronic-disease management programmes for America's elderly. For example, PacifiCare, a health insurer based in California, uses modem links with patients suffering from congestive heart disease to check daily on whether they are taking their medicine.

The most ambitious project is under way in Britain. At present, notes on patients are often still held on paper; electronic information is fragmented in locally based systems, and there is a great deal of duplication. The aim is to replace this with a comprehensive national electronic system, costing £6 billion ($11 billion), making it the biggest civilian IT project in the world. By 2007, all prescriptions will be created and transferred to pharmacies electronically. By 2010 the system will provide fully integrated access to patient records for appropriate health-care professionals, wherever they work.

These plans hold out much promise, provided they can be implemented without the usual pitfalls of big IT projects. Experience of IT in other service industries suggests that it has plenty of potential to cut waste and raise efficiency in health care. But, even allowing for worries about patient confidentiality, why has it taken so long in health care? In the mid-1990s, a survey of 53 American industries ranked health care 38th in its expenditure on IT per worker. A similar picture emerged from a British survey of IT spending in 2000 (see chart entitled 'unhealthily low'). The banking sector spent nine times as much on IT per employee as the health sector.

This in turn prompts a broader question. The Institute of Medicine report said: 'Because of the high levels of waste in the current system, the committee sees no immediate conflict in the simultaneous pursuit of lower costs through efficiency and better patient experiences through safety, effectiveness, patient-centredness and timeliness.' The international evidence of waste and inefficiency suggests that this conclusion holds not just for America but for most other developed economies. So why have strenuous efforts to control medical costs failed to control all that waste?

Source: 'Wasting disease', *The Economist*, 15 July 2004.
© The Economist Newspaper Limited, London (15 July 2004).

Case Questions

1 Why is this evidence of waste and inefficiency a strategic issue and not simply a matter of operational efficiency?

2 Explain how a Total Quality Management approach should address these problems.

Further reading and references

Abernathy, W (1978) *The Productivity Dilemma: Roadblock to Innovation in the Automobile Industry*, Johns Hopkins University Press, Baltimore, MD.

Aguayo, R (1990) *Dr Deming*, Fireside Books, New York.

Bales, E (1992) 'Making Six Sigma and Quality a Part of the Curriculum', Presentation on Motorola's Quality Efforts at the Academy of Management Annual Meeting, Las Vegas.

Barney, J (1986) 'Strategic Factor Markets: Expectations, Luck, and Business Strategy', *Management Science*, **32**, pp. 1231–41.

Carnegie, A (1920) *Autobiography of Andrew Carnegie*, Houghton Mifflin, New York.

Cho, DS and Lee, DH (1993) 'Dynamic Integration of Cost Leadership and Differentiation', paper presented at the 1993 Strategic Management Society annual conference, Chicago.

Crosby, P (1979) *Quality is Free*, McGraw-Hill, New York.

Cusumano, M and Takeishi, A (1991) 'Supplier Relations and Management: a Survey of Japanese, Japanese-transplant, and US Auto Plants', *Strategic Management Journal*, **12**, **8**, pp. 563–88.

Deming, W (1986) *Out of the Crisis*, MIT Center for Advanced Engineering Study, Cambridge, MA.

Deming, W (1993) *The New Economics*, MIT Center for Advanced Engineering Study, Cambridge, MA.

Dierickx, I and Cook, K (1989) 'Asset Stock Accumulation and Sustainability of Competitive Advantage', *Management Science*, **35**, **1**, pp. 1504–14.

Doyle, P (2000) 'Value-Based Marketing', John Wiley & Sons, Chichester.

Eisenhardt, K (1985) 'Control: Organizational and Economic Approaches', *Management Science*, **31**, pp. 134–49.

Eisenhardt, K (1989) 'Agency Theory: an Assessment and Review', *Academy of Management Review*, **14**, pp. 57–74.

Freeman, RE (1984) *Strategic Management: A Stakeholder Approach*, Pitman, Boston.

Garvin, D (1986) 'Quality Problems, Policies, and Attitudes in the United States and Japan: an Exploratory Study', *Academy of Management Journal*, **29**, pp. 653–73.

Garvin, D (1987) 'Competing on the Eight Dimensions of Quality', *Harvard Business Review*, **65**, 6, pp. 101–9.

Ghemawat, P (1991) *Commitment: The Dynamics of Strategy*, Free Press, New York.

Gitlow, H and Gitlow, S (1987) *The Deming Guide to Quality and Competitive Position*, Prentice-Hall, New York.

Godfrey, AB (1993) 'Ten Areas for Future Research in Total Quality Management', *Quality Management Journal*, **1**, **1**, pp. 47–70.

Hayes, R and Abernathy, W (1980) 'Managing Our Way to Economic Decline', *Harvard Business Review*, **4**, pp. 67–77.

Ishikawa, K (1982) *Guide to Quality Control*, Asian Productivity Organization, Tokyo.

Ishikawa, K (1985) *What is Total Quality Control? The Japanese Way*, Prentice-Hall, Englewood Cliffs, New Jersey.

Juran, JE (1951) *Quality Control Handbook*, 1st edition, McGraw-Hill, New York.

Juran, J (1978) 'Japanese and Western Quality: a Contrast in Methods and Results', *Management Review*, **67** (November), pp. 27–45.

Juran, JE (1951) *Quality Control Handbook*, 1st edition, McGraw-Hill, New York.

Juran, J (1981) 'Product Quality – a Prescription for the West: Part 1: Training and Improvement Programs', *Management Review*, **70**, **6**, pp. 9–14.

Juran, J and Gyma, F (eds) (1988) *Juran's Quality Control Handbook*, 4th edition, McGraw-Hill, New York.

Kaplan, R (ed.) (1990) *Measurers for Manufacturing Excellence*, Harvard Business School Press, Boston.

Kaplan, R and Norton, D (1993) 'Putting the Balanced Scorecard to Work', *Harvard Business Review*, **71**, **5**, pp. 134–42.

Kohn, A (1986) *No Contest: The Case Against Competition*, Houghton Mifflin, Boston.

Leffler, K (1982) 'Ambiguous Changes in Product Quality', *American Economic Review*, **72**, **5**, pp. 956–67.

Mahoney, J and Pandian, J (1992) 'The Resource-based View Within the Conversation of Strategic Management', *Strategic Management Journal*, **13**, pp. 363–80.

Mintzberg, H (1973) *The Nature of Managerial Work*, Harper and Row, New York.

Moen, R, Nolan, T and Provost, L (1991) *Improving Quality Through Planned Experimentation*, McGraw-Hill, New York.

Parasuraman, A, Zeithaml, V and Berry, L (1985) 'A Conceptual Model of Service Quality and its Implications for Future Research', *Journal of Marketing*, **49** (Fall), pp. 41–50.

Pegels, CC (1995) *Total Quality Management*, Boyd and Fraser, Danvers, MA.

Pirsig, R (1974) *Zen and the Art of Motorcycle Maintenance*, Bantam Books, New York.

Porter, M (1980) *Competitive Strategy*, Free Press, New York.

Prahalad, CK and Hamel, G (1990) 'The Core Competence of the Corporation', *Harvard Business Review*, **68**, **3**, pp. 79–91.

Shewhart, W (1930) *Economic Control of Quality of Manufactured Products*, Technical publications monograph B-496, Bell Telephone Laboratories, New York.

Skinner, W (1969) 'Manufacturing – Missing Link in Corporate Strategy', *Harvard Business Review*, **47**, May/June, pp. 136–45.

Slack, N and Lewis, M (2002) *Operations Strategy*, FT Prentice-Hall, London.

Susman, G (ed.) (1992) *Integrating Design and Manufacturing for Competitive Advantage*, Oxford University Press, New York.

Taguchi, G (1986) *Introduction to Quality Engineering: Designing Quality into Products and Processes*, Asian Productivity Organization, Tokyo.

Taylor, F (1911) The *Principles of Scientific Management*, Harper and Brothers, New York.

Turnbull, P, Oliver, N and Wilkinson, B (1992) 'Buyer-supplier Relations in the UK Automotive Industry: Strategic Implications of the Japanese Manufacturing Model', *Strategic Management Journal*, **13**, **2**, pp. 159–68.

Walker, GE (2003) *Modern Competitive Strategy*, McGraw-Hill, New York.

Wernerfelt, B (1984) 'A Resource-based View of the Firm', *Strategic Management Journal*, **5**, pp. 171–80.

Williamson, O (1985) *The Economic Institutions of Capitalism*, Free Press, New York.

Wilson, DC (1999) *A Strategy of Change*, International Thomson, London.

Womack, JP, Jones, DT and Roos, D (1990) *The Machine that Changed the World*, Newson Associates, New York.

Zeithaml, V, Parasuraman, A and Berry, L (1990) *Delivering Quality*, Free Press, New York.

Chapter 21

Managing business value as a system: value creation from a systems perspective

Introduction

The term 'value' has been contested terrain for a number of years. For example, it has been used to describe **business value** (Parker and Harcourt 1969), **social value** (Carroll 1979) and as a term to replace the much maligned word 'profit' (Glautier and Underdown 2001). As we have seen in previous chapters of this book, over the past two decades, as a result of the globalization of trade and capital markets and the information technology revolution, the strategic attention of many leading companies has focused on the principle of generating and maximizing **shareholder value** for strategy evaluation and performance measurement. From this perspective, the primary task of senior managers is to act as agents for the shareholders and to maximize shareholder value (SVA) in financial terms, typically using an SVA discounted cash flow criterion. This allows shareholders to assess the value of their investment over time, using the rate of interest as the method of assessing the *time value* of money. For example, if the rate of interest is 10 per cent per annum, €1 invested now at 10 per cent will amount to €1.10 in a year. Or, conversely, the *value* of €1.10 a year hence is €1 now. Following Day and Fahey (1990), the SVA model can be depicted as:

- Purpose of strategy   ⟶   Maximize returns to shareholders
- Reference group   ⟶   Shareholders and proxies
- Decision variables   ⟶   Revenues, costs, investments and capital structure
- Level of analysis   ⟶   Company and strategic business unit
- Basis of measurement   ⟶   Share prices, market/book ratios and net present value of cash flows

Doyle (2000) argues that the adoption of SVA has eliminated much of the excess and inefficiency of capitalism in the decades of the 1960s and 1970s. We shall explore this claim later in this chapter.

While economists such as Friedman (1970) and Friedman and Friedman (1980) have stressed that business is in business to make profits and should not be expected and, indeed, is not best suited to do anything other than this, nevertheless, there is increasing recognition in today's environment that businesses cannot exist solely to make a profit. Henry Ford's much earlier statement is important here:

> Business must be run at a profit, else it will die. But when anyone tries to run a business solely for profit ... then also the business must die, for it no longer has a reason for existence.

Many writers (e.g. Freeman 1984) have noted that the actions of business affect not only themselves but also other stakeholders, with sometimes contradictory expectations, such as employees, managers, customers, suppliers, investors, governments and communities. They argue, therefore, that business must recognize its responsibility to those stakeholders and society as a whole. In essence, they suggest that there is a strong mutual interdependence between business and society. The responsibility of a business to society is to build and improve conditions for wealth creation through such things as commercializing new innovations, investing in new plants and facilities, creating new job opportunities, paying corporate taxes and minimizing negative social or environmental externalities. In turn, business depends on society to create and foster an environment in which business can fulfil its goals of wealth creation (AACSB 2003).

It is clear that the challenges for business, and its corporate strategists, go far beyond simple bottom-line profitability goals. Writers from MIT's Innovation Project (such as Malone *et al.* 1996) also point out some of the critical issues in managing and inventing organizations in the future. They include the need to understand how to tap into the complex sources of competitive advantage in the new economy, in environments where new skills, new sources of continuous innovation and increasing impacts of information technology create new ways of working and constant strategic change.

In consequence, arguably richer conceptions and theories of the firm are now emerging that encompass both the social and economic context of the firm and that seek to balance the 'doing well' and 'doing good' aspects of a firm's performance (Elkington 1997). In the end (*see*, for example, Kay 1995), the success of a company depends on how it meets and balances the often incommensurable and incompatible objectives demanded by its various stakeholders. Kay argues that the purpose of companies is to produce, in their own distinctive fields of capability, goods and services we want as individuals and as a society. The distinctive capabilities (*see* earlier chapters on the resource-based view of the firm) of companies are, in turn, embedded in their relationships with the social and commercial environments in which they operate. The argument is that organizations can succeed only by managing the totality of these relationships.

Kay's views prompt many of the arguments in this chapter. We seek to explore new theories and concepts of the firm from the perspective of the systems viewpoint – the 'web' of relationships, internal and external to the organization, which must be managed in order to create sustainable advantage and long-term wealth creation. Note that the strategy framework used in this book is a systems model and this discussion provides the overarching strategic systems model which links the various elements of the strategic plan together (*see* Figure 1.6). This chapter explores the following:

- The strategic systems framework as a lens for managing value as a system.
- Stakeholder theories of the firm.
- Learning theories of the firm.
- Adaptive theories of the 'living company'.
- Common issues such as trust, accountability and reputation that drive the firm's purpose.
- The role of intangible assets in creating value.
- The concept of managing value from a systems viewpoint.

21.1 **The strategic systems perspective**

> *How do we use the information gleaned about the parts to build up a theory of the whole? The deep difficulty here lies in the fact that the complex whole may exhibit properties that are not readily explained by understanding the parts.[1] The complex whole, in a completely non-mystical sense, can often exhibit collective properties, 'emergent' features that are lawful in their own right.* (Kauffman 1995)

---

[1] See, for example, the case study 'Microworld' at the end of Chapter 16.

As we outlined in Chapters 1 and 2, a *system* is a collection of parts that interact to function as a whole. The behaviour of a system depends on its entire structure, the relative strengths of the many connections among its parts at any point in time, and the manner and degree to which these connections change over time. **Systems theory** involves the study of living systems as integrated wholes whose visible properties cannot be reduced to those of smaller sub-units. Viewed from a systems perspective, the world consists of relationships and integration. Instead of concentrating on basic building blocks to learn about the properties of the larger system, the systems approach emphasizes basic principles of organization – how the parts are interrelated and co-ordinated into a unified whole. From that viewpoint, value-creating strategies emerge through learning about the system and can only be understood by analysing the system conditions that give rise to success and strategy innovation. We firmly believe that today's strategist should frame strategic thinking from a 'strategic systems' perspective (Bell *et al.* 1997).

From the systems theorist's perspective, a living system interacts with its environment through **structural coupling** – recurring interactions, each of which triggers structural changes in the system, such as when a cell membrane infuses substances from its environment into its metabolic processes, or when an organism's central nervous system changes its connectivity after receiving information. A structurally coupled system is a learning system. The structure of such a system continually changes in response to its environment. Consequently, adaptation, learning and development are key characteristics of the behaviour of living systems.

At the company level, organizations exhibit emergent behaviour – that is, they behave quite differently from how they would behave if their sub-units were independent of each other. According to Kees van der Heijden, retired executive from Royal Dutch Shell, who headed its Business Environment Division and was in charge of scenario planning:

> *Emergent behaviour is the outside behavioural manifestation of the internal mediating processes. In systems terms, it implies a hierarchical organisation, with the upper level guiding and constraining the actions at the lower. It is the constraints on the lower level members that creates the emergent behaviour at the higher level … If such constraints did not exist, lower level members would carry on as if they were independent and there would be no emergent behaviour and, therefore, no identity for the larger system.* (Van der Heijden 1996, p. 39)

The level of **complexity** inherent in an organization is a characteristic of the system's structure and is affected by the total number of its individual sub-units, the number of different layers in the structural hierarchy, the number of different business processes that perform business activities and the number and strengths of connections among all of these sub-units and between these sub-units and outside economic agents.

Beer (1981) has studied and written extensively about how to model the dynamics of complex systems such as today's business organizations calling such systems' perspectives 'exceedingly complex' (see Chapter 2 for a summary of Beer's five-level structure).

According to Richardson (1991, p. 187):

> *In Beer's view, every viable system is organised in such a hierarchy of five systems. Furthermore, complex viable systems are composed of viable sub-systems that again have this five-level structure. To be viable, a division of a firm should be organised this way. The entire firm as a set of inter-related divisions should also have the same sort of structure. A viable sector of an economy should have the same structure. Naturally, an entire national economy, to be viable, should be similarly organised. Viewed from the elevated level of the national economy, in the hierarchy an individual firm or sector operates at the level of systems one, two and three. The functions of its own high-level systems four and five are seen as part of the autonomic processes of the more aggregate system.*

To gain the appropriate level of understanding of a firm's business, industry and wider environment for the purpose of conducting a strategic analysis, we argue that strategists should direct their attention to the firm's systems dynamics – its strategic positioning within its environment; its emergent behaviours that impact its attained level of performance; the strength of its connections, or structural couplings, to outside economic agents; the nature and impact of any symbiotic alliances; the specific interrelationships and internal process interactions that dominate its performance; and potential changes in other reaches of the vast economic and social web that might threaten the viability of the client's strategies and niches. These systemic properties determine the strategic competencies and capabilities that enhance the **value** of the organization and that promote *changes in that value* over time.

Figure 21.1 depicts a firm as a complex web of interrelationships embedded within a broader complex economic web.[2] This complex web is what the strategist sees when looking through the strategic-systems lens. The strengths of the many interrelationships comprising this broader economic web reflect the extent of the organization's ability to manage its environment and therefore to **create value** and generate the cash flow needed to sustain growth. A fundamental understanding of the strengths of these connections provides a basis for development of expectations about the quality and creativity of the entity's strategies and its attained level of performance.

An example illustrates how, in an adaptive system, the relevance and strength of the interconnections changes over time (and how, in turn, value can be created or lost). Assume that the organization depicted in Figure 21.1 is a retail bookseller (such as Barnes & Noble or Borders in the USA or WH Smith or Waterstones in the UK) with a heavy capital investment in retail facilities located around the country. Now, assume that a new market niche emerges, involving the use of the World Wide Web in lieu of retail outlets to market and sell books.

---

[2] Figure 1.4 in Chapter 1 provides a simple picture and Chapters 3 and 4 provide a detailed description, of this complex economic web.

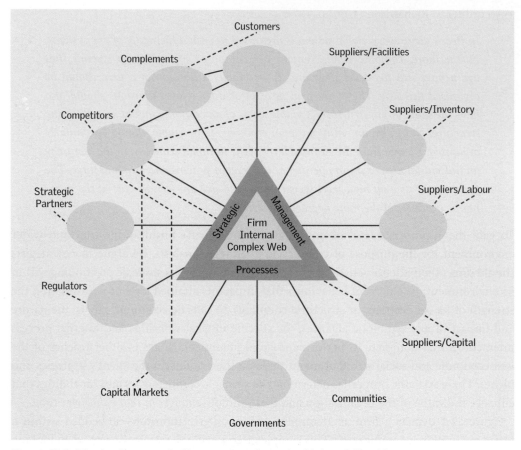

Figure 21.1 Viewing the organization as a complex web of interrelationships

New competitors such as Amazon.com occupying this niche offer access to much larger inventories than any retail outlet can stock, and can price their books at a substantial discount because of lower overhead costs. In addition, consumers can search these massive inventories using search engines provided by the new competitors and can access book reviews by other consumers available through these competitors' websites.

As the number of consumers connected to the World Wide Web grows over time, the connections between customers and competitors occupying this new niche are likely to increase in number. And, in turn, unless it adapts its own operation by moving into this new niche, the strength of connections between the original retailer and most of the other economic agents depicted in Figure 21.1 will diminish. For example, as the original retailer experiences a drop in demand, it will respond by reducing its own demand for facilities, inventory, labour and capital from suppliers.

21.2 The stakeholder management perspective

A particular example of a systems-type model is **Freeman's stakeholder theory**. Many of the stakeholders that have the potential to be most important to organizations are shown in Figure 21.2.

By definition, these stakeholders are individuals or organizations that have an interest in, or some kind of stake in, the firm's ongoing activities. Stakeholder analysis (Freeman 1984) is the process of identifying, understanding and prioritizing the needs of key stakeholders so that the question of which groups of stakeholders deserve management attention is addressed. The knowledge from this analysis is absorbed into the strategic framework, direction and management of the organization.

Clearly, the needs and goals of these stakeholders are sometimes in conflict with each other but stakeholder management is a never-ending task of balancing and integrating multiple relationships and multiple objectives (Freeman and McVea 2001). Some of the alternative stakeholder viewpoints are outlined in the following sections.

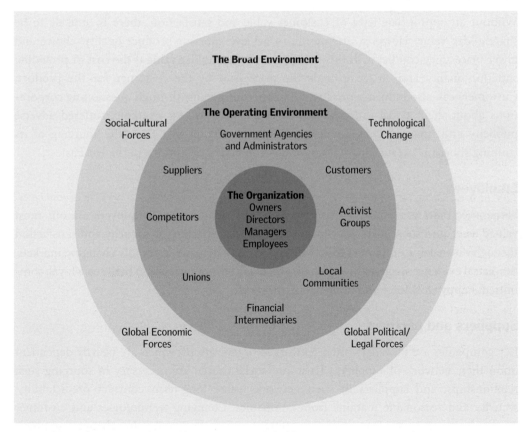

Figure 21.2 The organization and its primary stakeholders
Source: adapted from Harrison and St John, 1998.

Governments and local communities

Emerging conceptual frameworks that reflect changing societal expectations about the role of business in society can be seen in the following areas:

+ Socially responsible investment.

+ Corporate social responsibility (e.g. negative impacts arising from pollution and environmental damage – e.g. the *Exxon-Valdez* case and the Union Carbide Bhopal crisis).

+ Corporate citizenship.

+ Corporate governance.

+ Sustainability and the 'triple bottom line'.

Local communities, governments and non-governmental organizations try to ensure that organizations act in a socially responsible manner to maintain such things as a 'green' environment, ethical investing and a sustainable level of national resources.

Customers

Without an appropriate level of customer value and satisfaction, there is unlikely to be shareholder value. However, attempting to achieve superior product quality, choice and lower prices may conflict with the attainment of shareholder value if the cost of providing superior quality and choice exceeds the price paid by the customer for the product. Customers can also influence product purchase considerably through questioning corporations about their global sourcing and investments. Nike, for example, suffered adverse publicity and financial consequences from consumers, arising from the sourcing of its running shoes in 'sweat shops' with poor environmental conditions in the Far East.

Employees

Sometimes there is a strategic gap between statements such as 'employees are our most valued asset' and subsequent corporate actions which threaten job security and satisfaction through downsizing employees following shortfalls in demand in rapidly changing markets. Empirical evidence suggests, however, that there is a strong correlation between a loyal, committed, happy workforce and financial performance.

Suppliers and partners

Key companies are nowadays often networked organizations, which are heavily dependent upon their network of suppliers. Trust and social capital are necessary in sourcing such relationships, and suppliers in such networks value long-term contract predictability, security and reasonable margins from companies. Changing technologies and customer needs, however, may from time to time require companies to change suppliers.

These changes will create conflicts in relationships with suppliers that value network stability and corporate commitments but are also in competition with other supplier networks.

Shareholders

Shareholders are often depicted as a somewhat isolated but wealthy group of individuals who act in their own self-interest. However, through the activities of financial institutions and pension funds, most individuals in Western countries own shares in companies and have a very clear interest in ensuring that stock prices and shareholder value continue to rise in order to protect their future pension and social security provision. The rise in shareholder activism (e.g. CALPERS, the California State Pension Fund in the US, and Anthony Bolton of Fidelity in the UK) is probably more due to reaction to financial underperformance by firms than concern about their ethical or corporate responsibility activities, despite such recent corporate failures as Enron, WorldCom and Parmalat.

Freeman (1984) provides a model, a stakeholder grid, shown in Table 21.1, which classifies stakeholders on two dimensions: first, the nature of their stakes in the organization; and, second, the behavioural influence or power they have on the organization.

Businesses (e.g. Nike in shoe manufacture and Toyota in car manufacture) are already moving to organize themselves into networked form (see Chapter 12) and, in doing so, become the hub of a web or nexus of contracts enacted with many of the entities shown in the web of Figure 21. 2 and the stakeholder grid of Table 21.1. Clearly, the effective

Table 21.2 Freeman's stakeholder grid

STAKE		Formal or Voting (Contractual or Regulatory)	Economic	Political
	Equity	Internal stakeholders Directors Minority interests	External shareholders	
	Economic	Outside directors Alliance partners Tax authorities	Customers Employees Suppliers Competitors Creditors	Local communities Local governments Unions Foreign governments
	Social	Regulatory or government agencies	Financial institutions and financial community	National government Activist, lobbying groups Trade associations

POWER OR INFLUENCE ON BEHAVIOUR

Source: adapted from Freeman, 1984, p. 63.

management of the web of stakeholders is critical to wealth and value creation. Research evidence (see, for example, Mohr and Spekman 1994) suggests that effective partnerships are associated with the following:

- Strong quality of communication
- Joint problem solving
- Commitment
- Co-ordination
- Trust

Weak partnerships tend to adversely affect the hub organization's image and reputation in the marketplace.

Writers such as Senge (1998) stress and emphasize the role of processes of learning and adaptability in organizations with regard to understanding the pace of strategic change and in providing new ways of conceptualizing the business environment. Thus, strategists can frame strategic issues in terms of the web of customers, stakeholders, etc. in order to manage the business better (create more value). In the next section we examine the processes of building learning organizations that can create value.

21.3 Learning theories of the firm and value creation

Senge emphasizes the importance of what he calls 'adaptive learning' and 'generative learning' in organizations. Adaptive learning is similar to what Argyris and Schon (1978) call 'single-loop' learning in which individuals, groups and organizations adjust their behaviour according to fixed organizational goals, norms and assumptions. Generative learning, on the other hand, is akin to 'double-loop' learning, in which organizational goals, norms and assumptions as well as behaviour are all open to change. In Senge's terms:

> Increasing adaptiveness is only the first stage in moving towards learning organis-ations. The impulse to learn in children goes deeper than desires to respond and adapt more effectively to environmental change. The impulse to learn, at its heart, is an impulse to be generative, to expand our capability. This is why leading corpo-rations are focusing on generative learning, which is about creating, as well as adaptive learning, which is about coping.

Therefore, Senge is wedded to the idea of the firm both as a system and a social and knowledge web, which is conceptually very close to de Geus's framing of the firm as the 'living company' (1997). This 'living company' survives over the long term through such concrete factors as financial strength and stability, environmental sensitivity and adap-tation to change, and a strong culture, identity and value system which enables it to become a systematic, living organism that continually grows and reinvents itself. Leaders of such organizations are 'systems thinkers' who see the 'big picture' and focus more on understanding the underlying reasons and forces that contribute to change. Important skills for such leaders include:

- The ability to see the interrelationships and processes in systemic change.
- The recognition that problems in change result from poorly designed systems.
- The ability to recognize and understand the dynamic complexity of system problems, i.e. when the cause and effect of strategic problems are distant in time and space, and when the consequences of interventions over time are subtle.
- The ability to focus on areas of high leverage, i.e. systems thinking shows that small, well-focused actions can produce significant enduring improvements if they are in the right place.
- The avoidance of symptomatic solutions, i.e. 'quick fixes' or so-called 'band-aid solutions'. The best solutions rely on the ability to analyse the system and, thus, find enduring solutions. Enduring solutions create value.

21.4 Trust, accountability, reputation and value

From these perspectives, it seems that strategists must make a paradigmatic (or at least ideological) choice. This choice is between whether we should adopt the multiple objective goals of stakeholder and/or learning views of the firm, or adopt the primacy of shareholder value maximization (SVA) for optimizing the value of the firm as a system. The key argument against shareholder value maximization is that it ignores an organization's social responsibilities and fails to balance the different stakeholder interests. Doyle (2000, p. 23) and Sunderam and Inkpen (2004, p. 353) offer spirited arguments for the primacy of shareholder value maximization as the preferred corporate goal or objective. Sunderam and Inkpen summarize their arguments as follows:

- The goal of maximizing shareholder value is pro-stakeholder.
- Maximizing shareholder value creates appropriate incentives for managers to assume entrepreneurial risks.
- Having more than one objective function will make governing difficult, if not impossible.
- It is easier to make shareholders out of stakeholders than vice-versa.
- In the event of contract or trust, stakeholders, compared with shareholders, have protection (or can seek remedies) through contracts and the legal system.

Doyle's fundamental argument (2000, p. 24) mirrors much of the above reasoning. He argues stridently that social responsibilities are not the job of business. He notes that, in a market-based economy, the only social responsibility of business is to create shareholder value legally and with integrity. He believes that there are strong market-based incentives for value-maximizing firms to take into account stakeholder interests. They include:

+ The need to attract, retain and motivate key 'knowledge workers' and employees to ensure long-term competitiveness. This means paying competitive salaries to employees and offering safe and attractive workplace conditions.

+ The need to satisfy customers through new product development, quality and customer service.

+ The need to build trust, reputation and image with customers and society as a whole.

+ The requirement to undertake investments to create wealth and value and avoid investments undertaken to 'balance other stakeholder interests' for reasons of prestige and public relations, but not value creation.

+ The recognition that shareholders are generally pension funds, financial institutions and other societal institutions that require value-producing investments to meet their fiduciary obligations.

The alternative paradigm emphasizes the social role of organizations in society and argues that value emerges from conducting business in a socially responsible way. Such a perspective has many labels (such as corporate accountability or corporate citizenship) and in this chapter we will use the term **corporate social responsibility** (CSR) to cover the social and ethical roles of business organizations in society. In a basic way, laws already exist for some factors which affect the social good. Organizations are liable in law in many countries for the escape of dangerous substances, failing to provide adequate health and safety cover for employees and for rules about the manner in which accountability of business firms to investors and employees is met. CSR extends beyond this regulatory level. Originating in social and political theories, CSR argues three main points:

+ Organizational decisions should be centrally concerned with socially responsible alternatives.

+ The implementation of such decisions will help maximize profit (value) since customers will prefer to buy goods and services from ethical and responsible organizations.

+ Trust, reputation and image will be enhanced more by ethical and socially responsible strategic decisions than by maximizing shareholder value.

Carroll (1979) argues that organizations should be socially responsive since they are created by and sustained by society. Drucker (1993) argues that organizations should be given rights and duties in society in much the same way as individual citizens are (hence the term corporate citizenship). Increased image and reputation for the organization will help create value. As Rosenfeld and Wilson (1999, p. 353) point out, such value creation from the point of view of ecological responsibility is big business. Since the establishment of an international standard for 'green-ness' (ISO 14001) organizations have quickly recognized the value of being accredited. Shell and Xerox were accredited early and many other firms have publicly announced pro-environmental strategies (e.g. Elf, Union Carbide, Interplan, The Body Shop).

There are some enduring problems with the CSR value-creating perspective. First, it is theoretically very difficult to establish exactly what CSR is and what it is not. There is no agreed (or generally accepted) definition of what CSR is – other than organizations and decision makers should weigh the impact of their actions upon others. Second, the scope of CSR is difficult to determine. Should it apply to every organizational action and operation or to a selection of activities? Third, unless strategists are able to determine a clear view of what are societies' preferences and ethical priorities, then much of what is classed as socially desirable will remain either guesswork or subjective judgement. Arrow's (1963) 'general impossibility theorem' captures this neatly. He argues that if we exclude the possibility of interpersonal comparisons of utility, then the only method of transferring from individual tastes to broad social preferences that will be satisfactory (and defined for a wide set of individual rankings) will either be imposed or dictated by definition.

Nevertheless, the impact of CSR has been substantial and the 'triple bottom line' has reinforced the value-creating aspects of socially responsible performance by organizations. Aware of possible paradigm incommensurability between the SVA and the CSR perspectives, we suggest that, at least in some key aspects (intangible assets), a systems perspective can begin to integrate some aspects of CSR and SVA to create value. We explore this argument in the next section.

21.5 Intangible assets and value creation

Given the theoretical approach we have adopted in this book, we would suggest a marriage to shareholder value maximization and the strategic systems lens offers the strategist the best opportunity for managing the business system from a value-based perspective. Such a marriage will require close attention for the 'embedded firm' to maximize value from the system resources available to it. We regard the following three issues as critical intangible assets to the implementation of a systems model for value maximization – trust, accountability and reputation/image/identity.

Trust

This involves creating a strong sense of mission and values. Collins and Porras (1996) note that core values are enduring, essential tenets for those inside the organization. The core ideology consists of core values and core purpose, where core purpose is the 'raison d'etre' – the reason for being. Core ideology has to be authentic and is the 'glue' that holds the organization together over time. It is a consistent identity that all stakeholders learn to trust over time. For example, Hewlett Packard's core ideology was a code of ethics called the 'HP way'. It includes:

+ A deep respect for the individual.

+ A dedication to affordable quality and reliability.

+ A commitment to community responsibility.

+ HP exists to make technical contributions for the advancement and welfare of humanity.

A good example of trust in practice is shown in the following case box.

Case box: Johnson & Johnson and Tylenol

In 1982, Johnson & Johnson (J&J) found itself facing a corporate nightmare when bottles of its best-selling Tylenol were tampered with, resulting in several deaths. The corporation's immediate response was to pull all Tylenol off the shelves of retail outlets. Thirty-one million capsules were destroyed, even though they were tested and found safe. Although the immediate cost was significant, no other action was possible, given the firm's Credo. Authored almost forty years earlier by president Robert Ward Johnson, Johnson & Johnson's Credo states that permanent success is possible only when modern industry realizes that:

+ service to its customers comes first;
+ service to its employees and management comes second;
+ service to its stockholders, last.

Source: adapted from Senge, 1998.

As Senge notes, such credo statements may look like 'motherhood and apple pie' to those who have not seen how a clear core ideology can affect key business decisions. Johnson & Johnson's crisis management action in this case was based on the credo. It was simple, right and it worked.

Collins and Porras (1996, p. 67) quote Ralph Larsen, a former CEO of Johnson & Johnson, who puts it this way: 'The core values embodied in our credo might be a competitive advantage, but that is not *why* we have them. We have them because they define for us what we stand for, and we would hold them, even if they become a competitive *dis*advantage in certain situations.'

Accountability

A company must have in place 'systems' of accountability to measure performance outcomes for all relevant stakeholders in the system web of its corporate relationships and linkages. SVA on its own measures 'shareholder value', whereas the balanced scorecard approach (Kaplan and Norton 1996, 2001) in Chapter 18 introduces the viewpoint that firms need to develop performance measures along four dimensions – financial, customers, internal processes, and learning and growth – in order to achieve enduringly strong and balanced results along those multiple objectives and manage a strategy-focused organization.

More recently, Kaplan and Norton (2004) have added the notion of a 'strategy map' – a systems view of the organization – which maps the strategy, uncovers problems, monitors progress, identifies critical issues and communicates the strategy both internally to managers and employees and externally to investors, media, local and government communities. Critically, the strategy map incorporates a model to fit intangible assets: human capital readiness (e.g. skills), information capital readiness (e.g. databases) and organizational capital readiness (e.g. teamwork) into the balanced strategy approach. Ultimately, this is a strong attempt to provide a 'systemic' approach to discussing and investigating organizational strategy.

Reputation, image and identity

'Reputation, reputation, reputation – the one immortal part of man' (Shakespeare, from Othello).

The modern resource-based theory of the firm (RBV), discussed in Chapter 7, identifies a range of intangible assets including technology, patents, skills, etc. which, when combined with human and organizational resources, define the firm's core dynamic capabilities. A key set of intangible assets are the firm's **reputational assets** and these include the company name, its identity, brands, brand image and customer-based loyalty, the reputation of the firm's products and services, and the integrity of its relationships with the complex web or customers, suppliers, communities and governments. Many of the world's top brands (Coca-Cola, Microsoft, IBM, GE, Intel, Nescafe, etc.) are household names and help to develop a strong relationship of value, trust and goodwill with the customer. As we have recently seen, however, in the accounting industry, with the demise of Arthur Andersen, a hard-won reputation was easily dissipated and lost by the unethical and illegal behaviour of its employees. Therefore, a strong corporate reputation is a key strategic asset in managing value as a system.

21.6 Managing value as a system

What is critical from the strategic systems perspective is the ability to manage the organization strategically to maximize value. This requires:

- Strategy co-ordination – the strategy-focused organization.
- A clear objective of value creation and maximization.
- The ability to balance assets (e.g. trust, reputation, goodwill, etc.).
- The ability to balance financial measures.

◆ The ability to co-ordinate organization, operations and stakeholders so that the complex web of relationships works effectively.

As we have seen in this chapter, determining who the relevant business stakeholders and constituencies are requires a well-balanced understanding of the business system using, perhaps, Kaplan and Norton's concept of a strategy map. Value for customers results from customer satisfaction associated with product quality, choice and price. For shareholders and investors, SVA measures are appropriate. For employees, value may comprise such things as salaries, on-the-job training, stock options and job satisfaction. For suppliers, value may emanate from long-term corporate relationships and access to new technology and processes, as well as fair prices for their products. For governments and communities, value is measured by good corporate citizenship and social responsibility.

In addressing all these components of value – business strategy, customers, asset portfolios, organization and operations, learning and knowledge growth, supplier relationships, employees, local and government communities – the key skill is to treat them as a system and understand their context through the strategy map. In other words, by examining their interrelationships and treating the components of value concurrently and systematically, strategic decisions are examined relative to their impact on the other value components using SVA and balanced scorecard approaches. The strategy map, or systems diagram, then enables the manager to monitor and adapt strategy, develop organizational learning and growth and provide socially and financially responsible outcomes.

21.7 Summary and other issues in managing value

We continue to argue that the preferred objective for the corporation is the 'maximization of shareholder value', i.e. if an organization maximizes shareholder wealth in the long term, it will maximize firm value and enlarge the pie for all stakeholders. We recognize, however, that, as stated by Sundaram and Inkpen (2004, p. 371), 'All of us seek a path to a promised land in which accountable firms managed by ethical decision-makers create the greatest value for the greatest number of stakeholders'. This may occur using a shareholder value model, as we advocate, or through the development of a well-developed stakeholder theory, which is empirically supported (Freeman *et al.* 2004). In time, we may see such a theory developed but, in the meantime, some or all of the following issues are important in the process of managing the value of the business system:

◆ Would a company-wide ethical orientation (such as, for example, The Body Shop) or a strong commitment to corporate social responsibility constitute a key strategic resource in terms of the resource-based view of the firm? (*See* Wernerfelt 1984; Barney 1991.) In other words, is an ethical and socially responsible stance a non-imitable, unique source of sustainable long-term competitive advantage for the firm?

- Similarly, would strong organizational trust (Barney and Hansen 1994) create a long-term source of competitive advantage for the firm?

- Would core competencies and capabilities in business–government relations, such as the relationship between an ethical pharmaceutical company and the Federal Drug Administration in the drug-approval process, create a source of sustainable competitive advantage through effective management of the regulatory processes?

- Can a strong organizational identity or core ideology (e.g. Johnson & Johnson's credo) create an identity management competence for long-term sustainable competitive advantage?

- Managing value as a system requires a clear business model or 'Theory of the Business' (Drucker 1994). Drucker identifies four specifications about a valid theory of business:

  - The assumptions about environment, mission and core competencies must fit reality.
  - The assumptions in all three areas have to fit one another.
  - The theory of the business must be known throughout the organization.
  - The theory of the business has to be tested constantly.

    Throughout, Drucker has a systems-oriented view. He states 'when a theory shows the first signs of becoming obsolete, it is time to start thinking again.'

- As Yoffie (1988) points out, companies can strengthen their competitive advantage by forging closer ties with government. A political strategy may offer creative strategic choices in newly opened markets, such as in the dynamics of deregulated markets (e.g. rail, bus and utility companies in the UK).

In conclusion, we offer a couple of quotes and a case example from the challenging and controversial entrepreneur Anita Roddick, drawn from her book *Business as Unusual* (2000). Her stance on business challenges us all to examine the core values that drive business as a system and which create value.

> *One of our greatest frustrations at The Body Shop is that we are still judged by the media and the City by our profits, by the amount of product we sell, whereas we want, and have always wanted, to be judged by our activities in the larger world, by the positive difference we make. The shaping force for us from the start has not been our products but our principles.*

> *In terms of power and influence, you can forget the church, forget politics. There is no more powerful institution in society than business – I believe it is more important than ever before for business to assume a moral leadership. The business of business should not be about money, it should be about responsibility. It should be about public good, not private greed.*

Key terms

Business value *775*

Complexity *778*

Corporate social responsibility *786*

Create value *779*

Freeman's stakeholder theory *781*

Reputational assets *789*

Shareholder value *775*

Social value *775*

Structural coupling *778*

Systems theory *778*

Value *779*

Recap questions and assignments

1 What are the implications of the systems perspective for the work of a board of directors and the top management team? (refer back to the discussion on corporate governance in Chapter 17).

2 Does competition make it more or less difficult to apply a systems perspective? (refer back to the discussion in the previous chapter, pp. 760–2).

Online
Learning Centre

When you have read this chapter, log on to the Online Learning Centre website at www.mcgraw-hill.co.uk/textbooks/mcgee to explore chapter-by-chapter test questions, further reading and more online study tools for strategy.

Case 1 **Oh, the joy of the journey!**

I guess you'd call it one of those defining moments. The year was 1987. The Body Shop was still in its protoplasmic period, but the Confederation of British Industry had chosen us as Company of the Year. Which meant I had to pick up the award.

There, they sat, the captains of industry, the bankers, the analysts, the journalists, just about the entire British financial establishment, all lined up and holding their collective breath as I mounted the podium.

It was irresistible. Every provocative bone in my body was aching to act up. I'd prepared what I hoped would be a mildly inflammatory speech. When I showed it to my husband, Gordon, he advised me to challenge them all. I also showed it to Jilly Forster, a close friend who also happened to be our PR person. She told me I had to say what I'd written. As I started to speak, the tension was such that I could see tears streaming down her face. I could also see our brokers, sitting stoney-faced on either side of her.

What did I say? I stood up for entrepreneurs against the big corporations. I told these business titans they were stuck in the past. (I believe the phrase I used was 'dinosaurs in pin-striped suits'.) What else could I do? 'I've never met a captain of industry who made my blood sing', I declared – at which point I looked up to see Robert Maxwell walking out. For all I know he had another appointment, but still I felt a surge of pride. My blood did sing, thanks, indirectly, to Cap'n Bob.

That speech was a watershed for me. I had the optimistic sensation that The Body Shop way of doing business was the inescapable future.

In the decade or so that followed, the story got a lot more complex – 'richer', but darker too. History did 1800 flips. The Wall came down (so did Robert Maxwell for that matter). The maximalism of the 1980s surrendered to the minimalism of the 1990s. All the while, The Body Shop was growing into one of the most successful retailers in the world. And I found myself on an extraordinary journey, a journey which made me even more passionate about the urgent need for a new model of business. It was also a journey through a minefield, with every explosion a reminder – as if I needed one – of how fragile were the goals we'd set ourselves. That journey is the subject matter of this book.

Looking back from the vantage point of a new century, I can trace how the path I've taken has radicalized me. Whether it was a sally into the forests of Sarawak to photograph illegal logging or up the Amazon to set up the first direct trading link with the Kayapo, it gave me a glimpse of the way in which global corporations threaten to engulf life, not just in our society but also in the communities where businesspeople simply never go. The outrage I felt was no abstract emotion. It grew stronger the more I travelled, the more I met people forced to eke out a bare existence on the margins of the world, denied their fundamental human rights by the fickle voracity of the global business juggernaut.

I'd always known I was in uncharted territory, but sometimes the landscape I found myself in was so alien that the people I thought were friends were actually enemies – and vice versa. Talk about a recipe for paranoia. Life in a minefield isn't easy. There have been many dents in my optimism and challenges to my convictions – our libel action, our mistakes in the American market, that relationship with the Kayapo I mentioned – but this was ultimately a good thing. When you've had some years when everyone – including the stock market – says you can do no wrong, it's good to be reminded that you're running the same race as the rest of the world. What doesn't kill you makes you stronger.

Yet that sentiment is actually too harsh. Be kind, Harvey Keitel writes on Kate Winslet's forehead in the movie Holy Smoke. That's what I wanted to do to the business world – nurture a revolution in kindness. But underlying that ambition has been the recurring theme of my role in the company I founded, now that it has grown into such a huge and complicated organization. So this book actually has another subject as well. It is the story of how I managed to maintain some intimate part of myself – the original core, if you like – in a business gone global. I have had to constantly reinvent the role of the founder entrepreneur. That's tough when your natural tendency is towards a gleeful anarchy. There are no road-maps, no instruction manuals. Passion is your guide. Instinct tells you where to go when a challenge arises.

So this book is more than a chronicle of a decade at The Body Shop, more than a condensed manual for the wannabe business radical. It is also about one individual's attempt to marry the often impersonal wants of a successful business with the very personal needs of a successful businessperson. Despite the enormous constraints of a global company, despite the general intractability of life, I need to find new ways to push the limits of business, to change its language, to make it a force for positive change. **That's what I mean by business as unusual**.

Source: Anita Roddick (2000) *Business as Unusual: The Journey of Anita Roddick and The Body Shop*, Thorsons, London.

Case Questions

1 Discuss Anita Roddick's conception of a responsible business.

2 How do her guiding principles and values allow the business to grow?

3 What is the role of the founder-entrepreneur in the growth of a successful business?

Further reading and references

AACSB (2003) *Ethics Education in Business Schools*, St. Louis, AACSB International.

Argyris, C and Schon, D (1978) *Organisational Learning: A Theory-in-Action Perspective*, Reading, MA, Addison-Wesley.

Arrow, KJ (1963) *Social Choice and Individual Values*, Yale, Yale University Press.

Barney, JB (1991) 'Firm resources and sustained competitive advantage', *Journal of Management*, **17**, pp. 99–120.

Barney, JB and Hansen, MH (1994) 'Trustworthiness as a source of competitive advantage', *Strategic Management Journal*, **15**, pp. 175–90.

Beer, S (1981) *Brain of the Firm: The Managerial Cybernetics of Organisation*, Chichester, John Wiley & Sons.

Bell, T, Marrs, F, Solomon, I and Thomas, H (1997) *Auditing Organisations Through a Strategic-Systems Lens*, Montvale, NJ, KPMG Publications.

Carroll, AB (1979) 'A Three-Dimensional Conceptual Model of Corporate Performance', *Academy of Business Review*, **4**, pp. 497–505.

Collins, JC and Porras, JI (1996) 'Building Your Company's Vision', *Harvard Business Review*, **74**, September/October, pp. 64–77.

Day, GS and Fahey, L (1990) 'Putting Strategy into Shareholder Value Analysis', *Harvard Business Review*, **68**, March/April, pp.156–63.

De Geus, AP (1988) 'Planning as Learning', *Harvard Business Review*, **66**, March/April, pp. 70–5.

Doyle, P (2000) *Value-based Marketing*, Chichester and New York, Wiley.

Drucker, PF (1993) *Post-Capitalist Society*, Oxford, Butterworth-Heinemann.

Drucker, PF (1994) 'The Theory of the Business', *Harvard Business Review*, **72**, Sept/Oct, pp. 95–104.

Elkington, J (1997) *Cannibals with Forks: The Triple Bottom Line of 21st Century Business*, Oxford, Capstone.

Freeman, RE (1984) *Strategic Management: A Stakeholder Perspective*, London, Pitman.

Freeman, RE and McVea, J, (2001) 'A Stakeholder Approach to Strategic Management', in M Hitt, E Freeman and J Harrison (eds) *Handbook of Strategic Management*, Oxford, Blackwell, pp. 189–207.

Friedman, M (1970) 'The Social Responsibility of Business is to Increase its Profits', *New York Time Magazine*, September, pp. 32–3.

Friedman, M and Friedman, R (1980) *Free to Choose: A Personal Statement*, London, Secker & Warburg.

Glautier, MWE and Underdown, B (2001) *Accounting Theory and Practice*, New York, Prentice-Hall.

Grant, RM (1997) *Contemporary Strategy Analysis*, 3rd edition, Oxford, Blackwell.

Harrison, JS and St John, CH (1998) *Strategic Management of Organisations and Stakeholders*, 2nd edition, Cincinnati, Ohio, South Western Publishing.

Kaplan, RS and Norton, DP (2004) 'Measuring the Strategic Readiness of Intangible Assets', *Harvard Business Review*, **82, 2**, February, pp. 52–64.

Kaplan, RS and Norton, DP (1996) *The Balanced Scorecard*, Cambridge, HBS Press.

Kauffman, S (1995) *At Home in the Universe: The Search for Laws of Self-Organisation and Complexity*, Oxford, Oxford University Press.

Kay, J (1995) *Why Firms Succeed*, Oxford, Oxford University Press.

Magretta, J (2003) *What Management Is*, London, Profile Books.

Malone, TW, Scott-Morton, MS and Halperin, RR (1996) 'Organising for the 21st Century', *Strategy and Leadership*, **24**, July/August, pp. 6–11.

Mintzberg, H (1987) 'Crafting Strategy', *Harvard Business Review*, **65**, July/August, pp. 66–76.

Mohr, J and Spekman, R (1994) 'Characteristics of Partnership Success: Partnership Attributes Communication Behaviour and Conflict Resolution Techniques', *Strategic Management Journal*, **15**, pp. 135–52.

Parker, RH and Harcourt, GC (1969) *Readings in the Concept and Management of Income*, Cambridge, Cambridge University Press.

Richardson, GP (1991) *Feedback Thought in Social Science and Systems Theory*, Philadelphia, University of Philadelphia Press.

Roddick, A (2000) *Business as Unusual*, London, Thorsons.

Rosenfeld, R and Wilson, DC (1999) *Managing Organizations: Text Readings and Cases*, Maidenhead, McGraw-Hill.

Senge, P (1998) 'The leader's new work: Building learning organisations', in S Segal-Horn (ed.) *The Strategy Reader*, Oxford, Blackwell, pp. 296–312.

Sundaram, AK and Inkpen, AC (2004) 'The Corporate Objective Revisited', *Organisation Science*, **15, 3**, May/June, pp. 350–63.

Van der Heijden, K (1996) *Scenarios: The Art of Strategic Conversation*, Chichester, John Wiley & Sons.

Wernerfelt, B (1984) 'A resource-based view of the firm', *Strategic Management Journal*, **5**, pp. 171–80.

Yoffie, DB (1988) 'How an Industry Builds Political Advantage', *Harvard Business Review*, **66**, May/June, pp. 82–90.

Challenges in strategy: final thoughts and postscript

In this book we have presented a wide-range of analytical and theoretical models to help strategists frame their strategic problems and issues in an effective manner. These models provide concepts, theoretical frameworks and analytical approaches which strategists can use as 'lenses' through which to view their strategic problems and strategy formulation processes.

Indeed, as Ned Bowman (1990) convincingly argues, strategists must learn how to use these models and lenses as frameworks and as tools to promote clear and frank dialogue among members of the strategy team about policy options and strategic decisions. A classic, well-known book on strategic decision-making in the political arena, namely Graham Allison's (1971) *Essence of Decision – Explaining the Cuban Missile Crisis*, illustrates clearly processes of strategic dialogue. It convincingly demonstrates that the decision to block the Russian missile ships approaching Cuba emerged from a combination of rational analyses of the situation and the decision alternatives and of discussion and debate in the top team advising President Kennedy. Bobby Kennedy, the President's brother, acted as a 'devil's advocate' to bring out the alternative views of the military and political establishment that were instrumental in forming the eventual decision.

Similarly we believe that the field of business strategy needs analytical tools such as theories, concepts and frameworks supported by processes of dialogue and debate in the management team. This combination provides the basis for practical insights by managers and prospects for improving the quality of strategic decisions. The role of strategy academics, such as we who have written this book, is to develop the conceptual foundations for the practice of strategy and show how these relate to the realities of decision-making.

For its part, top management must take responsibility in leading organizations to establish a corporate context in which both creativity and foresight are emphasized and which regards strategic thinking as the essential process from which both 'unbounded' or 'blue sky' thinking emerges and also from which sound and sensible business plans are created.

But strategic thinking involves the unknown, the improbable and the unlikely. The track record of organizations, both public and private, is for this reason at least very mixed. Strategic decisions by their nature are highly idiosyncratic and situation-specific. Therefore what works in one context does not necessarily work in another. Thus, there are no convenient blueprints for action. Instead academics, consultants and strategy practitioners repeatedly emphasize the importance of strategic thinking. Strategy in this way is an intellectual discipline and the concepts, frameworks and tools developed by academics, consultants and practitioners are an aid to thought, dialogue and debate. They are not a substitute for them. For these reasons and others to do with the natural distance between academics and practitioners it is evident that strategy theory and practice are not always well connected. Indeed, Bettis (1991) notes that research in strategic management has not yet produced the volume of useful results expected by managers. While the strategy field has clearly advanced over the last twenty years – as evidenced by the rapid growth of both scholarly and practitioner journals in the field (to say nothing of the burgeoning number of books on strategy), research in strategic management has continued to leave gaps between what is known from an academic perspective and what is, or can be, prescribed to managers. The opportunity for all of us in the field, including students of strategy, is to try to bridge this gap between theory and practice. Without such a bridge, managers may start losing interest (and insight) into theoretical developments which do not seem, in their eyes, to either help to explain reality or to facilitate action designed to influence it.

As academics, our research is usually focused on examining data so that we can understand what has happened in the past and why. This is a useful endeavour from which many valuable analytical approaches can be developed. But, in addition, academics, just like managers, have a responsibility to assess future possibilities, examine trends, and debate the turning points and discontinuities of the future. In this postscript, we focus on three elements which we think are important and which can form a platform for research agendas now and in the future.

1 What do leaders do, why are they important, and what difference do they create?

2 How can creativity be achieved through strategy?

3 The development of concepts of 'unbounded' thinking in strategy formulation.

Leadership

Vision without action is a daydream. Action without vision is a nightmare. (Old Japanese Proverb)

In a challenging article, John Kotter (1990) examines what leaders really do. He points out that leadership complements management; it does not replace it. Good management is about coping with, and controlling, complexity. Whereas leadership, by contrast, is about establishing a direction and coping with change. It is clear from the themes developed in this book that the business environment in recent times has become increasingly competitive, complex, turbulent, and subject to rapid change. We have rehearsed many of the reasons for this throughout the book, including new forms of competition, new and occasionally disruptive technologies, the need for new strategic capabilities, and changes in accountability and regulation. All of these are also happening in a rapidly changing demographic, cultural and international context.

Kotter notes that coping with complexity and coping with change are characteristic activities of managers and leaders. Managers and leaders have three tasks in common; namely,

> *deciding what needs to be done, creating networks of people and relationships that can accomplish an agenda and then trying to ensure that these people actually do the job.*

First, in deciding what needs to be done *leaders* set direction and a vision for the future whereas *managers* set plans and associated budgets.

Second, in developing the capacity to achieve the plan, *leaders* communicate the direction and align people to commit to the direction whereas *managers* devise, organize and staff an appropriate organizational structure and system.

Third, in ensuring that the organization's goals and plans are achieved, *leaders* need to motivate and inspire people to follow the strategic direction, whereas *managers* seek to control and monitor the plans in order to reach appropriate targets from a 'balanced scorecard' perspective.

In essence, leaders need to develop a leadership culture which promotes values of adaptation to change and in which recruiting quality people to the organization is critical. It is then important to provide them with opportunities to learn by creating new business ideas, opportunities and risks. The simplistic metaphors of the leader as hero or as omnipotent dictatorial power are increasingly inappropriate in today's world. As Porter, Lorsch, and Nohria (2004) point out there are some important and subtle lessons for chief executive officers:

> *First, you must learn to manage organisational context rather than focus on daily operations.*

> *Second, you must recognise that your position does not infer the right to lead, nor does it guarantee the loyalty of the organisation.*
>
> *Finally, you must remember that you are subject to a host of limitations, even though others may treat you as omnipotent.*

These lessons create dilemmas for leaders, for instance to be coercive or to be democratic, to be authoritative or to be a coach, to be affiliative or to set the pace. These are increasingly important as the structural context in which businesses work becomes more fluid and more unpredictable, and as such, business organizations need to abandon comfortable structures on favour of experimental changes. The effect of leaders and leadership on strategy and strategy-making will become more significant and this will become a major challenge for business and for strategy academics.

Strategy and creativity

A keystone of strategy is innovation. However, a pertinent question to ask here is 'where do new ideas come from'. Typically, the simple answer is from people and human ingenuity. It is people who ultimately design new products, create new software, develop new businesses (e.g. Anita Roddick's Body Shop discussed in Chapter 21) or make existing businesses more efficient through management of the value-chain.

The key to creativity is the availability of high-quality creative individuals in the areas of science, engineering, architecture, education, art and music and more applied knowledge workers in the professional fields of law, business and medicine. From a macro-economic viewpoint (see Chapter 4), this requires an appropriate level of societal investment in both education and research and development in order to create an innovatory entrepreneurial culture. Recently Richard Florida (2004) has pointed out that countries such as Ireland, Canada, Australian, New Zealand and Denmark are spending more on R&D and higher education than either the US or the UK in order to attract and retain creative human capital.

New ideas tend to emerge from entrepreneurs (Drucker 1985) and it is from their highly individualised and personal cognitive maps (Porac and Thomas 2002) that new business ideas are sold to venture capitalists and new business arenas are formed (remember our discussion of entrepreneurs in Chapter 8). Drucker points out that it was through the linkage and integration of previously independent technological developments, i.e. audion tubes, binary theory, Jacquard punchcards and symbolic logic that the concept of the computer was created. Subsequently the modern computer industry with its many entrepreneurs such as Thomas J Watson, Steve Jobs, Tim Berners-Lee, Michael Dell and others, was created.

In all these cases entrepreneurs had to sell their creative visions and product concepts to other stakeholders who were often wedded to existing business models. For example, the business model of Jeff Bezos at Amazon.com needed to be sold to both venture capitalists and consumers. The rapid growth and success of Amazon has forced significant changes to the existing bookseller model favoured by Barnes and Noble in the USA and Waterstones in the UK. Something similar has happened in the internet world in EBay, ably led by the CEO Meg Whitman. This rapidly growing web-based trading network has forced a re-evaluation of auction trading. At a more mundane level the concept of 'Post-it notes' (essentially an adhesive piece of paper which did not adhere very well) at 3M was implemented within 3M's offices and office networks long before it was noticed and considered worthy enough to be launched as a new product by senior 3M managers. In summary, these examples illustrate the point that the strategy literature must more clearly incorporate into its frameworks entrepreneurial values such as the creative, cognitive and emotionally intelligent skills of the entrepreneur. Bill Gates at Microsoft, Herb Kelleher (Southwest Airlines) and Stelios (easyJet) in low cost airlines and Curtis Carlson the inventor of Xerography are all examples of entrepreneurs examined within the pages of this strategy text.

Unbounded thinking

Another characteristic of the entrepreneur is the ability to think 'out of the box'. Richard Branson at Virgin, Phil Knight at Nike, Nicholas Hayek at Swatch, Sochorio at Honda and others all exemplify the ability to think beyond current industry and competitive norms.

How can such 'unbounded' thinking be fostered? Gary Hamel and CK Prahalad's work, well represented in this book, offers concepts such as 'strategic intent', 'strategy as stretch and leverage' and 'strategy as revolution'. These exhort strategists to set 'big, hairy, audacious goals' (Collins and Porras 1996) and think outside current frames of reference in setting the company's vision. Indeed, Gary Hamel argues that it is through the activities of revolutionaries and innovators that sustainable competitive strategies are developed.

Chan Kim and Renée Mauborgne, 2004, advance the concept of *blue ocean strategy* to describe the existence of a previously unknown market space in which demand is created rather than fought over. One of their main examples is Cirque du Soleil – the French circus company. Despite a secular decline in the circus industry, Cirque has profitably increased its revenue over twenty times over the last ten years by reinventing the concept of a circus. This is an example of a company creating a 'blue ocean' by expanding the boundaries of an existing industry. EBay, on the other hand, is an example of a *blue ocean* created in a completely new fashion and defining a new market domain, namely online auctions.

More recently, the work of Johan Roos and his colleagues at the Imagination Lab in Lausanne, Switzerland has married creativity skills with blue ocean thinking. They use Lego blocks and Lego creativity play concepts with top management teams as a vehicle to enable them to think creatively about strategy in a systemic concept. The notion of developing unbounded thinking in organizations is a new and exciting area of study for the future.

As a final note . . .

We have identified a few important and novel themes in this postscript. In our view these are the areas in which strategic thinking and acting can develop both in theory and in practice. The five sections of this book were intended to provide an extensive examination of strategy as analysis and strategy as practice. The three new themes identified here will provide challenges for analysts to extend and develop their models to incorporate more subjective and imponderable characteristics. Similarly, strategy as practice needs also to extend its purview to move from a preoccupation with implementation and change to leadership, creativity and longer term perspectives.

Our other main goal in writing this book was to create for you a sense of enjoyment and fulfilment when you read it. In that respect, we hope that you enjoyed the content, organization, and the range of concepts offered here and are stimulated to think and act strategically as well as critically examine any organization in the future using the strategic systems lens presented in this book.

Further reading and references

Allison, GT (1971) *Essence of Decision: Explaining the Cuban Missile Crisis*, New York, HarperCollins.

Bettis, RA (1991) 'Strategic Management and the Straitjacket: an editorial essay', *Organisational Science*, **2** (3), pp. 315–19.

Bowman, EH (1990) 'Strategic changes; possible worlds and actual minds', in JW Frederickson (ed.), *Perspectives in Strategic Management.* New York, Harper and Row, pp. 9–39.

Collins, JC and Porras, JI (1996) 'Building your company's vision', *Harvard Business Review*, **74**, September–October, pp. 65–77.

Drucker, PF (1985) 'Innovation and Entrepreneurship', New York, Harper and Row.

Florida, Richard (2004) 'America's Looming Creativity Crisis', *Harvard Business Review*, **82**, **10**, pp. 121–39.

Kim, W Chan and Mauborgne, R (2004) 'Blue Ocean Strategy', *Harvard Business Review*, **82**, **10**, pp. 76–86.

Kotter, JP (1990) 'What leaders really do?' *Harvard Business Review*, **90**, **3**, pp. 103–11.

Porac, JF and Thomas, H (2002) 'Managing Cognition and Strategy', in AM Pettigrew, H Thomas and R Whittington (eds) 'Handbook of Strategy and Management', London, Sage, pp. 165–82.

Porter, ME, Lorsch, JW and Nohria, N (2004) 'Seven Surprises for new CEOs', *Harvard Business Review*, **82**, **10**, pp. 62–76.

Index